The Dryden Press
Sociology Publications

GENERAL EDITOR
WILLIAM J. GOODE
COLUMBIA UNIVERSITY

BY

JESSIE BERNARD

THE PENNSYLVANIA STATE UNIVERSITY

AND PUBLISHED BY

The Dryden Press

NEW YORK

SOCIAL

PROBLEMS

AT

MIDCENTURY

Role, Status, and Stress in a
Context of Abundance

Library of Congress Catalog Card Number: 57-8828

Second Printing, December 1957

COVER PHOTOS: American Community Builders, Inc., Park Forest, Illinois (top), and A. Devaney, Inc. (bottom)

SPECIAL ACKNOWLEDGMENTS

The author gratefully acknowledges the kindness of authors and publishers in granting permission to reproduce their materials. The following pages give acknowledgment to all holders of copyright from whose publications we have quoted. Page numbers refer to the bibliographic notes, where the sources are described.

Abelard-Schuman, Inc., 443

Addison-Wesley Publishing Company, Inc., 52

The American Academy of Political and Social Science, 271, 541

American Anthropological Association, 359, 382

The American Association on Mental Deficiency, 240

American Book Company, 35, 152

The American Chemical Society, 306

American Council of Learned Societies, 508

American Economic Association, 456, 464, 470, 471

American Institute of Public Opinion (Gallup Polls), 245, 268

American Journal of Public Health, 151

The American Scholar, 585

American Social Hygiene Association, 195, 199, 445, 541

The American Sociological Society, 84, 119, 151, 240, 306, 307, 334, 384, 452, 470, 507, 540

American Statistical Association, 34

Appleton-Century-Crofts, Inc., 198, 470, 540

Archives of Industrial Hygiene, 269

Archives of Psychology, 471

The Atlantic Monthly, 406, 444, 612, 634, 639

Barnes & Noble, Inc., 120, 153

Basil Blackwell, Oxford, 174

Peter M. Blau, 508

Albert & Charles Boni, Inc., 445

Ernest W. Burgess, 53

Business History Review, 509

The Canadian Medical Association, 269

Centre Daily Times, 215

Christian Children's Fund, Inc., 612

Christian Examiner, 119

The A. H. Clark Company, Cleveland, 175

John A. Clausen, 289

Columbia University Press, 151, 240, 385, 470, 478, 501, 502, 508

Cornell University Press, 199

Criterion Books, Inc., 639

Thomas Y. Crowell Company, 119, 152, 267

Louis Dolivet, 612

The Dryden Press, Inc., 120, 335, 540, 541

Durham Labor Journal, 507

Eastern Sociological Society, 270, 334

Ebony, 35

Everybody's Poultry Magazine, 289

Family Life, 406, 470

The Ford Foundation, 612

Foster & Stewart, Buffalo, 240

The Free Press, 69, 305, 333, 382, 443

The Fund for the Advancement of Education, 406

Genetic Psychology Monographs, 240

Ginn and Company, 151, 335

PREFACE

Before we venture into the forest of data dealing with our subject and focus our attention on the many trees we will be observing there—the individual problems of society—it may be well to look over a map of the whole terrain. The subject matter we will be discussing is so manifold and so absorbing that unless we keep a map in mind we may find ourselves observing only the discrete units and passing by their inclusive significance. And it is just as important to have a picture of this larger whole of which social problems are a part as it is to try to understand the problems separately and individually as they emerge, ramify, and dissolve or become transformed into different problems.

Later, some students will take more intensive courses in which specific social problems will be discussed. This book is not intended as a substitute for such specialized treatment. It is not a collection of separate, abbreviated little treatises. It is not a survey. It would not be very misleading to say that this book is as much about role and status as it is about social problems. By emphasizing role and status—the aspects that are common to social problems—rather than the medical, psychological, economic, and legal aspects that differentiate them, we hope to place all these problems within a genuinely sociological perspective. In a sense the problems are viewed as illustrations of sociological trends rather than as individual areas of substantive study.

For the central thesis of our study is, briefly, that although the social-problem ideology remains much the same today as in the past, based as it is upon a belief in the necessity and possibility of alleviating human suffering, the phenomena it deals with—the kinds of suffering to be alleviated—have changed. As a result of the abundance at last made possible by modern technology, the pervasive motif of social problems has changed from concern with mere survival—"poverty and dependence"—to concern with the malfunctions of role and status. The principal form that suffering takes in a context of abundance is not physical pain but anxiety.

World medical officers, to introduce an analogy, have developed the concept of "masked diseases." They have found that so long as the great mass diseases—infectious and nutritional—decimate a population, many other diseases are masked or remain latent. When these pandemics have been cleared away, however, the latent diseases have a chance to manifest themselves. When malaria is wiped out in an underdeveloped area, the morbidity and mortality figures come to resemble those of industrialized nations; the area, it is said, has been "Westernized." The degenerative diseases then become important in the statistics, but civilization does not "cause" them; it merely keeps people alive long enough to suffer from them.

In a similar way we might speak of certain social problems as latent or masked until other social problems are disposed of, thus making way for those "underneath." Thus in the 19th century, as industrialization concentrated whole countrysides of people into cities—one of the most spectacular phenomena in human history—the problems associated with scarcity were all-important. Poverty, the complex which we have labeled the slum-syndrome—all the ills that cluster around and are inherent in slum living—had to be conquered. Problems of role and status anxiety, even though present, were overlaid by these more immediately urgent ones. But in the United States of today people live better than they ever did—they live longer, are better fed, and their education and perhaps even their intelligences are superior. The technological system which has produced this abundance makes necessary patterns of relationship within the family and at the place of work that are different from those of the past, but it is by no means clear, to the observer or the participant, what these new patterns should be. The characteristic social problems are, as a consequence, not the same as those of even a generation ago. To a large extent they involve people who experience anxiety because of confusion—if not conflict—in their role and status relationships.

The problem phenomena with which we concern ourselves in this book fall into two major categories: (1) those that are, or result from, pathologies; (2) those that are, or result from, disorganization. The pathologies we deal with here are considered social because, whether or not they are social in their origin, they are always social—that is, role-impairing—in their effects; into this category fall the physical, mental, and emotional illnesses or disabilities (Part IV). But many problems involve no pathologies at all. They concern people who are as normal as the total population in every way. Their problems originate in the functioning of the social system. Change confuses roles, for example, and upsets established status relationships (Parts V and VI). Although anxiety is generated by these role and status changes, it is not extreme enough to produce pathologies.

At midcentury we find ourselves in ringside seats at one of the major dramas in human history: the extension of the social-problem ideology to the underdeveloped or formerly colonial areas of the world. The idea that suffering is not inevitable, that something can and should be done about it, that abundance is possible even for them—these are the quickening ideas that are transforming the fatalism of the underdeveloped areas. In these areas the characteristic social problems are still those that spring from scarcity—infectious and nutritional diseases, hunger, inadequate housing. These lands are experiencing the uprooting of populations and all the attendant problems which the more advanced nations faced earlier, in the 19th century. There are status problems also —race relations between whole world areas—and role problems associated with technological change. These can no longer be ignored by the student of social problems. Part VII of our study is therefore devoted to them.

The phenomena we deal with here are the concern of a number of special approaches, of which the sociological is only one. The sociological approach cannot and should not attempt to explain everything. A rigorous discipline was therefore imposed on the treatment here in order to hew close to the sociological line and not cross over into other areas. Thus, although the clinical psychologist, the psychiatrist, and the internist as well as the sociologist deal with pathologies which are social in their origins or effects, and although economists, political scientists, and legal theorists share our concern with disorganization, an effort was made to keep our discussion within sociological terms. There is a place for the so-called interdisciplinary or functional approach, and the almost exclusively sociological emphasis here is not intended to imply that other approaches are inferior. And since the distinctively sociological aspects of problems cannot always be understood except in the light of other specialties, the alternative approaches to our discussion have been accorded recognition. But it was felt that there was room for a distinctively sociological contribution couched as much as possible in the terms of its specific discipline.

The study of social problems can be either the most or the least theoretical specialty of sociology. It can be primarily substantive; that is, it can consist almost wholly of straightforward factual—usually statistical and case-descriptive—materials, with a minimum of theoretical formulation. There are, however, few things more perishable than statistical or even verbal descriptions of social problems. In a rapidly changing society their value becomes primarily historical within a few years after they are presented. Most research older than, say, a quarter of a century is unreliable not only because the findings are old but also because adequate techniques, or even concepts, for gathering and analyzing data have been available for so short a period. The study of social problems can, at the other or theoretical extreme, be largely methodological, emphasizing concepts and models rather than specific data. It can show the student how to view social problems. It can involve an analysis of the nature of consensus, of social order, of norms, of socialization, of conformity, of social bonds, of ideology, of progress, and so on. This book attempts to steer a course between these two approaches —or better, perhaps, to incorporate contributions of both. It contains a core of statistical, case-descriptive, factual data and in this sense it is substantive; but it also pays a good deal of attention to the general theoretical context in which these data are found, as sketched above, and in this sense it is methodological.

The writing of any textbook imposes a tremendous task of selection. Unless a book is to be encyclopedic in nature—in which event it may cease to possess the virtues of a textbook, whatever others it may gain—the author must discard much more material than he includes. The materials selected must have some logical coherence or the result will be a hodgepodge. The criteria that guided the selection of materials in this book are presented in Chapter 5; the thesis that guided their organization is presented above.

If the selection of materials has resulted in the omission of data on topics of special interest to the student, he will find enormous supplementary resources in the library. He will find that the specific facts change from year to year; but the major trends discussed here will prevail. He can use the conceptual framework offered in this book to organize data in any problem area of especial interest.

The conviction embodied in this book—and presented, we hope, convincingly—is that if we wish to understand the social problems of our time, rather than those of the past, we must interpret them in terms of the constantly changing role and status picture that now characterizes the second half of the 20th century. These changing problems of role and status are associated with an age of abundance; we are going to have to learn how to live with abundance even if this means a complete revision of our old role and status concepts.

In *American Community Behavior* the problems confronting American communities were analyzed in terms of the underlying processes that gave rise to them. Organization, competition, conflict, community disorganization, and dissociation were the major foci of attention. In this volume the point of view is more personal; the people themselves and the stresses they are subjected to are the center of interest. Instead of such organizational units as crescive and enacted norms, those of role and status are emphasized. Role and status problems are essentially problems of organization; they are also involved in competition and in conflict. The two books, although complementary, are wholly independent.

JESSIE BERNARD

SYNOPTIC TABLE OF CONTENTS

CONTENTS

PART V

Abundance and Social Disorganization: Family and Worker Roles

I

THE CONTEXT OF SOCIAL PROBLEMS AT MIDCENTURY: ABUNDANCE

An Old Theme: Suffering in an Age
of Scarcity

[6TH CENTURY B.C. MIDDLE EAST.] Men remove landmarks; they seize flocks and pasture them. They drive away the ass of the fatherless; they take the widow's ox for a pledge. They thrust the poor off the road; the poor of the earth all hide themselves. Behold, like wild asses in the desert they go forth to their toil, seeking prey in the wilderness as food for their children. . . . They lie all night naked, without clothing, and have no covering in the cold. They are wet with the rain of the mountains, and cling to the rock for want of shelter. There are those who snatch the fatherless child from the breast, and take in pledge the infant of the poor. They go about naked, without clothing; hungry, they carry the sheaves. . . . From out of the city the dying groan, and the soul of the wounded cries for help. . . . The murderer rises in the dark, that he may kill the poor and needy; and in the night he is as a thief. The eye of the adulterer also waits for the twilight, saying "No eye will see me"; and he disguises his face.—JOB 24 : 1–16.

[1421. PARIS.] . . . and every day and every night there were heard throughout Paris, because of the aforesaid high prices. . . . long complaints, lamentations, sounds of sorrow, and piteous cries . . .; for night and day cried out men, women, little children, "Alas! I die of cold," or "of hunger." And in truth it was the longest winter that one had seen for forty years; for at the fairs of Easter it snowed, it froze and brought all the misery of cold that one could imagine. And because of the great poverty that some of the good citizens of the good city of Paris saw being suffered, they went so far as to buy three or four houses which they made into hospitals for the poor children who were dying of hunger within Paris, and they made soup and a good fire and were well bedded down. And in less than three months there were in each hospital forty beds or more well equipped, which the good folk of Paris had given, and there was one in the Heaumerie, another before the Palais, another in the Place Maubert.

And in truth when good weather came, in April, those who in the winter had made their beverages from apples and sloe plums emptied the residue of their apples and their plums into the street with the intention that the pigs of St. Antoine would eat them. But the pigs did not get to them in time, for as soon as they were thrown out, they were seized by poor folk, women and children who ate them with great relish, which was a great pity, each for himself; for they ate what the pigs scorned to eat, they ate the cores of cabbages without bread or without cooking, grasses of the fields without bread or salt. . . .

Also, in this time the wolves were so ravenous, that they unearthed with their claws the bodies of people buried in the villages and fields; for everywhere one went, one found people dead in the fields and towns, from the great poverty, the dear times, and the famine which they suffered, through the cursed war which always grew worse from day to day.—James Bruce Ross and Mary Martin McLaughlin, *The Portable Medieval Reader.*

[20TH CENTURY. INDIA.] When Rukmani, who was the daughter of a village Headman, was 12 years old she was married to Nathan, who was only an illiterate tenant farmer. It was a social comedown, but it could not be helped. Dowries for Rukmani's three elder sisters had impoverished her family and left no choice. After the wedding the young couple rode in a bullock cart to Nathan's village and set up housekeeping in the mud hut with coconut thatch that Nathan had built himself. Their subsequent life. . . . [was] typical for peasants in a South India village. . . . The absolute poverty in which most Indian villagers are condemned to live is a grim and pathetic statistical fact to most Americans. . . . Rukmani does not even protest. She is not angry or bitter. Life for her was always a matter of fear and of ill-founded hope. Everything depended upon the rice harvest. Too heavy rains meant hunger; a drought meant famine. The new tannery came and disrupted the life of the village. And always there was the brutal fact to face that nothing could be done. The margin between not enough and starvation was too thin. No plans could be made. No steps to provide for the future could be taken. As Rukmani expressed it:

"The calamities of the land belong to it alone, born of wind and rain and weather, immensities not to be tempered by man or his creations. To those who live by the land there must always come times of hardship, of fear and of hunger, even as there are years of plenty. This is one of the truths of our existence as those who live by the land know: that sometimes we eat and sometimes we starve. We live by our labours from one harvest to the next, there is no certain telling whether we shall be able to feed ourselves and our children, and if bad times are prolonged we know we must see the weak surrender their lives and this fact, too, is within our experience. In our lives there is no margin for misfortune. . . ."

[RUKMANI'S IS] a terrible story of death and disaster and despair, of children dying of starvation, of a daughter becoming a prostitute to earn enough to feed her baby brother, of an old couple thrown off the land they did not own to become beggars in a temple. But somehow this is not a bitter, sordid or angry story. Rukmani's own attitude is not bitter. She remembers her love for her husband and children, the self-sacrifice of many people and little moments of joy and gladness.

Such anger as this book arouses must be the reader's in his reaction to a society that allows such conditions to exist. The conditions that ruled Rukmani's life were not just an inequitable system of land distribution and of callous exploitation of their fellows by money lenders. They were more basic than that.

Rukmani's life was cursed by ignorance—ignorance of everything that might have helped. She and her friends knew nothing of birth control and all too much about the necessity of having many sons. They knew nothing of hygiene, nothing of modern agriculture, nothing about the world beyond the boundaries of their village. . . . They were too isolated, too ignorant and too busy breeding, suffering and dying.—Orville Prescott, reviewing *Nectar in a Sieve* by Kamala Markandaya.

POVERTY, EXPLOITATION, murder, theft, adultery, technological innovation, homelessness, untimely death, natural calamities, war, famine—there is little in the catalogue of contemporary human misfortune missing from the above accounts. From long before Christ up to this very day, as they show, the same themes have recurred again and again. For human suffering and misfortune have a long history. Records of illness and pain are deeply etched in the bones of even prehistoric men. Dental caries, poliomyelitis, and arthritis exacted their price then as now. Plagues and epidemics have swept back and forth across the continents from time immemorial. Hunger has been no stranger to human beings. Premature death has for millennia left widows and orphans unprotected. Mental as well as physical illness has ravaged communities a long time. Injustice and exploitation of the weak have aroused resentment in prophets for centuries. Man's inhumanity to man has been documented from the beginnings of history. Men have forsaken their wives, parents have rejected their children, from at least Old Testament times. Perpetrators of crime appear in the first historical records. Corruption, war, exploitation, injustice—we have only to name the ill and evidence of its long history can be found. Natural forces wholly outside the social system as well as forces within it have wreaked havoc on man for thousands of years.

Variations of an Old Theme: The Impact of Industrialization

The 19th century exaggerated, and added new variations to, the old theme. If anything, these variations of the scarcity theme were worse, since more people suffered. The uprooting of millions of people from the land was unprecedented; the geographical movement of peoples was on a vast scale; the concentration of masses of human beings in industrial cities—these were new phenomena in human history. They created new ills for which there were no precedents. Now that time has intervened between us and the colossal first impact of industrialization on human adjustment in the 19th century we are beginning to see it in perspective; we find precisely the same kinds of stresses occurring today in underdeveloped areas of the earth under the impact of industrialization. We find the same slums, the same squalor, the same family disorganization, the same split between generations. The following account, written to guide those concerned with technical assistance programs in underdeveloped areas today, might just as well have been written about

5

the generations of immigrants and rural folk who came to the cities of the United States in the 19th century.

The peasant who comes to the city brings with him all the stability derived from a childhood spent within a traditional and coherent social order. His personality reflects that experience and he often withstands enormous pressures, and meets crisis after crisis with courage and imagination. It is not among the first generation immigrants from country to city, from agricultural country to industrial country, from simple levels of life to complex levels, that we find the principal disturbances which accompany technical change. Rather, it is in the lives of their children, reared in conditions within which no stable patterns have been developed, by parents who, while they may be able to weather the storm themselves by drawing on a different childhood experience, have no charts to give their children. Juvenile delinquency, alcoholism, drug addiction, empty, defeated, meaningless lives, lives which are a series of drifting rudderless activities, commitment to oversimplified political programmes which promise relief from their feelings of inadequacy and lack of direction—these are the prices which are paid. . . . by the disturbed members of the second generation.*

But the 19th century which so accentuated and exaggerated the scarcity evils of the past also inaugurated the means—abundant productivity—by which the old scarcity evils could be mastered. The 19th century witnessed a race between two tendencies inherent in industrialism and urbanism: (1) toward increased stress factors on the one hand and (2) on the other, toward the creation and accumulation of the wealth which, through science, could mitigate if not entirely eliminate many of them. The 20th century is seeing the implications of this abundance.

A New Theme: Abundance

It is only in the context of abundance that current social problems can be understood. Abundance, as we shall see, is relative; it can never be absolute so long as human beings can think of new things to want. Even in this relative sense it did not suddenly explode upon the social scene. There is no specific date we can point to and say, "That's when the age of abundance began." It has been almost two centuries in coming. It began with the technological revolution at the end of the 18th century.

Beginning at the top of the social system, abundance enormously enriched the so-called bourgeois class, but it took a long time for this abundance to descend the class ladder. And only now, in the middle of

* Margaret Mead, ed., *Cultural Patterns and Technical Change* (Mentor, 1955), p. 287.

6

the 20th century, is it beginning to reach the lowest levels of the social structure. The scarcity ideology—as embodied, for example, in the theory of the old Poor Law—persisted until just a generation ago; it was not supplanted until the 1930's. An ideology congruent with an age of abundance is only now in process of formulation.* We are beginning to come to grips with all the implications of abundance. Because of its enormous importance we devote Chapter 1 to a documentation of its nature and a summary of its concomitants and implications.

* If a specific date is called for, the work of J. M. Keynes entitled *General Theory of Employment, Interest, and Money* (Macmillan, 1936) could be said to establish the new theoretical framework or ideology of abundance.

1

The Nature, Concomitants,

and Implications

of Abundance

The Nature of Abundance

Early in the 20th century Simon Patten spoke of the transition from an era of scarcity to one of abundance. The human ills of the past were, he said, those of a deficit economy; those of the present, of a surplus economy:

> [There is a] difference between a society struggling to meet a deficit and one so well situated that thought can be centered on the equitable distribution of a surplus. In the one case the civilization must develop its traditions to keep the deficit as small as possible and eventually to overcome it, and in the other to utilize the surplus for common good, not to undermine energy and productive ability or to create parasitic classes, but to distribute the surplus in ways that will promote general welfare and secure better preparation for the future. The one type of society may be called a pain or deficit economy, the other a pleasure or surplus economy. All civilizations before the nineteenth century, like the primitive societies of the Western world to-day and the backward despotisms of the East, were realms of pain and deficit,

The Nature of Abundance

Some Concomitants of Abundance

Some Philosophical Implications of Abundance

in which the traditions and experiences of men were moulded out of the general menaces to life and happiness. When adjustment to nature was defective at many points and lacking altogether at others, forecasts of evil were proved true by the event, and men learned to expect calamity and disorder. . . . But are these sad endings the fit sequels of man's ill-doing in a one-time perfect world, as certain moralists have affirmed, or are suffering and defeat the outcome of the purely physical conditions of existence? If the latter, improvements in the environment will construct a new basis for civilization by lessening deficit and destroying the old status between men and nature. . . . A new agriculture means a new civilization. . . . Each gain upon nature adds to the quantity of goods to be consumed by society, and lessens the labor necessary to produce them. Improved conditions make better men, and better men improve conditions. . . .[1] *

The middle of the 20th century reveals what he meant and some of the implications.

There is, indeed, a "new agriculture," fabulously more productive than anything ever known before.

* Superior figures refer to notes found at the end of each chapter.

Yields per acre of 28 crops were 42 to 52 percent greater in 1948–1951 than in the ten-year period 1923–1932. Fruit crops, as well as feed grains, vegetable crops and cotton, have shown a remarkable rise in yields since 1936. Ten important fruits had average yields per acre 50 percent higher during 1948–1951 than their 1923–1932 average. . . . Over the twenty years from 1930 to 1950, average crop yields per acre for . . . 28 crops increased by 55 percent and over the twenty-three-year span from 1930 to 1953, they increased by more than 60 percent.

The same technological, educational and economic forces that were responsible for the increase in per acre yields during the 1930's and 1940's are still operative. A large part of the improvement in the yield of corn, wheat, oats, cotton, potatoes, tobacco and other crops will therefore probably continue, and yields per acre in 1960 could easily be about 15 percent greater than in 1950.[2]

A similar picture is revealed by industrial production. Factory productivity rose 4 to 6 per cent in 1954–1955; the increase in factory productivity was averaging 3 per cent a year before World War II. Output per man-hour in 1955 increased about 6 per cent over 1954.[3] Modern technology had doubled productivity in the United States between 1900 and 1950, half of this increase occurring after 1940, so that the prospect was that the rate would be even greater in the second half of the century. An economist who had examined eight careful forecasts of the future performance of our economy concluded in 1955 that they all "in general imply a doubling of the economy within the next 20–25 years and a near doubling of our living standards by 1975."[4]

As a result of this great rise in productivity in the United States, both personal and family income has greatly increased. Personal income doubled between 1919 and 1953, from $858 (in 1953 dollars after taxes) to $1,566.[5] Most of this increase has come in the last twenty years:

The years from 1935 to 1955 were marked by vigorous growth in both population and economic activity. The population of the continental United States increased by 36 million to 164 million. The gross national product in 1954, in dollars of constant purchasing power, was more than two and one-half times that in 1934 and almost double the 1929 product. Per capita disposable personal income almost quadrupled in actual dollars and almost doubled in purchasing power from 1934 to 1954. . . . The national output per employed worker has increased about 3 percent per year since 1934. This increase, together with the 50-percent increase in the number employed, accounts for the rise of more than 150 percent in the real national product in the 20 years. This last increase, in turn, permitted during the same period a rise in personal income of almost 170 percent in dollars of constant purchasing power. Even after the personal tax payments, which had increased many times, personal income per capita at 1954 prices was about 90 percent higher in 1954 than in 1934.[6]

Table 1 summarizes data for individual workers between 1939 and 1951, and Table 2, for spending units from 1948 to 1955. It was estimated that family income would rise to $5,010 in 1960 (in 1950 dollars).

TABLE 1

WAGE OR SALARY INCOME OF PERSONS, BY SEX, IN 1939, 1947, AND 1951

Wage or Salary Income	Both Sexes			Male			Female		
	1939	1947	1951	1939	1947	1951	1939	1947	1951
$1 to $999	60.0	27.7	23.6	52.8	19.3	14.1	79.0	45.5	41.9
$1,000 to $1,999	29.2	26.4	16.8	33.4	22.2	12.5	18.1	35.1	25.3
$2,000 to $2,499	5.3	14.9	11.3	6.8	16.4	10.2	1.6	11.6	13.5
$2,500 to $2,999	2.0	9.7	10.2	2.6	12.4	10.8	0.5	4.1	9.1
$3,000 to $4,999	2.4	17.9	29.7	3.1	25.0	39.9	0.6	3.1	9.7
$5,000 and over	1.0	3.4	8.4	1.4	4.8	12.4	0.1	0.5	0.5
Total *	100.0	100.0	100.0	100.0	100.0	100.0	100.0	100.0	100.0

* Total refers to persons who had wage or salary income.
SOURCE: Data for 1939 and 1951 from U.S. Bureau of the Census, *Current Population Reports—Consumer Income,* Series P-60, No. 11, Table 9, and data for 1947 from Series P-60, No. 5, Table 21.

TABLE 2

SPENDING UNITS DISTRIBUTED ACCORDING TO INCOME CLASSES, 1948–1955 *

Income Class	1948	1949	1950	1951	1952	1953	1954	1955†
	%	%	%	%	%	%	%	%
Under $1,000	14	12	14	13	13	11	10	10
$1,000–$1,999	22	18	19	17	15	14	13	13
$2,000–$2,999	23	23	21	19	18	16	14	14
$3,000–$3,999	17	20	19	19	18	18	16	16
$4,000–$4,999	10	12	11	12	15	15	16	15
$5,000–$7,499	9	10	11	14	14	17	21	21
$7,500–$9,999	{5	{5	{5	{6	4	5	5	6
$10,000 and over					3	4	5	5

* Based on a survey of approximately 3,000 spending units defined as "all persons living in the same dwelling who are related by blood, marriage, or adoption and who pool their incomes for major expenses." Because the units surveyed in successive years are not identical, some lack of comparability is present. Income level is for previous year.
† Data for 1955 are preliminary.
SOURCE: Board of Governors of the Federal Reserve System, "Preliminary Findings of the 1955 Survey of Consumer Finances," *Federal Reserve Bulletin,* March 1955, p. 251.

This high rate of productivity, both agricultural and industrial—matched, it might be added, by high productivity among service workers also, which is made possible by improved technology—is, then, the evidence on which we base the case for our emphasis on abundance. Abundance is not, to be sure, precisely the same thing as high productivity because if there are disproportionately large numbers of people to share the high productivity there is no abundance. And we should not overlook the threat to abundance in the burgeoning population of the world today (a point to be discussed in Chapter 24), for if population increases faster than productivity, even high productivity cannot create abundance.

So far as the United States is concerned at midcentury, however, present trends suggest that although population is indeed growing rapidly, productivity is growing even faster. One economist in 1955 pointed out that although population by 1965 would grow by 18 to 19 per cent, output would grow by more than 45 per cent, and that by 1975 population would have risen by only a third while output would have about doubled.[7] At this point, therefore, we shall assume that abundance in the sense of a growth in productivity greater than in population is a demonstrable fact, and proceed to analyze some of its most important concomitants.

We shall not at this point enter into a discussion of the nature of this growing productivity, that is, into the elements of waste involved in it which some observers emphasize. Nor shall we assume that abundance in the sense of satiety or surfeit is on the immediate horizon. We shall see as our discussion proceeds that abundance in the sense here used—a faster rate of growth in productivity than in population—raises standards of many kinds and thus is not always perceived as abundance. The fact, however, that abundance makes us more aware of deprivation does not obviate the documentable fact of relatively greater growth in goods and services than in people to share them.

And now to a consideration of some of the concomitants and consequences of abundance.

Some Concomitants of Abundance

The concomitants and consequences of this abundance in the United States have been profound, and it is only in the context of abundance that we can understand the nature of the stress factors which impinge on human beings today. In addition to changing the age structure of the population (by making it possible for more people to live longer) and thereby changing the nature of health problems, abundance in the sense of high productivity has had the following concomitants and consequences: (1) it has introduced a new principle of class organization; (2) it has led toward a leveling upward of income, education, occupational status, and consumption patterns; (3) it has raised the standards by which we evaluate living conditions; (4) it has substituted an ideology of abundance for an ideology of scarcity; and (5) it has changed the quality of the population, and the basis of personal character, from an orientation around production to an orientation around consumption.

New Principle of Class Organization

In feudal, agricultural society the fundamental principle of class structure was one based on scarcity. When there was not enough, and where production could not be greatly expanded with available technology, there could be a class of Haves only at the expense of a class of Have-nots. The allocation of scarce goods may have been based on any one of several principles,[8] but whatever principle was used, the net tendency was likely to be in the direction of a class of Haves and a class of Have-nots so long as there was not enough for all.[9]

But in an industrialized society capable of producing abundance this is no longer true. Where there is mass production and a mass market, the very existence of a class of Haves at the top depends upon the existence of Haves all down the line to buy the goods produced. Unless the mass market can absorb what the mass-production methods turn out, there can be no Have class at the top. An economy of abundance is possible only if the abundance can be widely shared. The reply to scarcity in such a society is not to find ways to distribute what little there is but to find ways to get rid of the scarcity itself. There remain many genuine issues between those at the top and those beneath them, but in one respect they have common interests: all profit from wide distribution of the goods created by high productivity.[10]

One student of the influence of abundance on American character has gone so far as to couple democracy with it, suggesting that it has been possible primarily because we could afford it, because we could level up without at the same time leveling down. The contrast which he presents between American and Old World attitudes might just as well be couched in terms of abundance and scarcity principles of class organization:

. . . the presence of more than enough . . . has . . . given a characteristic tone to American equalitarianism as distinguished from the equalitarianism of the Old World. Essentially, the difference is that Europe has always conceived of redistribution of wealth as necessitating the expropriation of some and the corresponding aggrandizement of others; but America has conceived of it primarily in terms of giving to some without taking from others. Hence,

Europe cannot think of altering the relationship between the various levels of society without assuming a class struggle; but America has altered and can alter these relationships without necessarily treating one class as the victim or even, in an ultimate sense, the antagonist of another. The European mind often assumes implicitly that the volume of wealth is fixed; that most of the potential wealth has already been converted into actual wealth; that this actual wealth is already in the hands of owners; and, therefore, that the only way for one person or group to secure more is to wrest it from some other person or group, leaving that person or group with less. . . . The American mind, by contrast, often assumes implicitly that the volume of wealth is dynamic, that much potential wealth still remains to be converted; and that diverse groups—for instance, capital and labor—can take more wealth out of the environment by working together than they can take out of one another by class warfare. European radical thought is prone to demand that the man of property be stripped of his carriage and his fine clothes; but American radical thought is likely to insist, instead, that the ordinary man is entitled to mass-produced copies, indistinguishable from the originals. Few Americans feel entirely at ease with the slogan "Soak the rich," but the phrase "Deal me in" springs spontaneously and joyously to American lips. This American confidence that our abundance will suffice for the attainment of all the goals of social justice is evident throughout the greater part of our national history.[11]

The principle we are emphasizing here goes even beyond this analysis. It states not only that abundance makes leveling up without leveling down possible, but that it makes such leveling up essential. Unless the results of high productivity *are* widely distributed, unless there is a mass market, the very basis of high productivity—mass production—is threatened.

There is, then, a twofold movement in our society: as a society we are on an upward-moving escalator, as we saw above; but, in addition, on that escalator those at the bottom are also walking up the stairs. Let's watch them.

The Leveling-up Process

In some areas the leveling-up process accompanying abundance has been associated with a less marked leveling-down process also, so that the net result has been in the direction of equalization, at least of a narrowing of the status gap. This leveling up and consequent drift toward equality is not necessarily inherent in modern technology. Modern technology might conceivably have been institutionalized on a stop-start basis—periods of depression alternating with periods of boom—so that instead of producing abundance it might merely have continued the era of scarcity, a privileged class enjoying the fruits of modern technology at the expense of an unprivileged class. That is, productivity might have

The people pictured above (and on the binding of this book) are well dressed and well fed; they probably live in comfortable homes. But has abundance eliminated stress from their lives? Though none of these people is worried about where the next meal is coming from, probably a good many of them wonder how they will be able to meet payments on the new car. None of the young mothers shown here has lost a child because of diphtheria or whooping cough, but many of them are concerned about parents afflicted with arthritis or cancer or arteriosclerosis. Though few, if any, among the young fathers and mothers doubt that they can see their children through high school, many of them worry about their ability to see them through college. None of the men is involuntarily unemployed, but many of them are nagged by the disappointment of having fallen all too short of their own vocational or professional aspirations.

Abundance, in brief, has unmasked problems that in the past were hidden behind problems of sheer survival. Abundance has raised our standards.

The social problems characteristic of the second half of the 20th century in the United States, in contrast to those of earlier times, have their incidence among people very much like those shown in the photograph reproduced above. *(Photo: A. Devaney, Inc.)*

been "averaged out" on a low level over a period of time rather than increased. We shall elaborate this point at greater length in Chapter 20. At this point we merely note that a leveling up and drift toward equality have, as a matter of historical fact, accompanied the new technology.

If we take four indexes commonly used as criteria of status—income, education, occupation, and living or consumption standards—we can document these trends objectively.

INCOME. Not only has the general level of income risen with increased productivity, as pointed out above, but in the second third of the century there has also been a tendency, however slow, toward leveling up of the income of those on the bottom.[12] Until the 1930's, there was a strong tendency in the opposite direction—that is, toward increasing concentration of income in the higher levels—but after that time, and especially in the 1940's, this trend was reversed.

The rise in aggregate personal income (1934–1955) was accompanied by substantial changes in the distribution of families and unattached individuals by income classes. When families and unattached individuals are arrayed according to size of income and grouped in fifths, it appears that there has been a distinct reduction in relative income differences since the mid-1930's. The share of aggregate income received by the top fifth declined from 52 percent in 1935–36 to 45 percent in 1953, while that of the lowest rose from 4.1 percent to 5.0 percent (by 22 percent). When comparison is limited to families of two or more persons, the gain in the share of the lowest fifth appears to have been considerably greater, with a rise of 45 percent by 1950.[13]

The relevant data are summarized in Table 3.

TABLE 3

DISTRIBUTION OF FAMILY PERSONAL INCOME AMONG QUINTILES
AND TOP 5 PER CENT OF FAMILIES AND UNRELATED INDIVID-
UALS RANKED BY SIZE OF FAMILY PERSONAL INCOME:
1935–36, 1941, 1944, 1950, AND 1953

Quintile	1935–36	1941	1944	1950	1953	Per Cent Change, 1935–53
Lowest	4.1	4.1	4.9	4.8	5.0	+22
Second	9.2	9.5	10.9	10.9	11.3	+23
Third	14.1	15.3	16.2	16.1	16.5	+17
Fourth	20.9	22.3	22.2	22.1	22.3	+ 7
Highest	51.7	48.8	45.8	46.1	44.9	—13
Total	100.0	100.0	100.0	100.0	100.0	
Top 5 per cent	26.5	24.0	20.7	21.4	20.7	—22

SOURCES: Selma Goldsmith *et al.*, "Size Distribution of Income Since the Mid-Thirties," *Review of Economics and Statistics*, 36 (Feb. 1954, Table 4); *Survey of Current Business*, 35 (March 1955), p. 20.

It will be noted that most of the change in income distribution occurred in the early 1940's, and this fact is further documented by comparing the per cent increase in average income of the several fifths between 1935–36 and 1941 with that between 1941 and 1944.

TABLE 4

PER CENT INCREASE IN MEAN INCOME

Quintile	1935–36 to 1941	1941 to 1944
Lowest	23	52
Second	28	47
Third	36	34
Fourth	33	26
Highest	18	19
Top 5 per cent	13	9

SOURCE: Selma Goldsmith *et al.,* "Size Distribution of Income Since the Mid-Thirties," *Review of Economics and Statistics,* 36 (Feb. 1954), Table 5.

Ignoring for the present the effect of income tax and social security legislation, we find that this trend toward equality was implemented by a complex of many forces. There was *fuller employment,* for one thing, which "had greater relative impact on the lower paid occupations than on the higher paid ones and thereby contributed to the narrowing of income differentials." [14] Within specific occupations, furthermore, there was a widespread *decrease in wage-rate differentials* which was relatively greater for the higher-paid occupations than for the lower.[15] The greatest relative gains in income were therefore experienced by the lower-paid occupations; the least, by the best-paid. Within the wage-earner class, for example, the lowest income third received more of the total amount paid in wages in 1949—15 per cent—than it had in 1939—11 per cent. Conversely, the top third had received 62 per cent in 1939, but only 54 per cent in 1949.[16] Thus, "even if variations in extent of employment are held constant and attention is focused on full-year workers, it is apparent . . . that the relative income gains were highest among the lower paid occupations. . . . Both the increase in employment and the decrease in wage-rate differentials operated to reduce the income gap between high-paid and low-paid occupations." [17] Some indication of the greater increase in wage-and-salary income among the lower occupational groups as compared with the higher may be gleaned from the figures in Table 5.

Another factor implementing the trend toward equality was the *movement of population away from the low-income regions and toward*

TABLE 5

RELATIVE INCREASE IN INCOME OF DIFFERENT
OCCUPATIONAL GROUPS, 1939–1950

Major Occupation of the Worker	Percentage Increase in Median Wage-and-Salary Income of Male Workers, 1939–1950
Professional and technical	114
Manager, official, and proprietor	95
Clerical	111
Salesworker	147
Craftsman and foreman	160
Operative	172
Service worker except private household	176
Laborer except farm and mine	175

SOURCE: Elizabeth E. Hoyt *et al.*, *American Income and Its Use* (Harper, 1954), pp. 107–108.

The median salary of the professional and technical group, ranked first in median income during 1950, increased by about 100 per cent from 1939 to 1950. The median salary of managers, officials, and proprietors and the clerical group increased by slightly less. The median wage of "laborers" increased by 175 per cent. The relatively greater increase in the wage-and-salary income of the low-paid occupations may have been compounded by two things: a greater decrease in unemployment for them than for the high-paid occupations, or a relatively greater increase in rate of pay.

high-income regions. "For example . . . from 1929 and 1939 to 1949 . . . the most noticeable shift in the distribution of populations among regions had been the expansion of the region which in 1949 had the highest per capita income. . . . Also . . . net migration from 1949 to 1950 was clearly away from low-income and to high-income regions. . . ." [18] At the same time the per capita income of even the low-income regions was increasing, more rapidly in fact than that of the high-income regions.

The equalization of income resulted also in part from *the relatively greater income increase among nonwhites as compared to whites*, a fact which we will document in greater detail when we discuss the Negro in Chapter 22.

The forces we have just enumerated—increase in employment, decrease in wage-rate differentials among occupations, movements of population, and decrease in racial wage differentials—had their chief effect in raising the lowest income levels. In addition, the *change in the occupational structure of the economy* (to be discussed below) also played a part in the trend toward equality since it was in the direction of increasing the better-paid—technical and professional—jobs and decreasing the less-well paid, that is, the unskilled jobs. The *increase in the number of workers per family,* which occurred disproportionately among middle-income families,[19] also tended to reduce the differential between them and the higher-income families.

To emphasize this leveling-up trend in income in no sense implies that income equality now exists or is ever likely to exist. We are still justified in speaking of lower and of higher socioeconomic classes as measured in terms of income. Nor does our emphasis imply that we are ignoring the large number of families—8,000,000 (excluding individuals) in 1954 [20]—who were in the low-income (under $2,000) brackets, or a denial of the necessity of meeting their needs.

These low-income families are, indeed, of especial importance in our study because it is among them that the incidence of pathologies and of disorganization is highest, either as "cause" or as "effect." (Pathologies and disorganization are discussed in Part IV and Part V.)

In some cases the income of these families is low *because the earner is still very young;* these are the newly married couples who can confidently expect increased income with time. These we may dismiss from consideration here. In other cases, quite the reverse, income is low *because the head is old.* Among families of two or more persons in 1952 almost a third—30 per cent—had heads who were sixty-five years of age or older, and the median age of the family head was fifty-four years.[21]

TABLE 6
COMPOSITION OF LOW-INCOME BRACKETS, 1939 AND 1947

	Percentage of Units with Income	
	Under $500 in 1939 *	Under $1,500 in 1947 *
All	100 †	100 †
Unrelated individuals	17	25
Husband-wife families	68	58
Women living alone or as heads of families	20	30

* The shift in base from $500 in 1939 to $1,500 in 1947 is intended to take into account the change in value of the dollar.

† Some "women living alone" are included also among "unrelated individuals" so that the totals add up to more than 100 per cent.

SOURCE: Herman P. Miller, "Factors Related to Recent Changes in Income Distribution in the United States," *Review of Economics and Statistics,* August 1951, p. 218.

These figures suggest that in 1939 the lowest income groups were composed largely of "normal" families in which the family head was either unemployed or underemployed. However, the same groups today are composed, to a much larger extent, of "broken" families, aged persons, and others who live on fixed income or who are unable to take full advantage of increased employment opportunities.

Increasingly, *low income is related to family composition.* Thus, for example, a comparison of family composition in the low-income brackets in 1939 with that of 1947 indicates that in the latter year there were more in the categories "unrelated individuals" and "women living alone or as heads of families" than there were in the earlier year.

If we label as "poor" all those with incomes under $2,000 as of 1949 we can analyze the composition of families which made up the "poor" of that year in somewhat greater detail. The largest single category was that of "unrelated individuals," who constituted 39 per cent of the "poor" as here defined. Among the families, as distinguished from these "unrelated individuals," the composition was as follows:

TABLE 7

COMPOSITION OF FAMILIES WITH MONEY INCOMES
UNDER $2,000 AS OF 1949

Composition	Per Cent
No earner	9
No earner apart from armed forces	10
Head a self-employed farmer or farm manager	12 *
Head self-employed in a nonfarm industry	6
Head an "other laborer"	3
Head a farm laborer or foreman	2
Head a female	9

* The status of this group should be interpreted in terms of the type of income reported. For these families income in kind is important, and the data are for money income only.

SOURCE: Elizabeth E. Hoyt *et al., American Income and Its Use* (Harper, 1954), p. 350. The total percentage in the table from which these figures are taken is 90, not 100. That is, 10 per cent are not accounted for.

Some families have low incomes because *the roles they perform are no longer needed* in our society. We refer here to low-income farm families, who still live in a scarcity situation. We shall have more to say about them in Chapter 20. Some families are poor because they belong to disadvantaged racial or ethnic groups, a matter to be discussed in Chapter 22.

Misfortunes and acts of God account for a residual proportion of the low-income families in any given year. Floods, fires, droughts, or accidents may precipitate families into the lowest income brackets even though they ordinarily have higher incomes. "In other words, an important minority of these . . . families consists not of the chronically poor but of over-$2,000 families who 'had a bad year.' " [22]

In addition, there are young and old families, not mentioned in the above analysis, and an indeterminate number of families who are poor because they are the *victims of the pathologies* we are to discuss in

Part IV. In a certain sense they are really not a part of the productive system. An indeterminate number of them are hardly even part of the social system. So far as the normal functioning of our society is concerned they are an enclave, "in" but not "of" the total group. They suffer from role pathologies of one kind or another which make it impossible for them to respond to abundance. From time immemorial they have been distinguished from other low-income cases by such epithets as the "unworthy" as contrasted with the "worthy" poor. Although they contribute a disproportionate number of persons to the population of jails and almshouses, they are primarily medical rather than economic, or legal, problems.

Although we emphasize the importance of abundance in lowering the income differential among income classes we cannot ignore another great pocket of poverty in our society at midcentury. The almost half a million American Indians who live on reservations are, in effect, in "underdeveloped areas" of the world and hence still in a condition of scarcity, with the social problems—poor health and nutrition, and ignorance—which characterize scarcity. A long history of treaty violation by the United States government has deprived them not only of land but also of water for the land they retained. They have been bypassed by abundance.

Despite major and glaring exceptions in the anomalous types of cases just noted, abundance has, by and large, been accompanied by a trend toward the leveling up of income. Many forces, as we have just seen, have been at work to produce this result—social security,[23] minimum wage and income tax laws not the least among them. As a result, the data just presented suggest that families are poor nowadays, when they are, primarily because they have no earner or a female earner (Tables 6 and 7), or because the earner is old (Chapter 19) or a member of a handicapped racial or ethnic group (Chapter 22).

EDUCATION. The proportion of people who have a high school education has enormously increased in the 20th century; and it appears now that a similar gain in the proportion who have some higher education is also in process. In 1919 only 62.6 per cent of the population aged five to nineteen was enrolled in school in the United States; in 1950, the proportion was 78.7 per cent. At the beginning of the century the average number of years of schooling was only slightly more than eight. It is now 12.1. The average young adult today has completed high school; his father probably had less than a year in high school; his grandfather probably did not get beyond grade school. In 1915 only 5.5 per cent of those eighteen to twenty-one were enrolled in colleges; in 1950, the proportion was 30 per cent.[24] In addition a large proportion of young people attend business and vocational schools.

Since literacy, sheer ability to read, seems to be a great divider in populations,[25] the difference between the most educated person and the person of average education at midcentury is probably less than the difference between the person of average education half a century ago and an illiterate person.

OCCUPATION. Modern technology has the effect of leveling upward the occupational structure of an industrial economy. Little by little it removes from the ladder the lowest rungs of unskilled workers. The man who had only brawn and muscle to contribute is gradually eliminated. In his place we have a semiskilled worker and a machine. More spectacular and perhaps more significant for our purposes is the tremendous increase in white-collar occupations. The son of a man who went to work in overalls carrying his lunch goes to work in street clothes carrying a briefcase. And now, with the introduction of electronic devices—the process of automation—it is predicted that the working force will be even more upgraded. Technicians and engineers will increasingly replace even many of the white-collar occupations as machines take over more and more clerical work. The modern industrial worker resembles the 19th-century industrial worker in hardly a single respect. He often looks and acts like a businessman. His leaders are likely to be college-trained men, middle class in point of view as well as in manner of life.

With the proliferation of new occupations and the degradation of others by great specialization, many status differentials based on occupation become blurred. There has always been an uncertain line between the small independent businessman and the skilled manual worker, and within the blue-collar occupations the upgraded skilled worker soon becomes a professional engineer. There is therefore confusion with respect to occupation as a basis of status. Only the extreme status positions—doctors, judges, unskilled workers—remain clear-cut. Industrial union organization also has the effect of blurring status distinctions; everyone in the industry from top to bottom, except management personnel, belongs to the same union. Invidious distinctions become more difficult to maintain under these conditions.

CONSUMPTION. Accompanying the above changes there has been a leveling upward in consumption patterns. A mass-production economy, as we saw above, demands a mass market. Goods must be produced in enormous quantities; they must be consumed in enormous quantities. Automobiles, television sets, refrigerators, and electrical appliances become standard in most families. They have to. For, as one business-man has put it, "without consumption, capitalism will crumble, and because of the consumer, capitalism has been replaced by a new system—'consumerism.' " [26] We must practice what J. M. Keynes has called "relentless consumption."

One student who has analyzed living standards concludes that in terms of a minimum standard "the rise in per capita income in the first half of the twentieth century seems . . . to have reduced poverty in cities as set by a minimum living income greatly, probably by 80 or 90 percent." [27] For urban wage earners and clerical workers with aver-age size families of 3.4, somewhat less than 9 per cent were trying to live on less than the cost of the minimum standard in 1950, as con-trasted with about 40 per cent in 1901. The same author presents data on future trends in living standards and concludes that increased pro-ductivity will continue to upgrade the standard of living of the working classes still further:

> If we think of social classes in the first half of the century as economic classes and in terms of the articles they can and cannot buy, then the working class as previously known will cease to exist and will move up to the middle classes as defined in terms of purchases. In other words, the working classes of tomorrow will have the standard of living of the middle classes of yester-day.[28]

And, continues this same author, barring a small proportion of people of mental inability, illness, prolonged unemployment not provided for in social security schemes, "we should expect poverty to disappear."

An advertising and marketing firm noted in 1955 that between 1948 and 1953 there was a 33 per cent increase in consumer take-home income, reflecting itself in an increase in food sales of 35.7 per cent.[29] And in the same year the E. I. du Pont de Nemours Company predicted a 20 to 25 per cent increase in living standards within a decade.[30] There was a gap of 6 per cent in 1950 between the amount of goods and serv-ices produced by our economy and the consumption needs of our popu-lation, as computed by a team of economists; the gap was expected to drop to 4 per cent by 1960.

> On the basis of the estimates of need . . . expenditures of $206.4 bil-lion in 1950, or 6 percent more than the amount actually spent in that year, would have permitted the small minority of substandard families and indi-viduals to achieve a "health and decency" standard of living without any modification in the living standards of the vast majority whose income were more than adequate to maintain such standards. In 1960, with the estimated cost of meeting total needs amounting to $251.9 billion (at 1950 prices), the margin between demand and needs would be reduced to 4 percent.[31]

Poverty, then, in the 19th-century sense hardly exists at midcentury in the United States. There are very few people who are hungry or cold in the winter. And even in these cases provision is increasingly being made to protect them from genuine physical suffering.

Rising Standards: The Relativity of Abundance

We spoke above of the relativity of both abundance and scarcity. We cannot emphasize this point too strongly. And implicit in the relativity of abundance and scarcity is the concept of a standard. A standard is a quantification of a value.[32] How much? How good? How well? These are questions for which an answer demands standards. How much, how good, how well in terms of what end? Should we be satisfied with a 70 per cent achievement? 50 per cent? 10 per cent? Can we speak of abundance in the United States when we do not have enough schoolrooms for our children or adequately trained personnel for mental hospitals or prisons or probation work?

It will be noted that we are here in the very center of one of the most basic ethical problems. We are dealing with goals, with values, with ends and aims. And abundance has had a remarkable effect on the levels at which we set our sights. One of its most important effects has been the continued raising of sights. And the end is not in view. There is no indication that we will ever say: We have achieved our goals, attained our standards, we can now sit back and rest. For we no sooner reach one level than we raise our standards. The standard which at one time seemed a desirable level comes to be viewed as too low a generation later. If the standard is a 40-hour week one generation, it becomes a 35-hour week the next; if one third of those able to profit by higher education actually go to college in one generation, the goal becomes one half in the next; if a car in every garage is sought in one generation, two cars become the standard to be achieved in the next, and so on. The carrot always dangles before our eyes; we never reach it, for as we move forward it is moved on just ahead of us.

This concept of standards is basic in our analysis. The abundance of one generation is the scarcity of the next. The satisfaction of at least the basic food requirements on a "subsistence level" in one generation is considered inadequate in another. Sheer survival becomes far too low a standard. "Psychological" satisfactions loom large in new standards. And as standards rise progressively away from the sheer survival level, status considerations loom larger and larger. We are always being reminded of the fact that in many respects the average consumer today "lives better" than even the nobility 150 years ago. But so long as others

of his contemporaries "live better" than he does today, the status differential is important. The average consumer evaluates his level of living
not in terms of the past but in terms of the present. It is his contemporaries—sociologists call his standard-setters his "reference groups"—who
set the pace. "When I was a young instructor living in a quonset hut,
doing my writing with a typewriter on my lap," says one leading psychologist, "I used to look forward to the time when I could live in a
house and have a study of my own. Now I do." But the payoff was not
what he thought it would be. "Everyone here lives the way I do." There
was no status rise.

Abundance, then, is relative. We shall illustrate this principle with
respect to six problem areas, namely: (1) income, (2) schooling, (3) race
relations, (4) housing, (5) care of the aged, and (6) social work.

INCOME. One economist has pointed out that over the last three
generations the proportion of all families judged to be living below the
level of decency has remained fairly constant—about one third—despite
the documentable evidence of improved levels of living. Charles Booth
in 1890, on the basis of a famous survey of London, concluded that
30 per cent of the families of that city were below the line of poverty.
During the depression of the 1930's we were also told that one third of
the nation was poorly fed, housed, and clothed. Recent statistics have
been similarly interpreted. This economist concludes that the constancy
of this proportion merely reflects that the standards have risen:

> Critics have charged that the apparent stability in the volume of inade-
> quate incomes results from shifting standards that change with the level of
> the average wage or the average income and they point out that even the
> poorest families today have comforts, unknown two or three generations ago.
> . . . The inevitable conclusion . . . is that inadequate incomes can never
> be eliminated in any final sense because we as human beings always tend to
> judge incomes below the average as inadequate. And if this conclusion is cor-
> rect, low incomes become a matter not of size of income but of the prevailing
> attitude toward distribution.[33]

It is low status or position in the income structure, in brief, according
to this economist, not poverty, which is viewed as a problem. The
"poor," indeed, we have always with us, but the standard of what constitutes being poor changes.

Abundance, by raising standards, sometimes in effect even creates
certain cases of "poverty." We referred above to the proportion of total
national income going to the several fifths of the population, and the
figures in Table 3 suggest that the lowest fifth is still receiving only
one ninth as much as the top fifth. This is, to be sure, relatively more
than it received in 1935–36; still, what kind of "equality" is this? Actu-

ally a raising of standards has blurred the picture here. For many of the income units in the lowest fifth of the income structure, having separate identity and any independent income at all was an improvement over earlier years. For example, in times of scarcity unemployed and older persons and young-married couples doubled up with others and therefore did not appear as income units in the low-income or "poverty" brackets. When social security benefits permit the unemployed and the aged to maintain their own homes, however, and young marrieds to set up housekeeping by themselves, despite the actual improvement in their status which such independence connotes, they swell the numbers in the low-income brackets. There is a strong movement to improve their situation even more. We are as shocked to find that 8 of the 42 million income units in the United States received less than $2,000 income (as of 1954) as we were to find the much worse conditions in the 1930's— or 1890's. Our standards have risen. The very fact that we are shocked demonstrates our higher standards.

The relative nature of income level emerges when we look at the situation from the point of view of families themselves. Two students asked a sample of the population: "About how much more money . . . do you think your family would need to have things that might make your family happier or more comfortable than it is now?" The more income these families had the more they felt they "needed"; thus, those with weekly incomes of $25 felt they needed $16 more, on the average; those with incomes of $50, $30; and those with $100 or more, $100.[34] There seemed also to be a tendency for those with more education to "need" relatively more. This tendency has been interpreted as arising from the fact that:

. . . additional schooling raised the standard of consumption so that people wanted more things, or wanted things more intensely, than they otherwise would. There seems good reason to believe, however, that the greater the amount of schooling, the higher is the income expectation of a group. Dissatisfaction with things as they are is in part caused by the anticipation of better things to come.[35]

SCHOOLING. A similar rise in standards has taken place with respect to the amount of schooling which it is felt children should have. The following statement about schools sounds strangely familiar. It was written in 1894.

We may here enumerate the more patent defects in the educational function, chiefly as it is performed in the United States: (1) large numbers of incompetent teachers, (2) conventional and unscientific courses of study, (3) wrong methods of instruction, (4) inadequate provision for urban school populations, (5) only brief schooling for large numbers, (6) lack of unity and coordination in the educational system as a whole.[36]

The difference between the above lament and current counterparts is that at that time average school attendance was only two years and in some districts children attended school only half a day because there was room for only half of the school population.[37] If we measured ourselves by 19th-century standards we would consider that we had "solved" the problem of education, or could quite easily do so. But we have raised our standards and we are as much exercised about our failure to meet these higher standards as 19th-century observers were about contemporary failure to meet the then current standards.

RACE RELATIONS. We have raised our sights in far subtler situations also. The goal in race relations, for example, is coming to be the abolition not only of objective status barriers but also of subjective barriers. There was a time when most Negroes agreed with the man who said, "I'd rather be a back-door Negro and be well fed than a front-door Negro and go hungry." [38] But at midcentury he is coming to be viewed as an anachronism. When the Supreme Court handed down its desegregation opinion in May 1954, it based its conclusion on status considerations and on social-psychological evidence as well as on legal reasoning. The standards for good schools included status as well as physical plant and equipment. Segregated Negro schools, even when they cost as much as other schools, were inherently inferior; they had a deleterious effect on personality and were therefore held to be bad.[39] Not only were Negroes not to be treated as inferiors; they were not even to be allowed to feel inferior. They were to be well fed *and also* to use the front door.

HOUSING. In 1950 the Committee on the Hygiene of Housing of the American Public Health Association made status considerations part of their standards for housing, stating that "the sense of inferiority due to living in a substandard home is a far more serious menace to the health of our children than all the unsanitary plumbing in the United States." [40]

CARE OF THE AGED. Standards for the care of older citizens have been raised to include status considerations also. It is not considered enough simply to provide for physical needs. Thus, in setting up the provisions for Old-Age and Survivors Insurance under the Social Security Act, the goal was not only to make provision for older people but also to protect them from status deterioration, even if it called for a policy which was not economically or financially the best one:

The Old Age and Survivors Insurance pensions, since they are payable only to those who have made a specific, identifiable contribution to a fund, have the appearance of having been paid for by the beneficiary. Such recipients can claim the pensions as a matter of right, without loss of status. . . . It is for purposes of maintaining the appearance of adequate prior accumulation of funds on behalf of each participant in the system that the "fund" system of OASI pensions was adopted, instead of using a pay-as-you-go system of financing, which had advantages from an economic standpoint.[41]

SOCIAL WORK.   In an age of scarcity the social worker spent a great deal of her time in sheer relief dispensation, in keeping her clients fed, clothed, and housed. Today she spends an increasing amount of time and energy in counseling and re-educating them, and in healing role relationships. So far as institutional care went, in an age of scarcity it was primarily custodial. In an age of abundance physical survival is taken for granted. The goal becomes role rehabilitation. We attempt not only to cure the illness or disability which produces impairment but we also attempt to reweave the person's role relationships.

In brief, abundance has enormously elevated the standards by which we judge the functioning of our society. We can afford more. The alleviation of sheer physical suffering was most urgent in an era of scarcity; the alleviation of "mental" or "social" or "status" suffering also seems important in an era of abundance. Increasingly, standards are raised to include the protection of people against the stresses associated with status as well as those associated with physical survival.

The Change from an Ideology of Scarcity
to an Ideology of Abundance

The change in standards just referred to was not only quantitative, but qualitative as well. It reflected a wholly new ideology with respect to suffering. Abundance made a more humane attitude toward suffering possible, as well as refining what should be considered suffering. In an age of scarcity people must steel themselves, become indifferent to suffering, to protect themselves from exposure to it.

Only in a very sheltered life of the sort made possible by civilization can one maintain a fine and serious sense of the tragedy of misfortune. In an environment in which tragedy is genuine and frequent, laughter is essential to sanity; such laughter is neither callous nor humorous. [In an environment of abundance] it is both . . . for behind the protecting curtains of ease and resource which civilization has woven we grow sensitive. For us to be indifferent to suffering is to kill in ourselves that sympathy without which we become dead to our fellows and ultimately to ourselves.[42]

In an age of abundance we can afford the luxury of "a fine and serious sense of the tragedy of misfortune."

We can trace the change in ideology from one of scarcity to one of abundance by contrasting the ideology underlying the Poor Laws with that underlying present-day social security legislation. The Elizabethan Poor Law of 1602 dealt with the old, the infirm, the helpless, infants, the lame, the impotent, the blind, the sick, the unemployed; it made the local parish responsible for their care. But since the psychology of the time was one of scarcity, the general idea was that all care should be as inexpensive as possible. Since there wasn't very much, pennies must be pinched. The theory and practice of the Elizabethan Poor Law were introduced into this country by the colonists and the psychology and philosophy of this law persisted until well into the 20th century. They were not completely discarded, in fact, until they were superseded by the theory embodied in the Social Security Act of 1935. The nature of the theory of the Poor Law may be summarized as follows:

Human nature is essentially bad, so that unless you make relief as difficult and as humiliating as possible, people will just naturally take advantage of you. There must, therefore, be means tests of some sort or other, that is, people must prove their destitution and be willing to pay the price in humiliation, or even sacrifice of civil rights, if need be. Those receiving relief must be kept below the level of self-supporting families because economy in the administration of funds is a prime consideration and the taxpayer must be protected against a potential horde of chiselers, or [even] "worthy" and "deserving" poor. He must be protected against the squandering of relief funds on swindlers; most people who need relief are inferior or deserve their misfortune, therefore there should be no "coddling" of clients. The strictures of Malthus on the demoralizing effects of the dole thus found embodiment in the policies of overseers of the poor. Public relief must be made as disagreeable, as punitive, and as unendurable as possible in order to reduce the numbers asking for it. Generosity would inevitably lead to abuse. Economy in the use of public funds, taken for granted as a good thing, demanded that the natural tendency for people to take advantage of generosity be curbed.[43]

In complete contrast to this scarcity ideology—which assumes that those at the bottom can be helped only by taking away from those above them—is the ideology implicit in social security legislation which emphasizes the importance and even necessity of maintaining income at all times. Maintaining income in low-income families is not viewed as charity or philanthropy or even generosity; it is a basic requirement of an age of abundance. Abundance itself may depend upon it. If, as one student says, "increasing our ability to sell more and better is a prerequisite to future business health," [44] there must be people with income to buy. Whether or not people are "worthy" or "deserving" is beside the point. They must have money to spend to keep the economy functioning properly.

If we are going to have an increase in employment opportunities we have to have an increase in consumption. That means not only an increase in the gross figure itself but an increase in consumption per capita or per family. From what does that kind of increase come? It comes from a rise in the standard of living. . . . We have to learn to sell better.[45]

This is not humanitarianism, this is not Christian love; this is the ideology of abundance.

Changes in Character Structure

Abundance has been accompanied by profound changes in the nature of the populations exposed to it. The average person used to be younger; there were relatively few old people. There used to be more children who were orphans because parents, especially fathers, died younger. People were more ignorant; few had gone beyond the elementary schools. Today, as we saw above, high school graduation is the rule. More people used to live on farms, or at least had a rural background; relatively few do today. More people used to work with their hands; there are many more white-collar workers today. More people used to be self-employed; today relatively few are. In addition, the cessation of large-scale immigration in the 1920's means that there are fewer foreign-born in the population today; practically everyone is native-born, many are third-generation.[46] All these demographic and socio-economic differences reflect themselves in the kinds of problems which are characteristic of the second half of the 20th century.

It is fairly easy to document the above-named concomitants of abundance with respect to population. But the effect of abundance on the subtler aspects of a people—character, for example—is much more difficult to assess. Has it had any effect at all? Are people today different so far as character is concerned than they were in the 19th century? If they are, in what ways?

There is one viewpoint which holds that wealth or luxury tends to render a people effete. Tradition has it that the conquerors of China were defeated by their own success; they were so coddled that they lost their ability to control. The case of the Roman Empire is also referred to to prove that wealth leads to decadence. Or the Old Regime in France. Are these analogies valid? What, exactly, are the effects of abundance on a people?

Actually we do not yet know, since abundance in the sense we are using it here is such a new phenomenon in the world. Instead of trying to find lessons in historical analogies we might invoke the experience of modern societies in different phases of the business cycle. Here we find that by and large such phenomena as divorce, death rates, crime, and juvenile delinquency tend to increase in prosperity and to decline in depression. Should we conclude then that the historical lessons are valid, that it is indeed true that "character" deteriorates with abundance? Some people have pointed out that high rates of crime, divorce, and the like are luxuries which we can afford only because or when we are rich, that if we were hard put to support our population we could not tolerate them.

But here, as in the case of historical analogies, there are inherent fallacies which show up when we examine the phenomena closely. We find, for example, that, contrary to the results referred to above, it is precisely in the upper socioeconomic levels that crime and divorce rates are lowest. Further, marriages and births, as well as divorces and deaths, go up and down with the business cycle. It cannot, therefore, be assumed that abundance in and of itself causes deterioration of character.

We must, then, discard both historical parallels and reasoning from the effects of the business cycle and begin fresh in our appraisal of the effect of abundance on character. Three recent analyses may be pertinent here: one by a historian, one by economists, and one by a sociologist.

The historian has attempted to demonstrate the effect which abundance has had on American character in a detailed way, and we shall draw upon his analyses in some detail later.[47] Here we call attention only to his conclusion that the American emphasis on equalitarianism, mobility, rejection of status, and permissiveness, as contrasted with authoritarianism, are all products of abundance.

Another study, by economists, of American income and its uses points out that in an era of scarcity, virtues and vices are assessed in terms of their contribution to production. Good traits of character are those which make for efficiency. This standard for judging people is part of the ideology sometimes known as the Protestant ethic. Those who abide by it are accorded high status; those who do not, low. But in an era of abundance, the old criteria do not operate well. When they persist, they may actually impede social functioning.

. . . the Puritan philosophy that hard work is and ought to be the criterion of status and respect prevailed in the America of the 18th and 19th centuries, and prevails in some parts of the rural Northeast and the Midwest today. Those who achieved economic competence could not claim so much social approval if they held to the philosophy that inherited mental or physical ability, childhood environment, or original endowment of property was an important determinant of economic success. By contrast, outside the area of Puritan influence, the old-family whites who owned slaves justified the social order which they preferred by urging an ideology in which mental and moral traits supposed to be derived from proper lineage were and ought to be the criteria by which social status and economic rewards are determined.

The Puritan doctrine of virtue through hard work served its purpose

"What do you mean, 'Abundance'?"

The farm work done by the father of this household can no longer support his family. Our economy does not need the contribution that the worn-out soil of his mountain farm can make, a soil not fertile enough to warrant the investment of much human energy. If he could be persuaded to train for a job in a nearby industrial center, his work would be more productive and his income would rise correspondingly. He and his family would come to share in the abundance of our economy. But he prefers the rural way of

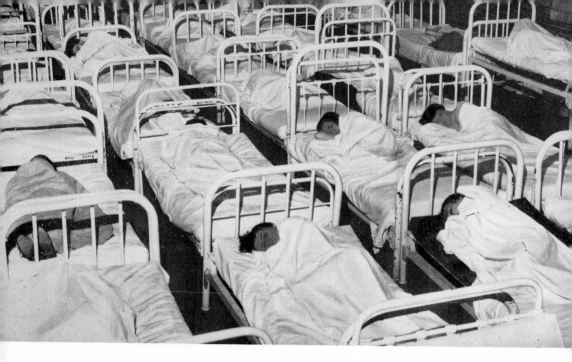

living. Urban life frightens him. Stability or status (in the sense of a feeling of belonging) is more important to him than mobility or ranked status (in the socioeconomic sense).

The comment "What do you mean, 'Abundance'?" might also be made about the overcrowding so common at midcentury. Custodial and treatment institutions of all kinds are acutely short of space. Many hospitals and prisons must care for several times as many persons as they were designed to accommodate. Personnel to staff these institutions is also in short supply.

Public schools are similarly overcrowded; at midcentury thousands of children must share desks and books. There are not enough classrooms or teachers. Nor is there enough good housing. Urban-development plans have led to the clearance of many slum dwelling units, but not all have been replaced by new housing projects. As a result, in the remaining slums crowding has actually

Can we speak of "abundance" when such conditions exist? worsened.

(United Press Photo; Ben and Sid Ross, Parade Publications)

well when it was the indispensable philosophy for a people bent on wresting from the poorly endowed land of New England the economic independence which was a means to high-order spiritual goals. But it lived in the culture until recently, diverting the social thinking away from an early consideration of ways to remedy the inhumanities to such members of an industrial society as were notably deficient in mental inheritance, normal family environment, educational opportunity, or ability to master the intricacies of finance and save to invest wisely for a protracted old age.[48]

There is, therefore, a strong tendency to modify standards and values in the direction of a more tolerant and generous orientation.

A third analysis of the impact of abundance on character structure, made by a sociologist,[49] points out that the abundance-related character is oriented around consumption rather than, as in scarcity-related character, around production. Its values are different. This author's general thesis has been summarized as follows:

> Prior to the attainment of abundance . . . people are concerned primarily with increasing production. In their own temperament this requires hard enduringness and enterprise; in their external concerns it requires concentration upon dominating the physical environment; in their personal economy it requires thrift, prudence, abstinence. But once abundance is secured, the scarcity psychology which was once so valuable no longer operates to the advantage of society, and the ideal individual develops the qualities of the good consumer rather than those of the good producer. He needs now to cultivate interests that are appropriate to an enlarged leisure, and, since he is likely to be an employee rather than an entrepreneur or to be engaged in one of the service trades rather than in production, the cordiality of his relations with other people becomes more important than his mastery of the environment. In his personal economy, society expects him to consume his quota of goods—of automobiles, of whiskey, of television sets—by maintaining a certain standard of living, and it regards him as a "good guy" for absorbing his share, while it snickers at the prudent, self-denying, abstemious thrift that an earlier generation would have respected. . . . In this process it would certainly seem that economic abundance plays a . . . critical part . . . in producing the transformation.[50]

Abundance, then, produces a different type of character than scarcity. There may be some question as to the inherent strength of this consumption-oriented type of character. Lacking the discipline which individually initiated and prosecuted work imposes on character, does it have enough stress resistance to withstand the tests of modern life? Some people wonder.[51] As yet we do not know, since this abundance-oriented character is still relatively new; it has not yet been subjected to severe test. It seems more easygoing than the highly motivated type of character which the work-oriented economy produces. Whether strong or weak, however, it does seem to be true that the character which goes with abundance is not the same as that which goes with scarcity.

Some Philosophical Implications
of Abundance

All the way through our discussion in this chapter we have found ourselves face to face with profound ethical problems. They were especially important in our consideration of standards and in our reference to the character changes associated with abundance. These ethical problems are in many ways unique in human history. We have not had enough experience with abundance to know just how to evaluate it. And the experience we have had has tended to result in a negative verdict, for when scarcity was the universal rule, as we pointed out above, certain people could be rich only at the expense of the many who were poor, and the implication was that wealth in and of itself was wicked.

The fact is, the great teachers of the past never faced the issue of great material abundance. It was not there for them to face. Men as a whole were too poor. These great teachers generally saw material abundance, in the hands of the few individuals who had it, as the enemy of spiritual growth; this naturally would be the case when the abundance of one man accompanied the poverty of a thousand others. It was natural for them, therefore, to condemn material abundance.[52]

And if, as was commonly believed, wealth made for effeteness, dissoluteness, lack of discipline, it was to be condemned. Vows of poverty were exacted of those who sought to live according to religious orders.

Leaders of Oriental civilizations—weighted down with centuries of poverty—have also sometimes spoken disparagingly of abundance or, as they labeled it, the "materialism" of the West. They, too, saw it as leading to moral and ethical deterioration. They were inclined to contrast Oriental spirituality with Western materialism much to the credit of the former even when it meant the deepest poverty for millions.

But today the consensus seems to be that abundance is desirable. Leaders of underdeveloped areas of the world hope to achieve it without having to take also what they consider to be its defects. Abundance is coming to be seen as an ally rather than an enemy of human welfare.

. . . the first half of the twentieth century . . . [will] be known in history not so much because of two great world wars as because it was during this period that mankind became aware of the possibility of a new freedom . . . the freedom for all mankind from destitution and disease. . . . During this half century, in certain portions of the world, in particular Western Europe and North America, the peoples confined within definitely limited areas have steadily improved in health and have attained continually increasing abundance of means of living. Men all over the world, as they have become aware of what is happening here, have caught a new vision. This vision is that for themselves also the specters of destitution and disease can be controlled.[53]

The implication of current economic, political, and sociological thinking is everywhere, then, that abundance is desirable. Since it results only when men and machines are employed in creating it, it has become a matter of national policy to keep them so employed in order to assure abundance. To be sure, we have by no means learned how to guarantee their continuing employment. We are in a machine which is speeding very rapidly through space while we try now this lever and now that pulley in an effort to steer, if not wholly to control, it. But the principle has been established that abundance is desirable and that it is a governmental obligation to underwrite it, or guide toward it.

Although abundance is, then, generally considered desirable, we should make clear that there is no implication in this acceptance of abundance that it is the same as Utopia or heaven or Nirvana or paradise. The term does *not* imply that mankind has now found the key to eternal bliss or that misfortune is a thing of the past. Indeed a major theme of the present study is that there are stresses associated with abundance no less than with scarcity. They may be different but that does not mean that they are less real. The well-fed, well-clothed, well-housed, rapidly transported, massively entertained modern man is just as capable of suffering as his forebears; and he has more years in which to exercise this capacity. The "pursuit of happiness" may be more precipitate now than formerly, but the goal is no less elusive for that. If we wished to dramatize the constant nature of suffering before the passing show of stress, we might ask: Is it any easier to watch obsolescent old people live than untried children die? A host of philosophical problems are implied in this question, perennial, unanswerable. Our task here is not to tangle with these imponderables, however. For time, not eternity, is our concern.

NOTES

1 Simon N. Patten, *The New Basis of Civilization* (Macmillan, 1907), pp. 9–17.

2 J. Frederic Dewhurst *et al., America's Needs and Resources: A New Survey* (Twentieth Century Fund, 1955), pp. 796–798.

3 Joseph A. Loftus, "Productivity Rise Is Noted in Nation," *New York Times* (May 27, 1955).

4 Julius Hirsch, ed., "Our Economic Future: 1955–75," in *New Horizons in Business* (Harper, 1955), p. 34.

5 Editors of *Fortune* magazine, *The Changing American Market* (Hanover, 1955), p. 261.

6 Lenore Epstein, Dorothy McCamman, and Alfred M. Skolnik, "Social Security Protection, 1935–1955," *Social Security Bulletin*, 18 (Aug. 1955), pp. 5, 6.

7 Hirsch, *op. cit.,* pp. 38–39.

8 Jessie Bernard, *American Community Behavior* (Dryden, 1949), pp. 89–94.

9 An anthropologist, Dr. Dorothy D. Lee, has been quoted as saying that complete equality was achieved among some of the less wealthy American Indian societies (*New York Times,* Aug. 30, 1955) but no such equality has ever been recorded in the history of Western societies.

10 Where the abundance is not taken off the market by consumers, as in agriculture, other techniques must be used to deal with it, including purchase and disposal by the government.

11 David M. Potter, *People of Plenty, Economic Abundance and American Character* (Univ. of Chicago Press, 1954), pp. 118–119.

12 In the second decade of the 20th century, the Italian social scientist Vilfredo Pareto concluded that "the distribution of income is a fixed datum in economics and that regardless of changes in economic conditions, short of a revolutionary change from a competitive to a collectivist society, the distribution of income is fixed in all places and at all times" (quoted by Herman P. Miller, *Income of the American People* [Wiley, 1955], p. 97). Perhaps the technological changes which have occurred since his time do indeed constitute the kind of revolution he referred to as necessary to modify the distribution of income. The relative stability in the proportion of national income going to the several fifths of the population over long periods of time (Table 3) might seem to confirm Pareto's law. There are limiting factors, however. For one thing, the composition of the lowest fifth varies with a great many sociological factors over a period of time, such as the marriage rate, doubling up of families, the age composition of the population, etc. (See *Income Distribution in the United States by Size, 1944–1950,* Office of Business Economics, 1953, pp. 24–25.) For another thing, the large proportion of national income going to the top fifth may be an artifact, since there is no ceiling to this top fifth. One or two extraordinarily high incomes have enormous weight in the total picture. At the other end, furthermore, the perennial incidence of disabling pathologies tends to keep the income level of the lowest fifth down, quite independently of the economic forces at work. We shall have more to say about the lowest fifth when we discuss the influence of abundance on standards.

13 Epstein, McCamman, and Skolnik, *op. cit.,* p. 6.

14 Miller, *op. cit.,* p. 118.

15 *Ibid.,* p. 119.

16 Herman P. Miller, "Changes in Income Distribution in the United States," *Journal of the American Statistical Association,* Dec. 1951, p. 411.

17 *Ibid.,* pp. 120–121.

18 Elizabeth E. Hoyt *et al., American Income and Its Use* (Harper, 1954), p 133.

19 Miller, *Income of the American People,* p. 122.

20 *Ibid.,* p. 133.

21 *Survey of Current Business,* 35 (March 1955), p. 20.

22 Editors of *Fortune* magazine, *op. cit.,* pp. 67–68.

23 Social security payments, which characteristically go to lower income groups, were 15 to 16 times greater in 1955 than in 1935; they accounted for 1.4 per cent of personal income in 1934, 4.0 per cent in 1954. (Epstein, McCamman, and Skolnik, *op. cit.,* p. 6.)

24 Dewhurst *et al., op. cit.,* pp. 379–380, 408.

25 This great dividing point seems to occur at about the fifth year of schooling, according to a study by Melvin Tumin and Arnold Feldman, "Education and Social Status in Puerto Rico," presented at the meetings of the American Sociological Society, September 1955. The army considers those with less than four years of schooling functional illiterates.

26 Robert A. Whitney, quoted in the *New York Times,* June 9, 1955.

27 W. F. Ogburn, "Implications of the Rising Standard of Living in the United States," *American Journal of Sociology,* 60 (May 1955), p. 543.

28 *Ibid.,* p. 546.

29 A. C. Nielsen Company, in a report based on United States Census Data. Reported in the *New York Times,* May 19, 1955.

30 *The Story of Creative Capital* (Wilmington, 1955).

31 Dewhurst *et al., op. cit.,* p. 931.

32 Bernard, *op. cit.,* Chapter 3.

33 Dorothy S. Brady, "Low-Income Families," Hearings before the Subcommittee on Low Income Families of the Joint Committee on the Economic Report, 81st Congress, 1st session, 1950, p. 475.

34 Hadley Cantril, *Public Opinion 1935–1946* (Princeton Univ. Press, 1951), p. 66.

35 Hoyt *et al., op. cit.,* pp. 171–172.

36 A. W. Small and George Vincent, *An Introduction to the Study of Society* (American Book Co., 1894), p. 293.

37 *Ibid.*, p. 294.

38 The Reverend H. H. Hunes, quoted in *Ebony*, August 1955, p. 74.

39 See Chapter 22 for a more detailed discussion of this point.

40 Committee on the Hygiene of Housing, *Standards for Healthful Housing: Planning the Home for Occupancy* (Chicago, Public Administration Service, 1950), p. v.

41 Hoyt *et al., op. cit.*, p. 279.

42 Elenore Smith Bowen, *Return to Laughter* (Harper, 1955), quoted in *Saturday Review*, August 27, 1955, p. 19.

43 Jessie Bernard, "Social Work," in Philip L. Harriman, Joseph S. Roucek, and George B. de Huszar, eds., *Contemporary Social Science*, Vol. 1 (Stackpole, 1953), p. 353.

44 Martin R. Gainsbrugh, "New Horizons in Business Research," in *New Horizons in Business*, p. 99.

45 Paul M. Mazur, "New Horizons in Distribution," *ibid.*, pp. 18–19.

46 The status implications of this fact are elaborated in Chapter 22.

47 Potter, *op. cit.*

48 Hoyt *et al., op. cit.*, p. 249.

49 David Riesman, *The Lonely Crowd* (Yale Univ. Press, 1950).

50 Potter, *op. cit.*, p. 70.

51 This point is considered in more detail in Chapter 17.

52 Hoyt *et al., op. cit.*, p. xx.

53 Arthur Compton, citing Arnold Toynbee, "The Case for Hope," *Saturday Review*, June 18, 1955, p. 47.

II

THE DIMENSIONS

OF

SOCIAL PROBLEMS

T HE THEORY of organization may be said to be a preoccupation of all the sciences, albeit the nature of organization differs markedly in the several specific areas of science. The physicist is interested in the structure of the atom and the molecules and in the way they are related to one another. The chemist is interested in the structure of elements. The biologist studies the organization of cells into organisms; he speaks also of "the web of life," the ecological organization of species with respect to one another; he analyzes aggregation, symbiosis, and parasitism, also.

The social scientist similarly sees such massive forms of organization as the tribe, gens, clan; he sees division of labor; institutions, classes, publics, associations, and face-to-face groups of many kinds. Economists, political scientists, sociologists, and social psychologists are all engaged in research concerning the fundamental nature of organization—formal, informal, conscious, and unconscious.

At one time social organization was explained in terms of a "social contract"; at another, in terms of a "gregarious instinct." Today such explanations are no longer considered necessary, since organization of some kind is considered a *sine qua non* of survival; it is a datum, something we begin with. There could be no human phenomena to study if there were no social organization for human beings to live in. Social scientists begin with the existence of organization and proceed to study the way it functions.

There are many conceptual tools for analyzing social organization. We have selected the two which seem most pertinent and useful for our purposes here, namely role and status. We view social organization as a network of roles. Since the theory of disorganization which we shall use in Part V implies derangement in role networks, it is essential that some theory of organization in terms of role be presented first. Chapter 2 directs itself to this end.

Social organization is also viewed as having the dimension of "height." "Height" implies ranked status, that is, status in a hierarchical sense. Since status changes are closely linked with social disorganization —or, if one prefers, social disorganization with status changes—Chapter 3 is devoted to a consideration of the status aspect of social organization.

Equally essential to our discussion is the concept of stress. Like organization, it, too, is a preoccupation of several disciplines. Medicine, psychology, and psychiatry, as well as the social sciences, each with its characteristic conceptual tools, concern themselves with it. We have built up our analysis of social problems around it. Because we rely so heavily on stress phenomena in our discussion we have devoted Chapter 4 to an overview of the relevant points.

All through Part II, as in Part I, we have to recognize two points of view: the objective or consensual and the subjective or experiential. When we spoke of abundance in Chapter 1, for example, we had the objective, measurable fact of increased levels of living, and also the subjective fact of higher standards for evaluating the levels. When we speak of institutional roles, we are going to have to recognize the objective or consensual definition of roles and also the individual or subjective conception of roles. When we speak of ranked status we are going to have the objectively measurable criteria and also the inwardly experienced ones. And when, finally, we speak of stress, we are going to have to make allowance not only for the objective or actuarial threat, but also for the perceived threat; not only for the consensual value of the object threatened, but also for the subjective value of the object threatened; not only for the objective reaction to the threat, but also for the subjective. The study of social problems, in brief, is both sociological and social-psychological, and Part II attempts to lay the groundwork.

2

The Role Dimension

of

Social Problems

A glance at the Table of Contents of this volume will show how heavily we lean on the concept of role in our analyses. The pathologies described in Part IV are viewed as fulfilling the criteria of social problems primarily because of the way they influence role behavior, and the confusion with respect to family and worker roles described in Part V is accorded weight for similar reasons. Because of this central position of the concept of role we devote this chapter to a brief introductory analysis of it.

Two Conceptualizations of Role

The concept of role has assumed major proportions in recent thinking in the social sciences, especially sociology and social psychology, but there is as yet no complete standardization of usage of the

Two Conceptualizations of Role

Some Distinctions: Role-playing, Role-taking,
Role Performance, and Role-acting

Role Performance and Personality

Role-related Problems

term. Thus it is not always possible to apply the research in one area to analysis of problems in another area. For our purposes we may reduce the several conceptualizations of role to two, one of which is exploited most extensively by social psychologists and one by sociologists. The first is a group-related conceptualization; the second is institution-oriented. Both kinds of role are conceived in terms of the functions they perform, as we shall presently see, and in this sense they are both functional. Both are required for our analysis.

Group-related Roles

It has been found in the laboratory that in any task-oriented group at least three functions must be performed if the group is to succeed. Ideas must be furnished, for one thing, and the interpersonal relationships must be maintained on a friendly basis in order to keep the members cooperative. There must also be leadership.[1] Experimental studies of task-oriented groups have shown that certain individuals tend to assume these several functions spontaneously, that is, without formal selection or even, for that matter, without formal recognition. An "idea-man" emerges to perform the function of supplying ideas for the group to work on. His concentration on the job to be done and the discipline his contribution imposes on the group may create resistance and hostilities in the other members. In order, therefore, to neutralize this resistance and keep the members working together to perform their assigned task, the function of hostility-dispersion must also be performed. The "social-emotional" or "expressive" role is taken over by another member. The leadership function may be performed by either the "idea-man," the social-emotional man, or by someone else.[2]

It is assumed that not only laboratory groups, but also stable real-life groups—boys' gangs, women's clubs, students' fraternities, social sets or cliques—tend to differentiate certain roles, similar if not identical to those which are differentiated in laboratory groups. These group roles have not yet been so thoroughly studied, however, as those in the laboratory. We are only beginning to appreciate the "helping role," which seems to play so large a part in many therapeutic groups. The alcoholic, for example, who helps himself by helping another, finds great resources in such a role. The persons who perform group roles contribute to groups. But the converse of this is also true, namely, *groups contribute to the persons performing roles,* as in the illustration of the alcoholic. The success of a group often depends, in part, upon its ability to furnish a suitable role to every member and the ability of the members to perform suitable roles with satisfaction.

Recent research has found, in fact, that group roles play an enormous part in the functioning of human beings. Group roles play a hitherto unrecognized part in human motivation. Military experience, experience with boys' gangs, with alcoholics, with drug addicts, with sex deviants, with recovered mental patients, with older men and women, have all pointed to the importance of group roles in influencing behavior. We are only now learning how to harness the powerful potential inherent in group roles.

Institutionalized Roles

An institutionalized role, as we shall use the term here, is a prescribed or specified integration of behavior patterns embodied in law, custom, tradition, convention, or other norm, which tells how certain functions are to be performed. Illustrations of institutionalized roles are: wife, mother, husband, father, teacher, pupil, physician, patient, lawyer, client, employer, employee, president, senator, judge, private, lieutenant, and so on. Two analogies may help us visualize the nature of institutionalized roles: an administrative agency and an athletic team.

Let us suppose that a new law has been enacted. An agency has been set up to administer it. The head of the agency has, with help, drawn up an organizational chart. Each position in this chart is—rather cynically, in a sense—known as a "slot." Each slot represents certain jobs that have to be done, or functions that have to be performed, in order that the agency achieve its goal. As the agency begins action it appears that new slots have to be created and new jobs are found that have to be performed. To do some of the work of the Chief Analyst, for example, a slot for Assistant Analyst must later be set up. It is found by experience that much of the work of the Assistant Analyst is clerical and does not require as much training or judgment as that of the Assistant Analyst, so Junior Analyst slots are set up, and later, Analyst Technicians, and so on. As the jobs to be performed increase, new slots are set up for them. It is all conceived in terms of slots or jobs to be performed. Not the individual who performs the job, but the function to be performed is the unit of organization.

The positions on an athletic team may also be thought of as analogous to institutionalized roles. Each member has a specified function to perform; every other member depends upon him to do it. A well organized team operates, as the popular cliché has it, like clockwork.

The above analogies may help us to visualize the institutional role system of any society. An institutionalized role is, figuratively speaking, a job description. But it differs from the usual job description in that it is not necessarily formally codified; it may be unwritten, embedded in the mores or in tradition or custom, crescive rather than enacted in origin.

The essential thing about a role, institutionalized or group, is *that it cannot be performed alone. It must always have a counterpart.* Thus confusion on the part of one role-performer spreads to those who are performing with him. We are surrounded, so to speak, by "prompters" who keep reminding us of our cues, for a role is always part of a relationship. Robinson Crusoe performed no role until his man Friday appeared. After that, both had roles, complementary to one another. A role is never a one-man performance, a solo, or monologue. It can never be performed in isolation: it must always be performed with respect to complementary roles, although, of course, the persons performing the complementary roles do not have to be physically present at all times.

Some Distinctions: Role-playing, Role-taking, Role Performance, and Role-acting

Because of the confusion which still characterizes role terminology,[3] we present here four terms to refer to quite different phenomena for which separate words are required: role-playing, role-taking, role performance, and role-acting. Role-playing is a diagnostic and therapeutic technique in which individuals are assigned certain roles to play in a specified situation and their behavior analyzed by trained observers.[4] On the basis of such observations it is often possible to determine how people will behave in social roles outside the laboratory. Role-playing is often educational to participants also; industry has found, for example, that sociodrama, in which a foreman plays the role of worker, is often helpful in increasing the foreman's insight and understanding.

Closely related to role-playing, but occurring in real life and often imaginatively, is role-taking. When one "takes" a role one puts oneself in another person's position to gain insight into the way the world looks to him in order to perform better one's own role vis-à-vis the other person. In common parlance, we put ourselves in the other person's shoes. The ability thus to take the role of other persons is believed to be closely related to good "social adjustment," and inability, with paranoid disorders.

It is a widely accepted postulate that the more roles in a person's behavior repertory, the "better" his social adjustment—other things being equal. Cameron and Margaret [*Behavior Pathology* (Houghton Mifflin, 1951)] have argued most convincingly that the absence of role-taking skills is influential in the development of paranoid disorders.[5]

We make a distinction between "performing" a role and "acting" a role, finally, to point up the difference between what the psychologists call "internalizing" the norms of our society and merely doing what we are supposed to do. Performing a role means that one performs a certain function in a group or does what one is supposed or expected to do in certain institutionalized role relationships without too much conflict. When all is going well we are not even aware of our role or that we are not just behaving "naturally" or "spontaneously." We and the role have, in effect, coalesced. But sometimes, as we shall presently point out, there is some conflict between our "selves" and our roles. We may, out of respect or fear of our fellows, try to do what the role specifies, but our actions are superficial, "hypocritical," artificial, even contrived.[6] We "act" rather than "perform" our roles.

In addition to these distinctions we shall find another one useful in our discussion, namely, that between "role definition" and "role conception." The first refers to the consensual specifications for a role as laid down in law, custom, mores, and other norms. The second refers to the way the individual interprets this definition. Institutions define roles; individuals conceive them in idiosyncratic ways. Individuals may differ among themselves in the way they conceive their roles even when these conceptions are based on the same institutional definitions.

Role Performance and Personality

Performance of group roles is probably closely related to the personality of those who perform them; it may almost be said that the personality selects, or even that it creates, its role. The performance of institutionalized roles, on the other hand, is theoretically independent of the personality of the person performing them. Actually, of course, there is no such independence. People color their role performance with their individuality. There are many ways of performing standard roles. Anyone who has seen the same play performed by different actors has found that the actors can almost remake the play according to the way they interpret the script. Shylock, for example, was originally played as a comic character; today he is the epitome of tragedy. The same lines may be spoken seriously or sarcastically. Old-fashioned melodramas, originally "tear-jerkers," are played today for laughs. Thus institutionalized roles also take on the coloring of those who perform them. So long as the functions assigned to the role are performed, such individuality is permitted, and people performing complementary roles learn how to accommodate their own performances. Indeed, if a certain amount of leeway were not permitted in the performance of roles an abnormal amount of stress might be generated. We are not to think of roles, therefore, as rigid straitjackets. A certain amount of slack is required to make them fit different kinds of people.

To make provision for the different ways different people perform specific roles some students distinguish *personal roles* in addition to functional roles—group-related or institutionalized roles. Actually these so-called personal roles are modifications of institutionalized roles; they are ways of trimming institutionalized roles to fit the individual performing them. One author has likened the institutionalized role to a script and the personal role to ad-libbing.

The distinction between cultural [or institutionalized] and personal family roles can be illustrated by assuming that for each role there is a script. In the case of cultural roles for women and other family members the scripts are uniform, like military manuals. In the old days a woman, upon marriage, took up the wife-and-mother role, scanned her script, and acted much as did other women playing from identical scripts. The counterpart of the personal family role is the behavior termed ad libbing. The actor in modern family dramas says in effect, "Yes, there are various scripts to choose from but since none quite suit me, I will ad lib when I please." A wife, for example, admits that in her script is written the duty to provide meals for her husband, but suddenly ad libs, "On Saturday night John has to take me out for dinner." Obviously it takes more than one person and more than one role to make a play. Personal roles come from unique family dramas in which others play personal roles. Parents confused and frustrated by mixed and blurred scripts begin to ad lib and thus confuse other members of the cast, including their children, who in turn ad lib.[7]

Although the kind of ad-libbing referred to above can, up to a certain point, act as a stress-reducing force, beyond this it can easily become a "stress-trap." The script goes by the boards, and the end result may be great confusion. In brief, if the role is too rigidly defined to allow for a variety of ways of performance, it can become a stress factor because it "goes against the grain" of people; but if it is too permissively or indistinctly defined—if too much ad-libbing is allowed—it can also become a stress factor by producing conflict in the performers and depriving them of the security of knowing what to expect from others. In the first case we have what we shall call "role impairment," in the other, "role confusion." Both may have untoward consequences.

Role-related Problems

There are in general three kinds of role-related problems. In one we assume a set of stable and clear-cut roles; the problem arises from impairment in role performance because of something in the make-up of the individual performer. In the second we assume competent people, willing and able to perform roles adequately; the problem now arises from confusion in the role structure of the society. In the third, there is either violation of institutionalized roles or the roles themselves are illegal. For lack of better terminology we label the first kind of problem "role impairment," [8] the second kind "role confusion," and the third, "role violation." [9]

Role Impairment

If everyone were assigned a suitable role, which he could perform with comfort and satisfaction, and if roles were clear-cut, stable, and congruent, there would be a minimum amount of anxiety associated with role. But this situation probably never prevails anywhere. Even under ideal conditions, as we shall see in Chapter 4, a certain amount of anxiety is generated in the individual in the course of normal socialization. But for some individuals the threats and consequent anxiety are minimal. They live in times and places which provide "scripts" they can act out with satisfaction. They learn how to perform their roles with comfort and ease; they fit their roles; there is little if any threat or anxiety involved. They are the "natural-born" mothers or "natural-born" fathers.

There are others, however, who find it difficult or impossible to perform at least certain kinds of roles. They are the square pegs in round holes. In some cases it is a matter of mere lack of skill or knowledge which, theoretically, could be remedied by training or education. In other cases, however, it is a matter of temperamental or constitutional *incongruence between role and individual*. In such situations people may chafe at the restrictions imposed upon them. They may "act out" their roles scrupulously; they do what is expected of them in their several roles. But at great cost, for there is some incompatibility between their "natural" selves and their roles.[10] Sometimes the anxiety generated by this incompatibility may accumulate for years and finally culminate in escapes of one kind or another.[11] The Parisian banker suddenly leaves his position and family and goes off to the South Seas to paint. Or the conservative wife of a famous aviator goes away to a distant island to find herself.[12] The friction between temperament or physical endowment and role demands varies from individual to individual, being minimal in some, intolerable in others.

In some cases the performance of role functions may be impaired *because people are ill*. They cannot carry on their expected activities.

(Often such people are assigned the role—or, rather, status—of patient instead of their usual role.) At the present time the characteristic illnesses which impair role behavior tend to be those of physical deterioration rather than, as in the past, of infection or malnutrition.

Sometimes the illness is "mental" in nature. Here role disturbance may be maximal. People may give up trying or never even try to act out their roles, or they may distort them or violate them to a dangerous extent. We call these cases "role pathologies."

And, finally, some people cannot perform roles, *because of mental inadequacy*. They just do not have the ability to do what is expected of normal people. Unless sheltered roles are designed for them, they, too, may become dangerous.

Since roles are always units or elements in a configuration of relationships, parts of a "cast," the failure of any one person to perform his role immediately impairs the role performance of those in his role network or cast. Others must take over the failing person's roles. New threats and anxieties are generated all around. Role impairment may thus be both "cause" and "effect" of stress; it may, that is, be either a reaction to stress factors or itself a stress factor.

Role Confusion

In general we may distinguish three kinds of role confusion: one results from lack of clarity in definition of the role, one results from conflict among the several roles a person must perform, and one results from "rolelessness," or absence of any accepted role at all.

LACK OF CLARITY IN ROLE DEFINITION. In a stable society, where change is so slow that to all intents and purposes it hardly occurs at all for any one generation, roles have a chance to "jell." There is consensus about what constitutes a "good father" or a "good mother," and so on. The role definitions or role conceptions are widely accepted; they are conceived in the same way by everyone. Nor are there many alternatives or choices. There is only one way to be a "good" father or mother. People are not confused about their roles; the script is clearly written. Little ad-libbing or improvisation is permitted. Whether or not people perform their roles well is another question, one we discussed above under impairment of role performance; they know, in general, what is expected of them. To this extent they are secure against anxiety.

But in dynamic and heterogeneous societies such *role clarity is by no means common*. Complexity brings with it many possible ways of performing almost any role. Except for a central core of role specifications much ad-libbing or improvisation is not only permitted but often required; the script is not spelled out.

What, for example, are the exact obligations of family members to one another today? of adult children toward their elderly parents? of parents to adolescent children? What, further, are the obligations of employers? of employees? of workers to one another? Millions of modern Americans would like to know. For not knowing creates a great deal of anxiety, not only in the person involved but, because of the interrelationships of roles, in those who perform complementary roles also. There is uncertainty about the roles of mother, father, husband, wife, son, daughter, employee, employer, and so on. Complementary roles cease to function smoothly as a unit. As a result, some people are never certain just what is expected of them and just what they can expect from others.

Since role definitions differ in different parts of the world and in different status levels, mobility—both geographical in the form of migration and social in the form of rising in the status hierarchy—may also become a source of anxiety. Parents and children may cease to have security in their relationships with one another when each is performing according to scripts written for different areas or different classes.

CONFLICT AMONG ROLES. Even when roles are clear in themselves, there may be conflict among them. "Stress may . . . result from frictions produced by the various, and sometimes incompatible, roles an individual has to play in his society, and by other 'stress-traps' in his culture, such as the conflicting norms and codes that spring from crosscurrents within the social milieu." [13] The role of worker may be quite clear; the role of wife may be quite clear; but there may be an inherent conflict between them.[14] Or there may be a conflict between institutionalized and group-related roles.[15] People find themselves acting in half a dozen dramas at the same time, hero in one, servant in another, character part in a third. Such role conflict may be a major factor in generating anxiety.

"ROLELESSNESS." Abundance has the effect in some cases of depriving people of any acceptable role whatsoever, and this can be the most anxiety-generating situation of all. There are no suitable roles for them. They are left out. They do not belong. The plight of older members of our society, for example, has been characterized as one of just such "rolelessness."

Society assigns to older persons in retirement what may be called a "role less" role. They are presumed to give up activity and be resigned to passivity.

Three reactions of older persons to this public attitude are: acceptance by some of the role of passivity, action by others to maintain or to regain an honorific position in society, and attempts by a third group to redefine the role of the retired person. Four of these new active roles are: reversion to a second adolescence in terms of having "a good time"; traveling as an expression of restlessness and mobility; excessive and feverish activity; and creativity.[16]

A similar diagnosis might well be made with respect to the adolescent in our society who has, by means of child labor laws, been kept from worker roles, as we shall suggest in Chapter 18. Even the middle-aged middle-class woman may find herself without roles. And the possibility that automation may deprive them of their roles is a source of anxiety to many workers.

When, for whatever reason, many people are deprived of work roles, we have what might be considered a kind of pathology. Such situations have occurred many times in human history because of technological or economic changes which forced people from the land or caused unemployment. And the fear of unemployment is probably a major source of anxiety even in an age of abundance.

Role Violation and Other Role Anomalies

Some types of criminal acts are merely symptoms of pathologies. The people who perform them are not normal. But other types of criminal acts are performed by people just as normal as anyone else. Crime is not in these cases a symptom of illness. It is role violation by people as normal as the total population. They violate trusts, they bribe, they may even kill, or hire others to kill.

In addition, there are certain anomalies which must also be considered. Some roles are illegal. Furnishing sex partners, operating gambling establishments, supplying narcotics—these are functions forbidden by law. They are institutionalized outside the law by crescive norms. The persons who perform them are criminals. They, like role violators, also constitute social problems.

Two Examples of Role-related Problems

Our concern in this book is primarily with two kinds of roles, namely family roles and worker roles. We close our introductory discussion here with an illustration of each kind, reminding the reader that most of the rest of the book is devoted to an elaboration of problems associated with family and worker roles in our society today.

The first example illustrates how changing sex roles have affected even the physiology of the human body; it deals with sex shifts in certain illnesses.

The phenomenon of sex shifts probably provides a statistical indication of the changes that have taken place in the "personality type" of sexes as a result of the social changes that led to "female emancipation" and to the "rise of the new woman." Thus certain of the psychosomatic affections which in the nineteenth century had preponderated in females (e.g. peptic ulcer, exophthalmic goiter, and perhaps essential hypertension) during the twentieth century occurred increasingly in males; whereas others that had preponderated in males (e.g. diabetes) occurred increasingly in females. These changes in sex incidence suggest, among other things, a developing neutralization in the psychological aspects of sexual distinction in that the personality type of males was apparently becoming in some ways more "feminine" and that of females more "masculine" than were their respective types in the nineteenth century.[17]

For millions of men and women the role confusion they must adjust to does not reach the level where it reflects itself in the physiology of their bodies; but it is great enough to generate a considerable amount of anxiety just the same.

The second example deals with the roles of the worker. In the 20th century role problems in the worker's life have come to vie with labor-management relations as a source of anxiety. The so-called "human-relations-in-industry" school of thought argues that more than wage increases is required to satisfy workers; they must have recognition as human beings also. They must derive satisfactions from the performance of their roles as workers. Union leaders agree that recognition as human beings is important; indeed, they argue that one of the most important rewards of unionism is precisely the feeling of value which membership imparts to the workers by giving them role satisfactions. The role basis of the workers' dissatisfactions has been elaborated by one industrial researcher as follows:

. . . the individual worker . . . has suffered a profound loss of security and certainty in his actual living and in the background of his thinking. For all of us the feeling of security and certainty derives always from assured membership of a group. If this is lost, no monetary gain, no job guarantee, can be sufficient compensation. Where groups change ceaselessly as jobs and mechanical processes change, the individual inevitably experiences a sense of void, of emptiness, where his fathers knew the joy of comradeship and security. And in such situations, his anxieties—many, no doubt, irrational or ill-founded—increase and he becomes more difficult both to fellow workers and to supervisor.[18]

Indeed, this author argues that these role problems—how to work in groups, how to cooperate, how to re-establish disintegrated role relationships in industrial enterprises—constitute "the social problems" of an industrial civilization.

The concept of role, then, both group and institutional, is one of the major sociological tools we shall use in our analyses. Later we shall apply three criteria—humanitarian, utilitarian, and dysfunctionality—to role impairment and role confusion and find that they do, indeed, constitute social problems. Before we do this, however, we turn to another concept of equal importance for our analyses, that of status.

NOTES

1 Robert F. Bales and Philip E. Slater, "Role Differentiation in Small Decision-Making Groups," in Talcott Parsons and Robert F. Bales, *Family, Socialization and Interaction Process* (Free Press, 1955), pp. 259–306; Philip E. Slater, "Role Differentiation in Small Groups," *American Sociological Review*, 20 (June 1955), pp. 300–310.

2 Other formulations of functional group roles are: opinion-giver, orienter, encourager, hostile critic, aggressor, and the like (K. D. Benne and P. Sheats, "Functional Roles of Group Members," *Journal of Social Issues*, 4 [1948], pp. 41–50). Also, initiator, coordinator, director, which correspond fairly closely to "idea-man," expressive role, and leader in the Bales-Slater formulation (Theodore R. Sarbin, "Role Theory," in Gardner Lindzey, ed., *Handbook of Social Psychology*, Vol. 1 [Addison-Wesley, 1954], pp. 232).

3 Walter Coutu, "Role-Playing vs. Role-Taking, an Appeal for Clarification," *American Sociological Review*, 16 (April 1951), pp. 180–187.

4 Nelson N. Foote and Leonard S. Cottrell, *Identity and Interpersonal Competence: A New Direction in Family Research* (Univ. of Chicago Press, 1956).

5 Sarbin, *loc. cit.*

6 Role-acting of this kind has been institutionalized in the East in the form of "ketman": "It is hard to define the type of relationship that prevails between people in the East otherwise than as acting, with the exception that one does not perform on a theater stage but in the street, office, factory, meeting hall, or even the room one lives in. Such acting

is a highly developed craft that places a premium upon mental alertness. Before it leaves the lips, every word must be evaluated as to its consequences. A smile that appears at the wrong moment, a glance that is not all it should be can occasion dangerous suspicions and accusations. Even one's gestures, tone of voice, or preference for certain kinds of neckties are interpreted as signs of one's political tendencies." (Czeslaw Milosz, *The Captive Mind* [Vintage, 1955], p. 51.)

7 Clifford Kirkpatrick, *The Family as Process and Institution* (Ronald, 1955), p. 183.

8 We speak of "role impairment" rather than "nonconformity" or "deviation" in our analyses because of the implications which have come to inhere in the last-named terms. At mid-century there was much concern being expressed that too much insistence on conformity was dangerous, that there was not enough recognition of the importance of nonconformity. The term "deviation" had come to be associated with communist heterodoxy or even heresy.

9 Chapters 8–14 deal with role impairment, including role pathologies; Chapters 15–20 with role confusion; and Chapter 21 with role violation.

10 Sarbin, *loc. cit.*

11 Leo W. Simmons and Harold G. Wolff, *Social Science in Medicine* (Russell Sage Foundation, 1954), p. 85.

12 Anne Morrow Lindbergh, *Gift from the Sea* (Pantheon, 1955).

13 Simmons and Wolff, *op. cit.*, p. 41.

14 Clifford Kirkpatrick has pointed out that the conflict between the role of women

as mother and as worker is basic to what he calls "the woman's problem," which he defines as "a lack of balance between woman's reproductive function and her work function, so complicated by individual differences and public opinion that there is confusion and unhappiness for herself and others." (*Op. cit.*, pp. 165–166; see also Chap. 8.)

15 Samuel A. Stouffer and Toby Jackson, "Role Conflict and Personality," *American Journal of Sociology*, 56 (March 1951), pp. 395–406.

16 E. W. Burgess, "The 'Roleless' Role of the Retired Older Person," paper read at the meetings of the American Sociological Society, September 1955.

17 James L. Halliday, *Psychosocial Medicine* (Norton, 1948), p. 66.

18 Elton Mayo, *The Social Problems of a Industrial Civilization* (Harvard Univ. Press, 1945), p. 76.

3

The Status Dimension

of

Social Problems

Status as an Aspect of Role

The term "status" is used in two quite different ways,[1] both of which are of special relevance to our discussion of social problems. We shall find these two kinds of status phenomena associated with many of the problems dealt with in this volume. We have already noted the increasing emphasis on status in our discussion of rising standards. We shall, in addition, find status a source of anxiety; we shall find it related to role pathologies; we shall find it used to interpret juvenile delinquency; we shall find it an integral part of the problems associated with age; we shall find it central in many work-related problems; and we shall find it the critical issue in the relationships between and among races and ethnic groups, both at home and throughout the world today. Because of the widespread incidence of status factors in social problems we devote this chapter to a brief outline of their nature.

When the term "status" is used with no qualifying adjective—such

Status as an Aspect of Role

Ranked Status

The Lower Socioeconomic Classes

The Stresses of Equality

as "high" or "low" or "socioeconomic" or "educational"—it has very much the same significance as "role." In fact, in this respect it is sometimes defined as the static or stable aspect of role; or, conversely, role is viewed as the dynamic aspect of status, as status in action, so to speak. Status in such a context refers to a secure position or place within a group. It has the same connotation as "face." Like other terms with the same derivation—"static," "stationary," "stasis," "estate"—the concept of status implies stability. It implies a secure position, however humble. Its most important characteristic is that it does confer this security. The person with status "belongs."

The problems which cluster around status so conceived are very much like those related to group role. In fact, so far as the subjective aspects are concerned, they may be identical. Loss of role may be traumatic primarily because of the resulting loss of status in the group. And such loss of status, as we shall see in our discussion of stress, may be considered worse than loss of life itself.

When mobility is substituted for status as a principle of social organization the repercussions on personality may be traumatic.

Denial of status deprives the individual of one of his deepest psychological needs. Few societies have ever attempted to dispense with it, and most of them have acted to assure the individual of a certain niche in society, even if they were not prepared to offer a minimum wage or a more abundant life. . . . Where status has been publicly renounced, individuals continue to manifest, in a variety of ways, a deep psychological craving for the certitudes which it offers. The hazards and insecurities resulting from absence of status have sometimes caused an impulse. . . . to "escape from freedom". . . .[2]

Status anxiety is said to be one of the most pervasive phenomena of the present time. The present has, indeed, been characterized as "the age of anxiety." We are not anxious about loss of life or limb; much of our anxiety today refers to loss of status. In this sense the problems associated with status security are critical.

Ranked Status

When the term "status" is qualified by such adjectives as "high" or "low" it has a significance almost exactly opposite to that we have just described.[3] There is now an implication of mobility, of change, rather than stability. Invidious distinctions are now implied.

The heavy emphasis which America has placed upon mobility. . . . necessitated. . . . [a] rejection of status, for the two are basically contradictory. Whereas the principle of status affirms that a minor position may be worthy, the principle of mobility, as Americans have construed it, regards such a station both as the penalty for and the proof of personal failure. This view is often pushed to a point where even the least invidious form of subordination comes to be resented as carrying a stigma, and certain kinds of work which are socially necessary are almost never performed except grudgingly.[4]

An understanding of the nature of ranked status involves analysis of the following variables: (1) the units involved in the status relationship; (2) the prerogatives or privileges of high status and the penalties of low status; (3) the criteria on which ranked status is allocated, whether functional or nonfunctional, whether ascribed or achieved; (4) the nature of the norms—legal or crescive—which regulate behavior in the several status ranks, and, almost inherent in these norms, (5) the covert or subjective behavior characteristic of the several status ranks.

The Units Involved in Ranked Status Relationships [5]

We may distinguish at least three kinds of units involved in status relationships: individuals in roles; groups; and aggregates. We use the term "individual in role" when referring to the individual in order to distinguish the phenomena which social psychologists describe as dominance and submission from those which the sociologist refers to as status.[6] Nor should ranked status among roles be confused with what psychoanalysts refer to as "feelings of inferiority." [7] It is true, of course, that individuals in different status levels may take advantage of the kind of situation that produces feelings of inferiority in others to enhance the status differential between them.[8] But these personality traits and feelings are not the same as status phenomena. Regardless of personality or feelings of inferiority, the role of employer has higher status than that of employee; that of parent, than that of child; of doctor, than that of patient; of teacher, than of pupil. The status, that is, inheres in the role relationship rather than in the relationship of individuals as such.

In addition to inter-role status, it is becoming common to distinguish *status groups* and *status aggregates;* that is, the units in the status relationship may be groups and aggregates as well as individuals in role relationships.[9] Status groups have some "consciousness of kind"; status aggregates do not. Status aggregates are classifications with respect to certain criteria imposed on the aggregate from the outside, not natural groupings. The outsider classifies people; people group themselves. Everyone with a college education, for example, or with incomes between $5,000 and $7,500 would constitute a status aggregate; but within each of these aggregates there might be many status groups.

One important criterion according to which people group themselves into status groups is their value system. A recent study has suggested time-orientation—to the past, to the present, or to the future—as an insightful classification for values.[10] If people depend on family, lineage, and the achievements of the past they have a great deal in common, whatever their income may be; similarly, those who are looking ahead, whatever their income, have a great deal in common, as have those who live in the present.[11] The accompanying scheme suggests, in a general way, how people tend to group themselves into status groups within any given status aggregate.

Any one of these units—individuals in roles, groups, or aggregates —may have either a superior or an inferior status with reference to any

TABLE 1

STATUS GROUPS BASED ON ORIENTATION TO
PAST, FUTURE, AND PRESENT

Status Aggregates Based on Criterion of Income	Values Oriented to Past	Values Oriented to Future	Values Oriented to Present
Low income	Elderly or retired, "genteel" poor	Young married people, ambitious members of disadvantaged groups	Lower class
Middle income	Marginal or fringe upper class	Middle class	Bohemian class
High income	Upper class	Upper middle class	Fast set, café society

other. For example, a motion-picture star, athlete, general, great scientist, or other outstanding person has high status vis-à-vis the aggregate which we call his "public." He is looked up to. A leader or officer or employer, similarly, has high status vis-à-vis his group, and is looked up to. A teacher has high status vis-à-vis her pupils. But sometimes a member has lower status than the group, as in the case of a servant in a household, a minority-group member of a higher-status group, or a person who "escapes from freedom" by submitting to some totalitarian group. And in the case of criminals, alcoholics, the feeble-minded, the unemployed, and the like, the individual has very inferior status vis-à-vis the total aggregate or public. He is looked down upon. Sometimes a group has higher status than an aggregate, as in professional groups, "old families," and the like; sometimes one group has higher status than another, as in one ethnic group vis-à-vis another. And, finally, one aggregate may have higher status than another: for example, one income grouping as contrasted with another.

Privileges and Penalties of Ranked Status

One of the most important privileges of high status in our society is the improved "life chances" associated with it. Infant mortality, longevity, health, education, occupational mobility, and the like are all associated with status differences.[12] Among the subtler prerogatives and penalties of status are the patterns of interpersonal behavior which may be specified. There may be, for example, servility, obsequiousness, groveling, abjection, fawning, or catering on the part of the inferior. The complementary behavior for the high-status person may include

arrogance, hauteur, or contempt. Or the pattern may be one of adulation on one level and condescension or patronization on the other; or
respectful admiration, even a reverential attitude, on one side and
patronization on the other. We shall have more to say later about the
penalties of low status.

The Criteria on Which Ranked Status Is Based

Some status relationships are inherent in the roles involved. Thus,
for example, the role that has the function of making decisions is inherently or intrinsically superior to the roles that are assigned the function of carrying them out, and the more general the decision, the higher
the status of the role that is entrusted with the function. This principle
of status is independent of culture; it may even on occasion subvert the
cultural principles of status allocation, as when the "power behind the
throne" takes over, relegating the "throne" to inferior status. This
principle is inherent in group structure.

There are, however, other principles of status allocation which
are not independent of culture or inherent in group structure. As a
result, the status of roles may change from time to time. Some healers
of the sick, for example, once had low status; bleeders and surgeons
were grouped with barbers. At the present time doctors and surgeons
have high status. The role of mediator of relationships between man
and God once had the highest status of all; it still has high status, but
by no means as high as in the Middle Ages, for example.

When the criteria on which status is based are such things as age,
sex, race, or lineage, we speak of "ascribed status." If, on the other
hand, status is based on the criterion of individual achievement we call
it "achieved status." In general, group status—which tends to be on the
basis of ethnicity, race, occupation, or lineage—is likely to be ascribed.
Status is assigned to aggregates on the basis of such criteria as income,
education, occupation, residence, consumption patterns or styles of
living, usually achieved or, at least, achievable by individual members.

When status is ascribed it is usually built into the social system,
institutionalized. For the upper-status individual this makes for great
security and the minimization of threat, but for the lower-status individual threats may be very great. The white man may exploit the
colored, the man the woman, the old the young, etc. When status is
allocated on the basis of achievement, however, there is no automatic
alleviation of stress; there may, as we shall see below, even be an increase. Achieved status must be won competitively, with all the stresses
implicit in such testing.[13]

The criteria of status should not be confused with the attributes of different status groups. Criteria are operational, part of the definition. But attributes—high or low IQ, good or poor health, for example—characterize people in the several status categories.

The status characteristics used as criteria may, in addition to being achieved or ascribed, be relatively stable or relatively changeable. Education, for example, although achieved, is relatively fixed. If we classify adults according to number of years of schooling they have had, they tend to remain in the same class the remainder of their lives. Some people, to be sure, do continue their schooling after they become adults, but most do not. Thus the personnel in the several classes based on schooling is fairly fixed. The people who are in one class when they are twenty-five will still be in it at age sixty-five. The same stability marks lineage as a criterion of status. A member of an old family at age twenty-five is still a member at sixty-five.

But income classes—and, correlatively, consumption-based classes—do not have the same stability of personnel. In the United States, at any rate, the common pattern, as we shall see in Chapter 20, is for income status to increase steadily up to middle age or beyond and then to decline. Thus a family which is in one income level at one phase of its life cycle may not be in the same level five or ten years later. There is, in effect, a succession of families sweeping through the several income levels, up and down. The relatively fixed pattern of income distribution commented upon in Chapter 1 does not, therefore, imply that the social structure is correspondingly fixed so far as individual families are concerned.

Nature of the Norms Regulating Ranked
Status Relationships

Some kinds of status are, as we saw above, intrinsic in the roles they are associated with; they are not necessarily institutionalized. Sometimes, furthermore, status is a spontaneous development, as when people exalt a baseball player or a singer or motion-picture star. But in many cases status depends upon institutional definition rather than intrinsic function or spontaneous response. In some societies, for example, certain individuals or groups have privileges because the law says they should have them. The norms regulating status are legal. In other instances, the norms regulating status relationships are crescive, based, that is, on custom and tradition or on the mores. Crescive norms may be stronger and touch human life more intimately than legal norms.

As a legal term, "status" refers to "the sum of the legal capacities of an individual, his powers to enforce legal rights and obligations either for himself or for others." [14] Status in this legal sense of rights and obligations may rest on any of the criteria specified above—age, descent, property ownership, or what-have-you.[15] Over long periods of time, religion, heredity, race, property, and sex have been discarded as bases or criteria for legal status in most advanced countries; there is, for example, in the United States at the present time equal legal status for all adults of sound mind and noncriminal record.

But crescive norms do not always agree with legal norms. There is no legal impediment to Negro residence in certain areas of a city, but Negroes are not privileged to live there. There is no law which forbids Jews to be admitted to certain clubs, but they are not admitted. One student, referring to the treatment of the Mexican-Americans in the Southwest, has said that if the rules that governed the behavior of the majority group were explicitly stated, they would be found to be unconstitutional,[16] as, indeed, the rules with respect to Negro segregation were found to be in 1954. There are no privileged classes in the United States in the sense of official ranks or status; but there are privileged classes in terms of unofficially or crescively enforced rights and obligations.

Since most of the legal battles associated with status have been won, it is in this area of crescively enforced status distinctions that stress situations tend to arise at the present time. Not only, as we saw in Chapter 1, should Negroes not be assigned an inferior legal status, they should not, according to the values made possible in an age of abundance, be made to *feel* inferior by crescively enforced norms. Not only is the Poor Law, which deprived paupers of legal rights, abrogated and replaced by social security laws, but, in an age of abundance, needy people are not to be made to *feel* inferior by crescively enforced norms. Freedom to exclude lower-status individuals, even in private social life, is being questioned.[17] Being made to feel inferior is an unpleasant experience; it is resented; it is associated with lower status. Indeed, it is one of the penalties of low status. And it is coming to be viewed as a kind of cruelty as serious as physical cruelty, if not more so. Hurting people's bodies has long been condemned by law; hurting their feelings, making them lose "face" or status, is coming also to be condemned.[18]

Status-related stress situations of the present are associated with achieved status whereas those of the past were those associated with ascribed status. In a system of ascribed status—on the basis of sex, race, lineage, or age—everyone was protected against the threat of loss of status; but those of lower status were more exposed to exploitation, infringement of liberties, physical cruelty, and death, and those of higher status, to war, intrigue, responsibilities, and the like. In a system of achieved status, the stress factors are likely to be those associated with role failure, inability to succeed, and status insecurity, and the kinds of cruelty are likely to be symbolic rather than physical. Further, if earlier centuries hacked away at legally sanctioned privileges and disabilities, the 20th century is attacking the crescively sanctioned ones, those sanctioned in mores, custom, tradition, and convention. And the attack is not only on the overt expressions of privilege and disability, but also on the subjective and attitudinal concomitants. The drift in an age of abundance is not only toward freeing people from overt acts of discrimination but also toward protecting them from being made to feel inferior.

The Covert or Subjective Behavior Characteristic of the Several Status Ranks

The subjective attitudes which accompany status may be marked by either friendly or unfriendly feeling tone. The high-status person may feel appreciation and satisfaction or contempt and resentment; he may feel affection and *noblesse oblige* or arrogance and hauteur. The low-status person for his part may feel respect, affection, and loyalty, or anger, hostility, and envy. If the basis for the status is spontaneous, the subjective concomitant is likely to be affectionate on the part of the low-status individual. If it is enforced by law the concomitant may become very great hostility.[19]

The discussion of units, privileges and penalties, criteria, norms, and covert behavior which we have just completed is summarized in Table 2 (facing page 66) instead of in paragraph form in order to help the reader see the relationships among them. Not all of these status situations are of equal relevance for our analyses here. It is a matter of great interest to know on what basis high status is ascribed to individuals by aggregates—indeed, these criteria may be taken as some of the most illuminating indexes of the values of a civilization. Sometimes it is great military prowess, or mystic qualities, or athletic talent. Sometimes it is ability to organize industry or to amuse the public.[20] It is also interesting to know on what basis high status is accorded to individuals by groups. And so on through all the units and their relationships.

But some of these status situations are far more relevant for our purposes than others, especially the status relationships among groups, particularly racial and ethnic groups, and among aggregates, particu-

TWO AMERICAN CAPITALISTS TALK THINGS OVER

In our dynamic system of People's Capitalism, nearly everyone's a capitalist, sharing in America's ever-increasing productivity

Are these two American capitalists talking discount rates and inventory turnover? Not on your life! They're more likely to talk about baseball or politics or last night's prize fight.

But, under this new economic system we have in America today—under People's Capitalism—they are just as truly capitalists as anybody you can find on Wall Street.

They own stock. They own life insurance. Their union has a pension fund. In each case their money is invested in the capital that creates his own job. This system needs a new name—because it's not old-fashioned capitalism. Its new name is *People's Capitalism*, because the people own it.

Almost 9,000,000 men and women, in all walks of life, in all parts of the country, own stock in American business.

103,000,000 people own life insurance, a good part of which is invested in stocks and bonds. In addition, savings accounts and pension funds are invested in industry.

American Can Company itself is a good example of People's Capitalism. The capital for Canco's research, for Canco's production of modern containers is provided by 48,000 stockholders. Many of them are employees of Canco, sharing directly in the profits resulting from their own work.

It's this "working for yourself" spirit that makes People's Capitalism grow faster, stronger—produce more for everybody than does any other system the world has ever seen.

AMERICAN CAN COMPANY (CANCO)

In many advertisements status symbols are used to sell automobiles, whisky, travel, and a host of other goods or services. The photograph in the advertisement reproduced above illustrates the middle-class status of a large segment of the American working population today, as well as the aspirations of the rest.

The two columns of copy in the advertisement read as follows:

Are these two American capitalists talking discount rates and inventory turnover? Not on your life! They're more likely to talk about baseball or politics or last night's prize fight.

But, under this new economic system we have in America today—under People's Capitalism—they are just as truly capitalists as anybody you can find on Wall Street.

They own stock. They own life insurance. Their union has a pension fund. In each case their money is invested in American business. So, you see, the wage earner supplies the capital that creates his own job. This system needs a new name—because it's not old-fashioned capitalism. Its new name is *People's Capitalism,* because the people own it.

Almost 9,000,000 men and women, in all walks of life, in all parts of the country, own stock in American business.

103,000,000 people own life insurance, a good part of which is invested in stocks and bonds. In addition, savings accounts and pension funds are invested in industry.

American Can Company itself is a good example of People's Capitalism. The capital for Canco's research, for Canco's production of modern containers is provided by 48,000 stockholders. Many of them are employees of Canco, sharing directly in the profits resulting from their own work.

It's this "working for yourself" spirit that makes People's Capitalism grow faster, stronger—produce more for everybody than does any other system the world has ever seen.

(Courtesy American Can Co.)

larly socioeconomic classes. These two status situations constitute the background of some of the most important social problems today. We shall mention here two of the ways status is related to social problems, namely, the relatively greater incidence of problems in the lower socioeconomic classes, and the stresses which the trend toward equality imposes on group and class relationships.

The Lower Socioeconomic Classes

We spoke above of the privileges of high socioeconomic status, especially the improved "life chances" which go with it. Conversely, there are the penalties or handicaps of low socioeconomic status, especially greater susceptibility to the pathologies we are to discuss in Part IV. The people in low socioeconomic status positions are greatly disadvantaged. Many of them are included among the so-called "slum-dwellers." We shall have more to say about them in Chapter 18. We refer to them here primarily to remind ourselves that the problems associated with slums are often the penalties of low socioeconomic status.

Low income, however, is by no means always identical with low status. We saw in Chapter 1 that the composition of the lowest fifth of the income structure is quite atypical. There are many unattached individuals in it; there are many older persons; there are families without earners; there are families suffering from the illness, disability, or unemployment of their earners; there are families headed by females or by individuals of disadvantaged racial or ethnic backgrounds. There are also young people just beginning, who can confidently anticipate greatly increased income with the passage of time. These young people, assigned to the low-income class on the basis of income, have few if any of the attributes of many others in the same class. They are not likely to show the same kinds of problems as the others we have listed.

The following analysis of low-income families at midcentury illustrates how complex the attributes of this class can be and why studies in which income alone is taken as a criterion of status so frequently show inconclusive results.

Low income consumer units do not consist of families that, except for the size of their incomes, are a representative cross section of the population. . . . For instance, there are included at the bottom of the size distribution consumer units that were not in existence during the entire year. . . . A young person who graduates from school in June, finds a job some time in the second half of the year, and sets up residence apart from his family, is a case in point. He is included in the size distribution in the income bracket corresponding to his part year income. But the smallness of this income is in no way evidence of poverty. Young couples establishing themselves in independent households during the year similarly affect the statistics. It is likely that ample earnings opportunities, high marriage and birth rates, and progressive alleviation of the housing shortage during the postwar years, as manifested in the high rate of new consumer unit formation, have given rise to a substantial number of low income units of this type. . . . A far higher proportion of unattached individuals is at the low end of the income scale. . . . A substantial number of aged and retired couples can be found at the lower end of the income scale. . . . It should also be remembered that there is a considerable turnover in the low income brackets. Many consumer units are thrown into these brackets as the result of short-run vicissitudes such as temporary sickness, unemployment, or business reverses. To many others— young people starting out in economic life—a low income status represents the bottom rung of the economic ladder which they confidently hope to ascend. While genuine privation may be involved in many of these cases, they nevertheless differ significantly from those that represent a chronic low income core.[21]

It is this chronic low-income core that is likely to constitute a large part of many of the social problems we shall discuss in Parts IV and V.

But even those who rise out of this low socioeconomic status do not thereby escape status stresses, for there are stresses of equality no less than of inequality.

The Stresses of Equality

In Chapter 1 we discussed the powerful leveling-up process which has accompanied abundance, pointing out that the net effect has been a movement in the direction of equalizing income, schooling, occupation, and consumption patterns. We did not there attempt to assess the results of this narrowing of status differentials. At this point, however, we point out that equality has its stresses no less than inequality, and they may even be exaggerated. The anxiety-increasing effect of diminishing status differences among people has been described as follows:

The factor of abundance . . . has constantly operated to equalize the overt differences between the various classes [and races] and to eliminate the physical distance between them, without, however, destroying the barriers which separate them. The traditional dissimilarities in social demeanor, in education, in dress, and in recreation made class [and race] distinction in the past seem natural and perhaps, in a pragmatic sense, justifiable, while the social chasm between, for instance, an upper class which attended school and a lower class which did not diminished the element of what might be called "invidious proximity." Where extremes of wealth and poverty, education and ignorance, privilege and exploitation prevail, resentment is directed against these conditions themselves and not against class [or race] distinctions, which are a mere recognition of the conditions. If the poor, the hungry, the ragged, the unlettered man complains, his complaint is not that he is excluded from select society, in his starved, ill-clad, ignorant condition; it is rather that he is denied decent food, decent garments, and a chance to learn. But when, living in a society that practices outward uniformity, he gains a satisfactory income, acquires education, dresses himself and his wife in the standard clothes worn by all the members of the community, sends his children to school—and then finds himself the object of class [and racial] discriminations imposed at close quarters and based upon marginal, tenuous criteria, which are, in any case, probably invisible to his eyes, then the system of classes itself, no longer natural, no longer inevitable, begins to seem unjust and hateful.

If this analysis is accurate, it means that abundance has brought about an entirely new sort of inequality. By diminishing the physical differentials, the social diversity, and the real economic disparities that once separated classes [and races], it has made any class distinction or class stratification seem doubly unfair and discriminatory. In proportion as it has solved the problem of class differentials, it has accentuated the problem of class distinctions.

Thus the goal of social equality in a classless society, which abundance seemed to make possible and which the mobility drive promised to achieve, has been sought at a substantial cost. By presenting an unattainable ideal as if it were a reality, the mobility drive has created damaging psychological tensions; by eliminating class [and racial] diversity without being able to abolish class [and racial] distinctions, abundance has only made subjective discrimination more galling, while making objective differentials less evident.[22]

The kinds of equality which abundance makes possible, then, no less than inequality, have their anxieties. The reduction of status differentials may exacerbate rather than mollify human relations. Unlike income which, by increasing productivity, can be raised in the lower brackets without necessarily lowering that of the upper brackets, ranked status cannot be raised or lowered except by lowering or raising that of others. Because status is always relative, high status is inherently in short supply; there cannot be an abundance of it; it is always in deficit. If one group rises, another must, in relation to it, decline.

When we combine a democratic social system with the existence of status differentials, however reduced, so that all children are permitted and expected to compete for high status on the basis of achievement, we probably maximize the possibility of anxiety. In a stratified society with fixed status, the talented person in low-status position is penalized: he is given no opportunity to rise to the level of his abilities. On the other hand, in a mobile society, with status achievable rather than ascribed, the person of average ability is penalized if he happens to be born into a low-status position, for he is expected to compete and succeed even against odds. As it affects the child, one student has analyzed the situation as follows:

The child in America is undoubtedly evaluated, to a greater degree than in most other societies, as an individual. But this does not take us out of the realm of invidious status distinctions. It takes us, rather, to a consideration of another status system, one in which children of different social levels may be and are directly compared in terms of the same set of "achieved" criteria. In this status system children of any social class may compete with one another and in this sense it is democratic. The cards are not dealt and the hands all played for him before the child appears on the scene. However, this democracy has certain important implications. To the degree that ancestry as such is scrupulously ignored, it means that any child may be legitimately compared, to his advantage or his loss, with any other child of the same age and sex. The child's "status universe," the people against whom he is measured and against whom he measures himself, is enormously extended. In "undemocratic" feudal and peasant societies, it is assumed that society is permanently divided into natural social divisions or orders. Corresponding to each of these orders is a different set of expectations or standards for evaluation of persons. The child of a peasant family is not "ego-involved" in his differences from the landlord's son. They are in different status universes.

In a society like ours, however, in which a child may be legitimately compared, *in terms of the same criteria,* with "all comers" regardless of family background, it does not follow that the ability to achieve these criteria is necessarily distributed without regard to family background and social class. Systematic class-linked differences in the ability to achieve will relegate to the bottom of the status pyramid those children belonging to the most disadvantaged classes, not by virtue of their class position as such but by virtue of their lack of the requisite personal qualifications resulting from their class-linked handicaps. In short, where opportunities for achievement are class-linked, status discontent will be generated to the degree that the status system is democratic, to the degree that the status universe is maximized.

· · · ·

The existence of "achieved" as well as "ascribed" criteria of status for children makes it possible for some working-class children to "rise above" the status to which the social class position of their parents would otherwise consign them. However, this does not make the situation psychologically any easier for those of their brethren who remain behind, or rather, below. Low achieved status is no pleasanter than low ascribed status, and very likely a good deal more unpleasant, for reasons we have indicated earlier; it reflects more directly on the personal inadequacy of the child and leaves him with fewer convenient rationalizations.[23]

The stresses of equality take their toll in race relations also. Thus one psychiatrist accounts for the higher mental illness rate among Negroes than among whites as a result of the rise of the Negro to middle-class levels without the security which accompanied his old status.

The Negro in Virginia is far better off economically and legally than ever before, but he is more closely segregated. He has lost the security of his own culture and is moving rapidly toward a middle-class white culture. This period of uncertainty and close segregation parallels the increase in the rate of Negroes admitted to the state mental hospitals of Virginia.[24]

So much, then, for the status dimension of social problems at this point. It will appear again and again throughout our discussion in the following pages. But before we continue, we must introduce still another concept which is basic to a thoroughgoing analysis of social problems, namely, stress.

NOTES

1 A third use of the term "status" is not relevant to our discussion here. It is used as a basis for classifying people into categories. In this sense we speak of employment status, citizenship status, mobility status, marital status, dependency status, and the like. It tells us in which pigeonhole any specific case falls.

2 David M. Potter, *People of Plenty, Economic Abundance and the American Character* (Univ. of Chicago Press, 1954), p. 106.

3 Sometimes a connotation of rank is implied even in the static conception of status. The term "esteem"—high or low—has been suggested to convey the invidious judgment made on good or bad role performance in any status, high or low. See Kingsley Davis, *Human Society* (Macmillan, 1949), pp. 93–94.

4 *Ibid.*, p. 105.

5 High-status units are sometimes called "elites." For an acute analysis of "the power elite," see the book of this name by C. Wright Mills (Oxford Univ. Press, 1956). The author analyzes groups who have high status in our society, namely: local society, metropolitan society, celebrities, the very rich, top executives, the corporate rich, military leaders, and political leaders. From his analyses it is clear that the existence of such elites poses problems, but they are moral and political rather than social problems.

6 Psychologists distinguish a personality trait which they measure on an instrument, the so-called A-S (ascendance-submission) test (Gordon W. Allport, "A Test for Ascendance-Submission," *Journal of Abnormal and Social Psychology*, 23 [July–Sept. 1928], pp. 120–121). This A-S test was incorporated in the well-known Bernreuter Personality Inventory. Ascendance seemed to be associated with feelings of superiority, of competence, of self-confidence; submission, with the opposite (A. H. Maslow, "Dominance, Personality, and Social Behavior in Women," *Journal of Social Psychology*, 10 [Feb. 1939], pp. 3–39).

7 A king, for example, may have feelings of inferiority—as, indeed, King George VII of England is alleged to have had—and a menial worker may have none at all. Feelings of inferiority tend to occur in normal people when they are in situations they are not qualified to deal with as well as others, or which they are unprepared to handle in the presence of others who are prepared. One experimenter, for example, matched children in play situations. Children who were originally submissive or lacking in dominance in a play situation were coached

in the use of new play materials. They were then paired with children originally dominant but who had not been coached in the use of new play materials. At first the formerly submissive children waited for the formerly dominant children to take the initiative and assume dominance. But when they saw that the children did not know how to use the play material they stepped in and assumed a superior position. They did not act—or, presumably, feel—inferior or submissive in the situation when they knew how to deal with it and the others did not. (George D. Stoddard, "The Educability of Emotional Behavior," *Educational Record* [April 1938], p. 165.)

8 Thus a woman of high status may make another woman feel inferior by displaying her own *savoir-faire* in a social situation and the other woman's lack of it. A favorite theme in literature is one in which a person of low status is given an opportunity to feel superior to a person of high status, as for example, in James Barrie's *Admirable Crichton*.

9 The culmination of years of sociological discussion with respect to the nature of status, especially as related to social class, is summarized by Harold W. Pfautz in "The Current Literature on Social Stratification: Critique and Bibliography," *American Journal of Sociology*, 58 (Jan. 1953), pp. 391–418; and Gregory P. Stone and William H. Form, "Instabilities in Status: the Problem of Hierarchy in the Community Study of Status Arrangements," *American Sociological Review*, 18 (April 1953), pp. 149–162.

10 W. Lloyd Warner and James C. Abegglen, *Big Business Leaders in America* (Harper, 1955), pp. 123–136. The present discussion does not follow the analyses presented by these authors; it was, however, suggested by them.

11 It is interesting to speculate what widespread adoption of a guaranteed annual wage might do to the time-orientation of classes who are now paid on an hourly basis.

12 These are summarized in Jessie Bernard, *American Family Behavior* (Harper, 1942), Chapter XIV. They were dramatized during the sinking of the "Titanic" when despite the "women-and-children-first" rule, the rate of loss of children in the third class was higher than that of men in the first class (Walter Lord, *A Night to Remember* [Holt, 1955]). It is interesting to note that differentials

analogous to those amongst human beings have also been noted among animals. The kind of rank observed among subhuman animals is individual, not governed by institutional rules; although it is stable, it has to be proved at all times. That is, it is not inherited. It is based on individual prowess in a limited area. It may become habitual for animals to accept the dominance of other animals, but the offspring of these non-dominant animals do not inherit this habit. Rank among animals is certainly a social phenomenon, but it is not a sociological one in the sense of being an institutionalized phenomenon. Still it is interesting to note that "information is accumulating to suggest that an animal's social rank may modify many of its activities and perhaps its productivity. Among factors reported to be affected by social status under certain conditions are rate of growth, egg production, milk production, mating activity, and number of offspring sired" (E. B. Hale, "Social Factors in Sexual Behavior of Turkeys," Progress Report 108, Sept. 1953, Pennsylvania State University School of Agriculture, Agricultural Experiment Station, p. 1). It also has been found that fowl "generalize" status relationships. That is, if a member of Species A is dominated by a member of Species B, it will take a submissive position with regard to other members of Species B, even without individual experience with the others. The Species A member, that is, "stereotypes" all members of Species B as "dominant." With limited numbers, say up to 12 or 15, it has been possible to create "classes" among fowl on the basis of these generalizations of individual experience, so that all members of Species A take a submissive position with respect to all members of Species B (unpublished study by E. B. Hale).

13 For a discussion of some of the stresses of competition, see Jessie Bernard, *American Community Behavior* (Dryden, 1949), Chapter 5.

14 Max Radin, "Status," *Encyclopaedia of the Social Sciences*, XIV (Macmillan, 1934), 373.

15 In Greece and in Rome there were official gradations in legal rights and obligations according to citizenship status. When these were found to be awkward to administer they were abolished and replaced by status ranks of *honoratiores* and *humiliores*. Under the feudal sys-

tem, three status levels or classes were recognized: the free, the half free, and the slave, in addition to administrative officials, great landowners, and the clergy. It was not until the 17th and 18th centuries that "a real break in the medieval idea of elaborate classifications and minute discriminations was initiated" (ibid., p. 376).

16 Ruth D. Tuck, Not With the Fist: A Study of Mexican-Americans in a Southwest City (Harcourt, Brace, 1946), pp. 90–91.

17 See the symposium, "Segregation and Integration in College Fraternities," in Social Problems, 2 (Jan. 1955), pp. 129–175.

18 See, for example, the Supreme Court decision, quoted in Chapter 22.

19 Strictly speaking, it is hardly correct to speak of subjective attitudes with reference to aggregates, since the aggregate has no self-conscious existence. The behavior of the aggregate is the sum of that of a large number of individuals and is not to be thought of as self-conscious. Sometimes an aggregate may be transformed into a group, as when a movie star's "public" organizes into "fan clubs."

20 Leo Lowenthal, "Biographies in Popular Magazines," in Radio Research 1942–1943, P. F. Lazarsfeld and Frank Stanton, eds. (Duell, Sloan and Pearce, 1943), pp. 507–520.

21 Supplement to the Survey of Current Business: Income Distribution in the United States, United States Department of Commerce, Office of Business Economics, 1953, pp. 5–6.

22 David M. Potter, op. cit., pp. 102–103.

23 Albert K. Cohen, Delinquent Boys (Free Press, 1955), pp. 85–86, 112.

24 David C. Wilson, quoted in Southern School News, June 1956, p. 13.

4

The Stress Dimension

of

Social Problems

The Concept of Stress

The concept of stress has come into vogue primarily in the study of disease, but it seems to offer promise of value in analyzing other kinds of situations also. We expand the concept somewhat, therefore, to include a wider range of responses than is usual.

In general we may define a stress situation as one involving threat; and we break it down into three component elements: (1) the stress factor, which threatens, (2) the value which is being threatened, and (3) the reactions, individual and collective, to the threat. This breakdown is purely for analytical purposes; in real life, stress situations occur as unitary wholes, not as separate elements.[1]

Sources of Stress Factors

Stress factors or threats may originate either outside or inside any particular social system. Those originating outside the social system

70

The Concept of Stress

The Changing Components of Stress Situations

Illustrative Stress Situations in an Age of Abundance

may, in turn, arise within the individual's own body as a result of biological processes—such as maturation or aging, the growth of extraneous tissues, and the like—or they may arise in nature. The latter include inadequate food supply, hostile climate, micro-organisms, drought, famine, invasion of insects, and similar natural catastrophes.[2] Modern science has been most successful in handling threats from these two sources.

Also outside the social system, but not in exactly the same category as nature, is the threat which results from conflict, that is, from "the opposition of a large alien group, which threatens the integrity of the other by force or by its sheer size and immediate presence."[3] Change, in and of itself, may constitute a threat: "New situations creating problems of adaptation not provided by traditional solutions to social problems may set in motion anxiety drives. Examples of such situations are sudden environmental changes, including contact with alien groups."[4]

But some, and for our purposes perhaps the most important, stress factors or threats are generated by the social system itself. In the first place, a certain amount of threat is implicit in the very process of socialization, "by which the individual as a biological creature with limited endowments is forced into roles assigned to him by society and pressed into the mold of its culture."[5] As a result of "the inevitable press of standardized socialization techniques" there is always a certain amount of so-called "free-floating" anxiety in most populations.[6]

Status also generates stress, for individuals as well as for groups.

The rankings of one's fellows in relation to oneself are roughly defined as *surrogates* or superordinates, *peers* or equals, and *subordinates*. These are the stationed agents of society in designated positions who react with or act upon the particular individual under consideration. Their relationships to him fall within a range of influence that may run from extremes of domination to abject submission. The surrogates exercise their power of domination by means of sanctions, and the subordinates, reciprocally, acquiesce. What may be called "antagonistic cooperation" operates up and down the line of relationships with the nearest approach to mutual and voluntary cooperation appearing between the individual and his peers, probably because of a wider range of equal powers and common interests.

The actions and reactions of these fellow-group agents, from their stations and with their prerogatives, produce pressures upon the individual. A combination of these can be overwhelming. These interactive relationships constitute the vital societal elements with which an individual must cope and upon which he must rely; first, in his initial helplessness and later on in life in his recurrent intervals of dependence, and, indeed, even in periods of stability and achievement. Thus, the very relationships that sustain him also threaten him and become highly surcharged for him with attitudes of confidence or fear, love or hate, and tendencies to approach or withdraw, to dominate or submit, and many other combinations in social relationships. Particular situations become repetitive and persistent, setting up recurrent stresses that may be manifest in the physiological process. And it is probably trite to emphasize that the cumulative effect of such tensions and physically taxing responses, even though subtle and hidden, can wear down and waste away the resources of the individual, and sometimes even wreck the organism.[7]

There may be, in addition, built-in threats in the social order, as when a privileged group may legally, or with the sanction of custom, tradition, and the mores, kill or enslave or imprison or exploit an underprivileged group at will or capriciously. Many millions of colored persons all over the world live in the shadow of this kind of threat every day of their lives. And in totalitarian regimes many white persons do, too.

Stress factors have differential impact in the several status levels of any given society, for "society imposes stress upon certain of its members as truly as it eases stress and provides security for others," and usually it does this on a status basis, as we saw in Chapter 3. It is important, therefore, to understand the nature of status-related stress factors whether the units involved are groups or aggregates or individuals.

The criteria of status may become "stress-traps," or threats, when they change. The landed aristocracy see themselves losing status in the rise of the *bourgeoisie*. Capital, not land, becomes the criterion of status. "Old families" are "distressed" at the rise of upstarts. Lineage is no longer a criterion of status.[8] A man may suffer a great deal of anxiety when the skills on which his status rested become obsolete.

> . . . a man may resolutely stand pat and upright, toeing the mark and meeting commitments stead-fastly, but find social relationships changing around him, perhaps depriving him of old positions and prerogatives or assigning to him new stations and activities. This alters his standing with others and creates for him new and unexpected stresses. . . . Any of countless social relationships that ebb and flow around the individual can at times upset his personal equilibrium and intensify stress.[9]

Whether the norms regulating status relationships are legal or crescive—customary, traditional, conventional—they may generate stress. Indeed, it may be more frustrating to tilt with crescive norms than with legal ones. Many of the stress situations in the past which dealt with legal privileges and prerogatives have been resolved. But at the present time, powerful forces are at work transforming crescive patterns of status relationships, especially those based on racial criteria. These changes are threats to large groups of people; and the attempt to embody these changes in law generates a great deal of anxiety in them.

If the institutionalized status structure, whether legally or crescively controlled, inflicts too great penalty on the lower-status level, it may be accompanied by great hatred. This hatred may operate as a stress factor for both the lower and the higher party of the relationship. Status envy and resentment based on status differentials may be strong stress factors.

A culture may create symbolic threats of its own. Belief in malignant forces in the outer world, witches and warlocks, the evil eye, a revengeful deity, a threatening cosmology, values too difficult to attain— these may be as threatening as floods and famines. Or the mere existence of complexity and confusion in a culture, however benign its ideology, may be one of the most threatening facts of all.

Stress factors, then, are threats which arise within the individual's body, in nature, in other hostile groups or social systems, in the functioning of a social system, or in a set of cultural values.

The first two of these sources of threat are greatly diminished in an age of abundance. Famine, plague, nutritional and many germ diseases are reduced from major to relatively minor significance as threats. It is comparatively easy to keep people alive and well and even properly nourished in an age of abundance. The threatening illnesses in an age of abundance are those of the later years—the so-called degenerative diseases. But this increasing control of nature as a generator of stress factors is counteracted by the invention of new man-made threats more catastrophic than anything Nature could do by herself. Atom and hydrogen bombs, for example, and guided missiles, are threats as all-encompassing as volcanic eruptions.

Abundance has not reduced the threat inherent in the existence of hostile groups; it may have greatly increased status as a stress factor. The increased schooling which abundance has made possible has allayed ignorance as a source of anxiety—witches and hostile forces in the world —but it has substituted wider knowledge as a source. We now have more to worry about because we know more. We are better informed about what is going on in the world and therefore feel more threatened by situations which we were protected from by our ignorance in the past.

But perhaps the most serious threat accompanying abundance has been the rapidity of change which renders stability and security almost unattainable. This is felt most deeply in the threat it presents to role relationships and hence also to status.

When we speak of stress factors as greater or less at one time as contrasted with those of another time, we imply that the threats can be measured. Can they?

In a certain sense threat is an all-or-nothing phenomenon. Either the ax falls or it does not. Actually, however, threat may be thought of as having degrees which may be measured in terms of probability, both objective and subjective.

Objective measurement of threat is its actuarial probability, or probability based on past experience. The people who live on the side of an active volcano live under threat of its eruption, and the degree of threat is measurable in terms of the likelihood of eruption.[10] But psychologists have demonstrated in laboratory experiments that even when subjects are given the objective probability of the occurrence of certain events they do not act on these actuarial probabilities, but on subjective probabilities, which may differ for every subject. Given a choice between five cents and a chance to win more than five cents, depending on certain given probabilities (determined by the throw of fair dice or the drawing of cards from a fair deck), subjects do not base their choices on the actuarial probabilities that would maximize their gains, but on what psychologists call "subjective probabilities."[11] These subjective probabilities vary from subject to subject, but they are usually measurably different from actuarial probability.

Such individual differences reveal themselves in other aspects of life also. Some people, for example, have much higher subjective probabilities for threat than do others. If the actuarial probability of contracting some germ disease is, let us say, one in five, their subjective probability is one in three, or one in two, or even, in extreme cases, one in one. If they hear of a single case of the disease in the community they behave and make decisions as though they were going to contract it. These are the people who are sure that it is going to rain the day of the picnic, that the plant is going to shut down, that there is going to be a depression next year, that war is just around the corner, and who act accordingly. In a pathological form, these people are sure that Negroes, Jews, communists, or Catholics have a well worked out conspiracy to overthrow the government; or, in an extremely pathological form, that everyone in their environment is plotting against them. These people are under much greater stress than others living under actuarially identical probabilities of threat. When the stress factor is another human being, the high subjective probability on which the distressed person is making his decision may actually invite or stimulate the very threat he fears. We have here a form of what has been called the "self-fulfilling prophecy."

The Values Threatened

Life, health, property, privilege, freedom, security, status, "face," honor, self-respect, opportunity, future prospects—all as related either to one's own self, to one's loved ones, or to one's group, or to all three— may be the values which are being threatened. A threat to any value may produce a stress reaction. When status is the threatened value, the reaction may be even more traumatic than when life itself is threatened. Indeed, many men have been known to prefer death to loss of status. And groups of men from time immemorial have felt as did Patrick Henry, who asked for death if he could not have liberty.

In analyzing threat we must recognize the difference between subjective value and objective or consensual value, just as we did between subjective and objective probability. One can take a ten-dollar bill into any bank or store in the country perfectly confident that it can be exchanged for two five-dollar bills. Two fives equal one ten. Similarly five ones equal one five. This kind of equivalence is basic to mathematics, measurement, and hence to all science.

But it has long been known that this objective or consensual equality does not correspond to subjective experience. Five dollars are not the same to the millionaire and to the beggar. The first five dollars is much greater experientially than the fiftieth. And now psychologists have been able to determine experimentally the difference between subjective value and objective value. To some subjects, for example, five cents lost has greater value than five cents won; and the sixth five cents won has less value than the first, and so on.[12]

Translated into life situations, we find great individual differences in subjective value for identical things. Two men with identical jobs, for example, may have altogether different subjective values regarding them; if the position is a promotion (gain) for one and a demotion (loss) for the other, the step down may be far greater to the man involved than the step up for the other.[13] Or, even for the same man, each step down the job hierarchy is much steeper than the identical step up. Threat, in brief, is different for different people, even if the same objective value is being threatened.

Reactions to Threat

It should be clear without elaboration that when a reaction to threat is successful, that is, when it eliminates the threat or at least reduces it to manageable proportions, there is no problem and we do not have to consider it here. A very large part of human behavior consists of the successful handling of threats of one kind or another. It is only when the reaction fails that a problem arises. Not all stress situations, then, produce suffering, are harmful, or are felt to be "distressing." Some people, in fact, even enjoy at least a limited or controlled amount of stress. They may seek it out in the form of, let us say, gambling or accepting reckless challenges. They like to pit themselves against unscaled mountain peaks or supersonic barriers or polar wastes. This kind of situation is, obviously, not our concern here either. We are concerned only with the kinds of stress situations which create problems for human beings. And we expand the concept of stress reaction here to include not only individual reactions but also collective reactions.

INDIVIDUAL. The individual reaction to threat is complex, taking place concomitantly on several levels: the physiological, the emotional, and the interpersonal or social. It may be conscious, deliberate, planned; or it may be wholly unconscious.

Physiological Stress Reactions. In studying disease the most important stress reactions, usually glandular in nature, are those of the vegetative system, especially the autonomic nervous system; [14] but stress reactions are possible in any physiological system.

The autonomic nervous system, involved in dilation of the pupils, secretion of saliva, slowing of the heart, production of perspiration, erection of the hair, and contraction of the blood vessels, indicated the occurrence of a relationship between internal bodily processes and feelings, attitudes, and emotions. Moreover the skeletal muscles and joints supported by both systems become extensively involved in such emotional and behavioral adjustments to threats, as is conspicuously shown by tremors, tics, twitchings, and spasms. . . . The glands are involved in chemical regulation of the body through secretion of specific substances into the blood stream, and prove to be responsive to the needs and purposes of the individual through delicate connections with the cerebrum and the autonomic nervous system. Thus, for instance, the adrenal gland, by the discharge of adrenalin in times of danger, helps to mobilize the body for action. . . . The common denominator of stress disorders is reaction to circumstances of threatening significance to the organism. . . . Protective reaction patterns are evoked in given individuals by threats of highly particularized significance.* It has been shown that these threats or situations evoke entirely different bodily responses in different persons, although when a threat evokes a particular adaptive pattern, the reaction often can be seen to include specifically related attitudes, feelings, and behavior.[15]

Emotional Stress Reactions. Paralleling these physiological reactions, or part of them in many cases, as the above statement suggests, are such reactions as those we label "fear" or "anxiety." "The concept of anxiety . . . designates simply the state of mind resulting from the anticipation of danger." [16] When writers speak of "stress reaction" without further specification, the implication usually is that they refer to anxiety. And in a certain sense this anxiety is the central core of any stress situation. A large part of medical practice has for its function the allaying of anxiety. We shall have a great deal more to say about anxiety later.

Role-related Stress Reactions. A third aspect or level of individual reaction to threat is social or interpersonal, or what we shall call "role-related." It takes the form of aggression, withdrawal, hostility, apathy, escape—too much or too little of expected behavior. There is a whole field of medicine—psychiatry—devoted to the study of pathological reactions to threat as shown in role behavior. Whatever specific form the role-related reaction takes, it involves some impairment in role performance, as we shall see in Part IV.

The threats to which early man was subjected were of such nature and duration that a hereditary adaptation to them could take place. That is, man's body developed reactions for dealing with such threats as wild beasts and immediate, visible dangers. An elaborate system of glandular reactions prepared the body for fight or flight. It doubtless took a long, long time to perfect these stress reactions, and generations were involved. In contrast, genetic reactions to the threats which human

* Cf. "subjective value" above.

beings have been subjected to in historical times have not yet developed. There have been relatively few generations of man subjected to the social and societal stresses of civilization, certainly not enough to have bred adaptive reactions into man. Man has retained the stress reactions evolved in his prehistorical life, even though many are now dysfunctional. Man's physiology, in brief, has not responded to abundance. The glands operate much as they did in the past. Abundance has not, for example, inhibited the adrenal cortex. The functioning of the body is much the same now as it always was.

The emotional concomitants of perceived threats—fear and anxiety —are also much the same as they were in the past. People have the same capacity for suffering or "distress" as their forebears. That they are reacting to different kinds of stress, threatening loss of different kinds of values, does not mitigate the anxiety. The daughter deprived of satin slippers feels no less frustrated when her mother points out that she had no shoes at all when she was a child. In an age of abundance, in brief, people acquire new things to feel anxious about; they retain their ancient capacity for anxiety.

COLLECTIVE. A study of animal behavior, including that of protozoa, has shown that even so simple a collective pattern as mere *aggregation,* or "huddling," enhances chances for survival.[17] An aggregation can withstand threats better than isolated organisms. In this sense we have a primitive collective stress reaction.

Among the higher animals a distinctively social dimension is added to mere aggregation or huddling. The *group* itself protects against threat, and the anxieties of the individual in the group are allayed. "Many of the real and supposed dangers of individuals are removed at least in part by the comfort of common participation in group-centered activities."[18] Just belonging to the group relaxes the anxiety induced by a threat. In this context we see the enormous significance of role and status as related to stress. Depriving the individual of his role and status robs him of the protection of the group and exposes him to threat.

Among human beings this social dimension becomes highly elaborated and institutionalized and standardized in *culture.*[19] "Whole groups in the course of past adaptive behavior may have developed the habit of making anticipatory responses to real or imaginary dangers in the presence of certain cues. . . . Assuming that anxiety states are painful, especially when experienced intensely, it is expectable that some opportunities are necessary to relieve tensions and to dispel them temporarily."[20] The group thus may create certain controlled ways of allaying anxiety, such as malevolent accusation, witchcraft, or scapegoating. Thus although institutions create their own threats, they serve also and

The function of an army is to kill or capture the enemy;
the role of every soldier is rigidly defined to implement this goal.
Countless rules, written and unwritten, specify exactly how he is
to behave under all predictable situations. An army is, in fact,
an integration of institutionalized roles.

But it is also something more. Behind the formal, institutional
structure there exists a vast amount of informal organization—
that is, countless numbers of small groups in which soldiers find
group roles within the context of their institutionalized roles. One
man, for example, can be counted on to contribute humor at critical moments, thus reducing stress. Another can be expected to

"stand up" to the sergeant, serving as the group's spokesman in verbalizing gripes. A third can be relied upon to entertain, and so on. Such group roles are not formally institutionalized; the army takes no official cognizance of their existence. But they contribute vitally to the efficiency with which the institutionalized roles are performed. If these group roles are satisfying, morale is good. Without the support of such group roles soldiers may even fail to shoot their guns under fire; in prisoner-of-war camps they may succumb to the stresses of "brainwashing."

Typical of an army is its rigidly defined ranked status system. The higher one's status the greater one's responsibilities but also the greater one's prerogatives and privileges. In addition to this ranked status, the soldier in his small face-to-face group enjoys another kind of status growing out of his group role. He belongs.

The kind of "social nourishment" that the men in the picture above are getting from their interaction in this game is almost as important as the physical nourishment provided at the mess hall.

Although civilian life is not so rigidly structured as military life, similar social processes underlie both. *(United Press Photo)* perhaps primarily as collective means—accumulated and standardized—for meeting stress factors. By their stability they furnish the security that allays anxiety. It is for this reason that anything that interferes with stability—rapid change, for example—constitutes a threat and can generate great anxiety.

We pointed out above that in the physiological, emotional, and role-related reactions to threats there had not been much change with abundance. But in collective reactions there has been a great change. Whereas formerly, in an age of scarcity, anxiety was allayed by magic, resignation, escape, or renunciation, abundance makes possible a different collective reaction. Abundance, with the burgeoning of science (itself both cause and result of abundance), renders the elimination or at least the minimization of threats a possible goal. Attempts are made to apply science to the control of threat. And it is this collective stress reaction—the humanitarian movement which gave rise to the concept of a social problem and also sparked many social reform movements—which we shall discuss in Part III.

The Changing Components
of Stress Situations

Every age has its own characteristic stresses to deal with. When we say "characteristic" we do not necessarily imply that these problems are the only ones or even that they are always typical. A typical problem is one that is widespread; a characteristic problem is one that is peculiar to a situation or circumstance, whether or not it is widespread. It distinguishes one area or period from another. A characteristic problem need not be widespread. Thus, for example, the Hollywood marriage is characteristic of present-day United States culture; it is by no means typical of marriage in the United States today. Gangsterism, similarly, is characteristic but not typical. The characteristic is what the caricaturist seizes upon. It may coincide with the typical, but it does not have to.

Has stress increased? In the 19th and even the 20th century many people argued that civilization itself increased stress. They imagined a happier time in the past when there was more security, more stability, less anxiety. They compared an unhappy present with a happy past. The question sometimes takes a slightly different form, and people wonder whether or not there can ever be such a thing as progress. They grant that we may have abundance, or at least more of everything than we used to have, but they wonder if man is any better or any happier for that.

To avoid many of the pitfalls involved in attempting to compare the present with the past, we couch our comparisons in terms of abundance and scarcity rather than in terms of historical trends. For the past is long and variegated. Indeed, there is no one "past." There are many. There is the prehuman past, the preliterate past, the past of Egypt, of Greece, of the Middle Ages, and so on. Because most of the people in all of these pasts were inarticulate, we have a very imperfect picture of the threats to which they were exposed and the anxieties such threats generated. And even when people were articulate, records are incomplete and inadequate; we are more likely to have a first-hand view of the stress factors operating on the upper classes than those impinging on the lower classes.

We are likely, further, to inject our biases into such comparisons. We sometimes, for example, compare an aristocratic culture of the past with the mass culture of today, to the disparagement of the present. If we compare the common man of today with his counterpart of the past, however, the picture changes, as the following statement suggests.

Many people think of London in the eighteenth century as the city Samuel Johnson loved, the city in which Garrick acted, Reynolds painted and Burke orated, the city where Lord Chesterfield set the tone of aristocratic society and the brothers Adam devised new forms of beauty in furniture and architecture. They are right to do so, but they are thinking only of the surface gloss that overlay London's sickening squalor, gross brutality and unparalleled crime. Hogarth's "Gin Lane," not Gainsborough's "Blue Boy," is typical of eighteenth-century London. . . . Thousands of new-born babies were left on the streets to die; people still were burned alive; public enthusiasm for hangings was insatiable; thousands of boys were thieves and thousands of girls 12 to 18 years old were prostitutes; the miserable slum dwellers stupefied themselves with gin; organized gangs robbed and murdered almost with impunity. Rioting mobs ruled the streets. Corruption was normal in that age. . . . [It] was easy, profitable, and therefore nearly universal.[21]

Can we say that the stress load was any lighter then than now?

By using "models"—of scarcity and abundance—rather than attempting to trace historical trends we avoid the assumption that we know more than we really do about the past.

We cannot say in every case that abundance has "caused" the changes we discuss here; usually there are many intervening variables. All we can say is that the changes do seem to fit the "model" for abundance. In many cases the ultimate "cause" of the change is the technology which has made the abundance possible. It might be said that the 19th century saw man attempting to reshape his institutions to fit the new technology, the 20th, attempting to reshape them to fit the abundance resulting from the technology.

TABLE 1
CHANGING COMPONENTS IN CHARACTERISTIC STRESS SITUATIONS

	Age of Scarcity	Age of Abundance
Stress Factors		
Role-related	Limited roles available, so greater chance for incongruence between endowment and role; * role disturbance relatively more common in younger age levels †	Conflicting roles ‡ Role anomalies (confusion, "rolelessness," anomie, etc.) §
Status-related	Germ illness, malnutrition, hunger; † fatigue, exposure, overwork; * unemployment; ¶ drought, famine, flood *	Status insecurity, achieved rather than ascribed status, status mobility, changing status criteria **
Values Threatened	Life (of self or loved ones or of group); senses (blindness, deafness, etc.); "limb" (paralysis, etc.); vitality *	Status, "face," security, confidence in role performance, etc.*
Stress Reactions	Individual	Same
	Physiological (e.g., glandular)	
	Emotional (anxiety)	
	Role (aggression, withdrawal, pathologies)	
	Collective ††	
	Aggregation ("huddling" together)	Same
	Social organization (groups, institutions)	Same, reform
	Cultural (symbols, magic, etc.)	Science

* Not discussed in this book except incidentally.
† Chapters 8 and 24.
‡ Chapter 15.
§ Role confusion, Chapter 15; "rolelessness" (youth, Chapter 17; aged, Chapters 4 and 19; handicapped, Chapter 9).
¶ Chapter 20.
** Chapter 3.
†† The use of the term "stress reaction" in this sense of collective behavior is figurative.

Illustrative Stress Situations
in an Age of Abundance

We introduced Part I with a description of some of the major stress situations characteristic of an age of scarcity. We close Part II with a few illustrations of the kinds of stress situations characteristic of an age of abundance, with the higher standards which it brings.

In 1954, a time of mild recession, a cross section of the American public was asked: "What kind of things do you worry about most?" Ten per cent expressed no worries about any problems; 80 per cent expressed worries about personal and family problems only. The remaining 10 per cent reported worries about world problems and other nonpersonal concerns, as well as personal and family problems. The largest single source of worries was personal business or family economic problems, reported by 43 per cent of those interviewed; health, of self or of family, was a cause of anxiety for 24 per cent. Other personal problems, largely in the area of family relationships, caused worry in 30 per cent.[22] The specific stress factors quoted in this study illuminate the nature of role- and status-related stress situations in an age of abundance.

For example: "How to make a living for my family is my biggest worry. We've got the new house now if we can ever get it paid for. . . ." Or, "I worry about my pension. Might not have enough to eat. Hard times now and no work. I want fixings for my new house, but things cost a lot." Not actual hunger and homelessness, but how to pay for the new house and fixings is the problem. Or: "How I'll manage to finance my way through college. . . ." ". . . How am I going to send my children to college?" Not grade school, not high school, but college is the standard. Most serious of all at the moment of recession was the anxiety about employment and unpaid bills.

Husband-wife relationships, parent-child relationships, in-law relationships—these are sources of anxiety also in an age of abundance, reflecting role confusion and uncertainty: "I worry about my husband living in another city from mine." "I wish my wife were a better housekeeper. When I was married I found out she was dirty and I had to come home and clean." "I worry about having the ability to raise my children to be God-fearing children. . . ." "It's the future of the children. I don't care for much in an economic way, as much as I concern myself with their contribution to society. What I'm trying to get at is that I want to provide them with a good perspective." "My 17-year-old son wants to marry and that really is bothering me." "Well, you know we

THE STRESS DIMENSION OF SOCIAL PROBLEMS · 83

have a girl 13 and the way things are—my goodness, the things that happen—I'm afraid to let her out after dark." "In-law troubles worry me most. Just trying to keep peace in the family and get along with my daughters-in-law. Otherwise I have no worries." "I worry about the care I'll get when I get older. I'd probably have to go into a home eventually." [23]

Even affluence has its stresses.[24] A woman who seems to have everything writes as follows of the stresses which threaten her integrity:

The life I have chosen as wife and mother entrains a whole caravan of complications. It involves a house in the suburbs and either household drudgery or household help which wavers between scarcity and non-existence for most of us. It involves food and shelter; meals, planning, marketing, bills, and making the ends meet in a thousand ways. It involves not only the butcher, the baker, the candle-stickmaker but countless other experts to keep my modern house with its modern "simplifications" (electricity, plumbing, refrigerator, gas-stove, oil-burner, dish-washer, radios, car, and numerous other labor-saving devices) functioning properly. It involves health; doctors, dentists, appointments, medicine, cod-liver oil, vitamins, trips to the drug store. It involves education, spiritual, intellectual, physical; schools, school conferences, car-pools, extra trips for basketball or orchestra practice; tutoring; camps, camp equipment and transportation. It involves clothes, shopping, laundry, cleaning, mending, letting skirts down and sewing buttons on, or finding someone else to do it. It involves friends, my husband's, my children's, my own, and endless arrangements to get together; letters, invitations, telephone calls and transportation hither and yon.

For life today in America is based on the premise of ever-widening circles of contact and communication. It involves not only family demands, but community demands, national demands, international demands on the good citizen, through social and cultural pressures, through newspapers, magazines, radio programs, political drives, charitable appeals, and so on. My mind reels with it. . . .

And this is not only true of my life, I am forced to conclude; it is the life of millions of women in America. I stress America, because today, the American woman more than any other has the privilege of choosing such a life. Woman in large parts of the civilized world has been forced back by war, by poverty, by collapse, by the sheer struggle to survive, into a smaller circle of immediate time and space, immediate family life, immediate problems of existence.[25]

These are the characteristic role- and status-related situations which engender anxiety in an age of abundance.

We have now reviewed the major concepts we are going to use in our analyses, namely, abundance, role, status, and stress. Each contributes an important facet to our presentation, albeit in different planes or dimensions. Before we proceed to an application of these concepts to the analysis of specific situations, however, we turn, in Part III, to a discussion of social problems as ethical and intellectual problems.

NOTES

1 The term "stress" in the literature is sometimes applied to the stress factor or threat and sometimes to the emotional stress reaction. The context is supposed to indicate which is meant. Actually the term, like "pressure," "tension," and "strain," is a physical analogy. Unfortunately there is no terminology operationally defined to refer to the kinds of phenomena we are dealing with here. Since neologisms usually impede rather than facilitate communication, the conventional terminology is used, but with some modification. The term "threat" is used to specify the stress factor and, except when some other level of reaction is referred to, the term "anxiety" is used to refer to the stress reaction.

2 Leo W. Simmons and Harold G. Wolff, *Social Science in Medicine* (Russell Sage Foundation, 1954), pp. 84–85.

3 Bernard J. Siegel, "High Anxiety Levels and Cultural Integration: Notes on a Psycho-Cultural Hypothesis," *Social Forces,* 34 (Oct. 1955), p. 43.

4 *Ibid.*

5 Simmons and Wolff, *op. cit.,* p. 40.

6 Bernard J. Siegel, *loc. cit.*

7 Simmons and Wolff, *op. cit.,* pp. 60–61.

8 Walter Lord, author of a book describing the sinking of the "Titanic"—*A Night to Remember* (Holt, 1955)—believes that an era ended in 1912, an era marked by excessive deference to wealth. The loss of children was relatively greater in third class than the loss of men in first class.

9 Simmons and Wolff, *op. cit.,* p. 86.

10 Certainty of misfortune may produce less anxiety than uncertainty of even a lesser misfortune.

11 The nature of probability has puzzled logicians and mathematicians for a long time. Some modern statisticians reject the classical formulation in terms of frequency and argue that there is only subjective probability. See L. J. Savage, *Foundations of Statistics* (Wiley, 1954).

12 D. Davidson, P. Suppes, and Sidney Siegel, "Some Experiments and Related Theory of Utility and Subjective Probability," Report #4, Stanford Value Theory Project, May 1955.

13 A study of upwardly and downwardly mobile salesmen showed that "persons downwardly mobile into a given occupation show higher job dissatisfaction (greater job mobility and higher income aspiration) than persons who are upwardly mobile into the same occupation" (Douglas M. More, "Social Origins and Occupational Adjustment," paper read before the American Sociological Society, Sept. 1955).

14 In the study of the psychosomatic or stress diseases, the term "stress reaction" is given a rather special meaning, namely, reaction of the adrenal glands. For a statement of the stress theory of disease, see Hans Selye, "The General Adaptation Syndrome and the Diseases of Adaptation," *Journal of Clinical Endocrinology,* 6 (Feb. 1946), pp. 117–230, and *The Physiology and Pathology of Exposure to Stress* (Acta, 1950). For the implications of sociological phenomena for stress, see Simmons and Wolff, *op. cit.*

15 Simmons and Wolff, *op. cit.,* pp. 21–25.

16 Bernard J. Siegel, *op. cit.,* p. 42.

17 For a summary of the literature in this field see Ashley Montagu, *Darwin, Competition, and Cooperation* (Abelard, 1952) and *The Direction of Human Development; Biological and Social Bases* (Harper, 1955).

18 Bernard J. Siegel, *op. cit.,* p. 43.

19 *Ibid.*

20 *Ibid.*

21 Orville Prescott, reviewing *Hue and Cry; The Story of Henry and John Fielding and Their Bow Street Runners,* by Patrick Pringle (Morrow, 1955), in *New York Times,* Dec. 20, 1955.

22 Samuel A. Stouffer, *Communism, Conformity, and Civil Liberties: A Cross-Section of the Nation Speaks Its Mind* (Doubleday, 1955), pp. 59–66.

23 *Ibid.,* pp. 60–65.

24 At one time pointing to the anxieties of the rich was used as a palliative for the poor. It was a favorite theme of Hannah More, for example. There is no such intent in the statement in the text. A popular entertainer, Sophie Tucker, was quoted as saying that she had been both rich and poor and that it was better to be rich. Hardly anyone today argues in favor of poverty as a happier state than wealth. But to recognize that wealth alone does not obliterate stress is not the same as arguing that poverty is better.

25 Anne Morrow Lindbergh, *Gift from the Sea* (Pantheon, 1955), pp. 25–27.

III

SOCIAL PROBLEMS
AS ETHICAL AND
INTELLECTUAL
PROBLEMS

"The literary articles . . . appeared in the form of a copious review of a work on Chinese metaphysics, sir," said Pott.

"Oh," observed Mr. Pickwick; "from your pen, I hope?"

"From the pen of my critic, sir," rejoined Pott with dignity.

"An abstruse subject I should conceive," said Mr. Pickwick.

"Very, sir," responded Pott, looking intensely sage. "He *crammed*
for it, to use a technical but expressive term; he read up for the subject,
at my desire, in the *Encyclopaedia Britannica*."

"Indeed!" said Mr. Pickwick; "I was not aware that valuable work
contained any information respecting Chinese metaphysics."

"He read, sir," rejoined Pott, laying his hand on Mr. Pickwick's
knee, and looking round with a smile of intellectual superiority, "he
read for metaphysics under the letter M, and for China under the letter
C, and combined his information, sir."—CHARLES DICKENS, *The Post-
humous Papers of the Pickwick Club*

No MORE THAN Chinese metaphysics do social problems lend
themselves to definition by separating the constituent elements of the
term and then reassembling them. In order to do justice to the unique
connotations of the term we ought to follow the *Time* magazine practice
of joining the words. We should speak of *socialproblems*. For the term
thus used refers to a special strand in the history of human thought and
can be understood only in this light. What has and what has not been
subsumed under the term cannot be deduced from any logical definition. What has and what has not been included as a social problem is a
matter of tradition rather than logic, and, as we saw in Chapter 1, tradition changes from time to time. The tendency at the present time is to
raise our standards, to include more and more in the concept.

A problem is defined in the dictionary as "a perplexing question,
situation, or person; a matter involving difficulty in solving, settling, or
handling." If it does not call for a solution or for settling or for handling
it is not a problem; if it is not perplexing it is not a problem. When,
therefore, we say, "Crime is no problem among the Shortecs," we may
mean any one of three things: (1) there is no crime among the Shortecs,
(2) they are so well organized that they know exactly what to do about
crime, or (3) they are so resigned to the existence of crime that they do
nothing about it, accepting it fatalistically. When we say, "Nose-thumb-

ing is a very serious problem with the Witecs but no problem at all with the Nartecs," we mean that the same phenomenon is differently evaluated by different people, calling for handling among some but not among others.

It is because of these anomalies that we have insisted on distinguishing between human suffering and misfortune on the one hand, and the concept of a social problem on the other. The fact that suffering and misfortune are not viewed as social problems does not mean that they do not exist. The concept of a social problem, itself a collective attitude toward human ills and therefore a sociological phenomenon of some magnitude, is fairly new, not more than 150 to 200 years old. The development of this important topic is our task in Part III.

In Chapter 5 we trace the history of the concept of social problems as a form of collective "stress reaction" to the trauma of the new industrial civilization, and on the basis of this review we establish three criteria which seem to characterize social problems. Chapter 6 canvasses the field of social problems viewed as intellectual problems: Why do they arise? It surveys the several conceptual frameworks in which answers have been proposed. And Chapter 7 reviews the kinds of answers that have been advocated to the question, what is to be done? It devotes special attention to the exploitation of group resources, to revolution, and, in greater detail, to social reform.

When we say that something is a *social,* as distinguished from, let us say, an engineering, problem we mean that it deals with the socius or individual-in-role-relationships; when we say it is a *problem* we mean we feel we must do something about it collectively because it involves great suffering or is costly to the community or is dysfunctional. Let us proceed to a development of this theme.

5

The Criteria of
Social Problems

In the Introduction to Part I we pointed out that although human suffering—pain and anxiety, we might say now—is very old, the concept of a social problem is relatively new. In Chapter 4 we saw that a new collective stress reaction appeared with abundance, one which emphasized reform—an attitude of doing something about stress rather than resigning oneself to it. And now we wish to elaborate this theme in greater detail.

We are viewing social problems now as intellectual and ethical questions. We want to trace the emergence of this new activist point of view, and we want to end, if we can, with a clear-cut set of criteria for judging a situation a social problem, that is, as demanding change or reform. The first part of our task in this chapter, then, is inductive; it is an attempt to generalize from historical evidence the nature of social problems. The second part, however, is deductive; it is an attempt to construct a "model" or set of specifications by which we can judge whether a situation *is* or *is not* a social problem in the sense of requiring change or reform. The traditional concept will serve as a starting point. But before we can begin our task, we must clarify a terminological difficulty.

"Social" and "Societal"

In most conceptualizations of social problems there has been a recognition of the sociological principle that "individual" and "society" are two aspects of the same unitary phenomenon, two ways of looking at the same thing. Sometimes the focus has been on the individual, sometimes on the society in which he lived. Thus both individual and institutional ("personal" and "social") disorganization or pathologies have been included in the concept.

It would be useful in our analyses if we could use different terms for these two aspects of the problems to be dealt with here. The adjective "social" is most apt for describing what sociologists used to call the "socius," or human-being-in-a-web-of-interpersonal-relationships. Currently the nearest term to that of socius is human-being-in-his-role-relationships. In this sense we would speak of the interpersonal or role relationships of people in groups as "social."

The term "societal," then, would be reserved for application to the society as a whole, to the system of groups and institutions which constitute an established order.[1]

In the light of such distinctions, we see that the concept of "social" problems, that is, the problems of interpersonal relationships or of relationships within face-to-face groups, is quite old, for "social" problems in this interpersonal sense are not difficult to formulate. Anyone can see that the widowed woman with dependent children will suffer unless someone takes care of her; anyone can see that the sick man must have help. In this personal sense, then, the concept of "social" problems is not new, but quite old.

The concept that is new is that of "societal" problems. It is by no means easy, as we shall presently see, to perceive human suffering or misery as a societal problem, that is, as something *that concerns others than those immediately involved*. It was this concept of societal problems that arose at the end of the 18th century. And it was this concept that was new. We are confronted at this point with a nice terminological dilemma. If we wish to be precise and accurate in our analyses we must speak of "societal" as well as "social" problems; but in so doing we will be inconsistent with customary usage. To resolve this dilemma we shall put quotation marks around the word "social" when referring to interpersonal problems, that is, problems of the socius, and use either *societal* or *social* without quotation marks when referring to the larger concept.

And what, exactly, was this new concept? Who created it? Why? It is to a discussion of these questions that we address our attention now.

The Traditional Concept
of a Social Problem

Anticipating our discussion, we answer the questions above as follows: The traditional idea of a social problem emerged first as an attitude of middle-class reformers at the end of the 18th and beginning of

the 19th centuries toward the stresses created by the new urban industrial order which developed as a result of the new scientific ideology
and a growing humanitarianism. The key ideas here are: (1) the stresses
that the new urban industrial order was creating, (2) growing humanitarianism, (3) scientific ideology, and (4) middle-class reformers. Each
deserves some comment.

The Stresses of the New Urban Industrial Order

The rise of the industrial towns around factories in the early 19th
century was a phenomenon for which none of the social institutions of
men were prepared. All of the old stresses remained,[2] exaggerated to the
nth degree—unspeakable poverty, long hours of work in poorly ventilated and lighted factories, the work in factories of women and small
children, ill health, wretched housing. The sheer magnitude of these ills
was unprecedented. Commission after commission in Great Britain documented the inhuman conditions under which people lived in factory
towns and city slums. The "culture" of these new industrial slums was
as alien to outsiders as the culture of a distant African tribe. Indeed,
even after half a century of reform legislation, one passionate observer—
the founder of the Salvation Army—wrote a book describing "darkest
England," comparing it with the "darkest Africa" on which Stanley had
just reported.

And what a slough it is no man can gauge who has not waded therein,
as some of us have done, up to the very neck for long years. Talk about
Dante's Hell, and all the horrors and cruelties of the torture-chamber of the
lost! The man who walks with open eyes and with bleeding heart through
the shambles of our civilization needs no such fantastic images of the poet
to teach him horror. Often and often, when I have seen the young and the
poor and the helpless go down before my eyes into the morass, trampled
underfoot by beasts of prey in human shape that haunt these regions, it
seemed as if God were no longer in His world, but that in His stead reigned
a fiend, merciless as Hell, ruthless as the grave. Hard it is, no doubt, to read
in Stanley's pages of the slave-traders coldly arranging for the surprise of a
village, the capture of the inhabitants, the massacre of those who resist, and
the violation of all the women; but the stony streets of London, if they could
but speak, would tell of tragedies as awful, of ruin as complete, of ravish-
ments as horrible, as if we were in Central Africa. . . .

The blood boils with impotent rage at the sight of these enormities,
callously inflicted, and silently borne by these miserable victims. . . . Those
firms which reduce sweating to a fine art, who systematically and deliberately
defraud the work-man of his pay, who grind the faces of the poor, and who
rob the widow and the orphan, and who for a pretence make great professions of public-spirit and philanthropy, these men nowadays are sent to
Parliament to make laws for the people. The old prophets sent them to Hell

—but we have changed all that. They send their victims to Hell, and are rewarded by all that wealth can do to make their lives comfortable. Read the House of Lords' Report on the Sweating System, and ask if any African slave system, making due allowance for the superior civilization, and therefore sensitiveness, of the victims, reveals more misery.

Darkest England, like Darkest Africa, reeks with malaria. The foul and fetid breath of our slums is almost as poisonous as that of the African swamp. Fever is almost as chronic there as on the Equator. Every year thousands of children are killed off by what is called defects of our sanitary system. . . .[3]

All the old ills, all the old miseries, all the old suffering were there, concentrated in great cities, exposed; they could not be hidden. The priest might cross the road in order not to have to look at one suffering person; but it was impossible to avoid seeing millions of suffering persons except by deliberate effort. Priest and good Samaritan alike had no choice. They had to face the fact of inhuman living conditions.

Growing Humanitarianism

There may have been a time when misery and suffering would not have called forth a reformistic response. But the rise of modern humanitarianism which abundance made possible had rendered indifference impossible for thousands of people. Primitive peoples may have looked with equanimity upon infanticide or the killing of the aged, or torture; but not since the 18th century have civilized men accepted these practices. The "fine and serious sense of the tragedy of misfortune," which we referred to in Chapter 1, had come to haunt many members of the more privileged classes in the 19th century as a result of the rise of modern humanitarianism.

The idea of love or charity or philanthropy is very old; it is embedded in Christian ideology. It is essentially personal. For many centuries people had been practicing this Christian virtue by helping the widow and orphan, by taking care of the sick, by protecting the weak. But humanitarianism was a more abstract ideal; it was societal as well as "social." Love and charity might suffice for dealing with the socius and his misfortunes but something more was needed when dealing with societal ills, something with a wider perspective, something more abstract.[4] Humanitarianism was the form this new ideal took.

Modern humanitarianism has its origins in the eighteenth century. The firmest believer in the guiding force of ideas can hardly refuse to see in economic and social conditions the necessary starting point of an explanation of its rise. The newly enriched middle classes largely determined the intellectual climate of the eighteenth century, although their accession to political power came somewhat later. The middle classes unlike the nobles were trained for peace and not for wars; they were not even accustomed to the blood of the hunting field. Success in trade and industry although consistent with exploitation of laborers turned ultimately on ability to cooperate with large numbers of men. Travel, which became easier and common, helped break down age-old feelings of tribal exclusiveness. The middle class was so numerous that anything like a class consciousness had to rest upon a broad and general sense of the value of human life; and the necessity of attracting the support of the lower classes made an appeal to more general notions of human rights inevitable. The religious wars were over, and the national wars had not begun. Men could devote themselves to the cause of mankind, if only for lack of a more immediate cause. Under these conditions the thought of the age came to humanitarian conclusions. Utilitarianism not only found men equally capable of feeling pain and pleasure but concluded that the pleasures of benevolence were high and lasting. The rationalism of the *philosophes* found cruelty and suffering out of place in a universe as neatly ordered as the universe of Newton should be. The sentimentalism of Rousseau asked nothing better than to expend itself in pity toward the victims of an unnatural and unnecessary civilization. The most effective expressions of Christianity in the period—Pietist, Wesleyan, evangelical—sought to alleviate suffering immediately, worked among the poor and humble and assumed functions of social service rare since the coming of the friars.[5]

Not everyone accepted the humanitarian point of view; it was, and still is, criticized, but "much of the opposition . . . is abstract; [even] those who find the humanitarian approach to life too soft, colorless or unimaginative can hardly lead a ruthless free-booting existence." [6] Whether it was accepted as a philosophy or not, it exerted a powerful influence. Sober and responsible people, reared in an atmosphere of humanitarianism, could not long contemplate the ills of the new social order with complacency. But neither Christian love nor humanitarian sentiment was enough. Reform might be motivated by humanitarianism; but it had to be implemented by science. A discipline known as "Social Science" emerged to guide the new drive toward reform.

Scientific Ideology

The philosophers of the French Enlightenment had been so impressed and exhilarated by the successes of the physical and biological sciences that they could see no limits to human progress. Human ills were, like other phenomena, susceptible to study and even, perhaps, to control by science. Anything was possible.[7] Even death might ultimately be conquered. Man himself was perfectible. Science could solve any problem; nothing in either the physical or the social realm was beyond its power. It was in this kind of intellectual atmosphere that the concept of social problems arose. It arose as part of the discipline known as Social Science, whose objective it was to find out what the laws of social life were, in order ultimately to apply them to the amelioration of the human lot. A counterpart to Social Science was the "scientific social-ism" of Karl Marx. Here we merely note the element common to Social Science and Marxism: the attempt to apply science to the relief of human ills. Marxism proposed to harness it to revolution, Social Science, to reform. In this atmosphere the concept of social problems emerged.

The Social Science movement was an effort to wed humanitarian-ism and science to achieve social reform. The stresses of the new indus-trialism which were disturbing the minds of men of good will called urgently for reform; the ideology of science made reform seem possible. What science had been able to do in the physical world it was equally able to do in the social world.

. . . the practical skill, which has almost exhausted its resources, in the ma-terial world, must apply itself to the reorganization of human society. That the social system is out of joint is only too obvious. Here are the vast masses of superfluous and unproductive wealth; there the crowded ranks of the suffering, the starving, the degraded, the enslaved, for whom no healing or restoring influence has even gone forth. . . . Grovelling toil, both among the sordid rich and the hunger-driven poor, must be made to relax its demands and to equalize its burdens, so that in all classes of society the mind and heart shall claim their rights and have their dues.[8]

Said one observer, describing the 1840's:

Dr. Channing . . . called for the reform of the drunkard, the eleva-tion of the poor, the instruction of the ignorant. . . . Horace Mann. . . . began a great movement to improve the public education of the people. . . . The rights of labor were discussed with deep philanthropic feeling and sometimes with profound thought. . . . The natural rights of women began to be inquired into, and publicly discussed.[9]

Another contemporary asked what meant those demands for reform which arose on all sides, what did "these movements among the people, these combinations of even workingmen to meliorate society" mean? [10]

And as late as 1909 the impetus had not yet spent itself. In that year the same reformistic drive was still being commented upon as char-acteristic.

The most obvious and open way which offers itself as an approach to the Social Question . . . is the way known as Social Science. . . . Histor-ically. . . . social science was the way of approach first selected by modern students. . . .

Never before [have] . . . so many people [been] concerned with the amelioration of social conditions and the realization of social dreams. The most conspicuous and disturbing fact of contemporary life is its social unrest. No institution of society—the family, the state, or the church—is so fixed in stability or in sanctity as to be safe from radical transformation. The growth of great industry, with its combinations of capital and its organizations of labor, the unprecedented accumulation of wealth in the hands of the few, and the equally unprecedented increase of power in the hands of many,— these, and many other signs of the time, point to new social adjustments, and awaken a new social spirit. It is the age of the Social Question; and those who have embarked on enterprises of social service and social reformation feel beneath their little ventures the sustaining movement of the main current of the time.[11]

Social reform, then, motivated by humanitarianism, was to be guided by science. It was, as we saw above, this effort to apply science to social reform which became crystallized in the discipline known as Social Science.[12] Social Science took many forms which we shall not deal with at this point. We focus our attention on only one aspect, the one that had the most immediate impact on social reform, namely the Social Science associations.

The National Association for the Promotion of Social Science was organized in Great Britain in 1857. It included over 1,500 members and associates, who held meetings annually, presenting papers on jurisprudence and amendment of law, education, punishment and reformation, public health, and social economy. A French Social Science Association was soon organized also, and in 1862 the first international congress of Social Science was held in Brussels. The departments of the international organization included comparative legislation, education, art and literature, charities and public health, and political economy.

In 1865 there was organized in Boston an American Social Science Association, whose object was "the discussion of those questions relating to the Sanitary Condition of the People, the Relief, Employment, and Education of the Poor, the Prevention of Crime, the Amelioration of the Criminal Law, the Discipline of Prisons, the Remedial Treatment of the Insane, and those numerous matters of statistical and philanthropist interest which are included under the general head of 'Social Science.' "[13] The constitution adopted by the newly formed organization stated its purpose as follows:

. . . to aid the development of Social Science, and to guide the public mind to the best practical means of promoting the Amendment of Laws, the Advancement of Education, the Prevention and Repression of Crime, the Reformation of Criminals, and the progress of Public Morality, the adoption of Sanitary Regulations, and the diffusion of sound principles on the Questions of Economy, Trade, and Finance. It will give attention to Pauperism and the topics related thereto; including the responsibility of the well-endowed and successful, and the wise and educated, the honest and respectable, for the failures of others. It will aim to bring together the various societies and individuals now interested in these objects, for the purpose of obtaining by discussion the real elements of Truth; by which doubts are removed, conflicting opinions harmonized, and a common ground afforded for treating wisely the great social problems of the day.[14]

The two streams which united to form the Social Science movement, one an ideal of science and one an ideal of practical reform, never really formed a single river. The members of the American Social Science Association who were interested in the theoretical emphases soon broke away and formed their own organizations—the American Economic Association, the American Historical Society, the American Sociological Society, the American Political Science Association. On the more applied and practical side, the National Prison Association, the National Conference of Charities and Correction, the American Public Health Association, and the Association for the Protection of the Insane and the Prevention of Insanity were split off. Among those who were interested primarily in immediate problems two trends were discernible: one exemplified by those who approached the immediate problems from a theoretical point of view and the other by those who approached them from an administrative point of view. The first tended to identify with sociologists; the second, with social workers. It is doubtful if the concept of social problems could have achieved adequate theoretical formulation without the perspective given by the universities. Their development of courses in social problems will now be sketched.

It was in the bosom of the American Social Science Association, so to speak, that the first courses in social problems were developed for university students in this country. The first teachers were members of the Association and although their courses all differed in specific details, they tended to resemble one another in their general Social Science orientation.

The earliest of these social problems courses appeared in the universities in the early 1880's. At Harvard the course, called Practical Ethics, covered "the problems of Charity, Divorce, the Indians, the Labor Question, Intemperance." [15] At Michigan there were two lectures a week on "the more direct social problems, such as Popular Education, the Labor Question, the Burdens and the Prevention of Pauperism, the Punishment of Crime, etc." [16] In 1884, under the leadership of President Andrew D. White, Cornell inaugurated a course by F. B. Sanborn which dealt with crime, pauperism, insanity, preventable disease, public vice, crime, punishment, and prison discipline.[17] Sanborn also taught at the Boston University School of Medicine a course which discussed: (1) the dependent and delinquent classes (including the physically defective, the idiotic, the crippled, mentally or morally abnormal, the insane, the inebriate, and unbalanced or "cranky" class, widows and orphans, the old and infirm, strangers in the country, unemployed persons, victims of fire, flood, or other calamity, the sick, the vicious, including the intemperate, prostitutes, vagrants, petty thieves, young offenders, the criminal classes, and inmates of institutions; (2) general and special duties toward the classes named; (3) the health of the community and of individuals as an agent in producing the dependent classes; (4) the anomalous position of the medical profession in regard to disease and vice; (5) the true character of a public establishment for a dependent class; (6) hospitals for the sick and the insane; (7) almshouses of the state or the municipalities; (8) maternity hospitals and the care of young children; (9) truant children and juvenile offenders; (10) prisons and their inmates; and (11) general remarks on the whole subject.[18]

The Yale Divinity School had a course on Social Problems in 1893 which included "the history of labor in England and America, with special reference to the origin of the present industrial classes and the present industrial difficulties; socialism, its theory of the state, and its economic analyses; pauperism and crime; the causes of pauperism, and the history of charity and poor-relief; the criminal classes, punishment and recovery of criminals, the prevention of crime." [19] And Columbia University introduced a course in the late 1880's by an outstanding statistician, Richmond Mayo-Smith, which included "moral statistics," that is, "statistics of suicide, vice, crime of all kinds, causes of crime, condition of criminals, repression of crime, penalties and effect of penalties, etc." [20] Johns Hopkins, to give a final example, offered fifty lectures in 1892–1893 on Current Social Problems in Europe, and lectures on charities and their administration; the work for Political Economy and Social Science in 1892–1893 included "particular attention to the family and its modern environment, together with the social problems of large cities." [21]

As the volume of available teaching materials increased with the accumulation of research and experience, the courses became more numerous and more specialized. Under the compulsion of academic pressures to be scientific, more stress was placed on analysis, less on reform and description. A less normative terminology was sought in an effort to demonstrate scientific objectivity.

Twenty-five years ago they were giving courses on "Dependents, Defectives, and Delinquents," bringing together a hodge-podge of miscellaneous data about many types of persons, problems, and social programs. Then came separate courses on "Poverty and Dependency," whose chief emphasis was economic; courses on "Criminology," stressing sometimes psychological factors in delinquency and sometimes the mechanics of handling offenders; courses on "Race Problems," "Immigration," and "Eugenics," which combined the treatment of biological and sociological problems with plans for social reform. More recently we have had courses on "Social Pathology," starting with individuals in trouble—physical, mental, or economic—and searching for the ways in which their personal difficulties were involved in social relationships. Latest of all there have been appearing courses on "Social Disorganization," devoted to the study of social groups, institutions, interpersonal relationships and processes through which these are disrupted or destroyed.[22]

These, then, were the original forerunners of modern courses in social problems. The contents were not logically defined. But once a tradition was established, an effort was made to give some logical, coherent definition to the concept. At almost every meeting of the American Social Science Association there was at least one paper which attempted to synthesize the variegated strands of the movement into a unit. They never succeeded. It was left to the textbook writers to continue the effort. We shall see what they did in Chapter 6.

The traditional concept of social problems, in brief, was itself a sociological phenomenon of some significance. It arose at the beginning of the 19th century from the wedding of the ideal of science with that of social reform, which went under the name of Social Science. It was an effort to meet the stresses resulting from the industrial revolution. It stated that the successful had obligations toward the failures, the intelligent toward the "witless," the strong toward the weak. The Social Scientists saw the fallacy of a laissez-faire policy. They were the people who defined the nature of social problems and set the standards for judging or for dealing with them. A social problem was any situation that these humanitarian men and women thought needed to be reformed. The specific contents of the concept became traditional, with a core of agreement, although they varied somewhat from time to time and from place to place, in peripheral contents.

Middle-Class Reformers and the Nature of the Traditional Concept of Social Problems

It will be noted that the conceptualization of social problems which we have been analyzing here was for the most part statocentric [23] or classbound; it referred very largely to "the dependent, defective, and delinquent classes," to a slum-underworld syndrome or complex. It was almost exclusively the "well-endowed and successful, and the wise and educated, the honest and respectable" giving attention to "pauperism and the topics related thereto," assuming their responsibility "for the failures of others." It included "the relation and the responsibilities of the gifted and educated classes toward the weak, the witless and the ignorant . . . the causes of Human Failure, and the Duties devolving upon Human Success." [24] It was not "the weak, the witless, and the ignorant" who created and elaborated the concept of social problems; it was not the people who suffered from the impact of the new technology who saw themselves as constituting social problems. It was, rather, people in classes which had been created or benefited by it.

Often they came into collision with the people who constituted the problems.[25] The moral standards of people in the slums were not the same as those of the people who wanted to help them. To the middle-class student of social or societal problems, almost everything about people in the lower socioeconomic classes seemed to require reformation and change. They saw "vice" and "degradation" in almost anything that was different from what they were accustomed to. There was often resistance on the part of the lower classes to the efforts of the middle class to help them.

The reformers came into collision with the upper classes also, for at the turn of the century it became evident to many middle-class observers that the attitude of the upper class was as much a social or societal problem as the behavior of the lower classes. Irresponsibility, arrogance, disregard for the public were, in their opinion, as serious as their counterparts—"vice" and "degradation"—in the slums. The 19th-century "capitalist"—whose crimes, incidentally, are still used to characterize "capitalism," especially in communist countries—had to be tamed and reformed as much as the criminal in the slum.

To say that the concept of societal problems was a middle-class phenomenon implies a certain amount of arbitrariness or relativity or even caprice, as though some other conceptualization were just as good, or even possible. Such an implication, however, is not justified.

It is conceivable that if lower-class persons had developed the concept of social or societal problems it might have been quite different from the one which actually developed. But the important point is this: the concept was possible only to people in the position of the middle class. It does not seem to be possible to see the structure of a society— let alone its problems—from the position the lower classes find themselves in. By and large, therefore, the people who are at the bottom of the social structure do not see the societal system as a whole.[26] They see individual people; they see families; they may even see large groups and specific associations. But they have only a hazy notion of a social structure as a whole.

This fact has been documented by several studies. It has been found, for example, that when researchers wish to get a picture of the status structure of a community those at the top are more likely to be able to furnish data than those at the bottom. This fact was interestingly shown in a study of the way a community catastrophe was reported to interviewers. Lower-class informants talked from their own point of view; they could not see the situation as it might look from any other point of view. They were statocentric or classbound.

Lower-class respondents make reference mainly to the acts and persons of particular people, often designating them by proper or family names. This makes for fairly clear denotation and description, but only as long as the account is confined to the experiences of specific individuals. There comes a point when the interviewer wishes to obtain information about classes of persons and entire organizations as well as how they impinged upon the respondent, and here the lower-class respondent becomes relatively or even wholly inarticulate. At worst he cannot talk about categories of people or acts because, apparently, he does not think readily in terms of classes. Questions about organizations, such as the Red Cross, are converted into concrete terms, and he talks about the Red Cross "helping people" and "people helping other people" with no more than the crudest awareness of how organizational activities interlock. . . . It is apparent that the speakers think mainly in particularistic or concrete terms. Certainly classificatory thought must exist among many or all the respondents; but, in communicating to the interviewer, class terms are rudimentary or absent and class relations implicit. . . .[27]

Another study of 134 Cambridge housewives found that the higher the status of the subjects the closer were their ratings of socioeconomic standing on the basis of 24 photographs of living-rooms correlated with a scale.[28] And in Denmark the ability to perceive status differences was also found to correlate positively with social status.[29] Thus, although the people with low status may have "class consciousness" in the sense of feeling exploited,[30] they do not have a very precise picture of the structure of a community or society. It is therefore understandable that they are not likely to recognize societal problems.

It is easy for anyone to see that disabling illness is a problem to the person concerned and to his family. It is more difficult to understand that it is a problem to the social order as well. Sometimes the individuals concerned do not realize that they constitute a societal problem. The criminal may be a problem to others; he is not necessarily a problem from his own point of view. The successful operator of an assignation house may not see herself or her establishment as a societal problem. Outsiders do. The mentally retarded could probably never rise to the conception of a social or societal problem, and certainly not of themselves as an example. Nor could the psychotic. A poverty-stricken family might know it had a great many problems; it might know it needed help. It is doubtful that it would see itself as an example of a societal problem. To comprehend the concept of a societal problem requires a high order of ability in abstracting. It requires the ability to see the social structure as an integral whole rather than as an aggregation of individuals. It is not easy to see the total incidence of social ills or their ramifications. We have the illusion of separateness, of insulation, of independence. Not all persons even in the position of the middle classes understand the concept of a societal problem.[31] It takes research and imagination to see the ramifications of most problems, to see that they are truly societal in their impact.

The first people, then, to see, conceptualize, and define the contents of societal problems were members of the middle class. Thus the concept of social problems as it emerged in the 19th century was a middle-class preoccupation, based on middle-class standards and ideologies. The justification for accepting this formulation lay in the greater ability of the middle class to view social life abstractly. It was precisely because they were equipped to see society as a whole that the middle-class Social Scientist or professor or social worker or researcher assumed the prerogative of defining the concept of social problems.

Reformers as Social Problems

We have emphasized the middle-class nature of the traditional concept of social problems and the middle-class background of the men who assumed the attitude that social ills must be corrected or controlled. To these middle-class reformers, both the lower and the upper classes constituted problems. And we have pointed out that it was probably possible only to those in this middle position to see social ills as social or, rather, societal problems.

But not all middle-class students of the subject shared the bias of these reformers. To those who espoused the laissez-faire philosophy, for example, the reformers themselves constituted a serious social problem. These reformers were, according to this point of view, actually causing more misery, incurring more social costs, and behaving more dysfunctionally than the people whose stresses they were attempting to alleviate.

It will be noted that the laissez-faire theorists shared the same ultimate values as the reformers. The differences between them lay in the methods they advocated to implement the values, in the answers they gave to social questions. It was not that the laissez-faire theorists were indifferent to suffering or to the social costs of stress; it was simply that they believed social welfare could ultimately be best served by allowing what they considered to be beneficent natural social forces to work themselves out without human intervention or bungling.

It is conceivable that if the laissez-faire philosophy had prevailed, the answer to social problems would have had an entirely different history. Courses and textbooks would deal with the horrible results of attempting to control the social process. But since the reformistic—now called welfare—point of view did, as a matter of historical fact, prevail, the statement of social problems is indelibly stamped with its middle-class die.

We have now completed the inductive aspect of our task; we have traced what was actually subsumed under the rubric "social problem," from the early part of the 19th century down to the 20th, as revealed in the documents of the American Social Science Association and in the several courses in the universities. We turn now to a more difficult task, that of setting up a "model," or drawing up a set of specifications or criteria which a situation must meet in order to qualify as a social problem. Before we do this, we ask whether there are any limitations to the concept?

Limitations of the Concept

The people who define social or societal problems—reformers, researchers, journalists, whoever—are, in effect, architects of the future. They are the ones who lay down the specifications of what has to be changed. They are like inspectors who report to management—the public, in this case—what is wrong with the machine or factory—the social order in our illustration. Theirs is obviously an extremely important function. No one appoints them to perform it. They are self-appointed.

But can *anything* be diagnosed as a social problem and therefore as demanding reform? Could reformers or "agitators" convince us that anything at all was a social problem? Or are there limits to what will be accepted as a social problem? The question is analogous to the question of political issues. Do the parties create campaign issues? Can they make anything they choose an issue? The answer here is clearly no. If a political party could create campaign issues it would also choose issues on which it had an advantage. It could go to the people on issues that it was sure to win on. Sometimes parties do try to keep issues alive long after they have ceased to be issues. They rarely succeed. An issue which was very successful in one campaign often can no longer interest the voters in the next campaign. It is the people, in a sense, who create the issues. Or, rather, it is a dialectic between party and people which creates the issues. The party, like a fashion designer, submits a variety of feelers to the voters. Some "catch on." Others fall flat. The clever campaigner is the one who knows how to pick the most popular issues and how to discern which side of the issue to espouse.

Similarly we may say there are limits to the kinds of situations which can be accepted by the people as social or societal problems. We saw in Chapter 4 that not all stress situations were defined as social problems. We see now that only those which seemed amenable to reform or at least to control were so defined. But many problems that could have been reformed were not accepted as social problems. Why? We shall present below the three main criteria which seem to have been applied to conditions in order to determine whether or not they were to be considered social problems.

In addition to these more or less objective criteria, there seem to be certain psychological factors involved in the definition of social problems. One textbook writer a generation ago commented on the almost morbid fascination some students displayed toward the problems they studied:

Some seem drawn to the study by a morbid curiosity as to the "down-and-outs" of society, the "slum-dwellers," the "submerged tenth." They seem positively to *enjoy* reading about misery, vice and crime, or visiting alms-houses, hospitals and prisons. They come to the study of social pathology in much the same spirit with which they read the "yellow" journals or gossip about the latest scandal.[32]

The enormous popularity of novels in which murder occurs reveals more than an objective interest in the topic. And the alcoholic is a subject of perennial fascination. Unhygienic dress, an inefficient calendar, and nonphonetic spelling, on the other hand, have not been accorded recognition as social problems despite the efforts expended in behalf of dress reform, calendar reform, and simplified spelling. We cannot completely ignore this widespread preoccupation with suffering, misfortune, and even sin. In order to qualify as a social problem a situation must apparently touch some emotional chord in the public.

But more is involved. In general, three reasons seem to have motivated people to conclude that conditions should be changed or reformed. To avoid the fallacies to which a discussion in terms of motivation is exposed, we shall instead speak in terms of criteria.

Criteria for Determining
What Constitutes a Social Problem

An examination of the history of the concept of social problems and of the literature which has accompanied it suggests that there have been, in general, three types of criteria—implicit if not explicit—which have been applied in determining whether or not any particular stress situation was to be judged a social problem, that is, one requiring reform.[33] One of these was a humanitarian-sentimental criterion, one was a utilitarian criterion, and one was a criterion to which we shall apply the term "dysfunctionality."

Humanitarian

The humanitarian-sentimental criterion of whether or not any specific stress situation should be reformed is whether or not it causes actual pain or suffering. According to this point of view, pain and suffering are intrinsically bad and therefore anything which produces them should be reformed, changed, or done away with. (Even those stress situations which are inherent in social living—those, for example, intrinsic to the socialization process—were considered social problems by some of the utopians who dreamed of communities where natural harmony might be achieved.) This may be labeled a "tender-minded" approach to the matter. It may vary all the way from the crude sentimentality of the impulsive "do-gooder," which one textbook described so pointedly a generation ago,[34] to the thoughtful weighing of values which borders on the utilitarian approach. As we have so frequently pointed out, the stresses that are defined as social problems in an age of abundance differ from those of an age of scarcity. "Relative deprivation" rather than "absolute deprivation" is likely to be the criterion in an age of abundance. The criterion of suffering comes to include not only the physical pain of illness and hunger or cold, but also the anxiety of status insecurity. One must not only have a role, one must also "enjoy" a role. Abundance raises the standard of the humanitarian criterion always higher.

It should be pointed out that although the existence of suffering—physical or social in origin—is taken to constitute a social problem, the absence of suffering does not necessarily imply the absence of a social problem. We cannot judge the merits of any situation by the adjustment people have made to it, for human beings can adjust to almost any stress situation. This does not mean that the situation is therefore good for human beings or that it should not be changed. After the Civil War, for example, many Negroes remained on plantations and lived out their lives as slaves. Change would have occasioned more stress than their low status. This did not demonstrate that slavery was not a social problem. The spirit of people can be so broken that they cling to their chains. Sometimes prisoners do not want their freedom. People who have lived their lives in slums may come to prefer them to better housing in better areas. The alcoholic may not "want" to be helped. Many mental patients are "happy." Some people in occupied areas look with dread upon liberation because change inflicts stress. The wide limits within which human beings can adapt themselves to stressful living conditions means that they may even come to be satisfied with hurtful ones. To argue from these cases that one should not try to improve conditions is fallacious. The test is not what people want who have been shaped to want what is inferior, but what people who are not involved want.[35] A person, it is argued, who has been reared as neither slave nor master would not choose to be a slave; a non-slum–dweller who had his choice between a slum dwelling and a clean home would not choose a slum dwelling. We cannot, therefore, the reformer argues, accept anything as a criterion of what is humanly desirable simply because it is possible for people to learn to adjust to it. It is this point of view— which often looks like an imposition of the reformer's standards on the rest of the world—that is likely to arouse hostility and resentment on the part of those he would reform.

Utilitarian

The utilitarian criterion specifies that a situation is a social problem not because it creates pain and suffering—physical or social—but because it imposes expenses on the rest of society, either official in the form of taxes or unofficial in the form of voluntary contributions. According to this criterion, anything is a social problem that, for example, interferes with business or disturbs the peace. Not the misfortune or the suffering or the violation, but its impact on others is the test of whether or not any particular situation is a social problem. Two individuals may behave in the same way; the behavior might be a social problem in one case, not in the other. Drunkenness, for example, would be a social problem in the lower socioeconomic classes because it would involve entanglement with the law and the community burden of taking care of the man's family; it would not be in the upper socioeconomic classes because there would probably be no entanglement with the law and hence no burden to the community. Sickness would be considered a social problem not because it causes pain and suffering, but because it slows down production or because it costs the taxpayer money. Crime is a social problem not because it produces suffering but because it is an economic burden on the community. Much of the popular—and even textbook—discussion of social problems is couched in terms that reflect this point of view, such as, "the costs to the community" in the form of "absenteeism," "reduced productivity," "property destruction," "custodial care," and the like. This might be labeled a "tough-minded" approach. Here again the emphasis may vary from that of persons who think in terms of "the greatest good for the greatest number" to that of the hard-boiled person who thinks only in terms of the costs to him personally. The utilitarian criterion of what constitutes a social problem—what should be reformed—merges almost imperceptibly into the criterion of dysfunctionality.

Dysfunctionality

The criterion of dysfunctionality defines social problems in the societal sense. The functioning, or even survival, of groups, societies, or of culture as a whole, is the central concern here.

Dysfunctionality may be considered analogous to stress in individuals. It implies a threat to survival. Anything that threatens a group—a nation, for example—society, or culture constitutes a social problem. But, in contrast to individual stress situations, the threat that constitutes the *social* problem is something within the group, society, or culture, not something outside it. An outside, or nongroup, threat is a political problem. It usually cannot be reformed. But an outside threat, as we shall presently see, may reveal many weaknesses or dysfunctional conditions within the group, society, or culture.

The criterion of dysfunctionality, though widely used, is difficult to apply strictly, for a number of reasons. We cannot reject it but we should recognize its limitations.

1. *We know little about what is and what is not dysfunctional.* Dysfunctional, first of all, to whom or what? A certain condition might be a threat to a group but not to the nation or society; or to a specific *status quo* but not to the culture; or to a culture but not to the individual members of the population. Certain conditions, for example, under the Old Regime in France and the tsarist regime in Russia were dysfunctional so far as the then existing *status quo* was concerned, but French and Russian population and culture were not destroyed by the revolutions that demolished the old social orders. The "fall" [36] of Rome, on

the other hand, resulted in the ultimate decay not only of a *status quo,* but also of a culture and a society, though not of the people as physical beings. Anything, of course, that wipes out whole populations is totally dysfunctional, destroying *status quo,* society, and culture along with the people. It is for this reason that anything that threatens the physical survival of people, such as epidemics, high mortality rates, and the like, is generally considered a social problem.

2. There is, also, the problem of the *degrees of dysfunctionality.* In our discussion of stress in individuals we invoked the concepts subjective value and subjective probability as tools for measuring the degree of threat. But they can scarcely be applied to groups, societies, and cultures. A condition might be mildly dysfunctional or seriously so; at what point should it be pronounced a social problem, that is, something to be changed, reformed, or abolished? And how can we measure the degree of dysfunctionality? The great ethical philosopher Immanuel Kant laid down the so-called categorical imperative, which stated that one should never do anything that one would not wish to become a general principle of behavior for everyone. Any swerving from this high standard would, according to such an imperative, constitute a social problem. But we know that societies can and often do continue to function even with large numbers of people behaving contrary to this principle.

The fact that societies continue to function even when they must carry a heavy load of illness, hunger, and general distress suggests that we need a concept which one student has called "eufunctionality," [37] or good functioning, as well as the concept dysfunctionality. If a society survives at all, it is functioning. But it may be functioning well or poorly, according to almost any criterion one wishes to use. Anything which helps it function well would be "eufunctional"; anything which prevented it from functioning well would be dysfunctional. At what point should we speak of a situation as dysfunctional or eufunctional?

3. This leads to the problem of *standards.* Even if a system is functioning satisfactorily, could not some of the elements which contribute to its functioning be better, cheaper, more efficient in terms of the goals sought? It has been argued, for example, that crime is functional, that it contributes to the functioning of a system in the sense that it increases solidarity among a group against a common enemy, the criminal.[38] Even if this were demonstrable in all cases—which it is not [39]—the question could still be raised, assuming that social solidarity were a thing to be achieved: Is crime the best way to achieve it? Is not crime really an expensive and therefore ineffective way to achieve this end? A similar argument might be made with respect to war, which was also once exalted by militarists for its contribution to solidarity and welfare, or to

poverty, once extolled for its contribution to strong character, or to ignorance or inequality or any other kind of social phenomenon whose contribution has been analyzed. Could the same contribution be made in less costly ways? In brief, to say that something is functional does not imply that something else might not perform the same function better. The more costly way of achieving a goal is dysfunctional. A thing is dysfunctional, then, not only if it impedes the achievement of certain goals but also if it contributes less, or at greater cost, than some substitute.

If it could be definitely established that any particular situation was indeed a threat to the social order, culture, or to the population dysfunctionality would probably be acceptable to most people as a criterion for judging it a social problem, that is, as something that required reform. Indeed, the concept of mores implies that the forbidden or proscribed behavior is bad for the group, a threat to its survival; and violation of the mores is almost always considered a social problem. Even preliterate peoples see violation of their mores as the concern of everyone, because such violation is felt to be dysfunctional; it might provoke the anger or vengeance of the gods or spirits. Crime, likewise, was everyone's problem because it was dysfunctional to the social order. Much of the intensity motivating the Inquisitions in medieval Europe or the theocracy of Colonial New England was a result of the conviction that heresy on anyone's part was socially dysfunctional, a threat, and therefore the concern of everyone. Permitting heresy to exist would destroy the community. The dysfunctionality of heresy, or violation of the mores, was accepted as a matter of faith. It was never subjected to test.

THE EVIDENCE FOR DYSFUNCTIONALITY.   It is, as a matter of fact, extremely difficult, at least within any one lifetime or any given system, to demonstrate unequivocally that any particular thing is harmful in the sense that it threatens a social system or culture. The available evidence for dysfunctionality may be divided into two kinds, that which is gleaned from history and that which is gleaned from contemporary or at least recent events.

1. The philosophy of history was one of the important forerunners of sociology and in it were set forth many theories to explain the rise and fall of civilizations.[40] Usually, however, they were couched in such general terms—"challenge and response," for example, or "sensate" philosophy—as to permit wide latitude in applying them specifically. The decay of past societies and cultures especially has fascinated students, and almost anything that people wished to condemn has been accused of producing these spectacular historical events. But most of

the factual evidence on the fall of social systems is ex post facto and not very scientific. As a result we do not know very much about what is and what is not dysfunctional within a social system. We know, as we pointed out above, that social systems seem to be able to function—if not to "eufunction"—under what we consider unjust or harmful conditions, as the description of life in an Indian village in the introduction to Part I illustrates.

The evidence for the decline of the Roman Empire is perhaps as good as any available, although even here there is so little control of the variables that scientific generalization is not possible. One student has summarized the reasons for the fall of the Roman Empire as follows:

But even in . . . [the] Golden Age of Roman imperialism grave defects in the constitution of the State and in the structure of society manifested themselves. In the next century (A.D. 180–284) of bad rulers, military insurrections, civil wars, popular disorders, plagues, pestilences, and famines, these defects became glaringly evident as radical and irremediable flaws, fatal to the well-being and even to the continuance of the body politic. What were they? Six may be singled out as most conspicuous. First, the Empire included within its far-flung bounds peoples so various in race and in civilization that it was impossible to weld them into unity; in particular, Celt-Ivernian, Latin, Greek, Oriental constituted four groups whose differences precluded complete fusion. Secondly, with a constitutional hypocrisy strange in a people so practical and so brave, the Romans refused to face the fact that the Empire was not a republic; they persisted in regarding the emperor as a mere composite official elected jointly and severally by the Senate . . . and consequently they made no rules for the succession; hence, with increasing frequency and in growing violence, the death of a principle precipitated conflicts of factions, furious rivalries, internecine civil wars, horrible assassinations. (Between A.D. 211 and 284 there were twenty-three emperors, of whom twenty were murdered.) Thirdly, the economic foundations of the Roman dominion were unsound; nearly half the population were slaves, productive industry was despised as servile, taxation pressed with extinguishing severity upon the middle class, the cities were infested with a lazy proletariat fed with doles, agriculture languished on gigantic latifundia. Fourthly, economic unsoundness was matched by a growing moral depravity; the character of the Romans was not able to stand the strain of early prosperity and power; the austere virtues of the fathers of the State gave place in their degenerate descendants to pride, cruelty, extravagance, self-indulgence, and lust; a debilitated bureaucracy had to face the tremendous problems of a world in transition. Fifthly, ignorance of science, and especially of hygiene and medicine, rendered the Romans helpless in the presence of devastating pestilences which made their permanent abodes in the fetid slums of the great cities, and issued thence with increasing frequency to ravage the Empire. Hence the population diminished not merely relatively as compared with the barbarians beyond the borders, but absolutely with accelerating rapidity. The horrors of pestilential death, moreover, began to haunt the spirits of the survivors, and to oppress them with the sense of an adverse and inevitable fate. Finally, religious disintegration set in; the Romans lost faith in the gods on whose divine aid their fathers had trusted in building up the State, and whose worship formed an integral part of the structure of the constitution.[41]

On the basis of such an analysis, the following situations or conditions might be generalized as dysfunctional to a social system: great heterogeneity or incompatible diversity; violent political conflict; underemployment, inequable taxation, slavery, doles; character defects; plagues and pestilences; and religious disintegration. But just how much each of these situations contributed to the decline of Rome we cannot determine.

2. The evidence from recent events is of three kinds: one deals with cultural dysfunctionality, namely the attempt of the Nazis to destroy Poland; the second deals with societal dysfunctionality, that is, the Soviet attempt to build up a new world; and the third deals with group dysfunctionality among prisoners of war.

a) When the Nazis went to Poland they wished to destroy the native culture or civilization. They did not wish to destroy the people because they needed them as workers, but they wished them to be cultureless, so to speak. The policies they followed, therefore, illustrate the conditions that are considered culturally dysfunctional. They allowed, and even encouraged, the situations that we view as social problems, as harmful to normal community life.

It is interesting to note that when one sets about to destroy a community one does just the opposite of what one does when one wishes to keep it functioning well. Thus, for example, one weakens the cohesion of the several parts of the community "by dividing them into more or less self-contained and hermetically enclosed zones . . . to prevent communication and mutual assistance by the national groups involved." In other words, one Balkanizes the community, a process which believers in the American ideal try to prevent wherever possible. One isolates leaders, exports them, or simply kills them. Primary education is encouraged because it can be used as a channel of indoctrination of the young; and the acquisition of certain skills is permitted because they are useful. But liberal arts training is forbidden, "since that might stimulate independent rational thinking." Religious sanctions must, of course, be thoroughly wrecked. One method is to introduce rival churches in order to undermine the authority of the constituted church, as was done in Croatia. Moral degradation must be fostered. In Poland, for example, "pornographic publications and movies were foisted upon the people. Alcohol was kept cheap although food became increasingly dear, and peasants were legally bound to accept spirits for agricultural produce. Although under Polish law gambling houses had been prohibited, German authorities not only permitted them to come into existence, but relaxed the otherwise severe curfew law." The economic life of the community is destroyed by expropriation, by forbidding certain kinds of work, and by finan-

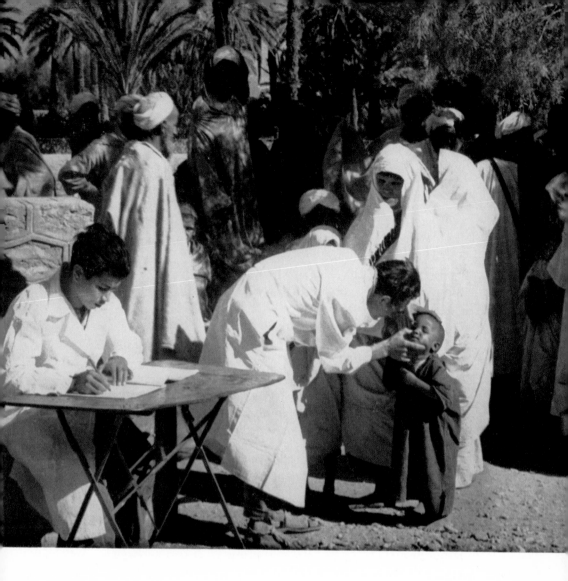

In the era of empire building, colonists used to refer
to the colored peoples of the world as "the white man's burden."
To be sure, much of their concern for the health and physical
welfare of colonial peoples arose out of political considerations,
but religious motives were also at work. Christian missionaries
found that in order to communicate their message effectively they
had to combat illness and poverty. Before long the colonizing in-
dustrialists made a related discovery: in order to assure themselves

efficient native workers, it was necessary to attend to health and housing needs.

Today, of course, the peoples of former colonial areas reject any implication of inferior status. They refuse to be condescended to. And the nations that formerly controlled their resources have come to view disease, poverty, and dislocations of industrialization and urbanization in underdeveloped areas as social problems that concern the entire world, rather than merely political or economic problems.

Doctors such as the one shown in the picture above are curing children of infectious diseases and raising life expectancy all over the globe. Such agencies as UNICEF (United Nations International Children's Emergency Fund) and WHO (World Health Organization) send out teams of health workers to help combat malnutrition, leprosy, diseases leading to blindness, and similar health problems wherever they find them.

One consequence of these medical services is that the peoples in underdeveloped areas are able to perform their worker roles with increased efficiency. In addition, the technicians who accompany the health workers teach new methods of agriculture and new technologies in factories.

Because of the better health of workers and the better technology they apply, productivity increases. But can productivity keep pace with the growth in population resulting from modern medical care?

Some people regard this race between productivity and population growth as the major social problem in the world today. Can we really have abundance, they ask, if we lower the death rate drastically without at the same time lowering the birth rate? Are we "plundering" our planet? *(Photo: World Health Organization, United Nations)* cial manipulation. Biological extermination took many forms: reducing the birth rate by keeping the sexes separated, chronic undernourishment, specific vitamin deficiencies, mass killings either in gas chambers or in concentration camps.[42]

Balkanization, isolation or destruction of leaders, deprivation of the liberal arts, destruction of religious sanctions, alcoholism, gambling, economic exploitation, reduction of the birth rate, chronic undernourishment—these are dysfunctional conditions, to be fought if one wishes to protect a culture.

b) The experience of the USSR illustrates societal dysfunctionality. It is illuminating because the leaders in the Soviet Union are in a position to attempt to do whatever they think should be done, so that presumably they weigh results of policy in terms of dysfunctionality, and their policies should reflect these results. In the early years after the 1917 revolution a great deal of sex freedom was permitted. The withering away of the family was anticipated. Marriage was simple; divorce was easy. But it apparently became clear in the 1930's that this way of organizing family life was dysfunctional for Soviet society, for at that time a great change, or reform, was introduced.

The crystallization of the new attitudes can be dated roughly, from 1935–36. Earlier social radicalism was denounced as a "Leftist" deviation, and the whole pattern of policy and of approved standards of behavior altered. Virginity was reinstated as a virtue, as was respect by the young for their parents; co-education was abandoned. The importance of stable family life was emphasized as a requirement for the effective functioning of the state, and divorce was made more difficult and expensive. Tax incentives were provided for the development of large families. And, in an act made notable because of a brief period of public discussion . . . abortion on other than medical grounds was made illegal in June 1936.*, [43]

Prostitution was attacked; [44] so, also, was alcoholism. The conditions which the West considered bad, needing reform—social problems, in brief—were found to be dysfunctional in that society also.

c) Group dysfunctionality is illustrated by the experience of prisoners of war. In their Report to the Secretary of Defense the Advisory Committee on Prisoners of War pointed out just how groups in prisoner-of-war camps deteriorated.

By design and because some officers refused to assume leadership responsibility, organization in some of the P.O.W. camps deteriorated to an every-man-for-himself situation. Some of the camps became indescribably filthy. The men scuffled for their food. Hoarders grabbed all the tobacco. Morale decayed to the vanishing point. Each man mistrusted the next. Bullies persecuted the weak and sick. Filth bred disease and contagion swept the camp. So men died for lack of leadership and discipline.[45]

* Abortion was legalized again in 1955 (*New York Times,* Dec. 1, 1955).

From this one gathers that absence of leadership, disorganization in the sense of role violation (every man for himself, mistrust, bullying), filth, and illness are dysfunctional to the groups involved, however functional they might be to their enemies.

DYSFUNCTIONALITY IN TERMS OF POLITICAL THREAT. It will be seen that there is no completely satisfactory approach to the concept of dysfunctionality—cultural, societal, or group—either through history or through recent events. The data on which these approaches rest, however accurate, are too equivocal and too indecisive to constitute the basis for a rigorously scientific concept. Are there any objective specifications for dysfunctionality which will eliminate these difficulties?

It has been suggested that dysfunctionality may be defined more clearly when it is seen against the competitive and conflict situations which prevail at midcentury among the great cultural traditions of the world. In brief, war—hot and cold—provides a setting in which we can set up specifications of dysfunctionality. Here three different approaches are possible.

"HOT WAR" AND DYSFUNCTIONALITY. A culture or a social system might be able to carry a heavy load of dysfunctionality so long as it remained unchallenged from the outside. Indeed, many have. They have survived despite illness on a vast scale, poverty, and a Balkanized structure—all these have existed in India for centuries. Such conditions may prevent the "eufunctioning" of a social system, but not its functioning, at least on a survival level. When such a system is challenged, however, or threatened from the outside, the hitherto merely dysfunctional elements become positive hazards, genuine threats to survival. The reasons given for the fall of Rome might not have destroyed Roman civilization if it had not been for the invasion of the tribes from the north. War, in brief, renders dysfunctional elements genuine dangers. This fact was invoked by the apologists of militarism and war; they argued that war forced nations to keep fit. It revealed dysfunctional elements to be social problems.

In the United States, for example, when 1,825,000 men were rejected for military service because of psychiatric disorders, and 600,000 were discharged for neuropsychiatric reasons, mental health could be seen by all to be a social problem of great magnitude. It was not simply that mentally ill people and their families suffered, or that it was expensive to take care of such patients; it was now a matter of the common survival of the whole group. Similarly, when a large proportion of young men were rejected because of physical defects, the health of the nation could be seen as a major social problem. For when a population is viewed in terms of military protective requirements in a threatening situation, it is a matter of great concern that it be healthy.[46] When discrimination against Negroes meant labor shortages and consequent slowing down of the production effort during the war, the prejudice which caused it was seen to be dysfunctional, even dangerously so. The uneducated were a drag on the Army, so the schooling of everyone was seen to be a social problem. The criterion of dysfunctionality, then, becomes more focused when we think of it in terms of a system being challenged or threatened from the outside. It also ceases to be statocentric or classbound. In thinking about social problems the whole population becomes the in-group; it is not one segment versus another. When social perception is limited to a class framework, it might be possible for members of the privileged classes to say that everyone should look after himself, and that the problems of others are no concern to them. But when social perception is not so limited and when a nation has to face an outside threat, all classes in the nation belong to the in-group and the welfare of all is a concern of all. Proponents of the ideology of mutual aid tried to make this point clear. In facing an outside threat, then, consensus with respect to social problems is more likely; the dysfunctionality criterion becomes more objective.

But dysfunctionality in wartime is a drastic criterion. It sharpens our thinking, to be sure, but it may overshoot the mark. We cannot apply the same tests in peace that we apply in a crisis. If we do we are in danger of setting up a so-called garrison state or a totalitarian regime, in which many other values are sacrificed to military efficiency.

"COLD WAR" AND DYSFUNCTIONALITY. The strategy and tactics of psychological warfare also provide clues with respect to dysfunctionality. It is the job of strategists in psychological warfare to locate weak spots in the enemy and to attack there. The communists, for example, are highly skilled in locating such sore spots—race relations, poverty, ignorance, labor-management difficulties—and exploiting them to the limit. Therefore, whatever can be used by one's enemies in a cold war or in psychological warfare is dysfunctional and hence a social problem.

Anything that puts one at a competitive disadvantage vis-à-vis an outside threat also becomes a social problem. Failure to achieve the maximum or at least optimum utilization of human talents was not defined as a social problem until very recently, and then only because the USSR was outstripping us in the training of scientists.[47]

WORLD PUBLIC OPINION AND DYSFUNCTIONALITY. The third approach to an objective specification of dysfunctionality has been suggested in terms of the "bar of world public opinion." According to this point of view, anything that puts us at a disadvantage in competing for world opinion is dysfunctional and hence a social problem. Anything is dysfunctional, that is, harmful, if it makes us look "bad" in the eyes of the rest of the world.

Problems previously taken for granted as purely domestic are now international in importance because of their relation to the world scene and because of the Soviet-American competition for the loyalties of other peoples. . . . A few examples may be cited to show how problems usually considered as *our own* have been raised to the international level.

One is the area of race relations. Incidents involving race relations are used to our disadvantage in a world where more than half of the inhabitants are colored and are becoming more sensitive to treatment accorded to them by the white peoples. Our government recognizes that our relations with other nations are injured and our power position jeopardized by evidences of racial discrimination.

Another factor of world importance is the state of our economy. We are so strong and influential in sheer economic strength that depression in the United States brings depression to large areas of the world, and prosperity here tends to bring it to the rest of the world. . . .

A third factor is the working of our democratic political system: the issues of civil rights and of honesty in government. All of these are intently watched by skeptical observers throughout the world and thus have a worldwide significance. . . . How other peoples regard our democratic system is significant in relation to the war for men's minds.[48]

It will be recalled that one of the objectives of our analyses in this chapter was a set of specifications or a theoretical model which would help us determine what constitutes a social problem, or a social situation that must be changed or reformed. We first canvassed the history of the idea of a social problem to gain a perspective on the original contents of the concept. We then set up three criteria which seemed to fit the historical data. With some modification, and despite their limitations, these three criteria have been applied here in selecting the materials to be discussed.[49]

Criteria for Selecting Social Problems for Discussion

The first criterion was tradition. As we saw above, certain social problems have been central in the concept from the very beginning. A discussion of them is expected in books and courses on social problems, and this expectation has been respected. The nature of these social problems changes, as we have so often pointed out: suffering becomes increasingly "mental," rather than physical; standards of what constitutes a problem are raised; the kinds of illness which are problems change; and so on. But the traditional core of "social problems" remains.

Most of the traditional social problems also meet the criteria of humanitarianism, utilitarianism, and dysfunctionality—with the limitations mentioned above. Physical and mental illness and disability (Chaps. 8-14); family relationships of men and women (Chaps. 15 and 16), in youth (Chaps. 17 and 18) and in old age (Chap. 19); work relationships of men (Chap. 20) and women (Chap. 15), in youth (Chap. 17) and in old age (Chap. 19)—all involve stress situations which may create anxiety, be costly to the community, and dysfunctional to the social system. Delinquency (Chaps. 14 and 18) and crime (Chaps. 14 and 21), similarly, are two other traditionally defined social problems which also pass the three tests. The relationships among minority groups and between them and the majority group (Chap. 22) were not originally defined as a social problem in the 19th century, but they became so defined in the 20th, and seem to pass all tests for such a definition.

Not traditional, however, is the discussion of social problems in an international setting (Pt. VII). The justification for including these problems lies in the fact that they tend at the present time to meet not only the humanitarian criterion, but, increasingly, the utilitarian and dysfunctionality criteria also.

The social problems, as distinguished from the political problems, related to religion have been dealt with only incidentally, as marginal distortions (Chap. 14); they are referred to also in connection with group-generated problems. Hatemongering and prejudice, not mere religious differences, constitute the social problems as here conceived. Most of the other problems associated with religion tend to be political, having to do with the use of tax monies.

The social problems related to education are dealt with in connection with youth (Chap. 17). The political, financial, and pedagogical problems of schools which plague us at midcentury are not included. The problems to be anticipated with respect to increasing leisure are referred to (Chap. 20) but not elaborated; they do not seem to fulfill the three criteria here established for social problems. Nor, finally, is the impact of the mass media dealt with here.

There are other important community problems which are not here discussed—consumer problems, for example—and their omission is not intended to imply that their seriousness is not recognized or that it is underestimated. Any book must be selective, and the basis for selection will necessarily exclude materials as important as any that are included.[50]

Before we pass on to a discussion of the "why" aspect of social problems, two points should be cleared up. One has to do with motivation and one with method.

Motivation and the Concept of Social Problems

We pointed out that there is both a subjective and an objective aspect to social problems: rising planes or levels of living which can be objectively measured and subjective standards or evaluations of poverty; institutionalized definitions of roles and individual conceptions of them; objective criteria of status and subjective status feelings; objective threats and subjective perception of threats. In addition, there is also a subjective or motivational element in the recognition or definition of a social problem.

Not everyone, as we pointed out above, can rise to the level of abstraction involved in stating social or societal problems. But even among those who can, not all do. Analyses of motives are usually fruitless. Motives may be irrelevant in any event. People often do injury to those they love with the best intentions in the world. Others with the worst possible motives may take actions that help their enemies. It is therefore necessary to evaluate motives and behavior separately. The work of reformers has often been impugned because of their motivation. Great reforms are sometimes discounted because they were accomplished by men with psychotic drives. It is, therefore, of only incidental significance to attempt to answer the question: Why do suffering, injustice, and handicap move some people, but not others, to define a situation as a problem, and to try to do something to help? Why are these phenomena viewed as problems by some, but not by others? Why does the priest walk past the wounded man on the road, turning his head not to see, wishing not to involve himself with the injured man who is not his concern? And why does the good Samaritan bind the man's wounds and take him to the inn and see that he is taken care of?

A psychologist might invoke love or sympathy to explain why some people judge situations to be social problems. And, of course, he would not overlook fear, either: fear that too much stress—suffering, injustice, crime—might lead to retaliation. Guilt feeling is a possible motivation also: why should I be privileged while others are not? Hate for authority might be deflected to hate for exploiters, that is, the motivation might not be sympathy for the oppressed but hatred for the oppresser.[51] Reform might be a sluice for all kinds of aggressive impulses.

Sociologists are more likely to think in terms not of individual psychological motives but in terms of role conceptions, such as duty, responsibility, obligation, *noblesse oblige*. One man conceives his role as a Christian or a nobleman or a responsible citizen; another conceives his role as a stranger, minding his own business: he is not a "do-gooder" or a busybody. Nor should the part that ideologies play be ignored. The Christian ideology has been a powerful force in motivating people to see certain conditions as problems; indeed, it has motivated them to see them as problems not only at home but all over the world, as we shall see in Chapter 23.

Can the Study of Social Problems Be Scientific?

If standards, motivation, and middle-class biases are so inextricably interwoven into the concept of social problems is it possible to be scientific in studying them? Is the concept inherently unscientific?

The Social Scientists, it will be recalled, insisted that the methods of science be applied to reform. To them the idea of science was almost as basic as that of reform. It hardly occurred to them that there could be any difficulty. They took it for granted that the scientific method was as applicable to social problems as to the physical sciences.

When social-problems courses were included in the university curricula, however, the theorists of the subject began to feel uneasy. Some of them became embarrassed or were ashamed of the reformistic antecedents of their subject. The value premises inherent in the concept troubled them. They wished to be rigorously scientific. Could they be, with such a concept?

In order to answer this question, some subtle strands of thinking must here be distinguished. So long as the students of social problems substituted moralistic judgments for careful observation and interpretation they could not be scientific. So long as they assumed answers instead of looking for them, they were not scientific. So long as their terminology reflected a condemnatory attitude toward people, they were not scientific.

But to say all this is not to say that it is impossible to be scientific about the study of conditions considered dysfunctional or, starkly, "bad." The analogy of medical science is apt. Medical research begins with the value premise that it is undesirable for people to be ill. No one denies scientific objectivity to most of the research on the illnesses of human beings. In a similar way it is possible to be rigorously scientific in studying other kinds of human social and societal ills. Some of the best scientific research in American sociology has dealt with crime, mental illness, and related subjects. The value premise on which research is begun in no way prevents the work from following rigorously scientific techniques.[52] Indeed, people with diametrically opposed value premises could attack the same problem and apply the same techniques and obtain the same results, whether they studied the state of the people's health, or the nature and extent of slums and blighted areas, or the incidence of family breakdown. Theoretically—not always actually, unfortunately—their results would be the same, but the interpretation and evaluation of them would be different. In brief, the application of science to the study of social problems is in no sense rendered impossible by the value premises embodied in the concept.

In this chapter we have attempted to deal with the question, What are the criteria for judging a situation to be a social problem? And we have concluded that there are at least four: the traditional, the humanitarian, the utilitarian, and the functional. In the next chapter we shall ask, Why do these problem situations occur?

NOTES

1 Efforts to make terminology reflect these distinctions have a long history. At Yale University, for example, in the 1880's and 1890's, William Graham Sumner, an outstanding sociologist, experimented with different titles for his course to give precision to the nature of its contents. And there have been sporadic efforts since that time. The use of the same term—"social"—to cover both interpersonal or group relationships and societal relationships may become quite confusing.

2 See, for example, the description of 18th-century London, page 80.

3 General William Booth, *In Darkest England* (Funk, 1890), pp. 13 ff.

4 See L. L. Bernard, "Conflict between Primary Group Attitudes and Derivative Group Ideals in Modern Society," *American Journal of Sociology*, 41 (March 1936), pp. 611–623.

5 Crane Brinton, "Humanitarianism," *Encyclopaedia of the Social Sciences*, VII (Macmillan, 1932), 545–546.

6 *Ibid.*, p. 548.

7 Not everyone agreed, of course. In England, for example, T. R. Malthus, a minister, pointed out that even if science improved the lot of the poor they would only increase the number of their children so that the end result would only be more miserable people in the world to suffer. This point is being made today also with respect to world populations, particularly in the underdeveloped areas, as we shall see in Part VII.

8 A. P. Peabody, "The Intellectual Aspect of the Age," *North American Review*, 64 (April 1847), pp. 286–287.

9 Theodore Parker, *Experience as a Minister* (1859), quoted by F. B. Sanborn in *S. G. Howe* (Funk, 1891), pp. 115–116.

10 O. A. B., "Education of the People,"

Christian Examiner, XX (new series, II) (May 1836), p. 168.

11 Francis Greenwood Peabody, *The Approach to the Social Question. An Introduction to the Study of Social Ethics* (Macmillan, 1909), pp. 28, 2–3.

12 See L. L. Bernard and Jessie Bernard, *Origins of American Sociology* (Crowell, 1943) for a history of the discipline Social Science.

13 *American Social Science Association, Constitution, Address, and List of Members* (1865), pp. 10–11.

14 *Ibid.,* p. 3.

15 L. L. Bernard and Jessie Bernard, *op. cit.,* p. 616.

16 *Ibid.,* p. 614.

17 *Ibid.,* pp. 620–621.

18 *Ibid.,* p. 621.

19 *Ibid.,* p. 640.

20 *Ibid.,* p. 641.

21 *Ibid.,* p. 643. A model course, covering 5½ pages, is presented *ibid.,* pp. 628–634.

22 S. A. Queen, W. B. Bodenhafer, E. G. Harper, *Social Organization and Disorganization* (Crowell, 1935), p. v.

23 Jessie Bernard, "Statocentrism: Proposing a New Term," *American Journal of Sociology,* 54 (Nov. 1948), p. 235.

24 There were other problems also, intensified if not created by the industrial revolution, in which the people who had the problems saw them as their own and attempted to do something about them themselves. The so-called "Woman Movement," the consumer movement, the agrarian movements, the labor movement, and reform movements among Negroes were among these efforts by people to deal with their own social problems in their own way and not wait for the "gifted and educated classes" to handle them for them. Sometimes the Social Scientists paid attention to this kind of problem also, but usually from the viewpoint of an outsider rather than a participant.

25 One study has documented this fact in connection with sexual behavior; it is alleged, for example, that a great deal of legislation concerning sex is an attempt of the middle class to impose its standards on the lower classes against their will. See A. C. Kinsey, W. B. Pomeroy, and C. E. Martin, *Sexual Behavior in the Human Male* (Saunders, 1948), pp. 389–393.

26 There is no implication intended in this statement that people in lower socioeconomic status levels are inherently inferior intellectually to others. They are capable of learning to see the total societal system but their vocabulary, system of concepts, and experience limit their perceptions.

27 Leonard Schatzman and Anselm Strauss, "Social Class and Modes of Communication," *American Journal of Sociology,* 60 (Jan. 1955), pp. 329–338.

28 James A. Davis, "Subject and Task Variation in the Perception of Status Symbols," abstract of paper read at the American Sociological Society meetings, August 1955.

29 K. Svalastoga, E. Høgh, M. Pedersen, E. Schild, "Differential Class Behavior in Denmark," abstract of paper read at the American Sociological Society meetings, August 1955.

30 *Ibid.*

31 Here, for example, is Mrs. Suburbia. She lives in a separate, individual home. It looks independent of others. Yet we can see that it is part of a vast and intricate pattern. There are electric wires entering this house; there are telephone wires; there is a television aerial; there are water pipes bringing water in and sewer pipes taking water out. All these physical things link her with the outside world. In addition, there are human ties, but we do not even have to refer to them. Seemingly remote conditions need only the channels we have listed here to involve Mrs. Suburbia and her family. It is not always easy to get Mrs. Suburbia to see that illness in slum areas involves her, that mental illness affects her even if none of her family suffers, that gangsterism has repercussions in her grocery bill, that any of the situations which we call social or, preferably, societal problems are really of any concern to her.

32 S. A. Queen and Delbert Mann, *Social Pathology* (Crowell, 1925), p. xi.

33 Some students avoid the difficulties inherent in a definition of social problems by discarding the concept and referring only to social disorganization. For an excellent statement of this point of view see R. E. L. Faris, *Social Disorganization* (Ronald Press, 1948). The fact remains, however, that there must still be a selection since not all social disorganization is included in texts which eschew the term "social problem." Furthermore, the very concept of social problems, with its inherent value judgments, is of great sociological significance.

34 S. A. Queen and D. M. Mann, *op. cit.*

p. xi. These writers refer to "those senti-
mental students who want to start right
out and do something for 'these poor
people.' They cannot wait to search for
the sources of trouble; they must go forth
at once with a basket of groceries or take
a collection for an orphan asylum. They
delight in giving alms, but refuse to examine the fruits of their 'philanthropy.' "
Philosophers refer to this as the "Socrates-
and-the-pig" problem.

35 Philosophers refer to this as the "Socrates-
and-the-pig" problem.

36 The word "fall" is placed in quotation
marks to call attention to the fact that
there was no simple, single event, such
as the sacking of Rome, which can be
labeled a fall. The fall occupied a long
period of time and it is doubtful if many
Romans at the time actually knew that
Rome had fallen. It was the historians,
many centuries later, who used the term
"fall."

37 Marion J. Levy, *The Structure of Society*
(Princeton Univ. Press, 1952), p. 56.

38 One sociologist, Emile Durkheim, suggested that crime served the function of
increasing solidarity in the group against
the common enemy.

39 Michael Eckstein, "Social Structure, Social Integration, and Crime," paper read
at the meetings of the Eastern Sociological Society, March 25, 1956.

40 Jessie Bernard, "History and Prospects of
Sociology," in *Trends in American Sociology*. G. A. Lundberg, Read Bain, and
Nils Anderson, eds. (Harper, 1929), pp.
8–10. See also Robert Flint, *Historical
Philosophy in France and French Bel-
gium and Switzerland* (Blackwood, 1893).

41 F. J. C. Hearnshaw, *Medieval Contributions to Modern Civilization* (Barnes &
Noble, 1949), pp. 22–23.

42 Jessie Bernard, *American Community Behavior* (Dryden, 1949), pp. 652–653.

43 W. W. Rostow, *The Dynamics of Soviet
Society* (Norton, 1953), p. 108.

44 Dyson Carter, *Sin and Science* (Heck-
Cattell, 1946).

45 Reported in the *New York Times*, August 18, 1955.

46 Newspaper reporters in the Belgian campaign of 1939 contrasted the pale faces
of the Birmingham clerks in the British
army with the sun-tanned faces of Hitler's men. The health of the German
youth had been a matter of concern to
Hitler; prewar Britain had shown no
such concern.

47 For example: "We must," said Chairman
Lewis L. Strauss, of the Atomic Energy
Commission, "in some manner insure

that those students with demonstrated
aptitudes receive the inspiration they deserve. This is a challenge to parents,
educators, industry, professional societies
and for Government at the Federal,
state, and local levels. It should be a
matter of national remorse that less than
half of our brightest high school students—those in the top 20 percent of
their classes—go to college, and only 2
percent of those judged capable of earning Ph.D. degrees do so. We go to great
lengths to conserve our forests and wild
life and waste the most valuable national
asset we have." (Quoted by James Reston
in an article entitled, " 'Cold War' and
Schools; An Analysis of How International Crisis Affects U.S. Policy on Aid
to Education," *New York Times*, December 5, 1955.)

48 Byron Fox, "The Cold War and American Domestic Problems," *Social Problems*, 1 (June 1953), p. 12. This point of
view is illustrated in the case of India
by C. L. Sulzberger, "Seeing Ourselves as
Others See Us," in the *New York Times*,
February 19, 1955.

49 Some writers consider it necessary to
specify that a number of people must be
involved before any ill can be denomi-
nated a social problem, although the
specific extent of the required incidence
is never defined. The position taken here
is that there is no human ill to which
one person is susceptible and other human beings not susceptible also. It is
impossible even to conceive of a unique
human ill or stress. Indeed, it is one of
the elements of sanity to recognize that
"we are not alone." No matter what the
problems are that any human being has,
there are others who also have them, or
have had them, or will have them. One
sick person may not be viewed as a social
problem; but if one person is sick, many
may become sick. The problem is the
sickness, not the sick person. That incidence or extent is an important measure
of the seriousness of a social ill cannot,
of course, be denied.

50 For a discussion of community problems
see Jessie Bernard, *American Community
Behavior* (Dryden, 1949).

51 See Rudolf Heberle, *Social Movements*
(Appleton-Century-Crofts, 1951), pp. 95–
97.

52 The value premises of current students
of social problems have been summarized
by Paul Furfey ("The Social Philosophy
of Social Pathologists," *Social Problems*,
2 [Oct. 1954], pp. 71–73) as follows:

The reproduction of the biologically fit should be encouraged by a eugenics program in so far as this is feasible. The growing child should be shielded from whatever can be detrimental to his morals and personality. Pre-school centers are desirable and primary education should be compulsory. Child labor can be dangerous. Parent education is a good thing. It is well to try to detect and treat behavior disorders at an early age. There should be good relations among the various groups that make up the community, for example, between Negroes and whites, between the educated and the uneducated, or between trailer folk and settled residents of a locality. 'Good' relations are those marked by cooperation and confidence, not by mutual suspicions, hostilities, misunderstandings, and resentments. Interpersonal relations should be friendly and individualized, a sense of belonging should be encouraged in all, and no one should be stigmatized as inferior on account of his ethnic origin. Planned recreational programs are a desirable means for encouraging friendly and relaxed interpersonal relations. Generally speaking, technological progress is a good thing; but the modern industrial system involves certain dangers that should be met by community action, for example, the dangers of excessive strain and fatigue, unemployment, and economic insecurity in old age. Economic pressure should not be used as a weapon against the worker. The standard of housing and nutrition should be raised. The benefits of modern medicine should be available to all. In particular, the community should organize to secure the early diagnosis and adequate treatment of mental illness; and to such illness no social stigma should be attached. Frankness in the discussion of sex is desirable. Our traditional code of sex ethics needs revision; this does not mean that sexual promiscuity can be tolerated, but rather that the code needs to be revised in the direction of a more relaxed, less guilt-conscious attitude. Government must not be arbitrary. In the interest of efficient government it is desirable to employ full-time, professionally trained personnel in administrative positions. Governmental planning for future development is also desirable. The social scientist should enjoy full freedom of teaching and research so that he can make his maximum contribution to the overall planning of society. . . . It is a philosophy perhaps most accurately called "humanitarianism." It places a great deal of emphasis on the dignity and worth of the human person. It condemns all cruelty and brutality. It demands for every man freedom to pursue happiness in his own way, provided he does not trespass on the equal freedom of his fellows. It is a reasonable philosophy, very critical of meaningless conventions and traditional social distinctions that lack a pragmatic basis. It is a kindly philosophy, tolerant of differences, more anxious to control by persuasion than by force. It is a secular philosophy, concerned with human welfare in this present existence and not taking sides on religious issues. Historically, it has its roots in the Enlightenment of the 18th century. Since that time it has undergone a good many modifications and today it is not a completely unified and consistent philosophy. However, the term "humanitarianism" is still definite enough to characterize that which is most distinctive in the social philosophy of American social pathologists.

6

Explanatory Theories
and Concepts

Long before human ills were viewed as scientific problems or as amenable to rational control they were puzzling intellectual and ethical problems. Why do pain and suffering occur? What causes them? This was the perennial problem of evil with which men had been wrestling for centuries.

Three Approaches

One possible answer has been, quite simply, It is God's will. A second explanation invokes nature, including human nature, as the cause. Certain things are "just natural"; they can be explained in no other terms. A third type of explanation attempts to be scientific—and it was this approach that was so new in the concept of social problems. It does not try to answer the basic question, why? in any but a superficial sense. It attempts only to find out what conditions are associated with what

Three Approaches

Textbook Conceptualizations: Social Pathology,
Social Disorganization, and Value Conflict

Pathologies as Social Problems

The Stresses of Disorganization

Historical Perspective on Social Disorganization

The "Causes" of Social Problems

Chance

situations. The explanations it offers of social problems are—ideally, if not always actually—tentative, undogmatic, and anthropocentric (drawn up from the point of view of man himself, not from that of some outside power or force). The scientific explanation for the existence of social conditions that cause stress does not deny an ultimate theological or metaphysical explanation; it merely proceeds on the assumption that it must ignore such an explanation if it wishes to deal with these conditions effectively. Scientific explanations may vary widely, as we shall presently see; they may make use of quite different conceptual interpretations; but they agree in that they all seek explanations in the data themselves rather than in outside forces.

Theological Explanations

Illness, crime, accident, premature death, drought, poverty, injustice, war—anything that happens can be interpreted as the expression of God's will. The story of Job is the classical case dramatizing the theory that the misfortunes of men have a divine purpose, however inscrutable to man. Here was an upright man, wealthy in goods and in the respect of the community. Then misfortune struck. He lost his children, he lost his wealth, he lost, finally, his health. He could not understand why all these evils should befall him. He had been a good man; there was no occasion for God to punish him so. His friends, basing their conclusions on human logic, insisted that he *must* have done something to deserve his fate. He should admit his guilt. But Job insisted that he felt no guilt. God finally spoke to him and Job came to a new understanding of God as inscrutable and gave up attempting to find a humanly reasonable explanation for his ills. God did what He did for reasons of His own, for reasons beyond mere human logic. It was presumptuous for man to demand that God conform to human logic, that His reasons satisfy merely human criteria of justice. Most people who subscribe to a theological explanation of human ills continue to seek a human logic in God's will. Unlike Job, they cannot accept what happens without an explanation which satisfies human conceptions of justice. For few people have learned Job's lesson. Most people insist that God be on their side, follow their logic, reason as they do. They are under compulsion to justify the ways of God to man.

The following account illustrates the way in which theological explanations of human misfortune, in this case, plague, have influenced political behavior.

In this year—1348—and in the following one there was a general mortality of men throughout the whole world. It first began in India, then in Taris (Tarus?), then it came to the Saracens, and finally to the Christians and Jews, so that in the space of one year, from Easter to Easter, as the rumour spread in the Roman curia, there had died, as if by sudden death, in those remote regions eight thousand legions, besides the Christians. The king of Tharsis, seeing such a sudden and unheard-of slaughter of his people, began a journey to Avignon with a great multitude of his nobles, to propose to the pope that he would become Christian and be baptized by him, thinking that he might thus mitigate the vengeance of God upon his people because of their wicked unbelief. Then, when he had journeyed for twenty days, he heard that the pestilence had struck among the Christians, just as among other peoples. So, turning in his tracks, he travelled no farther but hastened to return home. . . .

There died in Avignon in one day one thousand three hundred and twelve persons, according to a count made for the pope, and another day, four hundred persons and more. . . . At this time the pestilence became prevalent in England. . . . and people died as if the whole strength of the city were seized by sudden death. . . . The Scots, hearing of the cruel pestilence in England, suspected that this had come upon the English by the avenging hand of God. . . . And so the Scots, believing that the horrible vengeance of God had fallen on the English, came together in the forest of

Selkirk to plan an invasion of the whole kingdom of England. But savage mortality supervened and the sudden and frightful cruelty of death struck the Scots. . . .[1]

Preliterate peoples commonly interpret such misfortunes in terms of malevolent gods or spirits; and illiterate peasants even today sometimes protect themselves against misfortune by appeasing malevolent "evil eyes," and the like.

Among intellectuals the theological approach to social problems today is more sophisticated and subtle, but it is basically the same. One of the most powerful exponents of the Christian ideology in relation to social problems is Reinhold Niebuhr. He finds that exclusively secular attempts to deal with social problems have led only to even worse evils than those they tried to solve; and he believes the Christian Church is partly to blame.

. . . . the first task of the Christian Church is to interpret our sorrows and distresses, the agonies and pains through which the world is passing, and to recognize the hand of God in them. We must, as Christians, neither fall into complacency by evading the gravity of our experience, nor into despair and hysteria by interpreting the distress of our day as merely confusion without meaning. There is a divine judgment upon our sins in this travail of the nations and in this fall of nations and empires, in this shaking of historic stabilities and traditions. . . .

The Christian Faith is . . . unable to promise, as do secular creeds, some final historical redemption from all social evil. . . . This means that we must on the one hand strive to reform and reconstruct our historic communities so that they will achieve a tolerable peace and justice. On the other hand we know, as Christians, that sinful corruptions will be found in even the highest human achievements. . . .

We have . . . given some attention to the involvement of the Church and the churches in various sins and corruptions of modern society, whether these are expressed in racial pride, nationalistic idolatry, or economic and political imperialism. The Church, as well as the individual Christian, must see in the distress of our day the judgment of God which calls it to repentance and to a renewing of its mind. . . .

We have, furthermore, sought to draw some conclusions from the evidence on the social tasks which claim the special interest and service of the Church, and on the right strategy which the Church should pursue in seeking to conform to the injunction of our Lord to be a light to the world and a leaven in the world.[2]

It should be pointed out that the theological interpretation of social ills at the present time need not prevent those who espouse it from using scientific techniques in attempting to implement their goals. The Protestant Churches for many years, and the Catholic Church in recent years, have used scientific research techniques in determining the nature of the problems they were dealing with. Indeed, some of the earliest "research"—placed in quotation marks because it lacked modern techniques, but research nonetheless—in social problems was motivated by theological ideologies.[3]

Metaphysical Explanations

Metaphysical interpretations of human ills may take several forms. One is that it is the nature of man to behave in such a way that suffering and woe inevitably follow. Man is destined for evil. No further explanation for social ills is required. The seed of all evil lies in human nature, which cannot be changed. Under another interpretation the universe is assumed to be hostile to man. Nature is against him. Even if it is not, there are certain natural laws in social life, as in the physical world, whose violation means certain punishment, just as does violation of physical laws. Human misfortune and ills are the result of violation—witting or unwitting—of these laws. We may commiserate with human misfortune, but all we can do is recognize that it represents punishment for transgression of natural laws. Success, contrariwise, proves conformity with these natural laws. Whatever happens must be accepted as part of some great design. Nature pulls the strings and man is but a puppet responding. One of the purposes of Social Science was to determine the nature of these "natural laws" so that man could act according to, rather than against, them. As late as 1916 one author wrote of natural laws which must be obeyed: "If these natural laws, whatever they may be, are not taken into consideration, every plan and ideal for human betterment runs the risk of impracticability, or else of being brought to naught even after it has seemingly realized its purpose." [4] And almost thirty years later another writer complained of the persistence of this point of view:

There is a widely held belief in the existence of an over-all super-organic social system or organization which operates through large-scale social forces that govern our whole social life. . . . In both the textbook presentations . . . and in monographs . . . one finds either an explicit statement or a more or less implicit assumption that whatever happens in a society is to be viewed as the outcome of the operation of large-scale social forces, which, acting at a distance, produce all our social events. Whenever anything goes wrong in our society and the customary institutional practices of economics, politics, and social life fail to operate as expected, the statement is made that someone or some group has been violating or interfering with the operation of social forces or economic laws. Therefore, the only remedy for our difficulties is to conform to the requirements of this assumed social system and to accept the operation of these social forces with full recognition that they alone can bring resolution to our difficulties.[5]

The most important current form of metaphysical interpretations is one that invokes inexorable laws of history to explain and interpret the problems of any particular period. History takes the place of God. Here is how one author describes the process among communists:

I have known many Christians—Poles, Frenchmen, Spaniards—who were strict Stalinists in the field of politics but who retained certain inner reservations, believing God would make corrections once the bloody sentences of the all-mighties of History were carried out. . . . They argue that history develops according to immutable laws that exist by the will of God; one of these laws is the class struggle; the twentieth century marks the victory of the proletariat, which is led in its struggle by the Communist Party; Stalin, the leader of the Communist Party, [fulfilled] . . . the law of history, or in other words [acted] . . . by the will of God. . . .

Humanity devised effective measures against smallpox, typhus, syphilis; but life in big cities or giant collectives breeds new diseases. Russian revolutionists discovered what they claimed were effectual means of mastering the forces of History. They proclaimed they had found the panacea for the ills of society.[6]

With this belief in unshakable and already known laws of History, those who hold to this metaphysical point of view see "what is happening in the people's democracies [as] . . . necessary, even if temporarily bad." [7] Social problems in such a context can easily be defined in terms of resistance to History. And resistance to the established order is viewed as resistance to History; it can be wiped out with a clear conscience.

Our chief concern here, however, is not with either theological or metaphysical explanations of the occurrence of the ills which are viewed as social problems, but rather with the several attempts to explain them in scientific terms. Some of these have been in biological terms, some in psychological, some in cultural, and some in sociological terms.

Scientific Explanations

To simplify our discussion we shall combine the biological and the psychological approach as an "individual" approach, and the cultural and sociological approaches as an interactional or institutional approach.

APPROACHES BY WAY OF THE INDIVIDUAL

BIOLOGICAL. It should be pointed out before we begin our discussion that a biological interpretation is wider than one based on heredity alone. An amputation of a limb is a biological handicap; it is obviously not a hereditary one. An accident which destroys part of the brain is a biological fact; the resulting defect is not hereditary. Competitive stresses may stimulate certain glandular responses to the point where, let us say, stomach tissue is impaired. The injured tissue is a biological fact; it is not a hereditary condition.

There is always a strong temptation to explain what happens to people in terms of heredity. Why does he become a criminal? Because he was born that way. Why does he steal? Because he is a Negro. And so on. And when, especially in the 19th century, the evidence seemed so convincing, the temptation was particularly great.

The 19th-century perception of social ills, it will be recalled, was characteristically statocentric, that is, classbound or class-oriented. It was noted that these problems were not randomly distributed throughout the population. They were related to one another, they occurred together. Indeed, there is nothing about traditional social problems better documented than their tendency to cluster together. Careful studies of the distribution of problems in urban communities have shown that illness, recorded delinquency, crime, schizophrenia, paretic psychoses, alcoholic psychoses, gangsterism, family disorganization, and poverty tend to occur in certain areas. An intensive study of the families being cared for by social work agencies in St. Paul has revealed the same concentration of problems. A small nucleus of families was found to account for a large and disproportionate share of the load of these agencies.

Among the 41,000 families under the care of St. Paul agencies in November 1948, about 7,000—7 percent of the community's families—were dependent, nearly 11,000 had problems of adjustment, well over 15,000 had problems of ill health, and almost 19,000 were being served by public and private recreation agencies. . . . Some families had more than one kind of problem. . . . A group of 6,600 families, about 6 percent of the city's families, were suffering from such a compounding of serious problems that they were absorbing well over half of the combined services of the community's dependency, health, and adjustment agencies.[8]

These were designated the "multiple problem families," becoming the living symbol of that source of social infection which exists in every community, absorbing a high proportion of the time and energy of skilled practitioners, and constantly frustrating community efforts in the direction of prevention.[9]

The same thing is reported in other communities. Social ills seem to concentrate in certain families as well as in certain areas. Studies made in the 19th and early 20th centuries of a number of degenerate families—the notorious Kallikaks, for example, the Jukes, the Nam family, the Nolly family, the Dwellers in the Vale of Siddim—had seemed to demonstrate a hereditary basis for these facts.

And it was, indeed, precisely these facts, early observed, that seemed to give substance to the argument that social ills were basically genetic in nature. These problem people were, "obviously," of inferior genetic stock. They were poor, vicious, criminal, defective, insane, unemployable, or immoral because they had an inferior hereditary strain. Those who believed this argued for eugenic programs which would ultimately weed out the unfit and encourage the fit. They bemoaned the differential birth rate which seemed to be having a seriously deteriorating effect on the quality of the population. In both England and the United States, for example, it was—and still is—argued that the low birth rate among the higher occupational levels and the high birth rate among the lower levels reduces the average intelligence quotient generation after generation. "Typical estimates of this decline range from two to four IQ points." [10] In point of fact, interestingly enough—as we shall see in Chapter 10—children today may have higher IQ's than formerly. At any rate, there is no demonstrable proof of declining IQ.

The tremendous amount of emotion generated by the heredity-versus-environment discussion of social ills gives us a hint of its essentially nonrational nature. We now recognize that as stated—"heredity versus environment" or "nature versus nurture"—it was not a scientific formulation. Discussion therefore concealed within itself a host of ideological—religious, theological, philosophical—and temperamental biases. Of course, if an unequivocal answer to this controversy could have been found, it would have had profound bearing on policy for dealing with social ills.[11]

Current thinking on the subject does not deny the possibility of genetic factors in the etiology of pathologies and individual defect, but such factors are seen as operating in a very complex way. It is by no means easy to determine what is meant by genetic inferiority as applied to social behavior. We know that moral and social traits as such are not inherited. What *is* the relationship between genetic make-up and role performance in a social situation? Just how are moral and social traits related to heredity? to the social order? Until we have satisfactory answers to questions such as these, to view either "heredity" or "environment" as an answer to the question "why" is unrealistic. We shall have more to say about this when we discuss resistance to stress.

SOCIAL-PSYCHOLOGICAL. The psychologist, like the biologist, tends to explain social conditions in terms of individuals, but not necessarily in terms of heredity. He takes into account acquired as well as instinctive equipment and motivations. He studies the conditions that make individuals prejudiced, hostile, sadistic, authoritarian, revengeful, or emotionally disturbed. He examines the personalities of leaders. He places the compensatory mechanisms of men under scrutiny. He tries to find out how they view the world. In brief, he sees social ills as the result of the behavior of individuals, though always in a social context. If one could rear all children in a certain kind of family environment one could solve most social problems, even war. Crime, mental illness, mental deficiency, intergroup relations, housing, war, and labor problems are studied as assiduously by psychologists as by sociologists, but the approach of the psychologists is in terms of the individual.

At one time the accepted theoretical interpretation of the behavior of the individual was based on instincts. All human institutions were explained as expressions of such inherited mechanisms. The family, religion, economic life, government, war—everything was seen as the result of instinctive mechanisms.[12] The fallacy of the instinct approach was exposed in the 1920's.[13] If instincts are universal and present in everyone, then they do not explain the unique behavior of any specific individual. If, by training, they become unique and idiosyncratic, then they are never known until after the fact. After a person has done something we may then say he did it to satisfy an instinct; but we do not know his instincts, so conceived, until after he has done something to satisfy them. Instincts, then, explain either too much or too little.

At the present time the individual motivations with which psychological research is concerned are conceived of largely as social, rather than hereditary, in origin, but they are still thought of as capable of explaining most social behavior. Actually, however, no matter how carefully we study individuals, we can never "explain" the existence of poverty, of war, of technological change, of technological unemployment. The individual approach can help us understand a particular poor family, a particular soldier, a particular innovator, a particular unemployed man. But we need more than a clinical approach to understand the situations which produced them.

APPROACHES BY WAY OF SOCIAL ORGANIZATION: INSTITUTIONS AND CULTURE. This same association of social ills with lower-class living patterns convinced another set of thinkers that these problems were "environmental," not genetic, in nature. It was clear to them that people were vicious, criminal, defective, insane, or ill because they were poor rather than the other way round. Their answer was to eliminate poverty by changing the institutions.

The idea that social organization or society or institutions are bad has a long history. The Old Testament prophets, it will be recalled, thundered against the agricultural institutions which they found in Canaan.[14] The early Christian anchorite found the world so evil that he retired from it in order to save his soul, and religious sects have been following his example ever since.

Rousseau in the 18th century, on the other hand, painted the picture of "the noble savage" in contrast to the wickedness of civilization, which was corrupting. The philosophical anarchists argued that man was naturally good, but that he was corrupted by his institutions. Wordsworth had noted the trailing clouds of glory which the child soon lost as the prison walls closed in about him. A great procession of social reformers of the 19th century held essentially this point of view, albeit somewhat modified. The romantic socialists, the builders of socialistic communities, and even the Marxian socialists were in essential agreement on this issue. Not human nature but human institutions constituted the key to social ills. Reform institutions, and human nature would then emerge in its pristine purity.

In recent years this point of view has found proponents who speak of our society as sick,[15] delinquent,[16] lacking in sanity.[17] Not the individual but the society in which he functions is viewed as pathological.

There is a growing realization among thoughtful persons that our culture is sick, mentally disordered, and in need of treatment. This belief finds expression in many different forms and from a variety of professions. We have had, for example, *The Sickness of an Acquisitive Society,* by Tawney, and *Modern Education,* by Rank, wherein society, not merely the individual, is portrayed as the patient.

Anyone who reflects upon the present situation in which our Western European culture finds itself cannot fail to see that we have passed from the condition in which deviations from a social norm could be regarded as *abnormal.* Today we have so many deviations and maladjustments that the term "normal" has lost almost all significance. . . .

The conception of a sick society in need of treatment has many advantages for diagnosis of our individual and social difficulties and for constructive therapy. . . . Perhaps the most immediate gain from adopting this conception is the simplification it brings. Instead of thinking in terms of multiplicity of so-called social problems, each demanding special attention and a different remedy, we can view all of them as different symptoms of the same disease. That would be a real gain even if we cannot entirely agree upon the exact nature of the disease. If, for example, we could regard crime, mental disorders, family disorganization, juvenile delinquency, prostitution and sex offenses, and much that now passes as the result of pathological processes (e.g., gastric ulcer) as evidence, not of individual wickedness, incompetence, perversity, or pathology, but as human reactions to cultural disintegration, a forward step would be taken. At present we cherish a belief in a normal, intact society against which we see these criminals, these psychopaths, these warring husbands and wives, these recalcitrant adolescents, these shameless prostitutes and vicious sex offenders, as so many rebels who threaten society and so must be punished, disciplined, or otherwise individually treated. This assumption of individual depravity or perversity gives us a comfortable feeling that all is well socially, but that certain individuals are outrageously violating the laws and customs that all decent people uphold. It is, indeed, interesting to see how this conception of a social norm, with individuals as violators and frustrators of normality, runs through so much of our thinking.[18]

Cultural explanations are also currently popular. The cultural explanation of social ills views them as the result of certain patterned relationships imposed upon a fairly standard human biology and psychology. Men are much the same biologically and psychologically, regardless of race; but they become different because of the different values and ways of organizing social life to which they are subjected. Adolescence, for example, is a time of storm and stress in one culture; it is psychologically uneventful in another. Old age is viewed as a repository of wisdom in one culture, and is eagerly looked forward to. It is seen as a problem in another, and dreaded. Homosexuality is institutionalized in one culture, forbidden in another. Divorce occasions no trauma to children in one culture; it is very traumatic in another. One culture makes for widespread mental instability; another builds great mental stability. Even the illnesses to which men are susceptible vary from one culture to another.

It is certainly true that the social problems of an industrialized culture are different from those of a preliterate culture; but this fact alone does not give us much help or insight. Every culture "generates" its own kind of problems. But the experience of other cultures is not necessarily pertinent to our own. Since we cannot change our culture as a whole, but must operate within it, to say that our culture "causes" our social problems is not very helpful, except as it stimulates thinking and prevents it from falling into parochial, or absolutistic ruts.

Textbook Conceptualizations: Social Pathology, Social Disorganization, and Value Conflict[19]

We pointed out in Chapter 5 that it was left for the textbook writers to find a satisfactory theoretical framework for the study of social problems. Since most of the textbook writers were social scientists they tended to look to sociogenic forces rather than to individuals for interpretative concepts. It is interesting to note that they did not look to social organization as a source of stress; that might have implied a value judgment, a criticism of the *status quo*. And they were determined not to be guilty of value judgments.

The men and women who wrote the constitution of the American Social Science Association in 1865 had had no misgivings about the ethical or normative nature of social or societal problems. Nor were they mortified to recognize the fact that one of the prerogatives of middle-class status was the right—or obligation—to define what was and what was not a social problem. They gave lip service to the ideal of science, but they did not trouble themselves much about the implications of this ideal. They were too busy dealing with practical problems to worry about the theory involved.

But the men in the universities were under more compulsion to find a solid theoretical framework for their courses. And the difficulty was compounded because value judgments—inherent in the very concept of social problems as something that had to be changed or reformed —were considered unscientific. Two concepts—social pathology and social disorganization—seemed to side-step this difficulty. Other sociogenic forces, such as competition and conflict, were not highlighted. They were invoked tangentially, or smuggled in under the disorganization label.

Social Pathology

The textbook concept of social pathology was not the same as the concept of a "sick society" referred to above. There was no assumption that the social order was itself in a pathological state. Implicit in the textbook formulations, as the author quoted above pointed out, was a belief in a normal, intact society, and certain people as deviants.[20]

The earliest textbook use of the term "social pathology" antedated the concept of a "sick society" by a good many years. As first used, it was primarily a figure of speech, an analogy. It was, indeed, based on the so-called organismic analogy which viewed society as analogous to a living organism. The earliest textbook dealing with the subject defined social pathology as the "study of all phenomena which are apparently inconsistent with the best interests of society, and the determination of clearly abnormal or unhealthful structures and functions."[21] It listed as among the more obvious signs of social diseases: poverty, vice, crime, pauperism, physical disability, and social inactivity (that is, "selfish idleness"). Although this text recognized that "abnormal social arrangements and functions react upon individuals, offering opportunities for personal degeneration and unsocial conduct if not actually making them necessary," it also insisted that "diseased and abnormal individuals produce pathological social conditions." [22] Social pathology referred, that is, to both individuals and to "abnormal social arrangements." The implication was that the social order as a whole was itself "normal" but that there were certain pathological conditions in it. There was, however, no criterion established on the basis of which one could define a social arrangement as pathological and no standard to determine when this criterion became pathological. That is, there was no statement of a method for deciding whether or not a situation was "clearly abnormal or unhealthful" or "inconsistent with the best interests of society." The conditions listed above were merely assumed to be.

A conception of social pathology verging very closely on that of role inadequacy was embodied in a textbook originally published in 1905. It defined social pathology as "the maladjustments in social relationships."

> The term "social pathology" may be used to denote the social conditions which result (1) from failure of individuals to so adjust themselves to social life that they function as independent, self-supporting members of society, who contribute their fair share to its stability and progressive development, and (2) from the lack of adjustment of social structure, including organized ways of doing things and institutions, to the development of social personality.[23]

Still another concept of social pathology, offered in a book published in 1912, was based on social defeat.[24] The author of this volume recognized that whole groups might suffer from pathologies, giving the Crusades as an illustration; yet these pathologies were not necessarily dysfunctional. Mass hysterias or depression of spirits he recognized as social pathologies. But his main concern was with people who were "abnormal in that they fail to fit into the social organization."

> The fundamental difference between normal and abnormal men, whatever it may be for the individual, is essentially social in its manifestation. Normal men are self-directing, associate with their fellows, and by mutual assistance carry on the struggle of life. The abnormal classes cannot be trusted to direct themselves and must be cared for because in strength, in conduct, or in condition they are not properly related to the social group.[25]

The textbook conceptualization of social pathology implying a "normal" social order with specific pathologies in it persisted for many years. In another text called *Social Pathology*, published some thirteen years after the text just cited, the authors tell us that they were

> . . . interested in people whose scheme of life has broken down, who do not get on well with their fellows, who have no definition of their social situation on the basis of which they can proceed to deal with it. We are interested in these people not because we look upon them as inferior, not because we think

of them as having "character defects," but because in the midst of this rather complex civilization of ours they have lost their way or perhaps have never found it. We think of them as people who face problems of personal adjustment which they for some reason are not able to work out for themselves. Hence, when we call them maladjusted, we do not mean to express moral disapproval, but rather objective description.[26]

Here the emphasis is on the pathology of individuals, a pathology of human interrelationships. Another text, fourteen years later, also speaks of social pathology as the problems of human inadequacy and maladjustment.[27] In 1940, social pathology was conceived as anything which interfered with the ability of an individual to participate in the social process,[28] a definition which comes very close to the concept of role disturbance or pathology which we use in this book. Another conceptual device used by the textbook writers to escape the onus of normative judgment was the concept "social disorganization," sometimes used interchangeably with social pathology,[29] sometimes as a distinct sociological phenomenon.

Social Disorganization

The implications "normal" and "abnormal" inherent in the concept of pathology were discarded in the textbook concept of social disorganization. In a great four-volume study of the Polish peasant in both Europe and the United States the concept of social disorganization was elaborated and came to occupy a central position in the theory of social problems.[30] The authors of this study rejected the concepts of "normal" and "abnormal." [31] They concluded that "abnormality is mainly, if not exclusively, a matter of deficient social organization. . . . And from this standpoint, the question of the antisocial individual assumes no longer the form of the right of society to protection, but that of the right of the antisocial individual to be made useful." [32] The study documents "the tendency to disorganization of the individual under the conditions involved in a rapid transition from one type of social organization to another." [33] Some later texts in social disorganization viewed it in terms of deviation from a norm; [34] tension, conflict, or drifting apart; [35] broken or dissolved social relationships; [36] value conflict or lack of consensus.[37] In all cases the concept of social disorganization, like that of social pathology, has been applied both to individuals and to the social order; that is, both personal and societal disorganization are included in the concept.

An important variation of the disorganization theme has been the so-called social lag theory which views social problems as resulting from a gap between different aspects—usually material and nonmaterial or institutional—of a culture owing to differential rates of change.[38] It implies that at a given moment a culture is stable and well organized; the introduction of change into this stable social order disorganizes it and produces problems until all aspects of the culture can once more accommodate to the new situation and thus "solve" the problems. In the sense that it often takes a long time for human institutions to catch up with technological changes, there is profound truth in this theory, as our discussion will presently show. But if it is implied either that stability in social organization means absence of stress or even of pathologies, or that disorganization is the only source of stress, then historical evidence belies the implication. Stable social orders may be felt to be unjust; they may generate stress despite, perhaps even because of, their stability.[39]

Value Conflict

In addition to the social-disorganization and social-pathology conceptualizations of social problems, there arose in the second quarter of the 20th century the so-called value-conflict approach, which rejected both the earlier textbook formulations and laid its emphasis on the evaluations of social conditions made by various groups, rather than on the conditions themselves. According to this point of view conditions which are not themselves caused by value judgments, such as physical ailments and catastrophes, are not considered social problems. Such other conditions as crime and class-linked illness are social problems because certain mores and values conflict with other mores and values and thus prevent consensus with respect to treatment. It is this lack of consensus, not the conditions, which constitutes the social problem. And, finally, such issues as child labor, low wages and long hours, the status of unorganized labor or of the unemployed, divorce, and race discrimination are problems only because there is a conflict of values among different segments of the population.[40]

Although the value-conflict approach does lend itself to analysis by means of newly evolving mathematical concepts, there are many dilemmas and paradoxes inherent in this approach. We have attempted to skirt them in our discussion by making a sharp distinction between conditions and the concept of social problems, by setting up criteria for judging conditions to be social problems, and by selecting for discussion those conditions which conform to these specifications.[41] We saw in Chapter 5 that not everything that some people have judged to be a social problem has actually achieved that status by consensus. Contrariwise, not everyone agrees that the traditionally accepted social problems are social problems. This last condition need not, however, interfere with the general or consensual judgment. As we shall see in Chapter 6, those who have succeeded in arousing public action have, as a matter of historical fact, prevailed; the laissez-faire advocates have lost.

After this brief introduction to the major explanatory concepts which have been used in the study of social problems we turn now to a more detailed presentation of the concepts of pathology and disorganization.

Pathologies as Social Problems

What is the value of the concept "social pathology"? In order to answer this question we must make a distinction between the pathologies of individuals and the pathologies attributed to "social arrangements," and deal with them separately.

Individual Pathologies as Social Problems

With respect to individuals, it seems established beyond cavil that there are genuine pathologies, demonstrable scientifically, which are social in their impact. Physical illness, "mental" illness, and a large proportion of mental and physical defects are the result of pathological conditions in the individual, some inherited, some acquired, some of known etiology, and some of as-yet-unknown etiology. The social concomitants of these pathologies in terms of role impairment fulfill all the criteria for judging a situation to be a social or societal problem (Chap. 5). They cause suffering, they are costly to the community, and they are probably to some degree dysfunctional. In the sense that these pathologies disable people in their role performance we may legitimately speak of them as *social* pathologies. Part IV is devoted to an examination of such pathologies.

In some cases, to be sure, the line dividing the pathological from the nonpathological is a fine one. This is especially true in the role impairments for which the organic basis has not yet been determined, or which are wholly social or societal in etiology, or which reveal themselves not in a clinical, but only in a social, setting (Chap. 14). They are here viewed as pathologies, even if their etiology is uncertain, when they result in extreme role impairment.

At one time many of these problems with as-yet-indeterminate etiology were defined legalistically rather than in terms of pathologies. The current trend in thinking about them—possible only because of abundance—is, however, in the direction of medical rather than legalistic formulations: people are "ill" rather than "bad"; "patients" rather than "criminals." The present text accepts this conceptualization of social pathology.[42]

This shift in thinking from legalistic to medical formulations of social or societal problems is important. The status of patient is quite different from the status of the criminal. The patient is not blamed for his illness. He is treated in a different manner. In exchange for protection, care, and release from responsibility, the role of patient requires subordination, obedience, and inferior status (as measured by prerogatives). (Some criminals prefer to be treated as criminals than as patients; they would rather go to prison than to the "padded cell.")

When we speak of social pathologies, then, we are referring to pathologies in individuals which have widely ramified social effects because of the role impairment they produce, and we include pathologies for which the etiology is as yet undetermined if they result in role impairment.

Pathology of "Social Arrangements"

Whether or not we are justified in applying the concept of pathology to "social arrangements" as well as to individuals is another question. If we set up as our criterion of a pathological condition any social condition that "causes" pathologies in individuals we might be on firm logical grounds, but we would be on very shaky empirical grounds. The same forces, for example, that precipitate pathologies in some people are part of the values we prize most highly. Some of the increase in mental illness, for example, is a result of modern medical science which keeps people alive so long.[43] We could hardly label modern public health institutions as pathological. The competitive stresses that release so much creative activity in some people have deteriorating effects in others. Shall we for this reason label them pathological? Social pathologies in this sense are often the price we pay for some of our most cherished values. In the absence of acceptable criteria for judging social conditions pathological, the term remains analogical. At best it is but a figure of speech; at worst it becomes merely an epithet which we apply to anything we disapprove.[44]

In forswearing use of the concept "social pathology" in the textbook sense of "pathological social arrangements" we do not sacrifice the idea that there do exist certain stress conditions which create pathologies on a wide scale—unemployment, for example—and which are therefore major social problems, as we shall point out in Chapter 20. We simply feel that the application of the concept of pathology to such stress conditions is too ambiguous at the present time. We limit our acceptance of the concept, therefore, to the pathologies in individuals which have a limiting or disturbing effect on role performance or which reduce stress resistance.

The Stresses of Disorganization

The concept of social disorganization, like that of pathology, is accepted in this book, but, again, not without certain limitations. When the term "social disorganization" is used synonymously with "social pathology," the same criticisms hold for both concepts. When it is used as a descriptive rather than explanatory concept, moreover, there can be no criticism except that it adds nothing to our understanding. It merely gives a new label to old problems. When disorganization is conceived of in terms of deviance, it tends to overvalue conformity, implicitly if not explicitly. There is a kind of halo around conformity and almost any kind of nonconformity tends to be viewed as a problem.

It is a serious criticism of the concept of disorganization that it fosters a tendency to identify all disorganization with bad or at least disapproved or dysfunctional conditions,[45] for not all disorganization is necessarily of this kind.[46] Sometimes disorganization may be "eufunctional" rather than dysfunctional. One student, for example, has pointed out that in the Middle Ages, say from 450 to 1450, "the central social problem . . . was the emancipation of the slave, the elevation of the serf, the edification of the freeman, and in general the establishment of conditions which would render possible the liberation and the self-realization of the individual soul." [47] Given certain values, in brief, the disorganization of a *status quo* was a desirable goal.

For social organization, as well as disorganization, may generate stress. It may be exploitative, characterized by gross inequalities that create the stresses of poverty and illness in a disenfranchised class. Stability alleviates only one kind of stress factor; it may generate others. Indeed, the stresses associated with disorganization may seem preferable to those who bear the brunt of a social order which seems unfair to them.

Too great an emphasis on social disorganization, finally, tends to minimize the impact of such other sociological phenomena as those related to competition and conflict. Competition as well as organization and disorganization can be a major source of stress, especially when achieved status is a major value. Indeed, the concept of competition is almost inherent in the concept of ranked status.[48] And an explanation of social problems at the present time, especially those related to class and group relationships, must include the concept of competition rather than of disorganization.

Finally, conflict phenomena—social-psychological as well as sociological [49]—are not given adequate recognition as sources of stress when they are subsumed under the rubric "disorganization."

In brief, then, although the concept of disorganization is indispensable for an understanding of social problems, its use does not preclude the application of such other concepts as pathology, organization, competition, and conflict. Some social problems are created by pathologies of one kind or another; some are created by the stresses of the current *status quo* or organization; still others are a by-product of competition; and, finally, some result from conflict.

Historical Perspective on Social Disorganization

Social order, unlike a natural ecological order which may persist for centuries, is in almost constant flux. A stability which lasts even fifty years is phenomenal. And this was true even in times which seem so stable to us now, after many centuries, the Middle Ages. And in modern times, change is increasingly rapid. As early as the 16th and 17th centuries there had begun a "period of deep disorganization and distress, marked by the decay of old classes and the rise of new ones, by the rapid accumulation of wealth associated with a lamentable spread of pauperism," [50] as medieval agrarian society became transformed into modern capitalistic society. By the late 18th century and early 19th century the mass movements to the cities had greatly accentuated and accelerated this disorganization.

Class Aspects of Societal Disorganization

Two contradictory organizational trends accompanied the new urban industrial order which began to emerge. On the one hand there was increasing geographical or horizontal integration within nations.

Cities and towns, to be sure, had always been dependent on the country-side and to this extent had been integrated into the agricultural society. But in a predominantly agricultural society there had been a great deal of local autonomy in communities. Markets were restricted. People belonged to few publics. The society was only loosely integrated geographically. There was comparatively little communication among different parts of the nation. But with the new technology markets became larger and more interdependent; there was more communication; local communities became more tightly integrated into the larger society.

At the same time, on the other hand, there was decreasing societal or vertical integration. A kind of societal disintegration or dissociation [51] accompanied urbanization in the 19th century. Moreover, individuals were being cut loose from their old moorings.

It was not that the distance between the top and the bottom classes was necessarily any greater in the new social order than it had been in agricultural societies; it was rather that all except monetary ties between them were being severed. Under the old regime the lord and the serf were very far apart indeed; but the role of the lord required a strong feeling of responsibility, of *noblesse oblige*. It prescribed obligations as well as privileges, just as the role of the serf included rights to protection as well as obligations to serve. The feudal system was held together by these mutually binding ties or "feuds," that is, oaths. In the newly emerging industrial society, on the other hand, the upper classes and the lower classes were held together only by what Carlyle called the "cash nexus." The people at the top paid for the services of those at the bottom but assumed no further responsibility for them. The classes lived not only in different, but, indeed, in disparate, worlds.

Institutions which had grown up to meet the scarcity economy of agriculture survived and were assumed to fit the new economy. Thus in England, for example, there had never been such wealth; the banking, manufacturing and trading classes enjoyed a standard of living higher than had ever been known before, for the new wealth was being channeled upward to them via old institutions. But at the other end of the scale there had never been such extensive misery in the world before.

As the 19th century progressed, it looked as though industrialized societies were actually becoming polarized. The new technology seemed to be slicing societies into opposing status classes. The great problem was, if we may simplify so dogmatically, how to keep the new, urban, industrialized society from falling apart under the impact of machine technology, for "the creation of riches proved an easier task than their equitable distribution." [52] Karl Marx, in fact, predicted that the process of societal dissociation would continue until there would be only two classes, the *bourgeoisie* and the proletariat, and that ultimately they would come into open conflict and the proletariat would triumph over the *bourgeoisie.*

Social disorganization in this class sense has probably been stemmed. In the most mature industrial nation in the world, the United States, the rich, as we saw in Chapter 1, are probably becoming less rich and the poor certainly less poor. The middle class, far from disappearing as Marx predicted, is becoming the largest class of all. We should, in fact, speak of the middle classes in the plural because there are so many of them. Some of this reversal of disorganizing trends was probably the result of the efforts of reformers, many of whom went down into the slums to study, or even to live with, the depressed or submerged classes. They reported on what they saw and they made surveys; they did not allow the successful classes to forget how the other half lived—or died. All kinds of appeals were used—humanitarian, religious, patriotic, self-interest—to show that things could not continue as they were. They kept pulling at the sleeves of the classes which seemed to be drifting farther and farther apart from one another; they tried to re-knit the social ties, creating them when they did not already exist in the form of legal obligations or moral responsibility.

But the reversal of the disorganizing trend was probably inherent in industrialization itself, although it might not have been discerned in time if the reformers had not held the fort, so to speak, until all the implications of industrialization—especially the implications of abundance—became understood. The basic reason, perhaps, for the reversal of the disorganizing trend lies in the fundamental principle of class structure that is characteristic of an era of abundance, as described in Chapter 1.

Individual Aspects of Societal Disorganization

At the level of the individual, disorganization may reveal itself in differing degrees, ranging all the way from complete normlessness, technically known as *anomie,* to merely minor role confusions or disturbances. With the new social order old role and status relationships had, as we pointed out above, been dissolved. The 19th-century political theorist Henry Sumner Maine had pointed out that the basis of social relationships was in transition from status to contract. People were no longer born into permanent social relationships; they had to create them. Status was not ascribed; it was achieved. At first this was looked upon as a step forward. It freed the individual. He was no longer bound by his hereditary position. He could change. He could rise. Social ties

Is television bringing family members together? Here the Joneses have come to visit with the Smiths and they have brought their children. But are the parents and the children really together? The adults are amused; they know that what they see on the television screen is not true. Do the children?

Many people are concerned about the nature of the television programs to which children are exposed. Not so much the omnipresence of violence—violence has been a preoccupation of the folk mind from time immemorial—but the casual attitude toward it, disturbs some observers. It is alleged by some students of the subject that for children who already have motivation and patterns for criminal behavior, television may become a school for teaching techniques of crime. Other people express concern about the passive nature of television entertainment. With increasing leisure, they ask, will television usurp a disproportionate part of the waking day? Will it create a sponge-minded generation, all too willing to let others do its thinking and leading?

On the favorable side of the ledger, some observers look to television as one of the answers to the shortage of teaching personnel in the immediate future. A number of colleges in different parts of the country are already using closed-circuit television, and research is directed toward determining the most effective ways of utilizing it for this purpose. As to the use of the medium for adult education and general culture, even its confirmed detractors recognize the immense potentialities of television in making available to millions music, drama, discussions of ideas, and other intellectual experiences hitherto enjoyed by only a small proportion of the population.

As in every comparable development in the communications field, the television medium is as beneficial or injurious as its owners and viewers allow it to be. To what extent has it already ameliorated or aggravated the social problems characteristic of an age of abundance? *(Photo: Black Star)* were presumed to be more rational, bargained out, so to speak, rather than customary. Masses of men migrated to cities. There were population upheavals almost unprecedented in history in so short a time.

But the cost of the new freedom in time came to be seen as high. Large numbers of individuals were severed from permanent, reassuring, stabilizing group relationships. They were isolated; they were alone. They had no warm social nest, so to speak, in which they could assume that everyone was on their side. They received no automatic training in group cooperation, in working together for common goals. This absence of training in collaboration has been labeled one of the major social problems of an industrial civilization.

In the primitive community, or in the American and European communities of a century or more ago, group codes determined the social order of things and the direction of individuals' lives; the interests of the individual were subordinated, by his own eager desire developed from infancy, to the interests of the group; and in return the group gave him stability, an assured function, and opportunity for satisfying participation. It was an established society.

By way of contrast, the typical industrial community of today is an adaptive society comprised of individuals of varied origin, many of them moving several times from one group association to another in the quest of education and jobs. Difficulties of relating themselves to others and consequent solitariness and unhappiness characterize many of these people. Many come to a fundamental assumption that the world is hostile; some react by overaggressiveness, others tread too carefully; and groupings frequently form in an attitude of wariness or hostility to other groups. Social skill (that is, our ability to secure cooperation between people) has disappeared.[53]

This author believes that since we cannot turn back we must work out new ways of teaching people how to collaborate and that if we do not, technical progress will only lead to social chaos and anarchy.

In the extreme form of disintegration of the individual's social bonds—in *anomie,* that is—the effects of social disorganization on personality may be extremely deteriorative. Lacking the emotional sustenance which one normally derives from group support, the individual becomes socially and emotionally impoverished. New kinds of bondage emerge, not necessarily legal or official, but no less oppressive for that. So long as sheer subsistence problems overlaid the disorganizational ones, the latter did not become so manifest. Now that the most urgent of the scarcity problems has been solved, however, the nature of these disorganizational problems begins to stand out in greater relief.

We have now reviewed in summary fashion the major conceptual tools which have been used to explain the existence of human ills: individual pathologies (genetic or acquired), bad institutions, a sick society, a disorganized society, and the like. But no matter which set of concepts we use, many questions remain unanswered. Whether, for example, we picture the ills as the result of bad, defective, unsocialized, or vicious people or as the result of a bad, wrong, unjust or sick social order, anomalies remain. Not all people with presumably "bad" heredity become social or societal problems; nor do all people exposed to the same "sick" social order become social problems. The centuries of disorganization which we traced above went hand in hand with improved health, longevity, and education for most people, and not the reverse. Obviously there is a complex interplay of forces here. The theoretical problems involved in unscrambling all the variables—genetic, interactional, institutional, cultural—related to the causes of social ills seem almost insuperable.

Recently, as we saw in Chapter 4, the concept of stress has become prominent in the thinking of health researchers,[54] and along with it, the complementary concept of stress resistance. These promise to be useful in considering the questions which concern us here also.

The "Causes" of Social Problems

Whatever conceptual scheme one uses to explain the existence of social problems—that is, conditions which, because they cause suffering, are costly to the community, and are dysfunctional, are felt to require change—two quite different questions have to be answered. One asks why the conditions exist in the first place and the other asks why only some people succumb to them.

The Universality and Inevitability of Stress Factors

To the first question—why do the conditions which become social problems exist?—the reply is made here that stress factors or threats are inevitable, whether they arise within or outside the social system. They may change from time to time, as indeed they have. But in some form or other they persist. At one time, and even today in many parts of the world, inadequate food, cold, disease, and natural and societal calamities were major sources of stress, and the threatened value was life itself. At the present time in societies like ours, where abundance prevails, disorganizational stresses—status anxiety and role confusion, for example—probably predominate. Thus when one set of values becomes firmly established, new ones arise, and these in turn may be threatened. There is, therefore, a constantly emerging set of values, and with them come the stresses involved in the possibility of losing them. Stress conditions are, in effect, built into social life.[55]

Differential Stress and Stress Resistance

To the second question—why do some people succumb to stress and others not?—the reply is here made that (1) stress factors have differential impact on different segments of any given population, falling more heavily on some than on others; and (2) individuals under identical conditions of threat differ in their ability to withstand stress factors.

DIFFERENTIAL INCIDENCE OF STRESS FACTORS. We have already discussed this point under status and stress in Chapters 3 and 4. We saw that one of the penalties of low status was, indeed, greater exposure to threats of many kinds. There may be many contributing reasons why people in slum areas, for example, have greater mortality and morbidity rates than people who live in more protected areas, but the difference in exposure to stress factors of many kinds is usually enough to explain their greater vulnerability. We expect people exposed to larger "doses" of stress to succumb in larger numbers, even if they have, as a population, the same genetic composition. We would expect a regiment exposed to front-line combat duty to show more casualties than a regiment serving far behind the lines.

But even among those exposed to greater stress, not everyone succumbs; and in protected positions, some people in fact do. Where the "dose" of stress factors is greater we expect more people to succumb. But where the "dose" is about the same we must look to individual differences for an explanation.

DIFFERENTIAL STRESS RESISTANCE. When we analyzed stress situations in Chapter 4 we spoke simply of "stress reactions." This is a purely descriptive, non-evaluational term. It describes what people do in stress situations. But some students use explanatory or telic terms instead, such as resistance, fighting, defense, and so on. They speak of the body, for example, as "fighting" germs or "defending itself" against infection. When stress reactions are successful, when they ward off the threat, we speak of stress resistance. Stress resistance consists of those reactions which preserve the organism or which keep it well or, on a higher level, permit a person to continue performing his roles. For not only physiologists but psychiatrists as well have conceived the organism as actively defending itself against threats of one kind or another. One psychoanalyst views the ego as fighting on two fronts, inner as well as outer.

She distinguishes a number of defense mechanisms, according to the specific anxiety-situations which call them forth, such as: repression, denial, reaction-formation, fantasies, inhibitions, intellectualization.[56] We shall presently introduce sociological concepts also to explain stress resistance. But first let us examine the kinds of phenomena for which we are seeking an explanation.

QUANTITATIVE DIFFERENCES IN STRESS RESISTANCE: ENDURANCE. It is a matter of both common sense and scientific observation that human beings under the same conditions have different abilities to "take it." The mortality rate, for example, is higher for some peoples than for others. Some people succumb to illness more rapidly than others. Some succumb to fatigue, hunger, thirst, or pain more rapidly than others. Some people "crack up" or "break down" more rapidly than others. Some people "give up" or capitulate more rapidly than others. Some people "drop out" before others. Whatever the explanation for these quantitative differences in endurance, there is no doubt about the existence of such documentable differences.

Much of the best recent research on this subject comes from military experience. It was found, for example, that the average number of days that riflemen could withstand combat duty in the North African and Italian campaigns varied between two hundred and four hundred days. Prisoner-of-war data have also documented the differences in stress resistance among men. In these prison-camps men were subjected to stresses of many kinds—physical, psychological, emotional—to induce them to betray military secrets, engage in communist propaganda, or in some other way to collaborate with the enemy. Some held out to the end; some capitulated. The number who did capitulate is reported to have been one third in one study,[57] one half in another,[58] and 70 per cent in a third.[59] The sample which yielded the proportion of one third was not subjected to starvation, solitary confinement, or other forms of physical torture. The sample for which the proportion was one half, had been subjected to this treatment. "Out of 78 men under various forms of duress, 38 signed germ warfare confessions. Forty others did not. Both groupings were under coercion. Why did some break, and some refuse to bend?" [60] The third study found that 39 per cent signed propaganda petitions, 22 per cent made records, 11 per cent wrote articles, 5 per cent wrote petitions, 5 per cent circulated petitions, and 10 per cent did full-time propaganda work, even though 88 per cent of them rejected the contents of the propaganda they were spreading.[61]

The theories offered by the several disciplines to explain or interpret individual differences in stress resistance differ as much as do those invoked to explain or interpret other kinds of individual differences.

One common explanation is genetic. Some people, it states, are born more resistant to stress factors of many kinds, or to certain specific stress factors. Another explanation is based on the individual's early family experiences, especially with his mother or with his siblings in relation to his mother, or with his father in relation to her.

The phenomena we are dealing with are complex, and no single approach will cover them from every aspect. The geneticist, the internist, the psychiatrist, and the psychologist all contribute something. But none of them can give a complete explanation. No more can the sociologist. But he can contribute an analysis of the strictly sociological and social-psychological factors involved. A sociological explanation cannot pretend to substitute for other explanations, but aims rather to supplement them. It does not deny the contribution that heredity or early family experience make to "stamina" or "character" in stress situations; it is intended to add to, rather than to subtract from, what we already know, to point to certain factors which often go unnoted or remain but vaguely recognized under the rubric "environment."

Four sociological and social-psychological concepts are invoked here to help explain individual differences in stress resistance under identical circumstances: (1) role definition; (2) subjective value; (3) subjective probability; and (4) role conception and role support.

Role Definition. Sometimes roles are so defined that great resistance to threat is expected. If those who perform these roles conceive them as so defined they will tend to behave as anticipated. Two groups who began with identical stress resistance might behave quite differently if their roles were differently defined.

A vivid illustration of this fact can be found in the reported difference between Turkish and American soldiers during the Korean War.

. . . at least a third of Americans held in captivity died in captivity. These men evidently died from diseases, from the severe conditions of living that existed in North Korea, rather than from execution or torture or anything of that nature.

Yet several hundred Turkish soldiers held under approximately identical conditions of captivity survived almost to a man . . . [even though] they certainly were not, at the outset, in better physical condition than the American soldier. . . . Close questioning of these Turks about why they survived so well and lost so few revealed that the only possible explanation was the continuance among them of an extremely strict system of military organization and discipline. Thus, when a man became ill, a detail of soldiers was assigned to care for that man and ensure his recovery by any means possible. They often bathed, spoon-fed and cared for their sick and wounded with a tremendous degree of devotion. . . .[62]

The role of soldier was defined for the Turks in a way that called for this kind of mutual aid; it sustained them in their hardships and made it possible for all to resist the threats of their surroundings.

A knight or nobleman's role demanded more stress resistance than that of a churl. An officer's role demands more than that of his subordinates; a leader's, more than that of his followers.

We have no way of knowing whether the pain which one person feels is greater or less than the pain another person feels. But we do know that people differ greatly in the way they react to pain. We say, for example, that some people act like babies when they go to the dentist. They demand analgesics for the smallest job. Others can take extensive drilling and surgery without flinching. Some physical, perhaps even genetic, differences in sensitivity may be granted. But recognition must also be made of role definitions. Some role definitions permit more display of pain. Persons in some roles would feel shame and humiliation to show what would seem to them to be, in the light of the roles defined for them, "weakness." Role definition is probably of even greater importance in resisting social stress factors or threats than in withstanding physical ones.

Subjective Value. Even resistance to social stress factors may vary greatly according to the value threatened. We saw in Chapter 4 that the same thing may have quite different subjective value to different people. A threat to life may seem much more traumatic to some than to others. Loss of "face" or "honor" may seem more serious than loss of life to others. Such subjective values will be important in determining differential resistance to stress factors. One slum boy, for example, can "take" the stresses involved in going to school for many years because the subjective value of a professional career is very great; the boy in the tenement next door cannot, because his subjective values are quite different. The martyr or fanatic can take an inordinate amount of stress because the subjective value he is suffering for is so much greater to him than life or anything else. The blackmailer makes it a point to determine the subjective value of specific things to his victim in order to threaten where the resistance is weakest. So does the administrator of a prisoner-of-war camp when he wishes to "brainwash."

Subjective Probability. Doubtless this is also an important element in stress resistance. In common-sense terms, if we feel sure that help is coming, that the threat is of short duration, that our side is going to win, that rescue is imminent, that there is bound to be a let-up soon, we can resist longer. Contrariwise, if we see no hope for rescue, we may succumb more readily. Religion often supplies this kind of faith, and men with religious faith were found to be more resistant in prisoner-of-war camps than others.[63] St. Paul bracketed hope and faith with love.[64]

Role Conception and Role Support. As well as role definition, role support is important in rendering resistance to stress possible. Again we refer to the experience of prisoners-of-war. The man whose conception of his role as a soldier was supported by comrades resisted more stress than one who was cut off from such role support. The armed forces have also found, as we shall see in Chapter 13, that much of the soldier's morale depended on the role support he got from his buddies. In front of his fellow soldiers he held out; cut off from them he often succumbed to battle fatigue or to collapse of morale. In ordinary civilian life we experience the same need for role support. And a great deal of therapy today consists, as we shall see, of harnessing the powerful forces generated in groups for role-supportive purposes.

QUALITATIVE DIFFERENCES IN STRESS RESISTANCE. We are not to think of stress resistance as a unitary "trait" of personality. There are individual differences within as well as among individuals. One man, for example, is relatively resistant to the tuberculosis germ but not to the spirochete. Another may be relatively resistant to fatigue but not to the speed-up, and so on. During the 19th century, thousands of men who could not "take" the stresses of the new urban society moved out to the frontier; and, conversely, those who could not "take" the stresses of the frontier moved into the cities. People, in effect, "seek out" roles which they can fit into; they trim their sails or subjective values to the load they can bear. They look for role networks which will support them in their role performance.

Although succumbing to stress produces social problems, the opposite is not necessarily true. The mere fact that people do not succumb to stress does not mean that they may not become social problems. Sometimes stress resistance is really "borrowed" from others or is gained at the expense of others. The slum boy, for example, who cannot stand the stresses imposed by middle-class standards turns to the so-called "delinquent subculture" and there finds congenial role definitions, values, and role support. He survives, that is, he "resists" the stresses of a middle-class world, but only by fighting it.

The data on prisoner-of-war camps and military experience on which we have relied for analyses of stress resistance refer to exaggerated models of stressful life situations. Not many human beings are normally subjected to such compounding of stresses—restriction of movement, physical discomfort, food deprivation, sleep deprivation, emotional blackmail, withdrawal of role support, and the like. But we may use them nevertheless as illustrations of situations to be found in ordinary life. Life stresses do not fall with equal impact on all peoples; they are more severe among some groups and classes than among others. Both people and the incidence of stress among them are different.

It is conceivable that life stresses could become so severe that everyone would succumb; no one could survive them. It is said, for example, that under the impact of modern civilizations the peoples of some of the Pacific Islands just withered away. They felt no incentive to continue living. They lost their desire to reproduce themselves. Students of psychosocial medicine have also pointed out that something similar happens among coal miners when stresses become too strong to bear. Whole communities waste away.[65] Role definitions become blurred and, in any event, impossible to implement. Subjective values are rendered impossible of attainment. Subjective probability for disaster rises; and, since the whole community is affected, role support deteriorates.

But for the most part, life stresses fall differentially on different persons and segments in a population, and we expect those in the more stressful situations to show a larger proportion of victims. Many who might have succumbed in a less protected or less congenial environment do not, whereas others succumb who might weather the impact of less traumatic stresses.

We may summarize the theoretical conceptualization of "causes" on which this book is based, then, somewhat like this: stress factors are an inevitable part of human existence, arising both outside and inside a social system. The nature of stress differs from time to time, taking the form of food deprivation, cold, disease, and similar physical threats in an age of scarcity, but taking the form of threats to security and status in an age of abundance. These stresses do not fall equally on all members of any social system, but with greater weight on some than on others. Human beings have different degrees of resistance to stress, genetic and acquired. The geneticists have not yet ferreted out all the intervening variables between heredity and mental, moral, and social traits. Many of them are doubtless social in nature. So far as "environmental" variables are concerned, they probably operate through such phenomena as role definitions, subjective values, subjective probabilities, and role support. Although the succumbing to stress is now viewed as a social problem, the fact that people do not succumb does not mean that social problems are obviated, for there are qualitative as well as quantitative differences in stress resistance. The methods used—aggression, for example—may be injurious to other people and hence constitute a social problem.

The "causes" of social ills or distress, then, lie both in people and in the conditions of stress to which they are subjected.

Chance

Whenever we talk about causes we have to consider chance factors. When we speak of chance we do not imply that events are uncaused or capricious. We mean only that they are unique and nonrepetitive, and happen so infrequently that they could not be predicted nor reproduced. A chance combination of genes results in a defective child in a normal family. The boy "just happened" to be out of town the day his gang committed the crime that sent them to court. Or he just happened to come under the influence of the YMCA leader at a critical moment in his life. A "lucky" concatenation of circumstances saves one child from delinquency; or an "unlucky" one precipitates another into a delinquent's career. These chance factors can never be isolated in our research projects. All we can say is that no matter how refined our researches become, there are always negative cases, cases which go counter to the major trends. Religious people might speak of grace in such cases; superstitious ones, of luck. All the scientist can do is to make room for them in his recognition of chance factors. So far as almost any social ill is concerned, we may all say, "There but for the grace of God go I."

NOTES

1 Henry Knighton, "The Impact of the Black Death," in James Bruce Ross and Mary Martin McLaughlin, *The Portable Medieval Reader* (Viking, 1949), pp. 216–219.

2 Reinhold Niebuhr, "God's Design and the Present Disorder of Civilization." *The Amsterdam Assembly Series* (Harper, no date), pp. 24–28.

3 For example, General William Booth's *In Darkest England* (Funk, 1890).

4 Albert Benedict Wolfe, *Readings in Social Problems* (Ginn, 1916), p. 1.

5 L. K. Frank, "What Is Social Order?" in *Society as the Patient* (Rutgers Univ. Press, 1948), p. 286. The article originally appeared in the *American Journal of Sociology* in 1944.

6 Czeslaw Milosz, *The Captive Mind* (Vintage, 1953), pp. 199, 209.

7 *Ibid.*, p. 201.

8 Bradley Buell *et al.*, *Community Planning for Human Services* (Columbia Univ. Press, 1952), p. 9.

9 Carl E. Buck, Bradley Buell, and Roscoe P. Kandle, "Family Health in Tomorrow's Community," *American Journal of Public Health*, 41 (Oct. 1951), p. 1258.

10 O. D. Duncan, "Is the Intelligence of the General Population Declining?" *American Sociological Review*, 17 (Aug. 1952), p. 402. For a careful evaluation of the studies concerning this subject see pp. 401–407.

11 In general it has been found that people who are conservative in political ideology tend to believe in "heredity"; while those who are liberal tend to be in the "environmental" camp. See Nicholas Pastore, *The Nature-Nurture Controversy* (King's Crown Press, 1949).

12 The classical formulation of this point of view was that of William McDougall in his *Social Psychology* (Meuthen, 1906).

13 See, for example, L. L. Bernard, *Instinct, A Study in Social Psychology* (Holt, 1924).

14 Louis Wallis, *God and the Social Process* (Univ. of Chicago Press, 1912).

15 A. J. I. Kraus, *Sick Society* (Univ. of Chicago Press, 1929).

16 Milton L. Barron, *The Juvenile in a Delinquent Society* (Knopf, 1954).

17 Erich Fromm, *Sane Society* (Rinehart, 1955).

18 Frank, *Society as the Patient*, pp. 1–2.

19 The following discussion is not intended as an exhaustive review of the textbook literature. For an excellent summary of outstanding theoretical trends in textbooks, see Abbott P. Herman, *An Approach to Social Problems* (Ginn, 1949), pp. 9–49.

20 Frank, *op. cit.*, p. 2.

21 A. W. Small and George Vincent, *An Introduction to the Study of Society* (American Book Co., 1894), p. 267.

22 *Ibid.*, p. 270.

23 Frank W. Blackmar and J. L. Gillin, *Outlines of Sociology* (Macmillan, 1923), p. 463.

24 Samuel George Smith, *Social Pathology* (Macmillan, 1912), p. 3.

25 *Ibid.*, pp. 7–8.

26 S. A. Queen and Delbert Mann, *Social Pathology* (Crowell, 1925), p. viii.

27 James Ford, *Social Deviation* (Macmillan, 1939), p. 8.

28 S. A. Queen and Jeannette Gruener, *Social Pathology* (Crowell, 1940).

29 L. G. Brown, *Social Pathology; Personal and Social Disorganization* (Crofts, 1942); also James Ford, *op. cit.*, pp. 8–9.

30 W. I. Thomas and Florian Znaniecki, *The Polish Peasant in Europe and America* (Knopf, 1918).

31 *Ibid.*, pp. 8–10.

32 *Ibid.*, p. 80.

33 *Ibid.*, p. viii.

34 Ford, *op. cit.* This author approaches the Thomas-Znaniecki concept in his concept of underorganization (p. 9).

35 S. A. Queen, W. B. Bodenhafer, E. G. Harper, *Social Organization and Disorganization* (Crowell, 1935), p. 4.

36 Mabel Elliott and F. E. Merrill, *Social Disorganization* (Harper, 1950), p. 20.

37 J. M. Gillette and J. M. Reinhardt, *Current Social Problems* (American Book Co., 1937); John F. Cuber and R. A. Harper, *Problems of American Society: Values in Conflict* (Holt, 1948).

38 The lag concept was present in the concept of social pathology as well as in that of social disorganization. Thus one textbook pointed out that "pathological conditions in society may result from (1) natural lack of ability in individuals to keep pace with the changing ideals and institutions of society, or (2) from the failure of society to keep pace in its func-tional machinery with the changing conditions of social life." (Blackmar and Gillin, *Outlines of Sociology*, p. 463.)

39 In a certain sense the social disorganization concept, especially in the form of the social lag theory, is analogical to ecology. Students of plant and animal ecology have traced the destruction which can result in a natural order from a relatively minor change in the relationships among plants and/or animals. One begins by destroying a certain noxious weed and ends by destroying a useful bird; or one eliminates a pest only to acquire a much worse one. Some people tend to think of social relations and organization in a similar way: any given order is in delicate balance; if you change it, you dis-organize it and the result will be harmful. The fallacy of such an ecological analogy lies in the fact that ecological relationships are biological, based on heredity, worked out over long periods of time; new adjustments must also work themselves out by way of the genes, or by differentials in fertility, a long, time-consuming process. But social organization is not so fixed, certainly not genetic. Human beings are plastic; they change their groupings and their relationships and accommodations with relative speed. They do not have to wait for heredity. No human social order is as stable as an ecological order.

40 The value-conflict approach has been exploited especially by John F. Cuber, following Richard C. Fuller. See Cuber and Harper, *Problems of American Society: Values in Conflict.*

41 The importance attached by the author to the community problems associated with conflict may be measured by the amount of space devoted to this topic in a volume entitled *American Community Behavior* (Dryden, 1949).

42 In our presentation we have included in Part IV a discussion of the people who are social or societal problems because of some pathology, thus leaving us free in the rest of the book to consider only the problems dealing with those who are as normal as the total population.

43 There are anomalous situations which arise; for example, when elderly couples are given incomes of their own, so that they can live independently, their presence in the income structure increases "poverty" in the sense that they swell the low-income brackets, as we saw in Chapter 1. Here improved "social arrange-

ments" seem to increase the pathology of poverty.

44 The ambiguity of the concept when applied to social conditions was highlighted at a meeting of the American Public Health Association in 1955, at which Dr. Robert G. Foster of the Menninger Foundation in Topeka, Kansas, pointed out: "We have witnessed over the past few years changing cultural values, particularly with reference to our sex mores, divorce, marriage and the rearing of children. There is a difference of opinion among top-flight sociologists as to whether this is a normal progressive movement of social change for the better or whether this is the beginning of the end as it was in the Roman Empire." (Report in *New York Times,* November 15, 1955.) If there were clear-cut criteria of pathology, demonstrable to all, such difference of opinion would not exist.

45 One sociologist has said that "the conclusion seems inescapable that a high degree of social organization is associated with good mental health and a small extent of social problems. Conversely, a low degree of social organization is correlated with a high rate of mental disorders and of social problems." (E. W. Burgess, "Mental Health in Modern Society," in Arnold Rose, ed. *Mental Health and Mental Disorder* [Norton, 1955], pp. 8–9.) Such a conclusion may be warranted for the limited social scene this author is considering; but it would not necessarily hold as a general or universal principle. A high degree of organization may produce as much stress as a low degree. Indeed there are some social psychologists who hold precisely this point of view. See, for example, Floyd H. Allport, *Institutional Behavior* (Univ. of North Carolina Press, 1933), *passim.*

46 For a discussion of community disorganization, see Jessie Bernard, *American Community Behavior* (Dryden, 1949), Part IV.

47 F. J. C. Hearnshaw, *The Social and Political Ideas of Some Great Thinkers of the Sixteenth and Seventeenth Centuries* (Barnes and Noble, 1949), p. 9.

48 For a discussion of the nature of competition see Jessie Bernard, *op. cit.,* Chapters 3, 5, 7–12.

49 For a discussion of the distinction between social-psychological and sociological conflict see Jessie Bernard, *Remarriage, A Study of Marriage* (Dryden, 1956), Chapter 10. For a discussion of sociological conflict see Jessie Bernard, *American Community Behavior,* Chapters 3, 6, 13–21.

50 Hearnshaw, *op. cit.,* p. 9.

51 The concept of community dissociation implies, as in the concept of personality dissociation, the existence of two or more integrations occupying the same body. In personality dissociation we have two distinct personalities, two wholly separate integrations of behavior patterns, using the same body, either concurrently or alternately, as in the classic Sally Beauchamp case, or the fictional Dr. Jekyll-Mr. Hyde case. In community dissociation we have two distinct sets of institutions or cultures—class or racial—existing in the same area. See Jessie Bernard, *American Community Behavior,* Part IV.

52 F. J. C. Hearnshaw, *The Social and Political Ideas of Some Representative Thinkers of the Victorian Age* (Harrap, 1933), p. 16.

53 Elton Mayo, digest of *The Social Problems of an Industrial Civilization* (Harvard Univ. Press, 1945), n. p.

54 See, for example, Harold Wolff, *Stress and Disease* (C. C Thomas, 1953).

55 The above formulation is presented as a hypothesis which could, theoretically, be tested experimentally. Some readers may see in it simply another way of stating a theological or metaphysical proposition.

56 Anna Freud, *The Ego and the Mechanisms of Defense* (International Univ. Press, 1946).

57 Major William E. Mayer, "Why Did Many GI Captives Cave In?" *U. S. News and World Report,* February 24, 1956, p. 56.

58 Report to the Secretary of Defense by the Advisory Committee on Prisoners of War, August 1955. Present reference is to the *New York Times,* August 18, 1955, p. 11.

59 *New York Times,* June 21, 1956. See also *Look* magazine, June 26, 1956.

60 *New York Times,* August 18, 1955.

61 *New York Times,* June 21, 1956.

62 Mayer, *op. cit.,* p. 58.

63 *Ibid.,* p. 59.

64 1 Corinthians 13.

65 James L. Halliday, *Psychosocial Medicine* (Norton, 1948), Chapter 10.

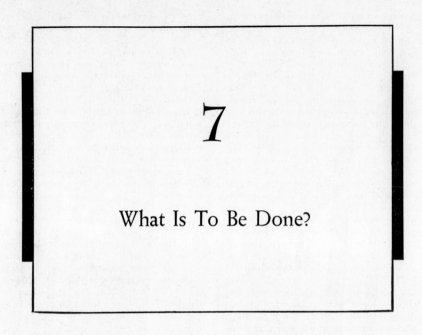

7

What Is To Be Done?

We have seen that it was the conviction that something should be done about them which transformed human suffering and misfortune into social *problems*. We have glanced at the criteria which determined what particular kinds of suffering and misfortune fell under the rubric *social* problems. Now we wish to focus our attention on what should be done, for it was not mere alleviation or palliation which was called for, but something more active, more positive. To see in perspective this new kind of "collective stress reaction" which abundance made possible—social reform—we begin with a brief overview of possible reactions to problem situations.

Before discussing the largely historical and descriptive aspects of our presentation, we turn to a theoretical and analytical consideration of the most fundamental questions of all: What are the possibilities of change with respect to social ills? What are the limits within which change is possible?

Can *Social Problems Be Solved?*

The Limits of the Possible

Policies Advocated

Acts of God

Can *Social Problems Be Solved?*

The answer to this question depends, of course, on how one defines
a solution. If the question is whether man can ever get rid of all stress
factors, or whether he can find a successful way to eliminate them when
they do occur, the answer can only be, No, there can never be such a
solution to social problems. If the question is whether man can keep his
standards or aspirations low in the face of abundance, so that new values
will not always be emerging which must be protected, the answer is,
Probably not.

But if we define solutions more modestly and make our specifications less sweeping, then we can say that some social problems have,
indeed, been solved and others are in process of solution. In the United
States today, for example, the problem of legal slavery has been solved.
The problem of waifs has been solved. The problem of the 12-hour

7-day week has been solved. The problem of child labor has been all but solved; the problem of the sweated industry has, also, been practically solved. The problem of some germ diseases and even of some of the virus diseases has been solved. And many of the same kinds of problems have been solved in other parts of the world today. The social problems of scarcity, in brief, are in process of solution.

But new problems constantly emerge because of new conditions and because of higher standards for judging social conditions. Hence there are always new social problems to take the place of the old. In this sense, social problems are not solved. They are replaced by new ones.

Lest our point of view seem too sanguine we hasten to add that it does not imply that there are no limits to what man can do to solve social problems, for there are.

The Limits of the Possible

The philosophers of the French Enlightenment saw no limit to the progress man could make once he applied the methods of science to his social problems; they conceived of man as infinitely perfectible and of nature as endlessly susceptible to man's control. In spite of the tremendous achievements of man by means of science we are not quite so optimistic at the present time. We do concede that there may be limits, although we are not altogether sure exactly where to put them. We know that man must always operate within the bounds of possibility. But where, exactly, are these bounds?

To some people—Malthus was one—the limits of what is possible seem close and breed great pessimism about social reform. They believe that the human species is trapped. They see only an endless succession of generations born, maturing, reproducing, and dying; they see man held down in the vise of his own nature. They see a world going through its fixed processes without change. Some of them are "determinists" in the old-fashioned sense of believing that everything has long been settled, that there is no "freedom," that man and nature go through their endless ballet to no point. There is little elbowroom for man to maneuver in.

Others, however, though also "determinists," in the sense that they believe everything that occurs is related to what went before, do not interpret the facts in the same way. They push back the limits of the possible and give man a much wider berth. They see the "laws of nature" as instruments or tools man must use rather than as shackles he must submit to.

To simplify the contrast: one person views gravity as a restricting force, holding man down when he might wish to fly. Another, however, views gravity as a force to use in, let us say, harnessing waterpower. One person sees the "laws of nature" as a restriction, preventing a different kind of society from developing, one in which human beings might be perfect, generous, angelic, unbound by the necessities of mundane existence. The other sees how the "laws of nature" may be used to serve man's ends. He accepts the existence of the limitations, and may even bemoan them, but he does not cry over them. One man is likely to say, sadly, "You can't change human nature." In the sense that we cannot change the fact that man is a symmetrical biped which must eat to live, be protected from dangers through a long infancy, reproduce in a bisexual manner, and eventually deteriorate and die, he is right. We cannot, that is, change these "laws of nature." No social reform movement, no revolution, can aim at a social order which requires a different kind of organism—say, one with three legs, eyes in the back of the head, or the ability to levitate. That would be outside the limits of the possible. We have to admit at the outset that the kind of creature man is is part of the rules of the game, just as the kind of planet we live on is. These are rules of the game and we have to play that game, not some other we might imagine.

But although there is no way to change the rules, there are many ways to play the game under these rules. We do not, actually, know the limits of what is possible. Many things become possible that were not possible before. It still remains true, for example, that if you are exposed to certain germs you will develop certain symptoms and perhaps die; but you do not have to be exposed to the germs. Or if you do, you can develop antibodies against them. It is still true that the body deteriorates with age; but the time at which this deterioration sets in can be delayed many years. It is still true that gravity holds bodies down; but we can fly as well as walk. It is still true that plants need water; but it is now possible to bring water to deserts. It is still true that the water of the ocean is unfit for agriculture; but it may soon be not only possible but also practicable to rid it of its salt. It is still true that men react to physical deprivation in certain dysfunctional ways; but physical deprivation may be eliminated. The rules do not change, but man learns to use them.

No solution to social problems is possible, then, which demands a different kind of human body or a different kind of planet. But within the limits of the possible—indeterminate as they are—many efforts have been made to "solve" social problems. And it is to a consideration of these efforts that we now turn our attention. We do not attempt any final answer here to the question we have raised in the title of this chapter, namely, What is to be done? All we do is outline the several policies that have been proposed to guide the search for an answer to the question and attempt to evaluate the relative success that has attended their application.

Policies Advocated

The policies advocated for dealing with social ills depend in large measure on which of the theories discussed in Chapter 6 is invoked to explain them. We referred in Chapter 4 to the several levels—physiological, emotional, interpersonal, and societal or cultural—on which reactions to stress factors take place. When we are dealing with social problems rather than blind reaction, policy of some kind is involved. The question then becomes an ethical one—What *should* be done—not a research or scientific one—What *is* actually done? The latter is important primarily because of the contribution it can make to the former.

In general, three strategies or policies with respect to stress situations are possible. One is to do nothing. Practice resignation, acceptance, *laissez faire*. Do not fight back. To those accepting a theological explanation of human ills, to fight back might be considered defiance of the gods. To those accepting a metaphysical explanation, meddling with natural laws is not only useless, but even dangerous or harmful. Those who advocate doing nothing are likely to be those who are not bearing the brunt of the stressful situation.

A second approach is to change the victim in order to help him to adjust to the problem situation. Repentance, penance, admission of guilt, reformation, and conversion are among the changes indicated in a theological conceptual framework. Conformity to natural laws, the forsaking of efforts to change the nature of things, and acceptance are the policies in a metaphysical framework. The scientific approach also includes policies which seek, by one method or another, to change the individual—his point of view, his definition of the situation, his role conception, his level of aspiration, his educational equipment, his subjective probabilities of threat, his subjective values—in order to help him "adjust," or fit in better in a social situation.

A third approach is to attempt to change or control the situational stress factor which creates the problem. Prayer, incantations, magic, and sacrifice may be used to appease or change the gods and spirits that are causing the trouble. Those who take a scientific approach are likely to attempt to change the conditions which are found to be associated with problems. Social reform movements aiming at legislation may be the solution attempted. Table 1 summarizes the techniques of adjustment which are likely to be used, based on the three kinds of policies—*laissez faire,* change the individuals, change the situation—and the three approaches to them—theological, metaphysical, and scientific.

TABLE 1
CLASSIFICATION OF TECHNIQUES FOR DEALING WITH SOCIAL PROBLEMS ACCORDING TO ASSUMED THEORY OF "CAUSE" AND OF "CURE" *

THEORY OF "CURE"	THEORY OF "CAUSE"		
	Theological	*Metaphysical*	*Scientific*
Do Nothing	Submit	Let history work itself out	*Laissez faire*
Change Individual	Penance, reform, absolution, etc.	Change "human nature," conform to natural laws	Counseling, psychotherapy, education, casework, groupwork
Change Cause	Prayer, magic, incantation	Change society, reform movements, revolution	Change society, reform movements, revolution

* This table may be viewed as a first step toward a payoff matrix in a "game" against nature.

Laissez Faire

It is perhaps anomalous to consider the policy of *laissez faire* in connection with social problems, since in effect the advocate of *laissez faire* denies the very existence of social problems, that is, of conditions that must be changed. But because the advocates of social action have always had to face strong opposition from believers in *laissez faire,* a statement of the do-nothing position is in order. Indeed, the policy of *laissez faire* is as much a policy of doing something as any other. The decision not to act is as fraught with consequences as the decision to act.

The justification for the laissez-faire policy has taken several forms. There were those, such as Herbert Spencer and his followers, especially W. G. Sumner in this country, who argued that the misery and suffering which were considered social problems by some people were really a necessary part of the social process. It was natural selection in operation, and should therefore not be interfered with.

This great cosmic force, they argued, should be permitted to work through its natural course without let or hindrance. Interference with it could do only harm. Reform, not the conditions themselves, would lead to social disorganization. Suppose laws were passed favoring this class of inferior people; they would prosper at the expense of superior people. There are, furthermore, great unforeseen consequences of such tampering with the social system. The end achieved might be different from that sought. The elimination of one evil would only entail another that might be even worse. Do not interfere with the struggle for existence. Let it weed out the incompetent, those who cannot successfully compete.

Similar is the point of view that says, in effect, anything that is, is right. A situation might seem bad to an outside observer, but the very fact that it exists proves that it is performing some function in the social system and therefore should not be changed. The implication is that any function being performed is a necessary one and hence an acceptable one. This argument might take a theological cast: God knows what He is doing. He would not allow it if He did not wish it to be. The argument might be formulated in metaphysical terms: if it is natural it must not be interfered with. It might even be stated in scientific or functional terms.[1]

Another argument buttressing the laissez-faire attitude can be traced to the early 19th-century reaction against the French Revolution and its concomitants. The radical shattering of the Old Regime had ended in disorder and destruction. The break with the past had been disastrous. Participants in the Romantic movement retreated into the medieval past for solace. But the political leaders set up the principles or philosophy of conservatism, which was, in effect, a cult of the past in the form of tradition. No set of social institutions could ever be perfect. The bonds which hold men together in society are essentially non-rational, based on sentiment. Destroying them does not mean that they will be reconstructed on rational grounds. It means only that they will be replaced by another set of institutions, no more rational. And in the meanwhile there will have been great disorder and disorganization. Stability and continuity with the past are more important than the reform of any evil. Even a bad social order is better than no order at all. The conservative philosophy, therefore—espoused most brilliantly by the British leader Edmund Burke—was one of leaving things alone, of preventing change.

All three of these apologia for *laissez faire* persist today. But the proponents of this approach have had to give way little by little. It is for them no longer a matter of *laissez faire* versus doing something, but a matter of what is the least one can do? For, as a matter of historical fact, it is the activist "do-something" philosophy which has won out. Despite the protests and cogent reasoning of the laissez-faire theorists, the actual course of history has been in the direction of attempting change. Even the laissez-faire theorists have become reconciled to at least a minimum amount of change.

But what form should change take? Should the change be in individuals? in the social order? And if in the social order, how should the change be brought about? by revolution? by piecemeal reforms? Let us review these alternatives in order.

Change the Individuals

Christian strategy is based, essentially, on changing individual human beings. Individual souls are saved one by one, case by case. Sometimes the work is done individually, as when the minister prays with the parishioner. Sometimes it is done in large groups, as in revivals. Sometimes it is done on a mass scale, as when an evangelist like Billy Graham seeks a great moral awakening, or when the Moral Rearmament Movement makes a world-wide appeal. In any event, it is an effort to solve social problems by changing individuals.

A great deal of psychiatry, social work, and professional counseling is based on the theory that the way to deal with social problems is to change the personality of the individual involved. Emotional re-education is used so that he will respond to the stresses of his environment without too much disturbance. He is trimmed, so to speak, to the milieu in which he has to function. In some cases, such a policy often works well. And perhaps in cases where there is no hope of changing the stress situation which produces the problem, there may be no alternative to "adjusting" to the difficulty.

A *reductio ad absurdum* of this approach was once described by the Polish author Stanislaw Ignacy Witkiewicz. Since his book was a satire, everything was upside down: the problem people were upper-class, not lower-class people, but their problems might have occurred anywhere. The "solution" to their problems came in the form of a pill —ominously like the tranquilizing drugs now used on disturbed people —which "adjusted" people so well that they went down in defeat perfectly happy. But let the story speak for itself.

The action of the book took place in . . . Poland, at some time in the near future. . . . Decadence reigned at a time when Western civilization was said to be threatened by an army from the East, a Sino-Mongolian army that dominated all the territory stretching from the Pacific to the Baltic.

. . . at that moment, a great number of hawkers appear in the cities peddling Murti-Bing pills. . . . A man who used these pills changed completely. He became serene and happy. The problems he had struggled with until then suddenly appeared to be superficial and unimportant. He smiled indulgently at those who continued to worry about them. . . . A man who swallowed Murti-Bing pills became impervious to any . . . concerns. . . . He no longer considered the approach of the Sino-Mongolian army as a tragedy for his own civilization. He lived in the midst of his compatriots like a healthy individual surrounded by madmen. More and more people took the Murti-Bing cure, and their resultant calm contrasted sharply with the nervousness of their environment.

The epilogue, in a few words: the outbreak of the war led to a meeting of the armies of the West with those of the East. In the decisive moment, just before the great battle, the leader of the Western army surrendered to the enemy; and in exchange, though with the greatest honors, he was beheaded. . . .[2]

There is constant controversy with respect to the individual approach to social problems. Should one attempt to "adjust" people to their environment even if the environment is bad? Should one accept the *status quo* and trim one's sails or should one attack it?

Obviously these courses of action can overlap. And as a matter of fact most people accept all three; differences are largely a matter of emphasis. Even those who believe in changing individuals may argue that the best way to do this is by changing the world they live in, immediately or remotely.

There are three levels, one might say, at which one may attempt to change the situation. The lowest, that is, the one nearest the individual himself, may be called the group approach; the next, somewhat more removed, may be called the social-reform approach; and the most abstract, the total-revolution approach. The first of these is also the newest; the other two represent ideologies which have flourished since the end of the 18th and beginning of the 19th century. The total-revolution approach advocated a complete renovation and reconstruction of society from the ground up; the social-reform approach, piecemeal change.[3]

Change the Situation: The Group Approach

One of the most interesting results of recent research and experience is a recognition of the therapeutic forces available in the interaction of people in groups. A so-called group approach has therefore emerged which attempts to exploit the powerful forces generated in group relationships for the purpose of helping individuals.

One of the first demonstrations of what these group forces could do was the phenomenal success of Alcoholics Anonymous, organized in 1935. A Narcotics Anonymous was organized in 1950 to do for drug addicts what the other organization was doing for alcoholics. A similar organization in New York City called Fountain House and another called Recovery, Incorporated, attempt to help former mental patients by using the same group principles. There is also an organization—Courage, Incorporated—to help the physically handicapped, and still another for sex deviants.

A group approach has been found more functional in dealing with boys in delinquency areas than an individual approach which deals with boys as, in effect, living in a vacuum. It has become recognized that boys are not separate individuals but socii, persons with status and role in group relationships, and that to extract them from this social matrix does violence to their personalities. Increasingly, therefore, efforts are made to work with and through the natural groups in which the boys live. The parents of retarded children have organized in order to use group-generated forces to help them bear the exceptional stresses of their parenthood. The group is also being used to help probationers, those who are successful helping those just entering their probationary periods.

Even the problems of workers in factories are coming to be viewed as amenable to a group approach. And the armed services, on the basis of sociological research findings, have found that there are tremendous therapeutic reserves available in the group relationships of soldiers, in combat or in prison camps. As research sheds more and more light on the way groups function, how they contribute to the individuals who constitute them, and how role and status affect personality, more use may be made of the group approach in dealing with many social problems.

Change the Situation: Revolution

The total-revolution approach to the solution of social problems is illustrated by such great upheavals as the French Revolution and, more recently, the Russian Revolution. Both were massive attempts to refashion a total society. Until the 20th century, the French Revolution was the most spectacular effort in this direction. It was not surpassed until the period 1928–1934 in Russia, which "marked an impressive upheaval in politics and economy [and social life], probably one of the greatest in the history of mankind." [4] In both instances social structures were reconstructed from the bottom up.

Yet in both cases the stresses which generate social problems persisted. In the USSR, for example, crime not only continued; it even increased.[5] Housing was still a problem.[6] Waste and pillage remained.[7] Safety hazards in factories were problems.[8] Statistics on mental retardation and mental illness are not available, but the existence, if not the extent, of these problems is documentable.[9]

The following account of juvenile delinquency in the Soviet Union sounds not very different from behavior in our society.

> Juvenile delinquency, which appears to be a problem of major proportions, is characterized primarily by considerable drinking among adolescents and sometimes by the formation of gangs for criminal purposes. . . . Policemen will buy coal they know has been stolen by juvenile gangs; and armed railroad guards . . . often do not intervene when school-children loot railroad cars. In the schools, teachers are unable to stem the tide of juvenile delinquency or even to maintain discipline. There are countless examples of brutality inside and outside the schools (sometimes with fatal results), including the molesting of school personnel. . . .[10]

And the following appeal in an *Izvestia* editorial, July 29, 1954, indicates how serious the problems are considered to be.

> Soviet law regards hooliganism as a crime and punishes those who are guilty. But it is of the utmost importance that this antisocial phenomenon should be forestalled and that those who violate the rules of our way of life should be called to order in good time. The police authorities, who are called upon to maintain and strengthen public order, should act more firmly. But administrative and prohibitionary measures alone are, of course, insufficient. The struggle against hooliganism, in particular among young people and adolescents, should be carried out by the entire public, by trade union and komsomol organizations, schools and parents' committees, house managements and the soviet *aktiv*.[11]

And, finally, alcoholism appears to have resisted revolutionary reconstruction also.

> Hard drinking seems to be widespread among Soviet manual workers. Apparently it is considered, in some workers' circles, a sign of manliness and serves as a badge of acceptance. The worker who can blow one hundred roubles on drinks in one evening becomes something of a hero. . . . There have been reported cases when foremen discriminated against workers or refused to hire them if they did not pay them a tribute in vodka. . . . Drinking among collective farmers appears to be prevalent. . . . Holidays, the meaning of which, apparently, has been lost to most, often turn into drunken brawls during which, of course, none or very little of the field work gets done. . . .[12]

Another report corroborates this:

> During 1954 a campaign against drink and antisocial behaviour, especially rowdyism, became very widespread and insistent throughout the Soviet

press. . . . The translation below . . . is a typical homily on drink taken from a leading article in *Izvestia*. Many of the hundreds of other articles on the subject ring the changes on such titles as "Harmful inheritance from the past," "Injurious survival of the past." Like all other campaigns against undesirable tendencies and tendencies that are considered by politically dominant opinion to be undesirable, the past (which is invariably equated with "capitalism") is put as the source of the evil, and progress in the matter is defined as a struggle between the building up of a communist society and the survivals of the pre-socialist past. . . .

Strictly Observe the Rules of the
Socialist Way of Life
(*Izvestia* editorial, July 29th, 1954)

. . . We have not yet outlived attempts to separate home life from politics, and to regard it as a "personal matter," as though it had no connection with a man's public conduct, and as though it did not concern anyone, what a man did in his free time or how he behaved in public places and in the family, provided he fulfilled his obligations at work.

Let us take so harmful and shameful a survival as drunkenness. This unhealthy phenomenon has an adverse influence on industrial labour discipline, undermines the foundations of the Soviet family and causes numerous violations of the rules of socialist living. Alcohol has a harmful effect on the organism, thus lowering a man's working capacity. Workers, who misuse intoxicating liquors, stay absent from work and cause breakdowns, thus harming industry. In public places and at home drunkards cause scandals and morally shock their families, in particular, their children. There have been cases of serious criminal offences committed by people under the influence of drink. In short, people who are given to drink will everywhere—at their work, in the street and in their home—unavoidably come into conflict with society, as violators of its laws and rules . . .[13]

Similar conditions were also reported for Poland, where "authorities are engaged in a serious struggle against wide-spread alcoholism." [14] The official party newspaper pointed out that "social damage and loss caused by alcoholism, namely loafing and wastefulness, disease and hooligan assaults, are very great and must be counteracted." [15] Among the ways used to counteract alcoholism were: posting pictures of drunken workers being arrested by policemen; cessation of bonuses to store clerks and waiters for artificially stimulating the sale of vodka; changing the indulgent attitude toward drinking and brawling in public places; restrictions on (but not the prohibition of) the sale of alcohol. In brief, all these were social reforms.

It is interesting to note, according to one student, that the official Soviet explanation of such current social problems as alcoholism, juvenile delinquency, and crime follows closely the social pathology (in the sense of a pathology in the social structure), social disorganization, and lag hypotheses. These problems are vestiges, so to speak, of "capitalism." They represent a "lag." [16]

The author we are here citing uses more realistic arguments to explain alcoholism and delinquency, namely: (1) "the erosion of family functions that accompanies industrialization"; (2) the fact that young people today are members of the " 'war generation,' brought up without close parental supervision, under conditions of severe deprivations, often forced to fend for themselves without knowledge of a peaceful, normal life"; (3) severe stress situations, especially "excessive demands put on human beings and lack of commensurate rewards"; (4) lessening incentive to be sober on the part of the lower classes as social stratification increases; and (5) custom.[17] Nor does he overlook the greater availability of alcohol as food-handling trusts turn to the sale of alcoholic beverages in order to make the profits which are demanded of them.[18]

Whichever set of arguments is used to explain the persistence of social problems in the Soviet Union, however, it is clear that the total revamping of the societal system has not eliminated them or even, perhaps, reduced their incidence.

The failure of the thoroughgoing renovation inaugurated by the Soviet Union to root out social ills was disillusioning to men in the 20th century, as the similar failure of the French Revolution had been to men in the 19th. At both periods men of good will were forced to concede, albeit reluctantly in many cases, that the total-reconstruction approach—whatever other problems it may have solved—was not the answer to social problems. The stresses of life could not be extirpated by these means.

Change the Situation: Social Reform

In contrast to both the group approach, which is really only one step removed from the individual, and the total-reconstruction-of-society approach, is that through social reform. This attempts to change the stressful situation piecemeal, one thing at a time, with the full recognition that this is only a partial and limited way to deal with the stresses which create social problems. This approach is likely to take the form of a social movement which seeks to "educate the public" and to secure legislation.

A social reform movement may be viewed as an attempt to redefine roles and to reassess status relationships among groups or classes of the population. It is often a protest, a form of conflict.[19] It attacks some aspect of the *status quo*. It attempts to achieve its goal by passing legislation setting up certain responsibilities and obligations—new role definitions—which did not exist before, or by "educating the public" in new role and status relationships, or by both.

Social movements have been classified as *value-rational* in nature if they are motivated by a belief in the absolute desirability, rightness, and goodness of their goals; as *emotional-affectual* if they are motivated by resentment against conditions or people or by love for a leader; and as *purposive-rational* if motivated by expectation of personal advantage.[20] For our purposes, those that fall into the first category are most important, that is, the value-rational reforms in which the people who participated were not those who were going to profit by success. They saw evils which they wished to rectify. They exposed what they considered wrong. It was not the handicapped, for example, who initiated the reform movements which led to their improved care. It was not prisoners who started prison reform movements, nor children who instigated juvenile courts. It was not the dependent women who agitated for mothers' pensions. And certainly it was not the venereally diseased who initiated public health programs in their behalf. Not the uneducated, but the educated, formed the movement which eventuated in the public school. Improved care of the mentally ill came at first from the well. Not until the 20th century did a man who had himself been ill become active in the mental health movement.[21] These social reform movements were no less significant or important because they were motivatd by humanitarian ideals rather than by self-interest, that is, *value*-rational rather than *purposive*-rational.

We shall not here consider the many social reform movements which were purposive-rational in nature, that is, movements in which those who constituted them were going to benefit from their success. We shall not discuss such examples as the labor movement, which was by and for workers in this country (with a minimum of leadership from intellectuals or middle-class humanitarians, as contrasted with Europe); or the woman's rights movement, which was for and largely staffed by women; or consumer, cooperative, or agrarian movements.

Although social reform has a long history in many parts of the world we shall limit ourselves here to a brief survey of social reform in the United States.

THREE PERIODS OF REFORM IN THE UNITED STATES. There have been three periods in the history of the United States which have been characterized by a stepped-up tempo of social reform, namely, the 1840's, the 1900's, and the 1930's.

THE 1840's. With respect to the first of these periods it was once said that no Boston dinner party was complete in the 1840's without the initiation of some reform.

The columns of advertisements in a newspaper might announce for Monday night a meeting of the antislavery society; Tuesday night, the temperance society; Wednesday night, the graham bread society; Thursday night, a phrenological lecture; Friday night, an address against capital punishment; Saturday night, the "Association for Universal Reform." Then there were all the missionary societies, the woman's rights societies, the society for the diffusion of bloomers. . . . the land reformers—a medley of movements that found the week too short.[22]

These midcentury reform movements, recognizing that almost everything was wrong with the life pattern of workers, sought, in addition to the more or less esoteric reforms listed above, to change almost everything. Their goals included public education, abolition of imprisonment for debt, mechanics' lien laws to protect wages from the bankruptcy of employers, banking reforms, reform of the compulsory militia system, and credit reforms.[23] The slavery issue braked the momentum of this reform exuberance, but after the Civil War it began again, coming into full force in the first years of the 20th century, this time with a new set of objectives.

TURN OF THE CENTURY: MUCKRAKING. We shall observe the turn-of-the-century period of reform primarily through the eyes of researchers of one kind or another, especially a group of men who came to be known as "muckrakers," journalists, for the most part, who devoted their energies not to the securing of specific legislative measures but to "educating the public."

The process of educating the public is one of the basic steps in any social reform movement, since presumably no sweeping change can be imposed on people without preparing them in advance by indicating the evils to be remedied, the rationale to be used, and the benefits to be anticipated. To succeed in redefining role and status relationships a social reform movement must change both public opinion and the law. It is both educational in its program and political in the sense of seeking legislation.

A number of ways of enlightening the people emerged in the United States in the 19th and early 20th century, such as the American Social Science Association, the so-called muckraking movement, the social survey movement, the Congressional investigating commission, and the research efforts of voluntary organizations. These furnished the educational tools needed to revamp the economy or institutional organization.

We have already referred to the American Social Science Association as one of the decisive forces in reorienting thought about social problems in the 19th century. It consisted of administrators, educators, professional men, and social workers, who saw at first-hand the casualties of the new technology and the new urbanism. They had the theoretical background to evaluate the operation of the economic and the social systems, and, in addition, wanted to do something about the evils they saw. They were not all primarily "action people" in the sense that they were pressure groups; they were explorers, people who articulated, thought through, and illuminated what was happening. They created an atmosphere in which reforms could be discussed objectively. Perhaps the most important contribution made by the Association was the matrix it furnished for the creation of the more specialized and professional organizations and the stimulus it offered to the setting up of courses in the universities.

Facts, and still more facts, were called for, especially statistical facts.[24] The monumental researches of Frederic LePlay in France and of Charles Booth in London had set a pattern which was followed on a large scale in the United States. Of special importance in this connection was the research and publication work of the Russell Sage Foundation, established in 1907. One of the advisers to the woman who endowed this Foundation had suggested "an institution primarily 'for encouraging inquiry and publication'—inquiry into the causes of ignorance, poverty, vice, and crime, and methods of dealing with them"; another had recommended "studies . . . in the field of curative and preventive philanthropy"; a third had said that "the first object of the fund should be investigation; the next education, chiefly by publication." [25] The legal adviser, Mr. Robert W. de Forest, concurred.

He shared the fresh enthusiasm of those early years of the twentieth century for hunting down the causes of poverty, disease, and crime, and discovering what could be done to eliminate or at least control those causes; the confidence that a large part of the "human wants and ills" in America was preventable, and therefore would be prevented if only the facts about conditions and remedies were generally known.[26]

The charter of the Foundation as finally set up specified that the income was to be used for "the improvement of social and living conditions in the United States of America" and that it could use "any means to that end" including "research, publication, education. . . ." [27]

A mere listing of the publications of this Foundation up to 1946 in such fields as recreation, education, child-help, charity organization, remedial loans, consumer credit, women's work, statistics, surveys and exhibits, social work interpretation, arts and social work, delinquency and penology, and the professions covers more than nine pages.[28] The great Pittsburgh Survey, published in six volumes between 1909 and 1914, exposed the living and working conditions prevailing in a great industrial center.[29] Other studies by this same organization, including such subjects as housing reform, workingmen's insurance, delinquency, homeless men, and city planning, revealed to the public some of the more distressing phases of American life. These studies were undertaken by serious reformers; they reached a public more limited than that of the muckrakers [30] (to be discussed below) but wider than that reached by the American Social Science Association and the professional societies.

Another great channel for reaching the public to "educate" it for reform was the Congressional commission, which drew on the skills and talents of professional researchers. The Industrial Commission and the Immigration Commission, to mention some of the important earlier ones, published huge volumes of evidence to show that industrial conditions were bad and that the entrance of immigrants into the country at the rate of a million a year was swamping American institutions, rendering them almost incapable of helping in the adjustment process. The Wickersham Commission in the 1930's and the Kefauver Commission in the 1950's publicized the problems of crime. The results of these great Commissions found their way into the popular press and became mines of information for those who had to deal with social problems. Other Congressional commissions furnished data for consumer-protective legislation, for social security legislation, and for labor legislation.

But perhaps the most characteristic form which "educating the public" took at the turn of the century was the so-called muckraking movement. It consisted of a band of high-caliber journalists—Upton Sinclair, Ida Tarbell, Lincoln Steffens, and R. S. Baker among them—who did an enormous amount of research and exposed to public gaze, in as spectacular or sensational a manner as they could, the evils they found in factories, slums, packing plants, mines, and industry. The magazines in which their work was published—*American, McClure's,* and *Everybody's*—had great circulations. The muckrakers rubbed the noses of privileged people in the muck of modern cities and did not let them forget the price that was being paid for progress by the underprivileged. They had tremendous impact on the conscience of the country.

Except in so far as muckraking was purely sensational, there lay behind it a real and often passionate sympathy for the under-dog. By and large the muckrakers were neither doctrinaire reformers nor hard-boiled economists; they were newspaper men with a generous interest in human nature, considerable confidence in American democracy, and a sportsmanlike desire for fair play.[31]

These journalists "exposed" labor conflict, the conditions of women in industry, child labor, the industrial status of the Negro and of the Chinese worker, and exploitative conditions in industry. Their contribution to social reform was not direct or immediate. They were not reformers in the sense that they offered programs of action. They helped the reformers primarily in making the problems dramatic and thus enlisting public opinion on their side.

. . . muckraking was a middle-class movement. Few of the muckrakers were in any way connected with trade unions; few of them wrote in the interest of trade-union development. As good reporters, they were on the watch for live stories wherever they could be found; as philanthropically minded men and women, they attacked injustice wherever they discovered it; but beyond that they did not go. . . . The muckraking movement was, for the most part, merely a special development of journalism in response to a special need, and. . . . derived its strength from the fact that the muckrakers did not attempt to prescribe remedies for the evils they depicted. . . .

Looking back on the muckraking movement, we can readily see that it was part of a larger social, intellectual, and political development. In the nineties. . . . the average man acquiesced in the methods of industry and commerce. Industrial expansion seemed as much a matter of "manifest destiny" as geographical expansion had seemed in the days before the Civil War. . . . For the poor there was sympathy and even charity, but few people stopped to consider the conditions which made poverty inevitable. The majority threw themselves into the struggle for wealth with as little consideration for abstract theories of right and wrong as the pioneers had shown in the struggle for land. Even those who were beaten in the struggle were inclined to look upon their defeat as produced by the very laws of nature, and not through the operation of controllable social forces.

Of course there were movements of protest in the nineties, but it was not until the next decade that there came a definite revolt against Big Business. . . . There came to be much talk about the "social conscience." Forward-looking men in the churches and in public life began to say that too much attention had been paid to the sins of the individuals. . . . Dr. Max Farrand holds that every twenty or thirty years a wave of "moral hysteria" passes over the country, and practices that were once regarded as proper and honorable come to be condemned and scorned. "Hysteria" may or may not be the right word, but it is true that, with almost the suddenness of conversion, the attitude of the American people toward industry and toward government underwent a complete reversal.

The expression of the attitude was twofold: exposure and reform. It is important to note that, taking the most conservative figures available. . . . we find the total circulation of the ten magazines which engaged in muckraking to run over three million. These periodicals devoted a considerable proportion of their space, sometimes as much as 20 per cent, to articles of exposure. . . . We have every reason, then, to suppose that the muckrakers touched in one way or another the great majority of American citizens.

Parallel with the muckraking movement went a political movement. . . . Muckraking was closely bound up with the progressive movement for reform. . . . The list of reforms accomplished between 1900 and 1915 is an impressive one. The convict and peonage systems were destroyed in some states; prison reforms were undertaken; a federal pure food act was passed in 1906; child labor laws were adopted by many states; a federal employers' liability act was passed in 1906, and a second one in 1908, which was amended in 1910. . . . eight-hour laws for women were passed in some states. . . . twenty states passed mothers' pension acts between 1908 and 1913; twenty-five states had workmen's compensation laws in 1915. . . . A great many important and valuable reforms were adopted, as the result, in part at least, of muckraking. What the muckrakers tried to do was necessary; the evils were there, and there was no hope of removing them until the public was aroused to a recognition of their existence. What they accomplished was significant; the public was aroused and conditions were improved.[32]

Muckraking as a phenomenon died down as the century progressed. There have been sporadic revivals, as in the 1920's, when a new consumer's movement arose to expose false advertising and false labeling; [33] but muckraking can no longer be said to be a characteristic attitude.

Popular journals do, however, concern themselves with social problems. Scarcely any of the major periodicals publish an issue in which some attention is not devoted to crime, delinquency, divorce, or mental illness. The tone is usually less shrill than formerly; the approach is usually one of "scientific" appraisal or "human interest" appeal.

THE 1930's: THE MANAGEMENT OF ABUNDANCE. The period of the 1930's introduced so many reforms that it has, with good reason, been called a period of genuine revolution. The social problems to which these reforms addressed themselves may have been in the same areas as those of a century, or even two centuries, earlier, but they were not the same problems. Goals were higher. Standards were higher. A new ideology pervaded the attack. The people to be dealt with fell into exactly the same categories as those with which the ancient Poor Laws had had to wrestle: the "poor," the old, the "infirm," and "helpless," "infants," the "lame," the "impotent," the blind, the sick, and the unemployed.[34] But instead of looking for the cheapest way to provide for these unfortunate classes of people, the 1930's saw adequate provision for them not only as a governmental responsibility but also as an economic necessity. The social security legislation which was drawn up recognized that these people had a right to help; they did not have to come begging, humiliated, as pariahs. Their status did not have to be reduced to that of "pauper."

In general, the characteristic social problems of the 1930's had to

do with the management of abundance, how to keep the machines producing, how to distribute their product. The major social reforms were
those embodied in social security legislation, in full employment legislation, and in housing legislation. Income maintenance and, if necessary, subsidization of housing became major goals.

SOME THEORETICAL IMPLICATIONS OF REFORM.   The significance
of social reform movements is theoretical, we should point out, as well
as substantive. They tell us something about the way societies function.
In spite of the evidence of the past, there are still people who argue that
reform, especially by means of legislation, is impossible.

Reform legislation attempts purposive control or direction of social
behavior. The people who promulgate or enact laws are aiming at
some goal; they know, or think they know, what they want and they
are trying to achieve it by means of legislation. How much can they
achieve? There is still some uncertainty as to what and how much can
be achieved by legislation as contrasted, for example, with education,
and especially when dealing with the mores, as we shall see in Chapter
22. For the process of legislation itself, as well as the position of law in
a social system, is bound by crescive or customary norms. In some societies the opponents of a bill may be liquidated, if, indeed, they survive
to express opposition. Thus even the process of legislation, as well as the
resulting laws themselves, is subject to crescive limitations. But that
legislation does achieve some measure of success seems to be documentable from history.

There is sometimes a tendency to exaggerate either the broad social
forces which operate to produce problems or to exaggerate the influence
of those who achieve great ends in "solving" them. The social reforms
of the 19th and early 20th centuries show that human beings do shape
and influence the direction of social change. There is nothing contrary
to nature or history in any of this. Reform movements were as "natural" and, indeed, as "inevitable" as the evils they sought to deal with.[35]

Acts of God

The above discussion of "cures" or solutions of social problems has
dealt primarily with sociogenic problems, that is, with problems which
have their genesis in human beings and their interrelationships and
institutions. For "theogenic" or "aleatogenic" social problems, the so-
called Acts of God, or accidents, such as disasters and mutations, the

solution seems to lie in creating organized ways or institutions for dealing with them. Since in the present state of technology we cannot prevent earthquakes, typhoons, or droughts, the only thing we can do is insure ourselves in advance and have organizations ready to move in at once to take care of the victims. In this sense we "solve" certain social problems by the use of disaster relief and rehabilitation organizations.

We have now, in effect, concluded our discussion of social problems. We have distinguished human suffering and misfortune, which are as old as mankind, from social problems, which are relatively new. Social problems, we concluded, are situations which for humanitarian, utilitarian, or dysfunctionality reasons are felt to demand positive, usually reformistic, action on the part of society. The situations which call for such action change from time to time. In an age of scarcity they were likely to involve physical pain and sheer physical survival; in an age of abundance they increasingly involve stresses associated with role and status. The remainder of our book is, in effect, merely illustrative of these general principles. It describes in more detail specific kinds of social problems: in Part IV, those involving role impairment, caused by pathologies; in Part V, those involving role confusion and role and status anomalies caused by social disorganization and change; in Part VI, group-generated problems; and in Part VII, those which are now emerging in other parts of the world.

NOTES

1 See Chapter 5 for further comment on this point.

2 Czeslaw Milosz, *The Captive Mind* (Vintage, 1953), p. 405.

3 Jessie Bernard and L. L. Bernard, *Origins of American Sociology* (Crowell, 1943), Parts V and VIII.

4 David J. Dallin and Boris I. Nicolaevsky, *Forced Labor in Soviet Russia* (Yale Univ. Press, 1947), p. 191.

5 *Ibid.*, Chapter 7.

6 A. Black, "Soviet Housing: Some Town Planning Problems," *Soviet Studies*, 6 (July 1954), pp. 1–15.

7 *Ibid.* (Oct. 1954), p. 169.

8 *Ibid.*, p. 164.

9 Joseph Wortis, *Soviet Psychiatry* (Williams and Wilkins, 1950), p. 128 and Chapter 7.

10 Mark G. Field, "Alcoholism, Crime, and Delinquency in Soviet Society," *Social Problems*, 3 (Oct. 1955), pp. 100–105.

11 Reproduced in *Soviet Studies*, 6 (Jan. 1955), p. 308.

12 Field, *loc. cit.*

13 *Soviet Studies*, 6 (Jan. 1955), pp. 307–308.

14 Jack Raymond, "Poland Combats Wide Alcoholism," *New York Times*, November 28, 1955.

15 *Ibid.*

16 Field, *op. cit.* pp. 105–106.

17 *Ibid.*, pp. 107–108.

18 *Ibid.*, p. 106.

19 For an analysis of reform as conflict behavior, see Jessie Bernard, *American Community Behavior* (Dryden, 1949), Chapter 29. For an analysis of social movements see Rudolf Heberle, *Social Movements, An Introduction to Political Sociology* (Appleton-Century-Crofts, 1951).

20 Max Weber, *The Theory of Social and Economic Organization,* translated by A. M. Henderson and Talcott Parsons (Oxford Univ. Press, 1947).

21 The people who constitute a problem, as we saw in Chapter 5, do not always see themselves as problems. The destructive child is no problem to himself, nor even, necessarily, to his family. But he is a serious problem to the neighborhood. The alcoholic may not seem a problem to himself, but he is a serious problem to his employer and his family. The senile parent may not consider himself a problem, but he is a serious problem to his children. The social injustice which ground down the faces of the poor in Old Testament times were hardest on the inarticulate poor, on those who went cold and hungry, who were dispossessed of their flocks and land. But it was to the Prophets that these ills became problems. The French Revolution was led not by the peasants who suffered most from the Old Regime, but by the middle class. The Russian Revolution was not led by the oppressed proletarians or peasants, but by middle-class intellectuals.

22 John R. Commons, ed., *A Documentary History of American Industrial Society* (Cleveland: The A. H. Clark Company, 1910–11), VII, *Labor Movement 1840–1860* (1910), pp. 19–20.

23 H. A. Millis and R. E. Montgomery, *Organized Labor* (McGraw, 1945), pp. 24–25.

24 For the history of statistics as related to social science in this country, see L. L. Bernard and Jessie Bernard, *Origins of American Sociology* (Crowell, 1943), Part XII. It is doubtful if any reform movement could even begin to organize today without a large mass of statistical information.

25 John M. Glenn, Lilian Brandt, F. Emerson Andrews, *Russell Sage Foundation 1907–1946* (Russell Sage, 1947), p. 5.

26 *Ibid.*

27 *Ibid.,* p. 11.

28 *Ibid.,* pp. 675–684.

29 The Pittsburgh Survey included: Elizabeth Beardsley Butler, *Women and the Trades* (1909); Crystal Eastman, *Work-Accidents and the Law* (1910); Margaret F. Byington, *Homestead; The Households of a Mill Town* (1910); John A. Fitch, *The Steel Workers* (1911); Paul Underwood Kellogg, *The Pittsburgh District* (1914); and Paul Underwood Kellogg, *Wage-Earning Pittsburgh* (1914). This exposé was a great blow to the city

of Pittsburgh, and it remained sensitive to such surveys for many years. In 1919 the so-called Interchurch World Movement made another survey of the steel industry and reported conditions little better than those reported by the original Pittsburgh Survey.

30 The Russell Sage Foundation also established a magazine, *Charities and the Commons,* which later became *The Survey* (1909). This publication reached a wide audience. "Its educational influence was also increased by a press service to leading papers in all parts of the country. It was adopted as regular assigned reading for many university classes." Glenn, Brandt, and Andrews, *op. cit.,* p. 224.

31 C. C. Regier, *The Era of the Muckrakers* (Univ. of North Carolina Press, 1932), p. 147.

32 *Ibid.,* pp. 156–157, 195ff.

33 For a brief summary of this muckraking movement, see Jessie Bernard, *American Community Behavior,* pp. 262–269.

34 Dorothy Marshall, *The English Poor in the Eighteenth Century, A Study in Social and Administrative History* (Routledge, 1926), p. 2.

35 The Marxists were always disturbed by the seeming paradox of their doctrine, which taught that the inevitable laws of history were working in the direction of polarizing society into two classes and that ultimately the proletariat would be victorious. Nevertheless, their doctrine attempted to mobilize the workers of the world to unite and strike off their chains. Why should workers have to do anything if society were moving, by inexorable laws, to their dictatorship? Stalin himself had to wrestle with this paradox in the USSR even in the 1940's. The answer he supplied was that men had to fulfill their roles in history purposively; it was not a passive matter of waiting for history to take its course: "Stalin viewed himself and the state he commanded as the instrument for driving History in the right direction, at the right pace, at the right time. The flow of Soviet policy was the reflection of this correct and purposeful interpretation of what should be done, in the light of Marxist-Leninist-Stalinist science of society. Within this framework, the function of each man in Soviet society was not simply to respond passively to his environment, but, rather, consciously to govern his actions so as to fulfill his part in the execution of the correct historical line. Theoretically,

within his own narrow orbit for action, the New Soviet Man would choose the alternative which would correctly fulfill his role in history." (W. W. Rostow, *The Dynamics of Soviet Society* [Norton, 1953], pp. 106–107.) In Western society, especially in Great Britain and in the United States, there was little appeal to inevitable or inexorable laws of history; there was a strong appeal, however, to "natural" social and economic laws buttressing the policy of *laissez faire.* But despite these appeals, reform movements began to emerge almost as soon as the problems themselves.

IV

ABUNDANCE
AND THE
SOCIAL PATHOLOGIES

We doubt very much that a population having more than this rate of mental illness [ten per cent of the urban population], in addition to the heavy load of chronic and acute disease found in [the] survey, could function as a society.—Report to the American Public Health Association, *New York Times*, November 16, 1956

PHYSICAL ILLNESS and disability can pass almost any test set up as a criterion of a social or societal problem. They cause pain and suffering, they cost money, and they are dysfunctional. With respect to the first two criteria there can be little doubt; but it might be argued, and, indeed, has been, that a high mortality rate is functional in that it limits population. Malthus, in fact, specified death as a major positive population check.

But not all illness is fatal, and if people remain alive they constitute a drag on the social system if they are not able to function because of illness. In this role-impairing sense, if in no other, physical illness can be said to be dysfunctional. As evidence we need only point out, as we shall in Chapter 24, that controlling the mass diseases in underdeveloped areas of the world produces almost magical improvements in productivity as a result of more adequate performance of worker roles.

Most of our discussion in Part IV will deal with illnesses which do not have high mortality rates. For in an age of abundance it is not the pathologies that kill people in large numbers that are characteristic, but those that result from keeping people alive a long time.

Although we shall be concerned primarily with the sociological aspects of illness and health, we cannot omit at least passing reference to some of the cultural aspects.* If health were entirely a matter of germs, or of tissue pathologies, it would be much easier to deal with. Actually it is part and parcel of the cultural pattern of a people.

* For a detailed analysis of medical care as an aspect of culture, see Lyle Saunders, *Cultural Difference and Medical Care* (Russell Sage, 1954).

Every human society faces the prospects of sickness and each one has developed its own general cultural adaptations for it, which constitute its solutions. There are identifiable concepts about disease and its origins, sets of prescriptions defining what can be done, and usually by whom, along with standard patterns of sentiments, attitudes, and emotional overtones to guide both the patient and his associates. There are also equipments and precautions, ritualistic safeguards, rational interpretations, and social compensations for both the sufferer and his involved fellowship.[*]

Healing is intimately tied up with religion; indeed the healing and ministering aspects of religion have been central in Christianity for centuries. It has been found in underdeveloped areas of the world that the introduction of scientific treatment of illness may be greatly handicapped if proper recognition is not made of local religious, or magical, modes of thought.

It is often difficult to change cultural practices—diet, for example—which militate against good health.[†] It is often equally difficult to change healing practices—resort to patent medicines, for example—which are ineffective. From the point of view of treatment, such cultural tabus as those which have restricted the diagnosis and treatment of certain diseases are also significant. The venereal diseases are the most spectacular illustration, alcoholism being only slightly less so. "Mental" illness has only recently ceased to be thought of without shame, and a similar change from shame to understanding is under way for mental defect.

Other cultural concomitants of illness are those which find expression in fashion. In the 19th century, for example, slight ill health in women was looked upon as an evidence of refinement or "delicacy." The most glamorous heroine of the 19th century, Camille, died of tuberculosis. Languor was sexually appealing. At the present time neuroses are referred to as the fashionable disease for *littérateurs*. Allergies are also fashionable.

Culture makes its impact in other ways also. Industrialization brings its own occupational diseases. It also brings the abundance which makes science possible. Everywhere we turn, then, in the discussion of illness as a social problem we find evidence of cultural forces at work.

In Chapter 8 we select two diseases to illustrate the problems associated with infectious diseases, the Black Death, or plague, and the venereal diseases. The first illustrates the disorganizing effect of a great mass disease on whole societies—whether it is dysfunctional or not might be mooted, depending on whose interests one were considering. The second illustrates the way infectious diseases, which impair role fulfillment, are handled today. Other infectious diseases, such as tuberculosis,

[*] Leo W. Simmons and Harold G. Wolff, *Social Science in Medicine* (Russell Sage, 1954), p. 74.
[†] Carl E. Taylor, "Country Doctor in India," *Atlantic Monthly*, June 1956, pp. 44–48.

poliomyelitis, and the common cold, remain with us, but they are not given detailed attention here.

Chapter 9 deals with the physically handicapped. In Chapter 10 role impairment associated with low intelligence is studied. Chapter 11 examines the addictions, especially alcoholism. We have already seen, in Chapter 7, that alcoholism has been remarkably resistant to reform and revolution. Abundance changes the attack on the addictions from a legal to a medical one. This cultural "revolution" may make more headway against them than other more drastic reforms. In Chapter 12 the so-called stress diseases are described. Since the history of these illnesses is not well known, we cannot tell in all cases how much of the increase in their incidence is related to abundance and how much to improved diagnosis. The change to a relatively greater incidence of anxiety states, as contrasted with the hysterias, suggests, possibly, that having more to lose in an age of abundance—or "age of anxiety"—we have more anxiety about losing it. The "mental" illnesses (Chapter 13) have increased not because more young people become affected but primarily because abundance keeps so many more people alive long enough to reach the age brackets where they are susceptible. The "antisocial" (discussed in Chapter 14) have pathologies which are not always revealed in the clinic; in many cases one must scrutinize a whole life pattern in order to make a diagnosis. The symptoms—in some cases called "sociopathic" —are revealed in the social relationships of the patient in the community rather than in the diagnostician's office.

The pathologies we study here fulfill all our specifications for social problems. They are "social" because they disturb role relationships and "societal" because they also affect the whole society; they are problems because, on humanitarian, utilitarian, and dysfunctionality grounds, they call for a solution, and are viewed as solvable.

8

Abundance
and the
Infectious Diseases

The Impact of Disease on Civilizations:
The Black Death

The first part of this chapter is devoted to a description of the impact
of one of the greatest killers in history, the so-called Black Death, as an
illustration of the way a disease with high mortality rates can affect
whole societies. Although few diseases, even in an age of scarcity, had
the decimating effect of the Black Death, other diseases—typhus fever,
smallpox, malaria, yellow fever—did have similar, if less extensive,
effects. The "fall" of Rome has been attributed in part at least to the
inroads of malaria. And we have no record of the perhaps hundreds of
preliterate and even nonliterate peasant villages all over the world
which must have been obliterated by germ and insect-borne diseases in
man's long history. Even as late as 1918 the civilized world was exposed
to an influenza epidemic which killed millions of people and disrupted

The Impact of Disease on Civilizations:
The Black Death

The Changing Nature of Health Problems

The Public Health Movement

Illness and Role

The Venereal Diseases

the ordinary functioning of institutions. By and large, however, the high-mortality infectious diseases do not belong to an age of abundance. They are characteristic primarily of an age of scarcity.

The end of the Golden Age of Athens has been attributed to the effect of the plague. Thucydides described the stress of disorganization in Athens when it was seized by the Black Death in 430 B.C. A modern writer summarizes the account as follows:

Despair seized the people, and with it a total disregard for all ordinary standards of life and conduct. No one knew how soon life would leave his body or how long he would be the possessor of riches. People indulged in all kinds of licentiousness. Murder, rape and rapine were rampant. The populace lost all reverence for the gods and for the laws of society, since they saw that both the pious and the wicked perished alike. . . . Certainly the plague, which destroyed one third of the people and struck down their leader, was a decisive factor in the downfall of Athens and in the extinction of the Golden Age.[1]

The dysfunctionality of this great epidemic so far as the Golden Age in

Athens was concerned is scarcely debatable, if Thucydides' account is reliable.

The Black Death returned in the 14th century. It is estimated that more than 13,000,000 people died of it in China; India was almost depopulated. Pope Clement VI reported that more than 42,000,000 persons succumbed to it. Of course, since there were no statistical records in those days, no figures can be taken as accurate. The mortality, nevertheless, however judged, was without doubt enormous. The results for life on this planet, in fact, have been compared with those of a modern war.[2]

Whether the 14th-century Black Death was dysfunctional depends on the point of view. It had a profound effect on the old feudal system and contributed to the abolition of serfdom. As landowners died, property changed hands with disorganizing frequency. The death of workers in large numbers meant that those who survived could demand compliance with their own terms. Some idea of the impact of this great epidemic on the social structure of England may be gleaned from the following account.

Meanwhile, the king ordered that in every county of the kingdom, reapers and other labourers should not receive more than they were accustomed to receive, under the penalty provided in the statute, and he renewed the statute from this time. The labourers, however, were so arrogant and hostile that they did not heed the king's command, but if anyone wished to hire them, he had to pay them what they wanted, and either lose his fruits and crops or satisfy the arrogant and greedy desire of the labourers as they wished. When it was made known to the king that they had not obeyed his mandate, and had paid higher wages to the labourers, he imposed heavy fines on the abbots, the priors, the great lords and the lesser ones, and on others both greater and lesser in the kingdom. . . . Then the king had many labourers arrested, and put them in prison. Many such hid themselves and ran away to the forests and woods for a while, and those who were captured were heavily fined. And the greater number swore that they would not take daily wages above those set by ancient custom, and so they were freed from prison. It was done in like manner concerning other artisans in towns and villages. . . .

After the aforesaid pestilence, many buildings, both large and small, in all cities, towns, and villages had collapsed, and had completely fallen to the ground in the absence of inhabitants. . . . In the following summer (1350), there was so great a lack of servants to do anything that, as one believed, there had hardly been so great a dearth in past times. For all the beasts and cattle that a man possessed wandered about without a shepherd, and everything a man had was without a caretaker. And so all necessities became so dear that anything that in the past had been worth a penny was now worth four or five pence. Moreover, both the magnates of the kingdom and the other lesser lords who had tenants, remitted something from the rents, lest the tenants should leave, because of the lack of servants and the dearth of things. Some remitted half the rent, some more and others less, some remitted it for two years, some for three, and others for one year, according as they were able to come to an agreement with their tenants. Similarly, those who received day-work from their tenants throughout the year, as is usual from serfs, had to release them and to remit such services. They either had to excuse them entirely or had to fix them in a laxer manner at a small rent, lest very great and irreparable damage be done to the buildings, and the land everywhere remain completely uncultivated. And all foodstuffs and all necessities became exceedingly dear. . . .[3]

The impact of the Black Death has been credited with marking the end of the Middle Ages and the beginning of another era, with giving rise to the Renaissance, and even—by decimating Church leadership and disillusioning the populace with regard to the Church, which was revealed to be helpless in the face of the plague—with leading to the Reformation.[4] Even if one discounts much of this assessment of the effect of the Black Death, one must still credit great social changes to it.

One might argue that some of these changes were desirable for at least some segments of the population and to this extent not dysfunctional to the whole society, however dysfunctional they were for the specific *status quo*. In reply, however, one might ask, as we did in Chapter 5, Was this the best way to accomplish these changes?

Other infectious diseases have also played their part in history, as the following statement points out.

Disease has played a dominant role in the destiny of the human race. . . . It has defeated armies, paralyzed trade, altered the economic life of nations. It has wiped out old castes and created new ones. It has destroyed explorers and colonizers, scattered their settlements and determined the ownership of continents. . . .[5]

Fatal disease, then, not only causes suffering and is costly, but also can be shown to be dysfunctional to specific social systems or to a specific *status quo*. It may, as the population theorists argue, serve a necessary function in holding down numbers—we shall have more to say about this in Chapter 24—but there is no proof that it always serves in this way. In the cases we have used to illustrate its impact there may have been no overpopulation to begin with. Fatal disease may also, as the eugenically minded argue, have been functional in wiping out inferior or less resistant stocks: "It has destroyed old races and cleared the terrain for new ones which were hardier, more resourceful and more intelligent." [6] It is doubtful, however, if it functions in this way at the present time. It is doubtful, in fact, if any of the alleged benefits of fatal diseases could not be achieved more effectively and more efficiently by other means.

Because in an age of abundance the high-mortality infectious diseases become less and less significant as social problems, we devote no

more attention to them in this volume, except briefly in Chapter 24.
But illness, even when it is not fatal, may cause suffering, cost money,
and be dysfunctional in the sense that it interferes with role performance. And it is precisely the nonfatal, role-impairing illnesses which
characterize an age of abundance. Before we examine the role-impairing
illnesses in more detail, however, we present data to document the
changing nature of health problems which comes with abundance.

The Changing Nature of Health Problems

Nowhere is the contrast between old and new social problems more
spectacular than in the field of health. Old diseases are mastered, but
new ones emerge. The mass diseases—infectious and nutritional—are
conquered; industrial and degenerative and stress diseases increase.

There are no frontiers to our health problems, only a succession of
horizons. When medical and social advances cross one horizon a vista of new
problems stretches ahead. Diseases which have been submerged or ignored
in the preoccupation with the mass diseases assume a new importance which
is sometimes only relative but is often real. When a country has advanced
so far as to get effective control of infections and contagious diseases, when
insect-borne diseases have been eliminated and efficient sanitation has ban-
ished the water-borne diseases, degenerative and "stress" diseases assume
new proportions. Industrial development brings new medical hazards such
as silicosis. More infants survive with congenital weaknesses. The conflicts
and anxieties, which the intensity and urgency of an advancing society can
create, may increase the extent of mental ill-health.[7]

Civilization apparently also "causes" some illnesses by the physical
conditions of living which it fosters, quite apart from stress. Lung cancer, for example, seems to be such an illness. It now kills more people—
22,000 a year—than tuberculosis does; and its incidence is increasing.
It more than quadrupled between 1930 and 1955.[8]

The most interesting illustration of the way a "new" disease may
reveal itself, once its competitors have been eliminated, is the story of
poliomyelitis, one of the most recent to come under control.

"New" diseases such as poliomyelitis appear to emerge. "New" is so
written because evidence of this disease is found in the Egyptian steles of
the eighteenth dynasty (1580 B.C.); but it has acquired a new prominence
in recent years, due partly to improved diagnosis but also, probably, because

it was previously masked or inhibited by the mass diseases. Indeed it looks as though this disease . . . is a levy on a rising standard of living, for the rising curve of poliomyelitis is closely related to the rising curve of prosperity. It has so far reached its highest epidemic proportions in the well-to-do countries of America and Europe and is relatively frequent among the well-to-do classes. It has occurred in recent years in poorer countries in Asia and in Latin America but it may be a case of a virus which, without the competition of other infectious diseases, acquires a new virulence in the advanced countries.[9]

The major health problems in the industrialized nations of the world are no longer, then, the so-called mass diseases. They are the health problems associated with the degenerative diseases of age, which result from the increasing age of their populations, and the stress diseases, which result from anxieties and strain. The accompanying figure, comparing the mortality rate from degenerative diseases in underdeveloped and in developed countries, might be used to compare the old with the new pattern of disease in any modern nation.

The results of keeping populations alive into the older age brackets are vividly portrayed also in the increase shown in the proportion of all deaths from the degenerative diseases. The following figures illustrate what happens in even short time-spans; in less than a decade, for example, deaths from diseases of the heart and circulatory system and from cancers and tumors rose almost 10 per cent.[10] And even since 1949 large strides have been made in still further reducing the death and morbidity rate from infectious diseases.[11]

TABLE 1

PERCENTAGES OF DEATHS FROM DISEASES OF THE HEART AND
CIRCULATORY SYSTEM AND CANCERS AND TUMORS

Country	Earlier Year	Percent	Later Year	Percent
Australia	1940	49	1947	58
Canada	1941	46	1948	53
Denmark	1941	45	1948	55
New Zealand	1940	49	1949	58
Sweden	1940	51	1947	59
Switzerland	1940	49	1949	59
United Kingdom (England and Wales)	1940	48	1947	59
United States	1940	49	1948	58

SOURCE: United Nations, *Preliminary Report on the World Social Situation* (United Nations, 1952), p. 31.

Death rates do not tell the whole story. With advancing age there is a great increase in chronic illness. And perhaps the most disturbing of

FIGURE 1

Comparative Mortality [at Midcentury] from Degenerative Diseases in Underdeveloped and Developed Countries

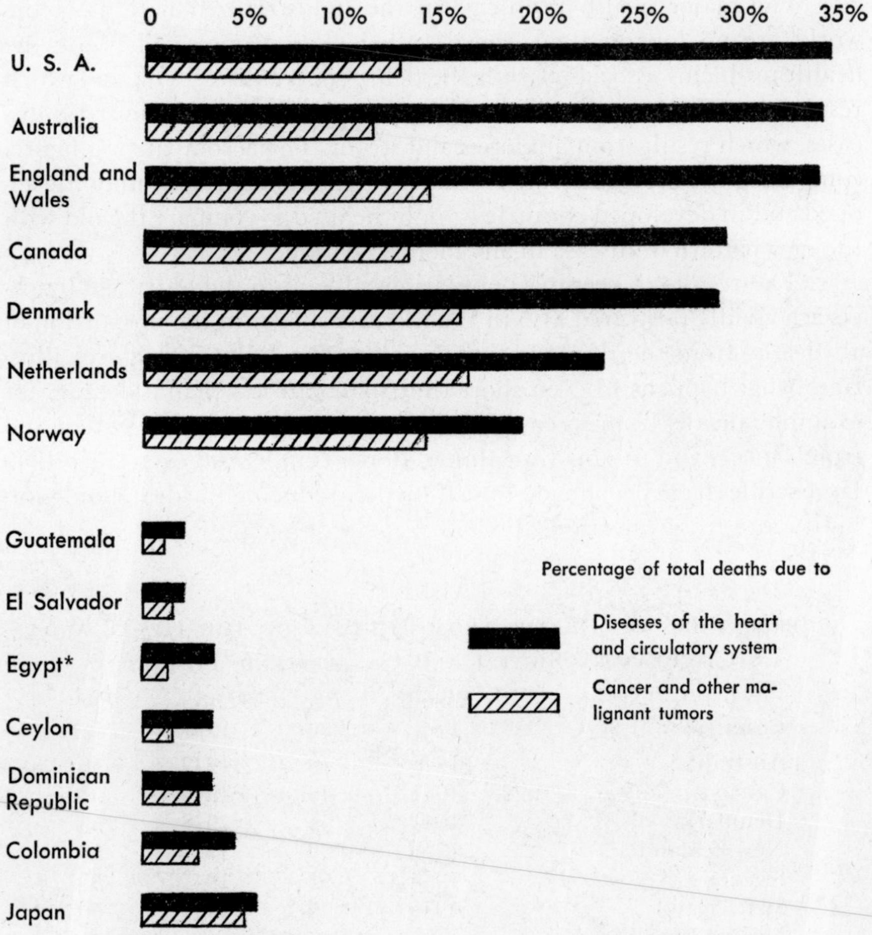

| | 0 | 5% | 10% | 15% | 20% | 25% | 30% | 35% |

U. S. A.

Australia

England and Wales

Canada

Denmark

Netherlands

Norway

Guatemala

El Salvador

Egypt*

Ceylon

Dominican Republic

Colombia

Japan

Percentage of total deaths due to

Diseases of the heart and circulatory system

Cancer and other malignant tumors

* Areas with health organizations

SOURCE: United Nations, *Preliminary Report on the World Social Situation* (United Nations, 1952), p. 30.

all are the senile dementias which increase the hospitalized population.

Abundance may also be responsible for physical "softness" which, though not fatal, had become a matter of such concern that in 1955 a conference was called to plan ways of combating it.[12]

The contrast between the diseases of scarcity—the mass germ and nutritional diseases—and those of abundance—the degenerative diseases—reveals itself also within any one society, albeit on a vastly reduced scale. Even in our own society, for example, contagious diseases such as measles, whooping cough, chicken pox, diphtheria, and scarlet fever occur at an earlier age in poorer urban areas than in better ones.[13] A study in the 1930's found that people in the lower socioeconomic levels tended to be ill more often, more seriously, and longer than people in the higher socioeconomic classes.[14] And, significantly, the differences between the upper and lower socioeconomic classes were greater in the diseases—infectious and nutritional—for which medical science has developed preventive and remedial measures. They were least marked in those degenerative illnesses for whose prevention or cure there are as yet only inadequate techniques.[15] A more recent study of health as related to class also highlights the effect of socioeconomic status.[16]

The Public Health Movement

Much of the credit for the conquest of the mass diseases is due to the public health movement which applied the new scientific findings to the health problems of modern cities. Thousands of people had been uprooted from the land and catapulted into industrial towns and cities. These earliest industrial towns were little more than hovels erected around the mills or factories. The factories themselves were dreary frames thrown up to protect the machinery. They were dark and poorly ventilated, and the machines were not guarded, so that accidents were common. The people who first came to the British factory towns to work were not the thrifty, but the less successful. They were not accustomed to living in towns and it took a long time to teach them how.[17]

In the meanwhile, as the towns grew into cities, problems of sanitation became pressing. The elementary services, such as an adequate water and sewage system, had to be provided, as well as some protection against infectious diseases. But as in any enterprise involving masses of people, sanitation was, it became evident, a social as well as a medical and an engineering problem.

The public health movement was inaugurated by social reformers, not by doctors. As early as the 18th century, John Howard had worked for the improvement of sanitation in prisons. In the middle of the 19th century, another pioneer, Lord Ashley, the Earl of Shaftesbury, sought to improve sanitation for the protection of the health of industrial workers also. But the greatest of the pioneers was Edwin Chadwick, whose *Report on the Sanitary Condition of the Labouring Population of Great Britain* in 1842 raised the question whether much sickness might not be preventable and whether much poverty might not be the result of sickness. This report had great influence throughout the civilized world. The sanitary reforms it suggested were carried out between 1848 and 1855 in the United Kingdom by John Simon. The foundation he laid down became the administrative basis for the public health movement. The assumption underlying the movement was that illness was an economic burden on the community and was to a large extent preventable.

By the beginning of the 20th century the concept of public health in the United States had been extended to include not only the negative aspect of prevention, but also the positive one of fostering good health practices in the life of the individual. Hence education became a primary aspect of its program. In addition, public health work came to include efforts to secure better housing, better zoning laws, better transportation to open up new residential districts in cities, better roads to reach remote rural areas with health services, and even improvement in agriculture and in the handling of foods.

Increasingly, public health officers recognize the social as well as the purely medical aspects of their work. This recognition has radically changed their approach to some community health problems. For example, they now see that "a whole complex of social . . . factors . . . underlies the extent of irregular sexual intercourse and thus directly controls the incidence of venereal disease; [and] the same is true of the problems of alcoholism and of drug addiction. . . . Tuberculosis cannot be controlled in a household where there is overwork or not enough to eat. Any social or economic organization or force which helps to eradicate poverty is a contribution of primary importance to public health." [18] Increasingly, also, some non-germ illnesses are coming to be seen as social reactions, that is, as reactions against social stress factors (Chap. 12).

The two germ diseases specified above—tuberculosis and the venereal diseases—are coming increasingly under control. In Pennsylvania in 1954 for the first time on record tuberculosis did not figure among the first ten causes of death. The same was true in Idaho, Iowa,

Nebraska, North Dakota, Utah, and Wyoming.[19] In some communities tuberculosis hospitals are being closed or turned over to other uses. Because of their intimate relationship with moral behavior, the venereal diseases, like alcoholism and other addictions, have to be dealt with in special ways. It is interesting, as we shall note below, that progress in conquering these diseases depends as much on the application of sociological principles as on the application of medical ones.

Illness and Role

Since illness always has some effect on behavior it will tend to influence role performance to some extent. The high-mortality infectious diseases disturb role relationships, as we saw in the accounts of the Black Death above. The dysfunctionality of low-mortality illnesses lies primarily in the effect they have on role performance rather than, as in the case of the high-mortality illnesses, in the effect they have on population survival. They do not decimate populations, but they do interfere with role relationships.

It is obvious . . . that physical misfortunes not only cripple or otherwise handicap the individual as an organism, but also frequently disrupt his life as a group member and as a personality. Anyone, for instance, who suffers blindness, loses the use of his legs, or endures a long-term physical ailment is unable to play his accustomed role in society, and he may also undergo a change in personality. In varying degrees his relations to his milieu are disturbed and altered.[20]

Even transient illnesses can disturb role relationships, temporarily at least. It is in this light that our discussion of illness and of handicap proceeds.

We have already seen that when a person becomes ill he is assigned a special role, that of patient. In this role he exchanges freedom, autonomy, and self-direction for control, but at the same time he gains protection, freedom from responsibility, and care.

All over the world, as far as we know, whenever a member of society shows recognizable symptoms of illness, fails to meet his obligations as in health, takes to his hammock or cot, complains and waits for others to minister unto him, his customary roles in the group are changed, along with some of the rights and duties associated with these roles, and other sets of privileges and performances come into effect. Thus, a generalized set of sick rules begins to function for those most closely involved, the patient himself and the responsible members designated to take over. It is practically impossible for a sick member to escape, even if he should choose to do so, the impact of his culture's "universals," which are designed to deal with the general problems of disease and possible death.[21]

Some people find the role of patient insufferable; they prefer almost any other role. They chafe under control. They dislike being patronized. They fight the restrictions imposed by the role. But other people welcome it. They gladly surrender autonomy and freedom for the peace and protection of the sickbed. In some cases it is an honorable, or at least not a disgraceful, way to escape from role responsibilities. Increasingly, resort to this avenue of escape is itself viewed as a type of pathology. The extension of the definition of the patient role to include many persons formerly viewed as wicked or as criminal is one of the major results of an age of abundance. We can afford to treat them as medical rather than moral or legal problems.

In general, men may tend to reject the role of patient more than women, perhaps in part because it puts them in such a subordinate position to the doctor who gives orders and to the nurse who executes them. But many women also reject it. Perhaps extreme rejection of the role of patient is as pathological as extreme desire for it.

Our chief interest here, however, is in the impact of illness on ordinary role performance, for normal role relationships are disturbed when a person withdraws from the performance of his roles to take over the role of patient.

Certain distinctions among illnesses may prove useful to us here. They are based not on the etiology or "causes" but on the nature of their role-effects. For purposes of treatment or social policy it is important to know whether the cause of an illness is a germ, a lesion, a family-social-cultural relationship, or a fear. But for our purposes here it will make only minor difference whether a man is incapacitated because of a physical or a "mental" illness. In fact, for our purposes, there is little value in such a distinction. So long as an illness affects role performance it is a problem, whatever its etiology.

We distinguished in Chapter 2 between role impairment and role confusion, the first referring primarily to the conditions in the individual which made role performance difficult and the second to conditions in the outer world which made it difficult. Our concern in Part IV is with role impairment.

Some illnesses, for example, impair role performance but do not prevent or wholly distort it. We speak in this case of simple role impairment. Slight colds, chronic fatigue, heart disease which is not incapacitating,[22] and the mild anxiety states represent this type. Some illnesses produce role pathologies. In some cases these pathologies take the form of role distortion. Obsessive fears, for instance, all-pervasive hostilities, persistent aggressiveness, and suspicions produce such distortions of role. In some cases the pathologies are so severe that the patients can perform no roles at all. They may have to be hospitalized. In the case of mental defect, we may have a form of role incapacity.

Some illnesses—alcoholism, for example—may begin by merely impairing role performance but end in complete role incapacity or pathology. Others may remain mere role impairments for many years. We have selected as an illustration of infectious diseases the venereal diseases. They may merely impair role performance in their early stages; but in the later stages, especially in the case of syphilis when it attacks brain tissue, they may eventuate in paretic psychosis, resulting in a form of role pathology.

The Venereal Diseases

History

The first authenticated records of syphilis in Europe date back only to the 15th century. Reportedly it was spread by the armies of Charles VIII of France upon their return from Naples. At that time it was a disease of the lower classes, something like the itch. Some twenty years later, when Francis I had succeeded to the throne, it had climbed the social ladder. The king himself was infected.[23]

Not until about 1520 was the sexual character of the infection recognized. But the attitude toward sex was so lenient that no stigma attached to syphilis. In fact, "the attitude of the upper classes towards syphilis became decidedly frivolous in the *siècle galant*. . . . In a century of great sexual licentiousness syphilis was taken as an unavoidable little accident." [24]

With the rise of the middle class, however, came a changed attitude toward syphilis. The middle class condemned sexual licentiousness; at least the appearance of virtue was demanded. "By adopting such an attitude the bourgeoisie claimed to be better than the nobility and therefore entitled to power. But it also endeavored to compensate for the ruthlessness of the economic system that it was constructing on the ruins of feudalism." [25] In the 18th and 19th century, therefore, victims of syphilis or gonorrhea were shamed and disgraced. Infected people hesitated to go to physicians for help; they went instead to quacks. The treatment of venereal diseases has therefore suffered from peculiar handicaps.

Only recently has the fallacy of attaching stigma to these diseases become apparent. The very words—syphilis and gonorrhea—were tabu for newspapers until a few years ago. The venereal diseases are now recognized as a threat not only to the individual himself but to society at large. New approaches have therefore been experimented with. Figure 2 and the legend accompanying it trace the incidence of venereal disease for half a century.

Trends

The decline in syphilis in Europe and in the United States began a century ago and, with the exception of periods of war and civil unrest, it has continued to decline. As a result, deaths from syphilis have decreased 50 per cent since 1940. Infant mortality caused by syphilis has been reduced by 92 per cent since 1933. Admissions to mental hospitals of patients suffering from syphilitic psychoses have declined drastically.

If the rate of first admissions to mental institutions because of syphilitic psychoses were still at the 1941 rate of 6.6 per 100,000 people, there would have been admitted to state mental hospitals during 1950, 9,914 patients. . . . instead of only 3,751. We may assume that venereal disease control from 1941 to 1950 prevented 6,163 persons from becoming neurosyphilis casualties, in 1950.[26]

The long-time trend down does not, of course, preclude fluctuations up as well as down, the rate being higher for some years than for others.[27]

The reasons for the long-time decline in venereal disease rates are both biological and sociological. They have been summarized as follows:

The fact that the character of syphilis has changed from a virulent acute type of infection to one of great chronicity suggests that by a process of gradual adaptation (1) the virulence of the syphilis organism has decreased, while (2) individual resistance to the disease has increased. Other important factors in the decreasing incidence of syphilis are attributed to (3) the progressive improvement in socioeconomic conditions and (4) the application of modern public health control measures.[28]

Some of the decline in the incidence of venereal diseases shown in Figure 2 must be attributed, as the above statement points out, to strictly biological forces: to the decline in virulence of the syphilitic organism and the increased resistance of the human organism. Some of the credit is due to the abundance to which we have so often referred. But in addition, some credit is also due to the application of sociological principles in the epidemiological approach through case-finding.

FIGURE 2
VENEREAL DISEASE INCIDENCE RATES,
NAVY AND MARINE CORPS, 1900–1949

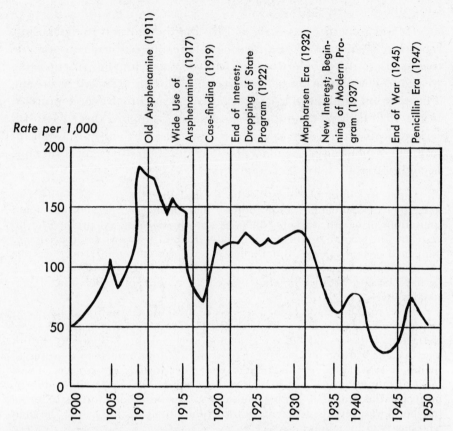

SOURCE: Department of the Navy, Bureau of Medicine and Surgery, Medical Statistics Division. (From A. Frank Brewer, "Dangers of the Antibiotic Cocktail in VD Control," *Journal of Social Hygiene,* 39 [Oct. 1953], p. 303.)

"[Figure 2] shows that the same sort of phenomena has occurred each time a new drug and new interest has been generated in the control of the venereal diseases. (This graph is based on Navy morbidity, probably the best statistics we have in America.) Note that reported cases of venereal disease steadily increased from 1900 to 1910—when use of old arsphenamine started—and lasted until 1916, the first deadline in our 50-year period. World-wide publicity was given Ehrlich's discovery and thousands of people sought therapy. Interest waned because of cost, toxicity and a relatively high mortality. With the discovery of neoarsphenamine, again widespread interest was aroused because of lessened toxicity and greater ease of therapy; it lasted until 1922, the end of World War I and the beginning of the first venereal disease control program in this country. Ten years then intervened with little interest, and sporadic work was done. Treatment was given when requested but with little casefinding either by the profession or by demand of the public or health officials. History repeats itself with the advent of mapharsen, still less toxic and more easily administered. In 1932 mapharsen was developed, and the Navy and civilians immediately started its experimental use. Again great interest was aroused in the venereal disease program. In 1935 with Social Security grants we developed the modern venereal disease programs with active case-finding. This period lasted through the war to 1945. Post-war dislocation occurred, with an increase of the venereal disease rates. Then in 1947 began the penicillin era. The same general trend can be observed over a 50-year period." (*Ibid.,* pp. 303–304.)

The Application of Sociological Principles:
Case-finding

It was recognized as early as 1917 that in addition to diagnosing, reporting, quarantining, and treating venereal infections it was imperative to locate the people who had had contacts with the patient being treated.[29] The patient himself was recognized as but one link in a chain. The question was how to locate the other links? Little was accomplished in the 1920's; there was no national financial support, there were still serious problems of diagnosis and treatment, and there was a difficult problem of holding patients for the long duration of arsenical therapy. In addition, there were social barriers:

First and most obvious was the natural unwillingness of patients to name their sexual contacts. And beyond that barrier lay the viewpoints and limitations of health workers. Then, as now, it was no great problem to investigate the sexual partner of the individual with syphilis if the partner happened to be a spouse. But we had a very profound reluctance to probe into the sexual life of the person with syphilis much beyond the marital tie, perhaps because further delving seemed an unwarranted invasion of personal rights.

This reluctance was only one aspect of the national traditions and social attitudes which barred successful search for contacts. Unaware of the real character of the sexual behavior of most venereal disease patients, health workers ascribed the reticence of patients in naming contacts to a feeling of shame or to a bona fide inability to remember casual sex partners. These rationalizations, which impeded a realistic approach to VD epidemiology, protected the prejudice deep in most of us against the informer . . . the busybody who reveals damaging information about his associates, the man who boasts of his conquests.

Perhaps of more importance, they expressed a profound distaste for the idea that many persons among us had a large number of casual or promiscuous sexual contacts within a short period of time.[30]

Little by little these social-psychological difficulties were overcome. It became clear that until cases were actively searched out, public health programs would be mere holding operations. A new vocabulary, a new set of epidemiological practices, finally emerged. Top priority was assigned to the interviewing of all lesion cases of syphilis to secure the names of all contacts, to find these contacts, and to bring them in for diagnosis and treatment.

The interviewer gets information on every contact and records it on a form. If the contact lives in the jurisdiction of the health department, the form is routed directly to the local investigator. If the contact lives in an adjacent local health jurisdiction, the telephone is used to initiate the case-finding action. If the contact lives in a different state, telephone or telegraph carries the information to the investigating unit, the form following by mail. "The investigator who goes out to find the contact must know his community and the groups of which the contacts are a part. He must know their hours of work and play, their haunts as well as their addresses, the focal points at which they congregate and the persons who know them and whose leadership they respect. He must be discreet to avoid violations of confidentiality, tactful to prevent embarrassment of contacts by family or friends, and alert to circumvent the reluctance of some contacts to come to the health department." [31] The investigator never uses intimidation or threats of legal action; he uses all his skills to secure voluntary cooperation.

The results of this epidemiological approach have been judged successful. As contrasted with reported gonorrhea in men, which declined only 37 per cent between 1947 and 1953, the minimum incidence of syphilis declined 78 per cent. An approach similar to that used in syphilis has therefore been developed for case-finding in gonorrhea also. Here time is of the essence. Contacts must be investigated within seventy-two hours, the length of protection of penicillin, so that the patient will not be immediately reinfected. All contacts during the six days before onset of clinical symptoms must also be located. The procedure is similar to that in syphilis control, but at a faster pace; telegrams are sent to all contacts on the day of the interview, requesting them to report immediately to the venereal disease clinic; an investigator seeks all contacts who do not receive a telegram. He personally seeks all those who do not respond to the telegram within twenty-four hours. All contacts who are reached are examined and treated. Within five working days, about 70 per cent of the contacts within the "speed zone" are being examined and treated.

There is evidence that immunity to syphilis develops in some people after penicillin treatment, and hope is expressed that in time there may be an immunization injection to protect against it; but not all students share this hope.[32] Whether control will take this form or some other, however, it does appear that syphilis as a major scourge is, like so many other infectious diseases, in process of attrition.

So much, then, for the infectious diseases which ravaged populations in the past. If our intent were to be encyclopedic rather than merely illustrative, we would include also discussions of a disease such as tuberculosis, which is not only dysfunctional to whole groups—notably among the Indians today—but also impairs role relationships. But since we have to be selective in our materials we merely point out that in general the same principles hold for the other diseases as for those we have been emphasizing here, namely: with the application of the science which abundance makes possible the high-mortality infectious diseases tend to come increasingly under control so that they become less and less a threat to whole societies. Infectious diseases, even when their mortality rates are reduced, remain social problems because of the role impairment which they, like all diseases, involve.

In the remaining chapters of Part IV our attention will be focused on pathologies which, so far as is now known, are not necessarily the result of infection but which, nevertheless, make themselves felt in the social order because of their effect on role relationships.

NOTES

1 Ralph H. Major, *Disease and Destiny* (Appleton-Century, 1936), pp. 3–4, 6.

2 *Ibid.*, p. 23.

3 Henry Knighton, "The Impact of the Black Death," from James Bruce Ross and Mary Martin McLaughlin, *The Portable Medieval Reader* (Viking, 1949), pp. 220–222.

4 Major, *op. cit.*, p. vii.

5 *Ibid.*

6 *Ibid.*

7 United Nations, *Preliminary Report on the World Social Situation* (United Nations, 1952), pp. 29–31.

8 Dr. Lester Breslow, chief of the Bureau of Chronic Diseases, California Department of Public Health, in a report to the 82nd National Conference of Social Work, reported in *New York Times,* June 3, 1955. Certain occupations were especially vulnerable: mining, smelting, welding, asbestos work, painting, metal fabrication, and restaurant cooking.

9 United Nations, *op. cit.*, p. 31.

10 *Ibid.* In 1955 a 50 per cent increase in the incidence of cancer in the United States was predicted in twenty-five years by the National Cancer Institute, as reported in the *New York Times,* December 24, 1955. About every third infant born would develop cancer if 1955 rates continued.

11 In the decade 1945–1955, for example, antibiotics, cortisone and other steroids, and Salk poliomyelitis vaccine were developed. New diagnostic tests for uterine cancer were also developed; and fluoridization of water for reduction of tooth decay in children was introduced. New treatment for epilepsy and for rheumatic fever were reported. Prevention of blindness in premature babies and the prevention of kernicterus, a nerve disease of infants, were made possible in this decade. Gains were made in the prevention of both infectious and degenerative diseases, but probably greater ones in the first than in the second. (*New York Times,* December 21, 1955.)

12 It was reported that more than half of the men called to service in World War II had failed to pass the physical fitness tests. It was further reported that 56 per cent of American children had failed on a minimum fitness test, while only 8 per cent of European children had so failed. Suggested solutions included plans to encourage more participation in sports and less spectatorship. (*New York Times,* July 12 and September 7, 1955.) In South Africa abundance was also reported as having lethal effects: "Too much eating, too much loafing—and too-demanding wives—are killing off South African men," said a newspaper report, continuing that "either they ate to excess, did not take enough exercise—or their ambitious wives were always trying to force them to get ahead in the world." (*Ibid.,* June 7, 1955.)

13 Barkev S. Sanders, *Environment and Growth* (Warwick, 1934), p. 283.

14 National Health Survey, Bulletin No. 2, *Illness and Medical Care in Relation to Economic Status* (1938), p. 2; G. St. J. Perrott and S. D. Collens, "Relation of Sickness to Income and Income Change in 10 Surveyed Communities," *Public Health Reports,* Vol. 50, No. 18 (May 1935); and G. St. J. Perrott, "The State of the Nation's Health," *Annals of the American Academy of Political and Social Science,* 188 (Nov. 1936), pp. 140–142.

15 Sanders, *op. cit.*, p. 289.

16 Earl Lemon Koos, *The Health of Regionville* (Columbia Univ. Press, 1954).

17 See Robert Owen's own account of New Lanark, Scotland, for some of the problems of personal sanitation in the early industrial towns in his *Life of Robert Owen* (Bohn). See also G. D. H. Cole, *Robert Owen* (Little, 1925), pp. 77–78.

18 C. E. A. Winslow, "Public Health," *Encyclopaedia of the Social Sciences*, 12, (Macmillan, 1934), pp. 647–650.

19 *Newsweek*, August 29, 1955, p. 68. There were 76,291 institutionalized cases of tuberculosis in the United States in 1950. In 1909 there were 156 deaths per 100,000 population; in 1950, 22.5; in 1954, 10.5.

20 Leo W. Simmons and Harold G. Wolff, *Social Science in Medicine* (Russell Sage, 1954), pp. 111–112.

21 *Ibid.*, p. 75.

22 The role effects of heart disease were studied in forty-six adult males, thirty to sixty years of age, living in Minneapolis. It was found that both worker and family roles were affected, particularly in the lower occupational levels. Where changes in occupation took place they were generally downward. "The effects on interpersonal relations was to bring about: a reorientation of expected roles; a realignment of the power and authority structure in the family; in some cases, temporary periods of family disorganization and interpersonal conflict; all of which served to aggravate an already difficult social situation." (Leo G. Reeder, "The Effects of Heart Disease on the Family's Socio-Economic Status and Interpersonal Relationships," presented before the Society for the Study of Social Problems, August 1955.) A detailed study of other chronic illnesses would doubtless find similar effects.

23 Major, *op. cit.*, p. 302.

24 Henry E. Sigerist, *Civilization and Disease* (Cornell Univ. Press, 1943), p. 77.

25 *Ibid.*

26 J. K. Shafer, "The Outlook for Venereal Disease Control," *Journal of Social Hygiene*, 39 (May 1953), p. 199.

27 A survey of 44 major cities in 1954, for example, found local syphilis epidemics in the early infectious stage in 18 states. The rate had gone up in 20 states. Gonorrhea rates were up in 36 states and in 23 major cities. One out of every 200 teen-agers became infected in 1953. (*New York Times*, February 23, 1955.)

28 A. Frank Brewer, "Dangers of the Antibiotic Cocktail in VD Control," *Journal of Social Hygiene*, 39 (Oct. 1953), p. 301.

29 "A frightening aspect of syphilis," a report by three public health organizations in 1955 pointed out, "is the swift geometric progression of untreated infection in a population. In Greensboro, N. C., for example, a six-week epidemic involved 101 persons, of whom more than half were teen-agers. A single infection in West Point, Ga., involved 211 persons within six weeks. Seventy of them contracted syphilis." (*New York Times*, February 23, 1955.)

30 J. K. Shafer, "American Venereal Disease Control Problems, with Emphasis on Their Epidemiology," *Journal of Social Hygiene*, 39 (Nov. 1953), pp. 358–359.

31 *Ibid.*, pp. 364–365.

32 Brewer, *loc. cit.*

9

Role Impairment:
Physical Handicap

Trends

There are probably millions of children in the United States who have never seen a hunchback; this deformity was once fairly common. A large number have never seen a clubfoot. For modern medicine has learned to prevent many of the formerly crippling and disabling illnesses and to correct many it cannot yet prevent. The work of the World Health Organization is reducing the number of blind persons in underdeveloped areas of the world, as we shall see in Chapter 23, just as modern medicine has already done in the West. Hope is being held out that the crippling forms of poliomyelitis will be conquered shortly.

But modern civilization introduces new ways to cripple people. Wars can still leave millions of people—civilians as well as soldiers—disabled. Radiation sickness could affect untold numbers. Modern industrial machines can destroy arms, legs, feet, and hands on a grand scale. The modern automobile has been called a weapon of death; an

Trends

Extent

Twofold Nature of the Problem of the Handicapped

The Handicapped in the Role of Worker

Status Aspects of Rehabilitation

The Handicapped in Family Roles

Role Aspects of Rehabilitation

enormous number of casualties are attributable to it each year. The modern home is the most dangerous place so far as accidents are concerned; they are four times as frequent in homes as on highways.[1] And raising the standard of housing will not necessarily improve its safety: "If every home boasts a swimming pool or a wading pond, home drownings will become more frequent. With more individuals owning their homes, the do-it-yourself movement will grow and the number of accidents in home workshops will increase."[2] So far as some causes of physical handicap are concerned, in brief, there is improvement; with respect to others, however, there is none at all.

Some infants are born with sensory or muscular abnormalities. Some persons are victimized by illnesses that leave their senses or their muscles impaired and that render them bedridden or chronically incapacitated so far as normal role performance is concerned. Traffic and occupational accidents take their toll in the form of lost limbs and senses. War leaves another sizable segment of the population with physical handicaps which impair role performance. It is to the social problems that these pathologies create that we now turn our attention.

Extent

On an average day in 1954 ". . . probably more than 9 million persons of all ages were disabled—unable to work, attend school, keep house, or follow their other normal activities because of a temporary or permanent physical or mental incapacity." [3] Not all of these 9 million were disabled for long periods, but a sizable number were. If we limit our discussion to those with disabilities of at least six months' duration, the number as of 1954 was estimated at 5.3 million.[4] These cases of long-term disability constituted about 3.3 per cent of the total civilian population of the United States. About 4.1 million were non-institutionalized cases and about 1.2 million were in institutions.

As could be expected the institutional population—inmates of resident institutions, such as mental and tuberculosis hospitals, homes or schools for the mentally and physically handicapped, homes for the aged and dependent, homes and hospitals for the chronically ill, and penal institutions—had a greater prevalence rate of long-term disability than the noninstitutional population—72.1 percent as against 2.6 percent.[5]

TABLE 1
ESTIMATED NUMBER OF PERSONS IN THE UNITED STATES WITH DISABILITIES LASTING MORE THAN SIX MONTHS ON AN AVERAGE DAY IN 1954
(*In Thousands*)

AGE GROUP	PERSONS WITH DISABILITIES LASTING MORE THAN SIX MONTHS		
	Total	*Non-institutionalized*	*Institutionalized*
Under 14	250	200	50
14–64	2,900	2,140	760
65 and over	2,160	1,760	400
Total	5,310	4,100	1,210

SOURCE: Alfred M. Skolnik, "Estimated Prevalence of Long-Term Disability, 1954," *Social Security Bulletin*, 18 (June 1955), p. 21.

The age distribution of the long-time disabled shows a disproportionate number, expectedly, in the older age brackets, as revealed in Table 1.

Almost 2.2 million or more than two-fifths of all persons with protracted disabilities are estimated to be in the group aged 65 years and over. They comprise 15.7 percent of the aged population, compared with the 2.9 percent disabled for more than 6 months among the group aged 14–64 and the 0.56 percent among children under age 14.[6]

The proportion of all disabled who are long-term cases is increasing relative to the proportion of short-term cases:

With the rise in the proportion of the aged in the population, and the ability of modern medicine to prolong the life of many disabled persons, the number of persons with long-term disabilities (more than 6 months' duration) has been increasing more rapidly, both absolutely and relatively, than that of persons with short-term disabilities. In 1935, it is estimated, the long-term disabled comprised about half the 6 million persons incapacitated on an average day, while by 1954 they numbered an estimated 5.3 million or almost 60 percent of all disabled persons.[7]

Twofold Nature of the Problem of the Handicapped

Income Maintenance

The problem which arises in connection with the handicapped is twofold in nature. One aspect has to do with providing income for those who cannot work; the other has to do with re-establishing role relationships, or rehabilitation. Of these, the first is by far the simpler to deal with. Indeed, as the following summary indicates, the problem of providing income may be on the way to solution.

Public provisions to offset the actual or potential wage loss among these millions of persons and their dependents have been extended somewhat in the past two decades. In 1935, protection through public programs was confined to work-connected disabilities under State and Federal workmen's compensation laws, to service-connected and non-service–connected disabilities under the veterans' and Armed Forces programs, to sickness and disability under programs for employees of Federal, State, and local governments, and to special programs for the blind in about half the States.

Since that time, both permanent and temporary disability benefits have been provided under the railroad retirement system, and temporary disability insurance programs for industrial and commercial workers have been adopted in four States. Federal grants for aid to the blind were provided under the original Social Security Act and in 1950 for a new assistance program of aid to the permanently and totally disabled. . . .

The number of persons in the age group 14–64 with long-term total disabilities who are receiving some support from public programs designed to maintain income in case of disability has increased, it is estimated, from something less than 200,000 in 1934 to about a million in 1954, or from about 1 in 10 in 1934 to about 1 in 3 such persons in 1954.

Insurance benefits for extended disability were paid in December 1954 to about 266,000 persons (some of whom were aged 65 or over) under the railroad retirement and public employee retirement systems. There were 224,000 persons receiving assistance under the program of aid to the permanently and totally disabled and 102,000 receiving aid to the blind. These figures contrast with the 33,000 receiving aid to the blind in December 1934. Additional disabled persons and their dependents receive payments under the aid to dependent children and general assistance programs. There has also been a large increase in the number of persons receiving veterans' compensation. About 470,000 totally disabled veterans under age 65 are now receiving veterans' benefits, compared with 100,000 in 1934. (The large number of veterans receiving benefits for partial disabilities is not included in these figures.) With the aging of the veteran population of World War I, the growth in the number of recipients of non-service–connected disability pensions has been particularly striking. The veterans' and public assistance programs are bearing the brunt of the public burden of income maintenance for the long-term totally disabled.[8]

In 1956 the Social Security Act was amended so that a person who becomes disabled at, let us say, age fifty, no longer has to wait until he is sixty-five before he is eligible to draw retirement benefits.

In evaluating income maintenance we must not forget the effect of rising standards. We once thought it satisfactory for handicapped persons to make their way by begging or by selling pencils or by other means we now consider degrading. No matter how many benefits the physically handicapped receive, so long as these benefits are less than the amount of income the unhandicapped receive, we shall probably consider the disabled a problem.

Re-establishing Role Relationships

But to maintain income is easier than to create or re-establish satisfying role relationships. For most handicapped persons it is not enough simply to be kept alive, even on a generous level. They want to perform dignified roles; they want to maintain as nearly normal relationships as possible. And those who have worked with handicapped persons have noted that morale—to be referred to below—is by far the most important factor in rehabilitation. The government can, and does, offer rehabilitation opportunities; [9] but it cannot force people to take advantage of them nor can it restore role relationships.

Two kinds of role trauma are especially serious in the case of hand-

icapped or disabled persons, namely those associated with the role of
worker and those associated with family roles.

The Handicapped in the Role
of Worker

It was estimated in 1955 that two million handicapped persons
were employed and that at least another two million more were capable
of being employed. About 275,000 persons were being added to the
number of disabled every year. These two million handicapped persons
were ready to perform work roles in a satisfactory manner. But a role,
it will be recalled, is always a reciprocal relationship. The performance
of any role demands the performance of a complementary one by another person. It is not enough, therefore, to rehabilitate the handicapped worker. He must be accepted as a worker by employers and by
other workers. Almost as important, therefore, as individual rehabilitation is the effort to convince employers that handicapped workers are
employable.

Among the efforts in this direction are organizations such as the
National Committee on the Employment of the Physically Handicapped. They are analogous to the organizations working to reduce or
even eliminate prejudice and discrimination with respect to other
groups with different kinds of handicaps—dark skin, for example, or
names with many consonants. The Committee just named, like these
other organizations, offers prizes for "the handicapped man of the year,"
for essays by high school students on the progress made in employment
of the handicapped, and for distinguished services in behalf of the handicapped. The ideal is to achieve equal opportunity for those who are
physically different in that they are handicapped as well as for those
who are physically different in race, sex, or age. For the physically handicapped have many of the characteristics of a minority group. As President Eisenhower pointed out:

It seems to me that we might extend [equality of opportunity] at least
within our hearts and minds, to include . . . any who may be somewhat
physically different or handicapped so long as that person can be made a
useful member of society.[10]

Unions are also interested in this aspect of the problem of the
handicapped. In our discussion of the nature of roles we used the illus-

tration of the "slot." The task of the head of an agency is to find a person who can fill the given "slot," that is, do a given job. The job is paramount; the individual who does it is secondary. But some students of the subject, especially those who represent the worker's point of view, suggest that it is just as logical to fit the job to the worker. Jobs, they argue, can be redesigned if necessary to make optimum use of the labor force just as it is, even when it includes those with handicaps.

Jobs are currently designed with only a moderate amount of interest in the characteristics of the potential employees. The stress is on finding the right persons for the job since it is generally assumed that the job requirements are relatively fixed. But that hypothesis is unwarranted. Jobs have been changing in their basic nature. Moreover, jobs can be designed to suit the people to be employed. The opportunities for profitable employment could be greatly extended by so doing.

A short review of the nature of job demands discloses that they have been responsive to human ingenuity. Some job changes resulted from technical innovations and new systems of production. Mechanical and electrical power have been substituted for human effort and judgment.

Even more significant has been the willingness of management in the past to adapt methods to the nature of the work force. Where children and women were employed, machines and jobs were altered to their size and physical capacity. In recent years, jobs at which women are employed are specially set up for them to eliminate much heavy manual work. Where there has been an abundance of unskilled labor, jobs have been kept at a level appropriate for such persons. When the numbers and proportions of the unskilled declined, employers revamped the jobs to justify the employment of higher-paid and better-trained personnel. On the other hand, where shortages of skilled and professional personnel have been felt, their jobs have been analyzed and broken down and the less-skilled segments have been assigned to persons trained for specialized tasks.[11]

The inevitable corollary is, of course, that the same process of job redesigning might well be undertaken in behalf of the physically handicapped. Jobs, by slight redesign, may be rendered performable by the blind, by those with limb disabilities, or by those with hearing defects.[12]

Even organizations representing the employers' point of view are now showing interest in seeing that the disabled find employment opportunities; the employment of rehabilitated workers is reflected in lowered governmental expenses in taking care of the disabled. The National Association of Manufacturers, for example, surveyed the situation and concluded that employment of the disabled was a profitable undertaking. Safety, attendance, turnover, and productivity records show the rehabilitated worker to be a good risk.[13]

Evidence is available from other sources also that rehabilitation of the handicapped is beneficial to the economy as a whole as well as to the

Handicapped? Yes, of course. But the extent of this child's handicap will depend upon the kind of care—broadly social as well as merely medical—that he receives. With the proper prosthetic device, he should be able to learn to perform an economically productive role satisfactorily.

Right now he is watching the "hands" of a man who went beyond success in mastering a worker role and who has become the champion of others similarly handicapped. Sharing the same problems sometimes gives handicapped people the strength to win their own battles for independence.

It is of course easy to recognize the handicap resulting from loss of a limb or of the senses. Other handicaps, no less role impairing than these, may be far more difficult to diagnose and remedy. Some people are emotionally "crippled" and are therefore severely handicapped in performing their roles. Other people are unable to perceive social relationships; they are as handicapped as those who are physically blind. There are, also, people who are handicapped because they "care" too much or because they cannot "care" enough.

Because roles are always reciprocal and are part of a configuration, anything that impairs the role performance of the individual —whether it be physical, emotional, or mental handicap—has repercussions among the others in his role network. They cannot perform their roles adequately if he does not perform his.

Re-establishing role relationships is therefore coming to be seen as of equal importance with physical rehabilitation in advanced programs for dealing with the handicapped. *(United Press Photo)* individual employer and the worker. In 1954, for example, of the 56,000 persons who were rehabilitated by state and federal agencies, not counting the Veterans' Administration, 12 per cent had never worked and 75 per cent were not working when their rehabilitation began; of those who were working, the total earnings were $16,000,000. All were in temporary, hazardous, unsuitable work. At the end of the rehabilitation program all were working in jobs that fitted them and they were earning $104,000,000. A study in one highly industrialized state, Pennsylvania, documented in more detail the economic benefits resulting from rehabilitation. Of 3,337 handicapped citizens, 44 per cent had originally been dependent upon their families for support; 15 per cent were dependent on insurance benefits; 11 per cent were receiving special assistance; 20 per cent were living on part-time wages; and the remaining 10 per cent were dependent on some other source of assistance. After retraining and placement, their wages increased 450 per cent, from $1,277,000 to $7,021,000, or to about $2,104 each.

Vocational rehabilitation is a one-time expenditure. Therefore it is only good business to invest in the rehabilitation of handicapped individuals so they can become more normal, useful, taxpaying instead of tax consuming citizens.[14]

And, finally, the handicapped themselves are actively interested in promoting their re-incorporation in worker roles. The American Federation of the Physically Handicapped, organized in 1940, for example, plans to establish the Institute for Human Engineering in Florida, where handicapped persons will be able to secure medical treatment and vocational training or retraining.[15]

Great as the economic benefits are in terms of improved wages when the physically handicapped person is rehabilitated and restored to productive worker roles, they are no greater than the subjective satisfactions he derives from finding himself once more functioning adequately in the community, performing a normal role in the social structure.

Status Aspects of Rehabilitation

Performing a work role satisfactorily redounds to the improvement of status also. The man who has a job "belongs"; he is not an outsider. He has status in a group.

The importance of ranked-status as well as role-status considerations has been increasingly recognized in rehabilitation programs. There was a time when it was taken as a matter of course that a handicapped person would have to accept inferior status; at the present time—probably as a consequence of abundance—the attitude is that such lowering of status is not necessary, that rehabilitation should take as long as is necessary to prevent it.

A few years ago a representative of a life insurance company was investigating the application of a woman executive in a business organization, for sick benefits due under a policy insuring her against total disability existing for a definite period of time. Her illness had lasted longer than the ninety-day period called for in the policy, but it had not kept her bedfast all that time; and the question was raised as to whether she was totally disabled.

In the woman's mind there was no question. Serious nervous aftereffects still existed, as a real disability, for she wanted nothing so much as to get back to her desk to work she enjoyed. But the life insurance company's representative refused to take her word. He interviewed the doctor who had handled the case (the proper procedure) and, after asking a number of questions, finally asserted his opinion that the woman had not been totally disabled.

"She could have taken care of small children, couldn't she—wheeled them into the park and acted as a nursemaid?"

"Not my children!" the doctor said. . . .

The story illustrates the old-fashioned viewpoint . . . on illness or injuries that create employment handicaps. The old attitude which still prevails in too many communities was that the capable man or woman who met with accident or disabling illness that did not keep him bedfast permanently should accept demotion to any kind of job that would keep body and soul together, if he was financially unprepared to meet illness and pay his own way to the kind of recovery that would make him as capable as anybody else. The attitude of many persons around him was not that he should first be helped to make the best physical recovery possible, but rather that he must earn his own living as quickly as possible even if earning it meant a needless sacrifice of the better opportunities that had laid ahead of him.[16]

Abundance, in brief, now makes it possible for the community to support the disabled while they acquire the highest skills of which they are capable. Status degradation is not assumed as a necessary corollary of disability. Here, we note, is again illustrated the higher standards which come with abundance.

If the breadwinner is incapacitated, the shift in source of family income may mean status degradation for the whole family as well as for the disabled person himself. And this status degradation may be more traumatic than the handicap itself. Since a man's role network is an integrated whole, and not merely an aggregation of separate roles, his disability ramifies throughout his other non-work relationships also.

The Handicapped in Family Roles

The presence of a handicapped child in a family may distort all familial relationships. The normal children may be neglected; the disabled child may be over-protected. A disproportionate amount of the family income may be diverted to the care or treatment of the handicapped child. Increasingly, those who work with handicapped children —blind, deaf, crippled—find that counseling parents is almost as important as dealing with the child himself. Sometimes—and this is reported as especially true in the case of asthmatic children—parents aggravate the disability by their attitudes. When the child is taken from them he shows remarkable improvement.

But distortions in family role relationships may occur at any age. Perhaps they become most acute in youth. "Who can love me?" the disfigured young person asks. "Who would marry me?" the crippled youth asks. "I cannot permit anyone to marry me," the disabled young veteran says. "Such a marriage would only be based on pity. I will not allow myself to be dependent on anyone."

The anguish suffered by many of the handicapped is a favorite theme in popular art forms. The returned veteran, for example, who will not marry his fiancée because he is convinced she is willing to go through with the marriage only from a feeling of duty has been a central character in drama, novel, and motion picture. Another character is the person deformed in an accident who turns bitterly away from human contact.

. . . probably you have been lying in bed telling yourself that social life is at an end for you: you're a cripple, and no one will ever want to have you around again; you'll be in the way, you'll spoil the fun, you'll ruin the party, and so on, and so on.

"Of course"—your gloomy reveries continue—"one or two friends will stick by me. Good old Bill, good old Jerry, they wouldn't let a dog down. But, as for most of the others, I'm not going to watch them go through gestures that can only mean they are enduring my crippled presence because they feel sorry for me. No, sir! I'm not going to be an eye-sore in the parlor, the dining room, or on the front porch. I'll just crawl into my shell and save the world from showing the pity I will not, by God, endure from anybody!" [17]

We do not have exact figures to tell us what the marriage rate is among the handicapped; but that many do marry, and marry successfully, is a matter of common observation. The handicap itself may endear the person to another. In some cases the handicap may come in time to be completely overlooked. It is said that a truly unprejudiced person becomes unconscious of the color of a man's skin. Similarly we eventually forget the existence of a defect in those we love. The limp, the scar, the prosthetic appliance fade into unconsciousness. Here, for instance, is how it happened to one person:

> At first I thought I could not control myself. . . . I thought I could never bear to take the second look. But the second time it did not seem nearly the same; and by the time I got acquainted with the man I was actually at a loss to account for my first reaction. He really is a wonderful man, and you can't be in his presence long without *seeing* it." [18]

There is probably a selective process involved in the mating of handicapped persons; that is, deaf-mutes tend to choose others with the same defect. And probably only those unhandicapped individuals of great maturity and generosity would be willing to assume the obligations of marriage to a handicapped person.

If the handicap occurs after marriage there may be very serious role trauma, for not everyone has the resiliency to withstand the shock of the disability. And the role trauma may be more serious than the physical trauma. A gynecologist, for example, once remarked that the role trauma suffered by women when malignancy demanded breast surgery was greater than any other suffering they endured. Even though there were no visible disfigurements, the mere knowledge that they were mutilated caused great disturbance. When the disability is plainly visible and actually handicapping, the role trauma may be even greater. A study of paraplegics found that many men experienced "a dreadful apprehension at the thought of having to return home to their wives and family." [19] Some found it possible to establish good role relationships with women who were similarly disabled because "the demand upon their adequacy as a masculine sex partner is greatly reduced in this kind of attachment." [20] The female paraplegic cases did not seem so disturbed about sex relations with a non-disabled husband; but they did feel great concern over ability to bear children and hence their ability to perform the role of wife. [21]

Perhaps the commonest family-role crisis associated with disability is the one which results from the deterioration of age. The man has lost his worker role; the wife has not lost hers as homemaker. He must remain at home, severed from most of his former role relationships. The role of husband assumes a different pattern. It may take all the insight, patience, and understanding of the wife to see her husband through this role transition.

In fact, in all rehabilitation work the role performance of those in the disabled person's role network may be as crucial in the achievement of success as the behavior of the disabled person himself.

Role Aspects of Rehabilitation

In the case of the handicapped, as with all other people who present special problems, we find great individual differences in stress resistance. Some people take their handicap in their stride; others, with no greater handicap, succumb to demoralization. Some learn to live with their handicap; others become bitter and sullen. Some succeed in learning how to perform worker roles at the same level of difficulty as their original roles; others fail. Some achieve satisfactory family relationships; others become an incubus on all family relationships. Why? Why does one man sit on the street corner selling pencils while another, with an equal handicap, works expertly at a skilled job? Why does one man sit morosely at the window while another cheerfully shows the children how to carve a piece of wood?

A common explanation seeks the answer in the attitudes of the disabled themselves. But attitudes are not autonomous or self-generating. They reflect a pattern of role relationships. Without underestimating the importance of individual differences we wish here to emphasize the role factor in successful rehabilitation. We have already referred to the importance of working with employers and family members in all rehabilitation work. Success with them may make all the difference between success and failure in the rehabilitation process.

It sometimes happens, for example, that a handicapped person is successfully rehabilitated in a hospital or in a special setting where those around him understand the psychological and sociological hazards of his position. When he returns home, however, and finds himself surrounded by people who pity him or treat him differently or who make it impossible for him to perform his role normally, he may suffer a collapse in morale which undoes much of the good of the rehabilitation. This is another case where the performance of a role by one person depends on the correct role performance by those around him. One cannot perform a role by himself. One can only perform a role adequately when others are performing the complementary roles adequately also.

Here are two illustrations of the way in which role support influenced rehabilitation; in one case it was helpful, in the other, harmful. First, the successful one: *

Here is the true story of a man, married shortly before the First World War, who came home with a terrible facial disfigurement. He happened to be a scholar at heart, and his earlier training and the qualities he now developed permitted him, after a while, to work as he liked in a study in his own home. This meant that his only contacts with human beings would be with his own family unless he chose otherwise. A social life, he felt, was impossible, because he could not look in the mirror without thinking of his face as grotesque. On a few occasions when he encountered people, he saw shock and aversion in their faces.

It was only natural that he stayed away from mirrors as much as he could, and from people almost completely. But his wife . . . saw him many times, every day of her life, and he quickly ceased to appear grotesque to her. Was this merely because she loved him? Apparently not, for a couple of old friends . . . spoke to her about having the same experience. The man himself eventually knew they were speaking the truth, because he was exceedingly sensitive to his impression upon people and he saw with his own eyes that what they said was a fact—that he had soon ceased to cause any reaction of aversion in them. And so, one by one, new friends were permitted the intimacy of the home, and a normal, though limited social life has long been part of that man's existence.[22]

In the second case the wife impeded rehabilitation because she enjoyed her husband's dependence. To people who have always been self-reliant and independent it is severely galling to be in the position of having to be helped. Sometimes handicapped persons refuse any sort of help, help that would be casually accepted by normal persons, such as, for example, having an ash tray moved across a table. Sometimes they overcompensate for their disability and work harder than anyone else. But sometimes, as in this case, they find themselves reduced to helplessness in spite of themselves. They are pampered like children. Some women prefer the role of mother to their husbands to that of wife.

. . . many a woman finds a man's helplessness the very thing one side of her nature wants. Consciously or unconsciously she often tries to keep her disabled man petted and pampered into . . . helplessness. This is a deadly, a terrifying situation for an injured man. And in the struggle that must arise out of it in a strong man's soul, the people who offer him help become fiends who would keep him from his full manhood. Women, then, become his hardest problem. For just as it is easy for a woman to admire and love a man who rises above his disabilities, it is also easy for her to cripple a man with her so-called love so that he may never rise above them.[23]

So far as sex roles are concerned, it has been alleged that disabilities are more handicapping to women than to men because the role of husband depends more on ability to earn a living than on physical appearance, whereas the role of wife depends to a large extent on sex appeal, which a disability may mar. In other words, women are more willing to marry disabled men—provided the men can support them—than men are to marry disabled women.[24]

If a disability is so drastic as to transform a person's very conception of himself it may be impossible for him to respond to any role cues from those about him. No amount of role support can keep him buoyed up. Here is such a case:

The patient who had both suffered a loss of his sexual organs through surgery and acquired a permanent colostomy was certainly correct in his claim that he could no longer rely on his former conceptions of himself as a man and that he could not return to his young wife and son at home, to his fellow workers in the shop, or to his cronies in the club in quite the same relationship he had formerly maintained. His experience and treatment for carcinoma, as well as the disease itself, had transformed his adaptations to his environment as an organism and had also altered his associations as a group member and a person. These, indeed, proved to be his undoing in that he lost interest in living and decided to end it all. Thus, frequently it is not difficult to trace and document in detail the connection between what happens to the organism and its effect on the individual as a member of society and as a personality in his cultural milieu.[25]

In both worker and family roles, the psychological and social aspects of handicap may far outweigh the physical ones in rehabilitation. Counseling of the handicapped and of their families is coming to be viewed, therefore, as coordinate in importance with physical therapy and medical treatment. Indeed, the strictly medical phases of rehabilitation are probably easier than the psychological and social ones. Mending a bone is often easier than mending a role relationship.

As in the case of so many other persons with pathologies which impair or distort role relationships, the physically handicapped have organized to reap the benefits of group-generated morale. In 1955, for example, twenty-five former patients of the Institute of Physical Medicine and Rehabilitation of the New York University-Bellevue Medical Center formed Courage, Inc., "to help handicapped persons readjust to a productive, happy life." [26] The organization hoped to take in others from the same institution and other handicapped persons. Eventually, no doubt, similar units will be established elsewhere.

The pathologies we have discussed so far—infectious diseases and physical disabilities—affect role performance in a fairly straightforward way. The arm is missing; the vision is gone; the leg is crippled. But there are other pathologies which affect role performance in a somewhat different way. The body may be quite normal and yet incapable of normal role behavior. We begin our discussion with the social problems of the mentally handicapped. In some cases—which we shall characterize as mentally defective—there is a physical as well as a mental handicap. In others, however—which we shall characterize as mentally deficient—there is no physical disability; the handicap is not in the body but in the "mind."

NOTES

1 "Home Accident Picture Changing," *New York Times,* April 17, 1956.

2 *Ibid.*

3 Lenore Epstein, Dorothy McCamman, and Alfred M. Skolnik, "Social Security Protection, 1935–1955," *Social Security Bulletin,* 18 (Aug. 1955), p. 10.

4 Alfred M. Skolnik, "Estimated Prevalence of Long-Term Disability, 1954," *ibid.,* June 1955, p. 20.

5 *Ibid.*

6 *Ibid.*

7 Epstein, McCamman, and Skolnik, *loc. cit.*

8 *Ibid.,* p. 11.

9 Workmen's compensation laws gave some relief to disabled workers, but did not provide for rehabilitation. In 1918 the federal government passed a law which provided for vocational rehabilitation of wounded servicemen under the direction of the Veteran's Bureau; it aimed to see that men were trained for productive work. Between 1918 and 1920, twelve states also passed rehabilitation laws; in 1920 a federal law was passed establishing an agency under the Federal Board for Vocational Education to promote rehabilitation of civilians also. Federal funds were made available to states that had rehabilitation programs which met certain standards. In 1943 this law was amended to provide more generously for civilian programs. All veterans come under the jurisdiction of the Veterans' Administration program; but civilians come under the jurisdiction of the several states. "The central idea of the laws for both veterans and civilians is: A vocationally handicapped person should be made able to go into productive work unhandicapped by his present injury or illness as far as his economic future is concerned—if that is possible. All necessary steps toward that goal are provided for under the laws. . . . The laws for both civilians and veterans provide further for (1) vocational counsel in the choice of work at which a man may be under no economic handicap, or under the least possible handicap, (2) education, training, or retraining, as the case may be, for the work he is to perform, and (3) help in finding and getting himself placed in a suitable job when he is ready for it." (Edna Yost and Lillian M. Gilbreth, *Normal Lives for the Disabled* [Macmillan, 1944], pp. 79–80.) In addition to these federal and state laws, three laws were enacted by the 83rd Congress to assist those with long-time disabling injuries. One expanded the federal-state program; one provided for more hospitals and facilities for rehabilitation; and the third, one of income security rather than rehabilitation primarily, safeguarded old-age and survivors insurance status of individuals with long-time disabilities. The American Medical Association opposes federal programs of this type. A bill which was passed by the House in the summer of 1955, for example, was branded as part of a "piecemeal approach to socialization of medicine" by the *Journal of the American Medical Association,* July 1955.

10 Speech before a meeting of the Committee on the Employment of the Physically Handicapped, May 22, 1955, as reported in the *New York Times,* May 23, 1955.

11 Solomon Barkin, "Job Redesign: A Technique for an Era of Full Employment,"

in William Haber, Frederick H. Harbison, L. R. Kelin, and Vivian Palmer, *Manpower in the United States; Problems and Policies* (Harper, 1954), pp. 41–42.

12 *Ibid.*, pp. 44–50.

13 For a summary of research showing the record of the disabled with respect to productivity, absenteeism, turnover, and accidents, see Yost and Gilbreth, *op. cit.*, pp. 198–200.

14 Report by John R. Torquato, Secretary of Labor and Industry, as reported in State College, Pa., *Centre Daily Times*, September 29, 1955.

15 Paul A. Strachan, in a speech reported in the *Durham Labor Journal*, October 6, 1955.

16 Yost and Gilbreth, *op. cit.*, pp. 101–102.

17 *Ibid.*, pp. 31–32.

18 *Ibid.*, p. 33.

19 Stanley Berger, "Paraplegia," in J. F. Garrett, ed., *Psychological Aspects of Physical Disability* (Office of Vocational Rehabilitation, Publication 210, 1952). Abstracted in *Marriage and Family Living*, 16 (Feb. 1954), p. 77.

20 *Ibid.*

21 *Ibid.*

22 Yost and Gilbreth, *op. cit.*, pp. 32–33.

23 *Ibid.*, pp. 44–45.

24 *Ibid.*, p. 36.

25 Leo W. Simmons and Harold G. Wolff, *Social Science in Medicine* (Russell Sage, 1954), pp. 111–112.

26 *New York Times*, October 3, 1955.

10

Role Impairment:
Mental Handicap

Changing Attitude Toward Mental Handicap

We think little of it when we hear people say, in exasperation, "You idiot!" or "You imbecile!" or even "You moron!" Yet the overtones of contempt, irritation, annoyance, and even hostility, in these expressions reflect a widespread but by now anachronistic attitude toward the mentally handicapped.

Attention was first called to this problem in the early years of the century in a number of studies of families—the Jukes, the Kallikaks, the

Nam family, the Tribe of Ishmael, the Nolly family, the families of the Vale of Siddim—in which generation after generation of mentally handicapped men and women were incapable of meeting life tests without outside help. Their mental deficiency handicapped them morally as well as intellectually. They became criminal; they violated the mores; they were demoralized. They became an incubus to the normal community. In brief, these were wicked people, our enemies. We shall present evidence below to suggest that these families probably suffered from other kinds of disorders as well as mental retardation, but they were exhibited primarily as cases of mental deficiency.

Because these early studies were of inbred and therefore probably hereditary strains, the problem of the mentally handicapped first presented itself as a genetic one. It was assumed that all mental defect and deficiency was hereditary. The logical attack seemed to be, therefore, through eugenics, that is, through control of reproduction.

We are only now beginning to overcome an almost hysterical attitude toward the mentally defective child. We are only now beginning to attack the problem with the same calm spirit of research that we use in studying poliomyelitis or tuberculosis. Families are only now learning not to feel shame and disgrace, or even guilt, because of the presence in their midst of the mentally defective son, daughter, brother, or sister. Only now is the stigma being removed.

The formation of the National Association for Retarded Children, with local chapters, has done a great deal to change our attitude and to help families of retarded children bear their strain. The principle is similar to that used by Alcoholics Anonymous, although, of course, the personnel and problems are different. Families with retarded children come together to face their common problems, to work for community facilities for their handicapped children, and, most of all, to relieve their own emotional burden by sharing that of others with the same problem.

Mental Defect and Heredity

The reasons for this incipient change of attitude are many. Among them is the recognition that mental defect is not necessarily an indication of defective heredity, of skeletons in family closets. There is still no unequivocal evidence to indicate what proportion of all cases of mental defect is hereditary. But increasingly we are learning how much is not.

Sometimes mental defect and deficiency are caused by infections, before or after birth. About 11 per cent of all cases are the result of meningitis, encephalitis, congenital syphilis, and German measles in the mother during the first two months of pregnancy.[1] Sometimes defect and deficiency are caused by Rh-factor reactions in the mother; 3 to 4 per cent of institutionalized cases have such an etiology. What happens is that mothers who are Rh-negative, but who bear Rh-positive embryos, may develop antibodies which are then carried back to the fetus, causing blood destruction. Infants who survive the damage may some time later show serious symptoms, including mental defect.[2] Sometimes it is caused by X-ray treatment of the mother, either before or during pregnancy.[3] All told, some seventy diseases or conditions are known to cause or are suspected of causing mental defect or retardation.

Mongolism represents about 10 per cent of all institutionalized cases, but the etiology is not known. All that is known is that the age of the mother is usually older than that of mothers of normal children. Cretinism or malfunctioning of the thyroid gland causes a defect which may be curable by the administration of thyroid. Cranial anomalies—microcephaly, hydrocephaly, and macrocephaly—cause mental defect in about 2 per cent of institutional cases. They are not considered hereditary.

There does remain, to be sure, a sizable proportion of cases which cannot as yet be accounted for by infection, by developmental accidents, or by other known factors. In at least one type of case—resulting from Tay-Sachs disease—the cause is known to be an enzyme defect produced by a faulty gene.[4] But it accounts for only $\frac{1}{2}$ of 1 per cent of institutional cases.

It cannot be denied that some cases of mental defect are genetic in origin, but just what the proportion is cannot yet be specified. Genes for mental defect are probably widespread in any normal population. There are, that is, probably millions of people who carry such genes in their chromosomes. Only when they mate with people with these *same* recessive genes can the defect appear in the offspring. It is the greater likelihood of such pairings of defective recessive genes, incidentally, which is the rationale of laws prohibiting intermarriage of cousins.

Some genetic mental defect is doubtless also the result of mutations in the genes. Mutations or sudden changes in the genes occur with greater frequency than was once supposed. Thus two people with wholly normal genes may have a child with defective genes. This mental defect is hereditary in the sense that it is genetic, but it is quite beyond human control. Such mutations can occur in any strain, high or low in quality.

Some mental defect is genetic because both parents come from stock with defective genes. Cases of this kind first attracted the public's horrified attention, and for these the most appropriate remedy seemed to be sterilization—one might almost say *punitive* sterilization, because of the horror their behavior evoked.

Sterilization would doubtless be an excellent solution for a certain proportion of mentally retarded cases, for therapeutic, not punitive reasons. But sterilization would not prevent the cases that result from the chance combination of recessive defective genes in normal people or from genetic mutation in normal people. We can never locate all the defective genes in a given population; and if we could, we would find that we would have to sterilize a large proportion of the whole population if we wished to prevent them from contributing to the genetic pool.

Increasingly, mental defect is being attacked as a medical problem. The goal is to discover by all the research weapons available just what conditions produce mental defect in the child before and after birth and then, if possible, to learn how to prevent them.

Criteria and Classifications of Mental Defect and Deficiency

There are at least three levels on the basis of which mental defect and deficiency may be classified, namely: biological, psychological, and sociological. The first classifies it into hereditary and acquired defect and deficiency. So far as dealing with the problem is concerned, this classification is not very useful. Some inherited defects may be cured [5] whereas some acquired defects cannot. Or they may be classified in terms of defective types and physically normal but mentally deficient types, regardless of etiology. In the defective types the deterioration is general and extreme. They are the idiots and the imbeciles. A metabolic disorder may be the basis for the defect.[6] The normal types are deficient but not defective, that is, they are normal except in amount or kind of intelligence, however measured. They constitute about half (45 to 55 per cent) of all institutionalized cases and 65 to 75 per cent of all non-institutionalized cases. They are just like everyone else except that they are not so bright. One student labels them the garden variety.[7]

A second and widely used basis for classifying mental defect and deficiency is that of performance on intelligence tests. Investigators may specify different limits for various categories, but the principle is the same. Two of the classifications in terms of intelligence quotients are given in Table 1.

Reliance on measures of intelligence by test performance has been particularly great in the United States. It has been criticized by psychologists as encouraging a neglect of other equally important aspects of the individual's personality and as tending to arbitrariness in dealing with specific cases. It is inadequate because it is one-sided as well as arbitrary. It ignores the probable error of any single measurement and also the overlapping among the several grades of defect; it also discounts the fact that mental tests measure only one kind of ability.[8] It is also prob-

TABLE 1

INTELLIGENCE QUOTIENT CLASSIFICATIONS

TERMAN SCALE		WECHSLER SCALE	
Criterion	*Classification*	*Criterion*	*Classification*
IQ above 140	Near genius or genius	IQ above 128	Very superior
IQ 120–140	Very superior	IQ 120–127	Superior
IQ 110–120	Superior	IQ 111–119	Bright normal
IQ 90–110	Average	IQ 91–110	Average
IQ 80–90	Dull	IQ 80–90	Dull
IQ 70–80	Borderline	IQ 66–79	Borderline
IQ below 70	Feebleminded	IQ below 65	Defective
IQ 60–70	High-grade moron		
IQ 50–60	Low-grade moron		
IQ 20–50	Imbecile		
IQ below 20	Idiot		

SOURCES: Lewis M. Terman, *The Measurement of Intelligence* (Houghton Mifflin, 1916), pp. 65–104; David Wechsler, *The Measurement of Adult Intelligence* (Williams & Wilkins, 1944), p. 40. Since Terman first established his standards he has raised the criterion for genius.

ably incorrect to put the *defective* cases and the *deficient* cases on the same continuum, for they are qualitatively different.

Social scientists have criticized the tests themselves, pointing out that they are not "culturally fair," that they discriminate against children in low socioeconomic classes.[9] The use of such tests is justified in that they do test the kind of intelligence which correlates very highly with success in our society, that is, verbal intelligence, symbolic intelligence, and abstract intelligence; hence they are fairly good as predictive instruments, especially for academic counseling. But it is generally agreed, even among clinicians, that test results should be supplemented by other data before making judgments or classifications of children who do not do well on such tests.

One study, for example, attempting to discount the bias in standard mental tests, found that in "culturally fair" tests, children from the lowest socioeconomic classes improved with motivation more than children from the highest; and practice helped the low-status children more than the high-status ones.[10] Although these results do not deal with mentally retarded children, they are pertinent in our evaluation of tests as a criterion of classification.

From the sociological point of view, the test of role performance seems at least as important as the clinical test, if not more so, in classifying mental defect. One student has therefore attempted to draw up more inclusive criteria which take account of role behavior or "social competence" as well as of the results of clinical tests. He includes in his definition sociological, psychological, and medical criteria, as follows: social incompetence, mental subnormality, developmental arrest, presence of the defect at maturity, constitutional origin, and incurability.[11] He has worked out a Social Maturity Scale to complement the mental tests. The idea is that such a test helps the clinician to see more aspects of the individual's personality.[12]

In England, since the passage of the Mental Deficiency Act in 1913, social inadequacy, or what we would call inadequate role performance, has been the most emphasized criterion of mental deficiency. The best-known definition using this criterion is that of the British student A. F. Tredgold, who states that amentia is "a state of incomplete mental development of such a kind and degree that the individual is incapable of adapting himself to the normal environment of his fellows in such a way as to maintain existence independently of supervision, control, or external support." [13]

The National Association for Retarded Children uses a role-performance criterion and classifies retarded "children" into: dependent retarded, semidependent, and marginal independent. They are described as follows:

> About 160,000 retarded "children" in the United States or one (1) out of each 1,000 of the general population are so severely handicapped that they require constant supervision all their lives. Some cannot walk. Some cannot talk. Some respond to minimum social training. All deserve the nursing care and attention accorded a baby.
>
> Approximately 640,000 or four (4) out of every 1,000 people in the United States develop at less than one-half the normal rate. They need continuous supervision. Many can learn self-care, acceptable behavior and useful work under sheltered conditions.
>
> More than 4,000,000 children and adults, or twenty-five (25) out of every 1,000 Americans need special schooling. They can usually learn enough reading and arithmetic to meet daily needs. As youths and adults they require special help for vocational adjustment. Most can become self-supporting and capable of handling their own affairs with counseling.[14]

The first of these categories—the truly defective—corresponds to the clinician's idiots and imbeciles. These cases constitute a problem in that they require custodial care throughout their lives, for their condition is usually incurable, but they are not a serious problem so far as reproducing their kind is concerned. Their life expectancy is low, and, moreover, they are so incapacitated that no one would marry them even if they wished to marry. They can never compete in the outside world; even in a protected environment they may have difficulties. Kindly custodial care is about all that can be given to them. We shall say nothing more about them in this book.

It is the people in the other two categories—the clinician's morons and borderline cases, deficient but not necessarily defective—especially, perhaps, the third, who constitute the most serious social problem, not only because there are so many more of them, but also because the outcome of their care can be either very good or very bad, depending on the role support they receive from their environment.

The role performance, or social adequacy, criterion, as well as the clinical test, has also been criticized. In the first place, it is indeterminate; it may mean different things to different people. It implies a "normal environment," a concept which is vague and may be quite arbitrary. And, finally, inability to adjust to a "normal environment," that is, to perform adequately in suitable roles, is characteristic of a great many people who have excellent intelligence, as we shall see in the chapters that follow.

Extent and Incidence

There were an estimated 4 to 5 million mentally retarded "children" in the United States at midcentury, although the estimates vary according to definition.[15] But it is difficult to determine the community, sex, class, and cultural incidence of mental deficiency because of the differences in definition and criteria just discussed. Because of differences in role definitions, role demands, and in role support, mental deficiency is more apparent in some circumstances than in others.

In the past a normal farm family, for example, could, without too much difficulty, protect a mentally deficient child. Without compulsory school laws the deficiency, if the child were not too retarded, might never come to light. People would simply say that the child did not "take to book learning." He could do the simpler farm chores, even if he could not manage a farm, and that would be enough. He could perform a simple worker role. If he were mentally defective to the extent that he could not even learn to dress himself, he could still be taken care of in the home. He would simply represent one more chore for his mother. He would be accepted as a family problem. The neighbors would know that one of the Jones children was "queer," but then that was something that had to be accepted. People learned to take such acts of God in their stride. In a modern urban environment, however, this kind of family protection is all but impossible. The child's deficiency is detected as soon as he goes to school, or soon thereafter. And if he is seriously defective it is an almost impossible burden to take care of him in the home. There is no place for him. In allocating family financial resources it often becomes a choice between the normal children in the family and the defective one. Defective "children," whatever their chronological age, must therefore be institutionalized.

So far as true defect is concerned, there is probably little difference in class incidence. So far as IQ as measured by mental tests is concerned, there is abundant evidence that it is inferior in lower socioeconomic classes.[16]

It seems to the scientist anomalous that one person should be judged mentally deficient because he cannot perform his roles adequately and succeed in his environment, whereas another person is not so judged because he is protected and assisted. Let us, for example, assume two boys of equal "native ability," which, however, is not great enough to permit them to function independently in our society. One of them cannot keep up with his age-group in school. He does poorly on the tests which measure the kind of ability necessary to succeed in our society. He is, therefore, mentally deficient in terms of both IQ and social adequacy. The other boy, let us say, has wealthy parents. He learns to talk well, to be affable and pleasant. He does poorly in school, so a tutor is engaged for him. He never actually learns very much, but he is pleasant about it all, and even the tester tends to be lenient in grading his performance. This boy has learned from those around him how to look interested, how to listen as though he understood all that was being said. He does not read well, but he knows the importance of books. He can learn enough to behave acceptably merely from observing those about him. He is socially adequate for his role in this highly protected environment. He might even hold a job which primarily required him to be pleasant, to listen, and to turn over the decisions to someone else. Such a boy would not be listed among the mentally retarded. One boy's environment supplies the supports which make it possible for him to perform a suitable role; the other boy's does not. One might almost say that the poor boy's environment "forced" him to be mentally retarded by not supplying him with the supporting role props which his limited equipment required.

Cultural standards may also influence the criteria and hence the incidence of mental deficiency. In the 19th century intelligence in women was not highly valued, nor is it even today in many parts of the world. On the whole, women seemed, and probably were, less intelligent than men. They were encouraged to be so. Relics of this old attitude have survived, as reported by some college girls who say they occasionally "play dumb" in order to please their dates. When little Victorian Dora or Agnes—decked out in feathers, lace, and silk—stared prettily at a difficulty which confronted her, and shook her curls helplessly, she was considered adorable. Her helplessness in the face of an abstract problem was part of her charm. Her father would smile down indulgently at her, and if her husband occasionally sighed at her inability to handle money, keep records, or add a column of figures, he accepted this as a part of sweet femininity. The role of the middle-class girl as daughter or as wife was not defined in a way which demanded high intelligence. If she were good, she could let who would be clever.

But when her counterpart in the slum, with the same mental equipment, was unable to protect herself and became easy prey for anyone who cared to exploit her, the police caught up with her. She was diagnosed as "witless," and was institutionalized. Mental deficiency among the comfortable classes was hardly apparent when their culture defined the roles of women in a way which made few demands; it was all too discernible in the raw encounters of the slum. In this sense of adequacy of role performance, mental deficiency was sex-linked as well as class-linked in incidence.

"Social Adequacy": Role Performance of the Mentally Deficient

We present here two sets of data bearing on the role performance of mentally deficient subjects. One set, made familiar to readers of the 19th and early 20th century by studies of such families as the Jukes and Kallikaks, referred to above, depicts almost unmitigated degeneracy.[17] It was once taken as typical of all mentally deficient families. The other set, less familiar to most of us, illustrates modest but nevertheless genuine success in role performance.

Illustrations of Poor Role Performance by the Mentally Deficient[18]

The H——y Family

The father of this family was a laborer, very deaf. Accused by wife of having relations with daughter. He was said to be alcoholic. The mother, 48, admitted to Belchertown in 1932, with an I.Q. of 68. Attempts were made to improve her care of the family under the supervision of the S.P.C.C. for eleven years but she did not improve. She kept a filthy home, was sexually promiscuous, and had incestuous relations with son, who may be father of twins born in 1930. Her own husband requested her commitment to the institution following her arrest for neglect of home. This family has been known to welfare departments for years. Children of this family, Louis, Harry, and Ruby, were committed in 1930 to the Division of Child Guardianship. Louis, age 23, I.Q., 70. Was committed to Belchertown State School in 1934. In 1930, he was in court charged with incest with mother and sister, charge later changed to assault and battery. In court in 1933 for abuse of a female child, committed to County Jail and then to Belchertown. He escaped in 1934. Louise, 20, I.Q., 69. Was committed to Belchertown in 1934. She was in Juvenile Court as delinquent child, admitted having relations with father and brother. Had been in care of Social Service Division of Department of Mental Diseases where she was found to be childish and incompetent and was returned to aunt who found her unmanageable and requested her removal. Harry, age 18, I.Q., 47. Sent to this school in 1930. He was suspected of imitating incestuous acts he had seen at home. Has defective speech. Ruby —no information. Earl, 14, I.Q., 52, speech defect. Admitted to State School in 1931. Margaret, 9 years old, in care of Division of Child Guardianship. Said to be very backward. Her paternity is denied by father of this family. Winifred, age 7, I.Q., 63. Admitted in 1933. It is suspected that her own brother is the father.

The H——n Family

The father was said to be feeble-minded and lacking in responsibility. Never able to make a living for family. He was related through his mother with two other families at the state school. The mother was suspected of being immoral with star boarder in the home, whom she permitted to have relations with daughters for the sake of money. The home was kept in terrible shape. Mother and children caked with dirt and covered with vermin. Younger children said to have sores where rats nibbled fingers and toes. The children, as we know them at this school, consisted of Henry, age 41, said to be simple. He married and his wife was said to be not much brighter. Mentally incapable of earning a living and providing a home for family. Robert, 48, said to be feeble-minded. Sexually abused his sister. Emma May, 36, I.Q., 55. Had been sexually abused by boarder in home. Was committed to Wrentham State School in 1915, transferred to this school in 1923. Hattie, 33. Was in the care of Children's Aid Association from 1915–1919. Placed in many foster homes but did not do well. She was sent to Lancaster as a stubborn child because of instruction of younger children in sex matters and experiences with boys. Was paroled and again returned. Released in 1924 and became pregnant. She was committed to this school in 1926 with an I.Q. of 85. Discharged as not feebleminded but she has never gotten along well in the community. Married and deserted her husband for another man. She was diagnosed at the Psychopathic Hospital as a psychopathic personality without psychosis. Martha, 31, I.Q. 47. Admitted to this school in 1923. Sexually abused by brother. Rosie Ella, 28, said to be feeble-minded. Under guardianship of Children's Aid Association of Hampshire County. Laura Ellen, 26, I.Q., 76. Admitted to this school in 1923. Tried parole in 1937 but she did not adjust well and wanted to return. Alice, 25, I.Q., 49. Admitted to this school in 1923 and can do first and second grade school work. Lena May, 22, supposed to be the illegitimate child of a boarder in the parents' home. She has since died.

Another study of 141 defective families found the following anomalies:

1. There was a higher death rate in these families than in the general population, especially among infants. In 56 families, 115 children died before the age of 14, owing, the author believes, to inadequate care by the mothers.

2. Desertion, abandonment, separation, annulment, or divorce occurred in 28 of the 141 families, that is, in about one-fifth.

3. The housekeeping was reported as "flagrantly" bad in 37 per cent of the families.

4. Malnutrition was reported in 21 families.

5. There was illegitimate motherhood in 51 families, incest in 7, and prostitution in 14.

6. There were reformatory, penitentiary, jail, or prison records in 38 families.

7. At least one child was removed from parental custody in 20 families, presumably for neglect or improper guardianship.

8. Physical violence was habitually practiced in 20 families.[19]

It was on the basis of studies of role inadequacy such as these that the association of all kinds of social problems with mental deficiency was built up into a causal relationship.

But mental deficiency is not always associated with social inadequacy, or inability to perform suitable roles. Indeed, it is surprising how well some individuals, judged to be mentally deficient on the basis of tests, actually do in life. A number of follow-up studies have been made to see what happens to non-institutionalized children of low mental ability as measured by tests. These studies are in startling contrast to those just presented.

Illustrations of Good Role Performance by the Mentally Deficient

In one study of 206 children with IQ's less than 70 when in school, it was found that 33 per cent completed the 8th grade, three finished high school, and one even entered college. This particular follow-up was made during the depression, and it is therefore interesting to note that 27 per cent were wholly self-supporting even in that difficult time;

57 per cent were partially so, an astounding proportion when one considers that even many highly trained and intellectually competent persons were on relief; 8 per cent were totally dependent; and 8 per cent were in institutions.[20]

Another study traced 17 of the 166 children who had the lowest IQ scores in school, and who had been diagnosed as having little if any prospect of becoming self-supporting as adults. Sixteen years after this prognosis had been made, eight of the men were self-supporting, four of the women had married men who were self-supporting, and five were dependent on family or community. One of the boys, with an IQ of 58—"low-grade moron"—had a particularly illuminating history:

> One of the boys in this group who showed many delinquent traits in 1914 and had a history of feeblemindedness, insanity, and immorality, spent four years in the first grade, and after six months in the second grade, spent the remaining three and a half years in the ungraded class. . . . At fourteen this boy got a work permit and for almost ten years has been working steadily and successfully with an insulator company as a responsible inspector. . . . He is very proud of the fact that once when he was home on sick leave for a few days, they sent for him to come back because his substitute had spoiled several hundred dollars' worth of material in his absence. He says, "I was no good in school, but when I got married, I knew I'd got to dig out." There has been no further delinquency, although infrequently he goes on sprees. He has learned to read the newspapers through having become interested in athletics, but can write only his name.[21]

A third follow-up study was made in a quite different economic climate, during World War II.[22] It included 177 higher-grade subjects who were paroled from a training school for feebleminded children. The researcher divided his cases into those with IQ's between 50 and 75 and those with IQ's of 76 or more. He found that these subjects were not dependent on their family or friends for jobs; many worked above the unskilled level; most held their jobs for three months or more; the lower IQ subjects compared well with the higher IQ subjects; and there was no relationship between IQ and wages. In brief, these subjects had greater ability of certain kinds, not measured on mental tests, than one might have supposed.

One of the best follow-up studies was made in Connecticut on 256 non-institutionalized subjects with IQ's between 45 and 75, diagnosed as deficient. At the time of the study, the average age of the subjects was 24.5 years. The researcher found 129 non-morons of roughly the same socioeconomic backgrounds to serve as controls. She matched the two groups in beginning school age, chronological age, race, sex, country of birth, nationality, and father's occupation. Most of the subjects had IQ's of 65 or over. Her results included the following:

1. School Achievement: 81:6 per cent left school below the 8th grade; 8.2 per cent went to high school; one completed high school. This achievement was inferior to that of the non-moron subjects.

2. Commitment to State Institutions Among Families of Subjects: Almost twice as many families of the experimental group as of the control group had some record of institutional commitment, the proportions being 26.9 and 16.3. Of significance from the sociological point of view was the fact that 56.5 per cent of the families of the experimental group had records of commitments to correctional institutions as contrasted with 28.6 per cent of the control-group families. A startling conclusion in the opposite direction was that far fewer of the families of the moron group had records of commitment to mental hospitals than families of the non-moron group, the proportions being 34.8 per cent and 57.1 per cent.

3. Economic Status: :"The differences, by any possible test, between morons and non-morons with respect to self-support are actually so slight, and the patterns are so shifting, that the only possible conclusion is that both groups are in about the same status in this regard. Certainly the morons show no detectable signs of greater dependency upon others than do the matched non-morons."

4. Employment Level: "Fewer morons than non-morons, of both sexes, are employed in the three highest kinds of occupations: professional, semi-professional and managerial (1.2 vs. 10.4%). Many fewer morons than non-morons are employed in clerical and sales work (3.7 vs. 25.6%). About twice as many morons as non-morons are employed in domestic and personal services (6.1 vs. 3.2%), but approximately the same proportion are engaged in agricultural work (2.9 vs. 2.4%). Many more morons than non-morons are in the laboring occupations (83.7 vs. 56.0%), but almost as many morons as non-morons are skilled laborers (13.1 vs. 17.6%), although many more morons than non-morons are semi-skilled (54.9 vs. 31.2%) and unskilled laborers (15.7 vs. 7.2%)." Earning power was about the same in the two groups; the morons tended to remain in their jobs somewhat longer.

5. Work Performance: Employers rated both groups with respect to accuracy, speed, learning rate, judgment, learning ability, absenteeism, promptness, efficiency, and relations with other employees on a 4-point rating scale ranging from generally unsatisfactory to highly satisfactory. The moron group tended to get lower ratings than the non-moron group on reliability of judgment, absenteeism, tardiness, efficiency, and co-worker relations; but with respect to the other variables the results were inconsistent.

6. Family Background: The lower-class background of the cases of

feeblemindedness which appear in the records is vividly documented by the contrast in family background of the two groups in this study. The families of the moron group were found to have been broken by divorce or desertion more often than those of the non-moron group, more had records of commitment to state institutions, fewer were in upper occupational levels, a larger number needed relief by more than one agency, more work relief had been needed, court records were more common in parental families, more fathers and siblings had court records, and more were foreign-born.

Summary: "Our study reveals that morons are socially adequate in that they are economically independent and self-supporting; and that they are not serious threateners of the safety of society, but are rather frequent breakers of conventional codes of behavior. Their inadequate academic background and their relatively poor records of work performance offer support for Doll's estimate that 'the individual feebleminded adult may approximate the norm in one respect or another of (the) requirements of social desirability under favorable circumstances or for a limited time or after long standing habituations' in these particular respects; but Doll's further statement that their 'social success is at best temporary, marginal and precarious,' if taken as a general and unqualified judgment is, on our evidence, overdrawn. The morons we studied are, by and large, successful in their social adjustment within limitations, which are apparently imposed by their inferior mental capacities . . . Doll's remark . . . that 'they find some humble niche in society which they can fill without becoming such a social menace that society becomes gravely concerned about them' seems to fit the actual situation very well.

"Indeed, the present author feels strongly that most if not all morons are unjustly designated as 'feebleminded' in the literal sense. They may be subnormal in many respects, as compared to non-morons, but in many others they do not even show subnormality." [23]

Reasons for the Differences in Role Performance

How can we explain the differences in the two sets of data? Why was the role performance so poor in one set and relatively good in the other? The conclusion seems to be warranted that the differences shown between the mentally deficient who succeed in life and those who do not cannot be explained in terms of their mental handicap alone. It is suggested here that two explanations must be used, one referring to other than mental pathologies in those who perform their roles poorly and one referring to the supporting role network of those who perform their roles well.

The Personality of the Mentally Deficient

We are likely to be so impressed by mental deficiency that we tend to forget that these human beings have personalities also, that they have hopes and fears, frustrations and anxieties. Indeed, it is likely that because their frustrations are more frequent than are those of people with more ability to cope with problems, much of their handicap is emotional rather than intellectual. Anyone who has ever visited an institution for the feebleminded must have been impressed by the tremendous affection the inmates show. They cling to a visitor who shows a sympathetic manner. Their capacity for affection, at least on this surface level, seems inordinate. With such need for affection we can well imagine how devastating their experiences must be to them, rejected as they are likely to be.

Even a cursory reading of the first set of cases presented above suggests that these people were suffering from far more than mental deficiency alone. Symptoms of psychopathic personality, that is, inability to feel anxiety, seem prevalent also, as well as other disorders. In brief, the poor role performance of these cases seems to be associated far more with other pathologies than with mental deficiency alone.

It has been usual among clinicians to consign mentally deficient cases to institutions, on the theory that they were not good prospects for therapy. But one of the interesting results of recent research is that many of these patients are amenable to therapy. It has been found to be remarkably effective in some cases, even in those that were institutionalized. Some cases originally diagnosed as mentally deficient, in fact, prove themselves to be normal; and some which exhibited seriously delinquent, or at least antisocial, symptoms became more nearly normal in their behavior or role performance, even if they are not normal in intelligence as measured on tests.

How many and what etiological types of an institutional population are amenable to and can benefit from psychotherapy cannot be answered at this time because of the absence of the necessary research. What evidence is available suggests that a fair number of cases diagnosed as mentally defective are in need of and respond favorably to psychotherapeutic procedures.[24]

Not mental deficiency in and of itself, then, but mental deficiency associated with pathologies may explain the poor role performance of many individuals.

Supporting Role Network

Because of their handicap, many mentally deficient persons never get experience in proper role performance. But when sympathetic and supporting roles are supplied to them, they can and do learn complementary role behavior. In the training of the men in the Army's Special Service Units, to be discussed below, advantage was taken of group roles and group support. At first the men with low IQ were very shy, since they had never associated closely with other men. But "gradually the spirit of teamwork and cooperation . . . developed and within a few days the men . . . made an adjustment sufficient to enhance learning." [25] Their instructor remained with them twenty-four hours a day; he wrote letters for them; he gave them advice on their personal problems. He had a special role: he was their kind father. It paid off in their improvement.

Of two people with equal handicap, one succeeds, the other does not. We suggest that something in the role network in which they find themselves must explain the difference. Some light on this problem is cast by a study of young parolees from an institution for feebleminded women in Pennsylvania, which found that success or failure on first parole seemed to be determined on a chance basis. That is, with respect to all the variables studied—IQ, family background, medical record— there was no difference between those who succeeded and those who failed. The conclusion was drawn that these young women were at the mercy of their environments; they themselves contributed little to the success or failure of their lives. They responded to the stimuli that presented themselves almost indiscriminately.[26] With respect to a policy for dealing with the mentally deficient child, the implication is that the very things which make it difficult for him to learn in the first place also make it difficult for him to change. Thus, if he is not properly role-trained in early life it will be hard to effect a change in him in later life.[27]

Because of the differences in family background reported in the experimental and control groups in the Connecticut study referred to above, one critic of the study feels that the project is really a study of differences between morons coming from unfavorable backgrounds and non-morons coming from less unfavorable ones. Moreover, he considers that since unfavorable background influences intellectual efficiency and social adjustment, the differences reported cannot be considered the result of differences in intelligence alone.[28]

In any event, the contrast in life patterns shown by the two sets of data reported above demonstrate that mental deficiency in and of itself cannot be taken as proof of social or role inadequacy. The crucial problem appears to be one of finding roles in which those who are mentally deficient can perform satisfactorily. Some of the difficulties involved in the role performance of these individuals have been highlighted by a recent study of illiterate males, aged eighteen to twenty-six, in Louisiana and Texas.

The Illiterate in American Society[29]

The illiterate lives in a world with a minimum of symbolic expression; this limits the range and flexibility of his reactions. In his interaction with society he is likely to be the adapting individual; he must accommodate to it. He rarely has any choice in the range of possible roles to perform; he never prescribes the roles of others. Because of his handicap, the illiterate tends to withdraw from the larger world, where so much interaction is on a symbolic level; when he cannot withdraw, his mode of interaction is likely to be compliance, concealment of his deficiency, or substitution of some nonsymbolic technique for a symbolic one. Shame is the common lot of the illiterate, especially when there is no group support. Because of his handicap he is easily exploitable. "Credit buying, loan companies, pawnshops, soothsayers, faith healers, politicians, and patent medicine purveyors find a lucrative market in this group." [30] Because he is an outsider, he tends to create a separate world with others like himself. They develop a culture of their own:

. . . they change from unexpressive and confused individuals . . . to expressive and understanding persons within their own group . . . they express themselves in institutionalized terms. Among themselves they have a universe of response. They form and recognize symbols of prestige and disgrace; evaluate relevant situations in terms of their own norms and in their own idiom; and in their interrelations with one another, the mask of accommodative adjustment drops. Within the illiterate group the common manifestations of informal social behavior are apparent. The modes of expressive behavior, since they are to one another mutually intelligible, make possible the expression of aggression, approval, disgrace, and so on, which are inhibited in various ways in their interaction with literates. More clearly observable are certain institutionalized categories of behavior. Their religion tends to follow a pattern of emotionalism and physical expression with the relative absence of abstract arguments. . . .[31]

They are ostentatious and flashy in consumption because they are denied the symbols of success in the larger society. They live in the present; they do not have the symbolic resources for long-time planning. "Outside of a few sports, 'adventure' movies, and gambling . . . much of their recreation consists of 'doing nothing' in a group, petty arguments, and prank playing." [32] Are they salvageable for useful roles in the larger society? The experience of the Army in World War II is suggestive in this connection.

Military Experience

During World War II, 716,000 men were rejected by Selective Service draft boards on the ground of "mental deficiency." This was the equivalent of forty divisions. In the year following the outbreak of the Korean War, 300,000 men were rejected on the same ground.[33] These figures represent a rejection rate of 4 per cent of all men examined. It has been estimated that about 1 per cent of the population can perform only unskilled work, and then only in a protected environment, and that another 1 per cent can work only if they have special supervision. Thus 2 per cent of the population would fail to achieve a minimum performance standard because of intellectual deficiency. The Selective Service rejection rate was about twice that proportion.

An analysis of the distribution of these rejects soon revealed that most of them were southern Negroes; and that the rate of rejection was closely associated with the quality of schools available. "The rejection rates for 'mental deficiency' were, in general, the result of the quantity and quality of education available in the 1920's and early 1930's." [34]

When it became clear in 1943 that there was going to be a shortage of military personnel, a program was initiated to salvage as many as possible of these "mentally deficient" men. Special Training Units were established. Men were observed, to determine which ones could be salvaged and then to prepare them as quickly as possible for service.

An analysis of the results of the work of the Special Training Units was made by a team of researchers to determine whether the salvaged men had succeeded. The Army considered that the work had failed; the researchers did not agree. Of the more than 300,000 men assigned to Special Training Units, about 85 per cent graduated. The remaining

15 per cent were unable to absorb the instruction, which aimed at fourth-grade proficiency in reading, writing, and arithmetic. A sample of 400 men, half white, and half Negro, was selected for study. Of these, 57 failed to graduate. Of these 57, 6 were discharged for defects not related to their mental ability and should not have been inducted in the first place. Four received medical discharges for psychiatric reasons. Of the remaining 47, 1 was discharged for enuresis, 1 for being below minimum standards, 1 for a mixture of physical, emotional, and mental deficiencies, 1 for being derelict in duty, and 1 because of injuries.

The remaining forty-two non-graduates were separated honorably with the notation that they were inept and not adaptable for military service. Although the vast majority of the non-graduates were discharged because they were inept, a reading of their records makes it clear that a considerable number suffered from emotional disabilities as well. The fact that these men were discharged primarily because of ineptitude means that lack of adaptability for service was probably their predominant, but not necessarily their sole, handicap.[35]

In brief, these men were not necessarily any more deficient mentally than those who succeeded in graduating, but in addition to their mental handicap they also had other disabling difficulties.

An evaluation was made of the records of the 343 men who did graduate. The researchers constructed the following four-step scale to assess the over-all performance of 331 men for whom sufficient data were available.[36]

A soldier was rated "very good" if he reached the grade of sergeant and was also awarded a combat decoration, such as the Bronze Star Medal. He was assessed as very good even if he failed to achieve the grade of sergeant if he won an outstanding medal, such as the Silver Star. . . .

The "good" soldier was one who, regardless of his rank, served for a long period in combat and won the Bronze Star Medal, and whose record was free of negative factors such as serious disciplinary infractions or a serious loss of time due to excessive hospitalization resulting from his own misconduct. Some men were considered to have been good soldiers even though they were convicted by a summary court-martial for a minor offense such as speeding or for having been absent without leave for a very short period. A man who did not serve in combat was judged a good soldier if he achieved the grade of corporal, had two years of service with high efficiency ratings, and had no serious blemishes on his record.

The "acceptable" soldier was one who achieved no rank higher than private first class, whose combat or non-combat record was undistinguished, and who may have lost some time for disciplinary or medical reasons. Many served overseas only short periods or not at all.

The "not acceptable" group included, first, those who were discharged from the Army dishonorably or without honor, and second, those who were separated because of "ineptitude." These two categories accounted for twenty men. In addition, we found that twenty-one others had not performed acceptably. Some were discharged quickly because of mental deficiency or emotional disturbance, which, in the Army's judgment, rendered them useless. Some others who served until demobilization—and one who was even permitted to reenlist—had never given satisfactory performance. The factors considered in judging these men as not acceptable were excessive time lost from duty, court-martial convictions, excessive hospitalization, and unsatisfactory efficiency ratings.

The results of applying these standards were as follows:

Classification	Total N = 331	White N = 170	Negro N = 161
Very Good	9.0	12.3	5.6
Good	28.7	35.3	21.5
Acceptable	50.0	41.8	58.4
Not Acceptable	12.3	10.6	14.3

Comparison with a control group, made up by selecting the man of the same race whose serial number was next higher than that of the man in the experimental group, showed that the experimental subjects did not match the control subjects in achievement. Since it was not the aim of the Special Training Unit that they should match, the researchers believe the program was a success.

The question was rather whether any appreciable number would perform adequately and represent a clear gain to the Army. This question is answered unequivocally. Eighty-five percent of the graduates performed acceptably or better as compared to 90 percent of the control group. Clearly, at a time when the Armed Forces needed men badly, they were able with a small investment to turn many illiterates and poorly educated men into acceptable soldiers.[37]

The implication is that careful management of human resources can salvage a sizable proportion of people who otherwise would, in effect, be wasted or even become a charge on the community. A considerable proportion of the population that is functionally "mentally deficient" would not be if we knew how to deal with them.

Trends: Are We Going To Be Intelligent Enough To Survive?

Fears are expressed by some students of human intelligence that the differential birth rate of the various classes is causing a decline in the average intelligence of our population and that we may cease to be able to hold our own if this decline continues. This fear, if well founded, would certainly warrant consideration as a basic societal problem.

The line of reasoning which produces this fear is based on two kinds of data: one is the inverse relationship between birth rate and socioeconomic status and the other is the inverse relationship between family size (reflecting birth rate) and intelligence. The grounds for these fears have been carefully analyzed by one sociologist and found to be unsubstantiated. He finds, for example, that there is by no means consensus among biologists about the effects of differential fertility.[38] A second objection to the theory of declining intelligence lies in the inadequacy of the instruments used to test intelligence; they are not, as we saw above, "culturally fair." A third weakness in the theory is our lack of scientific knowledge about the genetic mechanisms involved in the transmission of intellectual capacity. One geneticist points out that there is a kind of genetic equilibrium in which the average level of intelligence remains constant. Statisticians have long been familiar with the so-called law of regression, according to which there is a tendency for the offspring of parents who deviate from the average in either direction to regress or progress toward the average. This same sociologist has taken other biological traits—height and longevity—which show the same kind of relationship to socioeconomic status as that shown by intelligence, and demonstrated that although, according to the logic used in predicting reduced intelligence in future generations, we should as a nation be becoming shorter in stature as well as shorter-lived, actually we have been becoming taller and longer-lived all the time.

Most amazing of all, however, is the fact that even some of those who predict declining intelligence actually find just the opposite. If anything, average intelligence as measured by tests seems to be increasing.

The final and most telling blow to the theory of intellectual deterioration is the fact that, not only does no direct evidence exist to confirm the existence of such a trend, but what direct evidence there is shows the opposite movement toward a *rise* in the average level of measured intelligence! The extent to which scientific partisanship can govern response to evidence is nowhere better illustrated than in the temerity of one author who entitled her paper "The Decline of Intelligence in New Zealand" only to confess in passing that her sample scored considerably higher on the IQ test than did the earlier standardization sample taken in the same community.

The three large projects which thus far have been specifically designed to measure the trend of intelligence report the same finding that no decline can be detected, and that, if anything, a rise has taken place. Cattell, who some years ago predicted a decline of one IQ point per decade, reports a positive difference of more than one point in favor of the 1949 group of 10 year olds in Leicester and Devonshire, compared to the previously tested 1936 group.

Collating results from retesting programs in a number of English school districts, Emmett finds that over an average elapsed period of 9.4 years boys' IQ's have changed at the rate of —.09 points per year, girls' at the rate of +.09 points. It is noteworthy that this investigator feels able to rule out the possibility of incentive and test-sophistication effects as working in the direction of an increase.

The most ambitious resurvey is that of the Scottish Mental Survey Committee which tested the entire year-group of 11-year olds in Scotland in 1947 for comparison with a similar study done in 1932. Some 70,000 subjects were involved. Although this study reiterates the familiar inverse relationship between intelligence and family size, the 1947 mean test score is found to be [the equivalent of] about two IQ points higher than the 1932 mean.[39]

To explain these results, grossly environmental explanations are used, and the sociologist who has analyzed all these findings then says, "Certainly, if the improved nutrition of the children is to be advanced as an explanation of their improved test scores, one would like to see some consideration given the possibility that the lower test scores of children from large families are due to their relative nutritional disadvantage compared to children from small families." [40]

Although the above studies are British, there is no reason to believe that the results would be different in the United States. Far from documenting a decline in human intelligence, then, the research findings seem to point in the opposite direction.

Further, as modern medical science learns to conquer diseases—meningitis, encephalitis, Mongolism—which produce mental defect, as distinguished from mental deficiency, the number of such cases should decline. To the extent that mental defect is associated with unfavorable life conditions or with diseases amenable to treatment—congenital syphilis, for example—it is probably being reduced. That new cases of mental defect will constantly appear in the population must, to be sure, be accepted; we still cannot locate all the defective genes, prevent mutations, or control reproduction to the extent necessary to eliminate all chance of such defect. There may be an irreducible minimum of mental defect in any large population.

But the fears of those who predict that we are going to be swamped by persons of low IQ do not seem to be warranted. If anything, the trend is toward a higher average IQ, as measured by tests, rather than the opposite, and toward a reduction in mental defect as medical science learns how to control the illnesses which produce it.

At this point we must inject a caveat with respect to the above analysis. It assumes that mankind will be intelligent enough in the first

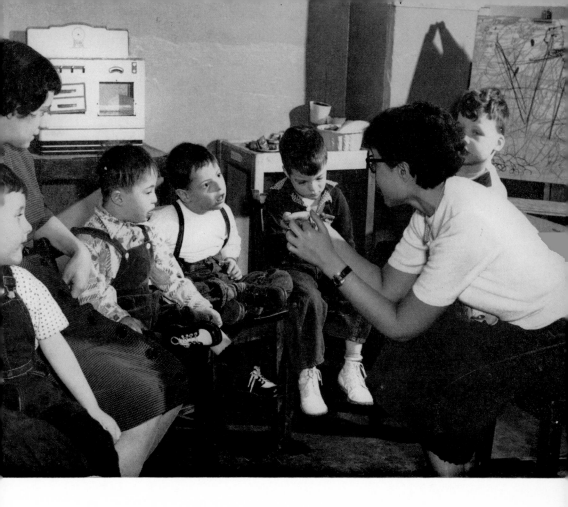

Any roles for these mentally retarded children?

In a relatively simple agricultural community they would, upon coming of age, have found suitable and useful worker roles that they could perform with satisfaction. To be sure, they would have been recognized as slow learners, but slow learning would not seriously have handicapped them as they performed certain adult worker roles requiring little skill and judgment. But in our complex and increasingly "automated" society, will there be suitable roles for these children when they grow up?

Children like the ones appearing in our photograph are more nearly at the mercy of chance than are children with greater intelligence. Whether or not they make an adequate adjustment to life will to a large extent depend upon the role network within which they find themselves. Trained by loving and patient teachers and protected by a network of supporting roles, these attractive children—physically as normal as other children—can become useful members of the community. Deprived of such training and protection they can become hazards, both to themselves and to others.

In its appropriation request for the fiscal year 1957 the Office of Education of the Federal Government specified improved education of the mentally retarded as one of ten areas important in the conservation and development of human resources. *(Photo: Association for the Help of Retarded Children, Inc.)*

place to control the uses of nuclear fission as applied to hydrogen and cobalt bombs. Radioactive dust, if it is not controlled, can in time have the effect of producing enough genetic damage to increase the mutations which produce defects.

. . . the impairment will usually be slight, or even unrecognizable, consisting of such traits as a slightly greater than average tendency to rheumatism or gastric ulcer, or high blood pressure, often not evident until the later years of life, or a higher requirement for some vitamin, or a slightly lowered I.Q. . . .[41]

What is the value, we might ask, of reducing defects by controlling the illnesses which produce them if at the same time we re-introduce defects by means of radioactive dust?

Although average IQ is not, as we have seen above, declining in any absolute sense, or even if it is rising, there is a distinct possibility that the demands being made on human intelligence by modern technology are increasing so sharply that the net effect will be the same as though IQ were, in fact, declining. We are already beginning to feel the pinch with respect to the highest talents. Not only the designing, but even the programming, so called, or "instructing" of a modern computing machine such as Univac, for example, demands abstract intelligence of a very high order. It is not inconceivable that in the not-too-distant future we will demand of the person with average IQ as much as we now demand of the person with superior IQ.

We shall have more to say about the social problems associated with high, as well as with low, intelligence when we discuss the position of youth in our society in Chapter 17. At this point, however, we resume our discussion of the pathologies, specifically, the addictions.

NOTES

1 Seymour B. Sarason, *Psychological Problems in Mental Deficiency* (Harper, 1949), pp. 204–207.

2 *Ibid.*, p. 214.

3 *Ibid.*, pp. 207–208.

4 *Ibid.*, p. 203.

5 The cretin, for example, can be brought up to normal in many cases by the use of thyroid extract.

6 There is some evidence, by no means as yet conclusive, that the chemical substance phenylpyruvic acid is associated with mental defect; it has never been reported in normal individuals but is often found in mentally defective persons. See Sarason, *op. cit.*, pp. 190–191.

7 *Ibid.*, Chapter 5.

8 For a critique of sole reliance on the IQ see *ibid.*, pp. 1–3.

9 Allison Davis, *Social-Class Influences upon Learning* (Harvard Univ. Press, 1950).

10 *Ibid.*, p. 87.

11 In some cases mental deficiency can be lessened or corrected altogether. As we saw above, for example, the cretin may sometimes be rendered normal by the use of thyroid extract. Glutamic acid has also been found to improve mental ability. One experiment was based on a group of children ranging in age from infancy to adolescence. "For six months the group was given glutamic acid and then tested with the Stanford-Binet, the Wechsler-Bellevue and the Rorschach tests. One boy who had an IQ of 45 now was up to 56. Another who began with an IQ of 131 now had jumped to 138. The IQ's of every child tested had increased. A study of 30 cases for one year showed a growth of mental age at twice the normal rate, with an average gain in the IQ of 11 points." (Arthur Jess Wilson, *The Emotional Life of the Ill and Injured; The Psychology and Mental Hygiene of Rehabilitation and Guidance* [Social Sciences Publishers, 1950], p. 45.) When IQ can be brought up to normal, the person cannot have been feebleminded in the first place, according to the Doll definition.

12 E. A. Doll, "The Essentials of an Inclusive Concept of Mental Deficiency," *American Journal of Mental Deficiency* 46 (1941), pp. 214–219.

13 A. F. Tredgold, *A Text-book of Mental Deficiency* (6th ed., Williams & Wilkins, 1947), p. 4.

14 "The Secret Child," pamphlet distributed by the Association.

15 Dr. Leonard A. Scheele, Surgeon General of the Public Health Service, estimated 4,500,000, as reported in the *New York Times*, March 18, 1955. Dr. Salvatore G. DiMichael, executive director of the National Association for Retarded Children, estimated 4,000,000 to be moderately retarded and 750,000 seriously retarded. The secretary of the National Catholic Education Association estimated that 2 per cent of the total school population were either slow learners or educable mentally retarded (*ibid.*). These figures compare with the estimates by the National Association for Retarded Children cited in the text, namely: 160,000 seriously retarded institutional cases; 640,000 less seriously retarded; and 4,000,000 marginally independent. Dr. Karl F. Heiser, consultant to the League for Emotionally Disturbed Children, estimates 8 million "handicapped persons," of whom 4 million are under twenty-one years; he estimates at least a million

seriously disturbed children in schools and at least 500,000 more who are too disturbed for ordinary schools and need a special program. (*Our Backward Children* [Norton, 1955].)

16 Davis, *op. cit.*, pp. 42–44.

17 Richard L. Dugdale, the author of *The Jukes, A Study in Crime, Pauperism, Disease, and Insanity,* has been discredited. His techniques of research were primitive and his results unreliable. His thesis was that crime and pauperism were hereditary. If his descriptions of the way the Jukes lived are taken as approximately correct, and his interpretations or explanations ignored, they may still have some value, despite the fact that his work is generally discounted at the present time. For a recent "exposé" see Samuel Hopkins Adams, "The Juke Myth," *Saturday Review,* April 2, 1955, pp. 13, 48–49.

18 G. McPherson, "Preliminary Consideration of the Heredity of Mental Deficiency," *Proceedings of the American Association on Mental Deficiency,* 42 (1936–1937), pp. 124–131.

19 C. H. Town, *Familial Feeblemindedness* (Buffalo: Foster & Stewart, 1939).

20 W. R. Baller, "A Study of the Present Social Status of a Group of Adults Who, When They Were in Elementary Schools, Were Classified as Mentally Deficient," *Genetic Psychology Monographs,* 1936, 18 (No. 3).

21 R. E. Fairbank, "The Subnormal Child— Seventeen Years After," *Mental Hygiene,* 17 (1933), pp. 177–208.

22 T. G. Hegge, "Occupational Status of Higher Grade Defectives in the Present Emergency," *American Journal of Mental Deficiency,* 49 (1944), pp. 86–98.

23 Ruby Jo Reeves, *The Social Adjustment of Morons in a Connecticut City* (Hartford: Mansfield-Southbury Training Schools, Social Service Department, State Office Building, 1948), p. 97.

24 Sarason, *op. cit.*, p. 310.

25 Eli Ginzberg and Douglas W. Bray, *The Uneducated* (Columbia Univ. Press, 1953), p. 72.

26 Unpublished study by Robert Clark and Jessie Bernard.

27 Sarason, *op. cit.*, pp. 310–311.

28 *Ibid.*, p. 112.

29 This section is based on Howard E. Freeman and Gene G. Kassebaum, "The Illiterate in American Society: Some General Hypotheses," *Social Forces,* 34 (May 1956), pp. 371–375.

30 *Ibid.*, pp. 373–374.

31 *Ibid.*, p. 374.
32 *Ibid.*, p. 375.
33 Ginzberg and Bray, *op. cit.*, p. 3.
34 *Ibid.*, p. 53.
35 *Ibid.*, p. 84.
36 *Ibid.*, p. 94.
37 *Ibid.*, p. 99.
38 Otis Dudley Duncan, "Is the Intelligence of the General Population Declining?" *American Sociological Review,* 17 (Aug. 1952), pp. 401–407.
39 *Ibid.*, pp. 405–406.
40 *Ibid.*, pp. 407–408.
41 H. J. Muller, "Race Poisoning by Radiation," *Saturday Review,* June 9, 1945, p. 11.

11

Role Impairment:

The Addictions

Alcoholism

As a Social Problem

The justification for considering alcoholism a social problem might rest on either the humanitarian or the utilitarian criterion. Alcoholism often causes suffering in the patient himself, and because it makes for role impairment, and ultimately role pathology,[1] the alcoholic's family suffers as much as, if not more, than he does. A recent study of 2,000 disorganized Catholic families in the Chicago Archdiocese—and there is no reason to suppose that they are different from non-Catholic families so far as the role effects of drinking are concerned—documents the way in which alcohol impairs family role performance.

The excessive use of alcohol bears in its train serious consequences for the family. To be specific, alcohol in any form costs money. It is not surprising, therefore, to find that drinking and nonsupport account for 37 percent of the cases in this category. Further, drinking often leads to physical cruelty

Alcoholism

Narcotics Addiction

The Compulsive Gambler

and abuse. At times, not only the wife but also the children are made to suffer physically. . . . Another result of drinking is the association with doubtful characters of the opposite sex leading to the presumption of adultery.[2]

The role-impairing effect of alcohol on the performance of work roles is suggested by the great, albeit indeterminate, amount of absenteeism in industry, especially on Monday mornings, attributed to excessive drinking over the weekend.

Alcoholism is also expensive to the community.

In any community, when 100 excessive drinkers learn how to remain abstinent and resume regular jobs, there is the increase in buying power represented by 100 pay envelopes. The families of these men no longer require support from welfare agencies. Courts and jails are relieved of a part of the load they carry. If another 100 men are kept at work six months in the year instead of several weeks, and make fewer appearances before the judge and the jailer, the financial saving alone justifies the effort and expense of maintaining rehabilitation services.[3]

It is impossible to reduce all the costs to dollars and cents, but if the costs of treatment, jails, accidents, and lowered productivity related to alcohol were added up they would doubtless be staggering.

The criterion of dysfunctionality might also be used, for although societies have been able to survive alcoholism,[4] it is doubtful if a machine-run society can function—or "eufunction"—with a high incidence of alcoholism. The arguments against alcoholism quoted from *Izvestia* in Chapter 5 were based on dysfunctionality to a large extent. The proportion of drivers involved in fatal accidents who are "under the influence" of alcohol at the time of the accident fluctuates between 5 and 9 per cent. And about one out of every eight traffic violators is "under the influence." A large proportion of pedestrians killed in motor accidents—almost one fourth—are also reported as having consumed alcohol.[5]

Alcoholism has a psychological, a medical, and a role aspect, as indicated in the definition of alcoholics given by the Subcommittee on Alcoholism of the World Health Organization: "those excessive drinkers whose dependence upon alcohol has attained such a degree that they show a noticeable mental disturbance, or an interference with their bodily and mental health, their interpersonal relations and their smooth social and economic functioning; or who show the prodromal signs of such developments." [6]

Alcoholism is, then, a role impairment, and ultimately a role pathology. On humanitarian and utilitarian grounds, as well as on grounds of dysfunctionality, it can be considered a social problem—that is, a situation calling for some kind of treatment.

Extent, Trends, and Incidence of Drinking and Alcoholism

EXTENT. One study in 1945 estimated that 60 per cent of the population fifteen years of age and over drank alcoholic beverages.[7] Another study in 1946 found that 17 per cent of the adult population of the United States were regular drinkers and 48 per cent were occasional drinkers, making a total of 65 per cent who were drinkers. The remaining 35 per cent were abstainers.[8]

In 1956 a summary of polling studies from 1945 on showed a marked decline in proportion of drinkers (see Table 1). Minor differences in definition or sampling procedures might account for the discrepancies between the figures given in the 1945 and 1946 studies and those reported in Table 1. The general downward trend since 1945 and 1946 may reflect a reaction from a postwar high, as there was, for

TABLE 1
Proportion of Drinkers and Abstainers in
Adult Population, 1945–1956

	Drinkers	Abstainers
	%	%
1945	67	33
1946	67	33
1949	58	42
1950	60	40
1951	59	41
1952	60	40
1956	60	40

SOURCE: Gallup poll release for February 19, 1956.

example, in the divorce rate.[9] Evidence for this is suggested by the slightly downward trend also in apparent consumption of alcoholic beverages from 1945–49 to 1950.[10]

It should be emphasized that the above figures are for drinking only. Not all drinkers are problem drinkers. It is estimated that about 6 per cent of all drinkers are problem drinkers.[11] And fewer—about 1.5 per cent—become chronic alcoholics, that is, develop the physical or psychological characteristics resulting from the prolonged and excessive use of alcohol which is known as alcoholism, as defined above.[12] On the basis of a survey of alcoholism in Kansas in 1954, the conclusion was reached that there were at least 21,000 problem drinkers, which was a rate of 15.8 per 1,000 adults (1.58 per cent) in the population.[13]

If we assume that the proportion of adults fifteen years of age and over who drink is 60 per cent, the number of drinkers as of 1955 would be about 68,116,200, since the estimated number of persons fifteen years of age and over in the United States population was estimated to be 113,527,000 in July of that year.[14] If we use 6 per cent as our basis for computing the number of immoderate drinkers, we find that there were about 4,086,972; and if 1.5 per cent of all drinkers were to become chronic alcoholics, there would be over a million.[15] Little wonder then that alcoholism has been called the No. 4 Public Health Problem in the United States today.

TRENDS. The long-term trend with regard to the use of alcoholic beverages seems to be that although an increasing proportion of people drink, they drink less and they tend to drink more fermented and less distilled beverages than formerly.

The most conspicuous features of the per capita rates . . . are the great decrease in the per capita consumption of distilled spirits and the great increase in the per capita consumption of beer. The superiority of rates based on the population of drinking age may be demonstrated at this juncture. Based on total populations the per capita rates for distilled spirits in the United States in the years 1850 and 1945 were 2.02 gallons and 1.46 gallons respectively, while the corresponding per capita rates for the population of drinking age were 4.17 gallons and 1.95 gallons. In the first instance the decrease is 27.7 percent but in the latter instance the decrease is 53.2 percent. The true characteristic trend is expressed by the rates per capita of the population of drinking age. . . .

A large consumption of distilled spirits and a small consumption of beer is generally an indication that the users are relatively few in number but individually heavy consumers. A large consumption of beer, on the other hand, is indicative of wide use and relatively small individual consumption. The fact that the consumption of distilled spirits in 1850 was 4.17 gallons per capita of the population of 15 years and over while the per capita consumption of beer was only 2.70 gallons would indicate that at that time few were moderate drinkers, but that the division was largely between heavy drinkers and abstainers. The early temperance societies then had a strong case and their contention that 3 out of every 10 users became chronic alcoholics dates from experience in the nineteenth century. Under present-day drinking habits, approximately 3 drinkers out of every 200 become chronic alcoholics.[16]

This drop in the rate of chronic alcoholics from three out of ten to only three out of two hundred is enormous, even for a period of a century, and could hardly be expected to continue. Some of the drop may be explained by the fact that there are high mortality rates [17] among heavy drinkers and therefore as the population grows older, they are weeded out of the older age brackets. The denominator, that is, grows larger as more people live to an advanced age, but the heavy drinkers are underrepresented in this older population because of higher mortality rates. But some of the decline reported by Jellinek may, as he says, represent a change in drinking customs, and a genuine decline in alcoholism.

INCIDENCE OF DRINKING AND OF ALCOHOLISM. Men are more likely to be drinkers than women,[18] although the number of women who drink is increasing. The proportion of drinkers seems to increase from low to high economic levels; the more educated seem to show a higher incidence of drinking than the less educated; more first- and second-generation Americans seem to drink than those of longer native background; and the incidence of drinking is greatest among Jews, next among Catholics, and least among Protestants.[19] Drinking occurs more commonly in those under fifty than in those over this age, more in urban than in rural areas, and more in New England and the Middle Atlantic States than in other parts of the country; it is least common in the South.

The above data refer to drinking, not to alcoholism. Alcoholism, like drinking, is relatively higher among men than among women. It is relatively lower, however, among such ethnic groups as Jews and Italians than among other ethnic groups. It tends to show higher incidence in large than in small cities.[20] In 1950 the highest rate was in San Francisco (4,190 per 100,000 adults aged twenty and over) and the lowest in Austin, Texas, and Charlotte, North Carolina (440 per 100,000 adults aged twenty and over in both cities). It is not urbanism per se which seems important but the ethnocultural composition of the population. Communities with large Jewish and Italian populations show relatively low rates of alcoholism.[21]

"OLD" AND "NEW" ALCOHOLICS: THE STATUS DIMENSION OF ALCOHOLISM. Alcoholism, like venereal diseases, was once so stigmatized that treatment was delayed, if ever even sought. Frequently, therefore, alcoholism was hidden, lied about, and locked up in the closet with other family skeletons. The professional man who was suffering from the illness was "indisposed" or "out of town." Only when it could no longer be kept under cover did it ever come to public attention. In the 19th and early part of the 20th century the problem of alcoholism was defined in terms of drunkenness, which is a legal and not a medical concept. As thus defined, it seemed to be a problem primarily of the lower socioeconomic classes. With the better perspective on the problem which modern research has made possible, however, alcoholism is no longer seen as primarily a lower-class phenomenon.

Alcoholism touches every level of society. The alcoholic has commonly been thought of as a person of limited intelligence and as a weak character. Actually the personality characteristics which appear to be associated with excessive drinking are human traits which have been common in every generation throughout history. . . . Alcoholism is not a respecter of family background, education, sex, intelligence, economic status or social position. Those who suffer from it include physicians, teachers, clergymen, lawyers, businessmen and housewives as well as skilled and unskilled workers and the shiftless, homeless vagrant.[22]

The above statement is confirmed by the results of the survey of alcoholism in Kansas referred to above. Most of the 21,000 problem drinkers —87 per cent—were men. The median age was between forty-five and forty-nine. About two thirds—64 per cent—were married; 39 per cent had dependent children. More than half—52 per cent—were in middle- or high-income groups. They were not transients, for 68 per cent had lived in their home communities more than five years.

But having made this statement, we must now point out that status seems to make an important difference in the form which alcoholism takes. Alcoholism in the upper socioeconomic classes is not the same as that in the lower. Alcoholism, in brief, is a complex illness which takes many forms.

One study of alcoholics comparing (1) 2,023 males in outpatient clinics in 9 different communities with (2) four groups of homeless men in New Haven and New York City found striking differences between them in family and in performance of work role.[23] Most of the clinic patients—80 per cent—had been married; of the homeless men, more than half had never been married and the rest were either widowed, divorced, or separated from their wives. Half of the clinic patients— 51 per cent—were still living with their wives; 36 per cent of those who had married were divorced, separated, or widowed. This rate of marital disruption was much greater than in the general population, but was remarkably low when compared with the 100 per cent disruption among the homeless men who had been married.

Performance of work role showed similar contrasts. Of the clinic patients, 62 per cent were steadily employed when first seen at the clinics; 60 per cent had records of steady employment for at least three years; 80 per cent had records of high-status jobs. Among the homeless men, on the other hand, there was no employment at the time of interview. Most had been without steady work for many years; some had never had anything but casual employment. Half had never done anything but unskilled work. Only 10 per cent had ever had white-collar, managerial, or professional positions.

The clinic patients lived in established households; most had lived in their present town at least two years; they were younger, almost half —46 per cent—being under forty and only 20 per cent being fifty or over. The homeless men were just the opposite. They had no residential ties; many were transients; only 20 per cent were under forty, while half were fifty or over.

All these differences were significant for the prognosis in treatment. The odds were heavily against the homeless men. But perhaps of equal importance was the difference in the clinical form which alcoholism took in these two groups of subjects. In the clinic patients it was a form which has been called "addictive drinking," and in the homeless men, "habitual symptomatic excessive drinking." The two kinds have been distinguished as follows.

. . . the identification of at least two distinct patterns of alcoholic behavior has emerged independently from several sources. The Subcommittee on Alcoholism of the World Health Organization has suggested that these categories be called "addictive drinkers" and "habitual symptomatic excessive drinkers."

For most addictive drinkers there is an impulsive drive to attain a maximum degree of intoxication from alcohol on nearly every drinking occasion. These people are seeking a peak effect from alcohol which the nonalcoholic has never experienced. Usually, once they start drinking they are unable to control themselves until this peak has been attained. The addictive drinker with a five-dollar bill will probably spend it for some form of beverage which will provide the greatest amount of alcohol in the quickest and most concentrated form, for in this way he can most successfully raise [the] level of alcohol . . . concentration [in his blood].

The addictive type of drinking pattern is most characteristic of patients seen in community alcoholism clinics. While there are some addictive drinkers among homeless men, it has been observed that a significant segment of these alcoholics fit the category described by WHO as habitual symptomatic excessive drinkers. They place their greatest emphasis on the duration of their drinking rather than on its intensity. They appear to be seeking a plateau. Given a five-dollar bill these men would not be likely to think how quickly they could achieve a state of peak intoxication, but instead would plan their drinking so that they could maintain a limited level of effect from alcohol for as long a period of time as possible. These plateau drinkers are seeking to maintain a limited alcohol-induced oblivion from the life around them. While under the effect of alcohol the vast gap between their own way of life and the rest of society seems less pronounced. They can acquire a feeling of well-being and accomplishment in the midst of poverty and degradation. They can overlook their lack of material possessions and forget their loneliness. Drinking also provides a certain status * in settings where the nondrinker is rare and may even be considered queer and avoided by others.[24]

These two clinical types correspond roughly to what used to be known as "misery-drinking"—"the quickest way out of Manchester is the gin-shop"—and "convivial drinking."

The status dimension in alcoholism has revealed itself also in the membership of Alcoholics Anonymous. Originally its membership was drawn almost exclusively from the homeless men in the population, the "last-gasp drinker," the denizen of skid row. More recently, however, it has begun to reach up into higher socioeconomic status levels.

There was a time when the organization known as Alcoholics Anonymous, which has become one of the greatest boons to the drunkards of the world, had a membership which was a little lopsided. On its rolls the Bowery was better represented than Park Avenue, a fact deplored by the organization's leaders. So, recognizing that the rich can become just as alcoholic as the poor, the organization decided to do something about it. Acting on its long-held tenet that only a sober ex-drunk can cure a down-and-out drunk, the A.A. leaders looked around for an ex-drunk with glamour and the ability to speak the Park Avenue language. They found it in an ex-drunk countess. The result: Park Avenue became as well represented as the Bowery on the rolls of A.A.[25]

* Status is here used in the role-related sense.

We must recognize, then, at least two rather different forms of alcoholism, each characteristic of a different socioeconomic level. The etiology and the prognosis of both are also different.

Etiology

NON-ADDICTIVE ALCOHOLISM. So far as the plateau or non-addictive type of alcoholism is concerned, the illness seems to be secondary to an all-pervasive dependency of long standing. The typical case is one in which the patient had little or no training in suitable adult family or worker roles in childhood or in youth. Here is the record:

Half of the men seen in the homeless-man studies had lost one or both parents by death before they reached the age of twenty, and the homes of many of them were disrupted by other factors. Most had left their parental family in their late teens and sought a substitute home in some employment situation providing board and quarters. Some joined one of the peacetime military services or the merchant marine. Not a few served with the Civilian Conservation Corps during the depression of the thirties. In all of these situations they found what can be called a highly institutionalized way of life. That is, the basic necessities of food, clothing, and shelter were provided for them, there was a fairly regular routine, and demands on individual initiative were at a minimum. After a few years of institutionalized living, at the crucial age period of perhaps 17 to 24 these men found it difficult to adjust to a more independent mode of living in a community. Having spent a number of years in a protected environment they had failed to learn many of the simple amenities for getting along in a normal society. Even the requirements involved with meeting their basic needs were wrought with insecurity. Furthermore, their contemporaries had married, become regularly employed, developed new interests, and progressed far beyond them. The histories of these men show a procession from one type of institutionalized living to another. Railroad and lumber camps, seasonal agricultural employment, work as attendants in public hospitals, casual laboring jobs in resort areas; all of these situations provided the basic food, clothing, and shelter while demanding little of the individual's initiative. In all of these situations drinking is found as a fairly common form of recreation or adjustment to a dull and isolated level of existence. As incentive diminished and health deteriorated, the men gradually became more dependent on missions or shelters or jails, at first between periods of employment and eventually on a fairly constant basis. The so-called skid row areas of our larger cities actually serve as a form of pseudoinstitutionalized setting for these men. Religious and public charities provide facilities for meeting basic needs, and society puts no demands on its skid row inhabitants. Thus, it is suggested that the homeless man has been caught in a spiral of ever-increasing dependency in which alcoholism of a nonaddictive plateau variety is a form of functional adjustment to his routine and low level of existence. When institutionalized living was studied, the histories of 93 percent of the homeless group revealed such a pattern; for at least 70 percent this pattern appeared dominant. . . .

Most of the homeless men studied do not appear to feel that they have a drinking problem. Many recognize quite frankly that alcohol is providing them with a means of going on from day to day and facing life. About 70 percent of one group of about 200 men stated with apparent sincerity and frankness that they desired no change in their drinking practices. Change for these men is frightening and full of insecurity and anxiety. The basic problem for a large segment of these men is one of dependency, not alcohol, and it goes far back in their lives.[26]

These are the men who appear in jails when they are younger and in almshouses when they are older; they are the "harmless drunks" who appear in police courts as petty offenders.[27]

This type of alcoholism, or drunkenness, engaged the attention of early students of social problems. Numerous studies were made to show the relationship between alcoholism and crime, poverty, and divorce.[28] The assumption was that the evils associated with it could be dealt with by legal means. This assumption is no longer accepted.

ADDICTIVE ALCOHOLISM. Quite different in etiology is addictive or peak drinking. Here physiological idiosyncrasies seem to play a large role in reaction to alcohol. We turn therefore to a more detailed discussion of some of the medical aspects of alcoholism.

About a tenth—9 per cent—of the admissions to state mental hospitals in Kansas in 1953 were alcoholic patients. The average length of stay was 61.8 days.[29]

The medical rather than the legal or moral nature of alcoholism may be seen by analyzing the way in which alcoholism operates. Let us assume a hundred men of identical moral character, will power, and responsibility. All are exposed to alcohol. After a period of time, varying for the different men, six of them will lose control of their drinking. Why? "It is impossible from present scientific knowledge to predict with certainty which individual in a drinking group will lose control of the ability to stop drinking if he continues to drink, and which one will remain stable. Will power or lack of will power is not the determining factor." [30]

There seem to be great individual differences in reaction to alcohol and in resistance to its neural depredations. Some people like alcohol and its influence more than others. Similar differences have been found experimentally among rats. In an experiment they were exposed to alcohol as well as to water. They could imbibe as much alcohol as they wanted, whenever they wanted. Some of the rats rejected it; they preferred water. But some imbibed a great quantity; they even preferred it to water.[31] The people who like alcohol will tend to use it more than those who do not care for it. But heavy drinking, even if controlled, if it lasts long enough "is believed to result in a breakdown of metabolic equilibrium, leading to uncontrolled drinking." [32] Theoretically it may be supposed that alcoholism could be induced in anyone, just as it is now believed that emotional or mental breakdown may occur to anyone if the stress is great enough. For any given amount of exposure, however, there are individual differences among human beings. Some succumb easily; others hardly at all. The destructive effects are small in some, great in others. When alcoholism has progressed beyond a certain point, organic damage often results from improper diet and the unhygienic living associated with prolonged drinking bouts.

So far we have been assuming that the one hundred men with whom we began our analysis were identical in character, psychological load, and conflicts. Those who became alcoholics had no more severe emotional difficulties than those who did not. But:

> There is also a relatively small group of drinkers in whom the pathological desire for alcohol appears practically at the beginning of their drinking career, instead of after many years, and can thus lead to a rapid development of alcoholism. Among these will be found certain types of psychopath (e.g., the volitionally weak and the impulsive personalities). It may occur also in certain cases of somatic or mental disorder (for instance, in postconcussion states, epilepsy, certain psychoneuroses, and oligophrenia). There is, however, a minority in this group who show none of these conditions and yet manifest a pathological desire for alcohol from the beginning of their drinking history.[33]

In such cases the alcoholism is secondary to some other illness. We spoke in Chapter 8 of the concept of "masked illness" which public health officers have developed. Similarly it may be said that alcoholism may mask other illnesses. We think we are dealing with alcoholism; actually we may be face to face with something different. It is true that in many cases the basic weakness might never have come to light if the patient had never exposed himself to alcohol, just as many of the men who broke down in battle would never have done so under normal situations. There are perhaps millions of abstainers who have personality difficulties just as serious as those of the alcoholic which will never incapacitate them, for:

Alcoholism, as a form of behavior, is [only] one expression of an emotional disturbance. There are numerous other socially objectionable ways of expressing inadequacy in coping with the stresses and strains of reality. Lying, petty thievery, seclusiveness, inability to meet competition, oversensitiveness, need for attention, impulsive aggression and other domineering traits—these are all commonly observed symptoms of lack of emotional adjustment which exact a heavy toll from the individual and his environment.[34]

But the mentally or emotionally unstable person who resorts to alcohol may distract our attention from his primary illness.

The number of persons suffering from severe mental illness, psychotic or prepsychotic states, who use alcohol because of their condition is unknown, but it is not insignificant. Too often excessive drinking obscures the symptoms of the basic disease. . . . In many so-called alcoholic psychoses the mental illness actually preceded the onset of excessive drinking. The florid alcoholism, in these cases, masks the underlying symptoms and makes the correct diagnosis difficult.[35]

There has been much discussion among students of alcoholism about the nature of the "craving" for alcohol. Is it a physiological phenomenon, like the craving for drugs in those who have become addicted? Or is it psychological? At the present time the consensus of specialists seems to be that during or immediately after a drinking bout, the "craving" for alcohol is indeed physiological in nature; the tissues of the body really suffer withdrawal symptoms which are alleviated by the consumption of more alcohol.[36] But after the bout is over the body returns to a normal condition. The piling up of tensions which then leads to a later drinking bout and "craving" for alcohol is not physiological but psychological in nature.[37] But psychological mechanisms alone do not explain the return to drinking.

In addition, a physiopathological condition (other than physical dependence) cannot be excluded as one of the factors which may lead to the resumption of drinking after days or weeks of abstinence.

In all alcoholics, regardless of whether they have an abnormal disposition or suffer from any acquired mental disorder, one observes a weakening of that part of the higher personality from which the inhibition of primitive tendencies derives. As a result, there appears a release of the primitive side of the personality. The pathological desire for alcohol therefore becomes more evident as the inhibiting forces weaken and ultimately fail.[38]

Exposure to Alcohol

None of this, however, explains the original exposure to alcohol. We are told that originally some uncontrolled drinkers drank to allay physical pain, some drank for the oblivion they achieved from painful experiences, and some drank as a stress reaction, to reduce tensions.[39] But perhaps the commonest motive is "social pressure." What is meant by "social pressure to drink?" Why should there be such pressure? First of all, it should be distinguished from cultural factors. There is probably little social pressure to drink where it is actively frowned upon or where it is widely accepted. Social pressure is probably most important at a time when there is a reaction against a cultural attitude of condemnation but when wide acceptance has not yet become secure. It is a complex phenomenon. In our society at midcentury, "drinking has an uncertain and changing status. While fewer people perhaps now regard it as a sin, it has not yet achieved the uncritical respectability of well-established patterns of social behavior." [40]

On the part of those who exert the pressure the motives may be of many kinds. Urging a guest to drink may be a way of demonstrating affluence. It may be a status symbol: "In certain circles a sense of social superiority is given by having a well filled cellar and a taste in wines of good vintage." [41] For many adults at midcentury, reared in families which disapproved of drinking, it is still a symbol of emancipation from parental control. For others it is a desire to remove the inhibiting or "wet-blanket" effect of a sober person among a group of drinkers.

On the part of those who accept the challenge, the desire to be polite may be operating; they do not want to seem like wet blankets or puritans, not yet emancipated from early 20th-century parental standards.

For both, a subtler process may be at work also. The person who is not afraid to become intoxicated in a group is demonstrating that he is secure and strong enough to be able to lower his guard and render himself helpless. He does not have to protect himself. He has nothing to hide. He can expose himself with impunity. Only persons who prided themselves on their security would be willing to take such chances. There is also pride in being able to hold one's liquor, in being able to drink like a gentleman, or in being able to outdrink others.

This kind of social-pressure drinking is quite different from solitary drinking. Although a person might conceivably be both a social drinker and a solitary drinker, the solitary drinker is less likely to be a secure person exhibiting his security by flaunting his defenses; he is more likely to be an insecure person who is afraid to reduce himself to helplessness in the presence of others, afraid of what he might reveal of his inner difficulties, hostilities, or fears.

The pattern of drinking is usually socially determined. In one study of 478 adults in the state of Washington in 1951 it was found that, in general, patterns of drinking were related to those of friends more than to those of parents. The drinking patterns of wives seemed to be determined by those of husbands.[42]

From our discussion so far it will be noted that the causes of addictive alcoholism are complex, involving cultural, social, and idiosyncratic physiological factors. Perhaps some of them may be visualized in the form of the accompanying paradigm. Any given population may be thought of as distributed along the continuum of two relevant vari-

Funny? Contemptible? Weak-willed? Do these clean, rather well-dressed middle-class people fulfill any of the specifications for the stereotyped alcoholic? Are they "worth" saving? Without help, these men and women might easily end up in a mental hospital suffering from alcoholic psychoses. They have in common an inability to control their drinking. If they drink at all, they drink to excess. Unlike so-called "plateau" drinkers, they want to control their drinking. That is why they are here listening to one of their fellows telling of his experiences. Their only protection against drinking is complete abstinence. But this is much easier said than done. How can you keep from drinking? These people have all admitted to themselves that they cannot do it alone; they need help. They help one another, they understand one another. Here is a group in which they have status. They belong. They can participate in this group without feeling inferior, different, or ashamed. They are surrounded by people who have struggled with the same problems they have. They draw sustenance from one another. There are group rewards to reinforce their new patterns of life.

In addition to such group rewards, Alcoholics Anonymous gives support to the new member struggling with his addiction by providing him with a "helper," a friend who will come whenever called to help overcome the temptation to drink. He will no longer be alone. Even more to the point, Alcoholics Anonymous will assign the helper role to *him* from time to time, so that he can help himself by helping others.

Alcoholics Anonymous was among the first organizations to harness the forces generated in group relationships for therapeutic purposes. Since its inception in 1935, many other therapeutic groups have modeled themselves upon its pattern.

Like all great forces, those generated in groups may be used exploitatively as well as therapeutically. The Communist party exerts a powerful hold over its members by way of its cells, which rely heavily on group roles to keep people in line. Criminal gangs use group-generated forces also. Some observers of the American scene at midcentury express great concern at the increasing dependence on groups that all of us show; one such observer—William Whyte, Jr.—advocates active resistance to group pressures. Do you agree? *(Photo by Pat Coffey, reprinted by courtesy of The Saturday Evening Post, copyright 1955, by Curtis Publishing Co.)*

PARADIGM OF THE CAUSES OF ADDICTIVE ALCOHOLISM *

	Strong appetite or liking for taste or effects of alcohol	Strong repugnance or disliking for taste or effects of alcohol
Have idiosyncratic susceptibility to alcohol	Most likely to develop alcoholism	"Latent" alcoholism present, but not likely to become manifest
Have no idiosyncratic susceptibility to alcohol	If drinking is long continued, metabolic changes may create idiosyncratic susceptibility, as above	Very little likelihood of developing alcoholism

* This paradigm assumes the same cultural background and the same psychological "load" for both categories.

ables, one involving the taste for alcohol or its effects and one involving the peculiar susceptibility or "allergy" which controls the body's reaction to alcohol. If a person has a strong taste for alcohol or its effects the chances are greater that he will be exposed to it than if he has no such taste. But unless he also has the idiosyncratic susceptibility to it, he may never become a problem drinker. If, however, he does continue to drink large quantities over a period of time, apparently tissue changes may occur which create the idiosyncratic reaction which may lead to alcoholism. The person who has no taste for alcohol, even if he has the idiosyncratic susceptibility—who is, actually, a latent or potential "alcoholic" in the physiological sense—will probably never become a problem drinker because, lacking an appetite for alcohol, he is not tempted to indulge in it. And, finally, the person who has neither the taste for alcohol nor the idiosyncratic susceptibility to it is the one who has very little chance of becoming an alcoholic, whatever other neurotic group he may belong in.

However it begins, and whatever the individual differences involved, alcoholism is a major public health problem, involving an estimated million people.[43] So long as attention was focused on drunkenness there was little headway made in dealing with it. It has been only recently that laymen as well as medical men have come to look upon alcohol addiction as a medical problem rather than one of defective character. Once the moral stigma was removed from alcoholism it became possible to deal with it more objectively.[44]

If it were possible to determine in advance who are the people who have the peculiar reaction to alcohol which makes them susceptible to addiction we might forewarn them and thus protect them from alcoholism, or we might develop antibodies through immunization. If we had clear-cut tests by which we could demonstrate to people that the use of alcohol would lead to alcoholism in their cases, we might, conceivably, avoid it in a large proportion of at least the normal cases. It might even become conventional for people to admit in advance that they were alcoholics and therefore must not drink, just as it is conventional now for people to decline foods because they have allergies. In the absence of such tests there is no way to be absolutely sure that one is not an alcoholic and the only way to be certain that one will not become a problem drinker is not to drink.[45]

Treatment

The 19th-century approach to alcoholism was legalistic. Although alcohol is an integral part of the culture of the underworld, the alcoholic is most likely to make his contacts with the law in the lower, rather than in the higher, courts where, on charges of vagrancy or drunkenness, he fills the docket. When deterioration has gone far, he is likely to constitute a large part of the flophouse, jail, and almshouse population. He accounts for a sizable proportion of the cases with alcoholic psychoses. These cases represent the so-called homeless-man type of alcoholism.

The futility of dealing with these men on strictly legal lines becomes increasingly apparent. Thus in at least one community—New York City—a special Social Court for Men has been instituted to handle cases of alcoholism with vagrancy.

"The effort is to change completely the judicial approach to the problem of alcoholism. The approach still is of course penal—we're dealing with the men as if they were criminals, and this despite the fact that it is generally acknowledged that alcoholism is a disease. Eventually I hope we'll be able to deal with the matter as a public health problem and not as a penal problem. Arraigning the men directly on Hart Island is a first step in this direction. Hart Island no longer has prison buildings—all the bars have been removed. By bringing them here directly we will avoid detaining them even temporarily in jail. We'll also end the regrettable practice of mass arraignments of men who are too drunk to understand either the nature of the charge or their rights. . . ." Intoxicated persons should not be accused of disorderly conduct, as most are. They usually are sodden and no threat to the public peace.[46]

This court urges men to avail themselves of spiritual counsel—chaplains of all denominations are available—and the services of Alcoholics Anonymous. The treatment is not rigid or standardized; some reject the new approach and are consigned to jail. Others are given suspended sentences. Some are interviewed by social workers, and plans for rehabilitation are worked out. Although no one claims that this new approach is a panacea, it is definitely a step in the direction of more discriminating and therefore more effective treatment. For many of the men who come to the Court the main problem is one of deep-seated dependency. They need to be taken care of. They have no role repertoire to fall back on. Cure is almost out of the question; there is too little to work with.

In general, it might be said that for those for whom alcoholism is secondary to some other pathology—not necessarily dependency—no treatment is likely to be successful. But for those in whom there is no underlying pathology and who have no more psychological load than others but do have the idiosyncratic reaction to alcohol which leads to addiction, certain kinds of treatment which support them in abstinence are successful. For although there is no known cure for alcoholism as yet,[47] it can be kept under control by complete abstinence.

In the late 1930's and early 1940's three new approaches to the problems of alcoholism appeared. The most spectacular was Alcoholics Anonymous, organized in 1935. It has a record of success in about two thirds of its cases, which is better than almost any other type of treatment. It invokes a religious sanction and relies heavily on the forces generated in group relationships. One of the most important aspects of its treatment is that of creating role relationships for its members. In order to remain "cured" members must spend some time helping others to stay sober. This is apparently just the kind of role that can be most therapeutic to the alcoholic. For once he is not in the position of the inferior, of the inadequate, of the failure; he is in the role of the helper, the one who can do something for someone else. These helping roles are assigned so that the helper and the helped are "matched" in status, for a homeless-man alcoholic could not be of much assistance to a Park Avenue alcoholic. In addition to reaching alcoholics in higher socioeconomic status than formerly, the organization now tries to help people before they become seriously ill. It is now reaching for the "menacing nuisance," the person who is just losing control of his drinking. The membership of Alcoholics Anonymous is a secret; some index of its size may be gleaned from the fact that the first edition of "The Big Book" sold 300,000 copies. It also publishes a monthly magazine, *The Grapevine*.

Community clinics constitute a second new approach. They began in Hartford and New Haven under the guidance and leadership of the Yale University Center of Alcohol Studies in 1944; by 1954 there were eighty such clinics in different parts of the country. Internists, psychiatrists, clinical psychologists, and psychiatric social workers work as a team in these clinics. Hospital facilities are usually available for acute phases of alcoholism; convalescent services and outpatient clinic guidance are available for those who are recovering. An effort is made to help the alcoholic re-establish his role relationships.

Such clinics are most useful for the addictive type of alcoholism; they are of little help for the non-addictive type. In fact, the non-addictive alcoholics avoid them.

For homeless men, treatment in an outpatient clinic presents all sorts of difficulties. In most instances they are without any type of permanent tie which would help them sustain contact. The outpatient clinic is severely handicapped in trying to work with such men by the fact that before it can even begin to consider their drinking problem it must try to solve their immediate economic problem—find them a place to sleep and some sort of a job and perhaps clothing. Furthermore, a majority of these men are not motivated towards accepting any "help" with their drinking problem. It was found that when a group of 50 homeless men were offered the services of the Yale Plan Clinic, only 10 were sufficiently interested to make even one visit to the clinic and none continued visits long enough to allow effective diagnosis or treatment. For many of these men the idea of a "clinic"—in a strange setting where people will be well dressed, where there will be close intimate contact with strangers, and where they may be examined and certainly will be questioned—is terribly frightening. They will go to considerable extremes to avoid such a situation.[48]

The third new approach takes the form of setting up voluntary and official agencies; in 1955 there were such agencies in about sixty cities, most of them affiliated with the National Committee on Alcoholism, founded in 1944. In 1945 Connecticut passed legislation providing for tax-supported education and treatment facilities and by 1954, forty-three states had such agencies. Educating the public with respect to alcoholism is a large part of the function of such agencies. In brief:

Activities directed against alcoholism. . . . centered in the police department, the jail and the divorce court, generally without success [are being supplanted] by medical-psychological treatment in combination with measures of rehabilitation [which] show promise of good results. People must be educated to the value of establishing tax-supported treatment facilities and encouraging preventive measures. The economic saving to the community will more than offset the expenditures entailed.[49]

It is interesting to note, finally, that in evaluating treatment, the criteria of adequate role performance are considered more important than abstinence alone. Thus:

The man who may have stopped drinking altogether but then becomes so difficult to live with that his wife left him and he lost his job would certainly not be rated as improved. On the other hand, a patient who had continued to drink would be rated as improved if his drinking pattern showed longer periods of sobriety and if at the same time he was developing insight and was considered an easier person with whom to live and work.[50]

Narcotics Addiction

As a Social Problem

That the use of narcotics is dysfunctional to a social system is shown by the almost universal attempts of governments to control it. It has been alleged that the Japanese used addiction as a weapon when they invaded China. And the same allegation is made with respect to the Cold War.

. . . opium has become a weapon in the cold war. The smuggling of narcotics into the United States has become a deliberate, organized and increasingly successful policy of world communism.[51]

The effect of narcotics addiction on role performance depends on a number of factors. The use of narcotics does not itself deteriorate the nervous system. The addict who has certain access to narcotics so that he does not have to worry about his supply may show little deterioration over a fairly long period of time.[52] A patient, for example, suffering from a painful and incurable disease who is ensured of a supply of drugs, who does not have to resort to crime to obtain them, and who is not in constant fear of being deprived or left unsupplied, may not be detected or known to be a user by his friends.

As a matter of fact, however, persons dependent on drugs often find them so expensive that role impairment of some kind is common. "Most addicts were known to medical and police authorities within two years after they contracted the habit. The average [daily] expenditures for drugs were about $10.00." The maintenance of addiction "is so expensive that most addicts cannot possibly maintain their supply of drugs without resort to vice. . . . From shoplifting and petty thievery, the addict quickly graduates to major crime." [53] The role impairments and pathologies so often observed in addicts result, then, in large part from the uncertainty of supply and the dependence on illegal sources of supply. As in the case of alcoholism, of course, the drug addiction may be a symptom of some other illness and the role impairment may be caused by this "masked" pathology as well as by the addiction. In any event, a certain amount of role impairment seems to characterize most known addicts.

Extent, Trends, and Incidence

The extent of narcotics addiction, like that of all problems which are related to illegal activities, is not exactly known. In 1955 the Federal Narcotics Commissioner estimated that there were about 60,000 narcotics addicts in the United States. Most of these cases were in New York (9,458), Illinois (7,172), and California (2,350).[54] These figures do not include persons who use marijuana, since it is not considered a habit-forming drug.

Whether or not drug addiction is increasing is difficult to determine since records are so incomplete. In 1877 the estimated number of addicts, as of 1874, was 251,936; in 1913, the estimate was 782,118; in 1915, it was 269,000; in 1918, 1,000,000; in 1920, 396,978; in 1924, 110,000; in 1925–26 there were 52,955 legally supplied cases and an estimated total of 88,964 cases. In 1931 it was still true that:

> There is no reliable information as to whether or not opium addiction is increasing or decreasing in the United States at the present time. Whatever the exact figures in the United States and other countries may be, the extent of opium addiction is sufficiently great to indicate the existence of a major medico-sociologic problem.[55]

The long-term trend would seem definitely to be down; but there are probably fluctuations up and down. The figure for 1955, for example, which gave a rate of less than 1 in 3,000, was considerably higher than the ratio—1 in 10,000—of those rejected for military service because of addiction in World War II; and this difference could not be wholly a result of the age composition of the military population since about half of the known addicts are in the 21–30 age group. The war period was considered the lowest ebb in the narcotics traffic since the enactment of federal control legislation in 1914. There has been a sharp increase in the use of drugs since the war, especially heroin.

We have already noted the geographic incidence—New York, Illinois, and California showing the highest rates. So far as age is concerned, the largest proportion of addicts—50.3 per cent—is reported in the 21 to 30 age group; 19.4 per cent in the 31 to 40 age group; and 13.1 per cent in the under-21 group. Reports of large numbers of juvenile users of drugs were not substantiated by the survey cited above, but data to be presented below indicate that drugs are widely experimented with in some gangs.

The public attitude toward drug addictions is very much like the attitude toward alcoholism before the 1930's. There is shame and disgrace associated with it. There *appears* to be a greater incidence of this pathology in the lower socioeconomic classes, where it cannot be hidden, than in the higher socioeconomic classes, where it can. Most of what we know about drug addicts, therefore, refers to a very biased sample. We do not know about the physicians, pharmacists, nurses, musicians, actors, entertainers, and others with incomes equal to the demands of the habit, or with access to supplies. They do not appear on police blotters or, therefore, in the records. For the present, then, we do not know the class incidence of drug addiction.

Exposure to Addiction

In some parts of the world exposure to addiction is not only widespread but is actually stimulated as part of a cultural pattern. The use of cocaine among workers in South America, for example, is encouraged in order to make them more exploitable.

Many writers are opposed to prohibition of the use of the drug [in South America] because they fear that serious labor and economic upheavals would result, since, while physically and mentally deteriorating effects eventually develop on continued use, individuals using it can subsist on a minimum of food while expending a maximum of energy.[56]

In most parts of the world, however, exposure to addiction is viewed as a serious problem, and an effort is made to protect people from it.

In the United States some people become exposed in the course of medical treatment; wars expose many others. The Civil War increased addiction so greatly that after 1865 it was called "the army disease." [57] Patent medicines at one time exposed people to the use of opiates. But nonmedical exposure is perhaps far greater today. "Association, curiosity, bravado" account for exposure in a very large proportion of cases.[58] In this connection a recent study of heroin use by street gangs in New York City is especially illuminating.[59]

The 305 members of 18 gangs were studied with respect to use of and attitudes toward the use of heroin. More than half—54 per cent— had never used either heroin or marijuana; one fourth were using heroin at the time of the study, and 5 per cent had stopped using it. By and large, the users were older than the nonusers. They were more delinquent, also, but this might have been related to the fact that they were somewhat older than the nonusers. The nonusers showed more opposition to the use of heroin and more hostile or derogatory attitudes toward regular users. But the nonusers who were in clubs in which more than half of the members were users were more tolerant of users than were those in clubs in which less than half were users. So far as gang activities were concerned, the nonusers participated more than users in "rumbles" (gang fights), but less in robbery and burglary. The users participated more in club-organized sexual delinquency, but less in active sports. The nonusers took more part in club dances and house parties than the users.

The picture that emerged from this study was something like this: during adolescence, that is, up to the age of eighteen, the gangs favor "rumbles," fighting, sports, and, in general, activities in which they can act out their problems. They gain security for their members by having them share experiences and by offering them the protection of the group. When the members become older, however, sports and other active programs begin to seem "like kid stuff" and are given up. Individual concerns, such as work and girls, become paramount, leaving less interest in gang activities. The normal young persons make the transition fairly smoothly. They withdraw from the gang, which now seems too juvenile for them, and take their place in the adult world, finding through their jobs and marriage new worker and family roles to take the place of gang roles.

But some members, it was found, could not make this transition. They became disturbed. They became anxious because others were succeeding, and no longer needed gang protection. But they still needed it and they were being deprived of it by the withdrawal of others. There was nothing to take the place of the old gang role and the old gang activities. Drugs offered a consoling substitute. They could forget girls, status problems, work; "they could remain children forever."

From this it appears that by the age of eighteen practically all the boys who live in gang areas of New York City have been exposed to the use of heroin. About half never themselves use it in spite of the "anything for kicks" tradition of gang culture. The gang itself does not exert pressure on its members to use heroin; more gang pressure was reported against its use than in favor of it. "Stay with us, we'll protect you" was the gang attitude. Interestingly enough, it was the actively delinquent gangs which most disapproved of users, partially no doubt because the use of heroin was a competing activity and detracted from more active pursuits. Gang membership per se cannot explain addiction. Some members succumbed, some did not. Why?

nals, but th
cuss them in

Althou
alcoholic or
of illness wh
persons gar
drugs do for
in a country

Miss A.
ticket. She h
could not b
founded by
deprived of
then did she
been unable
habitual che
you might e

There are
similar opia

The e
only neurot
one of mar
alcoholics,6
gambler is
common er
stant." 65

Unlik
pulsive gar
documente
establishme
reports of
the more l
from class
certain.

. . . th
by the arist
has attracte
it, gambling
pervasive ir
ment of mi
and numbe
have found

Etiology

The role explanation given above is very persuasive. The use of drugs was a solace, a substitute for gang activities for those who could not make the transition to adult roles, who clung to the role patterns of their adolescence. But the question still remains, Why did they select this substitute rather than some other?

And why is it that some recovered patients, when "the drug has been withdrawn . . . bear the incidental suffering, and when it is over . . . rejoice in their release and are not inclined voluntarily to use the drug again" [60] whereas others cannot relinquish its use?

In some cases resort to drugs is a symptom of some other pathology, just as alcoholism sometimes is. In these cases the true illness is something else and the addiction is a "mask." The phenomenon which demands explanation here is the original illness rather than the addiction.

But why do some seemingly normal people become addicts more readily than others? We may invoke here some of the same elements of stress resistance which were used to explain stress resistance among prisoners of war in Chapter 6. The subjective values of the person susceptible to addiction are such that the rewards of using the drug seem greater than those of not using it. His conception of his role may be defective. He may receive inadequate support from others in his role network in resisting the drug.

Sociological explanations of drug addiction in terms of role relationships contribute to our understanding of the etiology of this illness. But we need not dismiss the physiological explanations. Perhaps there is some physiological idiosyncrasy, similar to that reported for alcoholics, which renders those who have it more susceptible than others to the influence of drugs. We are not confronted with an either-or choice here; both sociological and physiological explanations may be accepted. They are not mutually exclusive. Until we have studied drug addiction in a truly random sample rather than primarily in status-biased ones, we will have to be very tentative in our etiological interpretations.

Treatment

The treatment of drug addictions is in much the same stage of development as was that of alcoholism until recently. Much of the difficulty of the drug addict is related to the cultural context in which the addiction occurs. He is viewed as an outcast, and comes in time to accept

Whether or not there is a long-time trend up or down in the extent of compulsive gambling there is no way of knowing, since there are no records. We do know that for many decades communities have had to grapple with the problems associated with gambling. But just as not all drinking is identical with alcoholism, not all gambling is identical with compulsive gambling.

Perhaps by analogy with the distinction made among alcoholics, we might speak of peak gambling and plateau gambling. In the peak type, the object is to bring oneself to a high peak of excitement as soon as possible, not to make the excitement last as long as possible. In the plateau type, the attempt is to spread the gambling over a period of time. Roulette, horse-race betting, and dice-throwing illustrate the peak type. Regular buying of numbers and lottery tickets, even weekly bingo games, might illustrate the plateau type. The first seeks an exhilarating effect, the second, a narcotic or daydream effect.

The compulsive gambler has been distinguished from the criminal and the percentage gambler so far as motivation is concerned, as follows:

Generally, the motivation of the compulsive gambler is self-destruction or rebellion; of the criminal gambler, rebellion; of the percentage gambler (the bridge or chess master, for example), the abnormal sublimation of the mock struggle for fear of the real one. The compulsive gambler must be a dare-devil, the criminal gambler must get something for nothing, the percentage gambler must have victory regardless of the intrinsic value of the reward.[67]

Psychoanalysts—Simmel, Freud, Reik, Laforgue, Jones, Bergler, Greenson, and Lindner—have analyzed the gambling neurosis in terms of: reversion to infantile ways of securing narcissistic supplies (food, love, comfort, and attention); pervasive conflict over or substitute for masturbation; seeking for oracular answers to questions which plague the patient; the eroticization of fear; the sublimation of oedipal aggression; unconscious aggression and self-punishment, rebellion against the reality principle embodied in logic, and psychic masochism; tension relief necessitated by infantile sense of danger; a method of warding off impending depression.[68] According to these students, gamblers seem to have in common these traits: great aggressiveness, unconscious hostility and resentment, chronic masturbation. Their aggression has been traced by one student to their relationships with domineering, moralistic, authoritarian fathers.[69] Whatever the etiology of this illness may be—infantilism, conflict, fear, aggression, masochism, rebellion—it expresses itself in ways that are likely to be destructive of normal role performance. Compulsive gambling is likely to be dysfunctional both to the victim's family and to the community as a whole.

The compulsive gambler shows role impairment especially in family relationships. He is likely to spend money on gambling that is needed for family use. Since gambling debts must be paid, he may resort to crime to pay them. The dysfunctionality of compulsive gambling cannot itself be documented; but the dysfunctionality of gambling as an industry is one of the best documented phenomena of community life.

Although gambling may not be criminal, its viciousness lies in the fact that it gradually corrupts city, state, and Federal Government agencies; it pays off regularly to political machines; it imports strong-arm men and gangsters to enforce its jurisdictions; it nominates and elects public officials; it constitutes a powerful and semilegitimate front for the underworld. On its heels come the harlot, the pimp, the pick-pocket, the narcotics peddler, the safe-cracker, the stick-up man, the blackmailer, the extortionist, the professional thief, the confidence man, the labor racketeer, the municipal fixer, the shakedown copper, the machine boss, the corrupt judge, and other paid protectors of crime less easily condoned than gambling.[70]

This is the environment in which the compulsive gambler is likely to seek the solution to his problems.

Compulsive gamblers rarely seek treatment for their illness. And if they do, they almost never continue the treatment until the end.[71] Since the compulsive gambler is not suffering from any form of poisoning, as the alcoholic or the drug addict may be, the medical treatment is exclusively psychotherapy.

We do not here enter into a discussion of the long history of gambling as a community problem, so picturesquely described in the quotation above, nor of the various legal methods that have been used to attempt to control it. In general, gambling as a business has, with specified exceptions, been forbidden by law. It continues to flourish, however, because, as pointed out above, there are enough occasional compulsive gamblers to support it at a profitable level and because, as we shall see in Chapter 21, there are enough men who find a congenial occupation in the administration of gambling as a business.

None of the remaining pathologies we are going to discuss in Part IV are the result of germs, as in the case of the Black Death and the venereal diseases, or of physical or mental defect or handicap, or of ingested poisons, as in the case of alcoholism and drug addictions. Rather, they are, as is compulsive gambling, the result of sociogenic forces operating in a particular cultural setting. First we shall discuss the so-called stress diseases and, after these, the mental illnesses. But there is no implication in the underlying logic of our presentation that the stress diseases are intrinsically related to the mental illnesses. The victims of the stress diseases are not mentally ill.

NOTES

1 About a tenth—9 per cent—of those admitted to state mental hospitals in Kansas in 1953 were alcoholic patients; the average length of stay was 61.8 days. "The Kansas State Commission on Alcoholism Activities in 1953–1954," *Quarterly Journal of Studies on Alcohol,* 16 (March 1955), p. 211.

2 John L. Thomas, S.J., *The American Catholic Family* (Prentice-Hall, 1956), pp. 220–221.

3 Raymond G. McCarthy and Edgar M. Douglass, *Alcohol and Social Responsibility, A New Educational Approach* (Crowell, 1949), p. 130.

4 The use of alcohol as a reaction to stress has been widely permitted in many cultures, and hence may be termed "functional." This is not identical, however, with alcoholism. It might be argued that even in such cultures some other way of performing the same function might be more effective and efficient.

5 McCarthy and Douglass, *op. cit.,* p. 125.

6 World Health Organization, *Expert Committee on Mental Health, Alcoholism Subcommittee, Second Report,* Technical Report Series No. 48 (Aug. 1952), p. 16.

7 McCarthy and Douglass, *op. cit.,* p. 48.

8 John W. Riley and Charles F. Marden, "The Social Pattern of Alcoholic Drinking," *Quarterly Journal of Studies on Alcohol,* 8 (Sept. 1947), pp. 265–273.

9 There was an opposite trend in Canada. The proportion of men who were drinkers jumped from 72 per cent in 1943 to 81 per cent in 1956; the increase for women was from 45 per cent in 1943 to 62 per cent in 1956. (Gallup poll release for February 19, 1956.)

10 The word "apparent" qualifies all recorded consumption figures because they do not take account of consumption of illegally manufactured and sold beverages. In the period 1945–1949 average consumption of beer and other malt drinks per capita was 18 gallons; in 1950 it was 17. Comparable figures for hard liquors were 5 quarts and 4 quarts; for wine, however, 3 and 4, respectively. (F. J. Dewhurst *et al., America's Needs and Resources* [Twentieth Century, 1955], pp. 134–135.)

11 McCarthy and Douglass, *op. cit.,* p. 58.

12 E. M. Jellinek, *Recent Trends in Alcoholism and in Alcohol Consumption* (Hillhouse, 1947).

13 "The Kansas State Commission on Alcoholism Activities in 1953–1954," *Quarterly Journal of Studies on Alcohol,* 16 (March 1955), pp. 210–211.

14 United States Census Bureau, *Current Population Reports,* P–25, 121 (Sept. 1955), p. 6.

15 A Gallup poll news release dated September 26, 1951, reported 57,500,000 drinkers twenty-one years of age and over. Dr. Karl M. Bowman, medical superintendent of the Langley Porter Clinic in San Francisco, speaking before the American Psychological Association, August 1955, estimated that there were 70,000,000 drinkers. He estimated that 5,000,000 drank to excess at times, a somewhat higher figure than the one here arrived at. He reported that 1,000,000 were alcohol addicts. (*New York Times,* August 31, 1955.)

16 Jellinek, *op. cit.,* p. 47.

17 Raymond Pearl, "Biological Aspects of Alcohol," *Encyclopaedia of the Social Sciences,* Vol. 1 (Macmillan, 1930), p. 622. "Heavy drinking . . . definitely reduces the expectation of life at all ages from thirty to seventy."

18 Male rats show higher preference and intake of alcohol than females. See M. Schadewald, G. A. Emerson, W. T. Moore, and B. M. Moore, "Voluntary Preference for Alcohol of White Rats after Gonadectomy," *Federal Proceedings,* Part I, 12 (1953), pp. 364–365.

19 Mark Keller and Vera Efron, "Alcoholism in the Big Cities of the United States," *Quarterly Journal of Studies on Alcohol,* 17 (March 1956), p. 69.

20 *Ibid.,* p. 70.

21 Riley and Marden, *loc. cit.*

22 McCarthy and Douglass, *op. cit.,* p. 187.

23 Robert Straus, "Alcoholism," in Arnold Rose, ed., *Mental Health and Mental Disorder* (Norton, 1955), pp. 441–447.

24 *Ibid.,* pp. 444–445.

25 John Haverstick, " 'The Big Book': Bible for Alcoholics," *Saturday Review,* August 27, 1955, p. 17.

26 Straus, *op. cit.,* pp. 445–446.

27 Irwin Deutscher, "The White Petty Offender in the Small City," *Social Problems,* 1 (Oct. 1953), pp. 70–73; Albert D. Ullman, Harold W. Demone,

Jr., A. Warren Stearns, and Norman F. Washburne, "Some Social Characteristics of Misdemeanants," *Eastern Sociological Society*, April 1956.

28 George E. G. Catlin summarizes some of these studies in "Alcoholism," *Encyclopaedia of the Social Sciences*, Vol. 1 (Macmillan, 1930), pp. 626–627.

29 "The Kansas State Commission on Alcoholism Activities in 1953–1954," *Quarterly Journal of Studies on Alcohol*, 16 (March 1955), pp. 210–211.

30 McCarthy and Douglass, *op. cit.*, p. 187.

31 R. J. Williams, L. J. Berry, and E. Burstecher, "Genetotrophic Diseases: Alcoholism," *Texas Reports on Biology and Medicine*, 8 (1950), pp. 238–256. Several interpretations have been made of the behavior of rats. One hypothesizes "that rats drink alcohol, at least in part, because of the emotional relaxation which results. Further, it might be expected that the greater the need for emotional relaxation, the more alcohol will be consumed." An alternative explanation hypothesizes "a nutritional basis for alcohol consumption, whereby deficiency, especially of certain vitamins, can result in an addiction to alcohol. Deficiency may occur even while animals receive a standard and presumably sufficient diet; such a deficiency results from genetic factors which determine an animal's ability to utilize the necessary nutritional elements in its diet." (W. N. Dember and A. B. Kristofferson, "The Relation between Free-Choice Alcohol Consumption and Susceptibility to Audiogenic Seizures," *Quarterly Journal of Studies on Alcohol*, 16 (March 1955), p 86.

32 R. G. Bell, "Blood Alcohol Levels and Toxic Drinking," *University of Toronto Medical Journal*, 30 (1953), pp. 133–139.

33 Formulation of the Joint Expert Committees on Mental Health and on Alcohol, " 'Craving' for Alcohol," *Quarterly Journal of Studies on Alcohol*, 16 (March 1955), p. 64.

34 McCarthy and Douglass, *op. cit.*, pp. 232–233.

35 *Ibid.*, p. 111.

36 M. Wellman, "The Late Withdrawal Symptoms of Alcoholic Addiction," *Canadian Medical Association Journal*, 70 (1954), pp. 526–529. "The late withdrawal symptoms as they occur in some alcoholics who give up drinking are described [as] . . . most severe during the first 6 months of abstinence; [they] diminish in intensity and frequency in the following months but may occur as late as after 5 or 10 years of abstinence. The syndrome consists of irritability, depression, insomnia, fatigue, restlessness and a 'sense of aloneness and distractibility.' Physical signs include a red face, heavy perspiration, elevated pulse and lowered blood pressure. There is confusion and occasionally anxiety. Thirst for alcoholic beverages is not a constant feature and is more common in patients aged over 30. The manner in which the withdrawal symptoms manifest themselves indicates that they 'have their foundation in the physical changes resulting from continued excessive drinking.' "

37 The Freudian theory attributes alcoholism to repressed homosexuality (Catlin, *op. cit.*, p. 625); a modern psychiatrist states that "it is rooted in a distortion of the early mother-child relationships" (Giorgio Lolli, "Alcoholism as a Disorder of the Love Disposition," *Quarterly Journal of Studies on Alcohol*, 17 [March 1956], p. 106). Since not all people who have these maladies become alcoholics, however, more research is needed for any psychological explanation.

38 Formulation of the Joint Expert Committees on Mental Health and on Alcohol, *loc. cit.*, pp. 63–64.

39 Bell, *op. cit.*, pp. 133–139.

40 Riley and Marden, *loc. cit.*

41 Catlin, *op. cit.*, p. 625.

42 John L. Haer, "Drinking Patterns and the Influence of Friends and Family," *Quarterly Journal of Studies on Alcohol*, 16 (March 1955), pp. 181–182.

43 The estimated number varies from about nine hundred thousand, if the Gallup poll figures for 1951 are taken as a base, to over a million, if computation is made on the basis of census figures.

44 At du Pont Company "the problem drinker's immediate supervisor refers him to the medical division, where he is examined. Attempts are made to explain to him that he has a disease which is interfering with his life and chance of success. Treatment is offered and he is urged to join Alcoholics Anonymous. If the patient does not recognize his problem during the course of three months, he is dismissed. Over a period of 10 years, 350 employees (65 per cent of those treated) have been rehabilitated. The total cost of the program is estimated at less than $100,000; total gains

cannot be measured." (T. H. Hogshead, "Problem Drinking in Industry," *Archives of Industrial Hygiene,* 9 [1954], pp. 526–529.)

45 McCarthy and Douglass, *op. cit.,* p. 111.

46 Chief Magistrate John M. Murtagh, as reported in the *New York Times,* September 20, 1955.

47 Medical therapy, especially antabuse, is used in some cases but is not considered a cure.

48 Straus, *op. cit.,* p. 444.

49 McCarthy and Douglass, *op. cit.,* p. 187.

50 Straus, *op. cit.,* p. 443.

51 Governor Harriman in a special message to the legislature, as reported in the *New York Times,* February 18, 1956.

52 Because of this peculiar characteristic of the drug addict, it has been proposed that known cases be supplied by public health clinics at moderate cost, in order to eliminate the necessity for criminal behavior to obtain supplies and also to eliminate the exploitative vender. Dr. Hubert S. Howe, chairman of the New York Academy of Medicine's Subcommittee on Narcotics, proposed such a clinic in New York City in 1955. He said: " 'The purpose of the clinics would be to keep addicts supplied with enough narcotics to meet their physical needs. In this way,' he said, 'they would become employable and would not be tempted to steal to pay black market prices to satisfy their craving.' Dr. Howe said a narcotics addict could be a useful member of society without being cured of his habit. He said the Academy's proposal faced the unfortunate reality that there is as yet no permanent cure for most addicts. Under the clinic plan, Dr. Howe said, patients would receive injections at the clinics and not be permitted to take narcotics home. They would have to agree to an examination to determine the amount they really needed, and would get psychiatric treatment, job placement aid and other help. Judge Goldstein said records of General Sessions for the last five years showed that 99 per cent of the convicted narcotics peddlers were also users. He said 30 per cent of those convicted of any crime were narcotics addicts. This showed, he said, how the need for money to buy drugs induces crime." (*New York Times,* September 20, 1955.) In addition to obviating the necessity of crime to pay for drugs, the clinics would reduce the in-

centive of venders to create new addicts or customers. The plan was opposed, however, as not feasible. It had been tried, both in 1919 and in 1929, and proved a "disastrous failure" (*ibid.*).

53 *New York Times,* January 4, 1955.

54 *New York Times,* June 3, 1955. The number of addicts was estimated on the basis of a five-year survey begun in January 1953, by the Bureau of Narcotics. By April 28, 1955, 28,514 had been counted. The report was by Dr. Harry J. Anslinger, Federal Narcotics Commissioner, to the Senate Judiciary Subcommittee.

55 C. E. Terry, "Drug Addiction," *Encyclopaedia of the Social Sciences,* Vol. 5 (Macmillan, 1931), p. 249.

56 *Ibid.,* p. 251.

57 *Ibid.,* p. 244.

58 A. R. Lindesmith, "A Sociological Theory of Drug Addiction," *Quarterly Journal of Sociology,* 48 (Jan. 1938), pp. 593–609; also his "The Drug Addict as a Psychopath," *American Sociological Review,* 5 (Dec. 1940), pp. 914–920. This author, who has made a thorough analysis of the sociological and social-psychological aspects of drug addiction, points out that in order for addiction—in the sense of a powerful motivation to obtain drugs—to occur, there must be a recognition of the relationship between the withdrawal symptoms and drug deprivation. If there is no such recognition the person suffers through the withdrawal symptoms or dies from the drug deprivation. If he survives the withdrawal symptoms he probably does not remain an addict. From time to time the medical literature reports cases of infants born with prenatally acquired addictions. They are treated like other addicts, with gradually tapered off doses of the drug until the symptoms disappear. Otherwise they might die. Such cases of purely physiological addiction are probably very rare.

59 Based on a paper presented by Eva Rosenfeld at the meetings of the Eastern Sociological Society, March 1956.

60 Terry, *op. cit.,* p. 247.

61 In 1939 the rate for deaths and suicides from the use of barbiturates was 3.2 per million population in the United States; in 1954, 6.5. In England and Wales the rates increased from 1.4 to 13 between 1939 and 1954. (*New York Times,* April 14, 1956.)

62 Robert M. Lindner, "The Psychodynamics of Gambling," *Annals of the American Academy of Political and Social Science,* 269 (May 1950), p. 96.

63 Case from the author's files.

64 Lindner, *op. cit.,* p. 96.

65 Albert H. Morehead, "The Professional Gambler," *ibid.,* p. 84.

66 Collis Stocking, "Gambling," *Encyclopaedia of the Social Sciences,* Vol. 6 (Macmillan, 1931), p. 557.

67 Morehead, *op. cit.,* p. 91.

68 Lindner, *op. cit.,* pp. 93–95.

69 *Ibid.,* p. 107.

70 David W. Maurer, "The Argot of the Dice Gambler," *ibid.,* p. 114.

71 Lindner, *op. cit.,* pp. 105–106.

12

Role Impairment:

The Stress Diseases

Psychosocial Medicine

In Chapter 6 we discussed the concept of social pathology, pointing out that some authors used this term to refer to certain situations within a society whereas others used it to refer to a society or culture or community which was, in their opinion, ill. At this point we introduce a discussion of what one student calls psychosocial medicine, which "is based on the application of the concepts of psychosomatic medicine to the illnesses of communities and social groups." [1] It refers actually to the illnesses of individuals, but to illnesses in which the etiology is often traceable to the community, not to germs or to nutritional defects: to illnesses which are, in brief, sociosomatic in nature.[2]

Although all illness is a sociological phenomenon, as we have seen, because of its impact on role and on the functioning of the social structure, the sociosomatic illnesses are sociological in a special way. They are, in fact, a kind of communication, a form of protest. They constitute

Psychosocial Medicine

The Language of the Stress Diseases

The Psychosomatic Illnesses

The Pseudo-Illnesses: The Hysterias

The Half-Illnesses: Mild Anxiety States

a language by themselves, with a vocabulary of symptoms and a grammar of incidence. It is only recently, and especially since World War II, that scientists are beginning to decipher this language, to interpret it to us, to tell us what these illnesses mean. The content of this communication gives a picture of our society today. Certain conditions in our society produce sociosomatic illnesses in large numbers of people; it is in this unique sense that we speak of social pathologies in this chapter.

The 19th century saw tremendous strides made in the conquest of the infectious diseases, the early 20th, in the nutritional diseases. The second half of the 20th century will probably see equal progress made in learning to master the sociosomatic illnesses, which until recently were "masked," or at least little attended to. Not all illnesses can be fruitfully approached by the concepts of psychosocial medicine; the mass diseases referred to above do not profit greatly by application of them.[3] But many other diseases may benefit.

The Language of the Stress Diseases

Any translation distorts the original to some extent. But if we could translate the messages communicated by the stress illnesses they would take some such form as this, for example: "The role you have assigned to me is intolerable; I cannot perform it with any satisfaction; I want some other role!" A study of 1,297 representative employees, mainly telephone operators of the New York Telephone Company, based on complete attendance and medical records, found that the average time lost by these women in 1950 was 22.2 days. But there was a large difference in health records between those who were satisfied with their roles and those who were not.

The well women had been content, comfortable and secure in their life situations. The ill women, however, had been made unhappy, insecure, and discontented by repeated frustrations, deprivations, unrewarded responsibility, and interpersonal conflicts throughout their adult lives. Nearly all of the well women were women who had had no great desire to be married and who had been quite content with a career as single women and telephone operators. They were individuals who were able to make friends readily. They were. . . . capable of diffuse emotional attachments. . . . Among these women there were many instances of profound loyalty and deep attachment to parents, brothers and sisters, or husbands, but the loss of these individuals from their lives led to no prolonged disturbance of their mood or behavior. . . . The group of women who were ill were quite in contrast to the group who had been well. This group of women had nearly all desired to be married and to have a family which was supported by a husband. They had gone to work as telephone operators with the idea that they would work for a few years, accumulate savings and a few worldly goods, and then be married and stop working. For one reason or another they had been frustrated in this goal. Some had been saddled with ill parents for whose care they were responsible. They had therefore felt unable or unwilling to be married and had continued in a state of resentment and frustration thereafter. Others had married only to find that their marriages soon dissolved. . . . Some of these women were left with young children to support. Several, because of their religious beliefs, felt precluded from obtaining a divorce or making another marriage. They had, therefore, returned to telephone operating as a necessary means of making a living. . . . As a group, they were women of ambition.[4]

Another message, communicated by the bodies of miners in British coal-mining towns during a long period of unemployment in the 1930's, might be translated as: "Give us a work role! You have robbed us of our status in work groups!" The following is an illustration:

Increasing unemployment consequent upon the decline of the heavy industries in Britain and the altering state of world economy deprived many miners of their occupational group and thus disrupted their social pattern not only for working but also for living. As mass unemployment was also a feature of the larger community, membership of a new occupational group was difficult to achieve. Emotionally isolated, the unemployed miners rapidly lost the sense of social purpose and the "life energy," being denied expression in life-constructive activities, became turned-in to attack both the "self" and the "society," that is, it became life destructive instead of life creative. A neat example of these phenomena is provided by Dr. R. S. Brock in his account of miner's nystagmus: "Whenever large numbers of men were discharged from a pit there was at once a rush to be certified [for public assistance]. Many of these men declared quite frankly that they could work if only they had a chance to do so, but, as they often added, a man must live. Yet having once been certified—the die having been cast—many of them proceeded to develop chronic neuroses and a depressed and melancholy state of mind.[5]

We hasten to insert an important caveat at this point. We should not conclude that the stress illnesses are deliberate, purposive, or voluntary in the usual sense. They do not constitute malingering, nor are they rationally selected as means to an end. Indeed, they bypass the "self." They are physiological responses to "sociopathogenic" forces. They are, as we shall see, "inept" physiological responses which were once "apt" ways of meeting old-fashioned stress factors. They are somatic as well as social in nature. And they communicate messages which the well-trained physician can understand, even when the patient cannot.

The Psychosomatic Illnesses

If a daily exposure of the blood stream to some chemical—say, lead poison—produces well-defined pathologies in the tissue of a given organ, we find this of routine scientific interest. If the chemical is injected not from the outside but from some other organ within the body we are amazed at the results. We speak of psychosomatic illness as though it were somehow unreal or imaginary, "all in the mind." Actually the pathologies are just as real, the lesions just as painful, whether the pathogenic agent comes from outside or from inside the body.

The human body, as we pointed out in Chapter 4, is prepared to deal with a great many threats or stresses from the outside world. It is prepared to act vigorously, or to lie low. It is prepared to respond to food deprivation for short periods of time. It can handle excesses, also. In brief, it has over many centuries, even millennia, learned "apt" ways of dealing with threats. The organism, however, often fails to distinguish a symbolic threat from a physical threat. "From all sides come signals that tee off protective reactions in him as an organism." [6] The individual generalizes all threats, psychosocial and symbolic as well as physical. His body gives the response which was originally apt but is "inept" in terms of modern threats. A person whose body is preparing him for physical combat when his struggle—usually a social one—requires inactivity is giving an "inept" reaction. He may ultimately find that his organs have suffered severe pathological effects.

In brief, man, feeling threatened, may revert to earlier responses that were once appropriate; he may use for long-term purposes devices seemingly fitted for short-term needs; or he may use as a defense against social or symbolic threats those that are more suitable for the realistic physical dangers. Protective patterns of all kinds are essential and life-saving beyond question when aptly used, but may prove costly when *ineptly* used or overused. They are well fitted only for the specific or fleeting emergencies in order that the individual may cope with exceptional dangers that threaten his survival. Although still "adaptive" in a sense, they are actually inappropriate for habitual or persistent patterns of response; and when so exercised they may damage the structures they were "designed" to protect.[7]

The inept responses may cause much more damage than the original threat.

There is a grammar as well as a vocabulary in this language of the stress diseases. The symptoms may occur in any of the bodily systems. There are, for example: (1) illnesses of the gastrointestinal system (such as duodenal ulcer, gastric ulcer of nonnutritional origin, mucous colitis, gastritis, and certain kinds of hemorrhoids and of gall-bladder disease); (2) those of the cardiovascular system (so-called effort syndrome or functional disorder of the heart, essential hypertension, coronary thrombosis, and cerebral hemorrhage); (3) those of the respiratory system (many cases of asthma, allergic rhinitis, and recurring bronchitis); (4) those of the genitourinary system (many cases of nocturnal enuresis, menstrual disturbances, leucorrhea, or even pyogenic urinary affection); (5) those of the locomotor system (some cases of "fibrositis," neuritis, sciatica, lumbago, rheumatoid arthritis, and certain non-traumatic cases of osteoarthritis); (6) those of the endocrine system (some cases of exophthalmic goiter, hyperthyroidism, diabetes, obesity, and myxedema); (7) those of the nervous system (certain kinds of migraine, anxiety states, and hysterias); (8) those of the blood (some kinds of non-nutritionally determined hypochromic anemia); (9) those of the skin (*alopecia areata*, prurigo, pruritus, urticaria, and seborrhea); and, finally, (10) those of the eyes (miner's nystagmus and some cases of chronic conjunctivitis and blepharitis).[8]

These illnesses, it should be re-emphasized, are not "all in the mind." They are very real; the tissues involved are injured (except in the hysterias). They differ from the mass diseases caused by germs, viruses, and malnutrition and from the degenerative diseases of age in their etiology, but not in the fact of their "realness."

The following illustrations show how the body, in the process of attempting to withstand threats, actually generates pathologies.[9]

Airways and Eyes. A patient who was reminded of her unhappy marriage burst into tears; when she expressed rage and desperation her nasal passages became swollen. Such reactions, continuing over a long period of time, may produce serious symptoms, including asthmatic manifestations. The nose becomes susceptible to infection, and chronic rhinitis, frequent colds, and sinusitis result. The defensive reaction to stress is sometimes one of weeping (washing away the foreign matter or the threat). Another type of defensive reaction is shrinkage and drying of the membranes; this is just the opposite of the shutting-out and washing-away reaction. The eyes may also show defensive reactions, such as weeping, washing away, and shutting out. "In short, the eyes and the airways can be demonstrated to react ineptly at times to socially derived stimuli."

Eating or Preparation for Eating. A common illustration of lesions is that of peptic ulcers. Here the tissues of the digestive system actually become ill because of secretions into the blood stream from glands which, innocently enough, "thought" that these chemicals were needed in the life struggle. The change in sex incidence of peptic ulcers is related to changing roles of men and women, to be discussed in Chapter 15.

Patterns of Ejection and Riddance. Two patterns have been noted here, one associated with fear, terror, abject grief, depression, and despair, which cause all gastric functions to slow down almost to a standstill, and the other associated with threats and assaults eliciting disgust and contempt, which, because of early experience, are associated with ejection. The ejection may take the form of either vomiting or diarrhea. "A person who is confronted by overwhelming environmental affronts, assaults, or demands may generalize the pattern of ejection and riddance. One who 'takes on more than he can handle,' who feels inadequate to the demands of his life situation, or is thwarted and filled with hatred, defiance, contempt, and suppressed or unconscious needs to be rid of a threatening situation, yet passive withal, may have bouts of diarrhea. . . ."

Skeletal Muscles and Cranial Arteries. Continued contraction of skeletal muscles in preparation for readiness to react—ineptly—to symbolic threats may cause headaches, backaches, and aches in arms and legs.

Over-all Mobilization and the Heart. The heart reacts to exercise in a certain adaptive way by increasing blood pressure and stroke volume, and by decreasing the ventilatory index. Some people find their heart behaving in the same way when they are under stress conditions. Ordinarily the heart returns to its normal functioning after the exercise is over, within about two minutes. Under stress, however, the heart does not return to its initial stage. Operating ineptly, the heart may suffer serious impairment.

The Large Bowel: Constipation. Sadness, dejection, or cheerless striving tend to inhibit the normal propulsive contractions of the large intestines: "it is as though the individual, unable to face and grapple with the threat, was nevertheless firmly 'holding on,' or tensely awaiting an attack that is indefinitely delayed. The individual so poised is not in a state optimal for defecation and may be inept in performance."

Basic Alterations in Metabolism. Even *diabetes mellitus* has been found to have a story to tell in some patients. Physiologically it is similar to the body's reaction to starvation. The psychosomatic form of this illness has been interpreted as a starvation reaction not to deprivation of food but to deprivation of love and security which, in infancy, are closely associated with food. "The diabetic patient reacts as though food and security were identical and develops a physiological reaction appropriate to starvation at a time when he is exposed to deprivations other than those of food."

Out of context, many of these physiological "messages" may seem farfetched. But increasingly medical practitioners are being trained to heed them. Illness may be viewed, almost without exaggeration, as a kind of social behavior.

Just as people develop different modes of communication, so different types of personality seem to be especially vulnerable to certain psychosomatic illnesses.[10] Two types of personality, the so-called "hysterical or histrionic" and the "obsessional," show characteristic kinds of role conceptions and consequently characteristic illnesses. The first seems to have a particularly strong necessity to obtain approval, attention, notice, or sympathy at any cost. This necessity may express itself in protean forms. Thus, the student we are following here points out, we have the hero, the hail-fellow-well-met, the devil-may-care type, the nice person, the resigned or saintlike martyr, and, if resentment develops, the chronic griper. The kinds of illness this type is susceptible to are the hysterias, either sensorimotor (paralysis, spasms, anesthesias or severe pains) or those of the autonomic functions over which there is some degree of voluntary control (eating, vomiting, breathing, coughing, constricting or relaxing the lower bowel).

The obsessional type includes those who emphasize ritualistic practices, such as never losing one's temper, always being clean, prompt, truthful, busy, dutiful, perfect, out of debt, self-controlled. Too great emphasis on cleanliness and tidiness has been found to be associated with colitis. If the role conception lays great emphasis on morality, honor, or religion, the illness may take the form of the so-called effort syndrome or functional heart disorder. If there is status anxiety or great preoccupation with security—economic or occupational—peptic ulcer may occur. Seborrhea, as in adolescent acne, may be related to obsessional preoccupation with work, the need to carry out role obligations by oneself, or to feelings of inadequacy which interfere with social contacts with others or with role performance. Coronary disease seems to be associated with unremitting work and the need to achieve or maintain "a subjectively evaluated role of authority or being on top." [11] Associated with rheumatoid arthritis there tends to be a role conception with a highly developed sense of duty, and abnormal requirements of self-sacrifice. People who are susceptible to this kind of illness seem to attract and be attracted to self-restricting life situations. The relationships and role definitions here listed are not, of course, invariable or absolute; they are common enough, however, to be significant.

Most of the characteristics embodied in the concept of psychosomatic illness may be summarized in a seven-point formula:

1. Emotion is a precipitating factor. The illness is related to some emotionally disturbing event.

2. Personality type, as we just saw, is related to specific kinds of psychosomatic illness; that is, certain kinds of personality seem to be especially susceptible to certain kinds of psychosomatic illnesses.

3. Sex ratios differ in the various psychosomatic illnesses; men are more susceptible to some, women to others, but these sex differences change over periods of time with changes in sex roles.

4. Psychosomatic illnesses in the individual are associated; they may occur together or they may alternate, or they may occur in sequence.

5. Family history shows a high proportion of cases with the same or associated illnesses in parents, relatives, and siblings. This tendency for psychosomatic disorders to occur in families is not interpreted as necessarily proving a genetic basis for their occurrence. Although cer-

tain sensitivities may be inherited, it is also possible that psychosomatic susceptibilities are acquired very early in life.

6. The course of psychosomatic illnesses is phasic, that is, they come and go. The patient recovers but has a recurrence some time later.

7. The prevalence of psychosomatic illness is associated with changes in the social life of the community; it rises and falls with changes in the structure and functioning of the community.[12]

The author illustrates his seven-point formula by reference to duodenal ulcer cases. In a study of some 200 people with peptic ulcers it was found that 84 per cent had become ill at a time when the patient was reacting to such upsetting stress factors as financial, occupational, or domestic difficulties. In a control group of persons with inguinal hernia—not a psychosomatic disorder—the illness was associated with emotional stress in only 20 per cent of the cases. The difference was statistically significant. (Point 1.) Deep-seated insecurity and dependence characterize the personality of patients with peptic ulcers. A majority try to overcome these feelings by overemphasized activity, efficiency, and independence; many become hard self-drivers. The actual breakdown tends to occur at times when threats to emotional security arise—through occupational or financial troubles—or when stresses caused by being in a position of authority bring anxiety or depression. A minority, the obviously dependent ones, tend to be easily provoked to bad humor or resentment and to use their ulcers to secure attention, or to excuse their inadequacies, or even to revenge themselves against society, whether in the form of individuals, associations, or the social order. (Point 2.) This illness was commoner among men than among women during the period between the two world wars. (Point 3.) Associated with it are migraine, hypertension, "fibrositis," and depression. (Point 4.) A family history of psychosomatic illness is reported to be four to five times commoner among the patients studied than among control-group cases. (Point 5.) This illness is phasic: the patient is cured for a while, then suffers a recurrence. (Point 6.) It increased in prevalence between the world wars. (Point 7.)

The incidence of psychosomatic illness varies with time, sex, community, age, and socioeconomic class. The data presented here are from Great Britain, but the same trends, with minor modifications, are considered representative of other industrialized societies also.[13] The hysterias, especially among women, declined between the two world wars; and with them, a disease known as mucous colitis, which had been prevalent until the first world war, practically disappeared. The author accounts for the disappearance of this disease of women in terms of the social emancipation of women which reduced the hysterias. But in contrast to the decline in the hysterias was the increase in anxiety states (diagnosed as "debility," "anemia," or "rheumatism"), in peptic ulcers and gastritis, exophthalmic goiter, diabetes, and hypertensive cardiovascular disorders. No data are available for trends in asthma, rheumatoid arthritis, or gall-bladder disease. Of these groups of illness, the anxiety states, gastritis, and peptic ulcer increased so markedly that in the years of the depression their incidence amounted almost to an epidemic.

Some psychosomatic illnesses which in the 19th century had occurred preponderantly in women (such as peptic ulcer, exophthalmic goiter, and perhaps essential hypertension) came, in the 20th century, to occur increasingly in males. Others, such as diabetes, which had formerly been found mainly among men, came to occur increasingly in women. The author we are following in our discussion suggests that these changes in sex incidence may mean that perhaps the personality type of males is becoming more "feminine" than in the 19th century, and vice versa, owing to modifications in sex roles.

When a psychosomatic illness is increasing, it tends to be most frequent in younger age groups; when it is declining, in older age groups. Thus, for example, when peptic ulcer was most common in females, in 1900, the age of maximum frequency or incidence was between twenty-five and thirty; in 1930 the age of maximum frequency was between sixty and sixty-five. Conversely, the peak for men, which was at about age fifty-five in 1900, was at about age thirty in 1930.

The psychosomatic illnesses tend to occur more frequently in urban than in rural areas. Socioeconomic class differences in deaths owing to psychosomatic illnesses may be summarized as follows:

TABLE 1

CLASS DIFFERENCES IN DEATHS

	Peptic Ulcer	Exophthalmic Goiter	Diabetes and Hypertensive Cardiovascular Disorders
Laboring Class			
Males	High		
Females	High		
Well-to-do Classes			
Males			High
Females		High	

SOURCE: James L. Halliday, *Psychosocial Medicine* (Norton, 1948), pp. 68–69.

We are warned to interpret these findings with reservations since death from peptic ulcer, for example, might result from lack of prompt medical attention or from nutritional defects, a quite different cause. The author does not feel, however, that the findings here reported can be explained away as results of different diagnoses over a period of time or among classes.

It has been suggested that the change in the incidence of some illnesses may be accounted for by new practices in child-rearing (to be discussed in Chap. 16) and by stresses associated with urbanization (to be discussed below).

The evidence seems convincing that the human organism does respond to symbolic threats with "inept" defense mechanisms—mechanisms that were evolved to deal with the threats to which it was subjected long before culture was developed. Applied to social and symbolic threats, these defense mechanisms often result in pathologies. The human body might, figuratively speaking, be viewed as a pressure gauge: the amount of pressure our society exerts on its members is indicated by the number of people who succumb to the stress illnesses.

The general theoretical basis for psychosocial medicine seems to be well supported, namely: human beings are socii, or social beings, as well as physical or biological beings; they have roles as well as bodies. They have certain status "needs" which are as urgent as their physiological needs. They must have constant support from the people in their social world, and their role networks must function effectively. When there is a disturbance in their social world which causes the collapse of emotional support they become ill, just as a breakdown in the sanitation system of a city may cause illness from infectious diseases.

There are two kinds of psychosomatic or sociosomatic illnesses which are of special importance, namely the hysterias and the anxiety states,[14] to which we now direct our attention.

The Pseudo-Illnesses: The Hysterias

We have emphasized the fact that in the psychosomatic illnesses we have just been discussing the pathologies are real, as real as those caused by germs or nutritional deficiencies. But sometimes there are symptoms with no physiological basis. The patient coughs as convincingly as though the tuberculosis germ were ravaging his lungs, but no lesions are present. He becomes as blind as though the optic nerve were severed, but the examiner finds that it is undamaged. He becomes as paralyzed as though the muscle were atrophied, but the muscle itself shows no abnormality. The symptoms are real enough, but their etiology is baffling. And the suffering is also very real. The patient seeks everywhere for a cure; he goes to grottoes with healing traditions; he seeks specialists in distant lands. He tries all kinds of therapies. Sometimes one set of symptoms suddenly disappears, but another set appears just as suddenly. False attempts at suicide are common.

If pathology were as objective a science as biology, it would make no difference to the patient which doctor administered treatment. But persons suffering from the kinds of illness we are here discussing go about "doctoring" with first one physician and then another. They are looking for the one doctor who can help them. They are, in a sense, clutching at the outside world, to maintain at least one sympathetic channel with reality. But they do not "really" want to recover.

Hysterical illnesses are sometimes interpreted as a substitution of the role of patient for the more arduous worker and family roles. Illness is a perfectly honorable escape from role obligations. This substitution is not planned, deliberate, or even conscious. The patient is completely convinced of his illness.

Hysterical illness has tended to decline in both civilian and military life.[15] Its incidence is greater in women than in men and in the lower socioeconomic status levels than in the higher. It is to a certain extent "a disease of the ignorant and the misinformed." [16] As people become better educated and better informed and, even more important, as they find resort to illness less necessary because of greater social tolerance of the weaknesses they had been trying to conceal, we may expect hysterias to be reduced to a minimum. It is reported, for example, that they have practically disappeared in England.[17]

But as the hysterias have declined in prevalence, a sister-illness, the so-called anxiety state, has tended to increase. Of the two the latter is perhaps the more serious.

The Half-Illnesses: Mild Anxiety States

Nature and Extent

The psychosomatic illnesses are genuine pathologies affecting the tissues. The hysterical illnesses are manifested by symptoms that have no physiological pathologies. There is still another kind of illness, the mild anxiety state, that shows symptoms but no organic basis. These symptoms indicate what we shall call, for lack of a better term, the half-illnesses.[18] The patient is obviously not well, in spite of the absence of evidence of disease. A large proportion—estimated at 30 to 60 per cent —of the cases which a general practitioner is called upon to treat show no pathologies. "Millions in our population have minor emotional illnesses which, while not necessarily incapacitating, are medically significant." [19] They do not necessarily cause the patient to be put to bed; he can still go about his business. But his role performance is perceptibly impaired. He has no clear-cut physical symptoms; he is neither well nor ill. When the doctor asks what is the trouble, he complains that he has no energy, is always tired, run down, and nervous. The tremendous appeal of advertisements of tonics, pills, vitamins, health foods, and patent medicines attests to the widespread incidence of this kind of twilight illness or marginal health.

Anxiety symptoms have been called "one of the most common ills of man" at the present time.[20] And one of the commonest characterizations of the middle of the 20th century is that it is "an age of anxiety," despite the fact that, in general, people today are probably healthier than ever. Anxiety states do not cause death, as germ diseases do. They may, however, become as crippling as the most virulent diseases.

Anxiety is by no means new in human history. Primitive peoples have their own anxieties.[21] Nor must we forget that in any society, in an age of abundance no less than in an age of scarcity, a certain amount of anxiety is—and, indeed, must be—generated in the very process of socialization, as we saw in Chapter 4. The absence of anxiety, as we shall see in our discussion of the psychopathic personality in Chapter 14, can be as pathological as an excess of anxiety. What seems to be important is the balance between provisions made by the society for stress reduction and the forces which make for stress induction.

As we have already seen, human suffering is the basis for the humanitarian criterion of social problems, and when hunger, cold, and physical pain have been mastered, anxiety becomes the major form which human suffering takes. Thus anxiety has been taken as one of the major factors about which our analyses have been organized.

Interpretation of Trends

But before we accept uncritically the reported increase in anxiety states we ought to examine the possibility that at least some of this increase may be in large part the result of changing role definitions and of raised standards.

CHANGING ROLE DEFINITIONS WITH RESPECT TO ANXIETY. In the 19th century worry seemed the natural condition of man. It was even provided for in many role definitions. Ladies often went into a decline, or pined away; these conditions would today be viewed as anxiety states. They were part of a role definition in the 19th century. The inculcation of fear was a large part of child-rearing and religious training. The relaxing of these old fears and anxieties is sometimes invoked as a cause of much delinquency today. Sin was a great preoccupation of many people. Biographies of 19th-century figures show much anguished wrestling with sin and temptation. Such expressions as "God-fearing man" and "fear of the Lord" suggest that a rather heavy load of anxiety was considered right and proper. Much psychoanalytic theory is based on the 19th-century fear which children had of their fathers. The role definitions based on a puritan ideology included anxiety as one of their concomitants, if not essential ingredients. No one thought of anxiety as even affecting roles, let alone as causing illness.

RAISED STANDARDS OF MENTAL HEALTH. Standards of mental as well as of physical health have been raised. Thus when F. D. Roosevelt formulated the four freedoms of the present, freedom from fear was given as much weight as freedom from want. Helping people achieve security has become a major goal of our society. We are more lenient about allowing people to express their fears and anxieties. In World War I, when the definition of the soldier demanded no fear, the symptoms of fear could not be expressed as such. They were therefore expressed in hysterias of one kind or another, especially shell shock. Today the role of the soldier does not require fearlessness; it allows the soldier to admit to himself that he feels fear. The symptoms are therefore more straightforward. In civilian life, also, we permit more admission of fears and anxieties. People talk more openly about what bothers them. They are encouraged to do so. Thus not only role definitions but also standards have probably changed, tending to contribute to the relative increase of anxiety with the decline in hysterias.

But we are not to interpret the increase in recorded anxiety states as meaning that everyone goes about with anguish in his soul. Many people do not even know that they suffer from anxiety. If asked what, if anything, they worry about, they say they don't worry about anything, as we pointed out in Chapter 4. Still we cannot dismiss the increased rates. We do know that more people drink alcoholic beverages now than formerly, even though they may drink less, and also that the use of sleeping pills has increased fantastically, as we saw in Chapter 11. Man's capacity for suffering has remained the same, even though the occasions for it are different. There is no longer the threat of famine, plague, evil spirits, witches, or malevolent forces mysteriously attacking in unforeseeable ways. It is rather the threat of such things as unemployment or hydrogen bombs which trigger anxiety states. The causes of anxiety are more likely to be social than physical.

Reasons for Increase

Many things have doubtless contributed to the paradoxical parallel trends of increased anxiety and abundance. For one thing, we have more to be anxious about today. It was once true that millions of people had nothing to lose but their chains. They have a good deal more to lose today.

But perhaps the major difference between the past and the present is the unbalancing of anxiety-induction and anxiety-reduction forces already referred to in Chapter 4. Even if occasions for anxiety have been multiplied by modern life, if there had been a corresponding development of anxiety-reducing forces, there might have been no net increase in anxiety states. Perhaps in time we may right the balance, but so far we have not.

One student of psychosocial medicine attributes the increase in anxiety to two sets of factors: the concomitants of urbanization and the societal and cultural disorganization which went with them. He cites as an example of the first of these forces the increasing separation of people from the soil as they left the farms and moved to the cities. Working on the land, with one's hands and with animals, is, in effect, an anxiety-reducing influence. In cities there is disregard of seasonal and diurnal and biological rhythms—what this student calls the "times and tides of nature"—and increasing regulation of life in terms of clocks instead. We do not think in terms of sunup and sunset, but in terms of 8 o'clock classes and 7 o'clock dinner dates. We must meet deadlines, pay bills at a specified time, work at the disciplined pace of the machine rather than according to the biological rhythms of our bodies. We are always racing against the hands of the clock. Fewer people, further, work creatively with their hands; they are thus deprived of the release which comes from manipulative creativity. And, finally, living in cities, he believes, demands more standardization and repression of individual expression.[22] Sheer physical crowding, without regard to its psychological or social aspects, may be a stress factor in and of itself.[23]

More important, however, from the point of view developed in this book is the second factor mentioned above: the societal and cultural disorganization accompanying abundance, especially in the form of the derangement of role and status patterns and of increasing rapidity of change in the structure of society.

Going home at last. Able to resume her role as wife, as mother, as sister. At first she will need follow-up care and protection. She will still have to have supervision. But at any rate she is out of the mental hospital. She is surrounded by normal living conditions.

It is a far cry from the situation two years ago when the broken-hearted husband brought her to be committed. For months she sat day after day in the hospital ward completely withdrawn from the outside world. The most terrible suffering of which human beings are capable had reduced her, and others like her, to almost vegetative inertness. She was unable to perform even the simplest of roles; she was too removed to be reached even by psychiatry.

Until recently the prognosis for such cases was all but hopeless. They could be kept alive but not much more. Today the situation is brighter. Chemical therapy, though not yet completely understood, has had the effect, if not of curing, at least of rendering many such patients accessible to treatment. Psychiatric treatment, recreational therapy, psychodrama, sociodrama, and other therapeutic procedures have thus been able to perform their healing function. Hundreds of patients like this young woman who might have had to spend years, or even a lifetime, in hospital wards are now able to re-enter the world outside. Their initial steps are, to be sure, like hers, tentative and experimental, but there is a distinct possibility that they can resume their family and worker roles, to a limited degree at any rate, if not completely.

But neither the hospital nor the psychiatrist can supply the last step in rehabilitation. That can be supplied only by the outside world. There has to be a suitable role and role network ready for the patient in order to make the treatment complete. This young woman is fortunate in having a husband who will supply the complementary role she will need. *(Photo: Ben and Sid Ross, Parade Publications)*

In 1860 the stratification of social classes was still fairly well defined and generally accepted. People "knew their place" and understood their standing, and they confidently worked, played, and strutted upon their apparently irrevocably allotted stage. In the years that followed, class warfare emerged. The old order was changing and indeed breaking, but a new order of reintegration had not yet emerged. The symptom of mass unemployment not only denied to the individual the emotional release of manipulative activity but also isolated him from society. Scales of relief admittedly provided him with the partial satisfaction of his basic material needs of food, clothing, and shelter, but these satisfactions alone were insufficient for an adult.

The need to be "safe"—whether against the outer threats of occupational loss, failure to be promoted, financial embarrassment, or social disapproval, or against the inner threats arising from frustration of the "life"—came to evoke a style of living regulated by obsessional mechanisms as a defense against evergrowing danger. . . .

There was a progressive increase of "inner insecurity," which . . . was a response to the progressive increase in the outer insecurity with respect to occupation, income, and status of the individual in the social setting.[24]

A physical organism which has been evolved over millennia to adjust to one kind of threat finds itself—suddenly, so far as human history is concerned—face-to-face with a wholly new kind of threat, not from nature but from "occupational loss, failure to be promoted, financial embarrassment, or social disapproval." To meet these threats it has only the old adaptive mechanisms. Anxiety is the net result.

Anxiety States and Role Pathology

Most people manage to control their anxieties. And most of them fulfill their role obligations. They have fun, they go fishing, they take trips, they go to ball games, they sail boats, they "do it themselves." Their role performance, in brief, is not impaired.

For some, however, the effort involved in keeping up role obligations becomes too great. The load imposes a heavy strain. So there comes a day when John Smith, for example, no longer goes to the doctor for treatment of his symptoms. He does not go to work, either. He sits in the rocker all day long. At first he may listen to the radio or look at television. After a while he may merely sit. Finally he does not even get out of bed. At first his wife is sympathetic; she discusses his illness with the neighbors. They know of a remedy or of a doctor who treats just such symptoms, and the wife, at her wit's end, relays the news to the patient. As time passes and conditions grow worse, with bills piling up, she becomes annoyed, then resentful at his apathy, his failure to respond, his refusal to do anything at all. The neighbors are beginning to gossip. Why does he just sit around all day and mope? She begins to nag at him. "The doctor couldn't find anything wrong with you; you're just lazy."

In most instances the wife seems to be the first person to recognize that something is wrong with the husband, but few wives are able to define what that "something" is. In the early stages they tend to see the husband's difficulty ("upsetness," "nervousness," "worry") as a reflection of character weakness, as a typical male response to illness or pain, or as a more or less natural response to great stress. Attempts are made to reason with the husband, and, especially with the neurotic or mildly psychotic husbands, successively to bolster him, shame him, comfort him, cajole him.[25]

But he says nothing; he just lies there. Then one day, seemingly no different from scores of others that have gone before, he jumps out of bed and tries to choke her to death. The hospital attendants finally arrive; he is declared insane and taken to the hospital. His illness is called a mental illness, or psychosis. Sociologically speaking, it is a genuine role pathology.

NOTES

[1] James L. Halliday, *Psychosocial Medicine* (Norton, 1948), p. 9.

[2] Leo W. Simmons and Harold G. Wolff, *Social Science in Medicine* (Russell Sage, 1954), p. 151.

[3] Even in the case of such a germ disease as tuberculosis, however, it has been found that stress may be an important factor. At the 50th annual meeting of the American Trudeau Society in 1955, a study was reported which showed that the lives of persons who became victims of tuberculosis were characterized by increasing distortion and maladaptation for about two years before the onset of the illness and that the personality of tuberculosis patients exhibited a characteristic pattern in response to stress. (*New York Times*, May 26, 1955.)

[4] Abstract of article by L. E. Hinkle and Normal Plummer, "Life Stress and Industrial Absenteeism; the Concentration of Illness and Absenteeism in One Segment of a Working Population," *Industrial Medicine and Surgery*, 21 (Aug. 1952), pp. 363–375, in *Marriage and Family Living*, 16 (Feb. 1954), pp. 78–79.

[5] Halliday, *op. cit.*, pp. 191–192.

[6] Simmons and Wolff, *op. cit.*, p. 121.

[7] *Ibid.*, p. 123.

[8] Halliday, *op. cit.*, pp. 46–47.

[9] Adapted from Simmons and Wolff, *op. cit.*, pp. 125 ff.

[10] Halliday, *op. cit.*, pp. 47–48.

[11] *Ibid.*, p. 51.

[12] Adapted from Halliday, *op. cit.*, pp. 47–48.

[13] C. P. Donnison, *Civilization and Disease*, (Williams & Wilkins, 1937).

[14] In much of the discussion which follows in this chapter and the next two chapters we shall be referring to illnesses which are the domain of the psychiatrist rather than the internist or surgeon or general practitioner. Our approach, however, is not that of the psychiatrist; therefore the materials are not presented in the conventional categories of psychiatry. The student is referred to the official classification of psychiatric disorders of the American Psychiatric Association, to be found in any textbook of abnormal psychology. In general, psychiatrists separate the major disorders into two categories, namely, the neuroses or psychoneuroses and the psychoses, the difference being largely one of degree of seriousness or incapacity. Three types of psychoneuroses are distinguished: hysteria, neurasthenia, and

psychasthenia. The psychoses are distinguished into those with known organic bases, such as alcoholic or paretic psychoses or psychoses associated with senile deterioration and those which result from mal-functioning of the organism. Of the so-called functional disorders, four are of major importance: schizophrenia, paranoia, manic-depressive psychosis, and involutional psychosis. Since our interest is not in the illness but in role impairment, we have not followed exactly the classificatory scheme used by the psychiatrists. It should be recognized that illnesses cannot always be neatly pigeonholed. The clinical description of a syndrome is a means by which the diagnostician may study a patient; but the patient does not necessarily conform to the model or type. In some cases it is not possible to make a clear-cut classification.

15 For the evidence in civilian life, see Halliday, *op. cit.*, pp. 112–120; for the evidence in military life, see David G. Mandelbaum, "Psychiatry in Military Society," *Human Organization*, 13 (Fall 1954), p. 10.

16 Winfred Overholser and Winifred V. Richmond, *Handbook of Psychiatry* (Lippincott, 1947), p. 172.

17 *Ibid.*, p. 171.

18 They used to be called "neurasthenia" or "psychasthenia"; the more modern term is "anxiety states."

19 J. F. Dewhurst *et al.*, *America's Needs and Resources: A New Survey* (Twentieth Century, 1955), p. 304.

20 Dr. Howard D. Fabing, former president of the American Psychiatric Association, in a paper read before the American Pharmaceutical Manufacturers Association, as reported in the *New York Times*, December 14, 1955.

21 Erich Drobec, "Zur Psychotherapie der Naturvoelker," *Sociologus*, 4 (1954), pp. 116–126. Abstract in *Sociological Abstracts*, III, No. 3 (July 1955), pp. 139–140.

22 Halliday, *op. cit.*, pp. 121–125.

23 In the case of poultry, for example, it has been found that crowding has a detrimental effect on the "birth rate," the morbidity rate, and the death rate. Summarizing experiments on fowl, one writer points out: "The smaller the floor space per bird, the smaller the egg production. This, of course, would be expected on general grounds. It was somewhat unexpected, however, that the larger the crowd in the pen the smaller the egg production, even though each bird in the two lots was allotted exactly the same floor space. . . . In an attempt to explain this phenomenon Raymond Pearl states: 'It is obvious that besides mere physical crowding another element is apparently involved, which element in our ignorance we may perhaps tentatively call psychological.' . . . Crowding not only increases the death rate and its twin, disease rate, but it also permanently affects the future of the survivors. . . . It has been demonstrated that the degree of crowding has a profound effect upon many, if not all, general and fundamental processes of life. . . . Crowding prevents the expression of the potential, latent, inherent vitality." (Carl H. Schroeder, "What's Space to a Chicken?" reprinted from *Everybody's Poultry Magazine*, November 1932, pp. 2, 3.)

24 Halliday, *op. cit.*, pp. 123, 125.

25 John A. Clausen, "Paths to the Mental Hospital," abstract of a paper given before the American Sociological Society, September 1955.

13

Role Impairment:
The "Mental" Pathologies

The Social Nature of Role Pathologies

If the term "social diseases" had not come to refer to the venereal diseases exclusively, it would have been the best one to apply to the so-called mental disorders. For the most important and characteristic aspect of these illnesses is the distinctively *social* nature of their symptoms. They are illnesses of role relationships. From the sociological point of view, indeed, the so-called mental illnesses are coming to be defined increasingly in terms of communication or isolation, role-taking, interpretation of stimuli, empathy, insight, and similar social concepts. The ill person misinterprets the stimuli which come to him from the social world; or he ceases to get the stimuli at all and therefore does not know how to behave. He is somehow or other cut off; or if he gets the stimuli and interprets them properly he reacts in a wholly inappropriate manner. He has lost the script.

There are many lesions of the nervous system which do not pro-

duce illness in role relationships. People become blind, deaf, or paralyzed; they show understandable disturbances from these misfortunes,
as we saw in Chapter 9. Still their social relationships remain within
the bounds of the normal, even though impaired. But there are other
lesions of the nervous system which do produce illness in role relationships. Paresis, for example, alcoholism, arteriosclerosis, and senile deterioration cause genuine illness in role relationships. The victims can no
longer fulfill their role obligations. They do not interpret social stimuli
properly; they do not react according to standard rules. It is not, then,
the presence of organic lesions which characterizes "mental" illness, but
the presence of role disturbances, or pathologies. If social or role relationships remain within the limits of acceptability, the person is not
considered "mentally" ill, whatever the pathology of his tissues or
organs. But if role relationships become disturbed, he is considered
mentally ill, whatever the pathology of his tissues.

The symptoms of role pathology have had a morbid fascination for normal people from time immemorial. In them they see in all their horrible details many of their own repressed fantasies of criminal behavior. Even when the symptoms do not take the form of criminal behavior, the derangements give us a glimpse into the vast complex jungle of the human mind, which most people find fascinating. We cannot understand; yet, in a way, we do. We come away with a new appreciation of the delicate balance which keeps people normal.

Sometimes the ill person retains his habits of speech, dress, eating, and sleeping, but he completely forgets his roles. He can function enough to keep himself alive. But he does not remember who he is. This sort of illness—which the psychiatrists call amnesia—illuminates the function of role. All the habits are maintained, but they are not organized or integrated into a role network.

Sometimes the ill person becomes obsessed with some idea; he is compelled to do certain things. Or he has strange fears, called phobias. He may be afraid of closed places, of open places, of high places, of germs, or of certain kinds of people. Common obsessions are guilt feelings, sex fantasies, revenge, and cleanliness. Common compulsions are ritualistic practices, drinking, and gambling; a less common compulsion is suicide.

All these symptoms have role-distorting effects. When people find their vision blurred they consult an oculist, have glasses fitted, and, if they are lucky, with the use of glasses their vision is brought up to normal. When people find their role relationships blurred or confused they may not know what to do about the situation.

We are to picture a party. Everyone knows and likes everyone else. Group roles are understood. There is much laughter and gaiety. One man makes a statement which he expects everyone to laugh at. No one laughs. He is a bit miffed, but passes it off. A few minutes later it happens again. And again. He begins to feel uneasy. Their failure to respond as he expects isolates him from them. If it happens often enough the experience can become alarming. The role network is not functioning properly. We are purposely exaggerating the simplicity of this situation because it is easier to empathize the problem in such a setting. After a while, if he still found himself not being laughed at when he expected to be—or, more seriously, being laughed at when he did not expect to be—he would begin to feel something was wrong. He would feel left out. If he were normal he would conclude that this group did not see things as he did, that their interests and tastes were different, and so on. He would, with no hard feeling, if with regret, look around for a group in which he would fit more comfortably, using as an index, for our purposes here, the fact that they reacted as he did to funny stories. This "matching" of individual and group goes on all the time. People and groups select one another.

But suppose that this man did not have the social skills or role-taking ability required to interpret the situation described above. For whatever reason, he interprets the lack of response of the group as hostility to him. If, because of his past experience, he assumes responsibility or blame for this hostility, he will feel guilty, inferior, inadequate; if he blames the group, he will feel resentful. Thus in this situation there are guilt feelings, anxiety, fear, and withdrawal on the one hand, and resentment, hatred, hostility, and suspicion on the other. He has committed an unpardonable sin. He is unworthy. He is wrong. He is not as good as other people. Or he is being persecuted and he must seek revenge.

Even if the group were actually snubbing him, a person with normal social skills or role-taking ability would take the hint; he would interpret their behavior correctly and resign from the group to seek another. He would probably feel bad, but he would recognize the facts. If he lacked social skills, however, he might interpret their behavior as threatening: they are leagued against him, they are trying to destroy him. We would call him paranoid.

People lacking in role skills are lost. They blunder about, run into obstacles, trip, and stumble. It is as if they had uncorrected visual defects. They have uncorrected defects in their social perceptions which are just as handicapping as uncorrected visual defects.

Not all forms of abnormal behavior constitute role pathologies. Some are mild enough or leave the patient with sufficient insight or role skills that he can continue to perform, or, at any rate, act his role, albeit with some impairment. There is enough role-taking ability left to enable him to view his own behavior as it looks to those in complementary roles and to apologize for it or laugh it off. Once his violent temper outbreak is past he feels sheepish or ashamed; he is sorry he lost control. Or at the end of a long period of morose withdrawal he explains that he has been feeling pretty low, but he has now "snapped out of it." Or after an exhibition of manic euphoria he "comes to his senses" and wonders why he made such a fool of himself. Chemical changes in his body impel him to behave in abnormal ways, but he can stand off and see himself as others see him. He can understand that his strange behavior requires explanation. He tries to find reasonable explanations. It is only when both the explanations and the behavior get too far off the beam that role relationships become pathological.

The Causes of Role Pathologies

When there are organic lesions in the nervous system, the role illness, however extreme, is not baffling. Such injuries can be diagnosed by standard laboratory procedures. They may not be curable, but they can be identified. For example, when the nerve fiber is damaged by paresis or alcoholism, or deteriorated by age, we can expect bizarre behavior, even if we cannot predict its form. But persons suffering from the most serious role illnesses, such as schizophrenia, do not exhibit such organic injuries. All that is known is that their several physiological systems do not function properly.

The human body consists of a number of systems. If all goes well they operate together as a well-disciplined team, each tending to its own business. They are guided in their integrated functioning by the nervous system, which is itself a complex of several systems. One, the voluntary nervous system, operates the large skeletal or striped muscles. Another, the autonomic system, operates the smooth muscles, including the glands. It is sometimes called the vegetative system because it performs the vegetative functions of the body and because it is not, after all, really autonomic in the sense of being independent. There is also a system of sensory perception, both for stimuli from the outside and for stimuli from inside the body. We might, figuratively speaking, call the voluntary nervous system the foreign office and the autonomic system the housekeeping agency or ministry of domestic affairs. The autonomic nervous system—phylogenetically much older than the voluntary system—is "intelligent" in its limited way. When the light is too great, for example, it automatically closes the shutters, that is, the pupils of the eyes. When the temperature is too high, it turns on the sweat glands. When the senses in touch with the outside world signal danger, it sees to it that sugar is released into the blood for immediate mobilization of the body for fight or flight, and so on. But it is very "stupid" in many ways, also. It has no way of evaluating the signals which are directed to it. It was evolved many millennia ago and has not become modified since. The sense organs report a threat. The best way to meet this particular threat may be to sit and think coolly and calmly for a while. But the autonomic nervous system, completely oblivious of the fact that threats in the modern world are likely to be not hungry wild animals but loss of a job or of status, goes about its ancient business, releasing chemicals into the blood which prevent cool appraisal of the situation and which even put a great strain on other systems to inhibit rash action.

The autonomic system can produce two quite different conditions in the body. In general, they are related to the sympathetic and the parasympathetic systems. On the one hand, the autonomic system can cause a greatly accelerated metabolism and—manic—activity; on the other, it can slow the body down or depress it to a very low, even stuporous, level of activity.

Normally there is fairly good cooperation between or among the several operations of the nervous system, as there is, also, between the nervous systems and all the other systems. But sometimes the works get out of kilter. The organism weeps at the wrong time, or laughs at the wrong time. It becomes uncontrollably excited, or, conversely, almost ceases to function at all, like a bear in hibernation. There is lack of coordination between the sensory apparatus and the central system, resulting possibly in hallucinations. Or there is misinterpretation of what is seen or heard. Quite possibly the several systems are normal in the sense of being free of pathologies or lesions, but they do not function together in a normal way.

We do not know yet exactly why these mishaps in functioning among the body systems occur. Some students consider them psychogenic or sociogenic, that is, the result of early disturbances in the socialization process; some consider them to have a physiological etiology as yet not understood.

As an illustration of the first of these theories we present the conclusions of one careful student of psychosocial medicine who traces the origin of such malfunctioning of the bodily systems back to the earliest experiences of the child. He finds, for example, that the several vegetative systems are peculiarly vulnerable to mishap at different periods of development, and that frustration at a critical time may leave weaknesses in the body which appear later under stress. During the first phase of emotional development—the first three months—the skin and the respiratory and gastrointestinal systems are most susceptible to damage. During the second phase, from six months to three years, dysfunctions of arteries, muscles, and bowels have their maximum frequency in the form of excessive anger flushing and paling, temper tantrums, pummeling, heel drumming, kicking, rigidity, and obstinate constipation. The third phase, from two to six years of age, is associated with increasing organization and broadened functioning of the cortex. Socialization accelerates; there is a strong drive to be approved and noticed as a person. Unstabilized innervations of the voluntary muscular and sensory systems may continue in the form of hysterical paralyses, spasms, anesthesias, and pains. Psychologically "the ego may fail to become firmly established in the sense that it remains labile, and the individual, not becoming, so to speak, fixed in his proper ego identity, changes his role with his life situation like an actor with different parts to play." [1] If there is undue frustration in the first phase the infant has little recourse except a state of withdrawal. If there is undue frustration in the second phase, this author continues, there may be a development of obsessional trends as a defense. If there is undue frustration in the third phase histrionic trends may develop, that is, an unusual necessity to obtain approval, attention, or sympathy. In brief, any particular bodily system may be thrown out of kilter at some critical moment in its development and as a result throw the whole body out of kilter at some later date.

We shall present more data on the way role and status are related to disturbed behavior below, but first a brief statement on physiological factors.

Evidence for the second explanation of mental illness—that it is caused by physiological factors—is beginning to accumulate. Recent research has shown, for example, that in persons who have been ill with schizophrenia for four years or longer there is a significantly low rate of oxygen use. Some chemicals related to epinephrine or adrenalin may cause disorders in the use of oxygen; others, notably glutathione, correct the disorder.

The possibility cannot be ruled out that some instances of what is called schizophrenia, may be caused by some as yet unknown substance related to a breakdown product of epinephrine.[2]

And a research group has found that lysergic acid may make an important semi-hormone—serotonin—unavailable in brain tissue, resulting in the development of the symptoms of schizophrenia; the drug reserpine seems to counteract the lysergic acid and releases this important semi-hormone for normal use.[3]

The discovery of such physiological causes of schizophrenia or of other illnesses does not rule out psychogenic or sociogenic factors. Since every case of mental illness occurs in an organism with a unique and characteristic history, the direction the illness takes will depend on past experience and habits. This point was dramatically illustrated in an experiment conducted with human subjects. Two men were given an injection of blood from a schizophrenic patient. Both became temporarily ill. But the striking fact was that they showed different symptoms. One became catatonic, the other, paranoid. In other words, the illness used behavior patterns already available.

Physiological reactions may be results as well as causes. That is, certain kinds of emotional reactions may occur so often as to produce chemical changes which in time erode normal checks and balances, just as certain chemicals produced by the glands may irritate the lining of the stomach and cause peptic ulcers. It is a matter of personal history whether the organ affected by the chemical changes is the stomach, the skin, the nervous system, or some other organ, and, if the nervous system, what the symptoms will be.

The fact, however, that chemotherapy is bringing about such promising results in dealing with role pathologies suggests that physiological as well as psychogenic or sociogenic factors must be used to explain the characteristic behavior of the "mentally" ill. We can no longer discount physiological causes, even though the form the illness takes may be determined largely by sociological factors.

Trends in Mental Illness

In mental health, as in physical health, the problems of the 20th century differ from those of the 19th. Because people live longer today they have a longer period in which they may succumb to mental illness or role pathology, or to the degenerative diseases. The mental illness of the older age groups is therefore relatively more common in an age of abundance than is that of the younger age groups.

It is commonly supposed that mental illness is increasing because modern civilization is too great a strain, imposing such severe stresses that fewer and fewer people can resist them. It was once estimated by the Metropolitan Life Insurance Company, for example, that one out of every twenty children born alive in the United States would succumb to a mental illness, one in fifteen seriously enough to require hospitalization. In 1955 the Hoover Commission task force on federal medical service raised the chances to one in twelve; [4] and in 1956, Richard M. Nixon stated it as one in ten.[5] These are frightening figures. But they conceal some ambiguities which must be taken into account in interpreting them.

They include, for example, life expectancies. Of course one's chances for becoming ill increase as life expectancy increases. One has a longer time in which to become ill. A more refined measure of expectancy of hospitalization has been provided, based on New York data for 1940.[6] This measure tells us what the chances in 100 are for admission to a mental hospital between any two ages; thus, for example, at birth the chances are 0.11 in 100 that a male will be admitted to a mental hospital by age 15; 0.43, by age 20; 0.92, by age 25; rising until the chances are 20.12 by the age of 90. At the age of 85, however, the chances are only 4.68 in 100—not 20.12 in 100—that a male will be hospitalized by the age of 90. In brief, it is misleading to speak of the chances of being hospitalized as though they were unrelated to longevity.

Actually, then, the increase in mental illness—which we shall document below—is an index not of the strains of civilization but of the protection which abundance offers, keeping people alive so much longer. Thus, although "patients with mental disorders due to conditions associated with old age account for an increasing proportion of all first admissions to mental hospitals [constituting] . . . one fourth of the total first admissions," [7] mental illness at the younger age levels has not, so far as we now know, increased, at least in the last century.

The evidence for this conclusion is based on a study which compared first-admission rates to institutions caring for the mentally ill in Massachusetts in 1840–1885 with rates for the present. On the basis of careful comparisons, and making allowances for differences in hospitalization patterns, it was found that:

1. When appropriate comparisons are made which equate the class of patients received and the conditions affecting hospitalization of the mentally ill, age-specific first admission rates for ages under 50 are revealed to be just as high during the last half of the 19th century as they are today.

2. There has been a very marked increase in the age-specific admission rates in the older age groups. The greater part of this increase seems almost certainly to be due to an increased tendency to hospitalize persons suffering from the mental diseases of the senium. However, there is a possibility that some of the increase may be due to an actual increase in the incidence of arteriosclerosis.

3. The 19th and 20th century distributions of age-specific rates, that is, the distributions of admissions by age independent of changes in the age structure of the population, are radically different. In the 19th century there was relatively a much higher concentration of admissions in the age group 20–50; and today there is relatively a high concentration in ages over 50 and more particularly over 60. This, of course, in no way affects the results summarized in paragraph (1) above.

4. Nineteenth century admissions to mental hospitals contain a larger proportion of psychotic cases and of severe derangement than do contemporary admissions. This is in part due to the more limited facilities of that period which tended to restrict admissions to the severer cases, and to the different distribution of age-specific rates.

5. Male and female age-specific rates show a greater degree of equality in the 19th century than today. This is largely due to the differences discussed in paragraphs (3) and (4) above.[8]

The fact that there has not been an increase in rates of hospitalized cases, age for age, does not in any way diminish the dimensions of the problem of mental, or, more properly, role, illness at the present time. It is, of course, comforting to know that the stresses of civilization are not increasing the rate of mental breakdown—if, indeed, they are responsible for it in the first place—but this fact does not lighten the load of caring for the mental illness which the increasing life span involves.[9]

And the load is heavy. Mental illness has, indeed, been called the No. 1 public health problem of the nation today. Whether it is increasing among young people or not, the rate of mental illness is staggering. Almost 12 per cent of the men between eighteen and thirty-seven, for example, were rejected by Selective Service in World War II because of mental and personality disorders, not counting mental deficiency or neurological defects. And between 40 and 45 per cent of army medical discharges were for psychiatric disabilities. Among the young, as well as among the old, therefore, the problem is immense.

There are no reliable figures on the full extent of mental illness at the present time, but the Hoover Commission task force on federal medical services, referred to above, estimated that in 1955 9,000,000 persons, or 6 per cent of the population, had some form of mental disorder, 10 per cent of whom probably needed hospital care.

Scattered indexes on the hospitalized population can also give us some idea of the magnitude of the problem. In 1952 there were more than 700,000 persons who were patients in nervous and mental hospitals on an average day;[10] in 1955, 750,000.[11] "Currently, nearly two fifths of the total bed capacity of the hospitals in our country is devoted to the care of mental patients, exclusive of beds in registered hospitals for epileptics and mental defectives which account for another tenth of the total."[12] The Hoover Commission task force pointed out that about a quarter of a million new patients were being hospitalized annually; 47 per cent of them were suffering from schizophrenia which required an average of thirteen years of hospitalization.[13] The number of persons needing prolonged care was increasing at the rate of 10,000 a year in 1955.[14] "In the past 20 years, the number of first admissions to hospitals for the long-term care of psychiatric patients has increased more than 60 per cent and the number of patients under care in these institutions has risen almost as rapidly."[15] As a result of these trends, the cost of operating tax-supported mental institutions in 1952—$600,000,000—was more than twice that in 1946. In 1956 Richard M. Nixon stated that the tax burden of mental illness was $1,000,000,000 and that the cost of private treatment of all illnesses with psychiatric implications amounted to another billion dollars, making the total cost $2,000,000,000.[16]

The crowded conditions in mental institutions, it should be pointed out, result not only from the increasing number of patients in the older age brackets who have disorders, but also from the fact that all patients, whatever their age at admission, now live longer, thus occupying beds for more years.

The increasing success of new types of treatment, especially chemotherapy,[17] suggests that we are on the verge of a breakthrough in this difficult field. The value of these new drugs, it should be pointed out, lies not primarily in any cures which they effect, but in rendering the patient amenable to psychiatric treatment. As a probable result of the use of these drugs, New York State hospitals for the first time in 1956 reported a reduction of 500 in the number of patients seeking admission and a 20 per cent increase in the number released.[18] And at St. Elizabeth's Hospital in Washington, D. C., the population in 1956 was the smallest in years—6,800 as contrasted with 7,200 in March 1954.[19] The use of the so-called tranquilizing drugs was making it possible to treat patients outside the institution.

For more than a century the states have assumed the responsibility for caring for severe cases of mental, or role, illness. In 1946, however, the National Mental Health Act was passed, which authorized grants of federal funds to the states to help them develop state and local preventive mental health services. Grants were also authorized for research and for training professional personnel in the mental health field. In 1951 all states had mental health programs, spending almost $2 for every $1 contributed by the Federal Government. The National Institute of Mental Health provides consultant services to the states and also works with them on related problems, such as alcoholism and drug addiction.

The Lessons from Military Experience

Data are now becoming available from military psychiatric records which give us new insights into the way role mechanisms operate in neuroses.[20] Combat experience is by no means the same as civilian experience; but the reactions of men in combat illuminate the stresses that go on in everyday life on a less exaggerated plane. The stresses of combat are more palpable, more concentrated, more intense than those of civilian life. The social structure of the army in which they must be met is different from that of civilian society; but the underlying mechanisms of stress reaction which military psychiatrists report from their studies are probably the same as those which occur in civilian life.

Military psychiatrists, on the basis of their experience with a million neuropsychiatric cases during World War II, changed their conception of normal and abnormal. The only difference they found was in tolerance of stress. With sufficient stress, anyone would break down.[21] The chief support in stress situations came from the bonds of the immediate social group and the social structure in which the soldier exercised his role.

> . . . environmental stress can be so great as to overcome the tolerance and adaptability of any individual. . . . every individual will manifest behavior of a neurotic or psychotic kind if subjected to great and long-continued stress. . . . the main supports for the toleration of stress and the principal defenses against it, for soldiers at least, lie in the soldier's primary group, his small and intimate group of friends, and in the social structure in which he plays his assigned role.[22]

One of the rather surprising findings of military psychiatric research was that persons known to be neurotic before entering the army performed about as well as any other men. The explanation offered is that in the army, as opposed to civilian life, they found group support which, in effect, "cured" them of their neuroses.

> What does seem to be undeniably established by the observations is that some men who had displayed inflexible and socially disadvantageous traits of neuroses in their civilian environment, managed to be fully competent and militarily useful even under the duress of combat. . . . This is not to say that psychotics or all patent neurotics can adapt well to military life and battle stress. But a considerable number of the men who had been unstable or who had stiffened neurotically in their civilian relationships, found in military society enough stabilizing influences and emotional supports to endure not only the usual adversities of training and garrison duties, but also the severities of battle. Presumably the specific traumas suffered in their former life situations were not touched off in the army; the strong primary group alliance which soldiers tend to form may have given them emotional bolstering they had not had before.[23]

It is the nature of this emotional bolstering which is of prime significance in attempting to diagnose, or even understand, many of the social problems of modern society.

> For the American soldier, a main psychic support lay in his primary group. The friends beside whom he fought, on whom his life might depend and whose lives might be in his hands, were most important in his conduct.

In their company, he found courage and incentive; together they could withstand the abrasion of combat for a "normal" period. Should this group of buddies be separated, and each find himself in the company of men he did not know—strangers for all that they wore the same uniform—his support and motivation tended to sink and his effectiveness as a soldier to droop until he could find himself with a set of buddies once again.[24]

If we translate this finding into civilian life we find ourselves faced once again with the "pathology" of modern societies which we referred to in Chapter 6. Many people do not have these group supports. They do not have group roles in families or tribes on whom their life depends, whose lives might be in their hands, in whose company they find courage and incentive, and with whom they can withstand the abrasion of life stresses.

In the army it was found that therapy was more effective if it used the group. Thus, "forward therapy" was more effective than withdrawing the casualty behind the lines or hospitalizing him.

If a combat soldier who becomes a psychoneurotic patient is not long separated from his group, if he is treated quickly and in the immediate vicinity of the fighting, he can—in the majority of cases—rejoin his buddies in a few hours or days, with little or no hampering carryover from his experience away from them. His friends take him back in, they help him resume his former role so that they may continue to bear their duty together.[25]

The fact that many of the men who became psychiatric casualties became ill only because the stress was so abnormally great, and not because they were inherently weak, is witnessed by the remarkable success of discharged veterans. The ability of discharged patients to succeed in life outside hospital walls has been documented by a follow-up study of a sample of World War II psychiatric casualties made five years after release.

In this study most of the veterans were interviewed by psychiatrists at follow-up. It was found that 85 percent of the men were gainfully employed, and all but a small proportion of these were in full-time employment. Two-thirds of them had had   psychiatric treatment after discharge from the service, and in only 2 percent had there been intensive or prolonged treatment by psychiatrists. Less than 10 percent showed evidence at follow-up of serious psychiatric disability.[26]

A later study by the Veterans Administration reported similar results. Ninety-three out of every 100 rehabilitated veterans were holding jobs and almost all of them liked the work they were doing. They were earning $15 a week more on the average than nonveterans in the same age group. Most of them—77 per cent—had at least one dependent and family responsibilities, showing that both family and worker roles had been successfully mastered.[27]

Among civilians it has been noted that neuroses were less frequent during times of war than in times of peace. It has been suggested that the group solidarity resulting from common danger supplied the support which protected individuals from illness. Speaking of Britain, one student points out "that in 1939 . . . the community found relief and even satisfaction on the outbreak of war." [28]

Status Aspects of Role Illness [29]

We have emphasized the role aspects of mental illness so far; but we can get some inkling of the contribution which status striving and status anxiety make to mental illness by considering some of the findings of recent research. It has been pointed out that many of the psychosomatic illnesses—especially peptic ulcers—result from the drive to get to the top. Coronary occlusion, as we noted above, is associated with "compulsive strivings for power and prestige." [30] One study comparing patients with psychosomatic symptoms and those with none found that although both groups reported about the same economic position for their families when they were children, the subjects with psychosomatic symptoms reported higher social than economic positions. A psychiatrist commented on this finding as follows: "These patients all want to be middle-class or better. This social position they want is economically expensive to maintain. They are knocking themselves out in the attempt!" [31]

In the above cases the stress resulting from status striving and anxiety is reflected in physical symptoms. Sometimes it has even more serious consequences. In a study of social mobility and mental illness in New Haven, Connecticut, comparisons were made between twenty-five cases of diagnosed psychoneuroses, twenty-five cases of diagnosed schizophrenia, and sixty non-patients in the middle class and in the lowest class. The middle class was composed of "proprietors of small businesses, white-collar workers, and skilled manual workers who are, for the most part, high school graduates. These people live in apartments, flats, and single family dwellings in wide-scattered residential areas." [32] The lower class was composed "almost exclusively of unskilled and semiskilled workers who typically have an elementary education or less and who live in the most crowded slum areas of the city." [33]

Achieved social mobility was measured by comparing class indexes of the parental family with that of the individuals themselves. In Class III, the middle class, there was a great deal of social mobility, and almost all of it was upward. Most important, the schizophrenic patients were the most mobile, the control group the least. The mentally ill subjects were, furthermore, more mobile than their brothers or sisters. The authors make the inference that "the psychoneurotics, and especially the schizophrenics, were over-achievers." [34] They had had to pay too much in effort and in other values for their achievement. Achieved social mobility was least in the Class V, or lower-class, subjects, and the relationship with mental illness was not so clear-cut.

Comparisons were then made between aspiration and achievement. Here again the results for the middle-class subjects were illuminating. They had not had as much education as they had wanted nor had they had as good jobs as they had aspired to.

The average class III psychoneurotic completed slightly more than one year of college, but he aspired to a college degree. The average class III schizophrenic completed two years of college, and he, too, wanted to finish college. The discrepancy between educational achievement and aspiration among the class III psychoneurotics and schizophrenics is significant. . . . All these [psychoneurotic] patients had worked hard to achieve their education. . . .

Every schizophrenic had [likewise] put forth great personal efforts to obtain his education. He was usually a good student; and he enjoyed school. Typically his problem was to get enough education to prepare him for the job he wanted. He worked upon the premise that if he could get enough education he would get the desired job, then he would be accepted socially, and his problems would be ended. Finally, he looked upon education as a panacea for his personal and social problems. . . . [The typical Class III schizophrenic] had over-aspired and over-achieved in the educational sphere, was not able to consolidate his educational achievement. The net result was excruciating anxiety over his failure to realize his job and status aspirations. . . .

When we turn from the educational to the occupational area, we find a definite discrepancy between the actual and the idealized. . . . Both groups [of patients] have moved in this generation from manual work into work that requires specialized training and reasonably smooth interpersonal relations. The men are employed as clerks, salesmen, and supervisors; the women are employed, or they were before marriage, as secretaries, elementary teachers, nurses, and technicians. Although the occupational achievements of both sexes have been substantial, their aspirations are far above their accomplishments. The men would like to be professionals, or in business for themselves; the women would prefer to be professionals, or married to professional men. The occupational reference groups of the patients include lawyers, doctors, professors, engineers, artists, musicians, and business executives.[35]

A similar pattern emerged for the Class V subjects. The psychoneurotics felt they could have had better jobs if they had had more education. "A good job meant a higher standard of living, and, if one lived well, what other problems could one have?" [36] The schizophrenics had all experienced educational frustrations.

Most of them were compelled to leave elementary school, at the earliest legal age, by a combination of economic circumstances and parental indifference, if not hostility, toward education. As adults they regretted their lack of an education.[37]

Occupationally, it will be recalled, the Class V subjects were semiskilled or unskilled workers; not one had realized his occupational aspirations.

They felt their jobs were unsatisfactory; they worried about how long they would last, the nature of the work, that they did not pay enough to meet the needs of their families, that there was no advancement, that the job carried no status, and so on through a long series of specific irritations. The jobs they aspired to were relatively modest ones, such as stationary engineer, machinist, a foremanship, clerical work.[38]

The authors of the above study do not imply that mobility and attendant status problems are the only or even the principal factors in mental illness. But they conclude that they were significant and feel that "the relations between status striving, anxiety, and mental health, deserves further intensive investigation." [39]

NOTES

1 James L. Halliday, *Psychosocial Medicine* (Norton, 1948), p. 98.

2 Dr. Mark D. Altschule, in a paper read before the Academy of Psychosomatic Medicine, October 7, 1955, reported in the *New York Times,* October 8, 1955.

3 National Heart Institute, reported in the *New York Times,* October 3, 1955.

4 Reported in the *New York Times,* March 8, 1955.

5 Reported in the *New York Times,* April 14, 1956.

6 Herbert Goldhamer and Andrew Marshall, *Psychosis and Civilization* (Free Press, 1949, 1953). Other studies with essentially the same conclusions, cited by the above authors, are: Henry B. Elkind and Maurice Taylor, "The Alleged Increase in the Incidence of the Major Psychoses," *American Journal of Psychi-* *atry,* 42 (1936), pp. 817–825; J. S. Jacob, "A Note on the Alleged Increase of Insanity," *Journal of Abnormal and Social Psychology,* 23 (1938), pp. 390–397; Harold F. Dorn, "The Incidence and Future Expectancy of Mental Disease," *Public Health Reports,* 53 (1938), pp. 1991–2004; Conrad Sommer and Harry H. Harmon, "Trends in Mental Diseases in Illinois, 1922–43," in *Trends of Mental Disease* (King's Crown Press, 1945), pp. 56–91; Ellen Winston, "The Assumed Increase of Mental Disease," *American Journal of Sociology,* 40 (1935), pp. 427–439. A contrary conclusion was arrived at by Benjamin Malzberg in *Social and Biological Aspects of Mental Disease* (Utica, State Hospitals Press, 1940), pp. 38–51.

7 "The Outlook for Mental Patients,"

Statistical Bulletin of the Metropolitan Life Insurance Company, 36 (April 1955), p. 1.

8 Goldhamer and Marshall, *op. cit.,* pp. 91–92.

9 "The Outlook for Mental Patients," *loc. cit.*

10 J. Frederic Dewhurst *et al., America's Needs and Resources: A New Survey* (Twentieth Century Fund, 1955), p. 304. The population in mental hospitals in 1950 numbered 613,628, distributed as follows: federal hospitals, 59,847; state, county, and city hospitals, 537,413; and private hospitals, 16,368. In New York state, 40 per cent were cases of arteriosclerosis and senile degeneration. Many county "homes" or almshouses or poorhouses are populated by mild cases of senile dementia.

11 Dr. Daniel Blair, Medical Director of the American Psychiatric Association, at hearing of House Interstate and Foreign Commerce Committee, as reported in *New York Times,* March 10, 1955.

12 Dewhurst *et al., op. cit.,* p. 304. All told, then, about half of the hospital beds were devoted to mental patients of one kind or another.

13 Dr. Leo E. Hollister, in a paper read at the New York Academy of Sciences, as reported in the *New York Times,* February 4, 1955.

14 Hoover Commission task force on federal medical service, *loc. cit.*

15 "The Outlook for Mental Patients," *loc. cit.*

16 *Ibid.*

17 W. H. Sebrell, Jr., "Chemistry in Chronic Disease Research," *Chemical and Engineering News,* 33 (May 2, 1955), pp. 1857–1858. "In the field of mental illness, several chemical substances are proving highly useful. . . . Chlorpromazine is said to be uniquely beneficial in symptomatic control of severe psychomotor excitement. . . . The reported results with manic-depressive and schizophrenic patients are particularly noteworthy. In manic states, psychomotor excitement is said to have been reduced, feeding problems disappeared, sleep was restored, and the patients became amenable to psychiatric approach. . . . The mode of action of chlorpromazine is still unknown. A therapeutic agent of great promise in the mental health field . . . is reserpine. . . . Reserpine produces a tranquillizing and sedative effect without hypnosis. It is useful in treating many conditions in which barbiturates are commonly administered, such as anxiety, tension, nervousness, and excitability. In schizophrenia, paranoia, and other neuropsychiatric conditions, several investigators report improvement after treatment for two months or more. . . ."

18 Governor Averell Harriman, reported in the *New York Times,* April 13, 1956.

19 *Newsweek,* May 21, 1956, p. 70.

20 Neuroses are less serious than psychoses.

21 The endurance of United States riflemen in certain North African and Italian campaigns was computed to average 200 to 400 combat days. See David G. Mandelbaum, "Psychiatry in Military Society," *Human Organization,* 13 (Fall 1954), p. 8.

22 *Ibid.,* p. 6.

23 *Ibid.,* p. 7.

24 *Ibid.,* p. 8.

25 *Ibid.,* p. 9.

26 "The Outlook for Mental Patients," *op. cit.,* p. 3. The study on which this report is based is by Norman Q. Brill and Gilbert W. Beebe, "Follow-up Study of Psychoneuroses," *American Journal of Psychiatry,* 108 (Dec. 1951), p. 417.

27 Reported in the *New York Times,* May 9, 1955.

28 Halliday, *op. cit.,* p. 123.

29 Not all anxiety associated with status is pathological. A comparison of school boys in the United States and England found American boys had more anxiety with respect to family and sibling relations, self-confidence, school, and material symbols of social status; the English boys had more anxiety with respect to relations to girls. The middle-class American boys had most anxiety, the middle-class English boys, the least. "Expressions of anxiety in both samples were interpreted as being roughly proportional to the institutionalized expectations of the two societies and to be non-pathological." (Joel B. Montague, Jr., "A Study of Anxiety as Revealed by Samples of English and American Boys, by Social Class," paper read before American Sociological Society, September 1955.)

30 Arthur Jess Wilson, *The Emotional Life of the Ill and Injured; The Psychology and Mental Hygiene of Rehabilitation and Guidance* (Social Sciences Publishers, 1950), p. 32.

31 Dr. Erich Fromm, quoted by Jerome D. Folkman, "Parent-Child Relations and Sensitivity to Stress," mimeographed copy of paper read before the Society

for the Study of Social Problems, August 1955, pp. 4–5.

32 A. B. Hollingshead, R. Ellis, and E. Kirby, "Social Mobility and Mental Illness," *American Sociological Review*, 19 (Oct. 1954), p. 578.

33 *Ibid*. Actually, these summary statements of class do not do justice to the care with which the criteria of class—occupation, education, and residence—were specified and quantified. See A. B. Hollingshead and F. C. Redlich, "Social Stratification and Psychiatric Disorders," *American Sociological Review*, 18 (April 1953), pp. 163–169, for more detail.

34 Hollingshead, Ellis, and Kirby, *op. cit.*, p. 581.

35 *Ibid.*, pp. 582–583.

36 *Ibid.*, p. 583.

37 *Ibid.*

38 *Ibid.*, p. 584.

39 *Ibid.*

14

Role Impairment:

The "Antisocial"

The illnesses we discussed in Chapter 13 are the kind which usually lead to hospitalization; they show symptoms which a doctor can diagnose in a clinic. But there are other illnesses which do not usually lead to hospitalization. The victims do not even seem to be ill. But they constitute just as serious a social problem as do the obviously sick patients in hospitals.

It is perhaps safe to say that it is the behavior of these persons which occurs to most people when they think of "social problems." For an indeterminate, though doubtless large, proportion of the people who become the clients of welfare agencies, who fill the ranks of the unemployable, who overflow jails, almshouses, and even prisons, who are haled into court for nonsupport, who shrug off their responsibilities by simply deserting—family, job, army—belong to the classes of ill persons we are going to discuss in this chapter. Their behavior causes suffering; it is costly to the community; and it is dysfunctional.

Suicide as a Symptom of Role Impairment

Not all suicides are symptoms of mental or role illness, for despite the claims of some psychiatrists that any suicide, for whatever reason, is evidence of illness, sometimes suicide does seem to be a rational way out of an intolerable stress situation. Why, asks the patient dying of an incurable illness, should I continue to be a burden to myself and to those I love? Why should I not relieve them as well as myself? On the other hand, suicidal tendencies are common symptoms in some mental or role illnesses in Western societies, and attempted *but unsuccessful* suicide, in fact, is characteristic of one particular pathology, the psychopathic personality. Whether it is a symptom of illness or not, it is—except when culturally prescribed—a symptom of role impairment.

Incidence and Trends

In general, suicide rates have been found to be higher among males than females, but the relative rate for females is increasing so that the ratio of 3 to 1 which obtained before World War I was reduced to 2 to 1 by the time of World War II.[1] The probability of suicide increases with age. It is commoner among Protestants than among Catholics, among whites than among Negroes, among lower occupational groups than among higher, among the divorced than among the married. It was once true that suicides were commoner in urban than in rural areas, but a study in Michigan in 1945–1949 showed just the opposite to be true; rural rates were higher than urban rates.[2] Within any one urban community suicides tend to be most common in zones of disorganization. In the United States they tend to be commoner on the West Coast than in other regions. The reported seasonal incidence varies from one study to another. A study based on French data in the 19th century reported a high rate in the spring and a low rate in winter,[3] and the same pattern was found in the United States. The Michigan study, however, found the highest rates in autumn and winter; and a Seattle study, to be cited below, found no consistent seasonal pattern at all, perhaps because weather differences are less extreme there.

The suicide rate seems to be declining, but this may be a cyclical phenomenon. In 1900 the rate in the United States was 11.5 per 100,000 persons; it rose to 17.8 by 1908. Then it declined and fluctuated around 16 until World War I. In 1920 it reached the low point of 10.2. After this it rose until it stood at 17.5 in 1932.[4] Since 1940 it has been declining again.[5] In Great Britain it reached the high point in 1935 and has declined since then.[6] In any event, there seems to be no long-time increase.

Some of the decline in the United States since 1940 has been attributed to the feeling of unity and solidarity fostered by war, and to high levels of employment. Some of it, however, results from the relatively greater increase of young than of old persons in the population, so that the base on which rates are computed includes larger numbers of the non-suicide–prone younger age levels.[7]

Suicide does not seem to be a pathology of an era of abundance. The number of suicides tends to go up in times of depression and down in periods of prosperity, although the correlation is by no means perfect. The rate, for example, began to rise steadily in 1925 even though this decade was, until 1929, a time of great prosperity. Since it does occur more frequently in the older age levels, it might increase if the birth rate should fall precipitously, so that the older people increased more rapidly than the young. But it is possible that if we learn enough about the role and status problems of older people the relatively high rate of suicide among them may be modified by proper planning.

If we are primarily interested in causes of death, successful suicides must be the focus of our attention, and the above data are the only relevant ones. But if we are interested in suicide as a symptom of role illness we must include attempted as well as completed suicides. A recent study based on Seattle data from 1948 to 1952 increased our knowledge of the incidence of suicidal behavior by including both completed or successful (468) and attempted or unsuccessful (1,055) suicides.[8] It has been found, for example, that, as seen above, the suicide rate for men is much higher than that for women. But when attempted suicides are combined with completed suicides, the rates for the two sexes are almost identical. That is, women as often have the urge to commit suicide as have men, but they are less effective in implementing the urge. Whether there is some unconscious inhibition which protects them from success might well be explored. The age incidence of suicidal behavior for women is also different from that of men. The authors of the Seattle study summarize their findings as follows:

1. . . . . Completed and attempted suicides in Seattle [showed] high rates in the central business district and contiguous areas and relatively low rates in outlying residential sections.

2. Although males predominate among completed suicides and females are more numerous in attempted suicide, total suicidal behavior is equally characteristic of both sexes.

3. For males, rates of total suicidal behavior tend to increase with age, while female rates of total suicidal behavior are highest in the early years of adulthood (ages 27.5 to 37.5).

4. Important differences were found in suicidal behavior by race. Chinese and Japanese have low rates of both completed and attempted suicides. Negroes and Indians have a low incidence of completed suicide and a high incidence of attempted suicide.

5. The highest completed and attempted suicide rates by marital status are for the divorced. Married people have the lowest rates for completed suicides, and the widowed have the lowest rates for attempted suicide.

6. The "white collar" occupations have lower rates of completed and attempted suicides than "blue collar" occupations.

7. No consistent patterns are found in seasonal and daily variations of completed and attempted suicides.

8. For both completed and attempted suicides, males tend to utilize more violent means and methods than females.[9]

•

Causes

Suicide is the most extreme reaction one can have to stress. Although, as we indicated above, "it may . . . occur in apparently healthy people in response to their meeting or envisaging a life situation in which all their accustomed social ties and aspirations are experienced as irrevocably destroyed," [10] it is usually considered a symptom of emotional illness. Calamities to which some people react with resolution, if not with fortitude, lead others to suicide. The actual suicide is therefore interpreted as resulting from the impact of the calamity on an already disturbed personality.

Hardships of various kinds, like unemployment, poverty, hunger and other deprivations; ill health, mental abnormality, physical pain and deformity, often induce thoughts of suicide. The loss of honor, position, freedom or love, as well as failure with its accompanying feeling of inadequacy, disgrace, sex difficulties and tangled personal relationships make death seem necessary as an escape. But ordinarily no one of these alone would drive a person to suicide unless he were already harassed by a serious emotional conflict. Usually external events merely intensify latent disturbances and provide the immediate provocation in any given case. . . . Fundamental forces are fear and anxiety, feelings of inferiority, hatred, aggressiveness, revenge, guilt and other mental disorders that prevent people from attaining emotional maturity.[11]

Some psychiatrists posit a "death instinct" which drives people toward self-destructive action, if not actually to suicide. Suicide is also interpreted by some as a method of turning aggression inward against oneself because one is too impotent to turn it outward against others.

Perhaps the most illuminating insights into the nature of suicide are those derived from the study not of the individual as an isolated entity but of his role and status relationships. One of the greatest monographs on the subject classified suicide into three types, namely: altruistic, egoistic, and anomic. Altruistic suicide occurs when an individual is highly integrated into one group but isolated from others. He is so identified with his group that he is willing if necessary to sacrifice himself for it. Or he may be overly responsive to the group, so that he becomes vulnerable to their disapproval. Now he may suffer anxiety not because of loss of status as a *fait accompli*, but as a pending threat. Egoistic suicide occurs among people who have lost close ties with any group. The ties which hold individuals securely in their group matrix have been dissolved. This kind of suicide tends to occur in areas where group ties are most brittle. The social bonds which give meaning and stability to human life are severed, leaving the individual alone, unsupported, without resources to meet life problems. There is no motivation to live. If people have no role relationships, no group status, they are deprived of any *raison d'être*. No one cares. The channels through which people normally derive their "social nutriment" are clogged; they are cut off from support. Anomic suicide, finally, like egoistic suicide, is associated with social disorganization. The individual has no group norms or rules to keep him in check.[12] Anomie or normlessness is a different aspect of what we have called role confusion.

Sometimes, of course, suicide is a culturally prescribed way to save "face" or status, as among the Japanese. This would correspond to altruistic suicide. Culture conflict has also been suggested as an explanation of the high rate of suicide, at least in the rural areas analyzed in the Michigan study.

The rural male suicide rate in Michigan is higher for both the native-born and the foreign-born white male residents for almost all age groups. Two factors have been suggested to account for this. First, as urban values and ideals become more widely disseminated in rural areas, the conflict in rural and urban values becomes more intense. This conflict offers greater possibilities for maladjustment and personal disorganization among rural people. Second, the data that have been presented in this paper indicate that the majority of rural white males who commit suicide are engaged in occupations which are characteristic of urbanized groups. Though they live in the country (including fringe areas) they are urban-oriented in terms of occupation and mental attitudes. Nonetheless, Michigan farmers and farm managers as an occupational group exhibit extraordinarily high suicide rates.[13]

But even if we accept this interpretation we must still use some intervening variable such as role disturbance to explain the suicide.

We have commented before on the therapeutic resources available in group relationships. The time may come when a Suicides Anonymous will attempt to do for those who are contemplating this most irrevocable reaction to stress what similar groups have done for other victims of role derangements.

Psychopathic Personalities

When we have used up all our psychiatric categories for classifying role pathologies, there still remains a sizable segment of the population whose members do not fall neatly into any of our pigeonholes. They do not show symptoms of physical illness, infectious or nutritional. They may drink excessively but there is more than alcoholism involved. They may not be clear-cut hospital or court cases, but still there is something wrong with them.

Confusion in Terminology and Classification

In a book published as early as 1835, the author, J. C. Prichard, spoke of patients who were suffering from what he called "moral insanity." [14] In 1891 the term "psychopathic personality" was introduced by J. A. L. Koch to cover cases which could not be diagnosed as having any specific mental disorder but could not be considered normal.[15] But in the term he also included other types of neuroses, so that it lacked precision, and covered a wide variety of pathologies. By 1900 the term "moral insanity" was discarded. In 1904–1905 Adolf Meyer separated the neuroses from Koch's psychopathic personality category, leaving only the psychopathic personalities, and labeled them as cases of "constitutional psychopathic inferiority." Since that time there has been a great deal of discussion and controversy with respect to the term. Some psychiatrists lump together a variety of disorders under the category psychopathic personality. Some insist on retaining a genetic etiology. Some insist there is no such thing as psychopathic personality. Because of the wide divergence of opinion, some students feel the term ought to be discarded altogether.[16] But whatever term is applied to these disorders—we shall continue to use the term psychopathic personality—the existence of people with the characteristic set of symptoms to be presented here is not denied by any close student of the subject.

What the Psychopathic Personality Is Not

We can perhaps best understand the nature of the psychopathic personality if we begin by telling what it is not. One psychiatrist has carefully distinguished the psychopathic personality from the psychotic, from the psychoneurotic, from the mental defective, from the ordinary criminal, from delinquents, from homosexuals and other sexual deviants, from the erratic man of genius, from the "injudicious hedonist" and some other drinkers, from the clinical alcoholic, and from the malingerer.[17] It is true that a person with psychopathic personality symptoms might also develop other illnesses; he might become psychotic, for example, or an alcoholic. But so might a person with peptic ulcers. And the original malady should not be confused with the newly acquired one. The psychopathic personality is in quite a different category from any of the above.

We may summarize some of the differences from other illnesses with respect to certain symptoms as follows:

ANXIETY. We have built a good deal of our discussion of social problems around the kind of human suffering which we call anxiety. We have seen that although a certain amount is necessary, indeed, an inevitable concomitant of socialization, an excess of anxiety may impair role performance and even cause pathologies. Now we see that its absence is as pathological as its presence in excess. If the schizophrenic or the depressed person or the anxiety-ridden person may be said to care too much, the psychopathic personality may be said to care not enough, if, indeed, at all. Whatever the mechanism is—chemical in the form of oxygen use, or psychogenic or sociogenic in the form of maladaptive behavior patterns—which produces in the body the chemicals associated with anxiety, it is defective in the case of the psychopathic personality. He is unable to care. Situations which for most people would generate embarrassment, shame, humiliation, or guilt feeling have no such effect on the psychopathic personality. He may become irritated, annoyed, or exasperated, but never genuinely ashamed.

It is highly typical for him not only to escape . . . abnormal anxiety and tension . . . but also to show a relative immunity from such anxiety and worry as might be judged normal or appropriate in disturbing situations. Regularly we find in him extraordinary poise rather than jitteriness or worry, a smooth sense of physical wellbeing. . . . Even under concrete circumstances that would for the ordinary person cause embarrassment, confusion, acute insecurity, or visible agitation, his relative serenity is likely to be noteworthy.

It is true he may become vexed and restless when held in jails or psychiatric hospitals. This impatience seems related to his inability to realize the need or justification for his being restrained. What tension or uneasiness of this sort he may show seems provoked entirely by external circumstances, never by feelings of guilt, remorse, or intrapersonal insecurity. Within himself he appears as incapable of anxiety as of profound remorse.[18]

OBSESSIONS AND COMPULSIONS. The psychopathic personality does not suffer from obsessions or from compulsive behavior. This is an important point because we sometimes hear of compulsive people erroneously referred to as "psychopathic" killers or arsonists or thieves. The psychopathic personality is not of that category. "In classical obsessive neurosis the patient recognizes his recurrent thoughts (that he may harm a love object) as nonfactual (perhaps absurd) and struggles with them in fear and anxiety. The schizophrenic accepts delusions as reality and, with little or no struggle or effort at rejection, may act upon them inappropriately or destructively." [19] But the psychopathic personality steals and lies cheerfully and even relaxedly, all the while comporting himself with great propriety; or he performs his antisocial acts with whimsicality, all in fun. When caught and brought to task, he cannot understand why people make such a fuss over what he has done.

PARANOIA. The psychopathic personality does not feel himself to be persecuted; he does not act suspicious. He shows no malice. He has, in contrast to even the masked schizophrenic, a "socially appealing presence, . . . warm, easy manners . . . a false promise of strong and superior character and human qualities. . . . The surface of the psychopath . . . all of him that can be reached by verbal exploration and direct examination, shows up as equal to or better than normal and gives no hint at all of a disorder within. Nothing about him suggests oddness, inadequacy, or moral frailty. His mask is that of robust mental health." [20] The absence of paranoia in the psychopath is the more remarkable because he actually has no understanding of why he is punished, when he is. So far as he can tell, people are unreasonable in becoming so annoyed with him. Yet he shows no persecution complex.

CRIME. The crimes the psychopathic personality is guilty of tend to be minor, rarely heinous—vagrancy, misdemeanors, drunkenness. They result from impulsive or merely whimsical behavior and do not require sustained thought and perseverance.

> Though he regularly makes trouble for society, as well as for himself, and frequently is handled by the police, his characteristic behavior does not include felonies which would bring about permanent or adequate restriction of his activities. He is often arrested, perhaps a hundred times or more. . . .
> But the psychopath. . . . usually does not commit murder or other offenses that demand major prison sentences. . . . Of course . . . persons showing the characteristics of those here described do commit major crimes and crimes of maximal violence. There are so many, however, who do not, that such tendencies should be regarded as the exception rather than as the rule, or better still, as a pathologic trait independent, to a considerable degree, of the other manifestations which we regard as fundamental. It is, of course, granted that when serious criminal tendencies do emerge in the psychopath, they gain ready expression, and that no punishment can discourage them. Psychopaths who commit physically brutal acts upon others often seem to ignore the consequences. . . . When the typical psychopath . . . occasionally commits a deed of violence, it is usually a casual act done not from tremendous passion or as a result of plans persistently followed with earnest compelling fervor. There is less to indicate excessively violent rage than a relatively weak emotion breaking through even weaker restraints. The psychopath is not volcanically explosive, at the mercy of irresistible drives and overwhelming rage or temper. Often he seems scarcely wholehearted, even in wrath or "wickedness." [21]

SUICIDE. The psychopathic personality shows a specific and characteristic immunity to suicidal behavior. He very rarely resorts to it, in spite of the fact that he often finds himself in a situation which would make normal people want to do so. Threats of suicide, on the other hand, are very common. And bogus suicide attempts are frequently made, with great cleverness and histrionics.[22]

So much, then, for what the psychopathic personality is not—anxiety-ridden, obsessed, compulsive, paranoid, violently criminal, or suicidal. Why, then, is he a social problem?

The Psychopathic Personality as Role Disturber

The essential pathology of the psychopathic personality—expressing itself in such symptoms as impulsiveness, whimsy, superficiality, lack of concern for mature responsibilities, lack of dependability, shallowness, deficiency of judgment, disregard for consequences, and the like—may be described as a complete inability to take another person's role. When we call the psychopathic personality "irresponsible" we are putting our finger on his precise defect; he cannot respond to the role cues of those about him. He functions in a kind of role vacuum. His social or role perceptions are defective. "He cannot put himself in another's place and realize how his actions may affect the other." [23] In this lack of responsiveness to the role cues of those about him, he throws them off balance also. It is therefore almost impossible for anyone to perform his own role properly vis-à-vis a psychopathic personality. There is a visual defect which cuts out the dimension of depth; people suffering from it see the whole world as a flat plane. The psychopathic personality has an analogous defect. He cannot perceive the moral dimension of social or role relationships.

The concept of the psychopath as one deficient in [role-taking] ability . . . is useful to the extent that it resolves and fuses the indeterminate number of descriptive statements . . . which could be given.

For our purposes, then, deficiency in [role-taking] means the incapacity to look upon one's self as an object . . . or to identify with another's point of view. The psychopath is unable to foresee the consequences of his own acts, especially their social implications, because he does not know how to judge his own behavior from another's standpoint. What might be called social emotions, such as embarrassment, discomfiture, loyalty, contrition, and gregariousness (group identification), are not experienced by the psychopath.

When confronted with disapproval, the psychopath often expresses surprise and resentment. He cannot understand the reasons for the observer's objection or disapprobation. The psychopath cannot grant the justice of punishment or deprivation, because this involves an evaluation of his behavior from the standpoint of the "generalized other," or society. The psychopath will violate others' wishes and desires because he does not conceive of his own actions as inimical to their wants. He forms no deep attachments because he does not know how to identify himself with another or to share another's viewpoint. He lacks control because he cannot anticipate objections which others will make to his behavior.[24]

It is not the suffering of the psychopath himself—he does not seem to suffer, in fact—which is so disturbing but rather the suffering of those who must live in his role network, the people he lies to, breaks promises to, deserts, steals from, embarrasses, brings shame upon.

The degree of the illness may vary from mild to serious. Those who suffer only mild forms may be merely nuisances; [25] those suffering serious forms may leave a wide swath of havoc in their social field.

The damage the psychopath can do is aggravated because, unlike the more obviously ill, he is not likely to be institutionalized. It is not always clear when the diagnosis psychopathic personality is justified. The normal people in his environment often hesitate to diagnose him as pathological. The normal person—precisely because he is normal and therefore sensitive to those about him and conscientious in his relationships—overlooks a great deal of irresponsibility because he realizes how easy it is to exonerate one's self by imputing blame to others. And those who are not in responsible role relationships with the psychopath may never have occasion to see the symptoms. If or when he falls into the hands of the law, he is often just strange enough to get off or to be sent to a hospital. But at the hospital he is just well enough to be dismissed. He thus falls between both penal and medical institutions and is released to continue his role-disturbing behavior.

The Psychopath's "Charm"

There is another characteristic of the psychopath which also multiplies his chances for damaging social relationships. The adjective "charming" is often applicable to him. No one who has ever visited a mental hospital is likely to think any of the inmates charming. Yet many psychopathic personalities are. Since they are not motivated by malice, hatred, or revenge; since they may know all the words of contrition and apology; since they feel no shame or humiliation or "loss of face," they often have an engaging innocence and spontaneity about them.

They are the pampered son who cannot understand why his father should care because he took the family car to Memphis and had a wreck on the way, since it was an old jalopy anyway; or the daughter who does not see why her parents should be so upset because she spent the night with some strange man in Washington; or the husband who wonders why his wife should be so annoyed because he left her for a wandering trip for a couple of months. The parents and the wife take the psychopath back with a kind of baffled exasperation. What can you *do* with a son, or daughter, or husband, like that? They do not mean anything wrong.

Many a psychopath is an attractive person, with winning ways and even charm when he (or she) wishes to use it. There is "something about him" that leads people to believe in him, to condone his faults, to keep hoping for his reformation. A parent holds on to a psychopathic child, covering his misdeeds and forgiving him "unto seventy times seven." A husband yields to a psychopathic wife, even though he knows her tears are false and that he has suffered tortures at her hands and will suffer them again. A wife endures poverty, wretchedness and even abuse from her husband, but cannot find it in her heart to leave him.[26]

These people know the words; they often have great verbal facility. Indeed, one student speaks of the psychopath as "semantically disordered." [27] He conceals his illness behind a "mask of sanity."

It may be precisely because he is so self-assured, so lacking in anxiety, so unafraid, so lacking in powerful drives, so willing to say he is sorry, that he appeals to people who lack his seeming freedom from inhibition, his spontaneity. In this may lie his "charm."

Extent and Incidence

No one knows how many psychopathic personalities there are in this country. One student estimates that they are more numerous than those disabled by any other recognized psychosis except schizophrenia; and he guesses the number to be about half the number of schizophrenics.[28] These cases may occur at all status levels. They are perhaps more likely to be protected from detection in the upper levels and therefore more likely to seem to occur in the lower levels. But nothing can be said with certainty with respect to incidence by class. They may occur among the bright as well as among the dull. Some may, in fact, be extraordinarily brilliant. But they may be very dull, also, or even defective. In general, however, it is not intelligence they lack but the ability to internalize role obligations.

Causes

Little by little physiological, as well as neurological, causes of extreme role illnesses like schizophrenia are being sought and found. But we have not yet found them in the case of the psychopathic personality. Some psychiatrists seek an explanation in heredity; but even so they do not specify in what kind of hereditary defect the illness inheres. What part of the body "inherits" such an illness? Other psychiatrists believe that early childhood environment explains the illness. The hostile and destructive aggression which is characteristic of all infants is not diverted into normal channels. Parental, especially maternal, rejection is seen to be the cause by many who work with children. Others point to the fact that "in the histories of these people, broken homes, poorly adjusted parents, alcoholism, mental disorder of one type or another, criminal behavior and similar conditions occur over and over." [29] But the same kinds of background factors are found in the histories of other people also. In many cases the home and family background is, so far as measurable factors are concerned, superior to that of the normal person. Why does the illness take this form rather than another?

Since one of the most characteristic symptoms of this disorder is the lack of the usual anxiety reactions it may be that there is some malfunctioning of the metabolic processes—perhaps in the use of oxygen—which is precisely the opposite of that which produces excessive anxiety. Ordinarily, as we have seen, anxiety is generated in the child in order to socialize him. For some reason such anxiety cannot be generated in the case of the psychopathic personality. Socialization is therefore defective. The psychopathic personality has unimpaired intellectual faculties; he can therefore learn what is right and wrong in terms of words. But this intellectual performance lacks the visceral dimension which is supplied by anxiety. Since he cannot himself feel anxiety, he cannot understand it in others. He is like a child who learns to respond to signs and cues in his parents—keeping out of their way when they are in a bad mood, for example—but who lacks any understanding of what these signs and cues really mean. The causes, then, so far as we now know, seem to be sociogenic, that is, they are to be found in the role relations of the child in his earliest years. However, it would not do to rule out biological causes—hereditary or acquired—since only certain people seem to respond in this particular way.

Treatment

Since so many of the symptoms of this illness are akin to the behavior expected in children, it may not be diagnosed until it is well advanced. And even when well advanced it may be difficult to diagnose. Because the psychopathic personality makes such a good impression in superficial relationships, the symptoms do not show up in a clinical examination. The whole life pattern must be scrutinized in order to arrive at a diagnosis.

Even after his illness has been brought to the attention of the community in the form of antisocial and even criminal acts, he is likely to escape treatment. How, for example, can prankishness be "treated"? If he does not deliberately defy the law but rather acts on an outrageous impulse, what can be done for him in a prison? If he has no hallucinations, no impairment in rationality, what can be done for him in a mental hospital? The psychopath can give all the right answers; he knows them verbally. The difficulty is that he cannot relate them to behavior. But how can this be dealt with in the hospital? Neither penal institutions nor hospitals are equipped to handle the psychopath, so he is shunted back and forth until he is finally released to continue his depredations.

The administrative officers of penal institutions attempt to have such individuals transferred to mental hospitals because they believe them to be mentally ill. Knowing how little they can do for them and what difficult problems they are, the superintendents of mental hospitals attempt to get rid of them as soon as possible and transfer them back to the prison as "not psychotic." Pushed from prison to hospital and back again, wanted in neither, the psychopathic delinquent is essentially the orphan of both penology and psychiatry.[30]

The first step, suggested by one student of the subject, is to gain acceptance of the idea that these people really are ill. Punishment has no effect on them, so that incarceration is pointless. There should be special provision made for them in mental hospitals, including supervised probation and parole. And, of course, much more research on this illness is needed.[31]

Delinquency as a Symptom of Role Pathology

Character and behavior disorders which lie between that of the psychopathic personality and genuine criminal behavior are classed as delinquency.[32] Impropriety or repeated misdemeanors rather than serious offenses are characteristic. It is commoner in young persons than in adults; if it continues into adulthood it is likely to indicate that the person is a psychopathic personality.[33] Practically every adult has had periods of delinquency. "During childhood and adolescence confused manifestations of revolt or self-expression are, as everyone knows, more likely to produce unacceptable behavior than in adulthood," [34] but most people outgrow them, and become "mature . . . well-adjusted people and happy and distinguished citizens." [35] Ordinary delinquency, therefore, "might be thought of as a relatively mild disorder with fair prognosis." [36] If, however, the delinquency is a symptom of deranged family conditions the prognosis may not be so favorable unless the parents are amenable to treatment.

We are speaking here of disturbed people, of people whose delinquency is a symptom of some fundamental role pathology. But perhaps by far the most important kind of delinquency is not a result of pathology, but of sociological forces in our society, which we shall analyze in Chapter 18.

Crime as a Symptom of Role Pathology

Criminal behavior may be either maladaptive, "a pattern of defeat," or adaptive.[37] When it is maladaptive it reflects an inability to learn from social experience or a grotesque lack of consonance between motivation and behavior; it is pathological. When it is adaptive it is rational, that is, as normal as the behavior of anyone else; it just happens to be illegal. We deal here with the first kind, in Chapter 21 with the second. The motivation of the criminals in these two categories is fundamentally different. In the maladaptive category the motivations have little relationship to the outside world; in the adaptive normal category they are as related to the outside world as those of anyone else.

Sometimes the pathological offenders are classified into the psychotic or criminal insane; the neurotic, characterized by compulsions; and the psychopathic personalities. Without regard to these psychiatric categories, we shall simply consider these offenders sick people whose symptoms happen to take the form of criminal behavior.

Compulsive Crimes

In addition to alcoholism, drug addictions, and compulsive gambling, which we have already discussed, the symptoms of these sick persons may take the form of other kinds of criminal behavior, such, for example, as compulsive stealing (kleptomania), arson (pyromania), sex crimes and offenses, or even murder. But there is little connection between the crimes they commit and any rational or reasonable motivation. They may not know themselves why they are impelled to do the things they do.

Some are, in effect, grown-up juvenile delinquents; they have a chip on their shoulder and spend their lives defying authority. They play a perpetual game of hide-and-seek with the law. The policeman is necessary to them; they must have someone to outwit or defy. Winning against him gives them their only avenue to a feeling of achievement.

Sometimes criminals want to be caught; they want to be punished for guilt feelings which often have an obscure origin.

Sometimes they are acting out an old drama which they can never resolve. The patient is under an inner compulsion to behave in these forbidden ways. He cannot help himself. If he has moments of lucidity he may not even remember his acts. If he does remember he may feel great anguish at his own behavior, as did the young man who wrote in lipstick on the walls of an apartment where he had just killed a woman an appeal for someone to catch him before he committed any more crimes.[38] Terrible as these compulsions are, they are perhaps psychologically no different from the mild compulsions many of us have except that the kind of behavior they call for is illegal.

Sex Crimes

One kind of forbidden behavior which is symptomatic of role pathology is sexual—incest, voyeurism, "unnatural" sex acts, and homosexuality. A relatively small proportion of persons guilty of these role-violating crimes are ever known to the police; one estimate places it as one in ten.[39] Most of those who are known have suffered acute anxieties long before they committed sexual offenses, and were first known for other offenses rather than sexual ones, suggesting that the sexual offense was but one symptom, and perhaps only incidental, in the illness.

Although the mere practice of homosexuality does in and of itself constitute role pathology, it is usually not until or unless it is preferred to heterosexuality or renders normal heterosexual behavior impossible or unsatisfactory that it is considered a psychiatric problem. Between a third and a fourth of the male population in the United States has been found to have indulged in homosexual practices at some time or other in their lifetime.[40] But in most cases these practices were not preferred to heterosexual contacts nor did they interfere with them. A study of an institutional population reported that homosexuals as a group had, in effect, been thrown back on homosexuality because they repelled women and could not afford to marry or pay for illicit sex relations; and in many cases they had themselves been seduced early in life.[41]

For most people it is easier to understand the male who assumes the aggressive rather than the passive role in a homosexual relationship because here the behavior lies along expected lines. It is more difficult to understand the male who prefers the passive role in such a relationship, who prefers, that is, to act and dress like a woman. This phenomenon occurs in many cultures; and in some it is institutionalized in the form of transvestitism. The male who prefers the female role is permitted to dress and act like a woman, and there is little or no ignominy attached to such role reversals.[42]

Counseling [43] and an organization which harnesses group forces, similar to Alcoholics Anonymous—known as the Emotional Security Program [44]—have been found useful in dealing with sexual criminals. In Brooklyn in 1955 an experiment was inaugurated for the treatment of the 200 to 250 persons arrested annually for indecent exposure.

The offender, who must admit his guilt and be ready to pay for psychiatric assistance, will receive medical and psychiatric examinations from the panel which will submit its findings to the District Attorney and the court. . . . Thirteen. . . . psychiatrists . . . will cooperate in the program. . . . It was hoped the program coud be extended to other types of offenders should this pilot program prove successful.[45]

Such experiments are surely steps in the right direction, for a strictly legal approach is as futile in these illnesses as it would be in treating cancer.

Prisoners: Is There a "Criminal Type"?

But the majority of pathological offenders in most communities are still processed in the traditional legal mill and come to constitute a large part of the prison and jail population, keeping alive that perdurable ghost, the Lombrosian theory that criminality is an inherited phenomenon.

One of the commonest remarks students make when visiting a penitentiary is that the prisoners *look* just like anyone else. They have a stereotype of a "vicious killer" or a "reckless bandit" and they expect to find scowling men with beetling brows. Instead they usually find many mild-mannered men, often smiling with pleasure at the sight of young visitors breaking the monotony of their day. They see condemned murderers who look no different from men they see every day in the street.

Is there, then, no criminal type? There has been a long history of attempts to find some clear-cut criterion which would differentiate criminals from noncriminals. In the 19th century an Italian criminologist named Lombroso thought he had found a criminal type, characterized by certain physical anomalies, which he labeled the born criminal. Lombroso explained this type as the result of an atavism which produced a more primitive type. The idea of a person born to be a criminal is anathema to those with a humanitarian or a free-will ideology. And so every generation of criminologists has, in effect, laid the ghost of Lombroso. But it continues to haunt the field. The more obvious stigmas of the criminal type which Lombroso claimed—receding forehead, asymmetrical development, deformities, irregular teeth, exaggerated facial bones, left-handedness, prehensile feet, outstanding ears, large jaws and cheekbones—are no longer viewed as important. But the search for physical differentia has continued. An American anthropologist studied 14,477 inmates of institutions, making more than a hundred physical measurements of them, and compared them with nonprisoners. He concluded that criminals were biologically inferior to noncriminals.[46] The fallacy lies in the fact that the institutional population is only a small fraction of the criminal population, and this fraction is not a random sample.

But the feeling persists that even though the prison population is not very different in the measurable indexes so far used, it is, somehow, different from a normal population in other ways. One observer, himself an ex-prisoner, who spent eight years in a penitentiary, concludes that:

> Convicts, however many exceptions there may be, are generally not mature, fully developed people. . . . Nothing could be farther from the truth than the notion that prisoners are a representative cross-section of the human population, who, through mischance or uncharacteristic impulse, happen to land in jail. For the most part, notwithstanding any number of incidental virtues that may be found among them, they are truncated personalities—a separate breed whose natural habitat is prison and who find an outlet for all of their limited facilities in prison surroundings. . . . A . . . relatively small percentage . . . are complete human beings capable of assuming the responsibilities of free citizens.[47]

This pronouncement is, to be sure, not buttressed by scientific tests and it is as biased in its sampling as any study of an institutionalized population. But it makes clear, in a forceful and vivid manner, the point we are emphasizing here, namely that there is a criminal whose behavior is pathological in nature though he may not be declared legally insane.

The nature of the "criminal" population at the local level may be gleaned from a number of studies. In one, a study of the misdemeanants in the Middlesex County House of Correction, Massachusetts, for example, it was found that by far the largest category of inmates—30.8 per cent—was guilty of drunkenness. These cases, further, were considerably older—40.0 years of age—than the nonalcoholics. They had averaged 176 arrests for drunkenness in 10 years. The second largest category of offense was nonsupport (13.8 per cent), but such other manifestations of role pathologies as vagrancy, assault, rape, narcotics law violations, and carnal abuse of a female child were also reported.[48] This study concluded that in general the inmates of the county jail are just in an earlier stage in their progress toward the almshouse. Another study of chronic white petty offenders in a small city found that their mode of adaptation to the world they lived in was to retreat. Although they had tried Alcoholics Anonymous, the efforts of this organization had been unsuccessful, probably because there was no one in the local chapter on a low enough social status level to serve in effective role relationships.

It is desirable that the petty offenders be organized under their own sponsorship in order that a socially acceptable sense of self may develop in a quasi-primary group situation and that their energies may be diverted into activities which will give them a feeling of belonging to the society from which they are rapidly becoming alienated.[49]

In any event, the usual legal or judicial procedure is pointless when dealing with these sick people; they are "criminal" in their own pathological way, not in the way defined by the law, for ". . . the petty offender is . . . a unique type of 'criminal' in that the behavior involved in his offenses is consistent and uniform and differs sharply from that of other kinds of 'criminals.' "[50]

We shall not here attempt to determine the origin of the personality disorder which leads to or expresses itself in criminal behavior. It may or may not lie in genetic factors; the present trend of thinking is likely to look for it in early family experiences. There is doubtless a complex interplay of both genetic and experiential factors. Our concern here is primarily to round out our discussion of role pathologies which find expression in criminal acts.

Divorce as a Symptom of Role Pathology

We saw in our discussion of alcoholism that although some alcoholics are married and living with their spouses, a disproportionate number of them are not. We saw above that suicide is more common among the divorced. In the county jail population just referred to, the proportion of divorced persons was higher than in a state prison population and strikingly higher than in the total population—12.9 per cent of the misdemeanants, 7.8 per cent of state prisoners, and only 1.6 per cent of the adult male population.[51] Nonsupport, which is in many cases tantamount to desertion, was also common.

Inability to perform family as well as worker roles seems to be one of the commonest characteristics of the people we are discussing here. For these people divorce and desertion are therefore likely to be ways out.

But having said this much it is important to point out that the reverse of the above statement is not true, namely that every person who secures a divorce is incapable of performing family roles satisfactorily. A study of remarriage after divorce shows that half or more of those who divorce are reported to have at least average success in a remarriage. The lack of success in the first marriage must therefore have resulted not from any pathology but from some team factor.[52]

Other symptoms of those who are ill may be far more damaging to family role performance than divorce, such as the inability to love one's children or even rejection of them, revealing itself in some cases in physical cruelty. In such cases the illness is often socially "inherited" by the child, that is, the deranged family situation transmits to or creates in the child a pathology as a result of the trauma experienced in the home.

Marginal Distortions

Prejudice: The "Authoritarian Personality"

In a competitive society the stresses may become very great; there is tremendous pressure to "make good." Sometimes the anxieties involved in "making good" express themselvest in illnesses of one kind or another, as we have just seen, or they are relieved by alcohol. Sometimes, however, they express themselves in irrational prejudices which can serve as a "mask for privilege," or in the so-called "authoritarian personality."

The factors which make for prejudice have been classified into (1) those which reflect a conflict of interest, (2) those which result from cultural conflict, and (3) those which are irrational, emotional reactions. Sometimes all three factors are operating. For our purposes here, however, the last-named is the most pertinent.

Many persons, driven by an inferiority or by a resentment complex, or by both, develop emotional trends of anxiety, insecurity, weakness in the sense of vulnerability, damaged self-esteem, or similar traits. Such persons are afraid not so much of members of other groups but primarily of themselves: of their conscience, of freedom, of solitude, and of change. To overcome these characteristics certain defense mechanisms are employed, among which group prejudice has been found to be one of the most important. Many such persons look for a simple cause of all their troubles, worries, and sufferings.[53]

These people seek a scapegoat. And sometimes this mechanism becomes so vital a part of their psychic make-up that to deprive them of it might be really traumatic. They maintain their balance by pushing against others.

The authoritarian or prejudice-prone personality has been conceptualized as a new "anthropological" species which has come into being with modern industrialism.

> In contrast to the bigot of the older style he seems to combine the ideas and skills which are typical of a highly industrialized society with irrational or anti-rational beliefs. He is at the same time enlightened and superstitious, proud to be an individualist and in constant fear of not being like all the others, jealous of his independence and inclined to submit blindly to power and authority.[54]

He is a potential fascist.

Unlike the person who approaches the differences which become issues in conflict with a rational and analytical point of view,[55] the authoritarian personality reacts with irrational emotions, especially fear and hate. One series of studies of prejudiced people found such devices as projection, displacement, and rationalization common among them.[56] In general, prejudiced persons have the kinds of fears that other mentally disturbed persons have but instead of being directed toward such things as closed places or open places or snakes or mice they are directed toward other human beings who appear to them as threats. An indeterminate proportion of our population suffers from these fears and hostilities, constituting a sort of latent reservoir for fascistic, racist, or hate-mongering movements.

Obsessions: "The Bureaucratic Boss"

Another marginal role distortion which may have wide repercussions on social health is obsessive behavior in persons with authority. When most social organization was in small units, obsessive behavior in any one person did not ramify widely; it was more or less limited to the units in which it occurred. But in a society functioning through great bureaucratic organizational units, obsessive behavior in any position affects a large number of people. A bureaucrat with an obsessive personality may become a serious threat to the whole organization.

Individuals who in a market economy were able to live out these [obsessional] trends in such manifestations as hoarding, gaining, accumulating and building up many resources may readily find in the necessarily enlarged bureaucracy of a service state substitutive liberation for these trends in such manifestations as methodical power seeking, perfectionistic planning and regulating other persons in terms of systems. And as obsessionals cannot stand the impediment of the free play of their personality trends, being rigidly unadaptable, they experience as upsetting any evidence of spontaneous vitality and creativity in persons who fall within the ambit of their official authority. Accordingly they feel such persons as "dangerous" and "unsafe," and endeavor to suppress or stultify them, thereby reducing the total creativity and bringing about further deterioration in social health.[57]

These people are not sick enough to require hospitalization; but they are sick enough to create a vast amount of disturbance in those with whom they deal, with consequent damage to social functioning. They must have conformity at almost any cost.

The Marginally Dependent

There is another class of persons who hover on the fringes of pathology, but who, with some assistance, can keep within the limits of passable role performance. When we were discussing alcoholism in Chapter 11 we noted that there is a characteristic pattern of life for some alcoholics which involves a long history of institutional living. There are some people who need this kind of protection. They feel most comfortable, most secure, most at ease living within an institutional setting. The armed services offer a congenial niche for them. They may be very intelligent, even talented, people. There is no necessary impairment of ability. In both the armed services and in religious orders, for example, there are men and women of the highest talents. They find the security of their positions congenial. People who live in and administer schools and hospitals may also find this mode of life satisfying. Some prisoners even prefer the confining walls to life outside. On a fairly low level the Salvation Army provides such a haven for the less talented, as do flophouses, shelters, and subsidized housing for homeless persons. These people, whether talented or of low intelligence, prefer to have someone else make the day-by-day decisions for them. They want others to provide shelter and food for them.

Such people do not become social problems, obviously, when they are performing their several roles adequately. It is only when they do not find the protection they need that they may slip over the line into true pathology. There is perhaps a large, though indeterminate, number of men and women in all the major cities who need some kind of institutional protection, not a hospital, not a prison, but a shelter of some kind in order to keep them from deterioration.

"Crazes"

So far we have been talking about the illnesses of individual human beings. In Chapter 6 we referred to the concept of a sick society or culture and rejected it; the application of such terms as "sick" and "sane" to societies or cultures was viewed as merely analogical. But there is an intermediate area in which individuals in groups or crowds or mobs or mass movements behave in ways which, if they were alone, would surely be judged as symptoms of psychiatric disorder. The so-called campus "pantie raids," in which young men in groups do things which would be considered abnormal if done as individuals, illustrate this phenomenon in a mild form. Individuals in mobs destroy, pillage, even kill. When the mob is dispersed and they return to their daily routines they may look back in amazement at their behavior.

Mass hysterias and frenzies were more characteristic of the past than they are today.

To estimate fully the force of these popular ebullitions in the Middle Ages, we must bear in mind the susceptibility of the people to contagious emotions and enthusiasms of which we know little in our colder day. A trifle might start a movement which the wisest could not explain nor the most powerful restrain. It was during the preaching of this crusade of 1208, against the Albigenses, that villages and towns in Germany were filled with women who, unable to expend their religious ardor in taking the cross, stripped themselves naked and ran silently through the roads and streets. Still more symptomatic of the diseased spirituality of the time was the crusade of the children, which desolated thousands of homes. From vast districts of territory, incited apparently by a simultaneous and spontaneous impulse, crowds of children set forth, without leaders or guides, in search of the Holy Land; and their only answer, when questioned as to their object, was that they were going to Jerusalem. Vainly did parents lock their children up; they would break loose and disappear. . . .[58]

The susceptibility of the Middle Ages to mass hysterias has been interpreted as the result of the dissolution of society and the abolition of the mores which stabilized behavior. The invading tribes took over Roman culture without really assimilating it; in effect they merely used it for their less civilized ends, so that "passion, sensuality, ferocity, superstitious ignorance, and fear characterized the age." [59] Groups of people went about whipping one another, or weeping wildly, or praying.

Mass phenomena took a somewhat different form in the 18th and 19th centuries. There were speculating frenzies, among the most famous being the so-called Mississippi Bubble and the Holland tulip-bulb craze. Many types of joint-stock companies were organized for all kinds of fantastic purposes; one had a charter which stated that no one was to know what its purpose was.

In the 19th and early 20th century lynching mobs and pogroms were characteristic; and race riots break out sporadically even today. Sometimes, however, the form these illnesses take is cold and calculated and therefore doubly shocking. When many modern Germans look back at the fantastic history of the 1940's when 6,000,000 Jews were scientifically killed it seems like a bad dream. The mass purges carried out by Stalin were repudiated by his successors, although the purge itself is considered by some inevitable in a totalitarian state.[60]

Mass hysterias, panics, and frenzies have many of the characteristics of pathological behavior. Role responsibilities are abrogated and since this affects a large number of people at the same time there is little enforcement of role obligations on one another. The result is a kind of holocaust. It is because of the possibility of such role abrogation when large numbers of people assemble that police permission and protection are usually required. Such mass behavior fulfills all the criteria of a social problem.

Some Implications of Role Impairment

That the people we have been discussing in this chapter are often social problems is scarcely debatable. But it might well be asked, Are they really ill? Are they really suffering from pathologies?

Are the Antisocial Really Ill?

It took a long time to recognize mental illness as an illness. Only the most serious types were at first recognized as pathologies, and "decades passed before the masked or cryptic schizophrene and the well-oriented, careful, and brilliantly reasoning paranoiac could count on so early medical attention as they receive today. We have not yet learned to distinguish such patients very readily and they sometimes remain without treatment or any protective social measures until their disorder is far advanced." [61] And we are only now beginning to view the less spectacular disorders as genuine pathologies.

As a result, the misbehavior which is so annoying, and even dangerous, seems to be willful defiance of the mores or the law, rather than a symptom of illness. We insist on punishment to fit the crime. We are infuriated at the idea of permitting these wrongdoers to escape responsibility for their behavior. It is almost impossible for a normal person to put himself in the position of the ill person. He can control himself, he can discipline himself, he can assume his responsibilities. Why can't everyone else? He interprets the ill person's behavior in terms of his own. If he acted in that way it would mean that he was deliberately trying to get away with something.

If punishment had any therapeutic effects on role-sick people, there would be some justification in using it. But nothing is more certain than that it has no effect. A legal approach to their problems is futile. It is not sentimentality that dictates a medical approach but, rather, sheer, hard practicality.

Not only a patient's welfare but that of the community must be given consideration in any step we decide to take. More and more as time passes we find symptoms and behavior formerly regarded as voluntary wrongdoing or the just results of sin being classed as disease. This does not prove that eventually all wrongdoing will be plainly revealed as disease and all conduct necessarily evaluated at a level in which good and bad are nonexistent. There are, however, indications that medical, legal, and social remedial steps are often useful in dealing with situations that we have not yet assayed and may never unanimously assay in formal terms of ethics.[62]

It may take time before the public learns to substitute pity for moral indignation; and it will not be easy, especially if the suffering of the sick person's victims has been great.

A second difficulty, in addition to that of viewing these people as ill, is the fact that they usually do not view themselves as ill and therefore do not willingly accept the role of patient. Because of the complementary nature of roles, if a person refuses to behave like a patient it is almost impossible to treat him as one.

A third difficulty, and almost the most baffling, is that of diagnosing the illness since as yet it must be made wholly on the basis of role performance. When should a person be judged ill? The problem is especially difficult in the case of the psychopath, but it occurs in obsessive cases also. It is because of the increasing urgency of making these diagnoses that the psychiatrist has become such a key person in our society today. He holds about the same responsibility as a judge. He is, in effect, a medical judge and his pronouncement is likely to be accepted by the legal judge.

The Antisocial and Democracy

Democracy is based on the assumption of a responsible electorate. Every man's vote counts as much as anyone else's. But a large, though indeterminate, part of the electorate consists of role-sick people, such as those discussed in this chapter. If they commit felonies and become convicted, they are, to be sure, deprived of their rights. But a considerable number remain at large. Not only are they unable to contribute to the functioning of a democracy but they may even act as a drag on its functioning. They sell their votes. They violate laws. Some are psychopaths, unable to understand why their behavior is wrong. Some are defiant: they have a chip on their shoulder. But democracy is also challenged by the obsessive conformist. He cannot bear to have people different, free, or spontaneous.

For it will be noted that just as some of the traits formerly labeled "bad" are coming increasingly to be labeled "pathological," so also are many traits formerly labeled "good." When "goodness" and "badness" are identified with the mores, it sometimes happens that the "good" man may be as pathological as the "bad" one. The rigid person whose virtue consists wholly in undeviating conformity with a fixed code may be no more normal than the spontaneous person who cannot understand why anyone should mind his nonconformity, or than the defiant person who understands all too well why people mind, and derives satisfaction precisely because they do.

The theory of democracy implies the ability to give and take, to make reasonable compromises. The obsessive person cannot; he must hew to the line. The theory of democracy implies, also, that people do not have to "escape from freedom" and seek security in thralldom to the group or to the state. Many role-sick people do.

Just how heavy a load of role-sick people a society can sustain we do not know. Nor do we know precisely how heavy our load is today. But that it can be reduced is the conviction of many persons working in the field of public health. And that it should be, is the conviction of men of good will in all fields.

NOTES

1 James L. Halliday, *Psychosocial Medicine* (Norton, 1948), p. 138. These figures are for Great Britain.

2 W. Widek Schroeder and J. Allan Beegle, "Suicide: An Instance of High Rural Rates," in Arnold Rose, ed., *Mental Health and Mental Disorder* (Norton, 1955), pp. 408–419.

3 Emile Durkheim, *Suicide,* translated by George Simpson (Free Press, 1951).

[4] Bessie Bunzel, "Suicide," *Encyclopaedia of the Social Sciences,* Vol. 14 (Macmillan, 1934), p. 457.

[5] Halliday, *op. cit.,* p. 138.

[6] Schroeder and Beegle, *op. cit.,* p. 409.

[7] *Ibid.*

[8] Calvin F. Schmid and Maurice D. Van Arsdol, Jr., "Completed and Attempted Suicide: A Comparative Analysis," *American Sociological Review,* 20 (June 1955), pp. 273–283.

[9] *Ibid.,* pp. 282–283.

[10] Halliday, *op. cit.,* p. 138.

[11] Bunzel, *op. cit.,* pp. 458–459.

[12] Durkheim, *op. cit.*

[13] Schroeder and Beegle, *op. cit.,* p. 417–419.

[14] *A Treatise on Insanity* (London: Gilbert & Piper, 1835).

[15] *Die Psychopathischen Minderwertigheiten* (Revansburg: Maier, 1891).

[16] Hervey Cleckley, *The Mask of Sanity, An Attempt to Clarify Some Issues about the so-called Psychopathic Personality* (Mosby, 1955), p. 550. In 1952 the term "psychopathic personality" was discarded in the *Standard Nomenclature for Diseases of the Psychobiologic Unit.*

[17] Cleckley, *op. cit.,* pp. 274–368.

[18] *Ibid.,* p. 384.

[19] *Ibid.,* pp. 390–391.

[20] *Ibid.,* p. 437.

[21] *Ibid.,* pp. 37–38, 293–294.

[22] *Ibid.,* p. 411.

[23] Winfred Overholser and Winifred V. Richmond, *Handbook of Psychiatry* (Lippincott, 1947), p. 185.

[24] Harrison G. Gough, "A Sociological Theory of Psychopathy," in Arnold Rose, ed., *Mental Health and Mental Disorder* (Norton, 1955), p. 279. In this quotation the term "role-taking" has been substituted for the author's "role-playing," since his usage of the latter term corresponds to our usage of the former.

[25] One mild form of psychopathic personality was lampooned in a *New York Times* editorial of October 13, 1955, as follows: "People who walk away with the Post Office Department's ball-point pens are probably the same ones who walk on the grass, pick flowers and go the wrong way on one-way streets when all the signs explicitly say not to. These same individuals, undoubtedly, pinch fruit to see if it is ripe, squeeze each piece of chocolate candy in a box to find one to their taste, ignore visiting hours in hospitals and cross streets against red lights. When they were young, these same persons possibly walked on wet cement or inscribed their initials for all posterity to see and grew up to cut dishonest corners on their income tax." Nothing heinous, nothing shocking, nothing "wicked"; there is merely an absence of responsibility or role sense or the ability to see their behavior in a social context. If they were ever called to account for their behavior they would doubtless apologize and say they were sorry—and wonder why under the sun anyone cared.

[26] Overholser and Richmond, *op. cit.,* pp. 187–188.

[27] Cleckley, *op. cit.,* p. 440.

[28] *Ibid.,* pp. 38, 543–548.

[29] Overholser and Richmond, *op. cit.,* p. 194.

[30] G. N. Thompson, *The Psychopathic Delinquent and Criminal* (Charles C Thomas, 1953), quoted in Hervey Cleckley, *op. cit.,* p. 509.

[31] Cleckley, *op. cit.,* Chapters 65–68.

[32] *Ibid.,* p. 297.

[33] *Ibid.,* p. 299.

[34] *Ibid.,* p. 300.

[35] *Ibid.*

[36] *Ibid.,* p. 297.

[37] Richard L. Jenkins, *Breaking Patterns of Defeat* (Lippincott, 1955).

[38] Lucy Freeman, *Before I Kill More* (Crown, 1955).

[39] *The New Approach, Sex Offender to Good Citizen* (Atascadero State Hospital, California, 1955).

[40] A. C. Kinsey *et al., Sexual Behavior in the Human Male* (Saunders, 1948), p. 664.

[41] John L. Gillin, *The Wisconsin Prisoner* (Univ. of Wisconsin Press, 1946), pp. 97–107.

[42] Margaret Mead, *Male and Female* (Morrow, 1949), pp. 129–131; Harry Benjamin, "Transvestism or Transsexualism," *International Journal of Sexology,* 7 (Aug. 1953), pp. 12–14.

[43] *New York Times,* October 18, 1955.

[44] Roswell H. Johnson, "Counseling the Homosexual Client," *Family Life,* 15 (Sept. 1955), pp. 5–6.

[45] *The New Approach, Sex Offender to Good Citizen.* Reported in *Newsweek,* December 16, 1955, p. 70.

[46] Ernest Hooten, *Crime and the Man* (Harvard Univ. Press, 1939).

[47] H. W. Hollister, "Why Prisoners Riot," *Atlantic Monthly,* October 1955, p. 67.

[48] Albert D. Ullman, Harold W. Demone, Jr., A. Warren Stearns, and Norman F. Washburne, "Some Social Characteristics

of Misdemeanants," paper read at meetings of Eastern Sociological Society, March 1956.

49 Irwin Deutscher, "The White Petty Offender in the Small City," *Social Problems*, 1 (Oct. 1953), p. 73.

50 *Ibid.*, p. 72.

51 *Ibid.*

52 Jessie Bernard, *Remarriage, A Study of Marriage* (Dryden, 1956).

53 Marie Jahoda, Morton Deutsch, and Stuart W. Cook, *Research Methods in Social Relations with Especial Reference to Prejudice* (Dryden, 1951), p. 367.

54 T. W. Adorno, Else Frenkel-Brünskik, Daniel J. Levinson, and R. Nevitt Sanford, *The Authoritarian Personality* (Harper, 1950), p. ix.

55 Jessie Bernard, *American Community Behavior* (Dryden, 1949), pp. 517–521.

56 Nathan Ackerman and Marie Jahoda, *Anti-Semitism and Emotional Disorder* (Harper, 1950); Bruno Bettelheim and Morris Janowitz, *Dynamics of Prejudice* (Harper, 1950); Leo Lowenthal and Norbert Guterman, *Prophets of Deceit* (Harper, 1949); and Paul W. Massing, *Rehearsal for Destruction* (Harper, 1949). These studies are summarized in Selma Hirsh, *The Fears Men Live By* (Harper, 1955).

57 Halliday, *op. cit.*, pp. 215–216.

58 W. G. Sumner, *Folkways* (Ginn, 1906), pp. 213–214. See also Henry Charles Lea, *A History of the Inquisition of the Middle Ages*, 3 volumes (Harper, 1888).

59 Sumner, *op. cit.*, p. 212.

60 Zbigniew K. Bryzezinski, *The Permanent Purge* (Harvard Univ. Press, 1956).

61 Cleckley, *op. cit.*, p. 511.

62 *Ibid.*, pp. 512–513.

V

ABUNDANCE AND SOCIAL DISORGANIZATION: FAMILY AND WORKER ROLES

"New occasions teach new duties; Time
makes ancient good uncouth."
—JAMES RUSSELL LOWELL, *The Present Crisis*

THERE HAVE BEEN many periods of great social disorganization in human history. Great plagues—as we saw in Chapter 8, for example— have shaken the foundations of social order; wars, invasions, famines, and great migrations have also. And if there had been analysts and researchers present to report the results, we might have had treatises on the social problems resulting from such disorganization. But the kind of disorganization which perplexes us today is the kind accompanying the rapid technological changes which in turn make abundance possible. We may easily imagine that the great technological revolution which took agriculture out of the hands of women and turned it over to men— when it was transformed by the substitution of the plow for the digging stick—was disorganizing in the sense that it modified role relationships. But few people were involved, the pace was probably slow, and the network of relationships disturbed was fairly limited. It is not abundance alone which produces the disorganization we are to discuss here but also the rapid rate of change, especially technological change, accompanying it.

The people we are going to discuss in Part V are not victims of pathologies, as were those we discussed in Part IV. They are as well as the rest of us. We remind ourselves at this point that we are talking of aggregates of people and that what is "normal" is not every single individual but the distribution of qualities in the population. They are within a range called normal. We cannot, in brief, explain their behavior in terms of pathologies, as we could the behavior of people discussed in Part IV.

In Chapter 15 we examine the change in the nature of the status problems of women between the 19th and the 20th century; we note

338

the effect the change in status has had on the relationships between the sexes; and then we proceed to examine in some detail the problems women face in the performance of their worker roles. In Chapter 16 we scrutinize the role of father and of mother, noting the provisions which the community makes for taking over the father's role of provider when he does not or cannot himself perform it, and analyzing in some detail the changes which abundance and urbanization have wrought in the definition of the maternal role.

Chapter 17 considers the family and worker roles of youth. The changes in definition of parental and filial roles which have come with abundance are presented, and some of the implications are examined. The current reappraisal of the worker role of youth is discussed, with some examination of the implications involved for schools. Because of the close connection between work, school, and delinquency, Chapter 18 attempts to clarify the trends in delinquency, placing particular emphasis on the status—rather than the psychiatric—dimension of this problem.

The role and status problems of the older members of our society are reviewed in Chapter 19, where it is pointed out that the improvement in standards which abundance has made possible has led us to be as dissatisfied with the position of older persons today as we were a generation ago, even though their status is measurably improved. They are more likely to be independent today, for example; but we want more for them now. We want more income, more work, better health. We want satisfying roles for them.

Chapter 20 is concerned with the worker roles of men, and the stresses which accompany them. The very special problems associated with criminal worker roles are considered in Chapter 21. The criminals we discuss there are not necessarily suffering from pathologies; their criminal behavior is not a symptom of any illness. They are as normal as the rest of the population except that they earn their living in illegal ways.

In brief, Part V is devoted to a fairly minute examination of social disorganization analyzed in terms of role and status changes as they have resulted from the abundance made possible by modern technology.

15

Status and Role Problems
of Modern Women:
Family and Worker Roles

The Pattern of Change

The following statement does not deal with role and status situations in an American community, although it might very well be said to describe situations quite familiar to many communities in this country. It refers, actually, to role and status problems in a Mexican village. It illustrates in an illuminating way—all the more illuminating because we can view it from a distance, uninvolved—the impact of technological changes on role and status relationships within the family.

Women are . . . more in conflict with traditional ways than are men. Husbands generally find themselves in a position in which they must conserve the old order of things in the home to maintain their control over the family. Wives tend to reject certain aspects of their role, particularly those which interfere with their freedom of movement and economic activities. The strong preference women display toward work which takes them outside the home, and their feeling of deprivation when they cannot leave the home,

The Pattern of Change

Status Equality: Legal and Crescive

Current Status Anomalies in Redefinition of Sex Roles

Sources of Role Conflict in Modern Women

The Worker Role of Modern Women

Role Conflicts of the Nonworking Wife

Conflict between Motherhood and the
Cultural Definition of the Feminine Role

Can We Prepare Women for Roles
of Wife and Mother?

are evidence of this. . . . The general reaction of women to pressure to conform is one of a sense of frustration and deprivation. The martyr-complex is widespread among married women, and in telling their life stories women are often so overwhelmed by self-pity that they break down and weep. They dwell on the sadness of their lives and the faults of their husbands; it is, they say, a woman's unhappy lot to suffer at the hands of men. Hostility toward men is quite generalized, and women readily and quite typically characterize all men as . . . very bad. . . .

The husband occupies a peripheral position within the home, his participation in family and household affairs being minimal. His work, except for . . . making occasional repairs to the house, is outside the home. For the majority of men, the home is a place where one eats and one's other physical needs are tended to. Men are away from home a good part of the day. . . . With the husband away, the wife is not only head of the family for long periods of time, but because of the low income she often has to find means to support herself and her children until his return.

Perhaps more important than his physical absence from the home is the behavior and attitude of the husband when he is there. Traditionally, husbands keep aloof from the petty details of the household. . . . In many families, particularly among couples who represent the older generation, the role of the husband gradually comes to be little more than that of punisher and provider. . . . There is little emotional dependency upon him. A large part of his status stems from the fact that he is the main source of support. . . . Despite the husband's role as provider, women are increasingly undertaking to contribute to the support of their families, even when the husband is a relatively good provider. . . . Many wives try to earn enough so as not to depend upon their husbands entirely. . . .[1]

In the Mexican village the technological changes which affect family relationships are such things as a new road, bus service to a nearby city, and the introduction of a corn mill.[2] In the cities of the United States changes might be more complex, but the pattern of change is very similar wherever it happens. New technologies result inevitably in new status alignments and new role relationships. This is social disorganization seen through a microscope.

It is our purpose in this chapter to examine some aspects of role and status problems associated with change as they relate to men and women in the United States in the second half of the 20th century. We are particularly concerned with the role conflicts of women in worker roles. We cannot, obviously, cover all such problems nor can we make an exhaustive examination of any one of them. We have selected for discussion, therefore, only some of the most salient, namely: the changes in the nature of status problems in the 20th century from those dealing with legal sanctions to those dealing with crescive—that is, customary, traditional, and moral—sanctions; the effect of sex role changes on the status of men; the worker role of women as related to familial roles; and the conflict between motherhood and the cultural definition of the feminine role.

Status Equality: Legal and Crescive

In the 19th century the woman's rights movement aimed at legal rights and privileges; it was primarily status-oriented. The position of women was likened to that of slaves; and the term "emancipation" was used with reference to women as well as to slaves. And, indeed, the movement to free the slaves was paralleled by a movement to "free" women. Women were, literally, second-class citizens. They suffered many legal disabilities both outside and inside the family. They were disenfranchised. Their legal existence was "suspended during the marriage, or at least incorporated and consolidated into that of the husband. . . ."[3] A militant woman's rights movement, together with a host of technological inventions—not the least of which was the type-writer—created a tremendous change in the status of women. At the present time there are few status differences between the sexes embodied in legislation. Whatever status differences now prevail are likely to be embodied in crescive—customary or traditional or moral—sanctions rather than in statutory ones. This does not, of course, make the problem any easier. It is often harder to fight customs, traditions, and mores than it is to attack laws. A husband's attitude or an employer's prejudices may be more effective than a law in determining status. Sometimes the aim of women's movements at the present time is to change these crescive norms by means of legislation, even if it involves reducing the rights of women.[4]

The old-style feminist was militant; she was carrying on a crusade. The modern woman is no longer militant; she does not have to be. Her fight is quite different from that of the 19th-century feminist.

Here is certainly a new-style feminist. She doesn't think of herself as a belligerent in a campaign for women's rights. You won't hear from her lips such telltale phrases of passionate involvement as "It burns me up to think that just because she is a woman . . ." or "It's a man's world. . . ." The absence of militancy is not surprising. Militancy belongs to an early stage of a social movement. Passion ran high when deep-rooted traditions were first attacked and new demands first proclaimed. But now the rights have been won. . . .[5]

The difficulty is, as the author we have just quoted points out, that rights require social as well as legal machinery for their implementation. It may do little good to have legal rights if it is too difficult to use them because of the absence of social machinery, in the form of appropriate role definitions. Role confusion and conflicts are so fundamental and so pervasive that they rather than status inequalities may be said to constitute the characteristic middle-class family problem in the second half of the 20th century. At the present time the problems that involve women are more likely to be concerned with role, status being incidental to the role difficulty.[6] But status stresses impinge heavily on men.

Current Status Anomalies
in Redefinition of Sex Roles

Before we turn to the specific role problems of women as they relate to the family, we remind ourselves of the fact, referred to in Chapter 12, that changes in the definition of sex roles have had profound impact, especially traumatic for men, on the status relationships between the sexes. Discussing the change in sex incidence of peptic ulcer over the past century, a recent analysis makes the following points:

If one wishes to speculate, it can be suggested that the "emancipation of woman" that has characterized western nations during the past half-century or more has placed a differential stress in man-woman relationships, with the "pace" of modern life adversely affecting the security of men more than that of women. The fact of significant change in sex ratio for the incidence of perforated peptic ulcers throughout western civilization does fit in roughly with the thesis of augmented social dynamics in disease. Even a brief survey of the corresponding transitions in the status relationships of men and women, especially in the middle socioeconomic classes, is provocative. Note-worthy would seem to be the change in women's attitudes toward men, augmented by profound changes in the social order that have resulted in urbanization, industrialization, and democracy in education, occupation, government, the family, and social life in general. This tide of change can be viewed as undermining the established statuses and emotional supports for man. His position of security and dominance in the family, which was en-trenched and reinforced by his culture and society and subscribed to in the nineteenth century by his women folk, especially by his wife, has been challenged and shaken in the twentieth century.

In the earlier period of male dominance, success and security for a woman were gained mainly through affiliation with men, especially by marriage. The period of maximum striving and competitive effort for marriage as her chief forte was between the ages of seventeen and twenty-seven, after which, if she had not married, resignation might replace striving as she took her place as a subservient figure in some relative's home. Thus, the cultural pattern for female success fostered stress in the years before marriage by strictly limiting her goals and denying overt expression to wider competitive efforts.

In contrast, man was freely conceded the "number one" position in the family circle, and his home was conventionally dubbed "his castle." Within a social matrix of uncontested male dominance he was permitted considerable emotional dependence upon his women folk, and, under cover of his position, he was able to give free expression to, and find support for, his emotional needs. His idiosyncrasies were indulged, his peccadillos tolerated, and his self-assurance reinforced.

With the change in cultural norms and codes, and with corresponding alterations in interpersonal relationships, the emotional reliance of man on his women folk has become more difficult to indulge and the fulfillment of these needs harder to achieve; his authority and freedom appear limited and his prerogatives curtailed. Environmental changes have swept away many of women's former obligations to him, and ambivalence on their part toward their remaining responsibilities seems significant in the altered domestic relationships. ·

While man's position of superiority and prerogative has declined in the domestic setting, his role of responsibility has not been reduced. A wife may become the major financial contributor to the home and gain power to make the key decisions, while unwittingly creating in her husband a conviction of inadequacy. If she attempts and fails in an occupational or vocational venture, she is justified by society in retiring to domestic duties and being provided for by her husband, while there is no such socially approved safety haven for him. And if he should fail to be as good a "provider" as neighbor Jones, he can be nagged and denied the emotional supports of his wife. Indeed, a wife's humiliation over her husband's failure to provide adequately, as measured by contemporary standards, has strong social approval and sanctions. While society's requirements of the male are essentially as stringent as before, the assured emotional supports of family life seem to have dwindled. Can it be that he resorts, and regresses in a sense, to earlier established patterns of eating and drinking or to the bodily reactions associated with the physiological preparation for eating and drinking, and may this be one of probably many factors that have tipped the scales in the sex ratio for peptic ulcers? [7]

The equalization of the sexes has, in brief, had the effect of lowering the status of men, with important repercussions in all aspects of the relationship between the sexes.

Many jobs which were once performed by men have been taken over by women. Secretaries, school teachers, and even riveters are women today; these were once male occupations. During both World Wars women learned to do factory jobs; plants were designed to accommodate women workers. On a more superficial level, as measured in tests of masculinity and femininity, one psychologist reports that unlike the situation reported by earlier studies, both men and women are now becoming more "masculine." [8] With these changes in role definition and the accompanying status upsets, there come difficult problems of adjustment for men and women to which there do not seem to be easy answers.[9]

It is important to remind ourselves that no one can be blamed for these changes. Angry tirades against a "generation of vipers" certainly lack cogency. The resentment against women which smolders so near to the surface in many men is certainly understandable; but it is hardly rational. Both men and women are victims of the changing nature of role definitions and conceptions in our society today.

Sources of Role Conflict in Modern Women

The sources of cultural role confusion may be summarized under three headings, namely: inertia, or lag between technological change and role definitions; the existence of a plethora of roles to choose among; and the incompatibility among roles themselves.

In American communities, as in the Mexican village described above, many old role definitions, suitable to a past social order, are no longer functional or "eufunctional"; yet they retain a kind of nostalgic, albeit anachronistic, vitality. New roles, fitting the current social structure, have not yet become firmly articulated or "jelled." Women are therefore caught between an impossible backward-looking definition of their role and a new one, as yet not completely established.

Women became a "social problem" because technological and social changes over the past century and a half have disturbed an old equilibrium without as yet replacing it with another. As a result, our society is a veritable crazy quilt of contradictory practices and beliefs. Some old attitudes persist stubbornly in the face of a new reality which has long since rendered them meaningless. New conditions have arisen which have not as yet been defined by public opinion—leaving human beings without guidance and protection. New goals have emerged without the social machinery required for their attainment. The old and the new moralities exist side by side, dividing the heart against itself. The present disharmony has a myriad of facets. Here a widow goes to work, leaving her children unattended because society still assumes that all mothers can stay home and take care of their children. There, a successful homemaker says apologetically, "I am just a housewife," thus reflecting the new demands upon women to be also achievers in the outside world. Again a woman, doing a man's job and supporting her aged parents, gets a lower wage on the old theory that women work for pin money. "What to do with the remaining third of my life?" asks a middle-aged woman whose housekeeping duties have been reduced by smaller families and modern inventions. "Was it worth it?" wonders a career woman who accepted her society's challenge to succeed in her career only to discover that success endangered her marriage. Economic forces drive a wife to take a factory job but, having done a day's work, she returns to her full round of washing, cleaning, and cooking. One can go so far as to say that whatever the woman does, whether she is single or married, a homemaker or a career woman, childless or a mother—each design for living has its own pattern of frustrations.[10]

We shall illustrate below the problems in each of these designs for living.

A second source of confusion is the large number of roles available to women today. As we pointed out in Chapter 2, the possibility of choice in a way undoes the good of clear-cut role definitions. There is less security. In an agricultural society, there are relatively few roles for young, old, male, female. Nor is there much choice among those roles which are open. There is only one way, for example, to be a good wife or husband or son or daughter. A certain amount of leeway may be permitted in the performance of the role, but the basic pattern is fairly fixed. All this is in contrast to the bewildering number of roles— and the many patterns to choose from in any specific role—open to women in a modern complex society like ours. There are, as we shall see, many ways of being a woman, a wife, or a mother, with resulting confusion and anxiety.

The multiplicity of roles now open to married women contributes to personality conflict in at least four ways. (1) One form of personality conflict arises from the fact that women have difficulty in choosing between roles. (2) Another form of personality conflict, based upon multiplicity of roles, is the frustration of the woman performing one role through duty and habit while longing for a different role. Many a capable woman, with talents fully equal to those of her husband, has become a neurotic housewife obsessed by envy of the woman who is a marriage partner. (3) Again, there may be personality conflict because of misunderstanding between husband and wife in regard to the role each expects the married woman to play. A woman expecting to be a wife and mother may find that her husband expects her to be a partner. This results in a conflict of loyalty within her own personality and in a personality clash with her husband. (4) Finally, there is the possibility of ethical inconsistency, in the sense of an unfair distribution of obligations and privileges. Since a privilege to the wife involves a certain obligation to the husband, any disposition on the part of the wife to claim the privileges of more than one role, without accepting the corresponding obligations, makes for unfairness in the marriage relationship. On the other hand, a woman who accepts the obligations of more than one role while being denied the corresponding privileges receives an unfair share of the dissatisfactions of marriage.[11]

And, finally, the incompatibility among the several roles a woman may be called upon to perform may be a source of conflict and stress. As we saw in Chapter 4 the "frictions produced by the various, and sometimes incompatible, roles an individual has to play in his society," [12] constitute one important source of stress. The demands of the role of worker may be incompatible with those of wife or mother; the demands of wife may be incompatible with those of mother.[13]

In the following pages we shall illustrate some of the role problems of women which result from these three sources of confusion. We remind ourselves that the problems here discussed cannot be attributed to pathologies in the women involved; we are dealing with normal populations. The source of the confusion is in the outer world, not in some illness in the women involved.

The Worker Role of Modern Women

Class Aspects

As early as 1865, in the first statements of the American Social Science Association, the employment of women was specified as a major concern. The role of the woman worker—there were more than 20 million in 1955, constituting 31 per cent of all employed persons—has widespread ramifications, both in the family and in industry. The problem, however, is diametrically opposite in low socioeconomic levels and in high.[14] In the low socioeconomic levels the problems have been those involved in protecting women from exploitation, from too severe physical strains, from too long hours. It was early recognized that if a woman were allowed to work too hard her role as a mother would be impaired. At the higher socioeconomic levels, on the other hand, the problem was to secure the "right" to work or to have a career. Since these problems are so different, we deal with them separately.

PROTECTIVE LEGISLATION FOR THE WOMAN WORKER. State laws passed before the Civil War limiting hours of work were unenforceable because all they stipulated was that women could not be compelled to work more than ten hours a day. Most women wanted to work longer because wages were so low; or they had to agree to if they wanted a job at all. It was not until 1911 that state laws—in California and Washington—were first successful in establishing an eight-hour day for women, and these laws applied only in manufacturing and mechanical establishments. Other laws followed assuring one day's rest in seven and forbidding night work. The federal laws of the 1930's in favor of labor —the National Labor Relations Act and the Fair Labor Standards Act, especially—applied to women, of course, as well as to men. And little by little states were beginning to comply with standards drawn up by the Women's Bureau of the United States Department of Labor.[15]

There have been recurrent efforts to equalize the status position of working women even if they involved reducing the rights which they now enjoy. Thus since 1923, at the request of the National Woman's Party, a constitutional amendment to abolish all discrimination in employment between men and women has been proposed every year. The movement to require "equal pay for equal work" gained momentum during World War II because of the demand for labor and the influx of women into the labor market. Since women do not usually do exactly the same work as men, however, laws demanding equal pay are difficult to enforce. Proposed legislation at the present time usually speaks of equal pay for "work of comparable character, the performance of which requires comparable skills."

A number of women's organizations as well as labor unions oppose such legislation on the grounds that it would deprive women of the protection they now possess and would not guarantee that substitute legislation incorporating protection for both sexes would be enacted. In order to meet this objection an amended form of the Equal Rights

Amendment, passed in 1950 by the Senate, provided that no "rights, benefits, or exemptions now or hereafter conferred on women" would be abrogated by the amendment.

There are other laws, which we shall discuss below, which have the effect of permitting mothers to remain at home to take care of their children rather than having to seek gainful employment outside the home. The theory is that she is more valuable in her role as mother than as gainful worker.

THE "RIGHT TO WORK." Quite different from the problems of the working woman in the lower socioeconomic levels are those of the middle-class woman. Forty years ago young women had to fight for the privilege of working. So far as at least the *unmarried woman worker* is concerned, that battle is over. Role definitions with respect to the unmarried woman worker are by now fairly settled. Young women no longer have to fly in the face of disapproval if they want jobs, as apparently many of them do. There is no longer any stigma attached to their working outside the home. The young working woman is an accepted part of the social scene. She constitutes an important public: magazines are published for her; there are fashions designed for her. She is not made to feel that she must choose between marriage and a career as she was made to feel some forty years ago. She does not have to choose. If she wishes she can have both, although she is more likely to talk about a job than about a career.[16]

There do, however, remain marginal role difficulties as holdovers from the middle-class generation of the parents of these young women. Obviously the young woman is reared for a different kind of role from that of her brother, but in one study of college women it was found that often there was danger that in this traditional role training there was excessive sheltering, so that the girl did not develop the independence, inner resources, and self-assertion required by life today. Further, this upbringing made the transfer of her loyalties to her husband difficult when she married. At the other extreme, some girls were trained for intellectual achievement even at the expense of the traditional feminine role. Or, perhaps even more demoralizing, parents presented conflicting goals for their daughters to achieve, neither of which was attainable without rejection of the other.[17]

The Worker Role of Married Women

If the worker role of the unmarried woman is now fairly clear, the same cannot be said for the worker role of the *married woman*. Here a veritable revolution has been in the making for some time. In the middle of the 20th century about a third—35 per cent in 1955—of all women of working-force age were actually in the working force. In 1890, the proportion was only 18.3 per cent.[18] More significantly, in the middle of the 20th century between a fourth and a fifth—22.5 per cent —of these working women were married, and by 1953 the proportion was 25 per cent; [19] in 1890 it had been 4.8 per cent; [20] even in 1940 it was only 15 per cent.[21] Between 1890 and midcentury the proportion of women gainfully employed who were married had increased about 500 per cent. In 1955 the number of working wives was 11,800,000, an increase of 600,000 over 1954. The number of single women—5,100,000 —on the other hand, represented a decline of 300,000 from 1954 and of 1,100,000 from early postwar years.[22]

Sometimes the disparity between role conceptions and reality takes on a disconcerting aspect. When occupational sacrifices have to be made, the wife is usually happy to be the one to make them; but unless there is some reward somewhere, the ultimate result may be disastrous. The young woman is willing usually to take an uninteresting job, if it pays well, even if it offers little prospect of advancement in order to make it possible for her husband to take a less well-paying job with good prospects. She is willing to give up her professional advantages in order to go where his future is best. It does not seem like a sacrifice: she wants to do it; she loves him.

She does not stop to think that, while the early sacrifices of the ardent young bride can be made with happy generosity, they will lead to later resentment when she discovers that she is an uninteresting person, unqualified for either self-respect or respect of others in a world that has moved ahead without her, where her own growth has been slowed and stunted. The husband will forget, in time, that it was she who helped him win success and grow beyond her very reach, that it was she who took upon herself the limiting routines and denied her own personal goals. . . .

[Successful] marriage can be attained today only if men can be convinced, can acknowledge intellectually that women are not inferior. "But . . . it is still hard for them to behave as if women were equals—difficult to admit that women's needs can (and perhaps should) cause them some inconvenience." [23]

A very thoughtful and penetrating study of a number of working wives uncovered many kinds of relationships between husbands and wives who worked outside the home. Some were extremely successful and satisfying; others were just the opposite. "The husband's attitude appears in our cases to be a crucial factor in the success or failure of the employed homemaker." [24] The results of these researches suggested that "happy adjustments can be made but whether they will be made depends, first of all, upon the norms held by the man and upheld by his milieu as to the proper role of women in marriage." [25]

The problems can be just as disturbing if the wife works when she does not really conceive her role as an earner. A study of 337 married couples at a midwestern university found, for example, that:

> Women who work full-time tend toward conventional conceptions and those who work part-time tend toward companionate conceptions of both husband and wife roles. And among women whose husbands are not employed, those who are not working full-time lean more . . . to the conventional conception of their own role and to their husband's as companionate than do those who are working full-time.[26]

In brief, the role confusions which characterize husband-wife relationships at midcentury may lead to problems whether or not the wife's role conception is in step with the emerging institutional definition of her role; and the same is true with respect to the husband.

The Worker Role of Mothers

The worker role of women is even more complicated when they attempt to combine it not only with that of wife but also with that of *mother*. One student of the family, in fact, finds that the core of the "woman's problem" today lies in the conflict between her maternal or reproductive role and her worker role.

> In attempting a precise definition of the woman's problem, one must recognize that the problem involves individual differences between women, a work function, a reproductive function, and public opinion in regard to status and functions. Since men likewise differ from one another, have capacities, and are susceptible to public opinion, one must look for some factor distinctive to women. The distinctive factor is the greater reproductive burden of women which is differentially hostile to a full expression of their work function. The woman's problem may then be defined as a lack of balance between woman's reproductive function and her work function, so complicated by individual differences and public opinion that there is confusion and unhappiness for herself and others.
> If there be a woman's problem it is because of the special difficulty that women have in working out a happy balance between their distinctive reproductive function and the work function which they potentially share with men. It is to be expected that the woman's problem acquires special significance when the movement of work from the home to the factory makes it more difficult to integrate the reproductive and the work function. The woman's problem arises when it is no longer possible to spin and rock a cradle at the same time in fulfillment of feminine destiny.[27]

So far as the woman of low socioeconomic status is concerned, it seems to be better policy to pay her to stay home and look after her children than to permit her to leave the home to take a job and thereby neglect her children. This was the rationale underlying the mothers' pensions laws and also the aid to dependent children provisions in the Social Security Act. And for a large proportion of mothers the use of their time taking care of the home is a better disposition of talent and effort than would be its use in an outside job.

For middle-class women, however, the desire for a job outside the home may be very strong, as we shall show presently. And the proportion of families where there are children under six in which the mother works outside the home seems to be increasing—from 11 per cent, for example, in 1949, to 15 per cent in 1955. There were 2,500,000 women workers with children under six in 1956.[28] The proportion of married women who work is 27 per cent; but it varies with the phase of the family cycle they are in.

During the first year after marriage about 40 percent of the wives have jobs away from home. During the second or third year, many drop out of economic activity to have children and the proportion of working wives falls to about 30 percent. For the period when women have children of preschool age (under 6 years old), only about 15 percent are labor force participants. After all of the children have reached school age, nearly one third of the wives are in the labor force.[29]

Among college graduates who were mothers, it was found that 9 per cent of those under thirty, 16 per cent of those in their thirties, and 27 per cent of those forty and over worked outside the home.[30]

We do not know, age for age, how many working women are mothers and how many are not. In a study of college women forty years of age and over, however, it was found that working wives were less likely to be mothers (60 per cent) than were housewives (85 per cent).

Several explanations suggest themselves. Women who are unable to bear children are more likely to work than are mothers. Involvement in a career may lower the desire for a family. Finally, the lower income of the working wife may hold the clue to the modest size of her family. We have just seen that it is only by holding a job, which she would generally have to relinquish if she became a mother, that the working wife brings up the family income to the level enjoyed by the housewives. Among college graduates the lower the income, the smaller the family.[31]

A great deal of concern is often expressed about the effect on children of working mothers. As we shall see presently the factors which determine the quality of motherhood at midcentury are far more basic than merely the worker status of women. All we shall do here, therefore, is point out that there is no unequivocal evidence that having working mothers necessarily damages children, at least in the middle socioeconomic levels. So far as business and professional women are concerned, a study of 100 cases in New York City even as long ago as the 1920's found that combining career and successful marriage and parenthood was possible. The following factors were associated with a successful combining of the roles of worker and mother: good health; good training and work experience before marriage; short and flexible working hours; good income, making the provision of good domestic help possible. The ability to restrict social activities without feeling deprived was also important. Of great moment was the attitude of the community: a reasonably favorable public opinion was necessary if motherhood and career were to be combined. Among the hazards of the working mother was jealousy of the child's nurse, a feeling of guilt and anxiety, and the tendency of the community to blame her for any mishap to the child.[32] There is little reason to suppose that the above results would not hold at midcentury also. Indeed, the combining of job and parenthood is probably easier at midcentury because in many families, especially those of the young generation, the husband-father contributes a good deal of help.

Role Conflicts of the Nonworking Wife

Even if the wife or mother does not work outside the home, she is by no means spared role conflicts. As we saw above, "whatever the woman does, whether she is single or married, a homemaker or a career woman, childless or a mother—each design for living has its own pattern of frustrations." [33]

What, exactly is the role of a modern wife? One study, on the basis of interviews and observation, distinguished two polar role types for both husbands and wives, one conventional and one companionate.

The conventional conceptual type of husband role revolves around the breadwinning duty of the man. His prestige and authority are dependent upon his working. In the home, it is his job to do the heavy (men's) work and to help out with other housework in emergencies, and to supervise and guide the children. The value of his education is vocational. His other activities are restricted to those that are defined as "male."

The counter-role of conventional wife is a conception of the wife role as subordinate to that of the husband. The physical care of house and children (as well as of the husband) is her forte. Education is considered as something nice to have but not very useful in marriage. It is wrong to work except for pin money for one's self or because of necessity.

In contrast to the conventional conception is the companionate conception of husband-wife roles which emphasizes personality needs of husband and wife and greater equality in the assumption of economic, household, parental, and social responsibilities. Education and employment are considered valuable for the personal growth of man and wife. Authority is not dependent upon income.[34]

If a woman is being held to the conventional definition of the role of wife, whereas she has, because of her background and training, a companionate conception, the possibilities of difficulty are great. If she has been trained for equality and independence, the conventional role may be a source of great stress.

Another student adds a third role, that of partner, to those of wife-and-mother and companion, and emphasizes the confusion and conflict which the existence of these different role conceptions may entail.

We shall distinguish between three roles provided in our society for the married woman, each role implying certain privileges and certain obligations.

The wife-and-mother role is the traditional role of the married woman. It implies as privileges security, the right to support, alimony in case of divorce, respect as a wife and mother, a certain amount of domestic authority, loyalty of husband and children. Corresponding obligations include bearing and rearing children, making a home, rendering domestic service, loyal subordination of self to the economic interests of the husband, acceptance of a dependent social and economic status, and tolerance of a limited range of activity.

The companion role is essentially a leisure class phenomenon. The privileges pertaining to this role include pleasures shared with the husband, a more romantic emotional response, admiration, funds adequate for dress and recreation, leisure for social and educational activity, and chivalrous attentions. On the other hand, it implies as obligations the preservation of beauty under the penalty of marital insecurity, the rendering of ego and erotic satisfaction to the husband, the cultivation of social contacts advantageous to him, the maintenance of intellectual alertness, and the responsibility for exorcising the demon of boredom.

Finally, the partner role corresponds to a new emergent definition of family relationships. The role entails the privilege of economic independence, equal authority in regard to family finances, acceptance as an equal, the exemption from one-sided personal domestic service to the husband, equal voice in determining the locality of residence, and equality in regard to social and moral freedom. The obligational side of the balance sheet would include renouncing of alimony save in the case of dependent children, an economic contribution in proportion to earning ability, acceptance of equal responsibility for the support of children, complete sharing of the legal responsibilities of the family, willingness to dispense with any appeal to chivalry, abrogation of special privileges in regard to children, and equal responsibility to maintain the family status by success in a career.[35]

The theoretical formulation just presented was illustrated in a study of the wives of some 8,000 business leaders. This study found four major roles performed by successful wives: the family-centered role, emphasizing home and child-rearing; the civic-minded-social-minded role, which demonstrated a husband's success by participation in community affairs; the role of valued consultant or even partner; and the role of the wife who carried on a career of her own. The second was the commonest and the first the next most common; but the wives who could combine both were the most successful. The third and fourth were the least common of all.[36]

Another study, this time of young married women, found their problems to be of many types, but two were especially significant, namely: (1) those of the housewife who accepts the conventional definition of her role but chafes at certain aspects of it, and (2) those of the housewife who rejects the conventional role definition and longs for a totally different way of life.

The first type of problem is personified by the overworked mother. "Overwork, tired muscles, constant and almost exclusive association with young children, monotony are among the frequently mentioned grievances." [37] No matter how much a mother may love her small children, their constant company may become an eroding experience unless she has respite from time to time. Their demands are endless. Lack of long periods of uninterrupted time is commonly complained of by mothers of young children. The isolation of the modern mother from stimulating contacts is also commented upon. If a woman performs her role properly, where is she to find the time and energy to prepare for the demands which will be made on her when her children are older? How can she keep up with her husband?

Some unsympathetic observers tend to discount the complaints revealed in such studies as those reported above. They attribute them to neurotic sickness in the women. But the author we are now citing finds a more satisfactory explanation in terms of role conception and definition and concomitant status stresses.

The extent of satisfaction with one's condition of life depends, in part, upon one's aspirations. An American workingman may, on occasion, be more disgruntled than a half-starved Indian peasant. Moreover, active discontent depends upon the ability to conceive a better alternative to one's present condition and upon the belief that unfair obstacles stand in the way of its realization. Mothers in colonial times who lost about one out of four of their babies in infancy accepted their grief as the natural lot of mankind. . . .

The feeling of intellectual deprivation presupposes certain aspirations. A woman of the low-income classes with an elementary school education, who is married to a skilled laborer, may not experience "intellectual stagnation." But [a college woman is likely to compare] her life to that of her husband. It is of no avail for the businessman husband to exclaim: "Do you think my job is any better? A lot of petty details and aggravations." His wife knows that despite his complaints he really considers business an occupation superior to housewifery.[38]

The homemaker who longs for a career may hate housework or feel like screaming after a day with the children; but even if she does not, or finds them actually pleasant, the appeal of a role outside may be greater than the appeal of the domestic role. The loss of economic independence which goes with the domestic role troubles many of these women. Equally painful is the disruption of a whole network of daily habits; thus the isolation and lack of stimulating companionship in the domestic role were felt by some to be conducive to "letting yourself go." They did not bother to try to look attractive. Not only daily habits, but the integration of habits into a total organization of life was involved in the transition from outside job to homemaking. "It is, therefore, not surprising that the sudden severance of an occupation should have brought a sense of disorganization and emptiness to some women." [39] Closely associated with the above changes was a break in group identification; women who work belong to a world of professional associates whose values they share and live by. They have roles in a work group. Severing these ties, changing "we" to "they," may be a traumatic experience, especially in the early stages, and leave the housewife feeling lonely and isolated. There was often a loss of self-esteem when the woman gave up her career, partly because she could no longer identify with a profession or firm, but also because of a feeling of loss of status; she felt that people who have no occupation do not amount to much. A sense of injustice often developed.

Conflict between Motherhood and the Cultural Definition of the Feminine Role

Students of eugenics have pointed out the inconsistency between the ideal of feminine beauty which prevails in our society and the biological requirements of maternity. They contrast, for example, the small bones, fragility, and general softness which characterize one main ideal of feminine beauty with the strong substantial frame suitable for childbearing.[40] Another student has contrasted, on the social rather than the biological plane, the incompatibility between what she calls cultural femininity and biological femininity. Her study was based on interviews with 246 mothers of newborn babies in a hospital. She concludes that cultural femininity has gained at the expense of biological femininity, and that the maternal role has suffered as a result.

1. Contrary to popular belief, women have lost status rather than gained status with the coming of the industrial revolution. When production moved out of the home, women became more dependent on their husbands' support. Women's childbearing and child care contribution to society became depreciated as children became economic burdens and the birth rate fell. Women's usefulness as teachers and supervisors of their own older children was greatly minimized as schools consumed more and more of the children's time. After women became less needed and important to family life, the divorce rate began to rise.

2. These changes made feelings of insecurity, inferiority, envy, and dependence part of the accepted feminine pattern. Actions which stem from such feelings are considered culturally feminine.

3. On the other hand, biological pressures put a premium on productiveness, activity, concerted effort, and aggressiveness in women. These biologically feminine characteristics are often opposite from those encouraged by our society.

4. [In] an exploratory study . . . set up to . . . test this reasoning, the most culturally feminine women almost always showed deep feelings of inferiority by saying they wished to be men; the least culturally feminine women very seldom felt so inferior that they said they wished to be men.[41]

This conflict—between the feminine and the womanly or motherly role—has, like the others here presented, profound implications for the definition, value, and performance of the maternal role. And therefore, it follows, equally profound implications for the kind of personality which the complementary role of the child tends to produce, as we shall see in Chapter 16. But before we pass on, a word with respect to the implications of our discussion so far for the education of women.

Can We Prepare Women for Roles of Wife and Mother?

The first lesson to be drawn from the above analyses is the complete futility of blaming women or preaching to them. There is no reason to suppose that women are willfully shirking their obligations and duties. The women of a hundred years ago in today's circumstances would behave as women behave today, and vice versa. It is just that the kind of role performance which was possible a hundred years ago is not possible at the present time.

Since so many current social and societal problems seem to point to family, especially mother-child, relationships as at least part of the etiology, the question arises: In the face of adverse environmental forces, can we actually prepare women in a meaningful way for their family roles? [42] At least one student of the subject believes that we can. She feels that college courses—for men as well as for women—can develop immunity to what she calls "culture shock," and it is conceivable that the kind of training she proposes might even be made available at the high-school level. Here is her analysis:

Confusion with regard to social norms is one . . . problem [adolescents bring to college]. Uncertainty about norms tends, in general, to pervade adolescence in our rapidly changing and complex society, but there are periods in which it is accentuated. The freshman year in a cosmopolitan college is likely to be one of them. It is one thing to know dimly, while one remains in the cozy shelter of one's family and social clique, that in some distant places foreigners entertain queer ideas. It is quite another to experience the indignation of a college roommate over a casual remark about the Negro or to sense the detachment of one's professor towards some unquestioned beliefs. . . . It is our inescapable destiny to live in a different kind of world, one in which rapid social changes have disturbed for all time the simple certainties of an earlier era. Paradoxically, one way to immunize the student against "culture shock" is to immerse her still deeper in the facts of cultural variability and to show her the amazingly diverse ways in which basic needs of family life have been fulfilled in human societies.[43]

College—and perhaps even lower-level schools—can also prepare the future wife and mother to recognize the social roots of personal conflicts. This recognition will not, of course, solve the conflicts; but it will furnish the detachment and understanding necessary for their solution. Courses, this author continues, can also help the student to understand herself. If she has resisted psychiatric explanations of personality, she may now find them acceptable under proper academic auspices. If she has accepted them too uncritically and found a neurosis under every relationship, she may have developed anxieties which proper teaching can help alleviate. Student counseling, she suggests, may also help. Romantic misconceptions may be dispelled. A study of the ordinary problems inherent in family relationships can help young people avoid conflicts about them. Most important, perhaps, courses in child development "in the setting of parent-child and sibling relationships should constitute the core of the college preparation for parenthood." [44]

We shall have more to say of parental roles in the following chapters, when we discuss the social and societal problems associated with motherhood and with youth. The problems become somewhat different when the parents are confronted with older children (Chap. 17) than when they are dealing with infants and small children. (Chap. 16).

NOTES

1 Oscar Lewis, "Husbands and Wives in a Mexican Village: A Study of Role Conflict," *American Anthropologist,* 51 (Oct.-Dec. 1949), pp. 603 ff.

2 ". . . women have been more affected than men by such technological changes as the building of the road, the establishment of bus service to Cuernavaca and the introduction of corn mills. These changes have also affected the relations between husbands and wives. Women began to patronize the corn mills over the objections of their husbands, and the success of the mills was . . . the result of 'the revolution of the women against the authority of the men.' . . . Since women are not so tied to the metate as they were, they are able to leave the house more freely. . . ." (*Ibid.,* pp. 606–607.)

3 William Blackstone, *Commentaries on the Laws of England,* 15th ed., Vol. I (London, 1809), p. 441. First published in 1765.

4 A 1955 bill, introduced by a Congresswoman from Oregon, Edith Green, provided under a double-penalty clause that any employer who paid an employee at a rate less than that paid for the same work to a person of the opposite sex would be required to reimburse not only lost wages but also an additional equal amount as damages.

5 Mirra Komarovsky, *Women in the Modern World, Their Education and Their Dilemmas* (Little, 1953), p. 96. Much of the discussion on the roles of modern women is based on this author's perceptive study.

6 The lack of concordance between traditional definitions of the feminine role and current realities produces disturbing stresses in the relationships between the sexes. Komarovsky, for example, reports young women confessing to "playing dumb" or "throwing the game" in order not to excel their male companions and thus humiliate them. (*Ibid.,* p. 86.) See also the discussion of the conflict between cultural and biological femininity at the end of this chapter.

7 Leo W. Simmons and Harold G. Wolff, *Social Science in Medicine* (Russell Sage, 1954), pp. 130–132.

8 "How People Change after Marriage," *Family Life,* 15 (Nov. 1955), p. 1. The following quotation is from a paper by E. Lowell Kelly read before the American Psychological Association, September 1955.

"To the extent that during this period the home has become more mechanized through modern appliances, and on the assumption that women find they like the mechanical aspects of home appliances, it is understandable that women should become somewhat more masculine in their likes and dislikes. . . . Perhaps our entire culture is becoming more masculinized all the time and while both men and women react favorably to these changes, men respond a little more than women."

An interesting side light on the "masculinization" of women in this rather superficial sense of interest in mechanical activities was given by men in the builders' supply business at a Home Show in Washington in 1955. "I can remember," one said, "when women wouldn't even come into our store. Now we have them in our home remodeling classes—nailing and sawing away." "I'll never forget the shock I got when a woman who said she was building a home told me she was installing the kitchen and bathroom equipment," said another. "She even dug the trench for the sewer pipe," he added. (*New York Times,* February 24, 1955.)

9 One author feels that the increasing masculinity of women foreshadows a decline of Western civilization. (George W. Henry, *All the Sexes: A Study of Masculinity and Femininity* [Rinehart, 1955].)

10 Komarovsky, *op. cit.,* pp. 48–49.

11 Clifford Kirkpatrick, *The Family as Process and as Institution* (Ronald, 1955), p. 164.

12 Simmons and Wolff, *op. cit.*, p. 41.

13 The conflict among incompatible roles has sometimes been resolved by greater specialization in role performance. In Athens, for example, different women filled different specialized roles. A well-born Athenian would have female slaves to do menial labor, a concubine to serve his physical comfort like a valet, a mistress to serve as sex partner, a wife to bear legitimate children, and hetaerae to offer intellectual companionship and stimulation. A modern woman is expected to perform all these—in many ways incompatible—roles herself, and others as well.

14 In 1950, 24.7 per cent of all female workers were in white-collar occupations, 55.3 per cent were in manual jobs, and 19.9 per cent were in agriculture.

15 "Most of the states failed by a wide margin to comply with these standards, though it was hoped that in time these goals would be approximated. [In 1950] the approved maximum 8-hour day or 48-hour week, with extra pay for overtime, was in force in 24 states and the District of Columbia, though in most of these states only manufacturing establishments were covered by the laws. Twenty-two out of the 48 states and the District of Columbia provided for a weekly day of rest. A lunch period was made mandatory . . . in 27 states and the District of Columbia. Only 8 states required rest periods of at least 10 minutes for each 4 hours of work, without lengthening the total work day. But 13 states prohibited night work for women, and only in some occupations. The Women's Bureau does not recommend prohibition of women's work in dangerous occupations, but rather regulations to reduce their hazards. In 1950, 17 states forbade employment of women in mining; some made it illegal in selling intoxicating beverages, or in specified hazardous occupations. Twenty-one states prohibited or regulated industrial home-work. . . . Twenty-six states and the District of Columbia had minimum-wage laws, generally inclusive in coverage. Compliance with this standard was more widespread than with most of the others. Discrimination in rate of pay because of sex was prohibited by 12 states. Two of these laws covered only manufacturing. The Women's Bureau recommends leave of absence for a specified period before and after childbirth, together with health insurance providing maternity benefits. Six states prohibited employment of women before and after childbirth." (George Soule, *Men, Wages and Employment in the Modern U. S. Economy* [Mentor, 1954], p. 79.)

16 In a study of college women, about a third hoped to work until their first child was born, stop for ten or fifteen years, and then resume gainful employment. (Komarovsky, *op. cit.*, p. 97.) The chances are very good that they will do just that, as we shall see presently.

17 *Ibid.*, p. 86.

18 A. J. Jaffe and Charles D. Stewart, *Manpower Resources and Utilization: Principles of Working Force Analysis* (Wiley, 1951), p. 164.

19 Paul C. Glick, "The Life-Cycle of the Family," *Marriage and Family Living*, 17 (Feb. 1955), p. 9.

20 Jaffe and Stewart, *op. cit.*, p. 172.

21 Glick, *loc. cit.*

22 United States Census Bureau press release, December 30, 1955.

23 Kate Hevner Mueller, "The Marriage Trap," *Mademoiselle*, September 1955. Quotation from press release.

24 Komarovsky, *op. cit.*, p. 185.

25 *Ibid.*, p. 186.

26 Annabelle Bender Motz, "Conceptions of Marital Roles by Status Groups," *Marriage and Family Living*, 12 (1950), p. 162.

27 Kirkpatrick, *op. cit.*, pp. 165–166.

28 C. I. Schottland, "Today's Children," *Social Security Bulletin*, 19 (May 1956), p. 4.

29 Glick, *loc. cit.*, p. 8.

30 Their occupations were mainly professional, especially teaching. The earnings of the husbands of these working wives were low as compared to those of the husbands of nonworking college women. The working wives had smaller families also.

31 Komarovsky, *op. cit.*, p. 168.

32 V. M. Collier, *Marriage and Careers* (Channel, 1926).

33 Komarovsky, *op. cit.*, p. 49.

34 Motz, *loc. cit.*, p. 136.

35 Kirkpatrick, *op. cit.*, pp. 163–164.

36 W. Lloyd Warner and James Abegglen, *Big Business Leaders in America* (Harper, 1955), pp. 120–123.

37 Komarovsky, *op. cit.*, p. 107.

38 *Ibid.*, pp. 117, 122–123.

39 *Ibid.*, p. 139.

40 Amram Scheinfeld, *You and Heredity* (Lippincott, 1939).

41 Niles Newton, *Maternal Emotions, A Study of Women's Feelings toward Menstruation, Pregnancy, Childbirth, Breast Feeding, Infant Care, and Other Aspects of Their Femininity* (Hoeber, 1955), p. 100.

42 In 1953 the American Council on Education established a Commission on the Education of Women to study women's education and the relations between education and the role of women in America.

43 Komarovsky, *op. cit.*, pp. 218–219.

44 *Ibid.*, p. 246.

16

Father and Mother Roles

The Dependent Child

Every year several million infants are added to the population. They are completely helpless: a day's neglect may mean their death. Their near-total dependence lasts for some five years; another five years of less extreme but still considerable dependence follow: after this period their dependence may continue for another five, or even eight or ten years.

We do not have to accept the theory that this prolonged period of infancy—which may be extended culturally but not curtailed—was responsible for the origin of society [1] in order to appreciate its enormous significance. The human infant is born unable to function on his own for a long time. This makes for great plasticity; he can learn instead of having to depend on inherited behavior patterns. The accumulation of centuries can be acquired; he can stand on the shoulders of preceding generations. But although the advantages are great, the penalties are commensurate with them if the care of the child is neg-

The Dependent Child

Importance of Parental Role Performance

Role Differentiation in Task Groups

The Role of Father as Provider

Public Programs for Dependent Children

The Unmarried Mother

The Role of Mother

The Role of Family as First Line of Defense

lected or inadequate. If the long period of plasticity is not used to — socialize the child along culturally accepted lines, there has been no gain but rather a loss in this period of prolonged dependence. During all the time of dependence someone must be responsible for the physical care and socialization of the child. The most natural assignment is to make the parents responsible, although in some societies it is the mother and her brother rather than her husband who have this responsibility.

Importance of Parental Role Performance

The reader will note that we do not use the familiar concept "broken home," or "broken family," in our discussion here. Despite the convenience of using the custom-hallowed term "broken home,"

the concept was sacrificed because it tends to blur rather than to eluci-
date the problems involved. It usually refers to families in which the
father or the mother is absent, because of death, desertion, or divorce,
or to children with neither father nor mother, for whatever reason. But
it is always recognized that even if both parents are present the family
may still be "broken," so far as role relationships are concerned. Research which has attempted to document the baneful results of broken
homes has usually been disappointing.[2] The fatherless home with a
strong mother may be better for children than the home with an alcoholic parent.[3]

Rather than use the concept "broken home," therefore, we have
preferred to apply the concept of role. Every child must have certain
roles being performed in his environment if he is himself to learn
suitable role behavior. One such role is the maternal, which supplies
affection and love to assuage the frustrations of socialization and make
them bearable. It makes no difference who performs this role for the
child. Usually the biological mother does, but this is not essential. Any
woman—or, indeed, any man—who can perform these role functions
satisfactorily will do. It is important that the role be performed; the sex
of the performer is irrelevant. Similarly, the role of father must also be
performed, a role of physical support and protection. Here, again, it is
not essential that the biological father perform the role. Anyone who
can, will do. The essential point, then, is not whether the child comes
from a broken home, but whether the parental roles are being performed adequately for him. As we shall see below, the mere presence of
two adults in the environment of a child does not guarantee that the
parental roles are being adequately performed. Nor does the absence of
one parent mean that his, or her, role is not being performed. For these
reasons, then, we base our analyses on role performance rather than
on the somewhat shopworn "broken home."

Role Differentiation in Task Groups

It has been found, as we saw in Chapter 2, that all task-oriented
groups tend to differentiate at least two kinds of roles, one of which has
been labeled "instrumental," or "task-oriented," and the other, "expressive."[4] If the family is conceived of as a group whose task it is to protect
and socialize the child, the "instrumental" role can be viewed as that of
the father and the "expressive" one as that of the mother. A study of

some fifty-six cultures found that, in general, the paternal role (whoever performed it) was defined somewhat as follows:

> [He] is boss-manager of the farm; leader of the hunt, etc. . . . the final court of appeals, final judge and executor of punishment, discipline, and control over the children of the family.[5]

And the maternal role, as follows:

> She is the mediator, conciliator, of the family . . . soothes over disputes, resolves hostilities in the family . . . is affectionate, solicitous, warm, emotional to the children of the family . . . is the "comforter," the "consoler," is relatively indulgent, relatively unpunishing.[6]

In our own culture, the role of father may be institutionally defined to include a great many characteristic responsibilities, but the duty to provide for his family is always one of them. This role obligation is more than a group phenomenon; it is also deeply imbedded in law, in tradition, and in the mores. There is no doubt that men are legally and morally obligated to support their families.[7] Being a good provider is considered an important attribute by women in evaluating men for marriage.[8]

Equally important is the role of the mother. The popular watchword today may be said to be *"cherchez la mère"* instead of *"cherchez la femme."* For example: 1,825,000 men are rejected for military service because of psychiatric disorders and another 600,000 are discharged for neuropsychiatric reasons. And 500,000 attempt to evade the draft and all war responsibility. It is said to be their mothers' fault. "The handwriting of 'Moms' looms large and plain." [9] Thousands of young people stream through our courts and clinics every year—the accusing finger is again pointed at their mothers.[10] Even some kinds of mental deficiency are attributed to long exposure to Kallikak-type family relationships.[11]

Many of the currently accepted theories of personality place great emphasis on parent-, especially mother-, child relationships in the earliest years. These relationships have, in effect, come to take the place of heredity as the great explanatory principle in much current thinking about personality. The role of mother therefore assumes special, pivotal significance, and the way it is performed becomes a matter of great concern. When it is badly performed it creates social and societal problems.[12]

Anything which interferes with the adequate performance of either the paternal or the maternal roles, therefore, fulfills any of the criteria which one may set up for social or societal problems. It will cause suffering; it will cast a burden on the community; and it is likely to be dysfunctional. Of the two roles, the paternal is easier to replace. And there have emerged during the last half century a number of programs designed to take over the support of dependent children when the father cannot or will not assume it.

The Role of Father as Provider

The role of father calls for a good deal more than mere physical support. He contributes a symbol of authority, a tie with the outside world, a model of male role behavior, and so on. In our emphasis on the provider aspect of his role we do not mean to imply that it is necessarily the most important. But from the point of view of social problems, it is failure in this aspect that is most likely to cause concern to the community.

Quite aside from all other traumatic aspects of death, of physical or mental illness or incapacity—including alcoholism—of desertion, of divorce, of unemployment, these situations have profound repercussions on children. They all precipitate serious dislocation in the family. Widows and orphans have been a charge on the community since at least Biblical times.[13] The family of the man unable to work must also be taken care of. If he is able to work but can find no work, some provision must still be made for the dependents. And even if he deserts his family or refuses to support them, the children cannot be made to suffer for the failure of their parents. Public provision is therefore now made for children in families with any of the above handicaps.

Although not all children without fathers need outside help, almost half of them do. A larger proportion of children than of adults need assistance because the leveling up of the population, which we described in Chapter 1, is slower in the case of children than of adults as a result of the differentials in the birth rate. Because families in the lower income brackets tend to be larger than those in the middle and upper brackets, more children have poor than well-to-do parents; more have less educated than more educated parents; more have fathers in the lower than in the higher status occupations.[14] Children, who constituted about a third of the total population in 1955, are poor as a class. And because mortality, divorce, and desertion, as well as illness and unemployment, are all more common in the lower socioeconomic classes, the children in these families are more likely to become community charges than are children of more privileged status.

The "broken" family was one of the major preoccupations of social

Mary Jones, who was a good student at college, is making an effective talk to an interested PTA audience, but her whole heart is not in it. "*Should* I have left the children this afternoon with that girl? Will I get home in time to straighten things out before I meet Jack at the station? Will I be too tired to help Jane with her costume tonight? Can I possibly get out of my responsibility for washing glasses after communion at Church next Sunday? Was it wrong of me not to ask Jack's boss over for dinner next week? Maybe I should take that job at Spence's. The extra income would help a lot. I could get a really good person to look after the children. And the mortgage could be paid off sooner.

But Sally says her job was what spoiled her husband. Would my job do the same thing to Jack?"

As the area for women's activities has widened—in business, the professions, and community activities, in particular—many women find themselves confused and harassed. Are women like Mary neglecting their roles as wives and mothers in order to perform civic, church, or worker roles? Do their children and husbands suffer because of their numerous outside responsibilities? Are there clear-cut guides to tell Mary how to behave?

Is there an inherent conflict among the many roles she is trying to perform?

Why does she feel that being "just a homemaker" and nothing more would lower her status and hence her self-esteem? *(Photo: The Providence Journal-Bulletin)* workers and of Social Science in the 19th century. "Drink, Desertion, and Divorce" was the name students used to apply to some of the earlier courses in Social Science or social problems. Just how to provide for the dependent child was one of the most difficult questions that faced the community. For a long time private philanthropic agencies bore the brunt of family care when there was no earner.[15] A complicated social-work organization was set up to locate and bring back—and punish—deserting husbands. All kinds of coercive techniques were tried. But it became evident in time that this approach was inadequate.[16] Early in the 20th century, therefore, the advocates of pensions for mothers began to place the responsibility for the care of dependent children in the hands of the state. It was not until the Social Security Act was passed in 1935, however, that state responsibility for dependent children became recognized and firmly established as a federal function.

Public Programs for Dependent Children

At the present time, in addition to local and state programs, dependent children may benefit from at least five federal programs: (1) from Title II of the Social Security Act, which deals with the survivors of deceased workers; (2) from Title III, which refers to unemployment benefits; (3) from Title IV, which provides for financial assistance solely on the basis of need without regard to insurance rights; (4) from Title V, which deals with services to children; and also (5) from legislation which provides benefits for the children of veterans. Theoretically these provisions should take care of any contingency that might arise from failure of a father to perform his role as provider. Actually, however, the administration of these laws can be only as generous as the community wishes it to be.[17]

The magnitude of the problems centering around impaired parental role performance may be seen from the fact that about 7,000,000 of the 54,500,000 children under eighteen years of age in 1955 [18]—more than one in every eight—were living either with only one parent or with no parent at all. There were 4,100,000 living with their mothers, 600,000 with their fathers, and most of the remaining with grandparents, older brothers or sisters, or other relatives.

There is no upward trend in the proportion of families without a father; but the reasons for his absence have changed. The death rate, for example, has shown a long-time trend downward; the proportion of paternal orphans in the total population therefore dropped almost 30 per cent between 1930 and 1950. The occurrence of incapacitating illnesses will undoubtedly decline at an accelerating rate as new "wonder" drugs are developed or discovered. The long-time trend in employment is up; an increasing proportion of the population is employed. But periodic declines in employment and chronic unemployment in depressed areas continue, even at midcentury.

As the death rate has gone down, the divorce and desertion rates have gone up. In the age brackets in which parents are likely to have children under eighteen, the proportion of marriages broken by divorce or desertion is far greater than the proportion broken by death.[19] It was estimated that in each of the early postwar years, between 307,000 and 382,000 children were affected by divorce.[20]

Paternal desertion is a perennial, and probably an increasing, problem.[21] Because of role confusion, referred to in Chapter 15, men often feel little if any responsibility for the care of their children. Hundreds of judges all over the country spend day after day reminding recalcitrant men that they are required by law to support their children. It is so easy to leave home, take a job in a distant city, and forget legal obligations. Unless the wife goes to court there is no one to make the husband carry out these obligations. The people he associates with certainly exert no pressure on him.

Divorce is a special case. The long-time trend over the past half century has been up, although the rate has fluctuated with the business cycle—going up in times of prosperity and down in times of depression —and with wars, being especially high immediately after wars. It reached an all-time high in 1946 and 1947; since then it has been declining. Will it continue to decline? One student answers this question as follows:

Probably not. Though our current rate (about 10 divorces per year for every 1,000 married couples) is far below what it was in 1946 and 1947, it is still more than twice what it was in 1900. The conservatism in family life that seemingly set in after World War II appears strong enough to have arrested the long-term increase in marital disruption, but not strong enough to diminish the rather high divorce rate that has become customary in our society and that rests on enduring changes.[22]

Not all of the children who are deprived of paternal support need financial assistance, but a substantial number do. In December 1954, for example, 3.3 million children were receiving some kind of financial support from a public income-maintenance program, not counting those in families receiving unemployment or disability insurance.[23] The father's role of provider was being taken over by some public agency.

Survivors' benefits were being paid at midcentury to half of all paternal orphans (about 950,000) and to 40,000 of 900,000 maternal orphans. The proportion of dependent children receiving *assistance* because of family breakdown resulting from causes other than death increased as the proportion receiving benefits because of breakdown resulting from death declined.

While orphans were declining in number and insurance payments were reaching an increasing proportion of them, the number of families broken by marital difficulties was on the rise.* In consequence, the need for assistance to such families was increasing, and a progressively larger proportion of the case load of aid to dependent children comprised those who had been deprived of normal support or care because of the continued absence from home or the incapacity of either parent. This trend is expected to continue, although there has been an increase in the proportion of families with fatherless children that receive aid to dependent children as a supplement to survivor benefits. At the end of 1954 there were more than 1.6 million children receiving aid to dependent children, of whom some 240,000 received aid because of the father's death.†,[24]

Programs administered by the Veterans Administration were providing *benefits* for 300,000 children under eighteen—15 per cent of all paternal orphans.

Admittedly the amount of support offered by these several insurance and assistance programs was not lavish. In May 1955, for example, the average monthly payment per family receiving aid to dependent children was only $86.71, ranging from $23.74 in Mississippi to $138.39 in Wisconsin. The average amount that a surviving child was receiving under Old-Age and Survivors Insurance was $36.42 per month; this does not, however, include benefits which a mother might also be receiving. The general trend has been in the direction of increasing generosity; it is often a matter of waiting for public opinion to catch up with what is possible.[25]

In addition to these benefits and assistance programs, there is also a three-pronged program set up under Title V of the Social Security Act which provides maternal and child health service, services for crippled children, and child welfare services.[26]

These programs, admittedly still inadequate—though tending al-

---

* The number of paternal orphans in the total population declined an estimated 30 per cent between 1930 and 1955; correspondingly the proportion of children receiving assistance because of father's death declined from 37 per cent in 1942 to 17 per cent in 1954. (Jay L. Roney, "Twenty Years of Public Assistance," *Social Security Bulletin,* 18 [Aug. 1955], p. 21.)

† In 1955 the total number of persons (including children) receiving assistance because of incapacity of father was .8 million; because of death of father, .4 million; and because of estrangement or other absence of father, 1.4 million. (*Ibid.*)

ways in the direction of greater liberality—are complex and complicated to administer; but they are far simpler than providing a substitute for the maternal role when it is lacking. They cost only money. The emotional care and socialization of the child—components of the so-called expressive role—demand a great investment of human personality. Before we turn to a discussion of the social and societal problems associated with the maternal role, however, brief mention should be made of the special case of the child born outside marriage in which both paternal and maternal roles are distorted.

The Unmarried Mother

The enormous significance attached to legitimacy in our society has been given as the basic reason for much of our efforts to control sex behavior. Kinsey has pointed out that "attempts to control such [illegitimate] pregnancies and to provide that children should have responsible parents were undoubtedly factors of considerable moment in the development of society's interest in controlling coitus outside of wedlock." [27] Because the child born outside marriage may lack anyone willing to perform the paternal role, the maternal role may be made very difficult for the mother.

Most of the dependency situations so far discussed have dealt with families in which the father is or was present, even if he was unable to perform the role of provider. There is, however, the special case of the child born outside marriage, the child whose family was never formed in the first place. Such a child is entitled to assistance under the aid-to-dependent-children provisions of the Social Security Act, and also, of course, to the child welfare services provided by that act. Increasingly, legislation and common law decisions work in the direction of ameliorating the status of the child born out of marriage; [28] more and more states—thirty-three, as of 1956—make no reference to legitimacy status on birth certificates.

As usual in any situation which violates the mores, our information about legitimacy is limited. We do know, however, that despite efforts to improve the status of the perhaps 1 child in 25 who is born outside marriage, he is under special handicaps. The stillbirth rate for the country as a whole among known cases of illegitimacy is almost twice as high (39.5 per 1,000 live births) as among legitimate births (20.5 per 1,000 live births), and in some states it is even higher. States differ in the legal claims which the child born out of marriage has on his father; some enforce none, whereas some require the father to give him the same care, support, and education as that given legitimate children. North Dakota and Arizona consider the child legal. Most children available for adoption are children born outside marriage; these children have, of course, all the legal claims on their adoptive parents that any child has on his biological parents.

The parents of unmarried mothers are more understanding today than formerly. There is probably less of the "don't darken our door again" attitude that used to characterize the parents of girls with children born outside marriage. But there is still stigma attached to the situation. We probably know more about the cases in which there are traumas associated with it than we do about those which are handled quietly by families.

It is commonly assumed that illegitimacy occurs most frequently among the lowest socioeconomic classes,[29] and this may be true. But whether or not relatively more of the babies born in low than in high socioeconomic classes are born outside marriage cannot be determined from the official records. Kinsey found in a sample of 2,094 single, white females who had had sex relations that there had been 476 pregnancies. About one in five (18 per cent) of the women had become pregnant one or more times. Since by the age of thirty-five almost half the women he studied (48 per cent)[30] had had premarital coitus, the total number of women incurring pregnancies outside marriage by the age of thirty-five must be fairly high (roughly, 18 per cent of 48 per cent, or 8.6 per cent). Not all these pregnancies are carried through to parturition. Many, no doubt, are aborted (the high stillbirth rate among children born outside marriage suggests the possibility of damage in attempting abortion). And some are presumably recorded as legitimate, especially in cases where the woman is older and able to afford private care, so that she can successfully represent herself as married.

If our prime interest is in the causes of illegitimacy, then it is important to recognize the class bias in most of the research in this subject. If our prime interest, however, is in the social and societal problems involved in illegitimacy, then we are justified in limiting our attention to the segment of the population which depends on the community for care and support. In thus limiting our attention, however, we should not suppose that we are dealing with the total question of illegitimacy.

The strong class bias in most studies of unmarried mothers in the past is documented by a study made in 1952 in California. The author of this study surveyed the literature over three decades and pointed out that in the 1920's, "immorality" and "mental deficiency" were greatly emphasized. In the 1930's, "broken homes," "poverty," "little education," and "domestic occupation" were stressed. In the 1940's cultural explanations were used; illegitimacy was an accepted pattern of life in a given subculture. Currently he finds that psychological processes are being used, the consensus being "that unwed motherhood is a product of unresolved parent-child conflict and represents an 'unrealistic way out of inner difficulties.' " [31]

Most studies in the past, however, were based on institutional or welfare or clinic cases and therefore do not represent all unwed mothers, so that attempts to explain the phenomenon which are limited to these cases do not necessarily apply to all cases. The author of the study here referred to went out deliberately to locate cases which would not bias his sample in the direction of lower socioeconomic classes. He does not claim that his cases are representative of all unmarried mothers, but they are important in that they counteract the usual bias in the opposite direction.

The findings reported in the present paper resulted from a deliberate attempt to sample unwed mothers who do not go to agencies, clinics or institutions. The data were based on a 71 percent response from 576 doctors who provided information on 137 unwed mothers delivered in private practice in Alameda County, California, during 1952.

The following findings suggest the need for more inclusive samples in studies of unwed motherhood and raise additional questions for future research. Of the 137 unwed mothers delivered in private practice:

83.9   percent were white;

51.8   percent were 22 years of age or older;

38.0   percent had attended or completed college and 34.3, 24.8, and 35.8 percent respectively of their fathers, mothers and alleged sexual mates had attended or completed college;

60.5   percent were employed in professional or white collar jobs or were college students, and only 8.8 percent were employed in semi-skilled or unskilled jobs;

36.5   percent of 74 who were working, received a salary of 251.00 dollars or more per month;

78.4   percent of those who came from out of the state to have their baby in California had attended or completed college;

50.0   percent of those who had attended or completed college were mated sexually with a man seven or more years their senior;

70.0   percent of those with less than a 12th grade education were mated sexually with a man the same age or not more than two years their senior;

90.0   percent of those who had attended or completed college were mated with an alleged sexual mate who had attended or completed college.

Occupational association appeared to be operative as a situational factor in some of the 89 cases for which occupational data were available for both the unwed mother and the alleged sexual mate.[32]

Since most cases like the 137 women analyzed in the above study would not be likely to appear in the usual sample of unmarried mothers, the phenomena they represent are not included in the conventional study. We are not to conclude, of course, that illegitimacy is necessarily as common in high as in low socioeconomic classes. But we should recognize that most of what we know about unmarried mothers is about unmarried mothers in distressed circumstances, and they may constitute a biased sample. As we pointed out above, however, from the point of view of social or societal problems rather than that of pure research, concentration of attention on these cases of distress seems to be warranted.

The Role of Mother

The role of mother is, as we saw above, pivotal in any society. In our own society nowadays a large part of personality is interpreted in terms of mother-child relationships in the early years. If mothers do not or cannot assume the care of their children it is extremely difficult to find satisfactory substitutes. The state cannot, as in the case of the father's role of provider, take over. The care of children cannot be successfully undertaken on a mass scale. One of the things we are surest about in this difficult area is that socialization in the earliest years must be accomplished on an individualized basis. Regimentation and mass methods do not succeed.[33] The kind of individualized care which children require cannot be bought in the market. People will offer it freely on the basis of love; they will even offer it on the basis of duty. But money alone will not evoke it.

Failure to perform maternal roles, as in the case of failure to perform paternal roles, may be the result of something in the woman herself or of something in the world she lives in.

Not all women have the skill, talent, temperament, or even the desire to assume responsibility for the care of children. Some are not well. Some are themselves dependent. Some are alcoholics. Some can hardly handle their own problems, let alone those of their children. Some are psychopathic personalities. Some are incapable of loving anyone. The mere fact, therefore, that there are two adults present in a family does not, as we pointed out above, guarantee that the parental roles are being performed. A mother who rejects, for example, may be just as damaging as one who deserts.[34] Indeed, it may be better for the child if a mother who rejects is absent rather than present. Any of the conditions discussed in Part IV may prevent women from performing their maternal roles satisfactorily.

In addition, however, even normal modern women, as we saw above, are sometimes accused of inadequate performance of their role as mother as contrasted with their grandmothers. Exactly what they are being blamed for is not always clear. For example, as contrasted with, let us say, a century ago, there is no proof that age for age any of the pathologies we discussed in Part IV have been increasing except, perhaps, one, anxiety states and psychosomatic illnesses resulting from them. Thus infectious illnesses are decreasing; the addictions may be also. Suicide is not increasing, so far as we know. We have no firm evidence for an increase in psychopathic personalities, or compulsive or obsessive criminals. If some marginal distortions are increasing, others seem to be declining. The evidence with respect to juvenile delinquency, to be discussed in Chapter 18, is not unequivocal. Thus although the way modern women perform the role of mother is quite different from the way women of the 19th century performed it, this change cannot account for any of the pathologies except, perhaps, the anxiety states.

This fact is, however, important enough to warrant some close scrutiny. Can we determine just what it is in modern maternal role performance which might help to interpret the increase in anxiety states? Can we put our finger on just what the difference is between modern motherhood and motherhood in the past? Two studies throw some light on this problem. In the first, the conditions of mothering in working-class homes in 1870 are contrasted with those of 1930. This gives us a picture of some of the differences which abundance has introduced into maternal role performance. In the second, the conditions of mothering in a remote mountain rural area are contrasted with those of a modern city. This gives us an idea of the difference which urbanization has brought about in maternal role performance.

Before we present these two analyses, however, a word with reference to specific child-rearing practices viewed individually in any one generation. Two studies have shown that in any given generation the effects of these practices on personality cannot be pinpointed. There are no clear-cut differences between children who were, for example, breast-fed and those who were bottle-fed, between those subjected to one form of toilet training and those subjected to another.[35] And yet a great deal of research on personality does lead back to early family relationships. When one takes a longer perspective than that of one generation one can see certain relationships between child-rearing practices and personality which seem significant, even though a cross-sectional analysis does not make them appear so.

Motherhood: 1870 and 1930

We saw in Chapter 12 that there has been a relative decline in the hysterias in the 20th century but that at the same time there has been an increase in the incidence of anxiety states. One student of psychosocial medicine has attempted to explain these trends in terms of the kinds of homes and maternal role performance which were characteristic of the 1870's and of the 1930's, and the differential effects they had on personality.[36]

Before the invention of baby carriages infants were carried about in their mother's arms. Women learned to cook and do other housekeeping chores with a baby in their arms or on their hips. They used to speak of lap babies and knee babies. The baby spent a large part of his time in close physical contact with his mother's body. Breast-feeding was almost universal; not until the end of the 19th century when the rubber supply became plentiful did bottle-nursing become widespread. The child nursed whenever it was hungry; mothers were available at all times. The mother carried the child in a shawl close to her body during the day. At night the infant often slept with his mother.[37] The infant was swaddled, sometimes even sewn up for months at a time; washing infants was considered dangerous. Bowel training was given little consideration; floors were bare and furnishings few, and toddlers could toilet themselves without injuring family property. There were many brothers and sisters, so that social life was plentiful within the family. Adults made no fuss over children. They were not expected nor encouraged to express themselves; they were to be seen, not heard. There was no compulsory education. The family was patriarchal. Thus although hygienically the home of the child in the 19th century was bad—lack of pure water and adequate sanitation, overcrowding—"viewed psychologically," this author concludes, "the child's environment was not so bad, in that during the early years emotional growth was largely permitted to develop and unfold in its own way and in its 'own good time.' "[38] Only in the custom of permitting the child to be seen but not heard was this a bad environment from the point of view of personality development. It may have had a bearing, this author believes, on the high incidence of hysteria in the Victorian period.

In the 1930's, this author proceeds, the child's family environment was quite different. Modern sanitation and hygiene reached all classes and drastically reduced the infant mortality rate; but the changes had consequences not foreseen. Breast-feeding was only partially practiced, if at all, by most women. And some time later canned baby foods partially replaced the bottle. A baby might be bottle-fed in his mother's arms, but when he is fed from a can he is more likely to be propped up in front of her, so that feeding is moved another step away from the mother's body. In the 1930's infants were fed on a schedule, not when they were hungry. Pacifiers and dummy teats, popular earlier in the century, were discarded as unhygienic. There was a minimum of body contact between mother and infant; shawls had disappeared and infants were transported in baby carriages. They slept by themselves. They were not picked up when they cried. They were bathed a great deal and kept clean; but they were also subjected to bowel training very early. Abundance showed itself even in working-class homes; household furnishings, carpets, and bedding had become more elaborate and expensive. They had to be protected from the child's soiling and exploratory activity.

In general, one might summarize these changes in terms of "the three c's—carriages, carpets, and cans"—the net effect of which was to separate the child from contact with his mother's body. Carriages took the baby out of the shawl for transportation purposes. Carpets symbolize abundance in the form of more expensive household furnishings which demand protection against the child's depredations, so that much of the content of the relationship between a small child and his mother came to have reference to training "not to touch." And, finally, canned baby food, as we suggested above, tended to put the child in front of the mother rather than next to her in feeding.[39]

In addition, other changes had occurred between 1870 and 1930. The social tendencies of the infant had less expression; families were smaller and homes more separated. The child was thrown more and more with his parents, "who began to feel they were never let alone, and their continuous reactive prohibitions and admonitions rendered the child inwardly insecure and outwardly 'difficult,' so long as it was unable to attain to the orderliness, tidiness, punctuality, dutifulness, and so on, demanded by the parents." [40] Because families were smaller, children become more precious; parents of small families felt they owed the child everything, whereas earlier the child had been taught that he owed his parents everything. Schooling was universal, and the child was sent away from his mother very early and required to compete at school. Family roles had been completely redefined. "Something entirely novel had developed—the attempt to base the family on the parental dyad, appearing in the role of pals, equals, and comrades." [41] The concept of God as the Friend of little children, which had succeeded the blood-and-thunder Jove-Jehovah, became attenuated for children, who saw the sky as a background for airplanes and who knew as a matter of fact that life could not maintain itself beyond the stratosphere.

Sex distinctions were neutralized. Indeed, the roles of father and mother tended to become so blurred that by the 1950's students of the family were warning against the possible dangers which might ensue. Fathers no longer offered the authoritarian support they had in the 19th century; in some extreme cases their role had been watered down into "mother's little helper."

Dr. Irene M. Josselyn . . . has sounded [a warning] against the tendency in some households to make dad into "mother's little helper." "I have no objection to the idea of fathers helping with everyday details of child care," Dr. Josselyn told us recently, "but I feel they should carry out whatever duties they wish to assume in their own way, as the competent, intelligent men they are—not as caricatures of women." When fathers are "used," she said, merely to do those tasks which mother would rather skip, the result might be that the child would cease to have a father. He would merely have a real mother and a substitute mother". . . .

Dr. B. D. Hendy, a British psychiatrist, argues father should not compromise his function of representing the outside world in the home or let himself become "a mere home bird, content all the time with his slippers and his pipe by the fireside." [42]

Hygienically, then, the 1930's provided a good environment; psychologically, the author we have been following argues, not so good. The attention the child received as a person protected him against tendencies toward hysterias, but the frustrations led to insecurity, unexpressed dependency, unexpressed resentment and hostility, and even obsessional trends. The full impact of all these changes, he predicted, would show itself in the 1950's.

Whether or not one accepts in detail the above author's analysis, the perspective in which he places the problem shows how futile it is to "indict" women for the changes which have been taking place in family life. It is not a generation of willful, headstrong, egocentric, ambitious women who have changed the family and, more specifically, the quality of mothering which women give, but a style of living which has made 19th-century mothering impossible. No one would dream of asking women today to carry babies close to their bodies a large part of each day, or to return to old dietary patterns, or to strip their homes of the modern equipment from which the child must be protected—and which must, in turn, be protected from the child—even if it does generate strains. Nor can we give up compulsory schooling or many of the other sources of stress. Mothers have to perform their role in the current scene, not in that of a century ago.

Rural versus Urban Definition of Mother Role

The comparison between mothering in 1870 and in 1930 which we have just presented points up differences in time, community being held constant. It was based on British experience. But there has been a concomitant change from rural to urban patterns which has been especially marked in the United States. We present here, then, a contrast between mothering in a rural setting and in an urban setting today. The study we cite conceals other than merely rural-urban differences— socioeconomic class, for example—but even if these are discounted, the contrast is startling. The child-rearing practices, or performance of the maternal role, in a mountain area which has retained a pre-industrial atmosphere show up in stark relief when they are contrasted with the changes which have taken place in an ultramodern city of the industrial age, New York.[43]

The author, who had been trained as a nursery-school teacher in Greenwich Village, went to the Tennessee mountains to open a nursery school there. The behavior of the children in Tennessee was so different from that of the New York children to whom she was accustomed that she made an analysis of the forces which produced these differences. Why, she asked, were the New York children so spirited, with such strong urges to rebel, and so vigorous and fearless in their expression of rebellion? Why were the mountain children so easy to handle? Why was there so little rebellion among them? Was there no maladjustment among them? What did their outwardly peaceful, placid behavior mean? Why were they so shy? Why was their play so undramatic? Why were they so much less creative than the New York children? So far as the mountain children were concerned she found:

Small babies are seldom out of their mothers' arms, and are nursed whenever they cry. Often they are not weaned until they are well along in their second year. Children are always to be seen with their parents at buryings, at P.T.A. meetings, at square dances. They are never left at home or put to bed early. Parents do not seem to expect their children to live on a schedule that differs very much from their own. Meals are the same for all members of the family, and even the youngest baby may have some of the chocolate pie if he wants it. Children live a life very close to that of their parents, a life involving few restrictions. Many boys and girls even drop out of school if they choose to.

However, children are taught to say "Yes'm," and are expected to obey their elders in matters that are considered important, such as behaving respectfully to grandmothers. They are whipped or threatened with whippings if they do not obey. Discipline is theoretically of the old "authoritative" kind, yet the actual routine of living is far from a strictly regulated one. . . .[44]

By way of contrast, the child in a modern city has quite a different role vis-à-vis his parents, especially his mother.

In city homes it is often considered not only necessary but advisable to put the children's bedtime and mealtime on regular schedules that may be entirely different from those of the adults; to limit the children's diet to the foods that are good for them though adults in the household may eat what is denied the children; to leave children at home when parents go out in the evening; and in other ways to expect the young members of the family to adhere to a special routine suitable for them.

Furthermore, many parents no longer believe in a disciplinary atmosphere that is authoritarian. They do not consider disobedience as much of a crime in their children as failure to grow in ability to control themselves.

And many of these parents have only one child. Many of them live in small apartments in the large cities. The mother works as well as the father, because she prefers to, and Ellen the maid takes Jerry out to the park to play in the afternoon.[45]

The result is a placid mountain child but a dynamic, often rebellious, city child.

Critique

The contrasts in mothering are undoubtedly real. Today the role of mother in an urban setting is indeed different from that of the past or of a rural environment. But the significance of the differences might well be mooted. Do these changes mean a deterioration in the quality of mothering? Is the kind of mothering which modern women offer their children inferior to that which women in the 19th century offered? There is no proof that it is.

The kind of mothering which the child of 1870 received may, it is true, have protected him from vulnerability to heightened anxiety states. But all this may mean is that his anxieties took the form of hysterical symptoms. We have only to read the cases on which Freud developed his theories to see what the Victorian family did to the personality of its children. The unexpressed and unexpressable hatreds which seethed in the bosoms of his patients do not compare favorably with the inner life of people today. The father who offered authoritarian support also caused frustration. Nor was the record of the 19th century any better than that of today with respect to the pathologies discussed in Part IV, as we noted above.

Nor was the personality of the individual reared in a rural area necessarily better than that of the person reared in an urban area. The author of the study reported above found that the mountain children, with limited experience of conflict and contact, with an easygoing, indulgent routine, did not as adolescents have enough strength to meet many of the problems of a modern, urban setting. The Greenwich Village child, despite his stormy childhood, or because of it, had the strength and ability to meet new situations.

None of this is meant to imply that the kind of mothering which children receive is not important. We know that early family relationships may almost determine many of the pathologies. The point we are making is that there is no documentable proof that there has been an increase in poor maternal role performance in the past century. In the past, as now, there has been a sizable proportion of men and women who have—for whatever reasons—inadequately performed parental roles. That the proportion is greater today would be very difficult to prove.

The changes in maternal role performance have resulted in more anxiety states and fewer hysterias, and they have also had profound effects on the character structure of people today, as contrasted with the past. We shall discuss this point in the following chapter. But first a word about the responsibility of the family with respect to the pathologies.

The Role of Family as First Line of Defense

Although we have referred to the fact that mental illness and crime are often attributed to violation of the maternal role by the patients' mothers, our emphasis has been primarily on normal relationships and their difficulties in a modern setting. We cannot, however, ignore the responsibility assigned to the family for taking care of deviants. Although, increasingly, communities, states, and even the Federal Government make available resources and facilities, and even assume responsibility, still the first line of defense remains within the family. The following excerpt describes the situation in a Southern town in the throes of industrialization; it refers to a pattern characteristic certainly of the immediate past and perhaps of the present in most American communities.

. . . there is no sense in which the community undertakes to make deviations from the behavior norms a community problem. The courts are adjudicating agencies to keep families from taking justice into their own hands. The police are arms of the court to enforce the peace and only reluctantly pick up individuals who are disturbing the peace. But the care and rehabilitation of disturbers of the peace, be they rowdies, drunkards, knife artists, seducers of womankind, or housebreakers, is not made a matter of community responsibility. It is regarded first of all as a *family problem*.

The family tends to make its own diagnosis of the problem. If the disturbance is by young children or by feebleminded adults, families tend to take no action regarding the deviants, treating them basically as nonresponsible. If it is possible to identify the problem as having a physical basis in some physical malformation, families will follow through with local physicians to specialists to undertake complete treatment. If, however, the trouble appears to be in the realm of overemotionalism, delinquency, or sexual misconduct, it is seen as evidence of *moral weakness* which requires much talk by family, friends of the family, ministers and doctors who encourage the person to mend his ways. He is assured of support and aid, may be prayed for, and every attempt is made to restore his moral strength.

Moral deviants divide between those coming from good families and those from poor white and Negro families. For the latter, rehabilitation is seen as a waste of time by the community and much greater toleration of deviation by these moral deviants is generated until they finally become too burdensome to be tolerated and are incarcerated or institutionalized permanently.

For all moral deviants there is a pattern of covering up, white protector covering up for his Negro dependents; white respected families covering up for their wayward members. Official admission of marital separations, applications for divorce, or insanity, is postponed by a system of circumventions. Pregnancies out of wedlock are disposed of by "trips to see our close kin." Alcoholic hangovers are defined euphemistically as "he's always indisposed after a party." Among the respectable sets in Eddyville, the labels of divorce or insanity were never applied. There was a great amount of social fiction about being "ill" or "having to go to the hospital for a check-up" which avoided clear-cut recognition of emotional illness. The more powerful the family the more protective it appears to be of its members and their reputations. . . .

Family care, in Eddyville at present, consists of accepting the responsibility for its members who are deviants, diagnosing their troubles, protecting them from criticism and punitive actions from others, and supporting them in their battles to regain the moral strength that it takes to be a responsible adult in the community.[46]

Parental roles, in brief, are still defined to include the diagnosis, care, and treatment of many of the pathologies discussed in Part IV.

For the most part our discussion of father and mother roles in this chapter has referred to small children. But parental roles are no less a problem during adolescence. We turn, then, to a consideration of parent-child relationships in youth as they reflect the influence of abundance, and then to the role problems of young people today.

NOTES

1 John Fiske, *Outlines of Cosmic Philosophy, based on the Doctrine of Evolution, with Criticisms on the Positive Philosophy* (Houghton, 1890), Vol. II, p. 344.

2 See Jessie Bernard, *Remarriage, A Study of Marriage* (Dryden, 1956), Chapter 12.

3 In a case reported by the Home Advisory Council of the Home Term Court of New York City, for example, the father was requested to leave the family as a therapeutic procedure: ". . . Helen wanted to return home but not if her father remained there. He could not refrain from subjecting her to both his seductive charm and his brutal anger. So Mr. S. yielded to the persuasive power of the judge and left home temporarily." Great improvements were reported in the family in the course of a year of counseling, especially in Mrs. S., for "once the destructiveness of her husband was minimized, it was possible to help build her ego." (Mimeographed case history.)

4 Talcott Parsons and Robert F. Bales, *Family, Socialization and Interaction Process* (Free Press, 1955), Chapter 5, "Role Differentiation in the Nuclear Family," by Morris Zelditch, Jr.

5 *Ibid.,* p. 318.

6 *Ibid.*

7 There is a trend in the direction of equalizing the role obligations of husbands and wives, so that some states also require women to support their husbands if the husbands cannot support themselves. The difference is, however, that men must support their wives even if the wives can support themselves, even, in fact, if they are wealthy; but wives are obligated to support their husbands only when they are unable to support themselves.

8 One sociologist, Talcott Parsons, goes so far as to say: ". . . a mature woman can love, sexually, only a man who takes his full place in the masculine world, above all its occupational aspect, and who takes responsibility for a family." Parsons and Bales, *op. cit.,* p. 22.

9 Dust jacket of *Their Mothers' Sons* by Edward A. Strecker (Lippincott, 1946).

10 For example, at a meeting on Delinquency and Crime, the director of the New Jersey State Diagnostic Center at Menlo Park, Dr. Ralph Brancale, said: "We find some of the most disturbing abnormal reactions leading to crime patterns seem to stem from pathological relationships between the child and his mother. This factor is probably leading to the most serious forms of delinquent behavior." (*New York Times,* August 19, 1955.) He said that conflicts resulting from father-child relationships were less likely to be serious because they came later in the child's life.

11 S. B. Sarason, *Psychological Problems in Mental Deficiency* (Harper, 1949), pp. 310–311.

12 In addition to the institutionalized parental roles, it has been found that large families tend to differentiate different group roles for the several children, such as: (1) the responsible one, (2) the popular one, (3) the socially ambitious one, (4) the studious one, (5) the family isolate, (6) the irresponsible one, (7) the sickly one, and (8) the spoiled one. The sequence of these roles is related to ordinal position, suggesting that each child tends to fit into a role related to but not identical with those already pre-empted. James H. S. Bossard and Eleanor S. Boll, "Personality Roles in the Large Family," *Child Development,* 26 [1955], pp. 71–78.)

13 In the Mexican village described at the beginning of Chapter 15, when children were asked to write themes "about what they liked best in each member of the family, they invariably said they liked the

father because he supported them. The comments of widows concerning the death of their husbands were all phrased in terms of economic loss. Thus one said with much feeling that at the time she had wished it had been her young son rather than her husband who died, because in that case she would at least have been sure of her food. Though grief over personal loss at the death of a husband undoubtedly is present in many cases, it is not required of wives to express this grief, and it is considered perfectly natural for them to emphasize the economic aspects of the loss." (Oscar Lewis, "Husbands and Wives in a Mexican Village: A Study of Role Conflict," *American Anthropologist,* 51 [Oct.-Dec. 1949], p. 606.)

14 The differentials referred to in the text are becoming attenuated, but they are still present. They may disappear in time.

15 In 1950 more than a third of the families with no earner included children under eighteen. (Elizabeth E. Hoyt *et al., American Income and Its Use* [Harper, 1954], p. 118.) The proportion was probably higher in the 19th century when men died younger and there were more children per family.

16 In 1955 the National Desertion Bureau, on the fiftieth anniversary of its founding, announced a change of name to Family Location Service. "The original name reflected the primary function of the agency when it was founded: to track down missing husbands and, largely by coercive procedures, bring them back to their families. Through the years this function broadened. The bureau has sought to 'sit down with' the husband [or wife] and with less emphasis on coercion, to strengthen the concept of responsibility. In effect, the service has moved from detection toward rehabilitation." (*New York Times,* October 25, 1955.) This change in emphasis reflects the transition, as in so many other problem areas, from a legalistic to a medical point of view.

17 For example, when the high divorce rates of the postwar years led to an increased number of children receiving assistance because of the estrangement of their parents, even though such families "represent only a small proportion of all . . . broken families, this evidence of social maladjustment [gave] rise to criticism of the program for aid to dependent children . . . [which] culminated in an amendment, effective in 1952, requiring that law enforcement officials be notified when children who have been deserted or abandoned by a parent are receiving aid to dependent children." (Jay L. Roney, "Twenty Years of Public Assistance," *Social Security Bulletin,* 18 [Aug. 1955], p. 21.)

18 It was estimated that in 1965 there would be 63,000,000.

19 For detailed data on this trend, see Jessie Bernard, *op. cit.,* Chapter 3.

20 Kingsley Davis, "Sociological and Statistical Analysis," in *Children of Divorced Parents* (constituting Vol. X, No. 15, of *Law and Contemporary Problems* [Summer 1944]), p. 719.

21 In 1940, 20 per cent of the children being assisted by aid-to-dependent-children provisions of the Social Security Act were in need because of the divorce, separation, or desertion of parents. By 1955, 60 per cent were in this category, and three fourths of these children had been deserted by their fathers. (Charles I. Schottland, Federal Social Security Commissioner, reported in *New York Times,* March 2, 1955.) Of the 2,600,000 children receiving aid-to-dependent-children grants in 1955, 800,000 had incapacitated fathers, 400,000 were paternal orphans, and 1,400,000 had fathers who were estranged from their mothers.

22 Kingsley Davis, "Divorce Downswing," *New York Times Magazine,* May 8, 1955.

23 Lenore Epstein, Dorothy McCamman, and Alfred M. Skolnik, "Social Security Protection, 1935–55," *Social Security Bulletin,* 18 (Aug. 1955), p. 10. About 5 per cent of these children needed help temporarily because their fathers were in prisons, sanitariums, or the armed services.

24 *Ibid.*

25 See note 17.

26 Martha M. Eliot, "Twenty Years of Progress for Children," *Social Security Bulletin,* 18 (Aug. 1955), pp. 25 ff. With respect to the maternal and child health services the program has been preventive in nature. It has included: "prenatal and postpartum clinics for maternity patients; child health conferences for infants and preschool children; health examinations of school children; immunizations of children against diphtheria and smallpox; dental inspections; public health nursing services in the home and in clinics; and nursing supervision of midwives." With respect to services for crippled children: "State agencies hold crippled children's clinics at varying intervals in different parts of the State. The physicians are specialists, who make examinations and give treatment in these clinics, in hos-

pitals, and in convalescent homes. . . . Many states . . . are including convalescent and foster-home care and nursing follow-up in the home. The definition of crippling is decided by each State, either by statute or administratively. . . . Since 1939 . . . there has been a steady increase in the number of children with other [than orthopedic] handicaps included in the State services. At present all State programs include children under age 21 who have a handicap of an orthopedic nature or who require plastic surgery. Over half the States have developed services for children with rheumatic fever. All States provide some services for children with cerebral palsy. Some include children who are hard-of-hearing and children with epilepsy. Many States include children who have eye conditions that can be helped by surgery." In 1954, 265,000 children were receiving services for crippled children. The third program—child welfare services—also aims at prevention: "When a child in his own home is having difficulty in making adjustments to his home, school, or community living, the child welfare worker tries to find the cause of the problem and to help him and his parents in solving it. These workers also aid children who are neglected or abused. They arrange, when necessary, for the care of children in foster family homes and in institutions. They assist unmarried mothers, many of whom are adolescents, with their problems, and in making plans for the care of their babies. They place for adoption children who must be permanently separated from their own homes. They help to make day-care plans for children of working mothers." As of December 31, 1954, 277,000 child en were receiving such services, of whom 41 per cent were living in their own homes. 42 per cent in foster family homes, and 17 per cent in institutions or elsewhere.

27 A. C. Kinsey et al., Sexual Behavior in the Human Female (Saunders, 1953), pp. 326–327.

28 Chester G. Vernier, assisted by E. Perry Churchill, Parent and Child (Stanford Univ. Press, 1936), pp. 3–4, Vol. IV of American Family Laws . . . (to Jan. 1, 1935).

29 Mabel E. Elliott and Francis E. Merrill, Social Disorganization (Harper, 1950), p. 146. The actual number of infants known to be born out of wedlock increased 150 per cent between 1938 and 1948. Some of this increase in numbers could be attributed to the rising number of total births. But even the rate increased; it was 80 per cent higher in 1948 than in 1940. See Helen L. Witmer and Ruth Kotinsky, eds., Personality in the Making (Harper, 1952), p. 177. The increase occurred among both white and non-white groups and in all age groups between fifteen and forty-four. See Lucy Freeman, Children Who Never Had a Chance. Public Affairs Pamphlet No. 183, New York, The Public Affairs Committee, 1952.

30 Kinsey et al., op. cit., pp. 326–327, 333.

31 Clark E. Vincent, "The Unwed Mother and Sampling Bias," American Sociological Review, 19 (Oct. 1954), p. 562.

32 Ibid., pp. 566–567.

33 Anna Freud and Dorothy Burlingame, Infants without Families (International Univ. Press, 1944).

34 David Levy, "Primary Affect Hunger," American Journal of Psychiatry, 94 (1937), pp. 643–652.

35 Harold Orlansky, "Infant Care and Personality," Psychological Bulletin, 46 (Jan. 1949), pp. 1–48; William H. Sewell, "Infant Training and the Personality of the Child," American Journal of Sociology, 58 (Sept. 1952), pp. 150–159; and also William H. Sewell and Paul H. Mussen, "The Effects of Feeding, Weaning, and Scheduling Procedures on Childhood Adjustment and the Formation of Oral Symptoms," Child Development, 23 (1952), pp. 185–191.

36 James L. Halliday, Psychosocial Medicine (Norton, 1948), pp. 112–121.

37 In some cases this practice led to smothering by so-called overlaying, but such accidents were not considered too serious; the law treated them as offenses, but not as crimes.

38 Halliday, op. cit., p. 115.

39 The separation of the child from the all-encompassing intimacy with the mother was illustrated in a study which contrasted the traditional definition of the maternal role, as depicted in the Madonna stance, with the current definition, as depicted in modern pictures. All the pictures of the Madonna, from the catacombs to the end of the 19th century—134 in number—were contrasted with 25 pictures taken from the March 1956 issues of three women's magazines, Ladies' Home Journal, McCall's, and Parents' Magazine. "In the traditional conception, the mother and child are more likely to be almost a

single symbiotic unit. The child is part of the mother. They seem to melt into one another. In the modern conception, on the other hand, the child is no longer part of his mother; he is a person in his own right. Both stance and attitude proclaim their separate identities. . . ." (Jessie Bernard, "Changing Familial Roles and Their Implications for Societal Stability," unpublished study.

40 Halliday, *op. cit.,* p. 117.

41 *Ibid.,* p. 118.

42 Dorothy Barclay, "The Men in Children's Lives," *New York Times Magazine,* June 19, 1955, p. 38.

43 Claudia Lewis, *Children of the Cumberland* (Columbia Univ. Press, 1946).

44 *Ibid.,* pp. xv–xvi.

45 *Ibid.,* pp. xvi–xvii.

46 Reuben Hill, J. D. Moss, C. G. Wirths, P. C. Daughterty, and T. W. Wirths, *Eddyville's Families* (mimeograph; Institute for Research in Social Science, 1953), pp. 419–422.

17

Social Problems
Associated with Youth:
Family and Worker Roles

How Old Is "Young"?

When the average life expectancy at birth was about thirty-five or even forty years, a young person of fifteen could scarcely be considered a child. When most of the work of the world was done by human muscle, and there was a lot of it to do, the strong muscles of teen-agers could not be wasted. When most people lived on farms, the adolescent was expected to contribute his share of responsible work. In an age of abundance, the life expectancy is stretched to seventy and young people of fifteen seem very childish; furthermore, pressure is exerted to keep them out of the labor market, so that they will not compete with their elders.

The age group from roughly fourteen to eighteen is in an anomalous position in our society. Young people of this age have attained their intellectual growth. Intelligence does not increase after this age. They are therefore as intelligent as their elders, as measured by

How Old Is "Young"?

Role Problems in the Families of Young People

Worker Roles of Youth

Education

Some Recent Recommendations

Youth and the Labor Market

tests, or at any rate as intelligent as they are ever likely to be. When change is occurring as rapidly as it is in our time, the experience of older people is little if any better for meeting current challenges than that of young people. There was much truth in the cartoon showing a father in front of his erratic television screen, calling to his wife: "Wake Johnny up to come and fix the TV set!" The young people of today come home from school to instruct their parents on what to do in case of an atomic attack. They have been reading about space travel ever since they graduated from Mother Goose; they take it as a matter of course that interplanetary transportation is just around the corner. It is an expected part of their world. In such an atmosphere the only superiority the older people have—experience—seems largely neutralized. Their experience is not necessarily germane to the problems young people face today.

But there is no functional place, no clear-cut occupational role defined, for these young people in the economy. They are physically superior to earlier generations in height and weight, and are better-fed. Yet, little use is made of this superiority. At eighteen they are old enough for military service. A century ago young men sailed in clipper ships. They were skilled fishermen or farmers; they were on their own. The annals of history are filled with young men who achieved great things. Benjamin Franklin left home at an early age to seek his fortune.

Young persons are sexually at the peak of their capacity but they are not in a position to marry. They are kept artificially young and immature, treated like children in a manner which is often grossly insulting to their potentialities. In some cases this is done by parents who do not wish to seem old themselves and who can retain an illusion of youth by preventing their children from becoming adult. In other cases it is done by well-intentioned people who wish to keep them in school or out of the labor market; after we have reviewed the history of child exploitation we will understand their solicitude. Whatever the reason, however, the result produces numerous anomalies. Many young people rebel against the false position they are placed in. They come to constitute a problem to themselves, to their families, and to others. And when we consider that most young people—because of the differential birth rate which means that a larger proportion of young people than of adults are in the lower income brackets—are in the poorer areas of the city, we can see how the problems of youth are compounded.

We shall consider only a selected number of social and societal problems which concern youth: family roles; worker roles, a subject inextricably bound up with that of our third topic, education; and, finally, in Chapter 18, delinquency, related not only to the first three but to almost everything else we consider in this volume.

Role Problems in the Families of Young People

Role Confusion

We continue here our discussion of family roles, which we began in Chapter 16, to note that at no age are family role confusions more puzzling than at the age of young adults. Just what is the role of the seventeen-year-old son vis-à-vis his father? What is the role of the father or the mother toward him? Is it possible for two generations of adults to live together successfully when there is so little crystallization of role obligations? The opportunities for mishaps are numerous. Several generations ago we saw some of these problems writ large in the families of immigrants in which the parental generation had role conceptions quite different from those of the children's generation. Today a similar situation exists between generations because of the rapidity of technological changes. It is almost as though the parents were immigrants from another culture, a point we shall pursue further below.

Yet, despite these intergenerational differences, both parents and children are locked in a kind of role vise. The son or daughter has the parents, in effect, "over the barrel." No matter what the young person does, the role of the parents requires that they assume responsibility for it. They cannot cut the son or daughter loose; that might have serious repercussions and cause them even more trouble. They have to accept whatever the young person does. Often they even stop trying to exert any influence—it seems so hopeless.[1]

But the parents, likewise, have a stranglehold on the young person. Since there is no functional worker role for him in the economy, he is at their mercy financially. He is dependent on them. He cannot escape from them. There was a time when young persons could leave home at a fairly early age to "seek their fortune." They could apprentice themselves or find a place on a farm or in a store. The economy was not so abstract and complex that they could not comprehend it and find a niche for themselves. Today when young people run away from home—as they frequently do in the lower socioeconomic classes—it is usually a precursor to serious delinquency.

Very often it would be to the young person's advantage if he could escape from his "home." One psychiatrist, after twenty years of counseling, expressed surprise that more children did not become delinquent. She said she found in them an "amazing capacity to tolerate bad parents, poor teachers, dreadful homes and communities." [2]

Character and Discipline in an Age of Scarcity and in an Age of Abundance

We likened the intergenerational problems in a rapidly changing society to those of immigrant families. We might think of the generation which grew up in the earlier years of the 20th century as immigrants from a culture based on an economy of scarcity; young people of today are growing up in a setting of abundance. Older people often hark back to the conditions of their own childhood as somehow or other ideal and view present conditions as bad deviations. We have not yet adjusted to the withdrawal of scarcity as a disciplinary force in shaping character. Some people wonder if without this discipline character can ever be made firm and strong. The following statement represents this view.

There can be no question that the improvement in the condition of the average man, with its increase in earnings, has contributed radically to the change in attitude of parents. Most of them overlook the part which strict discipline, scanty allowances, and hard work played in their moral and physical upbringing. Instead they are determined to give to their children what was denied to them. They buy them better clothes, provide them with larger allowances, enable them to participate in sports, to attend movies, to enjoy summer vacations, and to do all those things calculated to make life agreeable. They not only relieve them of the little tasks or chores which once were a part of a boy's life, but they even frown on the performance of any manual labor, particularly for hire. The industry that was once encouraged in youth as a virtue is now regarded as an interference with the right to enjoy life.

This generosity on the part of parents has had an evil effect on the generation upon which it has been lavished. The little gifts which once provided the great incentive to youth for obedience and industry are now without effect. What was once awaited as an act of kindness and generosity is now demanded as a right. . . . Instead of having its feet on the ground and being conscious of the stern realities of life, our younger generation has its head in the clouds and looks down on its parents as old-fashioned and out-of-date.[3]

The tone of the above statement makes it appear that parents somehow willfully planned it that way. Actually the parents were themselves responding to the transformation of the economy to one of abundance, with its demand for "relentless consumption." A parent can refuse a child's request on the basis that "we can't afford it," without arousing too much resentment; this is a fact the child must learn to face. But it is far more difficult to refuse a child's request on the basis of parental disapproval. Now there is room for argument, and the child may well feel that he is being mistreated if he cannot have something his parents can afford but refuse him on moral grounds.

And in an age of abundance, surrounded by exhortations to buy and spend—required, in fact, to buy and spend—the old character structure is out of place.

In the early days of our country, in fact until recently, the conventional moral dicta—exhortations to thrift and plain living, self-denial and self-sacrifice, meager consumption of economic goods—fitted our economic system. If we were to develop our resources we must have capital to do so, and if we were to have capital tomorrow it was necessary not to spend today. The popular literature of our early days is full of injunctions to abjure comfort and luxury. A penny saved is a penny earned, and the godly man is he who lives on as little as possible and saves the rest.

The virtues of Poor Richard were nine-tenths frugality. His doctrine was simple: labor and save. In the cold glimmer before dawn he breakfasted on oatmeal and beans and hastened to the fields or the countinghouse, where he spared neither himself nor others until everyone was exhausted by exacting toil. The financial returns from this labor Poor Richard put back into the farm or the business. He had all the satisfactions which follow the pursuit of virtue, and the nation profited as well.[4]

This work-and-save orientation, which is associated with the Protestant ethic, made for strong, if not lovable, character. It was a powerful discipline. Both parents and children accepted it. It served as the scaffolding for all other disciplines. Even the Soviet Union fell back on it in the 1930's in its desperate drive to create capital. It shapes the character which is best suited to an economy of scarcity.

But in 20th-century America the self-denial and self-sacrifice advocated by the judge quoted above is not only unneeded, it is positively dysfunctional for the economy as a whole. The economy depends on consumption, on taking off the market the enormous amount of goods which it can create. This fact has produced a revolutionary change in the role structure of modern society. It transfers a great deal of discipline from parents to peer groups.

One student of current American society has traced this change in detail. He has invented the term "inner-directed" to refer to the kind of personality which was oriented to productivity in an age of scarcity and the term "other-directed" to refer to the kind of personality which is oriented to consumption in an age of abundance. To achieve success, "personality," not character in the old sense, is important. One proves one's competence not by mastering tools and materials, but by making friends and influencing people. The inner-directed person has, figuratively speaking, a gyroscope inside him which keeps him properly oriented toward his goal, regardless of impinging interferences. The other-directed person, it might be said, has a radar which keeps him sensitive to cues from his fellows, who determine his goals. Peers rather than parents become the key people in the child's environment.

Under the new conditions of social and economic life parents who try, in inner-directed fashion, to compel the internalization of disciplined pursuit of clear goals run the risk of having their children styled clear out of the personality market. Gyroscopic direction is just not flexible enough for the rapid adaptations of personality that are required, precisely because there will be other competitors who do not have gyroscopes. Inhibited from presenting their children with sharply silhouetted images of self and society, parents in our era can only equip the child to do his best, whatever that may turn out to be. . . .

Increasingly in doubt as to how to bring up their children, parents turn to other contemporaries for advice; they also look to the mass media; and

. . . they turn, in effect, to the children themselves. . . . They cannot help show their children, by their own anxiety, how little they depend on themselves and how much on others. Whatever they may seem to be teaching the child in terms of content, they are passing on to him their own contagious, highly diffuse anxiety. . . .

The loss of old certainties in the spheres of work and social relations is accompanied by doubt as to how to bring up children. Moreover, the parents no longer feel themselves superior to the children. . . . It may be that children today do not gain the strength that adults—no longer inner-directed —have lost. . . .

Despite the diminution of their authority, the parents still try to control matters; but with the loss of self-assurance their techniques change. They can neither hold themselves up as examplars—when both they and the child know better—nor resort, in good conscience, to severe corporal punishment and deprivations. At most there are token spankings, with open physical warfare confined to the lower classes. The parents' recourse, especially in the upper middle class, is to "personnel" methods—to manipulation in the form of reasoning, or, more accurately, of rationalizing. . . .

Finally, we must observe the change in the content of the issues at stake between parent and child. The more driving and tense inner-directed parents compel their children to work, to save, to clean house, sometimes to study, and sometimes to pray. Other less puritanical types of inner-directed parent want their boys to be manly, their girls to be feminine and chaste. . . . The large home could absorb enormous amounts of labor.

In the other-directed home, on the other hand, the issues between parent and child concern the nonwork side of life. . . . So parents and children debate over eating and sleeping time and . . . over use of the family car. . . .

The parental role diminishes in importance as compared with the same role among the inner-directed.[5]

When it is successful, the pattern of parent-child role relationships characteristic of the present time produces a flexible, outgoing, generous orientation in interpersonal relationships. A European cliché about Americans is that until about the age of eighteen, they seem older than their European counterpart; but that after eighteen, they seem younger. As children they have initiative, independence, and spirit, which makes them seem mature. As adults they are trustful, open, and do not play their cards close to their chests, which makes them seem young. At its best, the role system we have today produces young people who are self-confident. One has only to note the behavior of youngsters who appear before the public—on the television screen or at school programs—to see the aplomb with which they comport themselves. The agonizing shyness which used to characterize young people is rarely seen at the present time.

At its worst, however, the current role configuration results in disrespectful attitudes or even gross insubordination.[6] The young persons strut insolently to make very clear their contempt for teachers and other symbols of authority.[7] Like every sword, it has two sides. It can produce destructive as well as constructive character. The important thing seems to be to learn how to use it properly.

Worker Roles of Youth

The current position of young people in our society is an interesting illustration of the unforeseen results of social reform. It is also an example of the way in which good intentions may have dysfunctional consequences.

In order to understand the anomalies of our current conception of the worker role of youth we sketch here briefly the history of child labor and the social reform movement, which had as its objective the elimination of child labor where possible.

The first use of children in British mines and mills in the 18th century had been looked upon as a fine innovation. Here was work children could do, and it would keep them out of mischief. It was better than the workhouse or the poor farm for orphans. The following account may be overdrawn, but it describes the tradition which has motivated reformers to fight child labor for over a century:

. . . manufacturers wanted children, and they got them from the workhouses. It was not difficult to persuade Bumbledom to get rid of its pauper children, especially when its conscience was salved by the specious pretext that the children were to be taught new trades, as apprentices. "Alfred," the anonymous author of the *History of the Factory Movement,* gives a thrilling description of the horrible inhumanity and wickedness of this practice of sending parish apprentices, "without remorse or inquiry, to be *used up* as the cheapest raw material in the market." The mill owners would first communicate with the overseers of the poor, and the latter would fix suitable dates for the manufacturers or their agents to examine the children. Those chosen were then conveyed to their destination, closely packed in wagons or canalboats. Thenceforth they were doomed to the most miserable slavery. A class of "traffickers" in child slaves arose. These men made a profitable business of supplying children to the manufacturers. They deposited their victims in dark, dank cellars, where the sales to the manufacturers or their agents were made. "The mill owners, by the light of lanterns being able to examine the children, their limbs and stature having undergone the necessary scrutiny, the bargain was struck, and these poor innocents were conveyed to the mills." Their plight was appalling. They received no wages, and they were so cheap, their places so easily filled, that the mill owners did not even take the trouble to give them decent food or clothing. "In stench, in heated rooms, amid the whirling of a thousand wheels, little fingers and little feet were kept in ceaseless action, forced into unnatural activity by blows from the heavy hands and feet of the merciless overlooker, and the infliction of bodily pain by instruments of punishment invented by the sharpened ingenuity of insatiable selfishness."

Roger Blincoe, himself an apprentice who, at seven years of age, was sent from a London workhouse to a cotton mill near Nottingham, gives a harrowing but well-authenticated account of actual experience. He tells how the apprentices used to be fed upon the same coarse food as that given to the master's pigs, and how he and his fellow-victims used joyfully to say when they saw the swine being fed, "The pigs are served; it will be our turn next". . . . "When the swine were hungry," he says, "they used to grunt so loud, they obtained the wash first to quiet them. The apprentices could be intimidated, and made to keep still." Blincoe describes how, for fattening, the pigs were often given meat balls, or dumplings, in their wash, and how he and the other apprentices who were kept near the pigsties used to slip away and slyly steal as many of these dumplings from the pigs as possible, hastening away with them to a hiding-place, where they were greedily devoured. "The pigs . . . learned from experience to guard their food by various expedients. Made wise by repeated losses, they kept a sharp lookout, and the moment they ascertained the approach of the half-famished apprentices, they set up so loud a chorus of snorts and grunts, it was heard in the kitchen, when out rushed the swineherd, armed with a whip, from which combined means of protection for the swine this accidental source of obtaining a good dinner was soon lost. Such was the contest carried on for some time at Litton Mill between the half-famished apprentices and the well-fed swine." *

The children were worked sixteen hours at a stretch, by day and by night. They slept by turns and relays in beds that were never allowed to cool, one set being sent to bed as soon as the others had gone to their toil. . . . Sometimes the unfortunate victims would try to run away, and to prevent this all who were suspected of such a tendency had irons riveted on their ankles with long links reaching up to their hips. In these chains they were compelled to work and sleep, young women and girls as well as boys. Many children contrived to commit suicide, some were unquestionably beaten to death; the death-rate became so great that it became the custom to bury the bodies at night, secretly, lest a popular uprising be provoked.

Worse still, the cupidity of British Bumbledom was aroused, and it became the custom for overseers of the poor to insist that one imbecile child at least should be taken by the mill owner, or the trafficker, with every batch of twenty children. In this manner the parish got rid of the expense of maintaining its idiot children. What became of these unhappy idiots will probably never be known, but from the cruel fate of the children who were sane, we may judge how awful that of the poor imbeciles must have been.[8]

It was not until the devastating effect which this situation was having on the health of British citizens became clear that legislation to protect children began to be passed, in 1802. This legislation—the first

* See the description, in the Introduction to Part I, of Paris during the winter of 1421, when children competed with swine for food.

factory legislation ever passed—was precipitated by an epidemic in 1799-1800 ascribed to the wretched conditions in factories. The pauper apprentice system was broken up, but the "free" children who succeeded them were almost as badly off. There was no age limit below which children could not be employed; but hours of work were not to exceed twelve per day. In the United States, Alexander Hamilton in his "Report on the Subject of Manufactures" had argued that women and children should be employed in factories. But after the mechanics' lien and wage exemption laws were passed, the first important labor laws in most American states were those which restricted child labor. Until the Civil War children customarily worked twelve or thirteen hours a day in textile mills, coal mines, steel mills, and glass factories. Only in 1842 did Massachusetts and Connecticut establish a ten-hour maximum for children under twelve and fourteen. As late as 1880 few states regulated child labor in factories. But by 1900 practically every state had some legislation on the subject, however inadequate by modern standards.

But conditions remained bad even by contemporaneous standards. In 1906, for example, four-year-olds were working in canning factories in New York State and girls of five and six, in cotton mills.[9] Children of four and five were being seriously exploited in sweated industries, working at home.[10] Unless one understands how bad the situation used to be one cannot understand how strong the pressure had to be to protect children from exploitation and how loath people are to modify present conditions in the direction of returning young people to industrial work.

The elimination of child labor was the goal not only of reformers but also of organized labor.

. . . organized labor, reformers and women's organizations waged an increasing agitation for better standards and eventually influenced public opinion sufficiently so that by 1930 all states except four had passed child labor laws covering manufacturing establishments, and about two-thirds of the states had laws regulating child labor in other occupations as well.[11]

The motivation of the unions was not strictly humanitarian, being aimed at keeping young people from competing in the market and lowering wages.

By 1940 there were thirteen states with a minimum age of sixteen for employment; nine of them prohibited employment in factories of children under this age. Thirty states set the minimum age for factory work at fourteen. Street trades, considered most hazardous, were not regulated in twenty-seven states except by municipal ordinance; but ten states prohibited night work of certain kinds for boys and girls, and twelve more prohibited it only for girls. The situation with respect to child labor legislation at midcentury has been summarized as follows:

Standards were relaxed somewhat during World War II because of the great demand for labor, but state laws began to be tightened in 1945, and the early postwar years brought further improvements. In 1950, however, there was still room for advance. A comparison of the standards recommended by the Fourteenth National Conference on Labor Legislation (1947) and the actual situation reveals major discrepancies in state legislation. . . .

Twenty-three states (less than half of those in the Union) plus Alaska and Puerto Rico approximated the standard of a minimum working age of 16 years in any employment in a factory or in any employment during school hours, and of 14 years in nonfactory employment outside of school hours.

Few states fully met the recommended standard of a minimum age of 18 for employment in hazardous occupations, though many prohibited employment in some of these occupations. Twenty-one states had, as recommended, established an administrative agency to determine what occupations were hazardous for minors.

Only 15 states, plus the District of Columbia, Alaska, and Puerto Rico, had adopted the maximum 8-hour day for minors under 18 in any gainful occupation. Only 5 states and Alaska, and Puerto Rico enforced a maximum 40-hour week for minors under 18, though 7 others and Hawaii applied it to those of less than 16 years only. Some states had a 44-hour week.

Night work for those under 16 was forbidden by 23 states, the District of Columbia, Hawaii, and Puerto Rico, though only 10 of them met or exceeded the recommended standard in this respect. Recommended limitations on night work for those from 16 to 18 were observed by 13 states.

As a measure to aid enforcement of the law, it was recommended that employment certificates be required for minors under 18 in any gainful occupation. This recommendation had been adopted, though with some occupations excepted, by 23 states, the District of Columbia, Hawaii and Puerto Rico.[12]

Child labor as it was institutionalized by early factories and mines had almost certainly been dysfunctional from the point of view of the child. It had kept him from getting an education. He had been easily exploited. He had been allowed to enter blind-alley occupations. He had been permitted to engage in morally hazardous occupations. In addition, child labor had depressed the labor market; the competition of the child had kept wages down. Nothing had seemed more clearly a social or societal problem so far as the normative aspects were concerned than that of child labor.

As a result of state legislation and of the federal Fair Labor Standards Act of 1938, as well as of the rapid shift from agricultural to nonagricultural industries which has characterized our economy in the 20th century, the problem of child labor has been all but solved.

The proportion of children aged ten to fifteen in the working force has declined to about 5.3 per cent.

TABLE 1
ESTIMATED PERCENTAGE OF CHILDREN 10-15 YEARS OF AGE IN THE
WORKING FORCE, BY SEX, FOR THE UNITED STATES, 1870-1950

Date	Total	Male	Female
1870	13.2	19.3	7.0
1880	16.8	24.4	9.0
1890	18.1	25.9	10.0
1900	18.2	26.1	10.2
1910	15.0	21.7	8.1
1920	11.3	16.8	5.8
1930	4.7	6.4	2.9
1940	1.8	2.7	0.8
1950	5.3	7.8	2.8

SOURCE: A. J. Jaffe and Charles D. Stewart, *Manpower Resources and Utilization: Principles of Working Force Analysis* (Wiley, 1951), p. 168.

The enumeration of the occupational status of young workers is subject to error, but:

Despite the inadequacies in the available data, it is clear that there has been a downward trend over the last several decades in the participation of youth in the labor force. Indeed, there were apparently fewer children aged 10 to 15 years, inclusive, who were gainfully occupied in 1930 than there were in 1870; by 1940 the number was negligible indeed.[13]

With respect to those in the sixteen to twenty age bracket, there seems to have been no consistent trend so far as labor-force participation is concerned; in 1890 about half were in the labor force, in 1940, about a third, and in 1950, half were again reported as workers, including, however, those in the armed forces.[14]

Parallel with the movement to restrict child labor in the 20th century were laws increasing the compulsory school requirements. If education is a good thing, then everyone, it has been argued, should have as much of it as possible. In the United States thirty-seven states at midcentury required young people to remain in school until the age of sixteen; the others specified either seventeen or eighteen. Many of the children who would have been in mines and mills fifty years ago are in schoolrooms today.

As a result, the proportion of young persons enrolled in school has increased steadily since 1910. And it is expected to continue almost unabated.

TABLE 2

PER CENT OF POPULATION OF SPECIFIED AGE GROUPS
ENROLLED IN SCHOOL, 1910-1950

Age	1910	1920	1930	1940	1950
7–13	86.1	90.6	95.3	95.0	95.7
14–15	75.0	79.9	88.8	90.0	92.9
16–17	43.1	42.9	57.3	68.7	74.4
18–19	18.7	17.8	25.4	28.9	32.2

SOURCE: *Seventeenth Census of Population*. Vol. II: *Characteristics of the Population*, Tables 42 and 43.

But the increase in school enrollment and the reduction in child labor have not solved the new problems which have followed in their wake. These are of two kinds, one referring to the schools and one to the labor market. We shall deal here with the first of these problems. It has to do with the pressure on facilities created by mass education; the social waste of the talented; and the nonacademic youth.

Education

Pressure on Facilities Created by Mass Education

The improvement in schooling which has taken place over the past half century is, as we pointed out in Chapter 1, spectacular. And it has had far-reaching consequences. It has changed the character of many social problems. It has tended to reduce status differentials. It has increased the number of people in the middle classes. And the trend continues.

In 1900, for example, only 11.4 per cent of those fourteen to seventeen years of age were enrolled in secondary schools; in 1954, 79.9 per cent were. In 1900, only 4.0 per cent of those eighteen to twenty-one were in college; in 1954, the figure was 29.2 per cent.

With the enormous increase in population which has taken place since 1940 a very serious question exists as to whether or not facilities and personnel will be available to take care of such large numbers of children. By 1960 elementary school enrollments will be two thirds— 68 per cent—higher than in 1946 and 28 per cent higher even than in 1954. Secondary school enrollment by 1969 will be 70 per cent higher than in 1954. Where are the teachers coming from? Where are the

In addition to such ranked status as that based on income, education, lineage, occupation, and the like, there is the status based on personal appeal, or charisma. Successful generals, actors, entertainers, athletes, singers—sometimes even criminals, as in the case of Pretty-boy Floyd—may come to exercise great magnetic pull among those who idolize them.

As the society changes, so will the occupational types which are most likely to be given high status of this nature. Sometimes they are military leaders, sometimes religious, sometimes political. In 19th-century America they were likely to be captains of industry or financial wizards. Today they are more likely to be figures in the entertainment world. This change in heroes has accompanied the transition from production-centered to consumption-centered values.

Not only do different activities appeal more to the imagination of one generation than to that of another, but very different *personality* types may have charismatic appeal for very different age groups. In some circles the witty, disillusioned man of the world may arouse the greatest emotional response. In the picture above the thirteen-year-old girl expresses her adulation for a very different personality type. He seems to offer vicarious expression for the rebellion of adolescents against the adult world. In the case of these youngsters, rebellion takes the form neither of delinquency nor of ideological attack on the social system, but rather it takes the form of "crazes" such as the one that developed about Elvis Presley. In such youthful crushes and in warm and solidary diffuse relationships among friends of the same sex who share their enthusiasms, these youngsters take refuge—temporarily at least—against the comparatively harsher, impersonal, more disciplined adult world. *(United Press Photo)* classrooms coming from? Some people consider this the major social problem at midcentury.

We cannot measure the demands upon our people in the second half of the 20th century . . . by what was demanded of them at the beginning of the first half of this century. We are entering upon an era which will test to the utmost the capacity of our democracy to cope with the gravest problems of modern times—and on a scale never yet attempted in all the history of the world. We are entering upon this difficult and dangerous period with what I believe we must call a growing deficit in the quantity and quality of American education. We have to do in the educational system something very like what we have done in the military establishment during the past fifteen years. We have to make a breakthrough to a radically higher and broader conception of what is needed and of what can be done.[15]

This mass picture obscures two quite different problems which must also be wrestled with: how to find and conserve the talents of young people at the top of the talent pyramid and how to deal with the nonacademic young person at the base who has neither taste nor talent for academic learning. One concerns the waste of talent (which still persists) at the top of the intelligence scale caused by dropping out of school and the other has to do with the young person who is kept in school against his will.

Social Waste of the Talented

Before the concept of human resources or effective manpower utilization became important in our thinking, there was little concern expressed over the loss of potential talent in the population. But at midcentury the demands of the Cold War have made us sensitive to possible shortages of talent in at least one area, that of science and technology, if not in others. Students of the subject reported that the USSR was turning out technicians and engineers at a more rapid rate than we were. There were bottlenecks in our educational programs. We must salvage those bright young persons not being properly utilized. We must improve our science teaching and not permit it to be watered down to the level of the dull student. Talent-scouting was taken over by industry; research on ways of locating talent was undertaken. This search for talent and its maximum use may not properly qualify as a social or societal problem by either the humanitarian or the utilitarian criterion since there may be no suffering or high tax bills involved in wasted talent, but it does qualify as a societal problem under the criterion of dysfunctionality, since it is probably dysfunctional for any social system to squander its intellectual resources.

The United States wastes much of its talent. College graduating classes could be twice as large as they currently are, and with no less of quality. The potential supply gets drained off, in large or small amounts, all the way through the educational system. Practically all potentially good college students enter, and most of them finish, high school, but after high school the loss is large. Fewer than half of the upper 25 percent of all high school graduates ever earn college degrees; only 6 out of 10 of the top 5 percent do. Society fails to secure the full benefit of many of its brightest youth because they do not secure the education that would enable them to work at the levels for which they are potentially qualified. . . .

While the total number of college graduates is increasing, the demand for the best ones is increasing even faster. There are never enough men and women at the highest levels in any field. Yet there are people who do not attend college but who might with education attain those high levels. To identify them early, encourage them to plan on advanced training, and support them financially when that is necessary is a means of producing a qualitative increase in college graduates which would repay a large financial investment.

The question How many should go to college? is probably the wrong question; in its place should be written Who should go to college? If the nation seeks to make the best use of its intellectual potential, certainly pupils from the top intelligence brackets should have the opportunity for higher education. The fact that they would increase the total number of graduates is less important than the fact that they would be able to contribute more to the national welfare with higher education than without it. . . .

The brains of its citizens constitute a nation's greatest asset. From the minds of men will come future scientific discoveries, future works of art and literature, future advances in statesmanship, technology and social organization, in short, all future progress. Since there can be no argument over this proposition the practical problem becomes one of devising the best means of nurturing the talent which exists in the population. A nation which has had the ingenuity to conquer the air, to eradicate age-old diseases, to send radio messages around the world, to achieve a higher standard of living than has ever been seen elsewhere in the world can surely overcome the barriers of doubt, of unequal opportunity, of financial handicap, and of inadequate motivation and education which interfere with the fullest development of the industrial, educational, intellectual, and moral leadership which our kind of society increasingly requires.[16]

Of the problems involved in making the maximum use of talent—those of locating, motivating, counseling, and financing it—perhaps those dealing with motivation are the most difficult. The bright boy whose family and peers are apathetic if not antipathetic to education is not likely to want to make the effort involved in securing it. Nor are the problems of status differences in school easy to solve.[17] And equally ominous is the so-called anti-intellectualism of midcentury which has seriously challenged the status of the scientist and creative person.[18]

The Problem of the Nonacademic Youth

Serious as the problem may be of making maximum use of talented young persons, dealing with the young persons at the other end of the scale is no less difficult. Raising the number of years that must be spent in school has created the problem (almost equal in proportion to that of child labor) of what to do with the nonacademic young person. For not all children are interested in academic education or are able to profit from it. They have neither motivation nor talent for it. Vocational schools have evolved, but they have not solved the difficulty. Young people are kept in school when they are in every way ready to enter a more adult relationship with the outside world. In school they are constantly reminded of their inferiority. The school environment is hateful to them because it is a showcase for their inferiority. Every day they spend in school they are obliged to subject themselves to the humiliation of failure. They have no taste or aptitude for abstract or symbolic thinking. They are nonreaders—"failure in reading accounts more than any other single factor for behavior problems," [19] reported one study—and therefore show up poorly in literary or academic subjects. Yet they are made to exhibit their deficiency by attending school.

One of the most important . . . tensions derives from the compulsory education law itself. In September, 1936, it became necessary for a child to remain in school full time until his sixteenth birthday. Previously, the age limit had been 14, and even those who went on to high school were in a sense a selected group. Apart from the acute problem of continuation school. . . . the extension of the age from 14 to 16 altered drastically the school population. It forced thousands of adolescents into classrooms in which they demonstrated a variable but widespread reluctance to be educated.[20]

Many of these young people drop out of school as soon as they possibly can. But in the absence of guidance the same characteristics which made school difficult for them also make vocational roles difficult. One study of dropouts, for example, found twenty-two critical signs—presented as indexes, not causes—which tended to be associated with the dropping out from school of young people as soon as they became sixteen. They were:

1. A child who is unrecommended or passed on trial to the next grade.
2. A child who is 2 years older than his grade group.
3. A child who has a poor attendance and tardiness record.
4. A child who aggressively resists authority.
5. A child who has little or no interest in school.
6. A child who is reading below his mental age.
7. A child who has very low energy or is overactive, especially if a boy.

8. A child who has gone to many schools.

9. A child who is ignored or actively disliked by teachers.

10. A child who is ignored or actively disliked by pupils.

11. A child whose close friends are much older or much younger.

12. A child whose interests and friends are outside of school.

13. A child who is under psychiatric treatment.

14. A child from a broken home, especially if family has no meals together.

15. A child who is seriously handicapped physically.

16. A child who receives books and supplies from the board of education.

17. A child who is "different" in size, physique, nationality, or dress. A child with a split growth pattern; one who is biologically awkward and has an anachronistic pattern.

18. A child who is unable to do what the rest of the group does financially.

19. A child whose intelligence is 80 or below.

20. A child who is not in any extracurricular activities.

21. A boy or girl who refuses to participate in gym activities; refuses to get undressed or stands on the sidelines.

22. A child who feels inferior educationally in comparison to a brother or sister. Or a child who is ashamed of a brother's or sister's record.

It can be assumed that youth with these characteristics will find some difficulty competing in the labor market against other youth who are better adjusted to school and life. Although they find school boring and lacking in meaning, these youth need not less schooling but more. However, they are anxious to begin earning money in order to feel independent and begin to gain a place in the world of work which they feel they have been unable to gain in school. In short, this group is composed of workers who are marginal workers on two counts: (1) their youth; and (2) their lack of general, personal, and social adjustment. The second is often aggravated by a poor home and neighborhood background which offers little opportunity to develop qualities needed to get and hold a job.[21]

The seeming hodgepodge of critical signs indicates, in brief, that the child who drops out of school has status in no group, cannot perform his roles adequately, and is mentally, physically, or otherwise handicapped.

Not all nonacademic youth, however, are so severely handicapped. Some might be very useful in a garage, at a lathe, or operating a crane. They do poorly in school because they are confined in a routine which is meaningless to them, that makes little if any connection with life as they know it. One commentator has pointed out that youngsters who were flunking their shop courses in school were nevertheless very clever in making hand grenades, bombs, and guns.

School, then, for such young men—and young women—is little more than a custodial institution to keep them off the streets and out of the labor market. They feel themselves incarcerated. Their teachers are their jailers. These are not the words they use; but this is essentially what the situation adds up to for them. It would be strange indeed if they did not attempt to escape from this frustrating environment. Truancy is, in fact, one of the commonest forerunners of delinquency. Foot-loose, without responsibilities, free to roam the streets and byways of a modern city, there are endless opportunities for misadventure.

In some cases escape from an enforced endurance of humiliating failure may be all that is involved. Once this release has been achieved, there is a search for companionship in adventure. But sometimes the young persons want more than mere release from the restrictions of a hateful school environment. They want to get revenge, to express the frustrated rage that has been building up in them perhaps for many years, not only against the school but also against parents, siblings, persons in authority, the whole *status quo* which relegates them to such an inferior position. Theft is not always enough. Vandalism and destruction may give more satisfaction. Attacking people may be even better. The thin line between mischief and delinquency is crossed.[22]

Some Recent Recommendations

No one would argue seriously for a return to the old exploitative form of child labor which characterized the 19th and early 20th century. But some thoughtful observers feel that we ought to start afresh and review the whole problem of the role of young persons as workers. Exactly what form this role should take, how industry could be enlisted to help define it, or how the cooperation of unions could be enlisted are still unanswered questions.[23] But the pressure on the schools, especially in large cities, suggests that a new look at the problem is required. Young persons who were being initiated into industry, taking a useful place, earning some money, being treated as responsible human beings, it is argued, would be less likely to rebel or become delinquent. The child labor laws, designed to help children, have sometimes served, it is alleged by some observers, to injure them.[24]

On the basis of an extensive study of the relationship of work and delinquency, a Senate Subcommittee has therefore made the following recommendations, among others:

There . . . appears to be a certain cause-and-effect relationship in many instances between the inability of some youths to obtain employment and delinquent behavior. The subcommittee recognizes that the exact nature of this relationship is not fully understood and recommends that the Department of Labor, private foundations, and other groups support and undertake objective, scientific research in this area. This is a cause for concern to the subcommittee and a large segment of the public.

The subcommittee submits the following recommendations as possible steps in striving toward improving the situation:

1. There should be an expansion of work-school opportunities and experience through more educational experimentation in methods of using young people's part-time job experience for their educational and personal growth. This is especially needed for nonacademic pupils who are weak in the basic personal qualifications important for vocational adjustment. . . . This should be done without impairing the necessary protection for young people that has been gained through legislation in the past half century. The participation of youth in industry through work-school programs should be considered separate and apart from conditions of full-time independent employment of youth. . . . It is the opinion of the subcommittee that in many instances the inability of youth in this age group to obtain employment is a contributing factor to delinquent behavior.

2. It is recommended that . . . employment services be extended to all youth in part-time employment, summer employment, employment in work-school curriculum programs as well as in full-time independent employment. . . . It is recommended that the Department of Labor undertake . . . to provide consultant services to communities on programs to reduce youth unemployment and to better help youth to find a productive role in the labor market.

3. It is the opinion of the subcommittee that young people can perhaps be more effectively helped to find a place for themselves in the labor market in three ways and these should be carefully explored: (a) More part-time or combined school-work programs; (b) more effective vocational guidance and counseling in the school; (c) more adequate community facilities to bridge the gap from school to work and provide continuous guidance services.

4. The subcommittee recommends a significant expansion of guidance services within the school system of the Nation. . . . Specifically, attention should be given to the problem of identifying, developing, and conserving the professional, technical, and skilled manpower potentialities of the youth population of the United States. . . . Steps should be taken to broaden the school curriculum offerings in other ways for nonacademic pupils who lack the personality traits and responsibility needed for employability and successful vocational adjustment. . . .

7. The subcommittee has been concerned by the lack of firm knowledge concerning the social and psychological consequences of youth employment and unemployment, as well as by the absence of sound information about youths' career patterns, job satisfactions, and motivations. . . . It, therefore, recommends that appropriate agencies and groups. . . . support basic research studies in this important area of community life. Research is also needed to clarify the further relationship. . . . between school dropouts and delinquency.

8. The subcommittee recommends that . . . steps [be taken] to de-

velop and maintain effective programs and working relationships which insure more adequate guidance services in the schools, an orderly cooperative arrangement for the transition from school to work for youth leaving school and systematic and continuous vocational guidance and placement services for out-of-school youth who need them.[25]

Youth and the Labor Market

We spoke above of the need to use the labor of youth in an age of scarcity when all hands were required to wrest a living from a resistant nature. But we also referred to the effort of unions in more recent years to keep young people out of the labor market. The problem of youth in worker roles has reference not only to the young people themselves but also to the labor market as well. The question has been raised, for example, as to whether or not, or at least how, the labor market will be able to absorb the estimated one million high school graduates annually who are expected by 1965,[26] constituting the half who do not go on to college.

It is not the number that constitutes the problem. The problem will be one of quality. There are, and presumably will continue to be, great demands for top-caliber personnel, but will there be room for poorly trained people? As we saw in Chapter I, the lowest grades of workers tend to be erased from the occupational structure. Increasingly we need highly trained engineers and technicians. What about those who are unable to find a place in this technically demanding labor force? We used to wonder who would do the "dirty work" when everyone became educated. The question may become, Will there be any low-level work to do?

The lengthened shadow of the older segment of the population, which we have discussed before, reveals itself here also. Little by little persons sixty-five years of age and older have taken over many jobs formerly done by young people, such as newsstand salesmen, elevator operators, filling-station attendants, office messengers, stock clerks, and helpers in technical laboratories.[27] In a labor market that increasingly demands well-trained technicians and professional workers, what is to be the role of the inexperienced high school graduate?

It will be noted from the above brief résumé that we are at the present time in a process of redefining the role of the young worker; we are beginning to reappraise his status in our society. We are beginning to see that we cannot keep young people children when they are ready for more adult roles. The pendulum, which swung far in the direction of keeping children away from the labor market because of the reaction against the abuses of child labor, is now apparently swinging back in the direction of a supervised and controlled entrance into worker status, with great emphasis on counseling and guidance.

There is one aspect of the problems of youth today which at mid-century has caused special public concern: delinquency. We have already referred to it as a symptom of a pathology, in Chapter 14, and we have touched upon it incidentally in our discussion here of the worker role of youth. It is, however, of such importance that we devote the following chapter to it and, in particular, to the status dimension of the problem.

NOTES

1 One judge reported that frequently when he performed the marriage ceremony for two young people he asked them about their parents' attitude, and was shocked "at the number who reply, 'Whatever I do is all right with my folks.'" (Judge Elijah Adlow, "Teen-age Criminals," *Atlantic Monthly*, July 1955, p. 47.) Former President Truman, when asked about rearing children, replied that the best thing to do was find out what they wanted to do and then advise them to do it.

2 Dr. Lauretta Bender, senior psychiatrist at Bellevue Hospital, quoted in the *New York Times*, July 20, 1955.

3 Adlow, *loc. cit.*, p. 48.

4 Elizabeth Hoyt *et al.*, *American Income and Its Use* (Harper, 1954), p. xv.

5 David Riesman, *The Lonely Crowd* (Yale Univ. Press, 1950), pp. 48–55.

6 In a tabulation of various types of infractions by pupils in New York City academic and vocational high schools as of March 23, 1954, "gross insubordination" was by far the most common, accounting for 701 out of 1,654 offenses in the academic high schools and 190 out of 729 offenses in the vocational high schools. In the academic high schools the nearest runner-up was truancy, with 326 cases; in the vocational schools, truancy exceeded gross insubordination. (*New York Times*, May 24, 1955.)

7 Defiant smoking in washrooms and on school steps is another type of role violation reported by school authorities. (*Ibid.*)

8 John Spargo, *The Bitter Cry of the Children* (Macmillan, 1906), pp. 131–134.

9 *Ibid.*, p. 141.

10 *Ibid.*, pp. 173, 175, 181 ff.

11 George Soule, *Men, Wages and Employment in the Modern U.S. Economy* (Mentor, 1954), p. 76.

12 *Ibid.*

13 A. J. Jaffe and Charles D. Stewart, *Manpower Resources and Utilization: Principles of Working Force Analysis* (Wiley, 1951), p. 166.

14 *Ibid.*, pp. 166–167.

15 Walter Lippmann, quoted in *Teachers for Tomorrow* (The Fund for the Advancement of Education, 1955), p. 4.

16 Dael Wolfle, *America's Resources of Specialized Talent* (Harper, 1954), pp. 269, 276–277, 283.

17 Jessie Bernard, *American Community Behavior* (Dryden, 1949), pp. 203–206.

18 Wolfle, *op. cit.*, p. 282.

19 Report on delinquency by Henry Epstein, of New York City, reported in the *New York Times*, May 25, 1955.

20 *Ibid.*

21 J. Dan Hull, testimony in hearings before the Subcommittee To Investigate Juvenile Delinquency, *Youth Employment and Juvenile Delinquency*, Interim Report to the Committee on the Judiciary, 84th Congress, 1st session (Washington, D. C., 1955), pp. 228–229.

22 That this problem is not uniquely American is suggested by an address of the secretary of the *Komsomol* before the 12th Congress of Young Communists in 1955. He said: "Pupils are behaving abominably in public places, in the streets, even in the classroom. They insult teachers, parents, and other adults and above all they are giving themselves over to acts

of vandalism and hooliganism." (*Family Life*, April 1955, p. 3.)

23 One possible approach has been proposed by the New York City Congress of Industrial Organizations Council. In September 1955, it voted to explore "the feasibility of a plan to send labor union members into settlement houses to teach their trade skills to neighborhood youth. Delegates from twenty unions in the council unanimously approved a resolution to set up a committee to determine how the volunteer services of trade unionists could best be used in training youngsters to work with their hands. It is hoped that by making trades attractive to the young people a substantial contribution would be made in the fight against juvenile delinquency. . . . Since young lawbreakers do not typically come from the ranks of skilled, gainfully employed youth, it is clear that the labor plan has much to recommend it." (*New York Times*, September 28, 1955.) Reports of the results of this program have not become available.

24 "I have seen prosecutions under the Child Labor Law which did more harm than good. I have in mind particularly the owner of a cleaning and dyeing shop whose fifteen-year-old brother helped him after school and who was brought into my court for violating the Child Labor Law. If a young man is not as anxious to work as he might be, let us remember that laws like that have helped estrange him from habits of industry." (Adlow, *loc. cit.*, p. 48.)

25 *Youth Employment and Juvenile Delinquency*, Subcommittee to Investigate Juvenile Delinquency, Interim Report to the Committee on the Judiciary, 84th Congress, 1st session (Washington, D. C., 1955), pp. 37–40.

26 *Ibid.*, pp. 9–10.

27 *Ibid.*, p. 8.

18

Delinquency:
The Status Dimension
and Stress Resistance

Delinquency: What Is It?

Juvenile delinquency is a legal term whose definition varies from state to state. In general it applies to an offense committed by a child under a specified age—say sixteen or eighteen—which in the case of older persons would be considered a felony, or to any one of a specified list of misdemeanors. Not the act itself but the age of the person who commits it is the critical legal element.

It is, of course, fallacious to lump together the kind of mature—that is, rational, calculated, and planned—crime described by a Boston judge below, in which an eighteen-year-old engineered the theft of $10,000 worth of electrical equipment, and the kind of offense we usually think of as juvenile delinquency. At the other extreme, it is difficult to separate delinquency from other kinds of behavior, such as insolence, defiance, or impudence, which are psychologically and sociologically similar to delinquency, even if they do not technically or legally constitute delinquent behavior.

We present here the analysis of juvenile delinquency made by a recent student of the subject in terms of what he calls the "delinquent subculture." It deals with motivation and social structure rather than legally defined overt acts. It does not pretend to cover all juvenile crime; it does, however, describe what is characteristically considered to be juvenile delinquency.[1] This delinquent subculture is nonutilitarian malicious, and negativistic.

The stealing that gangs engage in is done just for the fun of it, not primarily to get some valuable object. It wins glory; it demonstrates prowess; it gives satisfaction. It is nonutilitarian.

There is no accounting in rational and utilitarian terms for the effort expended and the danger run in stealing things which are often discarded, destroyed or casually given away. A group of boys enters a store where each takes a hat, a ball or a light bulb. They then move on to another store where these things are covertly exchanged for like articles. Then they move on to other stores to continue the game indefinitely. They steal a basket of peaches, desultorily munch on a few of them and leave the rest to spoil. They steal clothes they cannot wear and toys they will not use. . . . Stealing is not merely an alternative means to the acquisition of objects otherwise difficult of attainment.[2]

Stealing is recreation, play, sport. But to say this does not explain why it offers so much fun to these boys, why they prefer it to more conventional recreational programs.

To explain this fact we must recognize that much of the fun results from the discomfiture of others which it entails and from defiance of taboos, for juvenile delinquency is characterized by malice.

Thrasher quotes one gang delinquent: "We did all kinds of dirty tricks for fun. We'd see a sign, 'Please keep the streets clean,' but we'd tear it down and say, 'We don't feel like keeping it clean.' One day we put a can of glue in the engine of a man's car. We would always tear things down. That would make us laugh and feel good, to have so many jokes."

The gang exhibits this gratuitous hostility toward non-gang peers as well as adults. Apart from its more dramatic manifestations in the form of gang wars, there is keen delight in terrorizing "good" children, in driving them from play-grounds and gyms for which the gang itself may have little use, and in general in making themselves obnoxious to the virtuous. The same spirit is evident in playing hookey and in misbehavior in school. The teacher and her rules are not merely something onerous to be evaded. They are to be *flouted*. There is an element of active spite and malice, contempt and ridicule, challenge and defiance.[3]

The delinquent subculture turns conventional standards upside down; it is negativistic.

The delinquent subculture takes its norms from the larger culture but turns them upside down. The delinquent's conduct is right, by the standards of his sub-culture, precisely *because* it is wrong by the norms of the larger culture. "Malicious" and "negativistic" are foreign to the delinquent's vocabulary but he will often assure us, sometimes ruefully, sometimes with a touch of glee or even pride, that he is "just plain mean."[4]

Other characteristics of the delinquent subculture noted by this author are versatility, short-run hedonism, and group autonomy. The delinquents do not specialize in any one kind of stealing; and stealing goes along with other property offenses, malicious mischief, vandalism, trespass, and truancy. They have no long-run goals; they do not plan activities nor budget time. They show no interest in activities which would require practice, deliberation, and study. They want to have their fun right now, not later on.

The members of the gang typically congregate, with no specific activity in mind, at some street corner, candy store or other regular rendezvous. They "hang around," "rough-housing," "chewing the fat," and "waiting for something to turn up." They may respond impulsively to somebody's suggestion to play ball, go swimming, engage in some sort of mischief, or do something else that offers excitement. They do not take kindly to organized and supervised recreation, which subjects them to a regime of schedules and impersonal rules. They are impatient, impetuous and out for "fun," with little heed to the remoter gains and costs. It is to be noted that this short-run hedonism is not inherently delinquent and indeed it would be a serious error to think of the delinquent gang as dedicated solely to the cultivation of juvenile crime. Even in the most seriously delinquent gang only a small fraction of the "fun" is specifically and intrinsically delinquent. Furthermore, short-run hedonism is not characteristic of delinquent groups alone. On the contrary, it is common throughout the social class from which delinquents characteristically come.[5]

By "group autonomy" the author refers to intolerance of outside restraints, resistance to efforts of home, school, or other agencies to control not only delinquent gang activities but also any other gang activities. The author makes very clear that:

It is not the individual delinquent but the gang that is autonomous. For many of our subcultural delinquents the claims of the home are very real and very compelling. The point is that the gang is a separate, distinct and often irresistible focus of attraction, loyalty and solidarity.[6]

There are, to be sure, other than gang forms of juvenile delinquency. But in general the above characteristics may be said to refer to a large, albeit indeterminate, proportion of all juvenile delinquency. It is this kind of delinquency we discuss primarily here. But first a word about trends.

What Are the Trends?

As in the case of all legally disapproved behavior, it is extremely difficult to measure the incidence or trace the trends in juvenile delinquency. How much delinquent behavior is there? How many young persons are delinquents? Is delinquency increasing? Is it, as sometimes alleged, climbing the social ladder, appearing more and more frequently in middle-class families? Is it becoming more violent? More serious? At midcentury there was a tremendous surge of interest in juvenile delinquency—almost a hysteria, some people thought—revealing itself in congressional investigations, scientific experimentation, popular articles, and radio and television programs. Still there were no unequivocal replies to any of the above questions. Equally competent students, approaching the subject from different angles, came to diametrically different conclusions.

Extent

With respect to the first three questions raised above, the answer is, We do not know. It has been estimated that at midcentury about 1 per cent of the students in a large city secondary school were delinquent and that about 5 per cent were vulnerable, skirting the ragged edge of delinquency.[7] On the basis of midcentury rates it was estimated that one child in every sixty would end up in a training school for delinquents.

The estimate that 1 or even 5 per cent is delinquent is probably conservative. As we shall see below, one study found that about a fourth of Chicago grammar school boys were recorded delinquents; [8] and another study of six-year-olds in the South Bronx, New York, judged about a third to be predelinquent.[9] The discrepancy between the estimates for the younger age groups and the secondary school estimates suggests that a large proportion of the delinquent acts of the younger children are not repeated. The children outgrow their delinquencies before they reach high school. But just what proportion of the young persons are delinquents even in secondary school we do not know.

The reason for our ignorance about the amount of delinquency and the trends over time lies in the wholly inadequate records on which knowledge would have to rest. For example, when a police commissioner in New York City reported an increase in arrests for misdemeanors among young persons he considered this a sign of increased efficiency: there were more policemen on the streets.[10] It did not necessarily mean that there was more juvenile delinquency. But if we were basing our analysis on the records we would have to report that there was an increase in delinquency. An even more spectacular illustration of the misleading nature of records occurred the following year when the same police commissioner reported an increase of 41.3 per cent in juvenile delinquency for the first half of 1956 over 1955, although the agencies specializing in the problems of youth said they had noted no such increase in their caseloads. They attributed the reported increase to better police enforcement.[11]

There are ups and downs in recorded delinquency: down in the depression of the 1930's, up during World War II, reaching a peak in 1943, a postwar recession, a sharp rise in the 1950's. But just what these recorded fluctuations really mean is by no means clear.

Whether actual, as distinguished from recorded, rates of juvenile delinquency are higher now than formerly we do not know. That the behavior of these disturbed and disturbing young persons is not a new phenomenon, however, is attested by a report of the Chief of Police in New York City over a hundred years ago—in 1849—in which he referred to:

. . . the constantly increasing number of vagrants, idle and vicious children of both sexes who infest our public thoroughfares, hotels, docks, etc.; children who are growing up in ignorance and profligacy, only destined to a life of misery, shame, and crime and ultimately to a felon's doom.

Their numbers are almost incredible, and to those whose business and habits do not permit them a searching scrutiny, the degrading and disgusting practices of these almost infants in the school of vice, prostitution and rowdyism would certainly be beyond belief.[12]

And a psychiatrist who based her conclusions on a study of delinquency throughout the world in 1905 "insisted that in the years 1860 to 1900 communities had to cope with exactly the same types of youth crimes as today [and] proportionately just as often." [13] The rise in standards which we commented upon in Chapter 1 affects children, as well as others. Thus "chronic or handicapping conditions or emotional disturbances . . . loom . . . large today—larger than ever now that acute infectious disease and most nutritional diseases have been conquered." [14] The child's mental health is a matter of great concern at midcentury; who ever thought of it fifty years ago? Because we are more sensitized to delinquency today we may find more of it.

Class Incidence

It is sometimes stated that juvenile delinquency is *moving up the social ladder*. Here, again, we have no way of documenting any such trend. It is true, as we pointed out in Chapter 1, that more and more people are middle class; we might therefore expect more delinquents to come from middle-class homes, middle class at least so far as income, if not values, is concerned. It is true that poverty in and of itself is not inherently related to delinquency. "The Cougars," says one observer describing a Brooklyn gang, "suffered more from boredom than poverty." [15] A child who, when asked where he had gotten a pistol, replied, "Oh, bought it from a friend for twenty bucks," can hardly be considered poverty-stricken. Nor can the members of a gang who wear blazers costing $20 with the club's name embroidered on them.[16] And yet there can be no denial of the fact that a disproportionate amount of recorded juvenile delinquency occurs in slum areas.[17]

Have Juvenile Offenses Become More Violent?

Some people allege that they have. But people have been alleging this for a long time. During the first decade of the century, for example, observers were already complaining that gang fighting was becoming more violent.

. . . gang warfare has become not the exception but the rule, and the violence and ferocity with which the small boys pursue their feuds excites the alarm of the entire neighborhood. "There has always been more or less fighting among the gangs of boys on the streets," a physician of long residence recently remarked, "but they are getting worse in character every year until now it seems that they will stop at nothing. They carry knives, clubs, and even, I have heard, revolvers. . . . They terrorize the neighborhood with their fights, breaking windows and injuring passersby with stones." [18]

And the following headlines show that offenses were very violent in the early years of the century:

**UPPER WEST SIDE DISTURBED
BOYS DISCHARGE RIFLES
—ONE MAN SHOT
AND WINDOWS BROKEN** *

**GIRL SHOT IN GANG FIGHT
SERIOUSLY WOUNDED WHILE
WALKING IN ELEVENTH AVENUE
—ASSAILANT ESCAPES** †

**BOY STABBED BY
YOUNG FEUDISTS
IS SECOND HURT** ‡

And one contemporary reporter pointed out that "rumors of boys being stabbed, shot, clubbed, maimed, and even killed are current everywhere, and there is good reason to believe that many of them are true. . . . There can be no doubt that many crimes are committed in these blocks which never reach the ears of the police. . . ." [19] Contemporary conditions always seem worse to the current generation of adults than those of the past.

Actually, the recorded offenses of young delinquents today, whatever they may have been in the past, are likely to be such non-violent ones as stealing, especially of automobiles in the case of boys, and being "ungovernable" in the case of girls. There is, to be sure, a large amount

* New York *Tribune,* December 18, 1911.
† *New York Times,* June 26, 1911.
‡ New York *World,* February 24, 1910.

of fighting today, as in the past, especially in middle and late adolescence; and occasionally serious injuries, even death, may ensue. But violence is not nearly so characteristic of crime in the young ages as theft.[20]

Perhaps the reason we have the impression of great violence among juvenile delinquents is that they do tend to be more violent than other young persons. For example, one author asked a group of college students to specify which of a list of 55 offenses with which delinquents had been charged they had themselves committed. Every one of the 437 college students had committed at least one of the offenses, the average number committed being 17.6 for the men before entering college and 11.2 after they came to college. Only two offenses—being of suspicious character and incorrigibility—were marked by no student. But there was a difference in the kind of offenses committed by the two groups. Public annoyance, traffic violations, and sex offenses were more likely to occur in the college population; vagabondage, theft, malicious mischief, dishonesty, personal affronts and injuries, trespassing, and encroaching on the rights of others were the counts against the court cases.[21]

Juvenile delinquencies, then, are probably no more violent today than they were in the past, but they are more likely to be violent in court cases than in cases which do not come before the court.

Whether or not juvenile delinquency is becoming more violent, it is alleged by some that it is becoming more serious, that we are not dealing with mischievous boys but with young criminals, and that much of what now passes as juvenile delinquency is actually mature crime that just happens to have been perpetrated by young persons. For example:

What makes the revolt of modern youth serious is that it bears little resemblance to what was once viewed as juvenile delinquency. There was a time when the difference between a bad boy and a playful boy was merely one of degree. Today the crimes of violence in which the young indulge can never be mistaken for boyish pranks. The many cases of malicious destruction of property that have entailed great loss to the public are not the cumulative consequence of youthful exuberance but the product of calculated and planned mischief. The many assaults with dangerous weapons, some of which have had fatal consequence, are the acts of irresponsible desperadoes which differ little from the planned attacks on society by adult outlaws.

More alarming are the thefts and holdups. The petty pilferings that once represented a boy's transgressions were largely restricted to doormats, ash barrels, and milk bottles. But in the past few years I have had an eighteen-year-old boy in my court who, while employed by a wholesale electric supply house, loaded $10,000 worth of electric equipment on a freight elevator, lowered the elevator to the ground floor, and then secured a truckman to cart away the loot. Three boys, all seventeen years of age, were before me charged with breaking and entering and larceny. After getting an automobile, these boys broke into a Surplus War Goods Store and carted away $3,500 worth of merchandise. Two others in the same age group looted the warehouse of a jewelry novelty wholesaler and carried away $6,000 worth of merchandise. After making their getaway they stored the loot in a safe place and canvassed the community until they found an operator of a jewelry store who would buy the goods from them. There is nothing "juvenile" about this kind of delinquency.

Recently four boys, all under twenty-one, brazenly attempted to secure the release of a sixteen-year-old girl who was in the custody of the Massachusetts Youth Service Board at the Lancaster School for Girls. This is not the first time that young desperadoes have attempted to force the release of inmates in correctional institutions. The bold daring revealed in these escapades merely reflects the cold-blooded indifference of modern youths to the penal consequences of their acts. Nothing is done halfheartedly. So far as youth is concerned, its war against society is total war.[22]

The contrast here between mature crime perpetrated by young adults and juvenile delinquency is valid; they are two quite different kinds of phenomena. But whether mature crime is increasing at the expense of juvenile delinquency might very well be questioned.

Frustrating as it is, then, we are obliged to say that we know very little about any of the trends we have been discussing here. In the absence of reliable records we cannot say unequivocally that juvenile delinquency is increasing (although it does fluctuate), that it is moving up the social ladder, that it is becoming more violent, or that it is more serious now than formerly.

Who are these delinquent members of the secondary school population? First of all, the majority is male. The exact sex ratio varies from study to study, but delinquency is anywhere from three to five times as common among males as among females.[23] We begin our discussion therefore with delinquent males.

Delinquent Boys

The questions we asked in the preceding section might be characterized as descriptive. We wanted to know what the facts were about juvenile delinquency. We turn now to a set of questions which attempt to explain and interpret these facts. These are analytical or theoretical questions. In descriptive questions, the data supplied by the answers are themselves important; in analytical or theoretical questions the data are not inherently important. They are important only to the extent that they can be used to explain or interpret underlying forces.

We now ask the following questions: Why is it that delinquency occurs more frequently among some young persons than among others, and why in some areas more than in others? And why is it that even in the so-called delinquency areas it occurs among some young persons and not others? We must explain why boys in slum areas are more likely to become delinquent than boys in other areas, and, also, why most boys in delinquent areas are not delinquents whereas some boys in middle-class areas are. The answer to the first of these two questions relies heavily on sociological concepts, the answer to the second, on social-psychological as well as sociological concepts.

The Causes of Delinquency

Before we proceed further we remind ourselves that we are now, by definition, discussing only normal young persons who are not significantly different from the total population. We saw in Chapter 14 that delinquent behavior is indeed at times a symptom of some kind of pathology, so that a certain proportion of delinquents may legitimately be classified as emotionally disturbed. They "act out" their illness; that is, their delinquent behavior is an expression of their inner disturbance. As in the case, for example, of Leo Hernandez, aged sixteen, who set fire to a three-story building because, he said, he "wanted to stir up a little excitement." [24] These psychiatric cases are in quite a different category from the delinquents we concern ourselves with here.

Even in the case of delinquents judged to be disturbed, however, there is great danger in evaluating their behavior as pathological or maladaptive. It may really be normal or adaptive for the setting in which it occurs. One student of the subject has shown, for example, that the young person in a slum culture learns certain kinds of behavior as naturally, as normally, and as adaptively as the middle-class boy learns exactly opposite kinds. Assessing the slum boy's behavior as pathological is, he believes, the result of a statocentric bias in the psychiatrist's point of view. This author uses aggression and sex behavior as examples. Middle-class children are taught to express their aggressions in the form of initiative or ambition; the slum child expresses them in unabashed physical attack. The expression of aggression the middle-class child learns helps him compete effectively at his own class level. The lower-class child is taught to strike out with his fist or with a knife, and to be sure to hit first. The slum child's expression of aggression is learned and approved and rewarded, just as the middle-class child's is; it is just as normal as similar behavior is in a frontier society.[25] So also some expressions of sexual activity are blocked in middle-class children, but permitted or even encouraged in slum children. The anxiety and guilt which the middle-class child acquires with respect to sex is considered normal; in a slum child it might be considered a sign of revolt against his class culture and hence a symptom of personality difficulty.[26] Thus although it is undoubtedly true that the delinquent is sometimes genuinely disturbed, it is fallacious always to interpret the forms which aggression takes in a slum area as symptoms of emotional disturbance.

In general, there are two approaches to the cause of delinquency. As we saw in Chapter 6, one is through the individual and one is through institutions. The first is likely to be espoused by psychiatrists and psychologists, the second, by sociologists and social psychologists. The first, or clinical, approach scrutinizes the delinquent and his family case by case, almost as though they lived in a vacuum. It views the delinquent as attempting to solve his individual problems through delinquent behavior as an individual. The sociological approach sees not separate and isolated individuals solving their individual problems in a vacuum, but rather groups of boys and young men taking over and using a cultural or institutionalized pattern they find ready-made in their environment, which grew up in the past for solving precisely the same kinds of problems. Both approaches are needed for a complete picture.

THE PERSONALITY OF DELINQUENTS. Can we explain delinquent behavior in terms of the personality of the delinquent himself? Is he different? Is he inherently "bad"? What is there about him that differentiates him from non-delinquents?

So far as we can judge, juvenile delinquents as a class show few if any distinctive differences from males who do not appear in the records. They are, so far as objective measurements go, quite normal. There are, to be sure, many fallacies in attempting to compare delinquent and non-delinquent populations because of the defects in records and because of differences in treatment and in vulnerability to arrest. One study, however, came as near as possible to eliminating this fallacy by basing its findings on detailed medical, neurological, anthropometric, and psychological reports on 997 boys in Chicago grammar schools. The boys were checked against the files of the juvenile court, the juvenile detention home, the criminal court, Board of Education records, truant-officer records, the police blotter, and special files of the Institute for Juvenile Research. About a fourth—25.9 per cent—were known delinquents. The results of comparing the delinquents and non-delinquents showed the following:

(1) The delinquent boys had a lower incidence of previous infections, and fewer surgical operations.

(2) Injuries of serious types were few, slightly higher among delinquents.

(3) General nutrition was good in both groups: 76.5% were normal or overweight. More delinquents were underweight, while overweight was equally distributed between the two groups.

(4) Serious organic defects were rare. (This was a culled, healthy school group.) Where pathology existed, e.g., heart diseases, it was usually in a nondelinquent.

(5) Heart-rate and blood-pressure response, used as a small index of autonomic stability in a stress situation, revealed: (a) the delinquents had a slower heart rate, (b) and lower systolic blood pressure, diastolic blood pressure, and pulse pressure. Delinquents were less "upset" by the test.

(6) Puberty and its precursory state were seen more often in delinquents.

(7) Hernias, inguinal and umbilical, were less common in delinquents.

(8) So-called stigmata of degeneracy, bizarre ears, palates, webbed fingers, etc. . . . as in the Lombrosan concept of a criminal type, were seen in only 5% of the total sampling and were found chiefly in the nondelinquents.

(9) Neurological defects, speech defects, and left-handedness were without significance.

(10) Anthropometric conclusions drawn from twenty-six basic measurements, seventeen derived indices, and ten descriptive observations showed little variation of the Caucasoid delinquent. The Negroid delinquents were grouped much closer to the mean than the nondelinquent.

(11) Studies of mental capacity would suggest that among the white boys the delinquents were of slightly lower intelligence rating. Since the tests measure, to some extent, scholastic achievement rather than intellectual power, one would hardly expect truants to keep pace with their fellows. Furthermore, tests of all groups in these blighted areas showed a steadily falling I.Q. as age progressed. . . . The falling I.Q. as age goes up reflects a failure of the boys in these areas to keep pace with the demands of the school curriculum. A study of the performance of boys removed from these areas and placed in foster homes would suggest that scholastic stimulation in the family setting is the important factor. The mean I.Q. of the boys removed to nondelinquent area rises.

[These conclusions are] reinforced by the findings of a much larger, carefully controlled study in the Chicago area. In the latter study, the delinquent boy is found to be in no way defective; he is not inferior to his nondelinquent fellow and often is more rugged and disease-resistant. In short, he is "equipped" to carry out the pattern of the area. He is one who "makes the team," which here is the gang, and delinquency is his sphere of activity and gratification.[27]

Similar results were reported in another study, which found that as compared with non-delinquents, delinquents were more likely to be of medium body build, that is, neither extremely tall and thin nor short and heavy; restlessly energetic; hostile in their attitudes; and direct and concrete in their intellectual expression.[28]

The inferior IQ of the delinquent boys is paralleled by a low average IQ of all boys—non-delinquent as well as delinquent—in certain areas. This is a fact that requires some discussion. We have already noted the difficulties which many of these young people have in school. Is it because of inherently inferior capacity? In some cases it doubtless is. But the cultural demands of the slum areas are different from those of better areas and often they are antischolastic in their effect. Thus a middle-class child is taught to fear poor grades, fighting, cursing, and aggressing against his teacher. The slum child, conversely, learns to fear being taken in by a teacher. If he does his homework it is a disgrace. If he happens to get good grades, he conceals rather than boasts about them.[29] In addition, the tests of intelligence place the slum-bred child at a disadvantage. This fact has been documented in great detail.[30]

None of this, however, gives us much insight into why the delinquent behaves as he does. All it tells us is that he is very much like other boys of his class. Such studies do tell us, however, what can *not* be used to explain delinquent behavior. We may not, that is, assume that delinquents as a class are physically or mentally inferior or pathological or abnormal. Some are bright, some are dull; some are strong, some are not; as a whole, they are about average, except in academic ability. And even here the evidence suggests that the lower average IQ has not a genetic but a class origin.

When we attempt to explain the non-delinquent, we will return to personality factors, but so far as physical and mental traits are concerned there is nothing extraordinary to differentiate between delinquent and non-delinquent populations.

We do know, however, that in general delinquents who appear in the records come preponderantly from certain areas of a city and that a large proportion come from disorganized families. These facts give us some clues.

STATUS DIMENSION. What, then, are the causes of delinquency in young persons? Any analysis of causes has to embrace conditions which have existed for a century, since, as we saw above, delinquency has been an urban problem for at least that long. This rules out such easy explanations as motion pictures, comics, or television. Almost everything has been invoked to explain delinquency: inadequate recreation, lack of religion, conflict between parents, parental indifference, working mother, poor family income, bad neighborhood, over-protected child, poor housing, low morals, abandonment of the child, separated parents, alcoholic child, improper school placement, mental deficiency, divorced parents, reading difficulty, physical illness, poor work record, and mental illness.[31] Since delinquent behavior may be a symptom of many things, it may have many causes.

One discerning analysis which has recently appeared makes our present status system responsible for the form which delinquency takes. We base our discussion here on this analysis.

The same status system, this theory avers, which places some people high and some low in the status hierarchy creates both delinquency and respectability.

> Our view . . . holds that those values which are at the core of "the American way of life," which help to motivate the behavior which we most esteem as "typically American," are among the major determinants of that which we stigmatize as "pathological." More specifically, it holds that the problems of adjustment to which the delinquent subculture is a response are determined, in part, by those very values which respectable society holds most sacred. The same value system, impinging upon children differently equipped to meet it, is instrumental in generating both delinquency and respectability.[32]

Status differentials, in brief, are at the base of what he calls the delinquent subculture, and a great deal of delinquency can be explained, he thinks, in terms of this concept.

Boys in lower socioeconomic levels, he points out, find themselves at an enormous disadvantage in a world which judges them by middle-class standards and goals. They live in a world they never made. In school, in settlement houses, wherever they are confronted with middle-class culture, they find themselves unprepared, made to feel inferior, left out. Shame and humiliation would be their constant lot if they did not protect themselves.

There are three possible solutions to this situation, each with its costs and rewards: boys may accept their lower-class status and make the best of it; they may attempt to assimilate the middle-class culture; or they may take over the delinquent subculture in which they can achieve high status from others like themselves, precisely by flaunting their nonconformity to middle-class norms, that is, by transforming their failure into successes.

Ultimately most young persons in lower socioeconomic status select the first solution. Most juvenile delinquents outgrow their delinquencies.[33] Relatively few become adult offenders. They grow up, come to terms with their world, find a job or enter the armed forces, get married, and indulge in, let us say, only an occasional spree. Even if they temporarily select the third solution, it is self-limiting.

It is the second and the third of the above solutions which will engage our attention here. We wish to explain the behavior both of those who do not and of those who do become delinquent, of those who take over the middle-class values and of those who wage war on them. We begin with those who choose the third solution.

THE DELINQUENT SUBCULTURE. A group exists which supports a culture designed in every way to comfort, or even exalt, those who cannot —often for reasons not of their own making—succeed in achieving middle-class values. The participant in this delinquent subculture finds many rewards.

> The delinquent subculture . . . permits no ambiguity of the status of the delinquent relative to that of anybody else. In terms of the norms of the delinquent subculture, defined by its negative polarity to the respectable status system, the delinquent's very nonconformity to middle-class standards sets him above the most exemplary college boy.
> Another important function of the delinquent subculture is the legitimation of aggression. . . . For the child who breaks clean with middle-class morality . . . there are no moral inhibitions on the free expression of aggression against the sources of his frustration. . . .
> The cavalier misappropriation or destruction of property . . . is not only a diversion or diminution of wealth; it is an attack on the middle class where their egoes are most vulnerable. Group stealing, institutionalized in the delinquent subculture . . . expresses contempt for a way of life by making its opposite a criterion of status. Money and other valuables are not, as such, despised by the delinquent. . . . But, in the delinquent subculture, the stolen dollar has an odor of sanctity that does not attach to the dollar saved or the dollar earned.[34]

Another student of the subject describes the rewards of gang life in terms of role as well as of status:

> The boy was essentially a waif. To him, gang life and its blandishments offered the missing elements. The older, sophisticated gang leader became the father figure. The gang itself was almost like a protective mother. It gave him a place to hang out or to sleep, warmth, food, and many actual pleasures. There were women, and there was money to be had. Loyalties were intense when one "belonged." Excitement was high, either in the actual delinquency or in the recounting of exploits. Life in the gang was secure, stimulating, and very gratifying, provided one made the grade.[35]

Such a gang or delinquent-subculture solution to a boy's status problems depends on the group in many ways. In the first place, the delinquent subculture would not be available to him if the group did not perpetuate itself. In the second place, the status he achieves by adopting the delinquent subculture exists only in that group.

The delinquent subculture offers him status as against other children of whatever social level, but it offers him this status in the eyes of his fellow delinquents only. To the extent that there remains a desire for recognition from groups whose respect has been forfeited by commitment to a new subculture, his satisfaction in his solution is imperfect and adulterated. He can protect his solution only by rejecting as status sources those who reject him. This too may require a certain measure of reaction-formation, going beyond indifference to active hostility and contempt for all those who do not share his subculture. He becomes all the more dependent upon his delinquent gang. Outside that gang his status position is now weaker than ever.[36]

The author we have been following does not claim that status problems provide the only reasons for participating in the delinquent subculture. One boy may be a member of a gang because it happens to be composed of his own racial or ethnic group, whereas the non-delinquent groups in the area are not. Another may join in self-protection, so that he will not be beaten up. In addition, others may join for quite idiosyncratic reasons—a sense of guilt, perhaps, which drives them to crime with the unconscious wish to be caught and punished, unconscious hostility toward a father against whom aggression is expressed through a substitute, or intense anxiety allayed by "flight into activity." But these psychiatric motivations exist throughout the social system; they find expression in the gang only in the delinquent subculture. What is important is the common core of status problems which gives stability and permanence to the delinquent subculture. Once it is established it can be used by boys for handling other problems as well as those based on status inferiority.

Not all problems are amenable to solution by means of the delinquent subculture; and not all persons are capable of interacting as the gang prescribes. Without group support, delinquent solutions may not arise, and socially less forbidden solutions may be worked out—including neuroses—although individually worked out delinquencies may also occur in such cases.[37] And, of course, we should not overlook the possibility that sometimes psychotic mechanisms may also be at work.[38]

This analysis of juvenile delinquency in terms of a delinquent subculture is very illuminating and contributes a great deal to an explanation of delinquent behavior in slum areas. But it must be modified and supplemented to make it applicable to other than socioeconomic status differentials. For not only socioeconomic status differences, but any kind of status differential might have the same effect on a boy's behavior. And, further, any analysis of juvenile delinquency must explain not only why it occurs more commonly in some areas than in others, but also why only some boys succumb and not others, even within the delinquency areas; why some boys, for example, select the second rather than the third solution referred to above. Before we turn to an examination of non-delinquency in delinquency areas, however, a word about the middle-class delinquent.

THE STATUS PROBLEMS OF MIDDLE-CLASS YOUTH. Any situation in which a boy found himself being made to feel inferior, or despised, might provide the motivation to seek compensatory status in a delinquent subculture. We have already referred to the anomalous situation in which his age-role puts the modern youth vis-à-vis his elders. This enforced or artificial subordination, as well as socioeconomic status factors, might motivate participation in a delinquent subculture. The essential thing about a delinquent subculture is that, by turning the enemy's values inside out, one not only achieves status but also gets revenge on the people who attempt to enforce them.

Middle-class young people at midcentury were in a peculiarly difficult situation status-wise with respect to their successful parents, quite apart from the artificial subordination referred to above. Their fathers had been able to make enormous advances over their parents who were newcomers to the city, either from rural areas or from foreign lands. These fathers often expected their own children to move up status-wise as rapidly as they themselves had. But it was much more difficult for a son to excel his college-reared father than it had been for the father to excel his foreign-born or farm-born parents. The competition of a son with a successful father which made the son seem inferior might lead the son to seek status in a delinquent peer group and thus to denigrate the values the father stood for.

A third problem which the middle-class boy may be trying to solve by means of delinquency, it has been suggested, is related not to status but to basic anxiety in the area of sex-role identification, as contrasted to the status problems of lower-class delinquent boys.

It must, however, be conceded that most of the indications of low status are determined by middle-class values, such as education and occupation. And it is more likely to be low socioeconomic status than other kinds of status differentials which triggers the need for protective status in a delinquent subculture.

The Causes of Non-delinquency

But why do not all young persons in delinquency areas become delinquents? Here we must invoke social-psychological as well as sociological factors. The sociological factor refers to the heterogeneity of the slum population. For, as we shall show presently, the people who live in slums are not all the same kind of people; they are as different from one another as are people in other areas. Thus young persons in the same area may have widely different exposure to delinquency and different needs with respect to the delinquent subculture.

The social-psychological factor refers to stress resistance. But we must examine the nature of stress resistance with some care. As we saw above, stress resistance in the form of bodily tolerance of physical stress cannot be used to explain non-delinquency since delinquents are, if anything, superior to non-delinquents in this respect. We must use instead the stress resistance associated with reference groups and role conceptions rather than with autonomic functioning of the body. First, however, we examine the variegated nature of slum populations.

DIFFERENTIAL EXPOSURE: THE HETEROGENEITY OF SLUM POPULATIONS. We sometimes speak of slum dwellers as though they were a homogeneous population, alike or at least similar in most respects. Actually, as we pointed out above, the people who live in slums are no more homogeneous than people in other areas of the city. In Chapter 1 and in Chapter 3 we saw how heterogeneous the low-income level is. So is the slum population. We may classify slum dwellers into at least four categories: the transient or transitional slum dwellers; the trapped slum dwellers; the residual or terminal slum dwellers; and the underworld. They differ from one another primarily in two basic criteria, their reference groups and their role conceptions.

TRANSIENT SLUM DWELLERS. The transient or transitional slum dwellers are people who are temporarily in slums because as yet they cannot afford anything better. Slum areas in most cities are just outside the business districts; they are in transition between use for residence and use for business. In the meanwhile, landlords do not care to invest money to keep them in good repair; they are holding them for the rise in value which they anticipate will ensue when business takes over. Rents per unit are cheap and therefore newcomers to the city, either from Europe or from rural areas, settle in these low-rent areas. Most immigrants were of this transitional category when they first came to American cities. These families had good morale. They were on their way up and out, and had goals for themselves and their children. Their reference group, that is, the group which furnished their standards, was that of their predecessors who had escaped the slum. They also meant to do so, in time. Their role conceptions were, in effect, middle-class even though their plane of living was lower-class. They were in the slum but not of it. They might need outside help from time to time, but for the most part they were able to make a go of things. Many outstanding people emerged from such slum backgrounds, notably the old East

Side of New York.[39] The children in such families would have less need than others for the delinquent subculture.

TRAPPED SLUM DWELLERS. The trapped slum dwellers are likely to be minority-group members who cannot find housing except in deteriorated areas even when they can afford housing in better areas. Many Negroes, Puerto Ricans, or Mexicans may fall into this category. They, like the transient class, may not be demoralized. Their goals and their reference groups may be outside the slum. No more than the transient dwellers are they of the slum, even though they are in it. Children from these families, then, are also protected from need for the delinquent subculture.

RESIDUAL OR TERMINAL SLUM DWELLERS. The residual or terminal slum dwellers may be of two kinds. They may be those who are too old to move out and too accustomed to their established way of life. Since they are not likely to have children in the delinquency-prone ages, however, we may dismiss them here. These terminal dwellers may also be those who are unable to make the grade up and out. These are the people who do not acquire skills, who are the last hired and the first fired. They are marginal, perhaps even demoralized. They may even have given up. The odds are too great against them. The families may be broken. A great many of the pathologies we discussed in Part IV are concentrated in these families. They are the "slum type." Their children, because they receive so little help from their families in meeting middle-class standards, are most likely to need the delinquent subculture.

THE UNDERWORLD. Because there are so many interstitial spaces in the slum there are great areas which are not open to social control. The people in these parts of the slum do not know their neighbors well; they do not scrutinize one another's behavior and subject it to the judgment of gossip. They keep out of one another's way. They protect themselves by not becoming involved in the activities of others. They exert no pressure on one another to conform to conventional mores. The absence of such interpersonal controls and the ease with which anonymity can be used to escape detection make these areas good places for criminals. And the slum dwellers cannot protect themselves against these inroads of the underworld. Because no other part of the city will tolerate them, the headquarters for underworld organizations and the hangouts of gangs tend to be in slum areas. The underworld is highly organized. There must be rooms for meetings of its boards of directors and for its communication systems. There must be an organized labor market or employment system. There are many jobs, and personnel are available in slum areas. There is also the drift of demoralized persons into these areas. The demoralized, the broken in spirit, the alcoholic, the psychotic, the alienated, the addict, the foot-loose, the isolated, the people without group bonds—all these tend to gravitate toward the slums. Flophouses cater to many of these.

The transient and the trapped slum dwellers find these members of the underworld as different from themselves in reference groups and role conception as do dwellers in better areas. They attempt to protect their children from exposure to the underworld, as families in middle-class districts do; but the terminal slum dwellers cannot.

"SOCIAL WATERSHEDS" IN SLUM AREAS. It is difficult for an outsider to see the "social watersheds" which clearly mark one slum block off from another so that one is infested with delinquent gangs and the other is not. A study of four slum blocks in New York City shows how widely such units may vary in almost every important sociological respect. The descriptive data may no longer be accurate for the specific blocks referred to, but they do illustrate the heterogeneity of slum areas and their impact on young people.

The extent of juvenile delinquency was far in excess of that formally recorded through arraignments in the Children's Courts. The nature of adult anti-social behavior directly affected the extent of juvenile delinquency. In such a block as Palm Street (1931), where the offenses of the adult population took place primarily among childless family and non-family groups, and consisted of carousing, gambling, and prostitution, there had appeared, as yet, no immediate effect on juvenile behavior. In such a block as Fleet Street, where family standards were good, where supervision over children was adequate and where there was no adult gangsterism, juvenile delinquency was minimal. But where there was either first-generation American young adult gangsterism, as on Tyler Street, or a concentration of demoralized old-immigrant family groups of chronic drunkards and ne'er-do-wells, with concomitant criminality and loose supervision over childhood, as on Parnell Street, there was excessive juvenile delinquency.[40]

From the above analyses it is easier to see why some boys in slum areas are less likely than others to need the delinquent subculture. They, like their families, are in but not of the slums. They have reference groups outside the slums; they are thinking in terms of other than slum goals and values. They conceive their roles in middle-class terms. They do not have to resort to the delinquent subculture in order to achieve status. They feel that they belong. Thus the boys whose families are just temporarily or accidentally in the slums but whose reference groups are outside will not, presumably, be as attracted to the delinquent subculture as the boys whose families are in the slums because they cannot make the grade out, and whose reference groups are composed of others like themselves. The use to which the delinquent subculture will be put, then, depends to a large extent upon the alternatives available for achieving status.

Factors relating to types of slum dwellers with differing reference groups and role conceptions give us one possible answer to the question, Why do some young persons in delinquency areas remain non-delinquent? These non-delinquents are not exposed to the same stresses as others—frustration and failure in attempting to achieve middle-class values with no support from family background—because they are protected by family background with middle-class reference groups and middle-class role conceptions.

Even in cases where such protection does not exist, however, some young persons do not become delinquent. All the factors which predict delinquency are present, yet they salvage themselves. Why? We are thrown back on a personality factor, one which we have called stress resistance.

THE PERSONALITY OF THE NON-DELINQUENT: DIFFERENTIAL STRESS RESISTANCE. Below are descriptions of six teen-agers who did not become delinquents. They were selected to appear on the *New York Times* Youth Forum because each had a background indicative of delinquency yet each had succeeded in spite of this handicap.

Robert Weinberg said that when he was 15 his father died, and he went to work as well as to school. His home was in a poor neighborhood, and others in the family became juvenile delinquents. "There came a time when I looked objectively at myself," he said. "I asked myself, 'Do you want to be a juvenile delinquent, to go to jail, to be a hood with your picture in the paper? Or, do you want to study, work and save money and make something of yourself?' Now, I am going to college, then law school, I hope, and into politics."

Theresa also came from a poor home, was often attacked by girl gangsters, and felt that her parents and her brothers and sisters "were all against me." "It was my minister who really helped me first," she said. "He got me interested in church work and encouraged me to study." She has just won a state scholarship to Cornell University where she will major in physics and intends to become a science technician.

Robert McDonald was born with a short leg that made him a prey to boy gangs of the lower East Side. "A teenage gang is out to take revenge on the world," he said. "They don't care what they wreck or whom they hurt. If you don't belong to a gang they all jump on you. I belong to a club, not a gang, but the police chase us just the same." Nevertheless, Robert is a good student and is going on to commercial art school and a career in advertising art.

Harry Frank is a refugee from Nazi Germany, where his father died in a concentration camp. Broken by troubles, his mother did not understand him and exercised no parental control, he said. "It takes strong will-power to stay out of gangs," he said. "The opinion of other teenagers is important to you." He is going into the Air Force after completing school and hopes to become a civilian aviation technician.

Iris Melendez was brought up by her stepmother who, she said, hated her and her natural mother. The Puerto Rican slum was no encouragement to struggle for a good life. She finally ran away from home, found shelter in a home for girls, now supports herself as a seamstress and will graduate soon as a dress designer.

Louis Moscatello was once a leader of a tough boy gang in East Harlem that boasted of several killings. "One day some of us said, 'What do we get out of this? If we want to be big shots there must be a better way.' So we worked on it and got ourselves elected to the Student Council at Franklin High School. We improved the service squads, installed music in the cafeterias, got 99 percent student participation in extra-curricular activities. Next election we had no opposition." [41]

These young persons could "take" the stresses involved in achieving middle-class values. They resisted the delinquent-subculture technique for achieving status. They took a harder way. What gave them the ability to resist an easier way to status and to choose a harder one? We say they were stress-resistant, they could work and study and delay gratifications. But just what do we mean by stress resistance? We saw above that we cannot be referring to physical reactions to stress since delinquents appear to be able to bear physical stress at least as well as, if not better than, non-delinquents. Nor can it be closely related to intelligence, although no doubt intelligence must have some bearing on it. Stress resistance of the kind which seems to be crucial must be related to reference groups and to role conceptions. We used such concepts in our discussion of stress resistance in prisoner-of-war camps, in Chapter 4; and the same phenomena must be present here. Stress resistance is a variable—a quality or a trait—for which we do not as yet have measuring devices or tests. But it seems most likely that it is a major social-psychological factor in differentiating delinquents and non-delinquents.

If, for example, we examine the above six cases closely we find that somehow these young persons took over middle-class values and standards, and then had the fortitude to strive to achieve them. "Do you want to be a juvenile delinquent?" young Robert Weinberg asked himself, "or do you want to study, work and save money and make something of yourself?" Do you, in brief, want to have a lower-class reference group or a middle-class one? The minister encouraged Theresa to study, a very middle-class kind of activity.

Just why the reference groups and role conceptions of these non-delinquents were different from those of the delinquents we cannot say at this point. The mechanisms by which reference groups make their impact are by no means clear. In some areas—sex behavior, for example—the data are quite surprising. It has been found that boys who later show great social mobility have the patterns of sex behavior which characterize the class into which they ultimately rise rather than those of the class in which they originate.

> In general, it will be seen that the sexual history of the individual accords with the pattern of the social group into which he ultimately moves, rather than with the pattern of the social group to which the parent belongs and in which the subject was placed when he lived in the parental home.[42]

As the author of the above statement points out, it would be understandable if boys consciously patterned their sex behavior according to the standards of their reference groups, "but considering that the boy in actuality knows very little about the sexual behavior of the social group into which he is moving, it is all the more remarkable to find that these patterns are laid down at such an early age." [43]

If we assume that other middle-class values make their impact in the same way as those regulating sex behavior, we must conclude that there are certain channels of which we are as yet not aware through which middle-class reference groups communicate their sanctions to boys in lower socioeconomic classes.

In Chapter 6 we referred to chance factors. They cannot be wholly ignored. The girl merely happened to find the minister who could exert influence on her. But why did not this minister have the same effect on other young persons? Why was this child susceptible and not others? As yet we do not know.

We conclude, then, that the causes of delinquency inhere in the total status system of our society. Some young persons, severely handicapped by family backgrounds which give them no help in striving for middle-class values and goals, would find themselves in constant shame and humiliation at their failure if they did not, in effect, create a world for themselves in which they could enjoy status precisely for their failures vis-à-vis middle-class culture. The delinquent subculture serves primarily as a means for achieving status. It may be used, however, for other reasons also.

The delinquent-subculture explanation of juvenile delinquency does not pretend to cover all kinds of delinquency, especially those which are basically symptoms of pathologies. It refers to the non-utilitarian, malicious, and negativistic behavior which normal young persons engage in as a kind of revenge for society's refusal to accord them status on any legitimate basis.

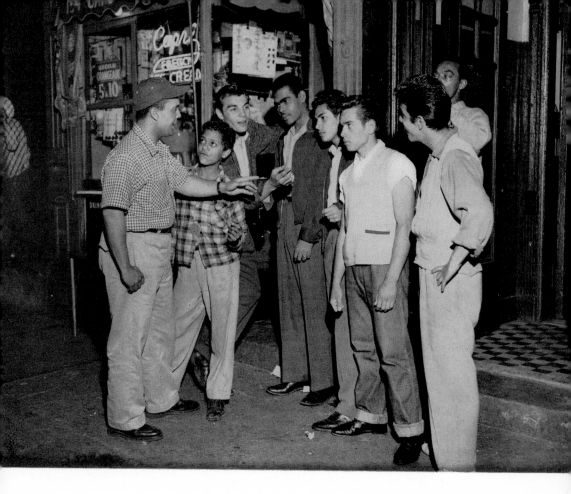

"Hey, maybe the guy's got somp'n at that!" says one of the young men. But it will take a great amount of convincing to overcome the suspicion and skepticism reflected on the faces of his friends. One of them thinks to himself: "The guy dresses like us, but you can see in his face that he doesn't belong."

These boys have been able to obtain the clothes and other outward appurtenances of middle-class status. Such material things constitute no problem—they require only money. The difficulty these boys face involves something harder to cope with: middle-class values and middle-class standards of behavior, which are usually acquired in the home. There is something about middle-class culture that makes them ill at ease. It is alien to them; it is something about which they know little in detail. Although they are young, vigorous, and good looking, virtually no one outside their own group admires them. Full of their own pride and spirit, they furnish one another with the recognition that is denied them by the larger society.

The Youth Board worker is an emissary from the middle-class world, but he does not come to them condescendingly as a do-gooder, emphasizing the status chasm between him and them. Nor does he come as a reformer, trying to make them over into middle-class boys. And certainly not as a policeman to watch, repress, and turn them over to the courts. He understands these boys and the social needs served by their gangs. He wants to retain what is good in their organization—since there is no other provision for satisfying the role and status needs of such boys as these—but he hopes to steer them clear of criminal activities. He may not succeed completely. In spite of all his efforts, they may still engage in street fights, vandalism, and pilfering. But if he can win their confidence he may prevent the shooting or the bombing which any one of these young men might otherwise perpetrate. The Youth Board worker and his agency will have contributed much to these young men if all he does is guide them safely across the troubled waters of youth without mishap. *(Photo: New York Daily News)*

What Is To Be Done?

The fact that delinquency is, for most boys at any rate, a self-limiting phenomenon does not detract from its seriousness for the community or even for the boy himself. There have, therefore, been many proposals for dealing with it.

The specific remedies proposed depend on the theory of causation on which they are based. As we saw above, almost everything has been used to explain it. And, indeed, almost everything—in the sense of the whole social system—*is* involved in "explaining" juvenile delinquency. Thus almost everything has been proposed to "cure it"—slum clearance, family discipline, more religion, and so on.

Actually, knowledge does not necessarily imply control in sociological problems. We referred above to the costs of any kind of change. Here is a statement of this principle of social costs as it refers to juvenile delinquency conceived as a product of the status system of our society.

How, for example, can we enable the working-class male to compete more effectively for status in a largely middle-class world or, if we want to cut into the web of causation at another point, how can we change the norms of the middle-class world so that his working-class characteristics do not relegate him to an inferior status? *If* these things are possible, we must then ask: What price are we willing to pay for this or that change? Since any social system is a complex network of inter-dependencies, any change designed to effect a reduction of delinquency may have all sorts of ramifying consequences. What consequences may we anticipate and are we willing to accept them? Many teachers, for example, are intuitively aware of the dilemma: to reward the "meritorious" and implicitly humiliate the handicapped, or to abandon this system of competition and invidious discrimination and abandon therewith a most powerful spur to the development of the kind of character most of us so highly prize. . . . The formulation of policy is a matter of choosing among alternatives and our choices must involve not only technical considerations but the balancing of social values.[44]

Most specific proposals for the control of juvenile delinquency fall far short of the total institutional change implied above.

Lip service is usually paid, in all proposals for dealing with juvenile delinquency, to the complexity of the problem and to the fallacy of supposing that any single or simple remedy exists. Yet simplistic remedies continue to be prescribed. According to whether the diagnosis is made in individual or in sociological terms, the approach is that of changing the individual or of changing the world he lives in.

We saw in Chapter 16 that the family is the first line of defense in any social-problem situation involving deviance. The family is supposed to diagnose the difficulty and deal with it according to accepted standards. One of the commonest and easiest remedies proposed for the control of delinquency, therefore, has to do with the delinquent's family, which is exhorted to exercise stricter discipline, more control, and severer punishment. The implication is that parents have willfully adopted a policy of leniency and permissiveness, with disastrous results.

> . . . a large portion of the delinquent group must be charged off as lost. They are the casualties of the new liberalism. The only hope for the future lies in the resurgence of the home as the basic institution of the modern world. We must recapture the spirit of the home which our parents and grandparents knew, and young people must be brought up and not left to bring themselves up. The position of the parent must be restored to its former place of authority, and the power to govern the household must be asserted with kindness when possible and severity when necessary. Then, and only then, will character thrive and the foundation be laid for a law-abiding society. . . . If society wishes to strike at the root of the evil, it must wage its campaign against those parents who refuse to discharge their responsibilities faithfully.[45]

And "We need more old-fashioned fathers and mothers," echoes Jersey Joe Walcott.[46]

It is certainly true that much juvenile delinquency is associated with unwholesome family relationships. But the problem is by no means simple. On the part of the slum family there is no studied abdication of control; the parents do not arbitrarily decide to give the child free reign. It is often simply impossible to exert the control called for. One study reported that:

> Supervision over children decreased with their age. The progress was from mother's lap, to the floor, the hall-way, the street hall-way entrance, the gutter, the street itself, the street corner, near-by play spaces, supervised recreations (in a fraction of the cases), and finally, to commercial recreations, and unguided pleasures and social activities outside of the neighborhood. . . . Supervision rarely involved an intimate contact with the social milieu of the child, and consisted usually of gross control over the time of home-coming and the avoidance of outstandingly disfavored individuals and places. Supervision for the youngest, save for those engaged in street occupations, such as shining shoes, and selling newspapers, emphasized the hours of home-coming and the restriction of play to the home block. Discipline usually consisted either of physical punishment or of loud threats of punishment. . . .
> The extent of parental control through supervision depended largely upon the cultural status of the family. Where there was disorganization in family life, control was least effective. Likewise in blocks where delinquency was greatest, controls were least effective.[47]

Among many parents, there was doubtless as much disturbance at their inability to control their youngsters as there was among the accusing critics. "After all," asks one psychiatrist, "who are these parents in 'bad homes?' Poor, unhappy people themselves." [48]

In the case of the middle-class pattern of role relationships discussed in Chapter 17 the plea that modern parents return to a past model implies a gross misunderstanding of the way roles operate. Even if they wanted to, modern parents could not perform the old parental roles. The performing of any role demands that the complementary roles be properly performed. If there is a hitch so that the roles do not dovetail or mesh, neither role can be properly performed. We saw in Chapters 16 and 17 that the current definition of parental roles has emerged in response to the conditions characteristic of an age of abundance, one which emphasizes consumption. The old virtues do not fit the new age. It is probably quite true that "a more widespread indulgence in luxuries and comforts than ever before is bound to witness a gradual disappearance of those primitive virtues which sterner and more sober generations nourished and applauded." [49] But the answer lies in determining and exploiting to the maximum degree the virtues which go with an age of abundance, rather than in attempting to revive the virtues which went with an era of scarcity. One of the commonest reactions of parents who have tried to control their children, and failed is, "What did we do wrong?" So far as they can see, they have performed their own roles strictly according to the script. They have acted as their own parents did. This kind of behavior succeeded with them. Why did it not succeed with their children? Their children are on a different stage.

Some people argue for severer punishment in the home, both lower-class and middle-class. But the case for this approach to the problem is extremely weak. The young people who appear in juvenile courts probably have had more severe punishment than their peers who never reach the court.[50] If the remedy were so simple, there would be little delinquency.

In dealing with the delinquent we may think of three general models of approach: the mass approach; the polar opposite to this, or the individual approach; and a modification of the individual approach, that of the group. The mass approach which deals with people in an undifferentiated manner is common. Proper institutional facilities are lacking in most communities. Young offenders are often placed in "shelters" or "detention homes," or even ordinary jails. Having already been damaged by emotional deprivation and status denigration they are subjected to even more. They learn from experienced inmates more about crime and how to commit it. If detention were successful there might be some justification for it. But it is not.[51] Furthermore it is expensive. It has been estimated that in New York probation costs about $250 a year per case; institutional "care," anywhere from $1,200 to $4,000.[52]

The wholly individualized approach is better, but even it does not necessarily produce positive results. The delinquent is, to be sure, a unique human being and has to be recognized as such. But he is also part of a social matrix: he performs roles, he has status in certain groups, he belongs to a certain system. To abstract him from it and act as though he could be treated in a vacuum is to fly in the face of all we know about the social nature of human beings. One experiment was undertaken to determine if proper individual treatment procedures could prevent juvenile delinquency. The theory was that delinquency was the result of family conditions, which could be helped by counseling, and of lack of recreational facilities, which could be remedied by furnishing them. The experiment was carried on in Cambridge and Somerville, Massachusetts. Beginning in 1935, the names of about 1,500 boys were referred by schools and agencies to the project. From these boys, 782 predelinquents and non-delinquents were selected. An elaborate matching process allocated 325 boys to a Treatment group (T) and 325 to a Control group (C). A specially selected staff supervised a program to help the T group; the C group was observed at the same time. Two surveys were made to evaluate results during treatment. The results were by no means unequivocal. Although 40 per cent of the subjects who entered the agency did profit from counseling, there was no proof that the counseling was effective in reducing delinquency. "Friendly counseling and provision of access to community facilities do not reduce delinquency. The usual group work services of a conventional character also appear not to have much effect on delinquency. . . . [Psychiatric treatment] is inadequate to overcome the influence of grossly unfavorable social conditions and is often unacceptable to families who live in the slums." [53]

Another experiment was attempted in two schools in the South Bronx, New York. In both schools groups of 125 children between $5\frac{1}{2}$ and $6\frac{1}{2}$ years were tested on an instrument designed by Sheldon and Eleanor Glueck to locate potential delinquents. Between 30 and 35 per cent were judged to be predelinquent on the test. In one school members of the Youth Board and other city agencies were working with the children in order to prevent delinquency; in the other school, no program was undertaken. The difference in delinquency rates would be taken as a measure of the success of the program. Five major areas were covered in the predelinquency test: the discipline of the boy by the father; the supervision of the boy by the mother; the affection of the father for the boy; the affection of the mother for the boy; and the cohesiveness of the family. The experiment was begun in 1953. Results have not yet been made public.

If we accept the delinquent-subculture hypothesis we can more readily understand why most approaches which begin with middle-class assumptions, middle-class goals, and middle-class points of view prove so ineffective. They exacerbate rather than mollify the conditions which make for delinquency in the first place. They point up the status inferiority of those they are designed to help. No matter how humanitarian, how generous, how well-intentioned, the very presence of "up-lifters" documents the status differentials between them and the young delinquent.

The approach which has seemed most effective has been one which accepts the delinquent in his social setting, deals with him not as an isolated or separate individual, but—as in Alcoholics Anonymous—attempts to exploit the strengths of group ties as they already exist.[54] It does not attempt to reform the delinquent; it does not attempt to make him over into a middle-class boy. It does not attempt to impose middle-class patterns of behavior on him. It accepts him for what he is, no more, no less. It aims only at reducing delinquency.

The first experiment in this new approach to delinquency took place in Chicago and was called the Area Project. It was instituted by Clifford Shaw, who had pioneered in the study of the sociological aspects of delinquency. The fundamental principle on which the project was based was that only the people in the area could do anything about delinquency. It works from the bottom up rather than the other way around. Most of the personnel come from the areas in which they work; they have no academic background; they may even have criminal records. The following is a description of the way the Area Project works.

Shaw . . . was convinced that delinquency, both juvenile and adult, is a product of social, or community, or mass forces—that it is a normal part of the ordinary life of low-income areas. This meant that the whole pattern of life-in-mass must be changed. Therefore the individual approach of probation and truant officers must fail. Further, Shaw believes that most mass-approaches so far attempted by various outside charitable, character-building, and welfare or settlement groups have failed because they were efforts to force reform on slum people from the top down.

In seeking a new approach, Shaw determined to try to work from the bottom up; to enlist the aid of the delinquents themselves, and of their neighbors, in combating delinquency. It was his belief that they, and they alone, could change the pattern of their own lives.

Shaw himself has moved into the background. . . . He fights institutionalization like the plague. . . . The people themselves, not outsiders, run the show. . . .

In 1932 Shaw selected for his first project the Russell Square community on the South Side. . . . The kids . . . are a problem. . . . Many of their fathers earn good money in the mills; the kids go in for crime less because of poverty, it seems, than as a result of the normal human longings for recognition and adventure which happen to be satisfied here by delinquent behavior. A child grows into petty thievery naturally, as children a few blocks up the lake shore grow into dancing school. Crime is simply a tradition, something you do when you're out with the other kids in the block. . . .

Shaw sent James F. McDonald, one of his staff members, into the area alone. McDonald had grown up on the South Side and knew the Russell Square community well. Quiet, twenty-seven years old, smallish, studious-looking, he went from alley to alley, mingling with the kids. They ranged from nine to eighteen years. Each vacant lot and corner and each section of the public park was ruled by its own gang—The Tigers, the Tomatoes, the Bush Walkers, the Baker Bears, and so on. The first time McDonald approached one gang, one of its graduates recalls, he bore a softball and a bat. At first the boys refused his invitation to play ball—"it was too easy, this guy bringin' us a ball an' bat"—but after a time he talked them into playing. Nevertheless, they regarded him with suspicion. "He's lookin' for my brudder," one said. Many thought he was a truant officer, or a plain-clothes detective, somebody connected somehow with hated authority; and however much he protested his unofficial status and his desire to be friends, the boys probably never would have trusted him but for one thing: he never squealed on them.

They wouldn't take him along when they went across the tracks to pick a fight with the Mexicans, or when they went out on their jobs—robbing or junking or stealing the copper gutters off the school. But they suffered him to hang with them because he was a good guy, and so before long he knew who was stealing what, and they knew that he knew, and they saw that he didn't tell on them. . . . He never lectured them on the moral or legal aspects of their enterprises. This tolerance was unorthodox welfare work, perhaps, but it endeared him to the boys. He encouraged them to form baseball teams and to organize into leagues (but they had to do the organizing themselves), and if they wanted to go swimming he arranged for the "Y" pool. . . .

All this time McDonald had been forming a local organization. He had been talking to some business men in the community about what he wanted to do, and they . . . formed the Russell Square Community Committee. . . . Gradually the Committee grew until today it includes about 125 active adults and about 700 contributing members. . . . The local residents run the show. . . .

What does all this add up to? What, in concrete terms, has the Chicago Area Project accomplished? . . . The rate of juvenile delinquency has declined in all but one of the six areas since Projects have been undertaken. . . . In . . . Russell Square and the West Side, the decrease has been striking during the period of the Project's activity. In each area the rate in 1940 was only about a third of the rate in 1930; in both areas the rate was cut approximately in half when the project took hold, and never again reached its former high. . . .[55]

Similar approaches in New York City have had similar results. More seems to be accomplished by rolling with the punch than by resisting it. In New York City, gangs sometimes consider it a mark of distinction to have a Youth Board worker assigned to them; it is a sign that they are tough and dangerous.

The "job man" . . . was a fellow, a few years older than most Mino-.taurs, who some time in 1951 began hanging out in bars, candy stores and other places frequented by the gang. He'd drop nickels in the jukebox, stand treat for beers or cokes, and openly courted the good graces of the gang mem-bers. Was he "queer"? Was he a cop? What was his game, anyway? For a while he was treated with undisguised hostility, later with suspicious toleration. He got jobs for a few of the fellows. Someone asked what was his racket, and he replied he was a social worker sent by the Youth Board to try to help the fellows.

"You mean you get paid doing this kind of stuff?" asked an amazed Minotaur. The youth worker was eventually accepted as a friend. The Youth Board sent other workers to the gangs with whom the Minotaurs fought. Soon other gangs began asking why they didn't have a worker assigned to them. This wasn't because they were getting soft; it was a matter of "rep." You just didn't figure as a real tough gang unless the Youth Board sent you a worker.

In this sort of climate, the youth workers make some headway, lose some ground, but somehow wind up making gains for law and order. The Minotaurs have in the last four years killed one boy in a street fight, shot three others and knifed several, none fatally. Two of their own members were killed, one shot non-fatally and several knifed.[56]

By conventional standards the above record would seem to spell complete failure. Yet, bad as it seems, it is not so bad as it might have been. Between 1947 and 1952 delinquency decreased in the eleven areas in which Youth Board workers operated; in 1953 and 1954 there was an increase, but it was much lower than the increase in other districts which had no Youth Board workers. Serious gang wars have been almost wiped out in areas where Youth Board workers operate.[57]

No one pretends, certainly not the youth workers or their leaders, that the youth-worker approach is a panacea for dealing with delin-quency. It does seem to be grounded more firmly than other approaches in adequate sociological theory, and it seems to be more successful than other approaches have been to date. It might be argued that it succeeds as well as it does because its aim is so low. To those who dream the American dream of abolishing delinquency, of turning every boy into a middle-class boy, of wiping out the culture which accompanies low status, the results may be disappointing. It may be said that in giving up the higher goals we have made a cynical capitulation to things as they are. There is some truth to this charge. We do sacrifice a bit of the American dream when we give up the ideal of turning the slum boy into a middle-class boy. Indeed American history for a long time has been the story of American schools turning generations of children of lower-class parents—immigrants, rural persons—into middle-class adults. For many today, this same process continues. And it may be that the youth-worker approach of rolling with the punches, of accepting the boys for what they are, will turn out to be a holding operation for this quarter-century, preventing conditions from getting worse until they can get better. We have yet to see what the age of abundance can do in clearing slums, healing pathologies, making opportunities, finding leadership, and minimizing the hurdles to achievement of middle-class values. Fifty years from now we will be able to evaluate the situation much better.

Delinquent Girls

It is estimated that girls are about one fourth as likely as boys to be recorded as delinquents. When they do appear in the records, the offense is most likely to be "ungovernability," and the next most likely, a sexual offense. Both are, for practical purposes, the same thing.

Although girls do not become gang members—only five or six female gangs were reported out of 1,313 in one study—they do associate with male gangs. For example, in connection with one New York gang,

there is a "debbie" (debutante) adjunct of about three dozen girls, aged 14 to 17. The sorority, not as tightly organized as the boys' club, has greater fluctuation of membership. The girls are the "steadies" for the gang's "sessions" (house parties and dances). Some carry their boy friends' knives and guns.[58]

Even when they have gangs of their own, however, they are not so likely to be delinquent in their behavior. The characteristic female delinquent today is the promiscuous girl.

Many promiscuous girls never become social or societal problems. There are, apparently, many of them. If we define as promiscuous a girl who has had sex relations with six or more men before marriage, the proportion found in one extensive survey was 13 per cent for all age groups taken together.[59] It was slightly lower for those born before 1900, and slightly higher (14 per cent) for those born after that date. The proportion varied, quite expectedly, with age at marriage, ranging from 9 per cent for those who married between sixteen and twenty, to 25 per cent for those who did not marry until the age of thirty-one to thirty-five. The author of the study here cited warns that these figures refer to a middle-class sample and therefore do not give a complete picture.

> . . . it should be pointed out . . . that the sample does not adequately represent the lower educational levels, and we do not have sufficient information to predict whether the data from those groups would show a greater or lesser promiscuity. Neither does the sample include histories of females who had done time in penal institutions, and our calculations show that group is much more promiscuous in its pre-marital activity. Consequently, the present record is based on only middle class and upper social level females.[60]

Sometimes the promiscuous girl does become a social or societal problem; that is, she becomes known to the police or to public agencies. She comes to their attention classified as a "prostitute." The term "prostitute" is a legal term and therefore not very illuminating from a research point of view. Some of the difficulties involved in the legal definition are elaborated in the following passage:

> By sociological and legal definition a prostitute is an individual who indiscriminately provides sexual relations in return for money payments. The practical interpretation of the term emphasizes the fact that a prostitute accepts a sexual relation with almost anyone, stranger or acquaintance, who offers to pay, and that the payment is in currency rather than in goods or services.
>
> It is impractical to confine the term to those persons who derive their whole living or any particular part of it from prostitution, for a very high number of the females who engage in such activities do so as a minor adjunct to their regular occupations. The person who is specifically paid for a single sexual relation is, for that particular occasion, a prostitute.
>
> The definition requires that payment for a sexual relation be in currency and be made for each particular contact. If the term prostitution were to be applied to all sexual acts for which either participant received some valuable consideration, it would be impossible to draw a line between the most obvious sort of commercialized prostitution and the relationships of every husband and wife. The girl who has to be taken to dinner or to an evening's entertainment before she will agree to intercourse with her boy friend or fiancé is engaged in a more commercialized relationship than she would like to admit. The gifts that are bestowed by males of all social levels upon girls with whom they keep company may be cloaked with fine sentiments, but they are, to a considerable degree, payment for the intercourse that is expected.[61]

The term "prostitute" should probably also include in its definition the contempt and disapproval which it connotes to millions, as well as the aura of glamor it has for other millions. Only the degraded prostitute is likely to appear in the records. The glamorous ones appear in fiction.[62]

Since the middle 1920's, the old-fashioned prostitute has been disappearing from the scene. Her place has increasingly been taken by the promiscuous girl. A study of some 500 delinquent women published in the 1930's showed the following percentages in different categories: full-time professional prostitutes, 7.1; occasional prostitutes, 42.0; one-man prostitutes or mistresses, 3.0; promiscuous adulteresses 6.6; one-man adulteresses, 6.6; unattached—widowed, separated, divorced, un-married—promiscuous women, 22.0; unconventional women, 8.6; doubtful girls, probably promiscuous, 2.3; not immoral, 1.8.[63] Less care-fully documented estimates during the 1940's, especially during the war, gave the proportion of "amateur prostitutes" as 80 to 90 per cent of the sexually delinquent population; and the *Journal of the American Medical Association* concluded that "the old-time prostitute is sinking into second place. The new type is the young girl in her late teens or early twenties." [64] She is probably much younger. In some cities, for example, the age at which agencies begin to work to rehabilitate girls is as low as twelve.[65]

There is no such thing as "the prostitute personality." The kind of girl who appears in the records by no means constitutes a representa-tive sample. The large number of promiscuous girls who marry and "settle down" are not in the sample. But the promiscuous girl who does appear in the record is likely to be from a disturbed family. One woman who has worked with promiscuous girls for many years describes them as follows:

> Prostitutes . . . have a common denominator—their inability to de-velop with another human being a relationship with meaning and continu-ity. The promiscuous girl has many men but not one on whom she can really count. . . . The girl who is sexually promiscuous does not permit herself to have any meaningful relationships, and finally she cannot have them. Her use of aliases, leaving her clothing hither and yon, frequent moving from one address to another—all these may suggest her need to evade police officers and family. But more likely they reflect her lack of self-respect, her inability to put down any roots or even to let her personal possessions have any real mean-ing. This is what is damaging to the girl and to society . . . for a human being to become so trapped in what she is doing, and so lacking in identity that she cannot or does not care what she is doing.
>
> Beneath the hard shell, the casualness or the sharp and ready humor of the promiscuous girl there is likely to be an unhappy, bitter person no longer in control of her own life. Many of these girls give a history of broken fami-lies. They could not bring their troubles into their homes. They could not get from home, school, church and community the resources to help them live creatively and usefully. Their sense of values is warped. They trust no one, not even themselves. They cannot bear themselves as they are. They cannot stop this self-destruction, this psychological suicide, until something or some-one on the outside puts a halt to their activities.
>
> Through these 10 years the type of girl we see has changed. There are fewer non-residents now, fewer girls who have left small towns to come to a

large city to work or to follow servicemen to neighboring camps. Those we see now are more likely to be residents, Baltimore girls. Some have been in state training schools. Some are adolescents defying parental authority, resisting the usual way for girls . . . in sex delinquency.[66]

As in the case of so many other categories of problems, the diagnosis which seems most appropriate is one made in terms of role disturbance. The promiscuous girl who appears in the records is incapable of performing suitable roles. And, again, the reason she cannot is that the proper opposing or complementary roles are not adequately performed by those around her—family, men, anyone. She cannot perform the role of daughter because such a role requires a corresponding role of mother.

The relation of people to each other as expressed in the family . . . is the milieu in which we live, in which we express our wants and needs, our hopes, our disappointments and our satisfactions. It is in relation to others that each of us finds his purpose, his definition. It is in our relationships that we create our democratic society—a society which requires not that we be like our fellow man, nor that we agree with him, but rather that we respect him for what *he is* and for his own unique place and role in society.

To carry this role—which we must carry as we give and take—we must have known a relationship which helped us find *our* own worth and dignity, *our* own importance as a human being. Most of us are able to do this because of the care and affection we had very early in our lives. If our parents failed to help us develop the ability to relate to another person, or if some catastrophe warps our ability to relate to other people and for the time being we cannot trust and "be" with other human beings, we are then unable to give and take in home, school or community in a socially useful and satisfying manner.

It is this—just this—which leads a person into anti-social behavior. Sometimes he expresses his frustration in mental or physical illness; more often—because he is unhappy and unable to get along in his family and community—in delinquent or criminal behavior. As he shifts from being responsible for his own conduct to railing against laws and limits, blaming others for his unhappiness, he begins to live against rather than with his fellowman. . . . When women get into this kind of anti-social activity they almost always become involved in sex delinquency.[67]

Future Trends

We saw above that with respect to trends from the past to the present we know very little; all we can do is make judicious guesses. The reason we are interested in these past trends is not because of their historical importance but because through them we can project future trends. In the absence of firm bases in the past, all we can do for the future, as for the past, is make guesses. The present section of our discussion should be read in this context. It suggests a number of guesses.

Looking at the situation coldly, some people might argue that if, as estimated, only 1, 2, or even 5 per cent of the youthful population actually becomes delinquent, we are not doing so badly. This, they might suggest, may be an irreducible minimum around which we may expect future rates to fluctuate. They would guess, therefore, that neither an increase nor a decrease in juvenile delinquency was to be expected in the future. The 1, 2, or 5 per cent might represent an ineradicable segment of the population so far as delinquency is concerned.

Others, viewing what seem to be increasing status stresses in our world, might argue that the future trend can only be upward. The "breaking point" of individuals may not change, but the stresses to which they are subjected will increase so that perhaps as many as 10 per cent will succumb. Even if we increase stress resistance, as we have increased height and weight, individual differences in stress resistance will remain, just as individual differences in height and weight continue. There is no likelihood that equality in talent, ability, physical endowment, mental capacity, or genetic composition will ever be achieved. But even disregarding rates—1, 2, or 5 per cent—so far as sheer numbers rather than rates are concerned, we may look to an increased number of delinquents as the children born in the forties and later reach delinquency-prone ages.[68]

Still others, finally, putting together bits of evidence from different sources, suggest that a long-time decline in the rate of juvenile delinquency is not impossible. To the extent, for example, that delinquency is based on personality distortions resulting from organic pathologies, improved techniques of early diagnoses and improved forms of chemical therapy will doubtless improve the prognosis of such cases. Since we do not know what percentage of delinquency is of this nature we cannot guess what the relative effect of such treatments will be.

To the extent that delinquency is related to status differentials in the social system, these observers might argue, changes now in process may have some impact. We saw in Chapter 1 that abundance has had a tendency toward equalization—of income, of education, and of consumption patterns—and that technology has complemented this tendency in the direction of equality by upgrading occupations. We are still far from actual equality; but the trend seems to be in the direction of a vastly increased middle class, with only vestigial classes above and below. There will doubtless be a great many middle classes; status within them will be unranked.[69] Whether or not the values which have characterized the middle class in the past—the value system sometimes characterized as the Protestant ethic—will persist in an age of abundance has been mooted, as we saw in our discussion of changing American character. We have already seen that the "inner-directed" type of character which went with an age of scarcity is being succeeded by an "other-directed" type, relatively noncompetitive, more consonant with an age of abundance. The "other-directed" type of character is more nearly like the type which has tended to appear in lower-status levels in the past. In brief, the character and value differences which have differentiated status groups may become greatly attenuated in an age of abundance. To the extent that they do, the status basis of delinquency should suffer attrition. The tendency toward equalization, however, as we have pointed out, is slower in the case of children than of adults because a larger proportion of children are in the lower socioeconomic levels. On the other hand, as we pointed out in Chapter 4, the reduction of status differentials may exacerbate rather than mollify relationships among individuals and groups.

As among the three guesses about future trends in juvenile delinquency—that it will remain constant, that it will increase, that it will decline—one's temperament will probably determine one's choice. Of this we can be fairly sure: as we get to know more about the nature of delinquency we will raise our standards, we will find more children who need help, and we will find them long before they commit delinquent acts.

So much, then, for the kinds of social and societal problems which are associated with youth in our society today. They are closely bound up with family and worker roles and with status differentials. And so, too, are the social and societal problems associated with the other end of the population pyramid, the older segment, but in a somewhat different way. We turn now to a consideration of these problems.

NOTES

1 Albert K. Cohen, *Delinquent Boys, The Culture of the Gang* (Free Press, 1955), pp. 25 ff.

2 *Ibid.*, p. 26.

3 *Ibid.*, pp. 27–28. The quotation from Frederic Thrasher is from *The Gang* (Univ. of Chicago Press, 1927), pp. 94–95.

4 *Ibid.*, pp. 28–29.

5 *Ibid.*, p. 30.

6 *Ibid.*, p. 31.

7 *New York Times*, May 24, 1955.

8 Benjamin Boshes, "Normal America in the Abnormal Setting." Reprinted by permission of the publishers, Abelard-Schu-

man Limited, from *Aspects of Culture and Personality* by Francis L. K. Hsu, Copyright 1954, pp. 97–99.

9 See also H. G. Geogh and D. R. Peterson, "The Identification and Measurement of Predispositional Factors in Crime and Delinquency," *Journal of Consulting Psychology*, 16 (1952), pp. 207–212.

10 Francis W. H. Adams, New York Police Commissioner, in a talk reported in the *New York Times,* July 25, 1955.

11 *Ibid.* July 30, 31, 1956.

12 *Ibid.*

13 Dr. Loretta Bender, senior psychiatrist of Bellevue Hospital, reported in the *New York Times,* July 20, 1955.

14 Charles I. Schottland, "Today's Children," *Social Security Bulletin,* 19 (May 1956), p. 21.

15 Stacy V. Jones, "The Cougars, Life with a Brooklyn Gang," *Harper's,* November 1954, p. 39.

16 *New York Times,* May 13, 1955.

17 Clifford R. Shaw and Henry D. McKay, *Juvenile Delinquency and Urban Areas* (Univ. of Chicago Press, 1942); Frederic Thrasher, *The Gang* (Univ. of Chicago Press, 1927); William Whyte, *Street Corner Society* (Univ. of Chicago Press, 1952); Cohen, *op. cit.,* Chapter 2.

18 Pauline Goldmark, *West Side Studies: Boyhood and Lawlessness* (Survey Associates, 1914), pp. 45–46.

19 Goldmark, *op. cit.,* pp. 53–54.

20 In the federal prison system in 1954, out of 4,728 offenders 21 and under, the commonest offense, after violation of immigration laws (1,521), was transportation of stolen motor vehicles (915). See *Federal Prisons–1954: A Report of the Work of the Federal Bureau of Prisons,* 1955, p. 74. Almost half of all "heists" of trucks are attributed to teen-agers. (Cargo Production Bureau of New York, reported in the press, July 16, 1955.)

21 A. L. Porterfield, "Delinquency and Its Outcome in Court and College," *American Journal of Sociology,* 49 (Sept. 1943), pp. 199–204.

22 Judge Elijah Adlow, "Teen Age Criminals," *Atlantic Monthly,* July 1955, pp. 46–47.

23 Cohen, *op. cit.,* pp. 44–45.

24 *New York Times,* May 31, 1956.

25 Allison Davis, *Social Class Influences on Learning* (Harvard Univ. Press, 1948), pp. 33–37.

26 *Ibid.*

27 Boshes, *op. cit.*

28 Sheldon and Eleanor T. Glueck, *Unravel-*

ing Juvenile Delinquency (Commonwealth Fund, 1950).

29 Davis, *op. cit.,* pp. 29–30.

30 Kenneth Eells *et al., Intelligence and Cultural Differences* (Univ. of Chicago Press, 1951).

31 A list submitted to a Temporary State Commission on Youth and Delinquency, White Plains, New York, September 1, 1955.

32 Cohen, *op. cit.,* p. 137.

33 Dr. Alexander C. Rosen, staff psychiatrist of the Contra Costa County (California) Probation Department, estimates that 80 to 85 per cent of all children coming to the attention of courts did not become serious adult delinquency problems. Paper read before the American Psychological Association, reported in the *New York Times,* September 2, 1955. "Gang life has no pull after age 19," says one Youth Board worker, quoted by Jones, *op. cit.,* p. 42.

34 Cohen, *op. cit.,* pp. 131 ff.

35 Boshes, *op. cit.,* p. 96.

36 Cohen, *op. cit.,* pp. 136–137.

37 *Ibid.,* p. 155.

38 One psychiatrist from the Mayo Clinic, for example, told a conference of the National Probation and Parole Association that "one or both parents often unconsciously permit or even foster delinquent behavior in their children. These parents . . . unconsciously enjoy satisfaction from the child's antisocial actions." (*New York Times,* June 22, 1955.) Another psychiatrist, from Western Reserve University, speaking to the American Psychoanalytic Association, pointed out that "children often misbehave to please their parents. . . . A delinquent child carries out acts that the parents themselves would like to do, but do not dare. . . . A mother . . . unconsciously may bring about in her child the behavior she consciously tries to prevent. . . . A child identifies himself not only with the idealized parent, but also with all the unconscious antisocial 'part' of the parent. Through 'nonverbal' communication between parent and child. . . . the child can sense parental pleasure at his provocative acts. . . . When a child acts to antagonize—by failing in school studies, stealing or lying—he may be aiming to please. . . ." (*New York Times,* December 3, 1955.) In such cases the parents probably lack the vigor or drive to engage in the delinquent subculture themselves, but secure, vicariously, the same status relief which the child enjoys.

[39] In a report of the New York City Housing Authority, the Chairman pointed out that 45,000 families had moved out of the housing projects over its twenty-year history to private apartments and homes of their own. These families were obviously not "slum dwellers" in the stereotyped sense. (*New York Times*, June 2, 1955.)

[40] Harry Manuel Shulman, *Slums of New York* (Boni, 1938), pp. 19–20.

[41] *New York Times*, May 18, 1956.

[42] A. C. Kinsey *et al.*, *Sexual Behavior in the Human Male* (Saunders, 1948), p. 419.

[43] *Ibid.*, p. 436.

[44] Cohen, *op. cit.*, pp. 176–177.

[45] Adlow, *op. cit.*, p. 50.

[46] *New York Times*, July 7, 1955.

[47] Shulman, *op. cit.*, p. 18.

[48] Dr. Lauretta Bender, senior psychiatrist at Bellevue Hospital, *New York Times*, July 20, 1955.

[49] Adlow, *op. cit.*, p. 47.

[50] At a meeting of the National Probation and Parole Association in June 1955, one speaker made the point that "in our western cultures people have been beating and abusing children for centuries and are still doing so. . . . I believe that those of us in child protective work have found no great reduction during the past ten years in the frequency of physical assaults upon children by parents or parental figures, acting in the name of character building or similar subterfuge. There still are bruised, welted and bleeding children as periodic exposés of institutions and prosecutions of parents for felonious assault reveal. I would expect 'back to the woodshed' advocates to deny any identification with sadism, but it is important to know what you are sponsoring when you encourage an increase in the frequency and severity of corporal punishment." (*New York Times*, June 22, 1955.) And the psychiatrist quoted above points out that studies of 8,000 of the worst cases of delinquency at Bellevue had shown gross deprivations of love, severe punishment and brutality at home, and enforced submissiveness and isolation, among other factors. (*New York Times*, July 20, 1955.) If punishment helped, these children should be paragons.

[51] Lowell J. Carr, *Delinquency Control* (Harper, 1940), pp. 177–180.

[52] *New York Times*, June 24, 1955.

[53] Helen L. Witmer and Edith M. Tufts, *The Effectiveness of Delinquency Prevention Programs* (Children's Bureau, 1954).

Present quotation from *Family Life*, April 1955, p. 3.

[54] Status factors may be exploited, as when one worker, finding that gang members "set great store by 'rep' or status," convinced them they could gain status by sponsoring a dance as well as by being the "baddest" gang. (Jones, *op. cit.*, p. 41.)

[55] John Bartlow Martin, "A New Attack on Delinquency, How the Chicago Area Project Works," *Harper's*, May 1944, pp. 502–512.

[56] Charles Grutzner, "Youth Gangs Spawned by Longing for Friends," *New York Times*, May 13, 1955. For a more detailed description see Jones, *op. cit.*, pp. 35-43.

[57] Jones, *op. cit.*, p. 42.

[58] Grutzner, *op. cit.*

[59] A. C. Kinsey *et al.*, *Sexual Behavior in the Human Female* (Saunders, 1953), p. 336.

[60] *Ibid.*, p. 292.

[61] Kinsey *et al.*, *Sexual Behavior in the Human Male* (Saunders, 1948), p. 595.

[62] For an inside account of prostitution as it used to be organized, by a literate madam, see Polly Adler, *A House Is Not a Home* (Rinehart, 1953).

[63] Sheldon and Eleanor T. Glueck, *Five Hundred Delinquent Women* (Knopf, 1934), pp. 89–90.

[64] Dyson Carter, *Sin and Science* (Heck-Cattell, 1946), p. 7.

[65] Mazie F. Rappaport, "After Ten Years: Helping Prostitutes Help Themselves," *Journal of Social Hygiene*, 39 (May 1953), p. 213.

[66] *Ibid.*, pp. 211–212.

[67] *Ibid.*, pp. 209–210.

[68] A federal report, assuming that the increase in reported juvenile delinquency between 1950 and 1954 was a long-time trend, pointed out the problem which increased numbers would pose for penal institutions: "When one considers this increase in relation to the predicted increase of more than forty percent in the nation's youth over the next ten years, the future possibilities of the youth-crime problem become truly alarming. . . . Those who operate correctional facilities for youths, both Federal and State, will face most serious difficulties in providing adequate treatment and training programs." (U. S. Department of Justice, *Federal Prisons, 1954* [Leavenworth, 1955], p. 3.)

[69] Gregory P. Stone and William H. Form, "Instabilities in Status," *American Sociological Review*, 18 (April 1953), pp. 149–162.

19

Social Problems Associated

with the

Later Years of Life

Age and the Characteristic Problems
of Abundance

All through our discussion of social problems we have seen the long shadow cast by older persons over our whole society. We saw that the problems they create are characteristic of an age of abundance, which makes it possible for so many of them to live so long. The characteristic pathologies, for example, change from those resulting from infections and faulty nutrition to those resulting from degeneration. The elderly rather than the young are largely responsible for the great increase in hospitalized mental illness in our time. We saw older persons taking jobs formerly done by young persons because their own jobs are taken from them.

It is difficult to appreciate the wide ramifications of the demographic changes which modern medicine has produced. They have created a population which never existed before in human history, one containing large numbers of older persons. We are only now in process of learning what to do about it. Our whole conception of age has to be changed. We must get used to the idea that older people are people too. In this chapter we explore some of the role and status problems of older persons in our society.

The Concept of a "Generation" and of a "Cohort"

The older generation at any historical moment has unique characteristics. The people who became sixty-five in the 1930's were different from those who will become sixty-five in 1965. They were born in the

447

1870's, not long after the Civil War. They had weathered great epidemics of diphtheria and influenza. They had been through the depressions of the 1870's, of the 1890's, of 1907, of the early 1920's. Most of them had been born on farms or in foreign lands. They had not had much schooling. Their *Weltanschauung* had been forged in a wholly different atmosphere from that of people born after 1900.

The concept of "social generations" or "political generations" was developed by French and German sociologists to explain differences in orientation between older and younger people. Older persons cannot be defined biologically or in terms of specific age groups, but must be thought of in terms of common experiences, sentiments, and ideas. Their orientation is a way of feeling and understanding, which is different from and even opposed to former, or newer, ways. It is a phenomenon of "collective mentality" and morality.[1] The historical scene during the time people are in their formative years, say, roughly, until their twenties, will determine the decisive experiences of any political or social generation. The concept of decisive, politically relevant experience includes the following elements: the general conditions of social life during the formative period—war, peace, prosperity, depression, stability, or unrest; the important political issues of the time; and the concrete political and social struggles, such as revolutions, rebellions, uprisings, strikes, or reform. The concept of social or politi-

TABLE 1

YEARS OF SCHOOL COMPLETED BY PERSONS TWENTY-FIVE YEARS OLD AND OVER, 1950

			PER CENT WHO COMPLETED AT LEAST: *		
Age	Median School Years Completed	8 Years of Grade School	4 Years of High School	2 Years of College	4 Years of College
Total, 25 years and over	9.3	70.8	33.4	10.6	6.0
25–29	12.1	84.8	52.2	13.9	7.6
30–34	11.5	82.4	46.1	12.4	6.8
35–39	10.5	77.9	39.5	12.3	6.8
40–44	9.9	74.6	34.9	12.7	7.4
45–54	8.8	68.0	28.2	10.3	5.8
55–64	8.4	59.7	21.4	8.0	4.5
65 years and over	8.2	53.2	16.7	5.7	3.3

* Excludes small percentage of cases (2.2 per cent of the total) for which years of schooling were not reported.

SOURCE: 1950 Census of Population: Preliminary Reports, Series PC–7, No. 6, May 13, 1952, Table 1.

cal generation does not imply that there are no differentiations within each generation, for obviously there are. "To have the same experiences in common integrates a generation into a social collective; but a generation may include several subdivisions, if the crucial experiences are met and mastered in different ways, for example, by different class groups." [2]

We may avoid the complications of the concept "social generation" —which is a psychological concept implying "consciousness of kind"—by using the demographic concept of cohort, which makes no such implications but deals with people as age aggregates. All the people within a given age bracket constitute a demographic cohort. The ages included within any given cohort may vary according to the intent. For our purposes here we shall think in terms of fairly wide age brackets, say twenty-five years.

The Cohort of Persons Sixty-five and Over at Midcentury and Later

The cohort of almost 14,000,000 people in the United States who are sixty-five years of age and over at midcentury reflects conditions prevailing at the beginning of the century. Because the rate of change was so rapid in the 20th century, those who become sixty-five years of age in the future will be, as a class, quite different. The social problems of "the aged" in the 1960's will refer to a different kind of population from that of the 1930's, 1940's, and even 1950's.

First, the older people will be more educated. The expected change in the composition of the older segments of the population is nowhere more striking than in educational attainment. Table 1 (facing) summarizes years of schooling for different age groups of the population as of 1950. It will be readily apparent that the segment of population becoming sixty-five years of age and over in the second half of the 20th century will be more educated. Inasmuch as life expectancy is greater in the upper socioeconomic classes, the relative proportion of persons with some college education will be even higher than that suggested by these figures. By 1990, then, barring a large influx of uneducated immigrants, we can expect that about one fifth of the older population will have had some college education. By that time it is conceivable that the younger segments of the population will have had more education than they have now, so that there may still be a differential between the younger and older segments; but the magnitude of the difference as shown in the table will undoubtedly be relatively much smaller.

The ethnic composition of the older population will be much different. At midcentury the median age of the foreign-born white population was 56.1 years. It was rising at the rate of about five years per decade; the median had been 51.0 in 1940. The foreign-born constituted between one fourth and one fifth of all those sixty-five years of age and over in 1950; this proportion will be far less in 1960. Of the children under five years of age in 1950, less than ½ of 1 per cent were foreign-born. Barring increased immigration, there will be almost no foreign-born in the older population when they grow up.

The occupational composition of the older population will be different also, reflecting the changes in occupational distribution which have been occurring in the 20th century. There will, for example, be relatively far fewer farmers, fewer unskilled workers, more professional persons, more white-collar workers, than now. One study of men sixty-five years of age and over in 1951 concluded that "the older men, in a sense, know the wrong trades. . . . The skills of older men are out of tune with contemporary needs. . . . The older craftsmen have skills for which demand has declined over the years." [3] It is true that we can expect continuing changes in the occupational composition of the total population, so that some older people will always find themselves with obsolete skills, but it is doubtful if the changes will be so drastic as in the first years of the 20th century. The jump from farming to urban industry, for example, is probably harder than the jump from one kind of factory job to another. At any rate, the skills of professional people "last longer" than mechanical skills.[4]

There is some evidence that the sex composition may be less unequal than it is now. But here the trends have to be carefully interpreted. We know that life expectancy for women is considerably greater than for men, and that the disparity has been increasing. Thus the mortality rate for women declined almost two-thirds, or 63.5 per cent—from 17.0 to 6.2—between 1900 and 1954, whereas the rate for men declined only one half, or 49.5 per cent—from 18.6 to 9.4—in the same period, a relatively smaller gain in the case of men than of women. The life expectancy of white women has increased 24.2 years since 1900, of white men, only 20.2 years.[5] However, as a British study points out, "the reduction in infant and child mortality has benefited boys more than girls, with the result that the [initial] preponderance of males, which was lost by the age of 10 in 1913, now continues up to the age of 30; in 1983 it is expected to continue up to 50." [6] Since the same reduction in infant mortality is being achieved in our population we may anticipate that there will be relatively more men in the older population in the future than now, but never, of course, more men than women. That is, when we can control the diseases and other causes of death that affect older persons as well as we control those that affect younger persons, and especially those that cause the death of more men than women—tuberculosis, accidents, suicide, and homicide—we may change the sex ratio in the older age brackets.

In discussing health, however, we are on more speculative ground. We are led to believe, though, that the science of geriatrics, applied to a generation which has benefited from improved knowledge about nutrition, which is using the many new drugs daily becoming available, and which is less worn out by hard physical labor, will be able to effect an improvement in the health of the older population so that the people who become sixty-five years of age in the future should be healthier than the older persons of today. Even today, in fact, we are told that we have many misconceptions about older people, based on past rather than current conditions.

> . . . much of the accepted data about old people . . . [were] gathered in institutions and hospitals. As a result they reflect the conditions of a limited group in late stages of deterioration and illness. An entirely different picture would be obtained by studying the whole aged population of today, which includes many who are healthy, well-adjusted and employed.[7]

One of the most important differences between older persons of even the immediate future and those of the past lies in the relative number of peers those of the future will have. All students of the subject have emphasized that some of the most serious hazards of the later years have been the loneliness, isolation, and frustration caused by lack of companionship and feelings of rejection. In the past there were not enough older persons to create a social system of their own, one which would furnish them a role matrix. But at midcentury they constitute about one twelfth of the total population, and hence can furnish such role matrices for one another. They can interact appreciatively; they are less dependent on younger persons for recognition; they have a peer group, no less necessary at their age than at any other age. One study of 468 older people, in fact, found that for those seventy years of age and over membership in friendship groups forestalled a feeling of "old age."

> . . . various mental states that characterize older people, and distinguish them from others, are actually precipitated by shifts in age identification from middle-aged to old. The important question consequently becomes: What are the social conditions that hasten or forestall such shifts in age iden-

tification? . . . [Group membership is an important factor.] Among people who are 70 and over clique membership makes a considerable difference for age identification. Only half of those who participate in a friendship group, but nearly two thirds of the others, consider themselves old.[8]

Meeting regularly with one another, the members of such groups achieve a sense of continuity in their lives; since all are aging together they give one another an illusion of changelessness. An illustration of this feeling is the practice of referring to themselves as "the boys" or "the girls."

Not the least difference between the "new" and "old" older generation is that the "new" older generation is going to be one that grew up with the automobile. Its members are at home behind a steering wheel. Neither figuratively nor literally will they belong to the horse-and-buggy days. The implications are important. Mobility will be greater. Already large numbers of them live in trailer homes on wheels. Mobility is a liberating force in their lives.

We have emphasized some of the main changes which we may expect in the future in the population sixty-five years of age and over in order to make clear how transitional the problems of this group are at the present time. But another important consideration must be recognized. "Old age" is going to begin later in life. The most striking rates of increase in the population are among those who are seventy-five years of age and over. There were more than four million at mid-century, an increase of 50 per cent over 1940. We may soon come to think of those in the sixty-five to seventy age bracket as still relatively "young," or in "late middle age," as compared with the increasing number who will be over that age. Thus although the problems now associated with old age will undoubtedly be attenuated so far as the years up to age seventy or even seventy-five are concerned, they will continue for a long time, but will center about an older age group. As life expectancy increases, the people who are considered "aged" or "senior citizens" or "older" will be in their eighties rather than in their sixties or even seventies.

As in the case of persons in other age brackets, role and status problems are major hazards for older persons. Family role problems center about widowhood and about the relationships between adults and their parents; worker role problems center about retirement or status degrading. Status problems also have to do with dependency. All are intimately related, and all are pervaded by ill health or the constant threat of it. It is almost impossible to discuss any one of the above problems without at the same time discussing all the others. We shall deal first with dependency status.

Status Problems: From Dependency to Independence

Dependency and ill health seem almost inherent in the definition, certainly in the connotations, of the concept of "the aged." When people are working at their jobs, in good health, and living with their wives or husbands, we do not think of them as members of the class known as "the aged." It is only when they can no longer take care of themselves that they come to be thought of as "aged." It is not fortuitous that, increasingly, we speak of "older age brackets" or "senior citizens," or use some other term rather than "aged," in speaking of older persons: for the dependent "aged" are rapidly passing from the scene. Dependency and the low status which accompanies it are disappearing.

Until the 1920's the main support for the older population was employment in agriculture, relatives, private charity, or the local community poorhouse. But the enormous increase in the number of older persons—from 3 to 14 million between 1900 and 1954—and the concomitant changes taking place in both the economy and in family structure rendered these means of support inadequate.

The spectacular decline of agriculture in the occupational composition of the total economy explains why agricultural employment is no longer available as a source of support for many older persons. The proportion of all male workers fifteen to seventy-four years of age who were engaged in agricultural occupations declined from 24.5 per cent

TABLE 2

MEDIAN AGE OF HUSBAND AND WIFE AT EACH STAGE OF THE FAMILY
CYCLE, IN THE UNITED STATES, 1950, 1940, AND 1890

Stage of the Family Cycle	Median Age of Husband			Median Age of Wife		
	1950	1940	1890	1950	1940	1890
First marriage	22.8	24.3	26.1	20.1	21.6	22.0
Birth of first child	—	25.3	27.1	—	22.6	23.0
Birth of last child	28.8	29.9	36.0	26.1	27.2	31.9
Marriage of first child	—	48.3	51.1	—	45.6	47.0
Marriage of last child	50.3	52.8	59.4	47.6	50.1	55.3
Death of husband or wife	64.1	63.6	57.4	61.4	60.9	53.3
Death of husband, if last	71.6	69.7	66.4	—	—	—
Death of wife, if last	—	—	—	77.2	73.5	67.7

SOURCE: Paul C. Glick, "The Family Cycle," *American Sociological Review*, 12 (Feb. 1947), p. 165, and "The Life Cycle of the Family," *Marriage and Family Living*, 17 (Feb. 1955), p. 4.

in 1930 to 14.9 per cent in 1950, and was expected to decline even more by 1960.[9] The improvement in technology which has made agriculture so productive—referred to in Chapter 1—has vastly reduced its manpower requirements; fewer men of any age, let alone those in their later years, will find useful work around a farm.

Dependency and Changes in Family Roles

The changes which have taken place in the family have been equally spectacular, and they are relevant in explaining why the care of older persons will no longer be assumed as a matter of course by grown sons and daughters. These revolutionary role changes in family structure are the result of basic demographic changes. Table 2 summarizes these role changes, which have been epitomized in the phrase "lengthened period of the empty nest." These "empty nest" years have increased because of earlier age at marriage, earlier age at birth of last child, earlier age at marriage of last child, and later age at death of spouse.

As recently as 1890 it was typical for one of the parents to die two years before the last of the children married. In 1940 the typical situation was for the first death of a parent to occur eleven years [and in 1950, almost fourteen years] after the last child had married. . . .

It is one thing for an unmarried child who is yet in the family to accept the responsibility for a widowed mother or to stay on to keep house for a widowed father, or to take on the responsibility for operation of the family farm. It is something quite different for a child who has been married [fourteen] years and has acquired his own home and children to take account of the fact that his widowed mother cannot carry on alone. In the latter case, the adjustment to providing for one's wife and own children with one's entire personal income will have been made. The exercise of authority free from restraints of parental guidance will have become second nature. In the [fourteen] years that have intervened, the last of the children to be married will have had ample time to surround himself with and become accustomed to the manner of life which is demanded in his present occupational class and to which it is quite possible the dependent parent would not become accustomed. If he has not risen in the world financially, he is then faced with the dilemma of refusing refuge to his surviving parent or sacrificing what he had planned to provide for his own children. If the decision is made in favor of the widowed parent, then the problem of family tension, involving authority over the children and the "new-fangled" ways of raising them, is the next hurdle. . . .

A combination of [certain] trends in family life and the decline in mortality rates have reinforced each other in creating . . . the lengthened period of the empty nest. First, in 1890 there was a larger number of children in the family; hence, some were born later in their parents' lives. Second, death of that parent who was first to die occurred at an earlier age in 1890 than in [1950]. Third, marriage now occurs at a somewhat earlier age than in 1890.[10]

The family-role difficulties of older parents are not wholly new; they were noted in the 19th century by foreign observers. But they were enormously increased by industrialism and urbanism, especially in the 20th century.

The accepted attitudes toward the old in early American society are reflected in *The Whole Duty of Man*, a popular manual widely read in the colonies. Children owed reverence, love, and obedience to parents. Regardless of the character of the parents, children were expected to aid them if weak, sick, or poor—partly because of moral or religious sanctions and partly in return for the previous support by parents. These moral precepts were much easier to follow when there were few alternatives to remaining in the vicinity of the parents' household, if not within it. After the establishment of our present government, with the development of the westward movement, the existence of alternative opportunities for young people in the form of the chance to pioneer on a farm of one's own, and the prevailing practice of dividing property among children, both tended to weaken kinship spirit. The marked familism that continued through the colonial period and the early days of independence was on the wane. By 1848 a European observer noted the difficulty met by farmers in their later years whose children had all left to establish their own hearths. Thus, even before the rise of industrialism and urbanization, beckoning opportunity was, in some cases, leaving the nest empty of children and marooning the aged parents.[11]

Old as the problem of the "empty nest" may be, it did not become acute until the 20th century, when family care became increasingly difficult to provide. It was seen that some kind of outside assistance was required. In 1923 the first state laws for old-age assistance which could pass the test of constitutionality were passed—in Montana and Nevada. And in 1935 the Social Security Act marked the assumption by the Federal Government of part of the load. Two separate provisions were embodied in the Social Security Act, one based on need and one based on earned rights or insurance benefits. The first implies a status of dependency; the second does not. The trend is in the direction of fewer people in the old-age assistance, or dependent, category and more in the insurance benefits, or independent, category.

Dependency: Old-Age Assistance

The Old-Age Assistance provisions of the Social Security Act developed out of the old Poor Laws. In the 19th century, institutions had been built for the blind, the deaf, the insane, and the retarded. But the destitute aged remained in the poorhouse or in county homes. In the

TABLE 3

Selected Data on Sources of Receipts, Persons Sixty-five Years of Age and Over, 1951

SOURCE OF INCOME	PER CENT HAVING THIS SOURCE		PER CENT OF AGGREGATE RECEIPTS OF GROUP	SIZE OF INCOME FROM SOURCE		PER CENT OF THOSE WITH INCOME, HAVING SOURCE IN AMOUNT OF		MEAN AMOUNT OF TOTAL RECEIPTS FOR THOSE WITH INDICATED PRINCIPAL SOURCE
	To Any Extent	As Principal Source of Income		Median Size of Receipts from Source	Mean Size of Receipts from Source	Less than $200	$2,500 or More	
Earnings								
Couples	60.3	42.1	63.8	$1,820	$2,514	7.1	37.5	$3,260
Unrelated males	37.6	22.8	51.6	1,323	1,885	10.8	24.4	2,082
Unrelated females	13.7	7.8	18.0	469	995	23.1	8.2	1,651
Assets								
Couples	26.1	8.6	9.4	517	822	23.0	5.9	2,268
Unrelated males	17.1	6.2	9.3	387	673	27.5	6.2	1,543
Unrelated females	21.5	12.6	26.4	509	851	15.7	8.7	1,236
Savings								
Couples	15.2	4.4	5.6	531	782	20.1	6.0	1,989
Unrelated males *	13.7	5.8	6.5	400	578	25.0	—	1,196
Unrelated females	13.7	7.0	15.1	472	681	20.4	4.8	1,187
Pensions								
Couples	36.5	22.6	16.0	837	1,001	7.0	4.2	1,536
Unrelated males *	35.0	25.8	21.3	654	780	5.5	1.8	913
Unrelated females	22.1	14.6	19.5	581	634	8.0	0.8	739
Assistance								
Couples	17.1	12.0	4.9	603	668	7.1	—	929
Unrelated males	26.5	19.3	10.9	468	512	8.9	—	539
Unrelated females	26.4	23.4	19.4	489	528	7.8	—	567

* Sample dangerously small.

SOURCE: Peter O. Steiner, "The Size, Nature, and Adequacy of the Resources of the Aged," *The American Economic Review*, 44 (May 1954), p. 657.

1920's, as we saw, states began to pass laws permitting counties to use public funds for the assistance of destitute aged persons. By 1929 eleven states had such laws. By 1934 there were old-age assistance laws in twenty-eight states, and these laws were mandatory in twenty-three states. "These state laws accepted by implication the theory that poverty in old age might be due to social influences rather than individual shiftlessness, though there was no acceptance of the idea that pensions were due to the old regardless of need." [12]

The Old-Age Assistance provision of the Social Security Act requires that recipients show need. It is based on a theory of relief. The recipients are not "paupers" in the degrading 19th-century sense; but they do have to pass a means test which is often extremely humiliating and which sometimes prevents people from seeking help.

The End of Dependency Status: From Assistance to Benefits

The Old-Age and Survivors Insurance provision of the Social Security Act differs in both theory and practice from assistance. It is an interesting illustration of the importance of status considerations in social problems at the present time. It was designed to allow the recipient to retain status. In theory he is entitled to his benefits as a matter of right because he has contributed to an annuity or retirement fund administered by the Federal Government. In fact, certainly in the earliest years, he received a great deal more than he had contributed. The question has been asked, "Would not a flat-rate benefit to everyone at a certain age, say 65, be more equitable, easier to administer, and, in the long run, more economical?" [13] The reply so far has been, Probably so, but the status distinction between the recipient of assistance and the recipient of retirement benefits must still be maintained.

The Chamber of Commerce of the United States has proposed extension of Old-Age and Survivors Insurance to everyone at age sixty-five, regardless of past employment history, and financing of the program on a pay-as-you-go rather than on a reserve-fund basis.[14] The future trend is undoubtedly in the direction of pension rather than assistance status for those sixty-five and over. Since February 1951, for example, the number of persons receiving assistance has been less than the number receiving insurance benefits. And the disparity is growing, as the assistance recipients decline in number and the benefit recipients increase. The time is approaching when there will be only insurance benefit recipients; the generation of assistance recipients will have passed away.

That it is the status rather than the amount of money which makes the insurance benefits preferable, reveals itself in the fact that as of January 1952, the average monthly payment for old age assistance was higher ($44.50) than that for insurance benefits ($42).[15]

In addition to insurance benefits provided for in the Social Security Act, there were retirement benefits available to older persons in railroad retirement legislation, veterans' compensation and pension programs, and public employees' retirement plans. By the end of 1954, an estimated one fourth of the total annual money income of those sixty-five years of age and over came from such public benefits.

The rapidly growing importance of social insurance as a form of income maintenance for aged persons needs no further emphasis. At the end of 1954 about 6.6 million persons, or almost half of all persons aged 65 and over, were receiving some income from social insurance or related public retirement or pension programs. Such benefits were the primary source of income for a large majority of the beneficiaries. In the aggregate, payments under the old-age and survivors insurance, railroad retirement, public employees' retirement, and veterans' compensation and pension programs were at an annual rate of about $4.8 billion, almost one-fourth of the estimated annual money income of all persons aged 65 and over at the end of 1954.[16]

TABLE 4

DEPENDENCY STATUS OF PERSONS SIXTY-FIVE YEARS OF AGE AND OVER IN THE UNITED STATES, 1937

Self-dependent	*35.1 per cent*
a. Current income from earnings, savings, real estate, and securities	27.8
b. Federal pensions	1.4
c. State and local pensions	0.8
d. Private pensions	2.2
e. Trade union pensions	0.1
f. Insurance annuities	2.6
g. Other resources	0.2
Dependent, Wholly or Partially	*64.9 per cent*
a. Federal programs	17.7
b. Organized private charity	0.1
c. Public homes and institutions	1.7
d. Private homes for the aged	0.7
e. Other	0.1
f. Friends and relatives	44.6

SOURCE: Marjorie Shearon, "Economic Status of the Aged," *Social Security Bulletin,* March 1938, p. 6, and August 1938, note, p. 7.

Besides these social insurance systems, private employer and union pension programs at the end of 1954 were paying about half a billion dollars in benefits to almost a million—950,000—aged persons, including wives. This constituted between 2 and 3 per cent of the estimated total income of all aged persons.

As a result of these benefit programs, the dependency situation of older persons is not so bad as it once was, and it is apparently tending to be ameliorated. A comparison, for example, of the dependency status in 1937 and in 1951, as shown in Tables 3 and 4, indicates that whereas in the earlier year almost two thirds—64.9 per cent—were wholly or partially dependent, in 1951 only 17.1 per cent of the couples and about 26 per cent of the individual males and females were dependent upon assistance. An increasing proportion of older persons are enjoying the satisfaction of independent status, even though, as we shall see below, their incomes are still low.

We are moving, then, in the direction of freeing older persons from the stigma of dependency on either children or public assistance. When Francis E. Townsend in the 1930's proposed that all persons sixty-five years of age and over be given a flat pension of $200 a month, he was considered by most people to be mad. The amount he asked—$200 a month—may still seem a bit visionary, but "taking the country as a whole, it is estimated that the average worker retiring in the future, and his wife, will receive something more than $100 a month." [17] The principle Townsend argued for is almost established, and the amount accepted as standard may some day approach his $200.

Deterioration of Role as Worker

It is, of course, a great advance when older persons can look forward to insurance and pension benefits upon retirement rather than to dependency status and assistance; but for many it is much better to work than to retire, even with a good income. There is much evidence to show that older workers do not retire if they can help it. Studies by both the Federal Government and by private pension funds show that "beneficiaries prefer to work." [18]

In our society a man's most significant role is that of worker. It is through his job that he relates himself to the world. There is hardly anything more catastrophic to the average man than losing this bond with his fellows. We shall elaborate this point in Chapter 20, but we raise it here because it is of crucial importance in the life of the older members of the population. Because of compulsory retirement or unemployment the older person is likely to be faced with loss of employment and all the attendant traumas. As one student says: "Older persons have insufficient incomes—in part because they do not have jobs. They are isolated, frustrated, and maladjusted—in part because they do not have jobs. They contain the seeds of a restive and irresponsible political group—in part because they do not have jobs. In short, ours is a job-oriented society, and it is not surprising that the whole complex of problems which accompanies aging should be related to the question of job or no job." [19]

Of the 63,000,000 workers in the labor force in 1953, 3,200,000— between 4 and 5 per cent—were sixty-five years of age or over.[20] This included 43 per cent of all men in this age bracket, and 10 per cent of all women. There is estimated to be in the future a downward trend in the proportion of older persons who work; from the 43 per cent of 1953, the decline for men will mean that by 1975 only about 36 or 37 per cent in the sixty-five-and-over age bracket will be in the labor force. For women, the decline is estimated to be much less, from 10 per cent to 9.5 per cent.[21] In 1920, 57 per cent of all men sixty-five or over were working; in 1950 the proportion was 45 per cent. The proportion of older men working has declined, then, from 57 per cent in 1920 to 43 per cent in 1953, and it is estimated that in 1975 it will be only 36 per cent.

In a study by the Bureau of Old-Age and Survivors Insurance, only 5 per cent of retired persons were found to have retired voluntarily. Loss and quitting of jobs because of poor health accounted for most retirements. The United Mine Workers found in the first five years of operation of their pension fund that only 10 per cent of their pensioners had stopped work for reasons other than layoffs or physical disability.[22] And data from the United Automobile Workers, International Ladies Garment Workers Union, and the International Longshoremen's and Warehousemen's Union show the same pattern.[23] One economist has estimated that if workers rather than employers were permitted to determine retirement age under private plans, there would be almost a million and a half more workers in the labor force.[24]

Compulsory Retirement

The setting up of pension and retirement plans illustrates one of the untoward and undesired consequences of social inventions. Although most people would much prefer to continue at their jobs as long as their health permitted, they are required to retire at a given age, and employers feel much less hesitant about forcing retirement when there is a pension plan to salve their conscience. Thus, for example, a University of Minnesota study found that almost all firms that had no pension plans—93 per cent, in fact—kept most or all of their wage workers even when they reached sixty-five and 87 per cent kept most or all of their salaried employees, whereas only 33 per cent of the firms that had pension plans kept their wage workers and only 26 per cent, their salaried employees.[25]

There is other evidence that older workers prefer to work. The Bureau of Old-Age and Survivors Insurance surveyed the work status of persons a year or two after retirement at four intervals of time. In 1940–42, 37 per cent were working; in 1943–44, when labor was in great demand, 55 per cent had work; in 1945–46, only 20 per cent had jobs; and in 1948–49, about 27.4 per cent had employment.[26] The implication is that the labor market, not the workers themselves, determined what proportion would be employed. The conclusion is that we are not making adequate use of the older worker.[27]

For those who hold that more use should be made of the older worker the problem seems to be one of convincing employers to keep their older employees or to hire older workers. An impressive literature on the merits of older workers has been written. One project, surveying the laboratory research on the employability of older persons, finds the results inadequate because of limitations of method. The authors conclude, however, that:

Experimental results indicate that when meeting a new task or performing one which is continually changing, older people tend to be slower at organizing the incoming data and the action taken in response. Where the task is such as to emphasize speed, accuracy may suffer instead, but there seems to be a fairly general tendency for older people to lay more stress on accuracy rather than upon speed.

Differences between individual performances appear to increase with age so that while there may be a substantial change of performance at a task when a group of older people is compared with a group of younger, some older people are likely to be found whose performances at many tasks are similar to those of people very much younger. . . .

The age distributions of those engaged on various classes of operations indicate fairly clearly that older people tend to be found on operations where speed is under their own control, or the main stress is upon accuracy and speed is of secondary importance. . . .

It seems fairly clear that many industrial skills can be maintained to an age far beyond that at which they can be learned at a reasonable speed, at least by the methods of training at present employed.[28]

On the basis of these findings and others like them, one union leader recommends that jobs be redesigned to make maximum use of older workers. Training methods, for example, should make use of past skills and experience. To make up for loss in sensory acuity, sensory stimuli should be magnified. Greater latitude should be permitted older employees to work out their own work patterns. Rest periods and vacations should minimize physical demands. Machines should do jobs demanding fast motion. Jobs requiring accuracy should be among the first redesigned for them. Jobs should take advantage of established skills, in order to maintain continuity in type of work.[29]

Health and the Older Worker

There is, however, a different point of view on this difficult problem. One study, based on a survey made in April 1952, concludes that 77 per cent of the older men are not in the labor force because they do not feel well enough to work. The author of this study feels that ill health and obsolescence, not the prejudice of employers, are the great factors keeping older workers out of the labor force. "A re-employment program could hardly meet the needs of these men or their families." [30]

A tabulation of the health status of older men as related to income level leads this student to the following conclusion:

. . . 74 percent of the men in units without incomes were not well enough to work while only 8 percent of the men in units with incomes of at least $5,000 were not well enough. Between these two limits there is a steady fall in the proportion not well enough to work. Furthermore, the percentage of men well enough to work but not in the labor force . . . does not vary significantly from income bracket to income bracket nor, for that matter, does the proportion of those interested in working but not working [vary from] the total number well enough to work. It is not differences in desire to work, then, which account for differences in labor force participation, but differences in the state of health. And, therefore, except insofar as income affects health, it is not income which determines the rate of labor force participation but rather the other way round: the level of income of the expenditure unit depends predominantly on whether the man is working.[31]

Translated into figures, this author finds that of the more than 3 million males over sixty-five not in the labor force, only about 200,000 want jobs and feel well enough to handle them. But 2,600,000 of these men do not feel well enough to work. This, he considers, is the hard core of the employment problem of the aged, and, he adds, "the various devices which have been suggested for persuading employers to retain older employees do not, in the light of these figures, touch the heart of the problem." [32]

The ill health of the aging population constitutes, therefore, a major social and societal problem of the second half of the 20th century.

Sure it's crowded, but at least you're not alone! There are other men like you around. No one acts as though you're just in the way. There isn't one of us who wouldn't rather be working at a bench or turning a lathe, but they say we're too old . . . .

Many of these men, despite their insistence that they are as well as they ever were, are too ill to work. But some are still capable of turning in a good day's work. Some were arbitrarily retired when they reached the age of sixty-five. Some have been unable to get work for many years.

Modern medicine keeps more and more people alive for a longer and longer period of time. "Old age" is being pushed back. We will soon come to think of men like those playing checkers in the picture above as being merely in late middle age.

The infant population is growing rapidly also, for when young people have good jobs they like to have children, and they do. The very old and the very young constitute the major "dependent classes" of the present time. Until at least the middle of the 1960's these dependent classes will constitute something of a problem, for the working population, those in the age bracket between twenty and sixty-five, will not increase as rapidly as they will. It is estimated, for example, that between 1955 and 1965 the total population will increase one fifth, but the population of working age will increase by only half that amount, and population actually available for gainful employment will increase by only 6 per cent. For the period between 1955 and 1975 population increase is estimated at two fifths, working-age population increase at less than one third, and increase in actual members of the labor force at one fifth. Can we afford to retire able-bodied workers at sixty-five? Can we maintain abundance if we do not conserve their health and ability to work? Can productivity increase more rapidly than population? Can we keep skills from becoming obsolescent with age?

But even if we merely postpone retirement, the time inevitably comes when people have to retire. Are they prepared for the trauma associated with giving up their worker roles? In some homes for the aged, much effort is now devoted to giving retired persons new, less taxing occupations in order to give them a sense of participation in the world.

The social and societal problems associated with the prolongation of life are so new that no precedents exist to help us solve them. And as the composition of the older segments of the population changes, the character of the problems changes also. Pictures like the one above will probably be anachronistic within a generation. *(International News Photo)*

Many older persons, far from being able to work, even intermittently, actually require custodial care. As we saw in Chapter 13, it is in large part because of the great influx of patients with senile dementias that mental hospitals are so overcrowded. But there are other chronic ill- nesses that can have equally devastating effects on the individual's role and status and also on his family. Sometimes family members must give up their own jobs in order to remain home to take care of a chronically ill older person. The result of having to care for such patients at home may be disruptive to the whole family. It has been proposed that insti- tutions be erected to remove this burden from these families.

Even if medical science through geriatrics learns to conquer the chronic illnesses of the later years, all we can reasonably hope for is a postponement of the ultimate ravages of time. Unless we can find a way to create people like the old one-hoss shay the poet tells us about, which ran perfectly until it collapsed, all at once, every part worn out at pre- cisely the same time, we will continue to wear out gradually, and for a large number of people this will mean lingering on for many years in a condition of chronic illness. It may be that more and more people will be able to work until seventy, or even seventy-five, but provision will always have to be made for those whose health does finally give way.

Occupational Degrading of Older Workers

Even among those who are well enough to continue to work, and who are not compelled to retire, the last years in the role of worker may be spent in jobs with lower status than that of earlier jobs.

We pointed out in Chapter 1 that our whole economy has been upgraded and is in process of upgrading many workers. And in the early career of most workers the direction of occupational mobility is upward. But for the older worker the direction of occupational mobility at midcentury is downward.

. . . the older members of the population have not only grown old; they have obsolesced. This is revealed in our survey in two ways. First, the occupational distribution of the older men is strikingly different from that of the entire male population. For example, 31 percent of the older men have farming as their longest or predominant occupation; the comparative figure for the entire male population over 13 years old is 13 percent. A second indi- cation of deterioration or obsolescence of skills is contained in the compari- son of the normal (as indicated by longest) occupation of older men with their last or current occupation. We found that although 39 percent of the older men interviewed gave professional, technical, and skilled trades as their longest occupation, only 33 percent gave such work as their final occupation.

At the same time that the survey revealed that aging was associated with a drift away from skilled occupations, it revealed a drift toward unskilled labor. Thirty percent of our sample give service, farm, and miscellaneous kinds of labor as their longest occupation; 38 percent gave these occupations as their terminal employment. There is a noticeable tendency, then, for the older man to be demoted even before he stops working. His skills become less effective and less valuable. . . .

The older men, in a sense, know the wrong trades. . . . The skills of older men are out of tune with contemporary needs. It seems safe to assume . . . that more refined data would show that many of the older craftsmen have skills for which demand has declined over the years.[33]

The professional and skilled workers tended to shift to service other than household and unskilled labor. But about 14 per cent of the men who spent most of their working lives in more highly paid occupations ended in these two kinds of labor.

There is a more optimistic side to this picture, however. Between half and two thirds of the men remained in their normal occupation until the end of their working careers. And some men did move up, especially professional and technical workers, into the managerial classification. About 12 per cent of the men who were not in professional, technical, managerial, or skilled occupations during the major part of their working lives finally graduated into these classes. We shall have more to say on this subject in the next chapter.

Despite these exceptions, however, "the data . . . show unambiguously . . . that men tend to be demoted to less skilled and less rewarding occupations before the end of their working careers, the signal exception being managerial occupations and proprietorship." [34]

Income

We noted in Chapter 1 that one of the concomitants of abundance is a tendency constantly to raise our standards. Having vastly improved the status of older people from one of dependence to one of independence we are now disturbed because their incomes are so low. There was a time when the almshouse or poor house or old folks' home or county farm—it was equally dispiriting no matter what it was called—was accepted as a matter of course. We relegated old people to it almost without qualms. Today we think that housing should be planned to fit the needs of older people.

The analysis of the lowest fifth of the income structure in Chapters 1 and 3 showed a disproportionate number of persons over sixty-five. For, as a result of unemployment, illness, occupational degrading, and compulsory retirement, the older segment of the population, even when inde-

TABLE 5
PERCENTAGE OF AGED WITH TOTAL RECEIPTS BELOW BUDGET LEVELS, 1951

	PER CENT BELOW		
Consuming Unit	"Emergency" Level *	Cash Equivalent Maintenance †	Total Maintenance ‡
Couples	27–31	39–44	45–50
Unrelated Males	33–36	47–50	52–58
Unrelated Females	50–54	65–69	71–75

* "Emergency" Level, 70 per cent of the cash equivalent budget.

† Cash Equivalent Maintenance, "budgets adjusted to estimate the average cash outlays typically required to provide the goods and services included in the total maintenance budget."

‡ Total Maintenance, see note 35 at end of chapter.

SOURCE: Peter O. Steiner, "The Size, Nature, and Adequacy of the Resources of the Aged," *The American Economic Review*, 44 (May 1954), p. 650.

pendent, is often left with inadequate income. These older persons have changed their status from dependence to independence, but we are no longer satisfied with this improvement. Now we want them not only to be independent but also to have an adequate plane of living.

Thus one student has applied certain yardsticks (based on budget studies for elderly couples developed by the Social Security Administration and the Bureau of Labor Statistics) to the incomes of older persons to see to what extent they came up to certain specified standards. Table 5 shows, as of 1951, the proportion of consumer units that fell below three levels: the emergency level; the "cash equivalent maintenance" level, which is a budget adjusted to take into account the "income value" of home ownership, home-produced foods, and remuneration in kind; and the total maintenance level.[35] It will be noted that a substantial proportion of all the units fell below the emergency level, which was 70 per cent of the cash equivalent level. Many elderly persons, apparently, live on a level far below that considered even minimum for them by current American standards. It is not, we remind ourselves, that they are any worse off than they once were, but that our standards are so much higher. We have no reason to suppose that they were any better housed or fed when they were dependent than they are now. To emphasize this point is in no sense to justify complacency with respect to the status of older persons at midcentury. The dissatisfaction we feel with the low income of older persons is as justified at midcentury as the dissatisfaction which was felt earlier with the care they received as dependents.

The "New" Older Worker

The data here, we remind ourselves, refer to the generation that was "aged" at midcentury. But the changes in the "aged" population of the future, which we pointed out above, will make a considerable difference in the worker role and status of the aged.

All the data we have presented on the aged refer to 1951 (or thereabouts). In an important sense, persons over 65 in 1951 were simply a segment of the American labor force as it existed forty to fifty years earlier, when they entered it. The males in this segment of the labor force, schooled in the first decade of this century, had a median of 8.1 years of schooling and the females, 8.3 (males over 75 had a median of 7.9 years of schooling and females, 8.2 years). Males and females of 20–21 years in 1950 had 12.1 and 12.2 median years of schooling, respectively; these youngsters are very unlikely 45 years from now to be replicas of the present crop of aged. Insofar as his behavior can be predicted from his educational status, the median youngster will be more likely when aged to continue working than his present-day counterpart. Also, his income will be higher relative to the median of all income receivers and will have been higher throughout most of his life.

I do not wish to suggest that, in any given age cohort, aging per se does not affect economic status. But I do wish to point out that the level of income after age 65 is strongly (and positively) associated with its earlier level. Highly educated workers are more likely to stay employed after 65 than others and hence to earn more. . . . Consequently, the general secular rise in educational attainment and the factors associated therewith are likely, of themselves, somewhat to ameliorate . . . conditions. . . .

Comparing interage income variations in a given year exaggerates in an economy such as ours the relative income disadvantage of the aged. Viewed against the background of the 1951 American economy, the economic status of the aged seems far worse than if, say, 1913 or 1929 were chosen as a backdrop; but it is in an economy of this older type that the aged lived most of their lives. In short, the inability of the aged to share equally in the fruits of economic progress, as well as an absolute decline in median real income with age, is responsible for their underprivileged position in the economy.[36]

The Aged as a Minority Group

As a result of all the role and status problems associated with the later years of life at midcentury, the older segment of the population may almost be considered a minority group. It has, like many such groups, visible stigmas which make detection easy, for it is difficult to mask the signs of age. It is definitely discriminated against, not only in employment but also in ordinary social intercourse. For example:

. . . the average oldster is not welcomed in younger groups. Sometimes his conservatism proves irritating, or his failing hearing or eyesight slows down the group movement. Frequently the middle aged have such deep-rooted fears about growing old that the presence of the aged in their social groups is disturbing to them. The result is that a group of their own is often the only place where the aging man and woman can find full social expression and acceptance.[37]

Older persons also resemble minority groups in the low level of their incomes, as we have just seen. And like some minority groups, because of intergenerational differences, they practically have different cultural backgrounds from the rest of the population. There is some tendency also toward residential segregation.[38] And like some minority groups they have tended to resort to political weapons to secure desired goals.[39]

Political Role

The wisdom of older people has traditionally been considered valuable. Even in our own Senate the theory is that, being older, the members will contribute sagacity and will act as a restraining force.

There is some question, however, about the relative amount of weight which the older person's judgment should be accorded in fashioning policy. It has been argued, for example, that with the increasing number of older persons in the voting population, the suffrage should be extended downward to the eighteen-year-olds to serve as a counter-balance. It has been argued that the United States may be at a disadvantage in dealing with other nations which have a more youthful leadership. And in some communities it has been argued that older persons, being property owners and taxpayers, often hold too restraining a hand over the purse strings when it comes to expenditures for schools and recreational facilities for young people.

The tendency for older persons to be conservative—except where their own interests are involved, as in the Townsend movement—has been documented recently in a study of attitudes toward the rights of nonconformists, especially communists. "Younger adults have consistently shown greater tolerance than older adults in public opinion polls on issues such as freedom of the press or free speech." [40] In a sample study of more than 6,000 men and women in all parts of the country and in all walks of life, it was found that "the older generation was less tolerant of non-conformists than the younger generation." [41] Although the higher level of education of the American public will make for greater tolerance in the older age groups in the future, nevertheless, even with the same amount of education, older persons tend to be more conservative than younger persons.

TABLE 6
FACTORS ASSOCIATED WITH HIGH SCORES FOR GOOD ADJUSTMENT IN OLD AGE IN STUDIES BY CAVAN, BY SHANAS, AND BY SCHMIDT

Factor	Category Favorable to Good Adjustment	Studies of Older Persons Cavan *	Shanas †	Schmidt ‡
Age	Less advanced	x		x
Nativity	Native—white	x	x	
Marital status	Married	x	x	x
Family relationships	High score		x	x
Living arrangements	Living with spouse	x	x	x
Friends	More than 25			
Intimate friends	More than 10	x	x	x
Health	Fair or better	x	x	x
Physical problems	Less than 4	x	x	x
Health score	High	x	x	x
Leisure-time activities	Six or more	x	x	
Organizations	Belong to one or more	x	x	x
Activity score	High—20 or more	x	x	x
Church attendance	Once a week or more	x	x	x
Feeling of permanent economic security	Yes		x	x
Age group	Thinks himself middle-aged		x	x
Discriminated against in life	No		x	x
Health compared with 10 years ago	No marked decline		x	x
Social status compared with 10 years ago	Same or upward	x	x	
Evaluation of marriage	Happy	x	x	
Unhappy periods in life	None	x	x	
Future plans	Yes	x	x	x
Belief in after-life	Sure		x	x

* Ruth Shonle Cavan, E. W. Burgess, R. J. Havighurst, and Herbert Goldhamer, *Personal Adjustment in Old Age* (Science Research Associates, 1949).

† Ethel Shanas, *The Personal Adjustment of 388 Cases of Recipients of Old Age Assistance* (Ph.D. thesis, Univ. of Chicago, 1950).

‡ John F. Schmidt, *Patterns of Poor Adjustment in Persons of Later Maturity* (Ph.D. thesis, Univ. of Chicago, 1950).

SOURCE: Ernest W. Burgess, "Personal and Social Adjustment in Old Age," in *The Aged and Society* (Madison, Wis.: Industrial Relations Research Association, 1950), p. 148.

Factors Associated with Good
Adjustment in the Later Years

Provision for independent status and adequate income, while of tremendous importance, is not the only necessity for successful aging. The older person continues to be a human being despite greying hair and faltering step. And, increasingly, recognition is being accorded to the social or role needs of older persons. What are the factors associated with good adjustment in later life?

In 1933 interviews with 170 men and 211 women, all receiving public relief, led to the conclusion that five factors were associated with "good adjustment and happiness, namely: good health, satisfactory social and emotional relations with friends and family, hobbies and out-side interests, living in one's own home, and some form of work or other useful activity." [42] A later study of older rural people in Iowa, including some who were financially independent and some who were financially dependent in status, found good adjustment to be associated with higher educational level, being married and living with spouse, good health, employment, no feeling that work is a burden, activities such as gardening, visiting, hobbies, and church attendance.[43]

The results of three other studies, summarized in Table 6, show that the chief factors associated with good adjustment tend to be good health; maintenance of roles (that is, marital and family relations) and friendships; leisure-time and other activities; membership in at least one organization; absence of discrimination or an unhappy period in life; conception of oneself as middle-aged rather than as elderly, old, or aged; [44] a feeling of permanent economic security; no lowered social status; plans for the future; church attendance; and belief in an after-life.[45]

Many of these factors associated with successful adjustment in the later years are expected to have an increased incidence in the future. More older persons, for example, will be native-born. As we keep peo-ple alive longer, married status will continue to a more advanced age. Health will presumably be better, at least until the very old age levels. Permanent economic security will be fostered by various kinds of an-nuities and pensions. As more people reach the older age levels there will be more friends available to them from among their own genera-tion. There will also be more organizations geared to the pace of older persons. In general, then, we may expect, on the basis of conditions now existing, that the adjustment problems of those in the older age brackets will tend to be mitigated. What will probably happen, however, is that the problems will merely be delayed, so that we will come to think of those in the sixty-five to seventy-five age bracket as in their later middle age; the "aged" will then be those in their late seventies and eighties.

NOTES

1 This discussion of "generations" is based on Rudolf Heberle, *Social Movements* (Appleton-Century-Crofts, 1951), pp. 118 ff. His discussion in turn is based on the work of François Mentre, *Les Générations Sociales* (Paris, 1920), pp. 186 ff.; Willy Hellpach, *Sozialpsychologie* (Stuttgart, 1946), p. 109; and Karl Mannheim, "Das Problem der Generationen," *Kölner Vierteljahreshefte für Soziologie* (7 Jahrg., Heft 2, Heft 3, 1938), p. 311.

2 Heberle, *op. cit.*, p. 118.

3 Robert Dorfman, "Economic Problems of the Aged: The Labor Force Status of Persons Aged Sixty-Five and Over," *The American Economic Review,* 44 (May 1954), pp. 637–638.

4 Thirty-nine per cent of one sample of men studied gave professional, technical, and skilled trades as their longest occupation; but only 33 per cent gave such work as their final occupation. For most of the occupations there was a demotion even before retirement.

5 Robert C. Cook, "Life Grows Longer," *Population Bulletin,* 11 (Dec. 1955), pp. 113, 110.

6 Quoted in *Family Life,* July 1955, p. 7.

7 Dr. Irving Lorge, before Gerontological Society, reported in *New York Times,* October 29, 1955.

8 Zena S. Blau, "Changes in Status and Age Identification," *American Sociological Review,* 21 (April 1956), pp. 199, 201.

9 A. J. Jaffe and R. O. Carleton, *Occupational Mobility in the United States, 1930–1960* (Columbia Univ. Press, 1955), p. 11.

10 Elizabeth E. Hoyt *et al., American Income and Its Use* (Harper, 1954), pp. 237–238.

11 *Ibid.,* p. 232.

12 *Ibid.,* p. 275.

13 J. F. Dewhurst *et al., America's Needs and Resources: A New Survey* (Twentieth Century, 1955), p. 451.

14 "Federal Security Program for the Aged," Chamber of Commerce of the United States, Referendum No. 93.

15 Dewhurst *et al., op. cit.,* p. 447.

16 Lenore Epstein, "Economic Resources of Persons Aged 65 and Over," *Social Security Bulletin,* June 1955, p. 19.

17 United States Department of Health, Education, and Welfare, Committee on Aging, "Aging, A Community Responsibility and Opportunity," p. 8.

18 *Social Security Bulletin,* January 1951, p. 15.

19 Robert Dorfman, *loc. cit.,* p. 635.

20 *Current Population Reports,* Series P-57, No. 128, U.S. Bureau of the Census, March 20, 1953.

21 *Current Population Reports, Labor Force,* Series P-50, No. 42, U.S. Bureau of the Census, December 10, 1952.

22 United Mine Workers of America, "Welfare and Retirement Fund, Report for the Year Ended June 30, 1952," Washington, D. C., p. 6.

23 Glenn W. Miller, "The Effect of Social Security on Manpower Resources," in William Haber, F. H. Harbison, L. R. Klein, and Vivian Palmer, *Manpower in the United States; Problems and Policies* (Harper, 1954), p. 54.

24 S. K. Slichter, "Retirement Age and Social Policy," in *The Aged and Society* (Madison, Wis.: Industrial Relations Research Association, 1950), p. 106.

25 H. Fox, "Utilization of Older Manpower," *Harvard Business Review,* November 1951, p. 43. See Jessie Bernard, *American Community Behavior* (Dryden, 1949), pp. 625–626, for another illustration of how provision for the older population had unforeseen repercussions.

26 Miller, *op. cit.,* pp. 58–59.

27 *Ibid.,* p. 59.

28 A. T. Welford and D. Speakman, "The Employability of Older People," in *The Aged and Society* (Madison, Wis.: Industrial Relations Research Association, 1950), pp. 200–201.

29 Solomon Barkin, "Job Redesign: A Technique for an Era of Full Employment,"

in Haber *et al.*, *Manpower in the United States; Problems and Policies* (Harper, 1954), pp. 48–49.

30 Dorfman, *loc. cit.*, p. 635.

31 *Ibid.*, p. 642.

32 *Ibid.*, p. 644.

33 *Ibid.*, pp. 635–636, 637–638, 639.

34 *Ibid.*, p. 639.

35 "The maintenance level is a level . . . that supplies for aged persons all those bare necessities of simple living customary among persons used to low incomes. There are few comforts, except . . . as energy, resourcefulness, and good management make pleasant and comfortable living possible out of bare necessities. The budget does not allow for saving. . . . It does not provide for emergencies of any kind or for major illness. . . . The budgets represent not an optimum level, but rather one below which aged persons could hardly be said to have a minimum of security." (Florence A. Armstrong, *Cost of Living for Aged Persons*, Federal Security Agency, Social Security Board Bureau Memorandum, No. 53, Oct. 1943.)

36 Melvin W. Reder, "Age and Income," *The American Economic Review*, 44 (May 1954), pp. 669–670.

37 James H. Woods, *Helping Older People Enjoy Life* (Harper, 1953), pp. 1–2.

38 Ruth Shonle Cavan, "Old Age in a City of 100,000," *Illinois Academy of Science, Transactions*, 40 (1947), pp. 156–159.

39 Lloyd H. Fisher, "The Politics of Age," in *The Aged and Society* (Madison, Wis.: Industrial Relations Research Association, 1950), pp. 157–167.

40 Samuel A. Stouffer, *Communism, Conformity, and Civil Liberties: A Cross-Section of the Nation Speaks Its Mind* (Doubleday, 1955), p. 105.

41 *Ibid.*, p. 107.

42 Christine M. Morgan, "The Attitudes and Adjustments of Recipients of Old Age Assistance in Upstate and Metropolitan New York," *Archives of Psychology*, No. 214 (1937).

43 Judson T. Landis, *Attitudes and Adjustments of Aged Rural People in Iowa* (Unpublished Ph.D. thesis, Louisiana State Univ., 1940).

44 A study of 499 men and 759 women, with median ages of 73.5 and 71.7 years respectively, showed that few of them regarded themselves as "old" or "aged." Of those 60–64 years of age, 54.2 per cent of the men and 66.6 per cent of the women considered themselves "middle-aged." Not until the seventies did they consider themselves "elderly." But even in the 80–84 bracket, only half of the men (51.6 per cent) and women (51.5 per cent) admitted being either "old" or "aged." Even among those in their nineties, less than 40 per cent considered themselves "aged." (Ernest W. Burgess, "Personal and Social Adjustment in Old Age," in *The Aged and Society* [Madison, Wis.: Industrial Relations Research Association, 1950], pp. 148–149.)

45 *Ibid.*, p. 147.

20

Problems Associated with
Worker Roles at
Midcentury

The Significance of Worker Roles
for Society as a Whole

Worker roles share equally with family roles in importance and significance both for society as a whole and for individuals. We shall elaborate below the importance of worker roles for individuals, but at this point we call attention to the importance of worker role performance for society as a whole. Aside from the fact that the very survival of a society depends on at least a minimum standard of performance of worker roles, and abundance, on a fairly high standard of performance, all the problems we have discussed so far are in some way related to worker roles. Illness and handicap, for example, are problems for the social order in part because they interfere with worker role performance. We saw in Chapters 15 and 16 how intimately worker roles are related to family roles for both men and women. We saw that

The Significance of Worker Roles for Society as a Whole

Industrial Workers Then and Now

Unemployment, the Great Role Destroyer

Underemployment: The Low-Income Farmer

The Status Problems of Workers in the 20th Century

it is through his role as worker that the husband and father serves as a link between the family and the total social order, so that anything which prevents him from performing his role as worker may have serious consequences for his family and hence for the community as well. We saw that among the most serious societal problems at the present time are those which center about the worker role of young people and of older people. And we shall see later some of the hazards which minority groups face because of discrimination against them as workers. It is because of the significance of the worker role for society as well as for the individual that the problems related to its performance warrant discussion here. We shall limit ourselves for the most part to consideration of male workers during their participation in the labor force since we have already discussed the worker-role problems of women (Chap. 15), of young people (Chap. 17), and of older persons (Chap. 19), and will refer to those of minority groups below (Chap. 22).

The problems associated with work vary from occupation to occupation, from status to status, from industry to industry. Only a generalized and over-simplified statement is possible here. We shall discuss first some of the changes which have virtually transformed the labor force over the last half century. Then we shall turn to a consideration of perhaps the most serious problem a worker has to face, unemployment, which destroys worker roles; and, finally, we shall give some attention to the several status problems of workers today.

Industrial Workers Then and Now

From "toiling masses" to "labor force," from "labor problems" to "manpower policies"—embodied in these contrasting terms lies a complete redefinition of the role of the worker and a reassessment of his status in the 20th century. As a result of a variety of changes—organizational, legislative, demographic, and technological—we have for the most part today a middle-class working population. It is no longer easy at midcentury to distinguish a group of blue-collar workers in street clothes from a group of business or professional men. Fewer and fewer workers show the stigmas of hard physical labor in their posture, skin, and general bodily condition. The leaders of unions in the middle of the 20th century are not the rugged fighters of the 19th century and early 20th century, but rather administrators or bureaucrats. Many of them have had college training, and those who have not are surrounded by advisers who have. On the television screen the union leader and the corporation vice-president with whom he is bargaining look very much the same so far as status symbols are concerned. This near transformation in the working force may be traced in part to the efforts of workers themselves and in part to certain changes which have taken place in our society and economy.

Organizational Changes

It took workers a long time to devise the best way to organize for their own welfare. The kind of organization we are familiar with—the union—seems so appropriate now that it is hard to believe it did not come into being spontaneously in its present form. But workers experimented a long time—and still are experimenting—before the union, as we know it today, was developed.

When workers first began to organize they fought for everything.

Since there seemed to be so many social evils in the early 19th century, they wanted to reform on a grand scale. Reforms ranging from mechanics' liens to the abolition of imprisonment for debt and provision for public school education were called for. As the century progressed, however, the objectives of workers came to be restricted to the rights to organize into unions and to bargain collectively rather than individually. They wanted, in effect, to add up their low individual statuses in order to reach the level of those with whom they had to bargain. After almost a century of trial-and-error tactics, American skilled workers hit upon the nonpolitical, craft type of "business unionism." This was a system of securing gains by their own economic power, especially the power inherent in the strike, not by means of political action or by means of legislation, which, indeed, they opposed. Some notable gains were achieved for the skilled worker. The policy of limiting political action to that of supporting candidates of either party who promised them most, seemed successful. So far as the skilled worker was concerned, the craft union was highly beneficial.

But for the millions of unskilled workers, the craft union was no solution. In 1935 the industrial type of union, more suitable for mass industries, was given great impetus by the formation of the Committee for Industrial Organization—later the Congress of Industrial Organizations—and by new federal legislation. Millions of unskilled workers—in the steel industry, in the automobile industry, in the rubber industry, among others—came to share the protection of unions and the benefits of their leadership.

Legislative Changes

There still remained millions of unorganized workers—always in the majority—skilled as well as unskilled for whom the union approach was not feasible. They needed protection by legislation, since they could not get it by union organization. Many states had experimented with legislation to protect labor—we have already referred to it in connection with women workers and will refer to it again below—but it was not until the 1930's that federal legislation was enacted setting wage-rate minimums and hour ceilings for all workers whose work passed in interstate commerce. Although many workers remained unprotected, a large and increasing number came under some kind of legislative protection.

In the second third of the 20th century the strategy of organized labor had changed from one opposed to legislation to one favoring it, especially legislation which protected the principle of labor organization, as did the National Labor Relations Act of 1936. The legal status of workers came to approach that of employers. Some people argued that it exceeded that of employers. Labor legislation and union efforts in the second half of the 20th century began to aim at keeping the legal status of union and employer roughly equal.

Demographic Changes

Workers today are no longer recruited to so large an extent as formerly from recent immigrants or from newly arrived persons from rural areas. They do not, therefore, have the handicap of foreignness, of strangeness. They are no longer Wops, Dagos, Bohunks, or Polacks. (The special case of the Negroes, the Puerto Ricans, and the Mexicans will be discussed in Chap. 22.) They have, furthermore, as we have already seen, had more years of schooling. More important, they do not have a tradition of docility. At midcentury workers in the South still retained the rural attitude toward work, one which concentrated on the job to be done rather than, as in a working force with a longer urban industrial tradition, on the job as a pawn in labor-management relations. Their rural work attitudes rendered them more docile, but this was expected to change as industrialization continued.[1] Workers today are demographically different from workers in the 19th century.

Occupational Changes

And, finally, because of the continuing technological revolution workers today are a more skilled class than they used to be; and their skills are different, more demanding. One of the most spectacular changes in the labor force is in its socioeconomic composition, even from 1910 on, as shown in Table 1. The proportion of white-collar workers almost doubled between 1910 and 1950, from 21.1 per cent of the working force to 38.2 per cent.[2] Professional and semiprofessional workers increased in that time from 4.4 per cent to 7.6 per cent, while the proportion of clerks and kindred workers rose from 10.2 per cent to 19.7 per cent. The proportion of laborers, on the other hand, declined. Farm laborers were less than a third as frequent in the economy of 1950 as in that of 1910—4.1 per cent as contrasted with 14.5 per cent. Skilled workers remained a fairly constant proportion, but the number of semiskilled workers increased, while that of unskilled workers declined.

The Census Bureau observed that "the social-economic status of the nation's labor force was rising rather rapidly from 1910 to 1940. The trend was definitely upward—definitely away from heavy, arduous, unskilled manual labor, and definitely toward more highly skilled manual pursuits and intellectual pursuits." Technological advances, which have made physical toil easier and contributed to the shift from production to distribution and service activities, the drift of women into gainful work and the spread of education all help to account for this upward trend in the social-economic composition of the labor force.[3]

TABLE 1
OCCUPATIONAL DISTRIBUTION, 1910–1950

Occupation	1910	1920	1930	1940	1950
NONAGRICULTURAL, TOTAL	69.0	75.2	79.0	82.8	88.1
White collar, total	21.1	25.6	29.9	31.3	38.2
Professional and semiprofessional workers	4.4	5.0	6.1	6.5	7.6
Proprietors, managers, and officials	6.5	6.8	7.5	7.6	10.9
Clerks and kindred workers	10.2	13.8	16.3	17.2	19.7
Manual, total	47.9	49.6	49.1	51.5	49.9
Skilled workers and foremen	11.7	13.5	12.9	11.7	12.8
Semiskilled and unskilled workers, total	36.2	36.1	36.2	39.8	37.1
Semiskilled workers	14.7	16.1	16.4	21.0	27.4 *
Unskilled workers	21.5	20.0	19.8	18.8	9.7 *
AGRICULTURAL, TOTAL	31.0	24.9	21.0	17.2	11.9
Farmers, owners, and tenants	16.5	15.5	12.4	10.1	7.8
Farm laborers	14.5	9.4	8.6	7.1	4.1

* From Ewan Clague, "Labor Force," *Scientific American*, 185 (Sept. 1951), p. 41.
SOURCE: A. J. Jaffe and Charles D. Stewart, *Manpower Resources and Utilization: Principles of Working Force Analysis* (Wiley, 1951), p. 190.

We may take the chemical industry as a case in point. The brief interval between 1947 and 1954 saw the ratio of production employees to professional, supervisory, clerical, and sales personnel decline from one half to only one third. And this upgrading of the labor force is likely to continue. Table 2 shows the occupational distribution in the labor force of males aged fifteen to seventy-four, for the period from 1930 to 1960. A range is presented for 1960, depending on the number of young men in military service, the first figure assuming few, the second, more.

In 1960, if conditions resemble those of 1940, there will be proportionately only half as many laborers as there were in 1930, and less than half as many farm laborers. Even if conditions resemble those of the depression year 1930, the proportion of laborers will be considerably less than in 1930. Conversely, the proportion of professional and technical workers in 1960 will be three fourths greater than in 1930. Continued upgrading of the economy seems inevitable. And automation, to be described below, is likely to accelerate it greatly.

As a result of all these changes, the workers who face management today are very different from those of the 19th and early 20th century.

TABLE 2

PERCENTAGE DISTRIBUTION OF MALE WORKING FORCE
BY OCCUPATION, 1930–1960

| Occupation | 1930 | 1940 | 1950 | 1960 Projections | | | |
| | | | | Based on 1930's Experience | | Based on 1940's Experience | |
				A *	A' †	B *	B' †
Professional, technical, and kindred workers	4.6	5.7	7.3	7.9	8.0	8.3	8.3
Farmers and farm managers	15.1	13.0	10.0	9.4	9.4	8.1	8.1
Managers, officials, and proprietors, except farm	9.6	8.7	10.3	9.3	9.4	11.1	11.3
Clerical and kindred workers	5.6	5.9	6.5	6.1	6.1	6.6	6.5
Sales workers	5.7	6.0	6.3	6.4	6.4	6.5	6.5
Craftsmen, foremen, and kindred workers	16.4	15.3	19.1	17.4	17.5	21.3	21.4
Operatives and kindred workers	15.5	18.4	20.7	21.6	21.6	21.2	21.2
Service workers	4.8	6.1	6.2	6.9	6.9	5.9	5.9
Farm laborers and foremen	9.4	8.3	4.9	5.9	5.7	4.3	4.1
Laborers except farm and mine	13.3	12.6	8.7	9.1	9.0	6.7	6.7
All occupations	100.0	100.0	100.0	100.0	100.0	100.0	100.0

* A and B based on assumption of few young men in military service.
† A' and B' based on assumption of many young men in military service.
SOURCE: A. J. Jaffe and R. O. Carleton, *Occupational Mobility in the United States 1930–1960* (Columbia Univ. Press, 1955), p. 11.

The Changing Definition of Management's Role

Because roles are always units in systems, changes in the definition of one role must be accompanied by changes in the definition of complementary roles. The representatives of management who deal with modern workers are quite as different today from those of the 19th and early 20th century as are the men they deal with. A wide range of responsibilities has been incorporated into the management role. From the role definition of the boss as an autocrat with no responsibilities toward the worker, to a role definition which includes an obligation to bargain with representatives of workers' organizations, responsibility for unemployment, for retirement, and in some cases even for recreation and family counseling, the role of management has come a long way in the 20th century.

Unemployment, the Great Role Destroyer

The Significance of Worker Roles for the Individual

Different as the modern worker is from his predecessor, he shares with him the terrible, haunting fear of unemployment. In a society where personality is organized around work, where a worker depends on his job for his very ties to the world, where his ability to perform his role as provider in the family rests on his job, anything that threatens that job is a catastrophe, not only economically but almost every other way as well.

Numerous studies by economists and sociologists have documented the tremendous dependence of workers on their jobs to give meaning to their lives. Take away a man's work and he feels isolated, frustrated, lost. His personality becomes disturbed. He loses "face" with his wife and children, no matter how hard they may try to protect him, especially if they can and do get jobs. Family relationships become strained. If unemployment lasts a long time bills pile up. Mortgages fall due. Installment payments cannot be made. Stress factors accumulate. The man's status rapidly deteriorates.[4]

Even when adequate income is provided by means of unemployment compensation, unemployment is very disturbing. Thus a recent study of the meaning of work among a national sample of employed men reports that:

. . . for most men having a job serves other functions than the one of earning a living. In fact, even if they had enough money to support themselves they would still want to work. Working gives them a feeling of being tied into the larger society, of having something to do, of having a purpose in life. These other functions which working serves are evidently not seen as available in non-work activities.

This finding that work has other meanings is consistent with observations of the effect of retirement and the effect of unemployment on men. If men work only for money, there is no way of explaining the degree of dislocation and deprivation which retirement, even on an adequate salary, appears to bring to the formerly employed. The particularly interesting results of this national sample study on the meaning of working are: (1) that working is more than a means to an end for the vast majority of employed men; (2) that a man does not have to be at the age of retirement or be immediately threatened by unemployment to be able to imagine what not working would mean to him; and (3) that working serves other functions than an economic one for men in both middle-class and working-class occupations, but that the non-monetary functions served by working are somewhat different in these two broad classifications of occupations. . . . To the typical man in a middle-class occupation, working means having a purpose, gaining a sense of accomplishment, expressing himself. He feels that not working would leave him aimless and without opportunities to contribute. To the typical man in a working-class occupation working means having something to do. He feels that not working would leave him no adequate outlet for physical activity; he would just be sitting or lying around. To the typical farmer, just as to the typical individual in a working-class occupation, working means keeping busy, keeping occupied. But work has a much more pervasive importance for the farmer. The boundaries between work and home life are not as sharp for him, and life without work is apt to be difficult to consider. . . .

It is through the producing role that most men tie into society, and for this reason and others, most men find the producing role important for maintaining their sense of well-being.[5]

Economists differ in their definitions of unemployment, but in general it refers to a situation in which a person is willing and able to work but cannot find a job. The people who are unemployable—the physically or mentally ill, the deteriorated alcoholic or narcotics addict, the psychopathic personality, the demoralized—are in a separate category. We discussed them in some detail in Part IV. The unemployed, as contrasted with these unemployables, are considered to be able to work, although the definition of "employable" varies with the requirements of the market. When there is a great demand for labor, employers find many persons "employable" whom they would reject if they had a wider choice. And, as we saw in Chapter 9, jobs may be redesigned so that persons formerly considered unemployable become employable.

Widespread unemployment passes all tests for a social and societal problem. It causes suffering; it costs taxpayers money; and it is dysfunctional to the *status quo,* often even to the whole social system. During the great depression of the 1930's, the *status quo* in all the affected nations of the world suffered; and in some—most notably in Germany —the whole social structure itself became a casualty.

Trends and Incidence

The long-time trend in employment, as we shall see presently, is upward so far as proportion of people in the labor force is concerned; but there are ups and downs so far as unemployment is concerned. There are no adequate statistics on the extent of unemployment before 1940, but there are estimates which run from 1900 to 1929. In 1908 and 1914, according to these estimates, between 5 and 7 per cent of the labor force was unemployed; in 1921, 11 per cent; in 1924, 4.5 per cent; and in 1927, 3.5 per cent.[6] These figures should be evaluated in light of the fact that when unemployment goes above 5 per cent it is considered dangerous.

Another series of estimates of unemployment for later years shows: 24.9 per cent in 1933; 14.3 per cent in 1937; 19.0 per cent in 1938; and 14.6 per cent as late as 1940. The demand for workers during the war reduced the figure to 1.2 per cent in 1944; demobilization increased it to 3.9 per cent in 1946; it reached 5.5 per cent in 1949; it fell to 5 per cent in 1950,[7] and below 3 per cent in 1955.

Unemployment is most likely to occur among unskilled workers. The next most vulnerable are operatives in factories, mines, and service industries. Less likely to be affected are clerical workers and salesmen. Proprietors, farmers, and professional persons are least likely to be affected. Workers in the construction and mining industries are very liable to unemployment; those in trade, transportation, communication, and government are less liable. Factory workers are in between.

In addition to this differential incidence by occupation and by industry, there is also a differential incidence by sociological characteristics. Even in times and in areas of high employment there are always some people who are unemployed. Who are they? What are they like? Why do they remain unemployed? What is there about them that makes them "unemployment-prone"?

A study of workers who received their tenth consecutive benefit check under the California Unemployment Insurance Act during the six-week period extending from November 24, 1947, to January 2, 1948, throws some light on this question. It found, for example, that they were unemployed in part because of something in their personalities and in part because of biases in the outside world.

It appears that the barriers to really full employment are both social and economic. They are social in that some part of the barriers undoubtedly stems from prevailing social attitudes toward segments of the population. This is probably most true in the case of the nonwhite worker and the aging worker, as well as in the case of women to a lesser extent.

The barriers are economic to the extent that the record of educational attainment, past work history and acquired skills indicates personal limitations in the performance of all but certain types of work. While the social attitudes previously mentioned may explain some of the prevalence of service and unskilled workers in our sample (especially among nonwhite and women workers), it is probable that mental, physical and temperamental limitations were present as well. Whatever the causes, it remains true that the pool of unemployed existing at high levels of employment was far from a random sample of the labor force as a whole.

On the basis of the evidence, the problem of making use of the marginal worker in the labor force seems to have two aspects. One part of the problem stems from what appears to be the existence of bias among the population as a whole toward the segments of the labor force found to be most prevalent in the fringe group—the nonwhite worker, the older worker and perhaps the woman worker. The other part of the problem stems from the distribution of work experience, skills, and possibly attitudes among the marginal workers themselves. It is certain that these two problems are interrelated to an unknown but probably substantial extent. In the individual cases where both social and economic barriers are operative, the elimination of either one singly would be of little value.

It seems probable that, in addition to social and economic "marginality," a third type exists. Some part of the unemployed are probably "marginal" in their attachment to the labor force. During all periods, but particularly during periods of high employment, some workers are lured into the labor market by a combination of good wages, abundant and convenient job opportunities and a relaxation of standards of performance. They operate in the labor market in a limited sense in that they are interested in particular types of work, in particular areas at particular time periods. . . . It is unlikely that a group of this type represented a major part of the total problem. . . .

The social and economic character of the problem of the unemployed-at-high-levels-of-employment has long been suspected and various remedies have been proposed. . . . In the absence of compulsion, the problem of eliminating unemployment . . . must include positive procedures involving the manipulation of social attitudes and the provision of training opportunities for considerable segments of the labor force.[8]

The most vulnerable workers, so far as unemployment is concerned, are those in whom are combined age, sex, racial, and industrial handicaps.

Those who have the least job security and the lowest paid jobs are under 25 or over 45 years of age; they are women and not of the white race; they are the casual and, especially the migratory, agricultural laborers. The least fortunately situated of all would be a person who combined these employment handicaps; on the other hand, the most fortunate would be a middle-aged white man working in a stable and expanding industry. Improvement of average levels of living depends on many developments, but among them looms large the diminution of handicaps arising from age, sex, race, and casual nature of employment.[9]

It will be noted that unemployment may be caused by social attitudes as well as by personal handicaps. But it may also be caused by forces quite independent of the individual worker or employer, by forces in the economy as a whole, unrelated to the individual himself or to his employer. For not all unemployment is identical in incidence, in extent, in duration, or in seriousness.

Kinds of Unemployment

Several kinds of unemployment have been distinguished, namely: transitional, that is, the unemployment which is often unavoidable between jobs; intergenerational, that is, the unemployment attendant upon the entrance into the labor force of young persons and upon the exit of those who are leaving it; seasonal unemployment, which is self-explanatory; cyclical unemployment; and technological unemployment. Transitional unemployment—involving about 2 or 3 per cent of the labor force at any particular time—is not a serious social or societal problem in times of high employment. Intergenerational unemployment we referred to in connection with youth and age. Seasonal unemployment can be mitigated by planning and by diversification, so that plant and equipment can be used for one purpose in winter and another in summer. Cyclical and technological unemployment pose the most serious problems, and we therefore discuss them in some detail. In addition to the above-named kinds of unemployment there is also the unemployment which results in so-called distressed areas when industries leave a community, taking jobs with them, or in certain industries which find themselves caught in technological or economic traps. We shall have a word to say of this also.

CYCLICAL UNEMPLOYMENT

THE EMPLOYMENT OF MEN AND MACHINES. It is quite true that through the creation of new goods and services technology in the 19th century made abundance possible. But technology is not a sentient being, with a will of its own, able to make decisions about its own use. There was nothing inevitable or automatic about abundance. Modern technology is productive only when the machines are working; abundance is not created by keeping them idle. Machines create wealth only when they are being used. And the decision to use them is a human one. It is not something that occurs as a matter of course. It is based on judgments, and these judgments in turn are based on ideologies and complex motivations. It is conceivable that technology might not be associated with abundance at all. It is conceivable that the use of technology might have been institutionalized on a start-and-stop basis, periods of unemployment alternating with periods of employment. If that had been the case technology would not have produced abundance; the economy of scarcity would have persisted in spite of technology. But the development of the mass market—usually attributed to Henry Ford —and the growing understanding of how a modern economy functions best—usually attributed to J. M. Keynes—have led to the institutionalization of the use of technology on a continually expanding basis rather than on a start-and-stop basis. The goal is to keep men and machines at work all the time.

The new technology, then, would not have been so enormously productive if it had not been guided by certain ideological principles. But these principles had to be learned and the tuition fee was high.

In the 19th century the accumulation of capital necessary for a modern industrial order was produced by the labor of workers. Very little of the new wealth went to them in the form of wages, just as little of the wealth created in the Soviet Union in the 20th century has gone to the worker in the form of consumer goods. It was only with the development of the mass market in the 20th century—itself an economic rather than a technological development, although technology made it possible—that the basic principle of modern, as contrasted with 19th-century, capitalism emerged. As we pointed out in Chapter 1, it became clear that the tremendous productivity of a modern economy depended on wide distribution of the goods it created. Unless there were enough buyers to take the goods produced off the market, the machines—in a profit-motivated economy—stopped. Unemployment ensued. Such stoppages in the economy have tended to come in cycles, and the unemployment which accompanies them is therefore called cyclical unemployment. We speak of such periods of unemployment of men and stoppage of machines as depressions.[10]

They are profoundly disturbing traumas to people and to institutions. The depression of the 1930's, indeed, created a crisis of such magnitude as to require a total reassessment of the role of worker and of the functions of government and of industry. The suffering of workers and their families has been documented in great detail. As a result the conviction crystallized that unemployment on such an unprecedented scale must never be permitted to occur again. This conviction was based, in part, on humanitarian ideals of long standing; later it was re-enforced by the Cold War. The USSR made no secret of the fact that it was waiting for a great depression with widespread unemployment to give capitalism its *coup de grâce*. Here was a challenge to American industry and to the American government.

GOVERNMENT RESPONSIBILITY. The challenge was answered by the assumption of responsibility by the Federal Government in the form of two pieces of legislation—the Social Security Act of 1935, which guaranteed income maintenance, and the Full Employment Act of 1946, which pledged the government to maintain employment.

Social Security Legislation. The Social Security Act of 1935 made provision for compensation to workers when they became unemployed. During the first 20 years of its operation it increased the number of persons covered from 19,900,000 to 41,000,000, and amendments are constantly being added to increase the number of persons protected, the amount of help they receive, and the length of time they are entitled to receive it. In the 1950's, furthermore, unions were beginning to win from industry the "guaranteed annual wage" which meant that industry would, in times of unemployment, add enough to what the worker received in unemployment compensation to bring his income up to about three fourths of his regular annual wage.

All this was to the good, so far as the worker was concerned. But it was recognized that social security legislation was only a palliative. It did not get to the heart of the problem. Unemployment payments, no matter how generous, are in no sense a substitute for a regular job, as we saw above. Even when they know that there will be money to pay the grocery bills, men still look with horror at the prospect of extended unemployment. Men must have more than bread alone.

The Full Employment Act of 1946. In 1946, therefore, a second answer was proposed in the Full Employment Act, which states that it is the policy of the United States to recognize the right of all Americans able and willing to work to "useful, remunerative, regular, and full-time employment" and to "ensure at all times the existence of sufficient employment opportunities to enable all Americans . . . freely to exercise that right," and that if private enterprise cannot, "it is the further responsibility of the Federal Government to provide such volume of Federal investments and expenditures as may be needed to assure continuing full employment." [11] This principle that "full employment"—at the present time unemployment at the rate of more than five per cent of the working force is considered dangerous—is a responsibility of the state is almost as revolutionary as the principles underlying social security legislation. It is, in effect, an effort to guarantee abundance and to protect the worker role of millions of people.

The objectives of public policy at midcentury, as embodied in the two laws just described, as well as in others, and in administrative procedures, have been summarized as follows:

1. To maintain a high-level employment which can provide job opportunities for all those willing and able to work.

2. To build and maintain a stable work force which is, at the same time, sufficiently mobile to adapt to the changing needs of a dynamic economy.

3. To utilize the labor force efficiently through proper matching of jobs with people, effective management, and the appropriate education, training, and development of people, and thus to raise the productivity of labor and the general standard of living throughout the nation.

4. To provide reasonable security against the hazards of illness, unemployment, disability, and old age.

5. To preserve and enhance the freedom, dignity, and worth of the individual both as a member of the labor force and as a citizen.

6. To provide the proper and necessary distribution of manpower between our armed forces and civilian work forces in order to maintain adequate national defense and a healthy economy.[12]

Items 4 and 5, it will be noted, are specifically related to the definition of the worker's role and preservation of his status.

It has, in brief become established governmental policy that it is a responsibility of the state not only to maintain income by social security programs but also to protect worker roles by keeping the machines in operation when private industry cannot do so. Whether or not we can actually keep men and machines producing at all times is by no means certain, for our situation in an economy based on modern technology is like that of a man driving a vehicle whose mechanism he understands only vaguely and imperfectly over unknown terrain with limited visibility. From time to time the vehicle begins to grind to a halt, but the causes may be different in every instance, so that although we can learn to avoid the things which produced the last breakdown we cannot always avoid the things which will produce the next one. The hope is that by the time the next major hazard begins to loom threateningly— a marked decline, for example, in the birth rate—we will know enough about the functioning of the economy to deal with it adequately. At any rate the principle has been established that both men and machines must be kept employed.

TECHNOLOGICAL UNEMPLOYMENT

IN THE PAST. In addition to cyclical unemployment there is what is known as technological unemployment, or the unemployment which results when skills are rendered obsolete by machines. From the beginning of the Industrial Revolution, workers have met the introduction of new machines with fear and hostility; at first they even attempted to destroy the new machines.

In Great Britain the new machinery aroused resistance among the workers it displaced. The introduction of the spinning jenny in 1767 was accompanied by a series of riots; in 1779 mobs of infuriated men sacked and burned the factories of Arkwright, the inventor of the water frame. Between 1811 and 1816 the famous Luddites conducted a well organized campaign of machine smashing in all parts of the country. At Blackburn in 1826 more than a thousand power looms were destroyed in three days as a protest against the factory system, under which half the town was living on public charity. In Germany the Silesian weavers rose in revolt in 1844 against the machine, and similar uprisings followed in Saxony and other districts.[13]

As a matter of fact, however, the increasing use of new technologies has benefited, not harmed, the workers. It has had no over-all effect on employment of men, but it has increased employment of women. These facts are indicated in the figures given in Table 3, which shows what proportion of persons fourteen years of age and over were in the labor force from 1890 to 1950.

TABLE 3
PERCENTAGE OF PERSONS FOURTEEN YEARS OF AGE AND OVER IN THE LABOR FORCE

Year	Total	Male	Female
1890	52.2	84.3	18.3
1900	55.0	87.7	20.4
1920	54.3	84.4	22.7
1930	54.5	84.1	24.3
1940	55.2	82.6	27.9
1950	57.5	83.7	32.1

SOURCE: A. J. Jaffe and Charles D. Stewart, *Manpower Resources and Utilization: Principles of Working Force Analysis* (Wiley, 1951), p. 164.

This does not mean that there are not pockets of unemployment resulting from the substitution of machines for men. The deleterious effects are likely to be especially great if such innovations coincide with cyclical unemployment. Thus one study showed that of 1,190 rubber workers laid off in 1929, 13 per cent were still unemployed after eleven months; and of those who did find work, two thirds were earning less—in some cases 50 per cent less—than formerly.[14] Another study, based on the experience of cigar workers between 1931 and 1937, showed that the average length of the period of unemployment when machines took over their jobs was one year.[15]

In the past, however, even though there were genuine hardships in specific cases, this did not mean that:

. . . increasing productivity must cause increasing unemployment in the working force as a whole. For a worker is never displaced by a machine;

he is displaced by other workers who build, maintain, and operate a machine. If production costs are reduced—and this is generally the motivation for the innovation—prices to consumers may be reduced and profits increased, thus tending to increase demand for other consumer and investment goods throughout the economy.[16]

AUTOMATION. But at midcentury technological changes involved not only better and faster machines for performing old functions; machines were being introduced that were also qualitatively different in the functions they performed. To be sure, for almost two centuries machines had been taking over the heavy, back-breaking work, and later even some of the monotonous manual jobs. What was new about technological changes at midcentury—so-called automation—was that now instruments were taking over tasks requiring judgment; they were taking over white-collar and highly technical jobs. The prospect of a plant operating wholly by machinery was no longer fantastic; in fact, a few such plants were already established, and there were some operations in other plants which were completed without the use of human effort. Devices based on the feed-back principle indicated to certain instruments when there was something wrong, and the instruments proceeded to correct the error.

A study of twelve cases in which automation had been introduced at midcentury, ranging from chocolate refining to railroad traffic control, showed that it had reduced the number of workers required anywhere from 13 to 92 per cent, with an average reduction in employment of 63.4 per cent.[17] Tobacco-workers estimated that machines had replaced 90 per cent of the workers on a given job; others reported reductions up to 50 per cent in the number of skilled workers required.[18]

Industries vary in their adaptability to automation. Oil refining, flour milling, and chemical production are most susceptible. Transportation, large-scale retailing, and some kinds of manufacturing can benefit from automation, but not so much as the industries mentioned above. Least susceptible are agriculture, mining, construction, small-scale retailing, and professional services.[19]

It was generally admitted that there would be some hardship in the short run for men whose skills were rendered obsolete or whose jobs were abolished altogether by automation. Much would depend on the rate at which automation was introduced. It was also pointed out, however, that since automation was coming at a time when workers were in short supply, its impact would be cushioned.

In the 1940's, some observers, carrying over the point of view of those who had lived through the depression of the 1930's, viewed with misgivings the large number of young people entering the labor force each year; they became fearful that there would not be enough jobs for them.[20] As it turned out, however, there was a shortage of young persons entering the labor force in the 1950's as a result of the low birth rate a generation earlier. And the high birth rates in the 1940's and the 1950's meant that there would be an increasing number of consumers in the next generation. The problem seemed to be one of getting enough young people to fill the jobs necessary to produce the goods demanded rather than one of getting jobs for the young people.

When, therefore, union leaders looked to shorter hours as an answer to automation, others looked to automation as an answer to the shortage of labor.[21] One student of the subject concluded that the working force during the 1950's and 1960's would grow less rapidly than the total population because of the relatively low birth rate in the 1930's, referred to above, and the high birth rate in the 1940's and 1950's. In 1955, he pointed out, every American worker supported himself or herself and $1\frac{1}{2}$ other persons in addition; in 1975 he would have to produce enough to support himself and $3\frac{1}{2}$ other persons at the 1955 standard of living.

Here, in summary, is the basic population structure within which the American economy will function during the next twenty years:

There will be a population increase of one-fifth in the next ten years.

But total population of working age will increase only by one-tenth.

Population actually available for work will increase only by 5 per cent.

And total hours worked by the whole economy in the course of one year may not increase at all.

And in the next twenty years, total population will increase by at least two-fifths.

Population of working age, however, will increase by less than one-third.

Labor force will go up by one-fifth, and total hours worked by 10 per cent.

And even more intensive employment, on a larger scale, of older people who are willing and able to work—however desirable in itself—would not materially affect these conclusions.[22]

Automation should, then, help to maintain productivity in the face of a relatively small labor force. But it will demand a redisposition of workers. Many more machine builders, machine installers, repairmen, machinery controllers, and programmers will be needed; also designers of new machinery, draftsmen, engineers, mathematicians, and logicians; and especially more managers to fill the new managerial jobs which automation will demand. In routine office work, jobs will be cut down; here unemployment will be marked. But, concluded this author, since these jobs are filled mainly by young, unmarried women just out of school and they are in short supply at this time, no undue hardship should ensue. These young women can be absorbed in other positions which now compete for them.

The really serious social problem is not employment but the need to upgrade whole segments of the population in very short time. Automation requires trained and educated people in unprecedented numbers. The quantitative need alone will be so great . . . that the eight or ten million college students we can expect fifteen years hence will be barely sufficient. One large manufacturing company (now employing 150,000) figures that it will need seven thousand college graduates a year once it is automated, just to keep going; today it hires three hundred annually.

But the need is above all qualitative—for better educated people. The "trained barbarian," the man who has acquired high gadgeteering skill, will not do. Even in routine jobs, automation will require ability to think, a trained imagination, and good judgment, plus some skill in logical methods, some mathematical understanding, and some ability well above the elementary level to read and write—in a word, the normal equipment of educated people. . . . If there is one thing certain under automation it is that the job—even the bottom job—will change radically and often.[23]

The problem here suggested highlights that discussed in Chapter 17 of locating the talented young persons and helping them get the highest training of which they are capable. On the other hand, it also highlights the problem of the person at the other end of the scale; can he be trained for these new jobs? For automation is going to demand an even higher quality of personnel than technology has to date.

Far from increasing unemployment, this student concludes, automation will require great stability of employment. Automation must have a fairly predictable, stable, and expanding market; otherwise it is not feasible. It cannot be turned on and off capriciously. Management will have to learn how to stabilize demand for manufactured products in order to stabilize production.

Automation should bring even greater stability to employment. . . . Management today still proceeds on the assumption that "labor" is a current expense which fluctuates, on the whole, with volume of production. Already this concept may be obsolete; in most large companies one-third or more of the employees are salaried; and of the hourly employees, a half or even two-thirds, in many industries, have to be kept on the job as long as the plant is open, regardless of output.

Under automation, however, the traditional concept will be untenable, if not dangerous. Labor under automation must be considered a capital resource, with wage costs being treated virtually as fixed costs. The essence of automation is its inability to adjust production to short-range economic fluctuations, except within narrow ranges. The number of people employed will therefore not fluctuate directly with volume, and the investment in the skill and training of workers will be much too great for the enterprise to disperse them, except in a situation of extreme peril.

Automation thus creates the opportunity for a high degree of employment stability—an opportunity that comes none too soon, since the social pressure for such stability has long been building up. This is partly a result of the American economy's success in making the worker "middle-class"; the most potent emotional symbol of middle-class status has always been the "salary" in contrast to the "wage." In part it is also the result of the disproportion between the rapid increase in total population and the slower increase in working population, and of the resulting labor pressure. But, in any case, the demands for stabilized employment and predictable income are certainly not inventions of the "power-hungry union bosses." They are the most important goals of the American worker.[24]

Whether union leaders or industrial leaders are right in their diagnosis of the effects of automation and in their prescriptions for dealing with it cannot yet be determined. If union leaders are right, they are likely to insist that the increased productivity resulting from automation be distributed in the form of a shorter work week, as we saw above. And if the goal of the thirty-two-hour or even the thirty-five-hour week is realized, a tremendous increase in leisure-time and recreational facilities will be demanded by workers. In any event, the productive capacity of modern machines when they are kept in operation is fabulous. The great problems are how to distribute the goods which these machines make possible and, more basic still, how to adjust our institutions to function successfully in an age of abundance. There are no precedents in history to help us.[25]

"SOFT SPOT" UNEMPLOYMENT. There is a special kind of technological unemployment which might be called "soft spot" unemployment. It occurs in industries when technological changes make it difficult or impossible for them to compete successfully with other industries. The coal industry, for example, was in distress for almost a generation; many textile towns in the North became distressed, as mills moved South.

In such communities, worker roles are erased on a broad scale; unemployment becomes endemic. People tend to resist moving to other areas where they could perform different worker roles; they prefer to wait for new industries to come in and create worker roles for them. In one community in western Pennsylvania most of the adults who remained when the coal mines closed down were just waiting for retirement benefits to begin.[26]

A similar situation exists in certain agricultural areas. Here technological advances also render many old worker roles obsolete. Men continue, however, to perform anachronistic roles; their plight is called "underemployment." It is different enough from technological unemployment in urban industries to warrant special consideration here.

Underemployment:
The Low-Income Farmer

In Chapter 5 we emphasized very strongly the urban nature of the social problems that attracted the attention of reformers in the early years of the 19th century. The great uprooting of populations from the soil which accompanies industrialization had its most spectacular effects in the great cities where the people settled. For many years people retained a nostalgic dream of an idyllic rural past which contrasted strongly with the disorganization and insecurity of the towns. The good life was a rural life. Cities were dens of evil and vice. It was the city, therefore, that engrossed the attention of the first students of social problems. We now know that rural areas have social problems also. The pathologies discussed in Part IV occur in rural as well as urban areas, and so does disorganization in the sense of technological changes which do violence to old role relationships. At the present time, for example, there is occurring a slow but inexorable elimination of certain agricultural roles in our society. As a result, one of the major problems is how to get the marginal farmer out of his agricultural worker role into an industrial worker role. The symptom of his disappearing role is given the euphemistic name "underemployment." [27]

During World War I a popular song asked how you could keep young men down on the farm after they had seen Paris. The problem seemed to be one of conserving the farm labor force, of stemming the population movement to the cities. Now we ask the question in reverse: how can we attract low-income farmers away from the farms, where their productivity and, hence, income is low, to industrial cities where their productivity and income would be higher. We shall see below that there are many problems associated with geographical mobility of workers. But there are also problems when there is too little mobility, when people do not shift from one area where they are not needed to another, where they are needed.

A government-sponsored study in 1951 reported that some low-income families were poor because the heads were too old or too young for optimum productivity, some because they had no male head, and some because the head suffered from disabilities. But more than a million farm families, as of 1945, the latest year for which data were available, had low incomes despite the fact that the head was able-bodied and of working age. Most—70 per cent—of these families were located in the South; 26 per cent were in the North; and 4 per cent were in the West.

No single explanation can cover all these cases. Sometimes they are dismissed as "shiftless" or as "ne'er do wells." Sometimes their plight is explained in terms of the social and economic values which prevail in their communities. We emphasize here, however, the role-related explanation: the economic or worker roles which these low-income families perform are no longer needed in our society. The enormous productivity of modern agriculture, which we referred to in Chapter 1, has decreased the need for many farm workers. They perform anachronistic roles.

Studies of population movements confirm this interpretation. In prosperous areas workers who are no longer needed in agricultural production migrate to centers where they can find industrial worker roles to perform. The low-income farm families do so to a far less extent.

There is here a vicious circle. Because they still live, in effect, under conditions of scarcity these families still suffer from the social problems that characterize scarcity: poor health, ignorance, inferior nutrition. And these conditions, in turn, serve as barriers to migration.

Rural communities made up of relatively small, low-productivity farms have poorer schools, have less capital to finance their children in finding jobs outside the community; they have less medical attention and often have inferior nutritional standards as compared with the more productive agricultural areas located an equal distance from industrial employment centers. These are the communities where underemployment has developed and persisted while the level of output per worker has increased rapidly in the balance of the economy. . . . Programs of improved education and health and increased communications with the outside world are basic to the long-run solution of this problem.[28]

The improved education suggested here applies especially to vocational training to equip many of these rural people for worker roles in industrial areas. It was estimated that during the decade 1950–1960, a third to a half of young rural persons in low-income areas would have to take up nonfarm occupations; training for such new occupational roles is a major problem.

So much, then, for role elimination by unemployment and "underemployment." But even when workers are performing their production roles, even when employment is secure and wages high, there still remain, or perhaps it would be better to say there then emerge many kinds of status problems which tend to be masked when legal status, wages, and working conditions seem to be the major difficulty. We shall review here four kinds of status problems: the legal status of workers vis-à-vis management; the status aspect of the role of worker; status and geographical mobility; and status and occupational mobility.

The Status Problems of Workers in the 20th Century

The Legal Status of Workers Vis-à-vis Management

The legal status of workers vis-à-vis employers in the 19th century was that of servant to master. Statutes, court decisions, the common law, custom, tradition—all defined the relationship between employer and employee in this way. It was taken for granted that the employer could make all the decisions about hiring, firing, working conditions, pay, and the like. That was the prerogative of ownership. The major problems of the industrial worker in the 19th century tended to be those characteristic of an economy of scarcity: exploitation in the form of long hours, low wages, unsanitary and unsafe working conditions, insecurity, and unemployment. The savings necessary for the accumulation of capital for industrialization came, as we saw above, from the labor of workers. Status problems were legal in nature and they were of secondary importance; improved status was a means to the end of improving working conditions.

As a result of the changes discussed above there has been a reduction in the legal status differential between workers and management. Increasingly, workers come to share the prerogatives of management. Complete elimination of status differentials is probably impossible; but that they have been reduced is a matter of record.

But to point out that the status problems of workers vis-à-vis management have been mitigated does not mean that there are no status problems for workers today. Status has become important in the 20th century not so much in the legal sense as in the sense of dignity, worth, and value. We shall here discuss two major status problems at the present time, one centering around the status aspect of the worker role and one centering around mobility.[29]

Toiling masses? Downtrodden, exploited workers? Modern technology and the abundance it makes possible are rapidly upgrading the labor force. Some of these men are better paid than workers in many white-collar occupations. They have high aspirations for their children who, they hope, will go to college.

Labor unions have helped to raise the status of workers. Now they have many of the problems of capitalists. Union leaders have vast welfare funds to administer, insurance plans to operate, and educational benefits to dispense. They must decide how to invest the money involved in these programs. They buy stocks and bonds, as other investors do. They acquire a vested interest in the capitalistic system. The very idea of fighting capitalism would be anathema to most of these workers. They are part and parcel of it.

As unions become large they often become unwieldy. The financial affairs of large unions have never been subjected to such close scrutiny as have those of businesses and corporations. Unscrupulous leaders may therefore take advantage of their relative freedom from control. Although most union officials are honest men, the racketeer is an ever-present threat. *(Photo: Brown Brothers)*

The Status Aspect of the Role of Worker

Students of labor problems had begun to point out long ago that there was a deep reservoir of hostility among workers which expressed itself in absenteeism, wasted material, slow-downs, high turnover rates, and the like. Clearly, something was wrong. It was something, further, which increased wages and improved working conditions, or improved legal status alone, did not cure.

At first this malaise was attributed to frustrated instincts, to the monotony of machine-tending work, to improper factory hygiene, or to fatigue. In the 1920's a series of studies undertaken by Elton Mayo, of the Harvard Business School, concluded that none of these explanations was adequate. Status problems were basic: "The studies of actual industrial situations which have been carried on show that the desire to stand well with one's fellows . . . easily outweighs merely individual interest and logic of reasoning." [30] The author concluded that the social problems of an industrial civilization were those involved in cooperation and that the kind of working together which had been almost automatic in preindustrial civilizations had been destroyed; therefore new ways of working together happily must be learned. This was the social problem of an industrial civilization.

This author cited two French thinkers, Frédéric Le Play and Emile Durkheim, who saw very clearly what was happening to society under the impact of industrialization. Le Play, a French engineer, studied the working and living conditions of workers over a period of twenty-five years and published his findings in six large volumes between 1855 and 1879. He contrasted, on the one hand, the simpler agricultural communities, in which family and kinship bonds related every individual definitively and unalterably to every other individual, with the industrial community, on the other hand, in which the stabilizing capacity of kinship ties had waned and individuals had lost their moorings and become restless and rootless. Emile Durkheim, a more academic student, made a study of suicide in which he found that it was inversely related to solidarity, and that solidarity itself was a casualty of industrialization. The individual no longer felt identified with his group. That is, he was no longer *solidaire* with a geographical community and with the people who lived in it. Social mobility as well as geographical mobility had the effect of further atomizing groups. At the extreme were found individuals who had no functional relationships with the world—the mentally (or role) ill, the suicide, the criminal.

Mayo characterized 20th-century social problems in terms of the breakdown of social relationships at two levels, individual and group, as follows:

> In a modern industrial society we . . . find two symptoms of social disruption.
>
> First, the number of unhappy [i.e., anxiety-ridden] individuals increases. Forced back upon himself, with no immediate or real social duties, the individual becomes a prey to unhappy and obsessive personal preoccupations. . . .
>
> Second, the other symptom of disruption in a modern industrial society relates itself to that organization of groups at a lower level than the primitive. . . . It is unfortunately completely characteristic of industrial societies we know that various groups when formed are not eager to cooperate wholeheartedly with other groups. On the contrary, their attitude is usually that of wariness or hostility. It is by this road that a society sinks into a condition of stasis—a confused struggle of pressure groups, power blocs, which . . . heralds the approach of disaster.[31]

The prescription suggested by Mayo was that the factory be seen, in effect, as a community and that each worker be given recognition as a member. He was to be treated as a worth-while human being; his group relationships were to be respected. He was to be accorded a worthy status.

Union leaders had also diagnosed some of the problems of the industrial worker as status problems. They knew that the worker needed more than improved wages. And one of the most important functions which the union performed was to give the worker a feeling of importance. He was a member of a strong group. Where unions were successful it became impossible for employers to push workers around, to violate their self-respect, to put them in positions of humiliation. In more recent times, workers are even permitted to participate in some of the work decisions.

It is not only within the plant that the status problems of workers are important. Workers also seek status in the community.[32] And some people feel that in their efforts to protect their new status they become overly conservative and anti-intellectual. One observer, viewing these trends, highlights some of the status problems of modern workers as follows:

> As a result of their difficulties and frustrations, our citizens suffer, consciously and unconsciously, from what can only be described as civil battle fatigue. . . . This all-prevailing discontent does not arise as during the 19th century from rebellion against entrenched wealth. The American people are more prosperous than ever, especially those who were formerly impoverished. These latter cannot be called middle-class groups; they lack the usual attributes of a middle-class culture. I can only describe them as *nouveaux riches* proletarians, whom I first discovered during my war journeys through our

industrial centers. Then these people, just off relief, had enjoyed bonanza war salaries for two years, yet they were very unhappy. "We thought all our troubles would be over if only we had enough money," they said to me. "But now we find that our troubles have just begun." They found that possession of gadgets and comfort was not enough.[33]

Status malaise has been used to explain the political behavior of workers, also. In France, for example, in spite of improved working conditions and standards of living, the proportion of voters who supported the Communist candidates remained fairly constant in the postwar decade between 1946 and 1956. It was 28.2 per cent in 1946, 26.5 per cent in 1951, and 25.6 per cent in prosperous 1956. One observer interprets this behavior as a status-based protest.

It seems necessary to conclude that there is no clear correlation between Communist votes and the standards of living of the mass of the people. . . . A non-Communist labor leader said . . . workers, although well paid, were treated about like machines if not rather worse. . . . He contended that the company, generous with its pay, neglected or opposed the unions; consequently, that the workers felt they were not treated with sufficient consideration. . . . The French worker is heir to a revolutionary tradition and a citizen of a republic upon whose official motto the word "equality" is inscribed as an apparent aim or promise. He lives in a country that has long prided itself upon representing humanism in all its aspects. He has thus been taught to consider that every individual possesses certain inherent rights which give him a kind of dignity that all must respect, however humble his social position. This dignity may be as important to him as his pay envelope, or so he feels at times. Therefore the attitude of management toward him and his trade unions is almost as vital as the wages it grants.[34]

Status in the role sense, then, tends to become a stress factor in the lives of many workers in an industrialized society, and their reaction to it may take the form of anxiety and hostility toward management. The solution to this particular problem is being sought both by management and by unions themselves.

There is one class of workers whose status problems are unique: the workers have no status in any community. We refer to the migratory worker, to whom we direct our attention at this point.

Status and Geographical Mobility

Both geographical and occupational mobility entail status problems. We leave occupational mobility for discussion below and concern ourselves here with the status problems that accompany geographical mobility.

Because of the nature of the role he performs in our economy, the migratory worker literally has no status in any community. He belongs nowhere. He is as much a "stateless person" as any European displaced person.

The migratory worker performs a vital role in our economy, as we have just said. He harvests many crops. He is needed, when he is needed, with great urgency. But when he has picked the cotton or the apples he is no longer needed, or even wanted. The community feels no responsibility for him. It wants him to get out.

The migratory worker is likely to be colored or, in many cases, foreign. Florida and the Southwest are usually the winter headquarters for these workers, and they then fan out, following the crops northward. From Florida, for example, there are several patterns of migration northward for the estimated 60,000 to 70,000 workers who, with their wives and children, make up this migrant worker population.

The white worker comes to Florida to supplement his wages and then returns home; if he is a year-round migrant he follows the Midwest migratory stream into Arkansas and Indiana and into Michigan. Negroes and Puerto Ricans follow the East Coast migratory stream, up through the Carolinas, the Middle Atlantic States, New York, and then back to Florida. The estimated 2,000 Texas-Mexicans stay in Florida. The so-called offshore workers from the Bahamas and the British West Indies work under contracts which protect them from exploitation, and then return home.[35]

In the Southwest some of the migratory workers are "Anglos" from the English-speaking culture, but the majority are Spanish-speaking—colonial Spanish, first- and second-generation Texas-Mexicans, and Mexicans not yet naturalized. There are also some Indians from the reservations.[36]

Wherever they are, however, they are regarded as aliens. No consistent effort is made to help them make use of available facilities or to teach them simple health and sanitation principles. Acute medical problems that interfere with working efficiency are tended to, but chronic problems go uncared for.

Because, as we said above, they literally have no status in the community migrant workers are not eligible for any of the ordinary services and benefits enjoyed by citizens established in the community. They cannot vote. They cannot receive assistance. They have the worst possible housing. Their health is often poor. Their children are often deprived of schooling. One boy had been in seventeen schools in five states before he finally graduated from high school.

The Federal Government is fostering efforts among the East Coast

States to work cooperatively in tackling the social problems generated by migratory workers. In the Southwest, as we shall see presently, an effort is being made to establish workers in settled places of residence, to transform them from migratory into seasonal workers in order to secure for them the advantages of status in some community. The sense of a meeting held to discuss these problems was that "since there is no such thing in our democracy as second-class citizenship we must plan our services to give the migrants the same opportunities as others." [37]

Among the obstacles to interstate efforts to help these workers are state residence laws, community indifference or hostility, the short stay in any one area which makes continuity of services impossible, low public financial resources, and confusion about responsibility for these workers. Another difficulty is sheer ignorance about the extent of the problem. The "free wheelers" never get into the records and are not counted. We just do not know anything about them. We shall refer to these migratory workers again when we discuss minority groups and their status problems.

Mobility also poses status problems, although of a quite different kind, for workers higher in the occupational ladder. Geographical mobility is more common among the higher occupational classes than among the lower—excluding migratory workers—and entails a constant re-establishment of status. These mobile people must re-establish roots, make new friends, and find a place in community activities. Although Americans have a great deal of skill and talent in resettling themselves, it nevertheless does pose some fairly difficult problems.

Occupational as well as geographical mobility is an important source of status anxiety for modern workers as opportunities for advancement are offered. This time we speak of ranked status rather than role-related status.

Status and Occupational Mobility

NATURE AND CRITERIA OF OCCUPATIONAL STATUS.   In addition to the upgrading of the whole economy which we described above, there is usually upward occupational mobility in the life of most individual workers also. It is as though they were walking upstairs on an escalator. But there is also downward occupational mobility, though on a far smaller scale. Status anxiety often accompanies both the upward climb and the downward descent. Indeed, some people feel that the status anxiety concerned with occupational mobility is one of the major social problems at midcentury.

When we speak of "high" and "low" status, of "upgrading" and "downgrading," of "upward mobility" and "downward mobility," we are thinking in terms of some sort of rank, as we saw in Chapter 3. The criteria of status rank may be objective and functional or they may be subjective. Within any organization—firm, plant, working unit—status may be said to inhere, as we pointed out in Chapter 3, in the decision-making function. Whoever exercises that function has higher status than those who implement it. And the more general the decision the higher the status. Thus the president of the firm has higher status than the third vice-president; the plant manager has higher status than the departmental supervisor; the supervisor, than the foreman. Among occupations status is proportional to income, education, amount of responsibility involved, and amount of skill required. These are objective criteria; they may be imposed from the outside. They may or may not correspond with more subjective criteria.

Subjective criteria of status have to do with prestige, respect, and honorific rewards.[38] Status based on subjective criteria is a very confusing concept. As one observer has pointed out:

. . . it is no longer clear which way *is* up even if one wants to rise, for with the growth of the new middle class the older, hierarchical patterns disintegrate, and it is not easy to compare ranks among the several sets of hierarchies that do exist. Does an army colonel "rank" the head of an international union? A physics professor, a bank vice-president? A commentator, the head of an oil company? [39]

Can status in the prestige sense be created to specifications? Or does it have intrinsic determinants? The experience of the USSR is instructive here. During the early years of the Revolution a certain order of prestige was decreed to different occupations. A study of Soviet school children in the 1920's reflected this attempt to create prestige patterns. Workers and peasants headed the list, and kulaks and businessmen, especially bankers, were last.[40] This was the official ordering of occupations. But in terms of actual privilege and rewards, the highest status has come to inhere in industrial administrators, in technical directors, in writers, musicians, dancers, and scientists.

In general, subjective criteria tend to follow those based on function performed. One study of 2,900 replies to a question asking for the respondent's personal opinion of the general standing of 90 occupations in the United States found that, in general, highly specialized training and a high degree of responsibility for the public welfare tended to make for prestige in occupations, whereas lack of skill requirements, low pay, "dirty" work, and little public responsibility characterized low-prestige occupations.[41] By and large white-collar occupations tend to have more prestige than blue-collar ones. And this is true even when many white-collar occupations differ from factory jobs in no other respect than that the worker wears street clothes instead of over-alls.[42] Manual labor has higher prestige value in the United States, however, than it has in countries with a feudal tradition. Most Americans do a great amount of tinkering, and a minimum skill with machinery is almost taken for granted. In countries where a leisure class has flourished, manual work is much less honored than it is here.

Still, in all studies of occupational mobility it is usual to assign low status to unskilled manual labor and high status to professional work. Our discussion here follows this convention.

There is this justification for talking of "high" and "low" status with respect to occupational levels. We know that "life chances" and opportunities are considerably better for children born to families in occupations ranked high than for those born to families in occupations ranked low. Whether prestige follows this pattern or not is immaterial.

TRENDS IN OCCUPATIONAL MOBILITY. A generalized picture of occupational mobility may be seen in the figures given in Table 4, which shows the occupational distribution of a cohort of workers at the beginning and at the end of their careers.

TABLE 4

OCCUPATIONAL DISTRIBUTION OF A COHORT OF WORKERS AT BEGINNING AND END OF THEIR WORKING CAREERS

	Occupational Distribution at Beginning of Career Per Cent	Occupational Distribution at End of Career Per Cent
Professional, technical, and kindred workers	5.48	7.59
Managers, officials, and proprietors	3.71	17.85
Clerical and kindred workers and sales workers	18.54	13.22
Craftsmen, foremen, and kindred workers	12.54	26.51
Operatives and kindred workers	30.92	19.83
Service workers	6.75	9.94
Laborers, except farm and mine	22.06	5.06

SOURCE: A. J. Jaffe and R. O. Carleton, *Occupational Mobility in the United States, 1930-1960* (Columbia Univ. Press, 1954), p. 52. The data are as of 1940.

TABLE 5

MEN CLASSIFIED BY MAJOR OCCUPATIONAL GROUP AT BEGINNING AND END OF WORKING CAREER

Occupation at End of Career	Total	Professional, Technical, and Kindred Workers	Managers, Officials, and Proprietors (Except Farm)	Clerical and Kindred Workers and Sales Workers	Craftsmen, Foremen, and Kindred Workers	Operatives and Kindred Workers	Service Workers	Laborers Except Farm and Mine
TOTAL	10,000	548	371	1,854	1,254	3,092	675	2,206
Professional, technical, and kindred workers	759	197	29	180	78	167	40	68
Managers, officials, and proprietors (except farm owners)	1,785	90	104	402	224	526	119	320
Clerical and kindred workers and sales workers	1,322	80	72	334	133	374	91	238
Craftsmen, foremen, and kindred workers	2,651	78	76	413	425	869	150	640
Operatives and kindred workers	1,983	55	53	308	236	680	126	525
Service workers	994	37	25	145	109	315	111	252
Laborers except farm and mine	506	11	12	72	49	161	38	163

SOURCE: A. J. Jaffe and R. O. Carleton, *Occupational Mobility in the United States, 1930–1960* (Columbia Univ. Press, 1954), p. 52. Based on data from *Labor Mobility in Six Cities* (Social Science Research Council, 1954) by Gladys Palmer.

In general the cohort of men here studied ended their working careers in higher occupations than those they began in. There are many more in the business and professional occupations at the end of their careers than at the beginning and far fewer in the laboring class.

But this general picture obscures important differences in specific occupational groupings. Table 5 presents greater detail. For example, of 548 men who begin their working lives in professional, technical, and kindred work, 197, or roughly one third—36.0 per cent—will end their working careers in this class of occupation; 90, or about 16.4 per cent, will end as managers, officials, and proprietors (except farm owners); and 14.6 per cent will end in clerical and sales work. There need have been no downward mobility in any of these cases. But the remaining third will end their careers in manual or service occupations. Some of these downwardly mobile men are doubtless the older workers we discussed in Chapter 19 who had to take lower jobs as they began to deteriorate with age. Some of these downwardly mobile men may be ill, handicapped, alcoholic, or disturbed. At the other end of the status scale, it will be noted that about 3 in 10 of those who begin as laborers move up to white-collar jobs, and an equal number move up to craftsmen jobs. Almost a fourth become operatives, and a tenth, service workers.

The general trends shown in Table 5 may be summarized as follows:

(a) In general those who begin their working careers near the top of the occupational order tend to remain there. Furthermore larger proportions of those who begin in such jobs remain in the same major occupation group in which they begin for their entire working lives than is the case among workers who start at the bottom of the occupational ladder.

(b) Of those who begin near the bottom of the occupational ladder, more move upward than downward; furthermore, more of them move upward than do men who begin toward the center of the occupational ladder.

(c) However, those who begin near the bottom of the occupational ladder and move upward do not move quite as far upward as those who begin at about the center. In short, comparatively fewer men who begin as lower white collar or craftsmen will move up the occupational ladder; those who do, however, will move into the top occupations, the professions and managerial groups. On the other hand, more men who begin as operatives and laborers will move upward, but comparatively few of them will reach the top occupations.[43]

There are stresses involved in all this mobility, whether down or up. One student of the subject has summarized them as follows:

Interpersonal relations pose a special dilemma for mobile persons, because attributes associated with socioeconomic status do not furnish unambiguous criteria of social acceptance. An analysis of this dilemma helps to explain some findings concerning attitudes of occupationally mobile people.

Difficulties in finding social acceptance among his new peers tend to prevent the mobile individual from assimilating their values fully, and place him in an intermediate position between his present and original class. But his lack of integration may also encourage overconformity. Which of these alternatives prevails seems to depend on the direction of mobility, class identification, and whether public or private conduct is involved. Moreover, the insecurity often affects certain attitudes directly, such as out-group hostility. Thus, the upwardly and downwardly mobile may have similar characteristics which contrast with those of the non-mobile.

The mobile person can adapt to his marginal position by associating with members of his old or of his new social class. If the former, the mobility experience is reinforced for the downwardly mobile with more fortunate middle-class associates, or the upwardly mobile with less fortunate working-class associates. If the latter, the mobile person ceases to be socially reminded of his occupational failure or success. Hence, shifts in style of life should be least evident, but the psychological impact most pronounced among those mobiles who continue to befriend members of their former class.[44]

THE STRESSES OF UPWARD MOBILITY. We saw in our discussion of schizophrenia in Chapter 13 that many of these patients were "overachievers"; their achievement had cost more than they could pay. They had worked their way up to a higher occupational level, but the stresses and strains involved in the climb had been too much for them. They had broken under the strain.

Sometimes upward mobility inflicts severe stress on family ties also. If a man moves up fast, for example, and his wife cannot keep up with him, the result may be disastrous.

The experiences of the man as he advances broaden and develop him. As he enters new and larger worlds he meets men and women whom he admires and respects, some of whom may become his friends and his models for status advancement. Their goals, values, and activities become his. His wife meanwhile often remains much what she was when they married and both were people of limited understanding and experience. Her social and personal equipment under these conditions often suffers when he measures her by his newly acquired standards. She may become increasingly isolated while he seeks elsewhere for companionship and intimacy. Divorces sometimes occur; her reveries may be filled unhappily with justified or unjustified suspicions and jealousies.[45]

Or there may be stress within the family if as the father moves up, his children move up faster. The child takes his position as a matter of course; he may be embarrassed by the reminders of lower-status origins in his parents. A comic strip—"Bringing Up Father"—based on this theme has amused millions of people for many years. Apparently many families recognized the situation as their own.

THE STRESSES OF DOWNWARD MOBILITY. Although perhaps to a lesser extent now than formerly, status tends still to be hereditary.[46] It is not that institutional rules prescribe that children inherit the status of their parents. Indeed, just the opposite is usually the case in modern societies. Nepotism, or the passing on of family privileges, is frowned upon. But the inheritance of status is no less real because it takes more indirect forms. The rewards of high status include the privilege of passing on some of the benefits to children. Further, children born into families with high status have a great head start over children born into families with low status. More than half the leaders of business in the United States at midcentury came from families of high-status.[47] The same is becoming true in the Soviet Union. The child of high-status parents has easier access to education. He has connections through his parents. Even more important, he has more intimate acquaintance with the world of success; he feels at home in it. He knows how it operates, and he has self-confidence. He belongs.

Despite the advantages of high status, some children fail in the sense that they become downwardly mobile. It does not take much imagination to picture the stresses such failure creates in the downwardly mobile person. He shows, for example, much more job dissatisfaction than the man in the same job who is upwardly mobile.[48] We know from many studies that mental illness is more common in the lowest occupational classes than in the higher ones. Many cases of this illness may be the result of the stresses and strains of low income, unemployment, and poor living conditions. But there is little doubt that a great many of them are the result of occupational role failure. Evidence for this conclusion may be adduced from the fact that occupational prestige was found in one study to be more significant for mental health than occupational income.[49]

Even if the man himself does not break under the loss of status in downward mobility, his family may become a casualty. The man may lose face with his wife and children. They may cease to respect him, or, even worse, come to pity or contemn him. If they remember their former higher status vividly, the contrast with their present condition is a constant source of irritation. The children may have to drop out of activities in which their friends engage. They may have to develop new reference groups.

The upper-class wife of the downwardly mobile man has special difficulties which cause great stress.

. . . well-born women may suffer from deep involvements with their families of birth making it difficult for them to play their proper roles in helping their husbands. Casualties, including divorce, suicides, and "social suicides," such as profligate sexual behavior, alcoholism, or marriage to a mate of evil or low reputation, often spring from these sources. Such women find it more difficult to free themselves from their past than do women of lowly birth because it is the custom of their subcultures to look to the past. Their whole significance and that of their social level are founded on their parents and ancestry. Difficult emotional adjustment to parents and ancestors can be "solved" for the mobile persons of low status by rejecting them and running away. Under the socially approved and rewarded ideologies of getting ahead and self-improvement, the basic rejection of their parents often can be disguised and their personal dissatisfactions masked and robed in a pretty costume. But the woman or man born to high status, with parents of distinction and social prestige, cannot follow such a familiar and well-marked path.[50]

Downward mobility, in brief, is a trauma of major import to both the individual and to his family.

Since status is always relative, occupational immobility may actually amount to degradation. If others are moving up, the man who is not keeping pace with them is actually falling behind them. We referred in Chapter 18 to the son who finds it difficult to compete with his successful father; he also illustrates a form of downward mobility. One must, like Alice in Wonderland, run fast in order to remain in the same place. This kind of competitive pacing is not so characteristic of industrial workers—they have, in effect, banned it by union contracts —as it is of so-called "junior executives," among whom the scramble for superior status is said to constitute a major health hazard.

Few would argue from the fact that there are so many stresses and strains involved in both upward and downward occupational mobility —the so-called open class system—that such mobility should be discouraged or curtailed, although some people do argue that we ought to teach people to trim their sails, to keep their levels of aspiration within reasonable limits. To others, however, such counsel seems "un-American." Ambition to rise in the world seems a virtue, whatever the costs. Whichever view one espouses, it is certainly important that we be aware of the hazards involved for both individuals and families in an open class system with great mobility and that we be prepared to minimize them.

So much, then, for the role and status problems of modern workers. They are, we saw, a different population from workers a century ago. We have noted the most serious of their worker role problems, those associated with unemployment and with underemployment. We have examined four kinds of status problems—legal, role, and geographical and occupational mobility— which characterize workers today. We shall have more to say about certain disadvantaged classes of workers—Negroes, Puerto Ricans, and Mexicans—in Chapter 22, but before we turn to them, we shall discuss criminals, giving a brief overview of worker roles which are illegal and worker roles which, though legal, often involve illegal behavior.

NOTES

1 James C. Worthy, "Organizational Structure and Employe Morale," *American Sociological Review*, 15 (April 1950), p. 173.

2 A. J. Jaffe and Charles D. Stewart, *Manpower Resources and Utilization: Principles of Working Force Analysis* (Wiley, 1951), p. 190.

3 J. Frederic Dewhurst *et al., America's Needs and Resources: A New Survey* (Twentieth Century, 1955), p. 730.

4 In the great depression of the 1930's a number of studies of unemployed men and their families were made which document the personality and family traumas accompanying unemployment. See, for example, E. Wight Bakke, *Citizens Without Work* (Yale Univ. Press, 1940); Mirra Komarovsky, *The Unemployed Man and His Family: The Effect of Unemployment on the Status of the Man in 59 Families* (Dryden, 1940); and Robert C. Angell, *The Family Encounters the Depression* (Scribner, 1936).

5 Nancy D. Morse and Robert S. Weiss, "The Function and Meaning of Work and the Job," *American Sociological Review*, 20 (April 1955), pp. 191, 198.

6 These figures are those of the National Industrial Conference Board. They are cited here from George Soule, *Men, Wages and Employment in the Modern U.S. Economy* (Mentor, 1954), pp. 28–29.

7 United States Bureau of Labor Statistics, *ibid.,* p. 29.

8 Joseph W. Garbarino, "The Unemployed Worker During a Period of 'Full Employment,' " Berkeley, Institute of Industrial Relations, Reprint No. 20, 1954, p. 31.

9 Soule, *op. cit.,* p. 44.

10 Depressions without unemployment are possible; they would be depressions in which people would suffer not because they had no jobs but because their incomes were severely cut by inflation. See Peter Drucker, "America's Next Twenty Years," *Harper's,* March 1955, p. 30. Depressions are sometimes distinguished from recessions, which are more moderate in extent.

11 Fortunately this law received no critical test of its efficacy; its major contribution was the establishment of an economic advisory committee which keeps the President informed about the condition of the economy as reflected especially in employment and unemployment rates.

12 William Haber, F. H. Harbison, L. R. Klein, and Vivian Palmer, *Manpower in the United States: Problems and Policies* (Harper, 1954), p. x.

13 Ludwig Lore, "Textile Industry: Labor," *Encyclopaedia of the Social Sciences,* Vol. 14, (Macmillan, 1934), p. 591.

14 Ewan Clague and Walter J. Couper, *After the Shutdown* (Yale Univ. Press, 1934).

15 Daniel Creamer and Gladys V. Swackhamer, "Cigar Makers—after the Layoff," WPA National Research Project, Report L-1.

16 Jaffe and Stewart, *op. cit.,* p. 267.

17 David G. Osborn, dissertation, University of Chicago, quoted by Joseph A. Loftus, "Automation Seen as Boon, Danger," *New York Times,* October 15, 1955.

18 *Durham* (N. C.) *Labor Journal,* September 15, 1955.

19 Walter S. Buckingham, Jr., quoted *ibid.*

20 This was the view of Seymour Harris, *The Market for College Graduates* (Harper, 1949).

21 Walter P. Reuther, president of the United Auto Workers, expected a thirty-two-hour week by 1965; and Otto Pragan,

of the International Chemical Workers Union, looked forward to a thirty-five-hour week at that time. Don G. Mitchell, president of Sylvania Electric Products, on the other hand, said that "the demand for goods would be so great that he doubted a work week of much less than forty hours by 1975, twenty years hence, unless we step up automation." (*New York Times*, Oct. 19, 1955.)

22 Peter Drucker, "America's Next Twenty Years," *loc. cit.*

23 Peter Drucker, "The Promise of Automation," *Harper's*, April 1955, p. 45.

24 *Ibid.*, p. 46. This author suggests that instead of selling its electrical appliances, a firm might sell a five-year service policy, lending appliances at a nominal rent, to be replaced with new ones at the end of that time, in order to have a steady market (p. 43).

25 Some books on social problems include discussions of the problems posed by leisure and recreation. These are, indeed, serious community problems, but they do not meet the criteria of social problems established in this book, except perhaps in connection with youth and age. One recent analysis of the problems associated with current productivity trends points out that we may be approaching a time when more than enough for everyone can be produced without paid work for more than a few. People, it suggests, will live until they are ninety; they will be able to retire at fifty; this will leave forty years of leisure. Can we develop the art of living to the point where people can make creative use of this leisure, or will they simply have that much more time to be bored in? These are the problems discussed by George Soule in *Time for Living* (Viking, 1955).

26 Jessie Bernard, unpublished study.

27 The discussion here is based on *Underemployment of Rural Families, Materials Prepared for the Joint Committee on the Economic Report* by the Committee Staff, 82nd Congress, 1st session (Washington, D. C., 1951). Other sources include: *Farm Policy Forum*, February 1953 and Spring 1956.

28 *Development of Agriculture's Human Resources, A Report on Problems of Low-Income Farmers*, prepared for the Secretary of Agriculture (Washington, D. C., 1955), p. 25.

29 See Chapter 3 for the distinction between the role aspect of status and the mobility aspect.

30 Elton Mayo, digest of *The Social Problems of an Industrial Civilization* (Harvard Univ. Press, 1945).

31 *Ibid.*, pp. 7–8.

32 The Steelworkers of America, for example, have since the middle of the 1940's financed workshops at universities in which community relations are included in the curricula and various methods of implementing union leadership are studied.

33 Agnes E. Meyer, "Learning and Liberty," the *American Council of Learned Societies Newsletter*, Spring 1955, p. 7.

34 Harold Callender, "The Red Vote in France: A Study of Factors that Impel Non-Communists to Back Party," *New York Times*, January 9, 1956.

35 Dorothea Andrews, "Moppets Who Migrate," *Children*, 1 (May-June 1954), pp. 85–91.

36 Ruth Boring Howard, "Better Health for Colorado's Migrant Children," *Children*, 3 (March-April 1956), pp. 43–48.

37 Kathryn Close, "Combining Forces for Migrant Children," *Children*, 1 (July-Aug. 1954), p. 152.

38 The terms "honorable" and "honorific" should not be confused. An occupation may be quite honorable but not honorific; street-cleaning would be a case in point. On the other hand, gambling on the stock market might be honorific, even if not honorable.

39 David Riesman, *The Lonely Crowd* (Yale Univ. Press, 1950), p. 48.

40 Jerome Davis, "Testing the Social Attitudes of Children in the Government Schools in Russia," *American Journal of Sociology*, 32 (May 1927), pp. 947–952.

41 Cecil C. North and Paul K. Hatt, "Jobs and Occupations: A Popular Evaluation," in Logan Wilson and William L. Kolb, *Sociological Analysis* (Harcourt, 1949), pp. 464–473.

42 C. Wright Mills, *White Collar* (Oxford Univ. Press, 1951).

43 A. J. Jaffe and R. O. Carleton, *Occupational Mobility in the United States, 1930–1960* (Columbia Univ. Press, 1954), p. 57.

44 Peter M. Blau, abstract of "Social Mobility and Interpersonal Relations," paper delivered before the American Sociological Society in joint session with the Rural Sociological Society, September 1955.

45 W. Lloyd Warner and James Abegglen, *Big Business Leaders in America* (Harper, 1955), p. 121. See also Jessie Bernard, *Remarriage, A Study of Marriage* (Dryden, 1956), pp. 128–129.

46 A study of the presidents and board chairmen of large nonfinancial corporations showed that the proportion who had inherited their jobs declined from 30 per cent in 1900 to 15 per cent in 1950. (Mabel Newcomer, "Professionalization of Leadership in the Big Business Corporation," *Business History Review*, 19 [March 1955], pp. 54–63.)

47 *Ibid.*, pp. 14–19.

48 Douglas M. More, "Social Origins and Occupational Adjustment," abstract of a paper read before the American Sociological Society, September 1955.

49 Robert M. Frunkin, "Occupation and Major Mental Disorders," in *Mental Health and Mental Disorders,* Arnold Rose, ed. (Norton, 1955), p. 153.

50 Warner and Abegglen, *op. cit.*, pp. 125–126.

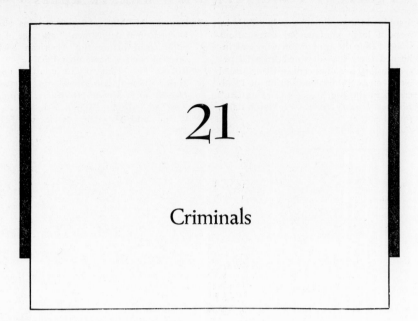

21

Criminals

Crime as a Social Problem

Abundance has not had much appreciable effect on crimes against persons. It has created new ways of killing people, but it has not changed the reasons for doing so. Abundance has, however, vastly increased the occasion for crimes against property. The sheer volume of property ownership has grown to enormous proportions and invidious distinctions seem to be more resented in an equalitarian than in a class-bound society. The invention of the automobile opened up a whole new area of crime. And modern economic and financial organization has created a vast new realm of crime. It is common at the present time to distinguish between traditional crimes—"old-fashioned" murder or stealing—and modern, especially white-collar, crimes. Most of what we know about crime and criminals has to do with the old-fashioned or traditional types; we are only now beginning to come to grips with modern types.

Crime as a Social Problem

The Extent of Crime

Trends

*Prison Populations as Clues to the Nature
of Criminal Behavior*

Classifications of Criminals

"Normal" Criminals

What To Do with Criminals?

Crime meets almost any standard one can set up as a social and a societal problem. It causes pain and suffering; it is enormously expensive; and most people consider it dysfunctional.[1] The fact that there is a law against a thing or a law requiring a thing proves that for at least an influential proportion of the population the thing is considered bad or necessary, and that the violation of the law is dysfunctional.

Throughout our discussion so far we have by deliberate design interspersed references to criminal behavior. In Chapter 14 we saw that many personality disorders involve, or have as their symptoms, some kind of criminal behavior. In Chapter 16 we referred, incidentally, to family desertion and to illegitimacy. In Chapter 18 we discussed juvenile delinquency. In our discussion of the slum-syndrome we referred to the criminal inhabitants of slums and to the underworld. The reason for this scattered treatment was to show that criminal behavior is not something separate, special, and different, but something that is interwoven through the whole social fabric. At this point, however, we assemble the data for an integrated approach to the social and societal problems associated with criminal behavior.

For reasons which we shall present below, it is impossible to describe the criminal population with any accuracy. Most of what we know about it comes from a study of convicted criminals, a sample biased in many ways, as we shall see. We can only peek at criminals, so to speak, through the crimes they commit, and even these clues are wholly inadequate.

The Extent of Crime

The Federal Bureau of Investigation reported that a major crime was committed every 13.9 seconds during the first 6 months of 1955. On each day of this period, 34 persons were killed, 255 were assaulted, 51 were raped, and 607 cars were stolen. According to the *New York Times* (September 25, 1955) there were, in addition, 3,714 larcenies, 167 robberies, and 1,405 burglaries every day. The actual number fluctuates from year to year—the above figures, for example, represented a decline (the first since 1948) from 1954—but it remains at about this level. For each 144 persons in the population a major crime is committed.

In spite of the seeming precision of the above figures, the true extent of crime is not known. The recorded and published data represent a minimum amount of crime, and they are only approximations.

In the first place, there are a large number of crimes—the exact number is not determinable—which no one except the perpetrator ever knows about. These may range from traffic violations to tax evasion, from violation of trust to murder which is made to look like natural death. Much of this violation of the law is done by people who are not "criminal" in the legal sense. This seeming paradox can be explained by referring to a study of 1,020 men and 678 women in New York City. They were asked if they had ever committed any one or more of 49 specified offenses. Almost all—99 per cent, in fact—of them had. The average number of offenses committed by the men was surprisingly high: 18; ministers reported the fewest (8.2 on the average) and laborers the most (20.2). Of the 49 specified offenses, 14 were felonies, that is, serious crimes as measured by the penalties attached to them by law. Sixty-four per cent of the men and 29 per cent of the women reported that they had committed felonies. Thus "the number of acts legally constituting crimes is far in excess of those officially reported. . . . Unlawful behavior, far from being an abnormal social or psychological manifestation, is in truth a very common phenomenon." [2]

Even if the crime is known, many crimes are not reported to the police either by the victim or by disinterested citizens.[3] The kinds of crimes most likely to be reported are: murder, rape, robbery, aggravated assault, burglary, larceny, and auto theft. Less likely to be reported are other assaults, forgery and counterfeiting, embezzlement and fraud, carrying or possessing weapons, sex offenses except rape, offenses against the family and children, violating drug laws, driving while intoxicated, violating liquor laws, drunkenness, disorderly conduct and vagrancy, gambling, and violating traffic and motor vehicle laws.[4] When crimes are not reported, the police officer must locate the violation without help. The number of such crimes located will depend on the number of police officers available to find them. Every driver who has speculated about the amount of policing on a stretch of highway will recognize the truth of this statement.

Still another disadvantage in depending on records for knowledge about the extent of crime lies in the fact that even if a crime is reported to the police, it does not necessarily find its way into the records. It may happen that a police system does not wish to make too bad a showing in its records of apprehension of violators. If there are too many reported crimes and too few apprehensions, they might reflect on the efficiency of the police.

Trends

Since we never know the exact extent of crime at any one time, we obviously do not know what the trends are over a period of time. In view of the large number of crimes which are never recorded or even reported, a tremendous increase in reported or recorded crime might take place without at all reflecting an increase in the actual amount of law violation. Increased efficiency or public pressure might make the figures swell into a "crime wave," when actually the total volume might remain fairly constant. The Police Commissioner of one great city, for example, considered it a mark of improvement in 1955 when there was an increase over 1954 in reported misdemeanors because it demonstrated better police service.

As for lesser crimes—misdemeanors and offenses—there was an over-all increase of 14.9 percent over the first half of last year, from 84,456 to 96,994. This increase is chiefly due to more policemen on the streets. Many misdemeanors occur every day which are unreported because there are no policemen at the scene. Today with more policemen on the streets many more misdemeanors are reported, and many more misdemeanor arrests are made in preserving the peace.[5]

There do seem to be fairly stable seasonal trends in different kinds of reported crimes. Burglary increases in December, January, and February; rape seems to occur most commonly in July; negligent manslaughter reaches a peak in December; auto theft is high in February; aggravated assault and murder are at their highest in July.

There seem also to be fairly stable sectional differences in reported crime, as shown in Figure 3.

The relatively low crime rates per 100,000 population for New England and Middle Atlantic states are consistent, although under-reporting in New York City is recognized as a factor in the generally low rates for the entire state. The relatively high rates of Mountain and Pacific states for crimes against property are also consistent. The South Atlantic, East South Central and West South Central states are consistently high on crimes against the person.[6]

The above information is helpful in trying to get at the nature of criminal behavior, but it is not very pointed. An examination of the people who perpetrate the offenses might be more helpful, but here also the roadblocks are great.

Prison Populations as Clues to the Nature of Criminal Behavior

We saw above that not all crimes which are committed are reported to the police and not all crimes reported to the police are recorded on the blotter. A large number of law violators are screened out of the known criminal population by these two sieves. In addition, not all crimes are cleared by arrests. Those most likely to be cleared are: murder, manslaughter, rape, and aggravated assault. Much less likely to be cleared are offenses against property, such as robbery, burglary, larceny, and auto theft.[7]

Even among those arrested, not all cases are prosecuted. For one reason or another charges may not be pressed. But even if the cases are all prosecuted, not all lead to conviction. And, finally, not all convic-

FIGURE 3

Geographical Distribution of Murder and Burglary, 1946–1952

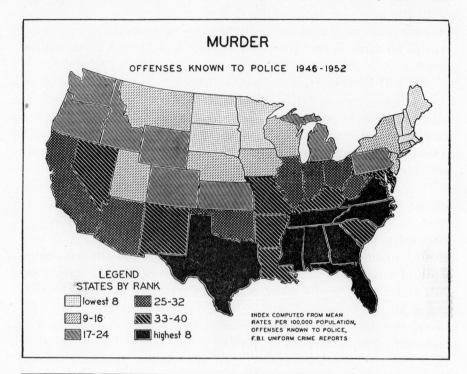

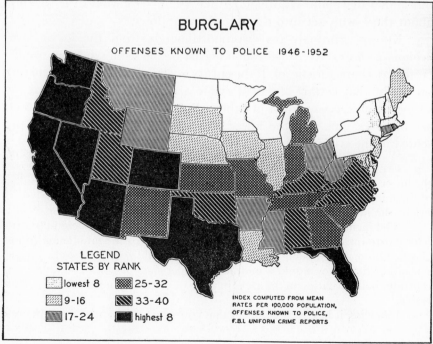

SOURCE: Lyle W. Shannon, "The Spatial Distribution of Criminal Offenses by States," *Journal of Criminal Law, Criminology and Police Science,* 45 (Sept.–Oct. 1954), p. 269.

tions lead to prison sentences. In fact, one study found that, as a result of all the sieves through which violators are screened, only about 3 per cent of all crimes known to the police—itself an indeterminate per cent of all crimes committed—led to commitment to a penal institution.[8]

It will be seen from the above overview that most of what we know about criminals is based on prisoners and hence is extremely biased so far as knowledge about criminals as a class is concerned; it is even more biased so far as information about people who violate laws is concerned. The only kinds of criminals we know much about are convicts and prisoners, and these are highly selected by the processes just described. Nor do we know the relative strength of these processes. If we did we could weight them and correct for the distortion which appears in the figures for the prison population as a sample of the total criminal population. The less than a fifth of a million (178,065 as of 1950) inmates in federal and state penitentiaries and the less than a tenth of a million (86,492 as of 1950) who fill municipal and county jails are not necessarily representative of criminals in general, much less of all law violators. Since we can never be certain that the nonprison population includes no violators, it is futile to compare prison and nonprison populations in an effort to find out how criminals differ from noncriminals. Recognizing, then, the wholly inadequate basis of our knowledge about criminals, we may summarize what little we know about those who get into the records, as follows:

Known criminals are disproportionately from the *lower socioeconomic classes.* Recorded crime is part of the slum-syndrome we discussed as characteristic of 19th-century social problems. And there is no doubt that certain kinds of crime are more characteristic of low socioeconomic classes than of others. But quite aside from this, there are other reasons why the lower socioeconomic classes are overrepresented in the criminal records.

Criminologists would admit by common observation that members of the lower classes are more liable to be acted upon by the police than members of the middle class or the class of greatest influence. Occupational analyses of urban offenders dealt with by the police lead to this same conclusion.

The members of the lower class in any society are more defenseless and have less resources and less influence than members of the middle and upper classes. Other things being equal, the police would suspect a lower-class person rather than they would a middle- or upper-class person. The police concentrate their activities on the areas in parts of town where lower-class persons reside.

Likewise, it has been observed that courts act differentially on the basis of class. A lower-class person has less chance to slip by the courts of first in-stance and the legal steps in the handling of offenders thereafter than does the upper-class person. Upper- and middle-class persons, because of their in-fluence and resources, are able to take full advantage of the loop-holes and technicalities of our legal machinery. Consequently, more severe justice may be unconsciously meted out to the poor man in our society.

Apart from the fact that police and courts act differentially upon the lower-class man as against the middle- and upper-class man, it is possible that some part of the higher crime risks for lower-class persons is owing to the fact that such persons are exposed to the more demoralizing and disorganizing conditions of living. They are more exposed to unemployment, overcrowding and bad housing, death, accident, disease, illiteracy, handicaps, and under-world traditions and institutions. [9]

The picture which emerges from the records, therefore, is by no means accurate with respect to class background. In recent decades we have been alerted to a category of offense which has come to be labeled "white-collar crime." [10] Falsification of reports, tax evasion, misuse of funds, concealed theft, and fraud occur among respectable businessmen. Corruption and graft are their counterparts in the underworld. It has been suggested, further, that if the private behavior of many upper-class persons could be as carefully observed and as accurately reported as that of the lower socioeconomic classes, there would even be as much sex crime as among lower-class persons.[11]

Men are overrepresented in the convicted criminal population. Both arrest and conviction data show a characteristic sex ratio for all kinds of offense. All offenses except prostitution are committed many times more frequently by men than by women, but the difference be-tween the sexes is greater for some than for others. The over-all ratio of men to women among persons arrested is about 9 to 1. But for some offenses the ratio is much higher than this. Rape, of course, is an all-male offense. But even for such offenses as auto theft, burglary, robbery, gambling, and violation of driving laws, the ratio of men to women arrested is very high; for example, there were 44 men arrested for every woman arrested in 1948 for the last offense in the above list, and 12 times as many men as women, for the fourth. Contrariwise, the ratio of men to women arrested for other offenses is less than the over-all ratio. The ratio of males to females arrested for sex offenses, vagrancy, disorderly conduct, violation of liquor laws, forgery, and counterfeiting was around 6 to 1.[12] Some of these differences in relative frequency of offense are due to innate sex differences, some to differences in oppor-tunity, and some to differences in police and court treatment. It has been suggested by one sociologist that the criminality of women has been vastly under-recorded, that an indeterminate but probably large number of murders of husbands and of infants are committed by women which are not diagnosed as murders but as natural death.[13]

A disproportionate number of committed criminals are *young people*. In the age group twenty to thirty, for example, there are almost twice as many arrested and convicted persons as in the total population.[14] In all age brackets from fifteen to forty-five there are relatively more in the arrested and convicted population than in the general population, although the disproportion is not so great as in the twenties. Crimes have characteristic age, as well as sex, incidence. Thus arrests for auto theft, burglary, rape, robbery, and larceny are likely to involve persons under twenty-five; whereas relatively few arrests for gambling, drunkenness, driving while intoxicated, offenses against the family and against children, or embezzlement and fraud are likely to involve persons under twenty-five. In the fifty-and-over age level, the proportion of persons arrested and convicted tends to be only about half that of the total population. Recorded crime, it has been often noted, tends to be a young person's occupation. As the population ages, the over-all rate of crime should decline, although not necessarily for the younger age brackets.[15]

The recorded criminal population is overweighted by *Negroes*. This large overrepresentation of Negroes has been attributed to their lower-class status, their greater vulnerability to arrest and conviction, and to cultural differences which make Negroes more likely to commit certain kinds of crimes—especially those most likely to be reported and cleared—than white persons. For just as different crimes have different sex and age ratios, so also do they have different race ratios. Homicide, assault, carrying and possessing weapons, receiving or buying stolen property, gambling, and liquor law violations are disproportionately high among Negroes; on the other hand, driving while intoxicated, auto theft, forgery and counterfeiting, sex offenses, drunkenness, embezzlement, and fraud are relatively less common among Negroes than among whites.

Nativity is no longer an important factor differentiating the criminal population. There was a time when the children of immigrants figured to a marked extent in the criminal population. But now the foreign-born have become a "ghost group," and their presence in the criminal population is negligible. They are now in the older age brackets in which crime is less likely to occur.[16]

A number of studies have reported that *feeble-mindedness* is more common among known criminals, especially women, than among the general population. But one study reported a disproportionate number of offenders in the higher intelligence ranges also.[17] We saw in our discussion of feeble-mindedness that many persons with low intelligence perform useful roles quite adequately. They may be more at the mercy of chance influences than persons of normal intelligence, but one can scarcely impute criminality to all feeble-minded persons or low intelligence to all criminals. Certainly the cleverest offenders are not caught so easily; and the perpetrator of white-collar crime, especially among respectable businessmen, is probably above average in intelligence. Intelligence is, in fact, associated with type of offense. The people found in local jails have low intelligence, on the average; those found in federal penitentiaries, high.

Classifications of Criminals

The social and societal problems presented by criminals do not fit any simple scheme or principle. When one considers the literally thousands of laws on the statute books, covering almost every aspect of human life, the impossibility of finding any single formula to fit violations of every law becomes clear. What, excepting the fact that both were found guilty of violating laws, do two such men as Alger Hiss and Frank Costello have in common? Or conscientious objectors and gambling-syndicate heads? Or panderers and Communist Party leaders? Or traitors and drug-pushers? All are criminals; all are different. It has been said that criminals have no more in common than have people who wear brown shoes.

There have been many attempts to classify criminals. The simplest is in terms of the seriousness of the crimes they commit: it classifies criminals as felons and misdemeanants. A felon has committed a crime which can be punished by imprisonment in a state institution for at least a year, or by death. A misdemeanant has committed an offense which carries a lesser punishment, such as a small fine or a short jail term. In addition, such a classification includes the traitor and the person who has violated a municipal ordinance, the behavior of the first being more serious than a felony, that of the second, less serious than a misdemeanor. Criminals may also be classified by the specific kinds of crimes they commit, into murderers, robbers, thieves, or burglars; or by the frequency of violation, into casual, occasional, episodic, or professional; or by the social context, into individual or "lone wolf," team, gang, or organization criminals.

We have felt that for our purposes the most functional classification is that based on whether the person is mainly a medical or a legal problem, that is, whether he should be assigned the status of a patient or of a criminal. In Chapter 14 we dealt with the first type; at this point, therefore, we limit our discussion to the second.

"Normal" Criminals

Having discussed the psychiatric aspects of certain kinds of criminal behavior in Chapter 14, then, we are now free to devote our attention to the "normal" criminal, to the men and women, that is, who are no more emotionally disturbed than the rest of the population. We cannot use a psychiatric explanation for the behavior we are here discussing. We have sieved out the cases in which crime was the secondary characteristic and personality disturbance the primary one. The people we are concerned with here are, as a population, just as normal as other people. We are not implying that every single person in this category is a model of normal mental health. The point is merely that we are to conceive of this population as having about the same distribution of intelligence, neuroses, height, and weight as the total population. It is in this sense that they are called "normal."

We may subclassify these normal criminals into as many categories as we wish, according to how detailed we wish them to be. For our purposes three may be sufficient: stress criminals; criminals in the role of businessmen; and white-collar criminals, or businessmen, professional persons, and public officials who perform criminal acts in their role of businessmen, professionals, or officials. A residual category would include those who commit crimes as a matter of principle, e.g., traitors and political criminals, but we shall have nothing to say about them.

Our main emphasis will be on criminals as businessmen, that is, on the people who perform the anomalous roles referred to in Chapter 2, and on white-collar criminals, or businessmen, professional persons, and officials who violate their roles. Anomalous roles are those which are forbidden by law and hence criminal by definition, yet which continue to flourish. The rewards for those who perform these illegal roles are usually great enough to counterbalance the chance of being caught and punished. The people who direct the gambling industry, for example, or the drug traffic, perform illegal roles. When people who are performing legal roles violate trust, or give or accept bribes, or cheat, or in any other way do violence to the subtle web of confidence on which group integrity depends, they are acting contrary to the definition or official specifications (if not their own conception) of their roles. When the role specifications which they violate are laid down by law, they are criminals, "white-collar criminals." Before we turn to a discussion of these two categories of criminals, we shall speak briefly about the stress criminal.

The Stress Criminal

Stress criminals may be subdivided into the casual, the occasional, and the episodic offenders. These men and women are law-abiding for the most part, and succumb to the temptation of law violation only under a certain amount of stress. The casual offender violates traffic laws because he is in a hurry, or parking regulations because he cannot be bothered to walk so far. The occasional offender may hunt without a license, or drive "under the influence." He may even, if the stress becomes intense, embezzle funds, forge a check, or steal a car. Often the occasional offender has not premeditated the crime; it "just happened" under some kind of stress.

Another kind of criminal behavior which occurs in normal personalities has been labeled episodic.[18] This is the kind of crime which any law-abiding person might commit under great stress. Most of us can understand the motivation which leads a man to kill his wife when he finds her in another man's arms, or which leads a man to kill someone who is blackmailing him. We understand that arbitrary and unjust treatment, without recourse to vindication, might lead to assault, if not to murder. Juries usually make some allowance for such stress-induced crimes. Most episodic criminals commit only one crime. This is the kind of crime which is likely to figure in fiction and in drama. We can all share the desire for revenge, the frustration, the feeling of hatred, or the greed which motivates this kind of crime.[19] Unlike the senseless killing of the psychotic, the crime of the normal offender often elicits in us the thought, There but for the grace of God go I.

Although the episodic criminal is the most important one in the popular or folk imagination, the criminals who make a career of crime are more important. Crime is their vocation. They make their living at it.

The Criminal in the Role of Businessman

It is often noted that criminals will sometimes do twice as much work to acquire their money as they would have to do to earn it honestly. But the point is that they like the work they do. They are skilled or talented in it. They prefer it to other kinds of work. These are the men and women who organize and run gambling syndicates; they direct the illegal drug traffic. Sometimes they direct organized prostitution. They are master bank robbers or swindlers. They smuggle. They are constantly on the lookout for ways and means to "make a fast buck." They look upon themselves as businessmen.

In order to understand the career criminal we must divest ourselves of moral disapprobation of his occupation and analyze it as we would any other. The planning and administration of crime is, as an occupation, probably on a professional level. It demands the same kind of talent as planning and administration in any other occupation or industry. People who can do it have high status in their group. They are the entrepreneurs. They have the same kinds of problems that other top-level businessmen have. They must often engage lawyers. In a large enterprise, accountants, or at any rate people who know how to keep records, must also be engaged. At the other extreme are those who engage in the least skilled occupations. As in other industries, there must be people who can do the heavy work—lifting, hauling, moving. Semiskilled and skilled workers also have their niche. Even murder demands more than sheer strength. Indeed, it rarely calls for brute strength; to be successful, certain skills are necessary. The organizational chart of a well-run criminal enterprise would probably not look very different from that of a legitimate enterprise. The one difference would be that, because it must always be on the *qui vive,* the tendency to fall into bureaucratic rigidity is doubtless much less.

We should not picture the people who make their living by criminal occupations as demoralized derelicts. They are often very proud of their talents and skills. They know intellectually that what they do is forbidden, illegal, even wrong. But they are not convinced of it. They do not consider themselves "bad people." It is simply that the kinds of things they can do well have no legitimate market. But they find recognition of their talents among their fellow professionals. A well-done job may call forth the admiration of peers. The man who does it may brag about it for a long time. There is as much satisfaction in this kind of homage as in homage won in legitimate activities. The successful pursuit of a criminal career may bring with it the same kinds of status reward as those won in respected occupations.

To illustrate the kinds of talent which lead to success in the profession of crime, several cases are presented here. The first kind of talent is one which is useful in gambling. The second is one involving great versatility, devoted, in this case, to swindling. And the third is one in which administrative skill is combined with ability to entertain.

PROFESSIONAL GAMBLER [20]

There are an enormous number of casual, occasional, episodic, and compulsive gamblers; [21] we are not concerned with them here. Our interest is in the men who make a living from gambling. These men have been classified into: the percentage gambler, the cardsharp or "cheaper," and the banker.

The percentage gambler may border on the compulsive, but he is an excellent illustration of the person with a talent which has no legitimate market. He is described here not because he is a common type, but because in him is illustrated a skill which has been devoted to illegal activities.

The percentage gambler—the bridge or poker expert, the crap-shooter whose brain is unusually agile at probabilities, the skillful player of any game in which skill is the dominant factor and the inferior player must lose in the long run . . . does not gamble in the usual sense. Unless he feels sure that he has an "edge," a better-than-even chance of winning, he does not bet.

The social status of the percentage gambler is even more variable than his psychological make-up. It depends partly on the social status of his game. . . .

The percentage gambler has a "feel" for probabilities—the talent that, when applied to cardplaying, is called card sense. It is difficult for an observer to escape the belief that this is an innate aptitude, rather than a result of application and tutelage. It is almost impossible to trick the percentage gambler into accepting a bad bet (that is, any venture in which the chances are that he will lose, rather than win, in the long run). Skill in most betting and gambling games depends not so much on ability to calculate probabilities as on an almost intuitive facility at translating the probabilities into terms of immediate advantage. The percentage gambler seldom knows anything of permutations and combinations, and he is usually not particularly good at arithmetic. Nevertheless, he could prevail, at most games, over professors of mathematics. . . .

The percentage gambler's approach to his profession is the typical underworld one. He has found that he has a measure of skill that he can exploit, just as the thug has found that he has an adequate quantity of recklessness; and each of them has despaired of the future at a respectable occupation. It should be noted here that criminal society in general has that sense of "percentage" characteristic of the percentage gambler; and also a reliance on hope that is characteristic of most gamblers.[22]

It is estimated that there are at least half a million cardsharps in the United States, ranging from the aristocracy among them, the prestidigitators, to the teams who rely on mechanical devices and collusive tricks.[23]

Then there is the banker who is not actually a gambler himself. He is the entrepreneur, the man who runs the gambling establishment. His talents are not those of the percentage gambler or the cardsharp but those of any ordinary businessman.

The banker is the man who owns or operates a casino—a gambling house. Essential to a proper definition of gambling is the consciousness of risk. One who does not accept risk is not gambling. The proprietor of a gambling house, by this definition, is no more a gambler than is a merchant, and certainly no more than an insurance underwriter; he lets his patrons gamble among themselves, expecting by experience and mathematics that a determinable portion of the money bet will remain with him. But he is or tends to become a "racketeer." He must bribe the law enforcement agencies if he would stay in business; therefore he must condone, protect, harbor, and associate with others who pursue illegal vocations by buying protection. . . .

The large gambling houses that are not connected with restaurants are, with few exceptions, operated by underworld groups who are implicated in other illicit enterprises. Small gambling houses are often opened by ex-gamblers who acquire the capital necessary to equip an apartment with the facilities for poker games, dice games, or any other form of gambling that does not require expensive paraphernalia. Such gambling rooms pay modest profits to the operators, and are seldom important enough to attract the attention of either the underworld or the police.[24]

Gambling in this commercialized form is one of the biggest industries in the country.[25] Its alleged head was Frank Costello. The same men who run the gambling syndicate are likely to be involved in other illegal businesses also. They have been called "vice lords."

We now present two people, a man and a woman, who carved out successful careers for themselves in criminal occupations. One was a swindler who "earned" something like $8,000,000 over a period of fifty years and the other was the most famous madam in recent times. Both illustrate the professional pride, the rationalization, and even the complacence of the successful careerist in crime, as well as the different kinds of talents that are used in illegal activities.

SWINDLER [26]

Analyzing my own actions in retrospect, I don't believe I ever had any basic desire to be dishonest. One of the motivating factors in my actions was, of course, the desire to acquire money. The other motive was a lust for adventure—and this was the only kind of adventure for which I was equipped.

The men I swindled were also motivated by a desire to acquire money, and they didn't care at whose expense they got it. I was particular. I took money only from those who could afford it and were willing to go in with me in schemes they fancied would fleece others. . . .

Lies were the foundation of my schemes. A lie is an allurement, a fabrication, that can be embellished into a fantasy. It can be clothed in the raiments of a mystic conception. Truth is cold, sober fact, not so comfortable to absorb. A lie is more palatable. The most detested person in the world is the one who always tells the truth, who never romances. If a lie is told often enough even the teller comes to believe it. It becomes a habit. And habit is like a cable. Each day another strand is added until you have woven a cable that is unbreakable. It was that way with me. I found it far more interesting and profitable to romance than to tell the truth. . . .

People say that I am the most successful and the most colorful confidence man that ever lived. I won't deny it. There is good reason why I am regarded as in a class by myself.

The fact is that I have played more roles in real life than the average actor ever dreamed of. The actor has a script carefully prepared for him in advance. I made my own script as I went along, depending upon my wits for any contingency.

Some small gesture that was out of character in the role I was portraying or the wrong answer to a question might have betrayed me. Fortunately for me, I always had the right answer and carried off convincingly the role I played.

To do this successfully—as I did for about half a century—I had to possess, first of all, a vast store of general information. Besides that, I had to know the rudiments of many professsions. If I played the role of a physician, I had to be in a position to use medical terms accurately. As a mining engineer, I had to know geology and mineralogy. As a broker or investment banker, I had to be up on the latest and most intricate financial matters. Perhaps the most important of all my qualifications was a good knowledge of the law. I kept well posted on this subject. Over the years, I have seen many new laws passed—most of them restricting the freedom of the individual. No doubt I was the inspiration for some of these statutes.

It is my hope that I will live to see the enactment of one more law—to mete out equal punishment for all who have larceny in their hearts. . . . I have never taken a dime from honest, hard-working people who could not afford to lose. But the victims of confidence games are usually people who are wealthy and can afford to pay the con man's price for the lesson. I ought to know. I've had dealings with some of the wealthiest men in the country. They had plenty of money, but they fell for my schemes because they were greedy for more. In my time, I devised some ingenious plans to relieve these people of part of their wealth, at the same time teaching them that it does not pay to be too voracious. . . .

I am now seventy years old and I look back over my career with mingled feelings. I have retired and I want to do what I can to promote harmony among my fellow men. For this reason, I decided to tell the inside story of my long and, I must admit, dishonorable career.

It is interesting to note the defenses such men build up in their own minds. This man's role, according to his own estimates, is not too far from the Robin Hood role. He wants to think of himself, at any rate, as social-minded.

MADAM

Our third illustration is of professional pride in a woman. She happened to have a remarkable talent for running a high-class brothel. She had a flair for serving as hostess. She was apparently a warm, vivacious, and energetic woman. In her own profession she had extremely high status. When she tried to transfer her talents to legitimate occupations—running a lingerie shop, for example—she was not successful. Not only did she earn much less money; as an "honest woman" she had lower social status. Men who enjoyed her company and patronized her illegitimate establishment would not associate with her when she was merely the manager of a store. There was much incentive for her to engage in the kind of business for which she had great talent and in which her status was high.

In an interview with a psychologist while in jail, she resented the implied condescension in the questions. She knew she had at least as much ability—albeit along different lines—as the psychologist.

I resented being treated like a child—and a backward child at that. If I was sane enough to conduct the most famous house in the biggest city in the world, smart enough to cope with cops and drunks, to amuse and be on friendly terms with people on the top intellectual and social levels, I didn't need advice from a girl who probably hadn't one tenth the human experience —clinical experience—I'd had.[27]

Attempting to explain her great success, she pointed out the high quality of the establishment she operated.

To me . . . my patrons were not just ambulatory bankrolls, but individual human beings—social acquaintances and often friends—entitled to the cordiality and consideration one extends to an honored guest. . . . If I have an angle . . . it's quality and consideration—the quality of my establishment and consideration for my customers. Bergdorf's and Bonwit's dress their windows attractively to pull in trade. I give my customers an attractive house. People in stores prefer to patronize good-looking, capable sales girls. I give my customers good-looking, capable hostesses. In the finest and most exclusive shops, the customers are treated as privileged friends of the management, their special likes and dislikes are tabulated, and they are given personalized service. Well, that's the way I try to run my business.[28]

She was proud of her clientele.

During these last peacetime years, I, as New York's premier madam, ran a close second to Grover Whalen as an official greeter. Whenever it was a

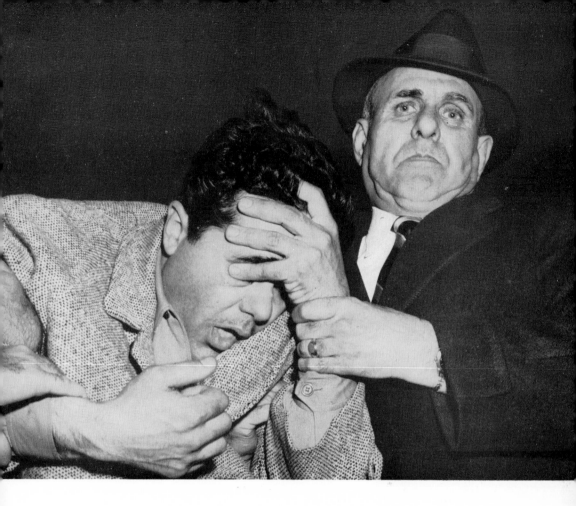

Why is this criminal ashamed? He tries to cover his face from the photographer, but not because he is suspected of taking part in a bank robbery. That would lower him in the eyes only of people like the readers and the author of this book, and he really doesn't care very much what they think. If the police had not arrested him he would have swaggered about in his world and enjoyed high status for his accomplishment. Apprentices and neophytes in criminal careers would have admired and imitated him. He would not have had to hide his head in shame.

But he was caught. In the eyes of the people who matter to him, therefore, he has failed. It is this proof of his ineptitude in his vocation, rather than the commission of a crime, that makes him feel disgraced. Not our standards, but those of his reference group, determine how he feels. He was not successful in his profession of crime. Fellow professionals will look down on him. He has the same reaction to failure that any business or professional man would have. He has lost face.

There is a large, albeit indeterminate, number of men like this one who make their living by crime. Could you tell they were criminals if you passed them on the street? *(United Press Photo)* question of providing a visiting V.I.P. with the more informal type of female companionship, I was usually appointed chairman of the sub-rosa entertainment committee, and, as a result, could boast a clientele culled not only from Who's Who and the Social Register, but from Burke's Peerage and the Almanach de Gotha.[29]

The product she marketed was of top quality, in effect, a kind of geisha girl.

> . . . my girls . . . were always beautifully groomed and lovely to look at and gay and responsive . . . always flattering . . . sympathizing. . . . Of course they were getting paid for it. . . .[30]

This woman, at the top in a criminal vocation, also bragged of her ideals:

> There were two . . . precepts which I applied to running my house: cleanliness is next to godliness, and honesty is the best policy. I was a fanatic on the subject of cleanliness. It was a must that both the house and the girls be immaculate. As for honesty, I considered it a keystone in my relationship with the customers.[31]

Like most professional criminals, this woman rationalized her occupation. She had always told her employees, "If you have to be a prostitute, be a good one. Well, the same applied to me. If I had to be a madam, I'd be a good madam. . . ." [32] She defined her role as socially useful and therefore justified.

> I had found that being cynical and half-hearted about my profession had worked out to the disadvantage both of my customers and myself. But if I could think of myself as fulfilling a need, as one in a long line which stretched back to the beginning of civilization, then, no matter what stigma attached to my calling, at least I was not "antisocial." I had a very definite place in the social structure. I belonged, I had a job to do, and I could find satisfaction in doing it the very best way I knew how.[33]

She also rationalized acceptance of expensive gifts on the basis that if others did, why shouldn't she? "Sometimes, my patrons made me handsome presents when they were particularly pleased with my brand of hospitality. And if I liked the man I would accept his gift. After all, if Washington officials can accept deep freezes, why shouldn't I grab off a little ice?" [34]

She also made much of the fact that "I never permit a girl to work for me unless she is already committed to the life." [35] She was proud that the girls who worked for her fared well. She felt especially proud of the initiatory experiences entrusted to her by fathers of young men:

> Often boys were brought to my place by their fathers. . . . They knew the physical and emotional damage that can result if a youth begins his sex life with some furtive, sordid episode which may forever make ugly and

shameful this aspect of human nature. They realized the importance of a satisfying and psychologically right initial sex experience, with nothing un-dignified nor cheap about it, and they relied on my tact and good judgment in selecting a congenial partner and putting the boy at his ease. I took a special interest in such boys, and was proud of their friendship and their trust in me. As they grew older, they often would discuss with me their future brides, and it was then I thought of them, rather sadly, as my own sons.[36]

Like the swindler presented above, Polly Adler conceived of herself as social-minded. She even viewed herself as performing an important role. She had to, in order to keep up her morale.

OCCUPATIONAL STRUCTURE OF OLD-FASHIONED PROSTITUTION. The criminal careerists just presented—the professional gambler, the swin-dler, and the madam—are the stars, the entrepreneurs, the highly skilled and talented. But as in any other commercial enterprise, there are a great many criminal jobs which call for less ability.

As an illustration of the complex division of labor which may be required in an illegal industry, we insert here, although it is of only his-torical interest at the present time, a description of how prostitution used to be organized. There were many roles that had to be performed, for traffic in sex was once a large industry. There were, for example, recruitment problems. Although some girls were always available, new "stock" was always wanted to replenish inventory. The traffic in women and girls brought recruits into the business who, without such effort, might not have entered.[37] In addition, business had to be solicited, for despite the argument that the demand for the prostitute's service is always great, under the old system there was competition for the busi-ness and men had to go out and hunt customers. The following descrip-tion illustrates how a great criminal industry was once organized.

Young people used to be exposed to open and flagrant commercialized prostitution. In most cities—large and small, from Maine to California—red-light districts or comparable conditions thrived. Houses of prostitution were also scattered through business and residential areas, usually within easy dis-tance of the main part of town. Streetwalkers patrolled the principal and secondary streets night in and night out. The back rooms of saloons were hangouts for prostitutes who openly accosted all comers. They took their trade to hotels or rooming houses nearby, whose owners or managers rented rooms exclusively for immoral purposes.

Steerers and ropers circulated about the tenderloins, directed trade to brothels and similar places, and boasted about the new stock that was always available. Very frequently they accosted their customers in full view of police officers on post, because they knew that those for whom they hustled had the green light to carry on their illicit activities.

Their accosting was open and above board, their sales talk similar to that of circus barkers.

Steerers got weekly salaries; other go-betweens got commissions on each customer they provided. Pimps lurked nearby in case a customer became obstreperous . . . and incidentally computed the number of customers the girls entertained to be sure that they were not holding out.

Tolerant municipal administrations permeated with graft and corruption made such conditions possible. Scarcely a person connected with the racket escaped without paying his or her way. The revenue that flowed into the pockets of corrupt politicians and law enforcement officials ran to millions of dollars. Vice districts became known as tenderloins after a police official who was placed in charge of a vice area in a large city boasted: "I've been eating chuck steak all my life . . . now I can afford tenderloin."

The owners of brothels—as well as procurers, pimps and some policemen—also grew wealthy. The prostitutes themselves, almost always in debt, eked out a mere existence . . . though they accommodated an average of 30 customers a day, and their daily earnings usually amounted to from $20 to $60.

Prostitution underworldlings always had their eyes on new stock and used every means to recruit it. Recruitment was not always easy; frequently they had to use strong-arm methods. Hardened prostitutes helped to induce and coerce green girls into the business . . . and taught them all the tricks of the trade.

Most brothels in the smaller cities harbored at least five inmates. Those in larger cities had as many as 10 or 20, and sometimes 30. Twenty-four hours a day, seven days a week, month after month they were on duty. Those who lived on the premises paid exorbitant rates for room and board and were compelled to buy necessities and knick-knacks from peddlers who split the overcharge with the operators. In addition, the inmates had to divide their earnings 50–50 with the operators of the houses.

In some cities the inmates lived at home and reported for duty in day or night shifts. They usually preferred late hours since they did most of their business after dark.

Frequently their pimps appeared on the scene to collect their earnings and then escorted them to hangouts where they compared notes with others in the racket and discussed their common interests.[38]

The status structure in this industry was as clear-cut as in any legal business. And the prostitute herself was usually at the bottom of the status structure, the most exploited, and the least likely to become rich.

The modern promiscuous girl is likely to have a more independent status. She is a call girl who makes her services available, as her title suggests, on call. But she is less likely to be exploited. After a few years she may retire, marry, and "live happily ever after," or at least uneventfully from the point of view of the law.

All of the criminals we have described and illustrated so far conceive of themselves as criminals and are so regarded by others. But there is a class of criminals—far more important than those so far discussed in terms of their impact on our society—who do not think of themselves as criminals and who are not so viewed by the public. Who are they? They are white-collar criminals, whose behavior we now examine.

The White-Collar Criminal

The counterparts to the criminal as businessman are the business and professional men who perform criminal acts. The kinds of crime which they perpetrate have come to be known as white-collar crime.

White-collar crime may be defined approximately as a crime committed by a person of respectability and high social status in the course of his occupation. . . . It excludes many crimes of the upper class, such as most of their cases of murder, adultery, and intoxication, since these are not customarily a part of their occupational procedures. Also, it excludes the confidence games of wealthy members of the underworld, since they are not persons of respectability and high social status.[39]

BUSINESS AND PROFESSIONAL MEN AS CRIMINALS. Fraud, violation of trust, and misrepresentation are characteristic forms which white-collar crime may take. During the war, black marketing and violation of price regulations were forms of white-collar crime. White-collar crime such as the illegal sale of narcotics by physicians or collusion with criminals by lawyers may also occur among professionals; or it may occur among government officials in the form of acceptance of bribes.

Most white-collar crime is financial in nature; its cost to the economy is estimated as several times greater than the financial cost of all customary types of crime.

The financial cost of white-collar crime is probably several times as great as the financial cost of all the crimes which are customarily regarded as "the crime problem." An officer of a chain grocery store in one year embezzled $600,000, which was six times as much as the annual losses from five hundred burglaries and robberies of the stores in that chain. Public enemies number one to six secured $130,000 by burglary and robbery in 1938, while the sum stolen by Ivar Krueger is estimated at $250,000,000, or nearly two thousand times as much. The New York Times in 1931 reported four cases of embezzlement in the United States with a loss of more than a million dollars each and a combined loss of nine million dollars. Although a million-dollar burglar or robber is practically unheard of, the million-dollar embezzler is a small-fry among white-collar criminals. The estimated loss to investors in one investment trust from 1929 to 1935 was $580,000,000, due primarily to the fact that 75 percent of the values in the portfolio were in securities of affiliated companies, although this investment house advertised the importance of diversification in investments and its expert services in selecting safe investments. The claim was made in Chicago around 1930 that householders lost $54,000,000 in two years during the tenure of a city sealer who granted immunity from inspection to stores which provided Christmas baskets for his constituents.[40]

The damage which white-collar crime inflicts financially is only part of its dysfunctionality; it is dysfunctional also in the effect it has on moral and social organization, an effect much more damaging even than ordinary crime: "White-collar crimes violate trust and therefore create distrust; this lowers social morale and produces social disorganization. Many of the white-collar crimes attack the fundamental principles of the American institutions. Ordinary crimes, on the other hand, produce little effect on social institutions or social organization." [41]

If a team of burglars entered every apartment in a housing unit regularly every month and took about six dollars from each one, there would be a tremendous hue and cry about a crime wave; the community would be alarmed. It would frighten everyone to think that such things could happen. But if the six dollars are taken in the form of an illegally authorized rent increase, no one thinks anything of it.[42] Such things are being done all the time by perfectly conventional businessmen, men we meet every day in the usual course of business. In an investigation of the Federal Housing Administration, for example, it was found that builders would falsify the estimated costs of building, secure government loans or mortgages in excess of the actual costs, and pocket the difference, or "windfall." Sometimes they would certify certain amounts as labor costs, as the law specified, and then pay less than the specified wage. Sometimes they would hold over construction costs and charge them to the first period of operation, thus showing that operating costs were high, and apply for increases in rent so that they could get the $6\frac{1}{2}$ per cent on their investment to which they were entitled. Sometimes they would persuade people to sign a contract with FHA for loans for home repairs at high rates; if they defaulted on the payment, the United States Government had to bring suit "against the victim of the fraud, and the victim of the fraud, of course, is rather upset that the United States Government is suing him instead of the fellow who defrauded him." [43]

But are these businessmen really criminals? Are their acts really crimes? Yes, says one student of the subject, in every respect except the procedural treatment involved in dealing with them.

With respect to the crimes themselves, he analyzes 980 decisions made against 70 large corporations. Of these, 16 per cent of the acts in question were clearly criminal by any test, since the decisions with respect to them were made by criminal courts and hence they were *ipso facto* criminal acts. But so were many of the remaining 84 per cent—621 out of 779—even though not adjudicated in criminal but in civil courts. These acts were prohibited by the State as injuries to the State and were punishable; they thus fulfill the two abstract criteria necessary in the definition of a crime. So far as the acts themselves are concerned, he concludes, there is no question that they are crimes as unequivocally as are ordinary felonies.[44]

Are these businessmen really criminals? This same author concludes that they are. He makes a point-for-point comparison of the white-collar criminal and the professional thief and finds much in common. Like the criminality of the professional thief, that of the white-collar criminal is persistent. Like the criminality of the professional thief, that of the white-collar criminal is much more extensive than the records indicate. Like the professional thief, "the businessman who violates the laws which are designed to regulate business does not customarily lose status among his business associates. . . . A violation of the legal code is not necessarily a violation of the business code. Prestige is lost by violation of the business code but not by violation of the legal code." [45] Just as the professional thief feels contempt for law, policemen, prosecutors, and judges, so does the white-collar criminal feel contempt for law, government, and governmental personnel, who are characterized as "snoopers." Like much of the work of the professional thief, the acts of the white-collar criminal are organized, either formally or informally through consensus.

Despite these similarities between the professional thief and the white-collar criminal, however, there are important differences between them. The professional thief conceives of himself as a criminal and so does the general public; he even takes pride in his criminal reputation. The white-collar criminal, on the other hand, thinks of himself as a respectable citizen and so does the public. The businessman criminals are considered by the courts to be "men of affairs, of experience, of refinement, and of culture, and of excellent reputation and standing in the business and social world." [46]

This difference between the professional thief and the white-collar or businessman criminal is a status difference, however, rather than a difference in the "realness" of their crimes.

The white-collar criminal does not conceive of himself as a criminal because he is not dealt with under the same official procedures as other criminals and because, owing to his class status, he does not engage in intimate personal association with those who define themselves as criminals. Furthermore, many variations are found in the identification of self with others even among those who conceive of themselves as conforming to the ideal type of criminal. The word "criminal" may be applied to all of them, but the essence varies. Prisoners generally constitute a hierarchy, with high-class confidence men at the top at present and with the "yegg" or safe-breaker at the top in earlier generations. One of these classes of prisoners does not identify itself with the others and those in the upper criminal class look with contempt upon the lower criminal class. They place in the lower class of criminals the small number of businessmen who have been convicted and committed to prisons for offenses such as embezzlement. The failure of a white-collar criminal to identify himself with other criminals is in part an instance of the general process of stratification and segregation among criminals.[47]

Although the businessman criminal does not conceive of himself as a criminal, he does recognize himself as a law violator and may even take pride in his cleverness in evading or violating the law and expect support, if not admiration, from his associates if he succeeds.

No more than the white-collar criminal himself does the public think of him as a criminal because he does not fit the stereotype. Here again the status dimension is important. These men have high status in the community; they have power. They do not look like "the criminal type."

Unlike the professional thief, white-collar criminals maintain an attitude of public adherence to the law; their violations are secret. The professional thief seeks the same end by concealing his identity, since the fact of his crime is clear and observable. Just as the professional thief resorts to aliases, the corporation criminal seeks secrecy by juggling corporate personalities and brand names. As the professional thief uses a mouthpiece to defend him against specific charges, the corporation criminal uses legal, advertising, and public relations experts not only for defense but also to influence public opinion and legislation in his favor.[48]

Like any other kind of nonpsychotic criminal behavior, white-collar crime is learned from people who define it favorably and in isolation from those who define it unfavorably.[49] An analysis of a number of documents written by white-collar criminals in subordinate positions shows that they came from good homes in good neighborhoods and that they had no records as juvenile delinquents. In some cases they were ordered to perform criminal acts by their employers; in other cases they learned from those in their own rank how to succeed by illegal acts. They learned specific techniques for violating the law as well as definitions of situations in which those techniques might be used. They developed rationalizing ideologies such as "business is business," or "we're not in business for our health." "These generalizations, whether transmitted as such or abstracted from concrete experiences, assist the neophyte in business to accept the illegal practices and provide rationalizations for them."[50]

The story is told of a small town which had a speed limit of thirty miles an hour. Ordinarily it paid no attention to enforcement. So long as moderate speeds were maintained through its streets, nothing was done. But when the town exchequer ran low and funds were needed, the constable would go out and arrest the first half dozen drivers he saw, fine them, and then return to his ordinary business. The law was kept on the books as a handy tool to use in case of need. Many such laws grace the books of all kinds of jurisdictions. So long as violations are not too blatant, or so long as public indignation is not too militant, enforcement is lax. But the laws are retained in case they are needed in a pinch.

Much business is therefore transacted on the margin of legality. So long as they can "get away with it," businessmen criminals will continue to engage in illegal practices.

Some businessmen may, however, be genuinely averse to the kinds of practices they feel they must engage in. They feel they are forced to, for competition is a hard taskmaster. The least scrupulous businessman sets the standard.

> A . . . problem posed by competition is its effects on character and personality. . . . Profit rather than production of goods is sought, and throat-cutting, unfair practices, shoddy workmanship are constant temptations. Businessmen often complain that they hate to do the things they are "forced to do" under the pressure of competition. They scorn themselves for doing what they feel they have to do. They suffer self-hatred and a sense of guilt.[51]

By a kind of Gresham's law—which states that bad money drives good money out of the market—low business standards tend to drive good ones out of the market.

And if the businessmen wish to come to some sort of cooperative agreement to protect themselves against being driven to practices which they object to, this is also illegal. A certain amount of criminal behavior is, in effect, almost built into a competitive economy.[52] The following is an illustration:

> A chemist who had been employed to advise this firm as to the scientific basis for claims in advertisements made the following statement regarding his experiences.

> > When I got members of the firm off in a corner and we were talking confidentially, they frankly deplored the misrepresentations in their advertisements. At the same time they said it was necessary to advertise in this manner in order to attract the attention of customers and sell their products. Since other firms are making extravagant claims regarding their products, we must make extravagant claims regarding our products. A mere statement of fact regarding our products would make no impression on customers in the face of the ads of other firms.[53]

Bribery is another of the major forms which white-collar crime takes. It is not necessarily bribery of public officials; it may be bribery of other businessmen. But bribery of public officials is a common offense. And, of course, the person who accepts the bribe is a criminal also. The usual name for this behavior is "graft and corruption." We turn to a brief discussion of the men who engage in this form of crime.

PUBLIC OFFICIALS AS CRIMINALS. Much crime, white-collar or blue-collar, is possible only because of the cooperation of public officials. Professional thieves learn which policemen they can bribe and which they cannot. Illegal businessmen, such as those who operate commercialized gambling houses, the illegal sale of liquor, and brothels, pay protection money to the police as a kind of license tax. The traffic violator flashes a bill in the face of the officer and expects to have his ticket torn up. Influential criminals have connections high in the power hierarchy and can see that pressure is put on law enforcement officers and even judges who are themselves honest.

Administrative as well as law enforcement officials may cooperate with criminals, more likely white-collar than any other kind. The following account of the career of a government official illustrates one such case; this man's career is also an interesting illustration of upward occupational mobility in the field of crime. With a flair for white-collar crime, he began at the lowest rung and gradually worked his way up. How typical or representative he is there is no way of knowing.

Clyde L. Powell was born March 2, 1896, at Salem, Mo.; served in World War I, having enlisted in September 1917, and being discharged in May 1919. He claimed 17 months' service in France and claimed attendance at the University of Missouri, engineering department, from 1914 to 1917 without graduation. Recent inquiry indicates there is no record of Clyde L. Powell attending Missouri University, Columbia, Mo., or the Missouri School of Mines, Rolla, Mo., during the period 1914–17.

The records of the St. Louis, Mo., police department reflect that a Clyde L. Powell . . . age 19 years, a bellboy, was arrested on March 29, 1916, for larceny from a dwelling. It is reported that this individual had two pawn tickets in his possession at the time of arrest. The records reflect he admitted these pawn tickets were for a ring and a pair of gold cuff links stolen from two different hotel guests. On May 2, 1916, the above-described Clyde L. Powell was sentenced to 1 year in the workhouse, and was paroled on the same date. The records of the circuit clerk for the criminal causes court, St. Louis, Mo., reflect that Clyde L. Powell, on May 2, 1916, upon entering a plea of guilty, was sentenced to 1 year in the workhouse for larceny of a ring valued at $25 from I. C. McNiece, of the Washington Hotel, St. Louis, Mo. It appears that this Clyde L. Powell was paroled on the same date, and ordered to report by letter to the judge. The circuit clerk's records show an application for pardon dated May 3, 1916 (same day as sentenced), and signed the same date. This application indicates the applicant, Clyde L. Powell, was born March 2, 1897; was employed at the Washington Hotel; and gave his home address as Salem, Mo. . . .

The identification record for one Clyde Lilbon Powell, Federal Bureau of Investigation No. 5180, reflected he entered the United States Army on June 4, 1917, at Kansas City, Mo. . . . The identification record reflects, further, that the same person was arrested by the Philadelphia, Pa., police department, on October 30, 1917, on a charge of larceny; entered a plea of guilty on November 8, 1917; was given a suspended sentence; and was discharged. The identification record shows this same Clyde Lilbon Powell was again arrested on January 12, 1920, by the Little Rock, Ark., police department, on a charge of suspicion. No disposition of this arrest is shown.

A search of the police records of the Little Rock, Ark., police department indicated one Clyde Powell of Salem, Mo., was arrested on January 12, 1920, for suspicion of passing bogus checks and was discharged. A notation on the records of the Arkansas police department indicates "now wanted Texarkana, Tex., and Dallas, Tex., bad checks." The identification record reveals this same person was again arrested, this time on August 19, 1922, by the Dallas, Tex., police department, charged with passing a worthless check. It appears he made a restitution and was released. . . .

The service record reveals Powell was unable to report for duty when called on January 15, 1918, because he was being held by civil authorities in the County Jail, at Chicago, Ill., for having passed a worthless check, at the Siegel Cooper Co. . . . The service record reflects, further, that Clyde L. Powell entered on active duty on April 15, 1918. The record indicates that Powell was absent without leave from December 14, to December 18, 1918, and received a summary court-martial sentence of confinement at hard labor for 2 months, and forfeiture of two-thirds pay. . . .[54]

The record continues with charges of embezzlement (St. Louis, 1917), failure to have a state automobile license (St. Louis, 1931), disorderly conduct (Washington, D. C., 1943), and falsifying his police record on a Civil Service form. By 1945, however, he was in the upper echelons of crime. As an official in a government agency on a salary of $6,083.46 in 1945, he could deposit $14,380 in the bank; in ten years, he could deposit $158,000 in excess of his government salary.[55] No income tax was paid on this amount. Crime paid him handsomely.

It is important to remember that the criminals we have been discussing in this chapter constitute a population as normal as the general population. They are not pathological. The stresses and strains to which they are subject are the same as those all the rest of the population are subject to. Nor can we explain their behavior in terms of "broken" homes, slum background, or deprivation. They are products of a concatenation of circumstances and can be understood only against the backdrop of modern civilization.

What To Do with Criminals?

As in the famous recipe for roast duck, the first step would seem to be to catch the criminal. But in our present ignorance of the wisest way to treat criminals this may not always be the best recipe to follow. A vast amount of petty violation is, as we have seen above, simply ignored. If a great deal of pressure is put on a police force it will catch many offenders. But what, under present conditions, is gained? When the City of New York was planning to raze the Old Bowery to make way for urban redevelopments, a great increase in arrests for vagrancy and drunkenness was anticipated by the police force. For when the alcoholics had no refuge like the Bowery to resort to, they would have to drink and sober up in respectable neighborhoods where there would be little tolerance of them, where they would be reported to the police and therefore arrested. The ordinary jail is in no way superior to the flop-house so far as helping the alcoholic is concerned.

The tendency is, increasingly, as abundance makes it possible, to deal with certain cases as patients rather than as criminals, as medical or psychiatric problems rather than legal problems. The behavior of the criminal is incidental; the basic concern is the personality disturbance. When the criminal behavior is thus merely a secondary concomitant of a deep personality disturbance, it is folly to assume that it can be dealt with effectively on so superficial a level as the law specifies. The futility, for example, of dealing with the alcoholic or the drug addict as a legal problem has been demonstrated again and again. The vagrants and the petty offenders who crowd the police courts and comprise a large pro-portion of all cases dealt with by the courts—the so-called degenerates—can in no sensible way be dealt with on a strictly legal basis. We lock them up in a purely ritualistic manner. It is no more than a gesture, a bow in the direction of legal theory. No one is fooled. Then we dismiss them to repeat their minor offenses. An indeterminate proportion of them are probably not salvageable at all by the time they reach the court. They have gone too far in the deterioration process, whatever may have been their original potentialities. It is all but useless to invest time and resources in trying to rehabilitate them. Occasionally a reli-giously motivated person achieves unexpected and remarkable results with these cases. The Salvation Army does. But for many the only thing that can be done is to offer them kindly custodial care. Jail farms have been proposed to take care of them and to protect others from being annoyed or disturbed by them. The idea is not that they would be punished, but that they would be sheltered, and the rest of society would be protected. For those who seem salvageable, psychotherapy, either individually or in groups, has been recommended, as suggested in our discussion of alcoholism.

At the other extreme, for the psychotic criminals or the criminal insane hospitalization is, without doubt, the indicated treatment. Here again the intent is not punishment but therapy, where possible, custodial care, and protection of others against their depredations until they are well enough to be released, if ever.

Between the petty offenders at one extreme and the criminal insane at the other lies the psychiatric case who cannot be pronounced psychotic, but who is, nevertheless, by no means normal. These are the people who constitute so large a proportion of the present prison population. For these unstable men, many of them at least mildly paranoid, who have obscure motivations which make them really want confinement, for the man "who swaggers in his walk, who shoulders a guard out of his path, who makes a theatrical production of his contempt for authority," [56] some kind of imprisonment may be the best we can do. These men "will respect strict discipline and not much else. And with absolute dependability they will interpret kindliness or a softening of discipline as a sign of weakness to be exploited." [57] Psychotherapy would also seem to be worth-while.

There still remains a large population of criminals and people who perform criminal acts—the distinction was made above—who are no different from the population we call normal. What about imprisonment for them?

The idea of imprisonment is relatively new, at least in the form of the penitentiary. The idea of the penitentiary is probably useful for only a small proportion of criminals—the casual or occasional or episodic —or for those who already feel guilty or remorseful, who share the moral values of the community. But they probably do not need a penitentiary in order to be made to feel penitent. In all likelihood their rehabilitation would be hastened if they could work out their guilt—"debt to society," as it is often phrased—and be relieved of it in normal settings. The chances are that they are not dangerous and not likely to continue to commit crimes. As it now operates, the penitentiary is simply a prison, a place for incarcerating men. As such it is not only ineffective in any but a custodial way, it is actually damaging to many. One study, for example, found that the chances of recidivism, or repetition of crime, increased the longer a prisoner had been confined.[58] Far from rehabilitating the prisoner, incarceration actually deteriorated him.

Imprisonment, modern penologists feel, should be only one, and perhaps not even the chief, of many techniques used in dealing with convicted persons. Those who seem susceptible to resocialization should be dealt with in more appropriate ways. Probation under skilled leadership, it is argued, should be used far more than it is, not only because it is cheaper—five men can be supervised on parole for what it costs to maintain one man in prison—but also because it is more effective. The warden of a state prison believed that one third of the inmates in federal and state prisons should be released. They were imprisoned for minor offenses and could do well on parole. Another third, he said, had relatively simple problems that could be taken care of in a fairly short time. The other third constituted the hard-core cases with serious social maladjustments; they needed long-term confinement.[59]

When we consider the background of career criminals, that is, the people who have been making their living in criminal occupations, the futility of much of our treatment becomes obvious. To make it vivid, suppose we were trying to "de-doctor" by imprisonment a man who had been making his living by the practice of medicine. His personality has been integrated about his work and his colleagues. Whatever status he has achieved has been in his profession. He thinks of himself in this role. All his contacts with people are as a performer of this role. He looks at the world through the prism of his work. Naturally, the first thing he does when we release him is to return to the profession he knows. This is his life. Similarly, it is not perversity or innate criminality that draws the criminal back to his old life; it is the attraction of the familiar, the accustomed, the congenial. Changing a man's occupation, especially if it is one in which he has a high degree of talent and success, is an enormously difficult undertaking. Everything that his former occupation furnished him in the way of status, achievement, distinction, satisfaction, and reward must be matched by some substitute occupation in order to make the transition possible. The person must be reintegrated around some new role.

So much, then, for criminals who, except for the fact that they violate the law, are not different, as a population, from the rest of us.

We have now completed our survey of the social problems resulting not from pathologies which are social in their repercussions but from role disorganization or from changes in the organization of society for which we are unprepared. The people we have been discussing in Part V are normal; the problems in which they are enmeshed are societal in origin, and the solutions, where they are possible, are to be sought in societal processes. No pills or wonder drugs or medical miracles can help us here.

So far our chief emphasis in discussing social problems has been on the individual, or rather on classes of individuals, although we have never lost sight of the fact that they are not separate or isolated individuals but always members of groups. The pathologies of classes of individuals (Part IV) and the family and work roles of classes of individuals (Part V) were our chief concern, although, of course, always in a social context. We have also emphasized the importance of group-generated therapeutic forces. But we have not emphasized the fact that problems are sometimes generated by groups also. It is to a consideration of such group-generated problems, especially those of ranked status, that we turn in Part VI.

NOTES

1 It can be argued that criminal activities perform a function in supplying a market for forbidden goods and services. But this does not mean that it is not dysfunctional for the economy as a whole. It can also be argued that the cost of getting rid of crime, or, at any rate, of minimizing it, would be greater than the gain to be achieved. The proponents of this point of view mean that the minimization of crime would involve the sacrifice of many of the things we value, such as individual freedom, competitive enterprise, and similar qualities.

2 James S. Wallerstein and Clement J. Wyle, "Our Law-Abiding Law-Breakers," *Probation*, National Probation Association, April 1947, pp. 107–112.

3 Thorsten Sellin has summarized the reasons why crimes may not be reported to the police as follows: (1) the offense may be private, such as blackmail, sex crimes, or abortion; (2) the injured person may not wish to have the offense discovered; (3) the inconvenience may be too great; (4) public opinion may not favor law enforcement and reporting would be considered informing, especially in such areas as gambling or prostitution; (5) some offenses are not reported because they are known only by the offenders themselves, such as carrying a concealed weapon, traffic violation, disorderly conduct, vagrancy; and (6) reporting of offenses varies with public sentiment. (Research Memorandum on *Crime in the Depression* [Social Science Research Council, 1937], pp. 69–70.)

4 *Uniform Crime Reporting: A Complete Manual for Police*, Committee on Uniform Crime Records (International Association of Chiefs of Police, New York, 1929), pp. 24–25.

5 Police Commissioner of New York City, reported in the press, July 25, 1955.

6 Lyle W. Shannon, "The Spatial Distribution of Criminal Offenses by States," *Journal of Criminal Law, Criminology and Police Science*, 45 (Sept.-Oct. 1954), p. 273.

7 The actual percentages in each of these categories vary from year to year and from place to place, but the same general tendency seems to persist. In New York City in 1955 the clearance rates were as follows: narcotic felonies, 95.2 per cent; murder, 87.3 per cent; felonious assault, 70.6 per cent; rape, 69.1 per cent; other felonies, 69.1 per cent; burglaries, 50.7 per cent; robberies, 47.0 per cent; auto theft, 34.1 per cent; grand larceny, 25.0 per cent. For all major crimes the clearance rate was 46.9 per cent; for misdemeanors, 62.9 per cent; for both combined, 57.8 per cent. (*New York Times*, July 25, 1955.)

8 Courtland C. Van Vechten, "Differential Criminal Case Mortality in Selected Jurisdictions," *American Sociological Review*, 7 (Dec. 1942), pp. 833–839.

9 Walter C. Reckless, *The Crime Problem* (Appleton-Century-Crofts, 1950), pp. 58 ff.

10 E. H. Sutherland, *White Collar Crime* (Dryden, 1949).

11 Reckless, *op. cit.*, pp. 59–60.

12 *Ibid.*, p. 62.

13 Otto Pollak, *The Criminality of Women*

(Univ. of Pennsylvania Press, 1950), pp. 13–14.

14 Reckless, *op. cit.*, p. 64.

15 Federal prisons dealing with youthful offenders anticipated a great influx because of the increase in the number of young persons in the population. (*Federal Prisons* [United States Penitentiary, Leavenworth, 1954], p. 3.)

16 The median age of white foreign-born in 1950 was 56.1 years.

17 Luton Ackerson, *Children's Behavior Problems* (Univ. of Chicago Press, 1931).

18 Morris Plescowe, *Crime and Criminal Law, Vol. II* (National Law Library, Collier, 1939), pp. 6–18.

19 See the discerning analysis of man's preoccupation with this kind of crime in John Van Druten's "Truth, Terror, and the Common Man," *Saturday Review,* June 25, 1955, pp. 9–10, 26. "The murderer, by his act, has put himself outside the ordinary pale. He will walk forever after with a stain of difference on him, or within him, whether he is known or not. He has done a thing that almost every one of us has at one moment wanted to do, and he has become branded in doing it. We want most desperately to know what that brand feels like. He was a normal man whom we would not have recognized had we met him in the streetcar as being any different from other men."

20 For a discussion of the community problems created by commercialized gambling, see Jessie Bernard, *American Community Behavior* (Dryden, 1949), pp. 538–541.

21 For example, it is estimated that the number of people who play the numbers game is eight million; who bet on athletic events and elections, nineteen million; who play dice and cards for money, twenty-two million; who play bingo, buy lottery tickets, take part in raffles, or participate in football or baseball pools, twenty-six million. Regular gamblers are estimated at fifty million. (Ernest E. Blanche, "Gambling Odds Are Gimmicked!" *Annals of the American Academy of Political and Social Science,* 269 (May 1950), pp. 77–80.

22 Albert H. Morehead, "The Professional Gambler," *ibid.,* pp. 82–83.

23 *Ibid.,* pp. 88–90.

24 *Ibid.,* pp. 81–82.

25 Estimates of the amount of money spent on numbers bets vary from just under 1 billion to 3 billion dollars a year; on bookmaking, 8 billion; on horse-racing, 1.6 billion; profits from slot machines are estimated at over half a billion. (Oswald Jacoby, "The Forms of Gambling," *ibid.,* p. 44; Louis A. Lawrence, "Bookmaking," *ibid.,* p. 46; Anonymous, "Slot Machines and Pinball Games," *ibid.,* p. 65.)

26 *"Yellow Kid" Weil, The Autobiography of America's Master Swindler,* as told to W. T. Brannon (Ziff-Davis, 1948), pp. 293 ff.

27 Polly Adler, *A House Is Not a Home* (Rinehart, 1953), p. 273.

28 *Ibid.,* pp. 319–320.

29 *Ibid.,* p. 328.

30 *Ibid.,* p. 336.

31 *Ibid.,* p. 320.

32 *Ibid.,* pp. 317–318.

33 *Ibid.*

34 *Ibid.,* p. 320.

35 *Ibid.,* p. 275.

36 *Ibid.,* p. 325.

37 Although prostitution in the old sense does not continue in the United States, it remains, as we shall see in Chapter 23, an international social problem on a world scale. The so-called "white-slave traffic" is not, therefore, a social or societal problem in the United States today, however serious it may be in other parts of the world. "One of the main reasons why international traffic in women and children is but a minor problem in the United States . . . is . . . the absence of licensed bordellos in this country. Neither the call-girl system, nor clandestine houses, and least of all the free-lance practice of the trade, lend themselves to the import and export of women on a large scale." (From *Vice, Inc.* [p. 21]. Copyright 1954 by Joachim Joesten and published by Ace Books, New York. All rights reserved.)

38 Paul M. Kinsie, "Prostitution—Then and Now," *Journal of Social Hygiene,* 39 (June 1953), pp. 241–248.

39 Sutherland, *op. cit.,* p. 9.

40 *Ibid.,* pp. 12–13.

41 *Ibid.,* p. 13.

42 The Committee on Banking and Currency of the United States Senate, making an investigation of the Federal Housing Administration, found that by the so-called "mortgaging-out process" tenants in the Shirley-Duke Apartments were paying $70 to $85 a year extra in rent and would continue to do so for 33 years. Hearings of the Committee on Banking and Currency, 83rd Congress, 2nd session, 1954, Part 1, p. 14.

43 *Ibid.,* p. 8. For an exposé of how these fraudulent contracts were solicited see pp. 480 ff.

44 Sutherland, *op. cit.,* Chapter 3.

45 *Ibid.*, pp. 219–220.
46 *Ibid.*, p. 222.
47 *Ibid.*, p. 223.
48 *Ibid.*, Chapter 13.
49 *Ibid.*, p. 234.
50 *Ibid.*, p. 240.
51 Bernard, *op. cit.*, p. 100.
52 This does not mean that white-collar crime is not also found in a Communist economy. See Chapter 7.
53 Sutherland, *op. cit.*, pp. 241–242.
54 Hearings of the Committee on Banking and Currency, 83rd Congress, 2nd session, 1954, Part 1, pp. 78–79.
55 *Op. cit.*, p. 3202.
56 H. W. Hollister, "Why Prisoners Riot," *Atlantic Monthly*, October 1955, p. 67.
57 *Ibid.*
58 Robert Clark, unpublished study.
59 Garrett Heyns, in a paper read before the National Probation and Parole Association, June 20, 1955, *New York Times*, June 21, 1955.

VI

ABUNDANCE AND
GROUP-GENERATED
SOCIAL PROBLEMS

Introduction

"New groups flood the city's blood stream, piling new tensions atop the old. 'Where will they live and where will they work?' we ask. 'Will they take over our homes and our jobs?' We ask these questions as if we have forgotten that not so long ago we were the 'they' about whose invasion another 'we' were so concerned."—*New York Times*, December 4, 1956

ALL THE PROBLEMS we have discussed so far may and indeed do involve individuals in all ethnic and racial groups, although with relatively different frequency. Pathologies and disorganization may impair or confuse role relationships in any ethnic or racial group. Illness is illness, whether it occurs in one group or in another. In this sense the problems so far discussed transcend ethnic and racial boundaries.

But some problems may be said to be generated by the very existence of ethnic and racial groups. We saw in Chapter 4, for example, that one group may be a threat to another and, therefore, a stress factor to the threatened group. We saw in Chapter 5 that heterogeneity may be dysfunctional for a society even when it is not a matter of one group threatening another. The very existence of diversity may, under certain conditions, generate problems. We saw in Chapter 14 that certain marginal pathologies in individuals, such as prejudice, may also result from group relations.

Ignoring the pathological aspects of group-generated problems, we may say that the essence of the difficulty is likely to lie in differences of role definitions among different racial and ethnic groups. An immigrant generation brings its culture with it; the children of that generation live marginally in two cultural worlds. It may not be until the third generation that an accommodation of the two occurs. The third generation learns how to salvage what it wants from the old culture and adapt it to the new. Role definitions gradually change until a new articulation is achieved.

Among the most difficult culture traits to accommodate are those associated with religion. Religion is almost by definition, certainly by etymology, the binding force which holds a group together. Those who share a religion share a great many common role definitions and conceptions. But these may differ from those shared by adherents of a different faith. Since all role performance depends on the complementary role performance of others, such varying role definitions and conceptions among members of different groups may constitute a serious handicap.*

Our concern in Part VI, however, is not with group-generated *role* problems but rather with the *status* problems associated with the relationships among groups in our society at midcentury. In our discussions so far we have dealt primarily with the status problems of individuals and classes of individuals, but groups have status problems also. And for groups there are stresses in upward mobility, as we shall presently see, as well as in downward mobility.

In Part VI, then, we direct our attention to some of these group-generated status problems. First we present the history of each immigrant ethnic group, showing the upward surge each has experienced in rising from the slums. We then turn to a consideration of the effect on old American families of the rise in status of immigrant groups. Inasmuch as status is always relative, if one does not rise while others do, one is, in effect, being lowered in status. We also examine some of the traumas which have accompanied the rise in status of the new American families.

Our main emphasis, however, is on the status problems of groups whose status relationships are complicated by racial differences, especially the Negroes, but also the Puerto Ricans and persons with Spanish surnames in the Southwest.

Finally, because of the importance of the slum and of housing in status relationships among groups, and because it has recently become a matter of government policy to assist in the upgrading of slum dwellers by means of slum clearance and urban redevelopment programs, we also devote some attention to this interesting movement.

* For a more detailed discussion, see Jessie Bernard, *American Community Behavior* (Dryden, 1949), Part III.

22

The Status Problems

of Ethnic and Racial Groups

The slums of any large American city have been the scene of some of the most dramatic episodes in the history of mankind. Hundreds of thousands, even millions, of people have passed through them and then up and out. Because this process sometimes took a century we often miss the drama inherent in this great story; if we could see it in fast motion it would be breathtaking.

Success Story: The American Saga

As successive waves of immigrants have swept into Manhattan and elsewhere in America, a rather clear-cut pattern of their experience and of the reactions of native Americans has been established. Most of the newcomers are poor, and hence forced into the least desirable sections of the city, from two to ten families often living in accommodations built for one. They are uneducated; the ways of the new city are strange and complex; the ways of yet another culture add to their strangeness and complexity; they are exploited by native landlords and sharks, and by some of their own countrymen who already "know the ropes." Entering the labor market, unlearned, unskilled, they seem at the mercy of economic forces. If the business cycle is on the up-turn, they are welcomed; if it is on the way down, or in the middle of one of its periodic breakdowns, there is a savage struggle for even the low wage jobs between the new immigrants and the earlier ones who feel they have a prior claim.

The new group huddles together for comfort in mutual misery, and then is accused of "clannishness." Yet the immigrant group itself is almost never cohesive, but is crisscrossed by economic cleavages, inter-village rival-ries, rural-urban lines, and sometimes by religious differences, educational rank, and vocation. But if the group as a whole has one visibly distinguishing characteristic . . . all members are usually lumped together by the "na-tives"; whatever distinguishing tag is given the group is applied willy-nilly to each and every individual in it.

The press and the politicians usually take the lead in influencing public opinion about the newcomers. Foreigners make news, which by definition has to do with the unusual. The more their manners and morals differ, the more newsworthy they become. No matter how bad the slum conditions in which the children of older immigrant groups live, they are not considered newsworthy, but slum conditions in which the children of newcomers live make the front page. High crime rates of slum dwellers as such are not news, but a few crimes committed by the recent immigrants may constitute a "crime wave." The conspicuous strangers become a convenient foil for attacks which give politicians publicity and the backing of the uneducated, the anxious nationalists, the professional patriots, and special interest groups.

The competition and conflict which mark the early years of former immigrant groups gradually give way to accommodation. Older established immigrant groups find that their economic and social status is not actually threatened by the newcomers; businessmen discover that the newcomers are among their customers; employers find that the strangers can do their work; unions find that language barriers can be overcome and that the immigrant in due course may become a loyal union member.

The new group itself begins to adapt to its new environment. English words and phrases begin to replace the mother tongue; some of the newcomers go to night school and learn the new language, new customs. and new skills. The birth rate, originally high because of ignorance and poverty, begins to decline. Finally the migrants begin a slow climb up the American occupational ladder. They establish businesses and churches, mutual aid associations and newspapers. They become citizens. The politicians then find that they are not a "menace to America" after all, but actually are bringing, just as their predecessors did, elements of new life and strength to "the greatest nation in the world."

Having gained acceptance, the newcomers begin a process of "assimilation." They become active outside their own group and occupation, in various civic, business, religious, and labor organizations. They are welcomed at community affairs; they mix with the "old timers" on a more or less equal basis; they have "arrived."

This pattern is subject to local variation by the stratification of each different community, but in general it has been followed by all major immigrant groups since the first wave 300 years ago.[1]

The dramatic rise in status which these ethnic groups have experienced as part of the history of group relations in this country has, as we suggested above, had the effect of lowering the relative status of old ethnic groups. For as the children and grandchildren of immigrant stock have risen, the "old American" families have not been able to maintain the wide status differential which once prevailed. In addition, all the forces operating in the direction of equality, which we referred to in Chapter 1 have reinforced the trend toward bringing ethnic groups nearer to one another so far as status is concerned. We turn first, then, to some of the results for old families of this reduction in status differential.

The Status Problems among White Ethnic Groups

The Status Problems of Old Families

We have already seen in Chapter 1 that as a concomitant of abundance most of the criteria of group status have been in process of erosion during the last half century, with resulting status confusion and status anxiety; and we have just seen that the history of all ethnic groups has been in the direction of rising status. Thus occupation, income, and education are all losing their value as clear-cut status differentia. Even life chances tend to become equalized, so that status differentials are less marked than formerly. The infant mortality rate in the slums, for example, is lowered, and schooling is encouraged and, where talent is present, subsidized in the form of scholarships.[2] More services are furnished to the underprivileged child now than before, so that although life chances are still unequal, they are more nearly equal now than formerly. The mass market has tended to blur many of the status criteria based on consumption. And one student of the subject has made the point that the great effort today in many areas of consumption is not to exaggerate differences but to minimize them. People do not wish to be conspicuously different in their consumption habits.[3] The Joneses have almost to be paid to set the pace in consumption.[4] Housing is an exception, but we defer discussion of this problem until later.

Lineage used to be a secure and dependable basis of status. But even this most honorific criterion of status has suffered attrition as more and more Americans have native-born parents and grandparents. When most people were immigrants or the children of immigrants, one could feel superior merely because one was native-born. But when almost everyone is native-born even this criterion loses its force. Lineage beyond a grandfather is a fairly perishable commodity. The immigrant accepts his inferior status as part of the price he has paid for mobility. His child may be made to feel inferior because of his close ties with the immigrant generation. But the grandchild of the immigrant cannot be made to feel inferior on ethnic grounds; he has relatively little consciousness of foreign ancestry. To old-line families it seems legitimate at the announcement of an engagement to note that one's forebears acquitted themselves with distinction in colonial times; but one can scarcely use this fact in everyday life, especially when others consider it irrelevant, and especially if one's present status measured in other criteria is low. Pretensions to the appurtenances of status merely on the basis of ancestry strike many as quaint or laughable—or even pathetic.

It was also easy to discriminate overtly against foreign ethnic groups when they were of the first generation; it was somewhat more difficult when they were second generation. When they are third generation—and it has been said that the characteristic American outlook is now that of a third generation—it becomes all but impossible. The grandchildren of even the "new" immigrants—that is, those from southern and eastern Europe, who came between 1890 and 1924—have, by and large, gone to high school, live in suburbs or middle-class residential neighborhoods, and have well-paying jobs. They have revamped their ethnic heritage so that it is quite "American." They behave like old-line Americans, talk like them, read the same periodicals, listen to the same radio and television programs, and, in general, live like them. What is more, they have achieved political power and learned how to use it. They have won many legal battles against overt discrimination in hiring, in housing, and in education. Not only are the outward signs on which overt discrimination is based gone, but, in addition, legislation is rendering more and more kinds of overt discrimination illegal. Prejudice and snobbishness are among the few techniques left for asserting status superiority.

The traumas which the upward climb of ethnic groups has inflicted on old American groups have been described as follows:

Consider first the old-family Americans. These people, whose stocks were once far more unequivocally dominant in America than they are today, feel that their ancestors made and settled and fought for this country. They have a certain inherited sense of proprietorship in it. Since America has always accorded a certain special deference to old families—so many of our families are new—these people have considerable claims to status by descent, which they celebrate by membership in such organizations as the D.A.R. and the S.A.R. But large numbers of them are actually losing their other claims to status. For there are among them a considerable number of the shabby genteel, of those who for one reason or another have lost their old objective positions in the life of business and politics and the professions, and who therefore cling with exceptional desperation to such remnants of their prestige as they can muster from their ancestors. These people, although very often quite well-to-do, feel that they have been pushed out of their rightful place in American life, even out of their neighborhoods. Most of them . . . have felt themselves edged aside by the immigrants, the trade unions, and the urban machines in the past thirty years. When the immigrants were weak, these native elements used to indulge themselves in ethnic and religious snobberies at their expense. Now the immigrant groups have developed ample means, political and economic, of self-defense, and the second and third gen-

erations have become considerably more capable of looking out for themselves. . . .[5]

As a result, many members of old American families, especially those
who are not so successful as the newcomers, experience great anxiety
with the relative decline of their status.

The Status Problems of New Families

Nor are the status anxieties all on the side of the old American
family, for there are stresses and strains in upward mobility as well as
in downward. The overwhelming social and societal problems of the
immigrant generations were those of scarcity. They came with few urban
skills. They could not speak the common tongue. They were easily
exploitable. They were herded into slums with only restricted contacts
with the outside world. No doubt status problems were potential and
implicit, but the most pressing problems were those of sheer survival:
housing and employment. Family disintegration had to be fought.
There was little time or energy left to worry about other problems.

But the problems of ethnic group relations in the middle of the
20th century are no longer these problems of scarcity and poverty; they
are primarily status problems. "In a country where physical needs have
been, by the scale of the world's living standards, on the whole well met,
the luxury of questing after status has assumed an unusually prominent
place in our civic consciousness." [6] The transformation of the nature of
social and societal problems of ethnic groups has been described as
follows:

New-family Americans have had their own peculiar status problems.
From 1881 to 1900 over 8,800,000 immigrants came here, during the next
twenty years another 14,500,000. These immigrants, together with their descendants, constitute . . . a large portion of the population. . . . In their
search for new lives and new nationality, these immigrants have suffered
much, and they have been rebuffed and made to feel inferior by the "native
stock," commonly being excluded from the better occupations and even from
what has bitterly been called "first-class citizenship." Insecurity over social
status has thus been mixed with insecurity over one's very identity and sense
of belonging. Achieving a better type of job or a better social status and
becoming "more American" have become practically synonymous, and the
passions that ordinarily attach to social position have been vastly heightened
by being associated with the need to belong.

The problems raised by the tasks of keeping the family together, dis-
ciplining children for the American race for success, trying to conform to
unfamiliar standards, protecting economic and social status won at the cost
of much sacrifice, holding the respect of children who grow American more
rapidly than their parents, have thrown heavy burdens on the internal relationships of many new American families.[7]

We should point out that in spite of the improvement in status of the foreign ethnic groups, an aura of prestige still lingers about Anglo-Saxon ancestry. Thus many persons of immigrant stock change their names in order not to handicap themselves in the race for success. One author has compiled a list of singers and motion-picture stars whose foreign names have been so changed.[8]

In brief, as one author points out:

Both new and old American families have been troubled by the changes of the past thirty years—the new because of their striving for middle-class respectability and American identity, the old because of their efforts to maintain an inherited social position and to realize under increasingly unfavorable social conditions, imperatives of character and personal conduct deriving from nineteenth-century, Yankee-Protestant-rural backgrounds. The relations between generations, being cast in no stable mold, have been disordered, and the status anxieties of parents have been inflicted upon children. Often parents entertain status aspirations that they are unable to gratify, or that they can gratify only at exceptional psychic cost. Their children are expected to relieve their frustrations and redeem their lives.[9]

Political Implications

Some students of political behavior at midcentury find the stresses and strains of upward and downward mobility described above reflected in political life. One observer finds that status considerations rather than interest considerations determine political behavior in an age of abundance.

Political life is not simply an arena in which the conflicting interests of various social groups in concrete material gains are fought out; it is also an arena into which status aspirations and frustrations are . . . projected. It is at this point that the issues of politics, or the pretended issues of politics, become interwoven with and dependent upon the personal problems of individuals. We have, at all times, two kinds of processes going on in inextricable connection with each other: *interest politics,* the clash of material aims and needs among various groups and blocs; and *status politics,* the clash of various projective rationalizations arising from status aspirations and other personal motives. In times of depression and economic discontent—and by and large in times of acute national emergency—politics is more clearly a matter of interests, although of course status considerations are still present. In times of prosperity and general well-being on the material plane, status considerations among the masses can become much more influential.[10]

Among the results of the status anxieties of both new-family and old-family Americans as analyzed above, according to some observers, has been the emergence of a sort of coalition of people lacking in status security—either because of downward or upward mobility—against what is, in effect, a new minority group, the intellectuals. The wave of anti-intellectualism in the middle of the 20th century, according to this point of view, was an expression of status insecurity among certain members of both old- and new-family Americans. The members of this coalition have been called variously "pseudo-conservatives" [11] and "irreconcilables." [12]

A Special Case: The Refugees

Although they did not constitute a social problem of great magnitude, the refugees in the middle third of the 20th century illustrate a special case in intergroup relations. At midcentury there were an estimated 250,000 to 300,000 of them in the United States, most of them— roughly four fifths—being Jews.[13] They differed from other immigrants in the high occupational status they had achieved in the countries of their birth. Indeed, their status degradation in this country was a major difficulty in their adjustment. Americanization for them involved accepting a lower status than they were accustomed to rather than, as in the case of former immigrants, advancing to a higher one. Among the refugees to this country since 1933 there were twelve Nobel Prize winners and a disproportionately large number of persons listed in *Who's Who in America* and in *American Men of Science*.

With the decline of differentials in other criteria of status among groups—income, occupation, and education—there has been a tendency to place more emphasis on housing as a status criterion. For this reason, among others, housing has become a critical factor in intergroup relations. We turn therefore to a brief statement of some of the problems involved in this area.

Housing and Group Status

It is true that in housing, as in other criteria, status differentials are narrowing. The difference, for example, between the servant-staffed mansion of the 19th century and the slum hovel was far greater than that between the exclusive and the nonexclusive suburb today. But despite the narrowing of the status gap in housing, or perhaps because of it, housing remains a great focus of social and societal problems in group relationships today.

Housing is still an all-pervasive index of socioeconomic status; it is as basic as occupation, income, or education.[14] And so far as its impact on group relationships is concerned, it is perhaps the most important index.

One reason place of residence is so important status-wise is that the place where you live determines how and how much your neighbors will police your morals. It determines, further, who will be the playmates—or gang mates—and the schoolmates of your children, who will be their probable reference group, and, more importantly, the young men and women they will be likely to date and later fall in love with and marry.[15] Willingness or unwillingness to accept a person as a neighbor is considered one of the measures of social distance. Indeed, the sociology of propinquity is the theoretical rationale for much segregation legislation.[16] Furthermore, since voting is on a geographical basis, the impact you have politically is closely tied up with the kind of neighbors you have and the district you live in. For all these reasons, housing is a major issue in intergroup relations.

Reliance on housing as a status criterion has curious implications. So long as occupation or income or education or consumption patterns could be definitively relied upon, one could protect his status individually. But when one depends on housing, he must cooperate with others to protect his status. His whole neighborhood is involved. One writer has analyzed the situation in terms of this transition from individualized social status to group social status as it refers to the neighborhood, as follows:

Difference in financial status was more noticeable in an earlier day through identification with tenancy or ownership, or through the tangible symbols, such as the mansion or the cottage, the Rolls Royce or the Model T Ford. But with tenancy no longer a sign of ignominy, with the rise of intangible personality that may never leave the vault, with stock houses as well as stock automobiles financed by installment buying, mortgages, and nominal down payments, and with boiler-makers now driving Cadillacs and debutantes Fords, identification of true status is much more difficult. Normally, this should be a sign of greater democratization of our society. It is not, because we have the increasing ascendancy of a *group* social status in place of the former *individualized* social status.

The growth of group status in neighborhoods has been accelerated by the tendency toward job stratification in the factories. Sometimes it may be a socially leveling factor. But sometimes, frustrated in their efforts to effect differentiation through their own talents or wealth, they have become more sensitive to attack upon their status as a social group. They function less like individuals than as an army. The same group of workers which accepts a Negro co-worker in a Detroit automobile plant and recognizes his equal vote at a union meeting is apt to be panic-stricken if that Negro moves into the group's suburb. The white worker has constructed two different identifications with the two different groups of which he is a member. He may fight for his Negro co-worker in the plant, but at home with his wife and with his neighbors and their wives he will fight the same Negro co-worker with fire and dynamite when the Negro tries to move into his neighborhood.

What is the social status the white worker defends in his neighborhood? It may be only the idealized image of his own eminence raised to the level of his idealized neighbors. He is no longer an individual but part of a faction. The moment the stereotyped minority moves in, the group concept is under challenge and the pang is felt simultaneously by the entire group. . . . In this reaction, neighborhood becomes as much a stereotype as the intruder— the neighborhood as envisioned and as it threatens to become. Though the neighborhood may be deteriorating the moment a minority enters, it is the "home and fireside," the refined cluster of homes that must be defended at all costs.[17]

One of the most spectacular phases of life at midcentury in the United States was the precipitate flight of urban dwellers out to the suburbs. One day cows are grazing peacefully in the fields; soon earth-moving tractors begin to churn up the soil; cranes and derricks move in; carpenters, bricklayers, and electricians soon follow; almost by magic a new housing development has grown up. Presently a shopping center is added, a school, a church. Some of these communities were transplanted ghettoes; some were destined soon to deteriorate into slums. Between 1940 and 1950 over nine million people moved into fringe communities. Baltimore grew only by 10.5 per cent, its suburbs, by 73 per cent. The communities around Galveston, Ogden, Oklahoma City, Washington, Sacramento, San Diego, San Francisco-Oakland, and Norfolk-Portsmouth had gained more than 100 per cent; those around Houston and Dallas, well over 50 per cent.

Much of this movement out of the city was by skilled and semi-skilled workers, clerks, small merchants, young professionals—largely the "new" middle class. Many of these new suburbanites were from cramped ethnic quarters, even slums, of the cities. They came to escape the noise, smog, dirt, and dangers of the city. But they also came for status reasons. There was prestige in owning a home, a kind of honorific elegance in the new houses. The suburb and the quest for status are considered by one student of current housing to be the contemporary counterpart to the 19th-century frontier as a force in shaping American personality.

In city after city, status depends on whether one lives on Swank Street or Blight Alley, and in suburb after suburb it depends on the status the suburb denotes. On Long Island, a man's status is plain when he lives in a public housing project or in Garden City. In Beverly Hills, California, certain street addresses tell whether the scenario writer earns $250 or $2500 a week. "One can no longer count on being known for what one is, but must declare visibly and substantially the symbols of one's class belonging. . . . The neighborhood left behind by this kind of competition for status may still remain desirable, but only to the families whose psychological standard of living and aspiring is lower."   .

Status has become more emphasized than ever since the rise of the suburb where social deterioration now affects value even more than physical deterioration does. Though Americans have always striven for vertical mobility, the emphasis had been on income or capital and the social limelight it generated. They made every effort to protect that status. But with the rise of income and the leveling of some social and economic groups, a different pressure set in for new marks of prestige and status. The neighborhood one lived in became a main index and new protections had to be devised to resist any assault upon it. The suburb and the quest for status are shaping the American personality of the future as the frontier once shaped the American personality of the past.[18]

This may somewhat exaggerate the status aspect of housing, but that it is important, especially in intergroup relations, is unquestionable. Housing is far more than shelter. It is an index of status and hence a critical issue in intergroup relations.

We shall have more to say about housing later in this chapter when we discuss the efforts of the government in slum clearance and urban redevelopment, but before we turn to this subject we direct our attention to the status problems involved in group relations where the complicating factor of race differences is present. We shall trace the processes by which three racial and ethnic groups—Negroes, Puerto Ricans, and Spanish-speaking people—are slowly climbing the status ladder, as during the preceding century their European counterparts did also. The process seems heartbreakingly slow when one sees the life these people live in slums and hovels; it seems—and has always seemed to contemporary observers—impossible that these people could ever rise above their circumstances. As we shall see presently, the same fears that have been expressed about all the ethnic groups during the time of their slum sojourn are now being expressed about colored groups. But with a kind of inexorable defiance of the prophets of defeat, like the other ethnic groups, the colored ones will in time rise. At least that has been the history of our country up till now, and there is no reason to suppose that it will be different in the future.

Race as a Complicating Factor
in the Status Climb

For many social and societal problems there is some question as to the extent to which they are biological, cultural, or sociological in origin. In the case of problems relating to racial minority groups the question is easily answered. They are purely sociological. Sociologically, race today is one of the most important problems in the world; biologically it is completely unimportant. It is not nearly so important, for example, as blood type or the presence or absence of the Rh factor. These biological differences might be lethal under certain conditions, such as transfusions, when the use of certain blood types might cause death. No one has ever built a system of group relationships on blood type; there are no prejudices and no discrimination against people who have blood type A or O or any other type. And if race traits were as invisible as blood type they would make no more difference in social relationships than blood types do. Race is biologically far less important than age or sex in determining behavior. Whether we could see the differences between young people and older people or not, these differences would be important determinants of behavior; young people would still be more active, more plastic, more preoccupied by sex. Whether or not we could see the differences between the sexes, men and women would still behave differently. Men would still run faster; women would still live longer. These differences are not cultural in origin nor are they sociological in origin. If we could not see race differences there would be no race problems as such. Sickness, handicap, role disturbance, youth, age, unemployment, and crime would be distributed randomly through the total population, not as now, selectively. Race makes a difference in our attitudes and behavior only when we recognize it. The unknown number of people who "pass" every year illustrate this conclusion. In the remainder of this chapter we shall discuss the status problems of ethnic and racial groups which are largely or partially nonwhite in composition.

As we consider the difficult problems involved in the desegregation of Negroes, it is well to bear in mind that they at least are part and parcel of American society. The American Indians who live on reservations illustrate a more severe kind of segregation. They live, in effect, in underdeveloped areas, and their problems—poverty, illness, ignorance—are the problems of scarcity, which we shall discuss in Chapter 23.

The Status Climb of the Negroes

The Bench Mark: Status After Slavery

Status, though sometimes masked by other problems, has always been central in Negro-white relations. The first major issue was that of slavery, an officially sanctioned, legally institutionalized status relationship which deprived the Negro of all civil and political rights. After the Civil War the status pattern of slavery was no longer officially sanctioned, but the status of the Negro remained that of "second-class citizen," or worse. The social problems of millions of freedmen were the chief focus of concern in the latter half of the 19th century. The struggle involved in trying to re-establish some kind of working arrangement between Negroes and whites was paramount. Accustomed to more than two centuries of accommodation on the basis of slavery, both races faced what looked like an almost insurmountable problem of accommodation on some other basis. Because the problem was being tackled in an era of scarcity, survival took precedence over everything else.

By the end of the 19th century it looked as though some kind of accommodation had been worked out on the basis of the "separate but equal" formula, that is, segregation. The two races could live together successfully if each kept in its proper place, the Negro's being, naturally, inferior and the white's superior. Segregation was the key to race relations, officially embodied in statutes in the South, unofficially embodied in practices no less binding in the North, during the first half of the 20th century. Implicit in segregation was discrimination, although it was not until the middle of the century that this fact was officially recognized.

But the segregation solution began to crumble in the second third of the century. It could not stand the test of court decisions, changed public opinion, and especially the challenge of world opinion as exploited in the Cold War by the USSR. Nor, apparently, could it stand the pressures of an age of abundance. In the late 19th and early 20th century status problems were subordinated to the problems of achieving anything at all. Any kind of school was better than none; any kind of job was better than none. Any kind of wage was better than none; any kind of house was better than none. The separate-but-equal formula could be flouted with impunity because the Negroes had to settle for almost anything they could get.

But as Negroes gained education and developed leadership, as the

What difference does it make, really, where you ride in
a bus? No difference at all, if you can sit wherever you choose.
But it makes a lot of difference if you are required by law to sit
in the back and are insulted if you refuse, or if you have to stand
when there are vacant seats up front. It made so much difference
to these men and women in Montgomery, Alabama, that they
chose to walk to work rather than subject themselves to the humili-
ations of segregation. Equality of status as measured by the privilege of sitting wherever they chose was more important to them
than their physical comfort. Their grandparents would not have
dreamed of aiming at this goal; a place to sleep, enough to eat,
clothes to keep them warm or dry, a job, elementary schooling

for their children—these were the goals they sought. But these are no longer enough.

Economic boycott is only one technique disadvantaged groups can use in their fight for improved status. In 1955 Puerto Ricans in New York invoked for the first time the provisions of the state's fair employment practices law. The courts have also in recent years tended to be on the side of those who were fighting to improve their status.

Boycotts, legislation, and court action, powerful as they are, are useless against the subtler forms of status degradation. A wealthy woman in one community gives $300,000 to subsidize a music center, but she is not invited to participate in the annual pre-Lent community celebration by the exclusive cliques that run it. She happens to be a Jew.

The history of racial and ethnic groups in the United States has been one of initially low status followed by a gradual climb, so that after several generations the status gap tends to become very narrow if it remains at all. Abundance tends to accelerate the status climb.

Narrowing the status gap among racial and ethnic groups may involve profound traumas for both the rising and the—relatively—declining groups. *(Photo: Grey Villet—courtesy LIFE Magazine. Copyright 1956, Time Inc.)*

demands of an age of abundance called for their skills, the minimum needs no longer seemed adequate. The great status differential between Negroes and whites was gradually lessened. Negroes made increasing demands for the implementation of their legal rights. The social problems centering about race relations at midcentury, therefore, were those of desegregation. The work of segregation had to be undone. The question was how.

So long as the status differential between the races was extremely wide, it was not too difficult to enforce segregation. It was a tolerable accommodation to a difficult situation. But the Negroes, although still behind the whites, are gaining rapidly. We can trace the closing of the status gap between the races on the basis of several indexes: education, income, occupation, and housing.

Narrowing of the Status Gap

THE EDUCATIONAL STATUS OF NEGROES AT MIDCENTURY. At midcentury the Negroes in the South had achieved a level of education which corresponded to that of white draftees of World War I.[19] They were, in effect, about a generation behind the whites. They were still contributing a disproportionate number to the illiterate population,[20] but they were in process of catching up with the whites.

> Racial inequalities are smaller today than a generation ago for all population segments at the eighth-grade level. At the high-school level inequalities diminished generally—the farmers of Arkansas, Louisiana, and Mississippi excepted. . . . At the fifth-grade level, however, racial inequalities in the younger populations approximate or exceed those of a generation earlier. . . . Racial inequality in completing at least eight grades has been declining for both urban and farm populations as increasing proportions of Negroes have shared more fully in the general American culture.[21]

There are great individual differences among the southern states in the amount of discrimination against Negroes as measured in disparity of educational achievement. A high degree of inequality exists where there is rapid educational progress for whites but where social distinctions between the races are great. Mississippi tends to exemplify this situation. In some cases the mass of whites and Negroes are equally unschooled; there are no status differences among them so far as education is concerned. All have low levels. But a small white minority does complete high school, thus distinguishing itself from practically all Negroes, as illustrated by conditions in rural Louisiana. Finally, where there is relatively little racial distinction and a high value is placed on education, the status differential as revealed in the lag of Negroes behind whites is small, as in Tennessee and Virginia. In general, the author we are here referring to concludes, the contrast between the races "has diminished markedly over the thirty-five years covered by the data, with southern Negroes today approximating the white situation of a generation earlier." [22]

TABLE 1

COMPARISON OF NEGRO AND ALL PUBLIC ELEMENTARY AND
SECONDARY SCHOOLS, SELECTED MEASURES,
1919–1920 TO 1949–1950

SCHOOL YEAR	NEGRO SCHOOLS *	ALL SCHOOLS	RATIO: NEGRO SCHOOLS TO ALL SCHOOLS
Average Number of Days Attended by Each Pupil Enrolled			
1919–1920	80	121	.66
1929–1930	97	143	.68
1939–1940	126	152	.83
1949–1950	148	158	.94
Average Length of School Term in Days			
1919–1920	119	162	.73
1929–1930	132	173	.76
1939–1940	156	175	.89
1949–1950	173	178	.97
Per Cent of Pupils in Secondary Schools			
1919–1920	2	10	.20
1929–1930	5	17	.29
1939–1940	10	26	.38
1949–1950	14	23	.61
Average Salary of Members of Instructional Staff			
1939–1940	$ 601	$1,441	.42
1949–1950	2,143	3,010	.71

* In 17 southern states and the District of Columbia.
SOURCE: Statistics of State School Systems, 1949–50, U.S. Office of Education, 1952, Table 1, pp. 28–29, and Table 36, p. 98.

Table 1 summarizes the trend of Negro education as the gap between it and white education is narrowed. Especially notable is the great speed with which secondary school attendance is increasing as compared with that of whites. Between 1919 and 1949 it increased something over twofold in all schools and sevenfold in Negro schools, a pace three times faster among Negro schools than among all schools. The Negroes were repeating in these thirty years the great push toward high school education which the whites had shown earlier. There is no reason to doubt that they will duplicate the push which the white population has shown toward higher education also.

Because of the enormous significance of leadership in any racial or ethnic group, it is interesting to note the relatively rapid rate at which Negroes already are entering colleges or professional schools. Thus in 1940, of those eighteen to twenty-four years of age who were in school, 30.6 per cent of the nonwhite students were in college or professional schools; in 1950, the proportion was 47.4 per cent, an increase of over 50 per cent. The corresponding figures for the white population were 61.7 and 78.8, an increase of something more than 27 per cent.[23] To be sure, the proportion of nonwhites in higher education was still only about two thirds that of the whites in 1950, but in 1940 it had been less than half. For all higher educational institutions, the enrollment increased 10.7 times between the beginning of the century, 1899–1900, and mid-century, 1950–1952; for nonwhite schools, it increased 28.4 times.[24]

These quantitative changes were impressive; but they did not necessarily mean qualitative improvement of equal extent. For Negro schools remained inferior to those of whites in most communities. They were so poor, in fact, that they may have had a deteriorating effect on Negro intelligence. Studies in Louisiana schools, for example, showed that the achievement gap between Negro and white children was less in the first grade than in the twelfth.[25] As Negro schools improved, so did the achievement of Negro children.

In 1947–48, 21.49 percent of sixth grade Negroes tested scored average or above [on the Otis Quick Scoring Mental Ability Tests]. By 1950–51 the figure was 22.12 percent, and by 1954–55 it was 28.55 percent. During the same eight-year span the percentage of tested Negroes scored as "mentally retarded" dropped from 30 precent to 17.48 percent. In the 1954–55 tests, for the first time, more Negroes qualified for the top category "average or above," than for any of the three lesser ones.[26]

But even with improvement, Negro schools were inferior.

Exposure to eight years of schooling did not therefore necessarily mean the same for a Negro child as for a white one. It was for this reason in part that so much importance attached to the epochal decision of the United States Supreme Court in May 1954 with respect to desegregation. The decision laid down that separate schools for Negro children were not and could not be equal to those of white children; "separate educational facilities are inherently unequal" were its very words.

But of equal if not even greater significance was the principle this decision laid down for governing intergroup relations. Wounds inflicted on the body had long been recognized as criminal. Now wounds inflicted on the mind and spirit were also considered to be wrong. Lacerating the "hearts and minds" of Negro children was as illegal as flogging. The scars of one were as serious as the scars of the other.

And, finally, this decision was revolutionary because it rested, in effect, on status, rather than on legal, grounds.[27] To segregate people was to place a stigma upon them; it placed them in a position of low status. To do this on racial grounds was unconstitutional.

Here is the critical passage in that famous decision.

> Does segregation of children in public schools solely on the basis of race, even though the physical facilities and other "tangible" factors may be equal, deprive the children of the minority group of equal educational opportunities? We believe that it does. . . . To separate them from others of similar age and qualifications solely because of their race generates a feeling of inferiority as to their status in the community that may affect their hearts and minds in a way unlikely ever to be undone. The effect of this separation on their educational opportunities was well stated by a finding in the Kansas case by a court which nevertheless felt compelled to rule against the Negro plaintiffs:

>> Segregation of white and colored children in public schools has a detrimental effect upon the colored children. The impact is greater when it has the sanction of the law; for the policy of separating the races is usually interpreted as denoting the inferiority of the Negro group. A sense of inferiority affects the motivation of a child to learn. Segregation with the sanction of law, therefore, has a tendency to retard the educational and mental development of Negro children and to deprive them of some of the benefits they would receive in a racially integrated school system.

> We conclude that in the field of public education the doctrine of "Separate but equal" has no place. Separate educational facilities are inherently unequal. Therefore, we hold that the plaintiffs and others similarly situated for whom the actions have been brought are, by reason of the segregation complained of, deprived of the equal protection of the laws guaranteed by the Fourteenth Amendment.[28]

The effect of this decision, regardless of how long it takes to bring about desegregation, will be to improve the quality of educational facilities for Negroes. Even if separate schools remain, the pressure to desegregate will force improvements, if for no other reason than as a delaying action.

OCCUPATIONAL UPGRADING. The Negro, along with all other workers, is being occupationally upgraded in the 20th century. Although a higher proportion of Negroes than of whites were still in agriculture in 1950, the proportion was declining. In 1940, for example, about a third of all nonwhite persons—32.6 per cent—were in agriculture; in 1950, only one fifth—20.0 per cent—were. The proportion of nonwhites in manufacturing rose from 13.4 per cent in 1940 to 24.0 per cent in 1950; for the total population the increase was only from 29.8 to 33.5 per cent.[29] Table 2 summarizes the occupational changes for nonwhite and all workers in the United States and in the South between 1940 and 1950. It will be noted that nonwhite persons in professional and technical occupations increased by a third—from 2.7 per cent to 3.6 per cent—in this decade; the increase for the total population was much

TABLE 2

PER CENT DISTRIBUTION BY MAJOR OCCUPATION GROUP OF EMPLOYED PERSONS IN THE UNITED STATES AND IN THE SOUTH, 1940 AND 1950

MAJOR OCCUPATIONAL GROUP	UNITED STATES				SOUTH			
	1940		1950		1940		1950	
	Total	Non-white	Total	Non-white	Total	Non-white	Total	Non-white
Professional, technical, and kindred workers	7.9	2.7	8.9	3.6	6.3	2.5	7.4	3.6
Farmers and farm managers	11.5	15.0	8.0	9.5	18.9	18.6	12.7	13.9
Managers, officials, and proprietors, except farm	8.3	1.4	9.0	1.5	6.8	0.8	8.5	1.2
Clerical and kindred workers	9.8	1.1	12.1	3.6	6.5	0.6	9.7	1.6
Sales workers	6.5	0.8	6.7	1.5	5.0	0.5	6.2	1.2
Craftsmen, foremen, and kindred workers	11.4	3.0	13.7	5.3	8.3	2.5	11.6	4.5
Operatives and kindred workers	18.4	10.4	19.8	18.7	14.9	8.9	18.0	16.1
Private household workers	4.6	21.3	2.6	15.2	6.7	20.8	3.7	14.7
Service workers, except private household	7.2	11.6	7.4	14.3	5.8	8.5	6.6	11.4
Farm laborers, except unpaid and foremen	4.3	11.0	2.8	6.4	7.1	13.1	4.3	9.0
Farm laborers, unpaid family workers	2.6	6.6	1.6	4.1	5.5	8.3	3.2	5.8
Laborers, except farm and mine	6.9	14.4	6.0	15.4	7.5	14.3	6.6	15.9
Occupation not reported	0.8	0.6	1.4	1.1	0.7	0.6	1.5	1.1

SOURCE: Adapted from 1950 census of population, Preliminary Reports, "Employment and Income in the United States, by Regions, 1950," Series PC–7, No. 2, April 11, 1951, Table 6.

smaller, from 7.9 per cent, that is, to 8.9 per cent. Clerical workers increased more than threefold among nonwhites, from 1.1 per cent to 3.6 per cent. Sales workers and craftsmen almost doubled, and operatives increased only slightly less. Farm laborers decreased by about 40 per cent, but other laborers increased slightly. Similar trends were noted in the South, and in addition in that region the proportion of managers, officials, and nonfarm proprietors increased by almost half.[30]

The Negroes were still several generations behind the white

population in occupational status, but the important point is that they were catching up.[31] Traditionally concentrated in agriculture and in domestic and personal service, the Negro occupational distribution is slowly approaching that of whites.

Nevertheless, for the present, the distribution of Negro workers reflects the conditions of the past. Any analysis of the least secure segment of the labor force, of the marginal workers, still reveals the Negro worker to be present in disproportionate numbers.

> In spite of the gains made by Negroes during and since World War II, they still, like women of all races, have less stable employment on the average than white men. Negro men in the years 1944 and 1946 averaged just about the same number of calendar quarters in employment covered by old-age survivors insurance as did white women; Negro women had less steady work than white women. . . . Negroes . . . are under a more severe economic pressure [than white workers] and the comparative instability of their employment is a clear sign that Negroes are among the less favored jobholders. Another sign is that the percentage unemployed is higher among Negroes than among whites, both in good times and in bad.[32]

Much of the occupational upgrading of the Negro worker resulted from the federal and later state and local fair employment practices legislation. It was found in World War II that discrimination against Negro workers was very costly. Skills were wasted. Labor shortages were aggravated. As a wartime emergency measure the Federal Fair Employment Practices Committee was set up in 1941 [33] forbidding discrimina-

TABLE 3
MEDIAN WAGE OR SALARY INCOME OF PRIMARY FAMILIES AND INDIVIDUALS WITH WAGE OR SALARY INCOME FOR THE UNITED STATES 1949 AND 1939*

| | Total | | Units Without Nonwage† Income | |
	1949	1939	1949	1939
White families and individuals	$3,138	$1,325	$3,501	$1,409
Nonwhite families and individuals	1,533	489	1,772	531

* " 'Primary family' refers to head of household and all other persons in household related to head by blood, marriage or adoption. If there is no person in household related to the head, then the head himself constitutes a primary individual not in a family. A household can contain only one primary family or individual. 'Primary families and individuals' is used with same meaning as 'families' in the 1940 census."

† Nonwage income includes payment in kind, housing (janitors, superintendents), and board.

SOURCE: U.S. Bureau of the Census, Current Population Reports, Consumer Series P–60, No. 7, February 18, 1951, p. 28.

tion against workers on the basis of race, creed, or nationality. This
measure expired with the emergency (1945), but states and municipalities began to enact similar measures, until at midcentury at least
seventeen states and eighty-six municipalities had them.[34]

TABLE 4

MEDIAN WAGE OR SALARY INCOME OF PERSONS 14 YEARS OF AGE AND
OVER FOR THE UNITED STATES 1939, 1949,* AND 1955

Color	Male			Female		
	1955	1949	1939	1955	1949	1939
White	$3,986	$2,735	$1,112	$2,065	$1,615	$676
Nonwhite	2,342	1,367	460	894	654	246

* U.S. Bureau of the Census, Current Population Reports, Series P–60, No. 7, February 18,
1951.

SOURCE: U.S. Bureau of the Census, Current Population Reports, Series P–60, No. 23, November 1956, Table 11.

THE WAGE AND INCOME GAP IS NARROWING.   As a result of greater
employment, of improvement in education and in occupation, and also
of the movement out of the low-paying regions to the better-paying
regions, especially to the West,[35] the income of Negroes has been approaching that of white workers. In 1937 the average wage of white
persons twenty to twenty-four years of age covered by old-age and survivors insurance was almost four times—3.6—that of Negroes in the
same age bracket; in 1946, this differential was reduced to less than half
that much—to 1.6.[36] Even for older workers, among whom educational
and training differences would be greater, the disparity in wages was
reduced from 2.6 to 1.8. Negro women did not show so much relative
improvement, but they did improve somewhat with respect to white
women.

TABLE 5

MEDIAN WAGE OR SALARY INCOME OF PERSONS WITH WAGE AND SALARY
INCOME, BY COLOR, 1939 AND 1947–51

	Total	Nonwhite	White	Nonwhite as Pct. White
1939	$ 877	$ 364	$ 956	38.1
1947	1,865	863	1,980	43.6
1948	2,017	1,210	2,323	52.1
1949	2,016	1,064	2,350	45.3
1950	2,133	1,297	2,481	52.2
1951	2,422	1,572	2,875	55.0

SOURCE: *Employment and Economic Status of Negroes in the United States* (U.S. Senate
Committee on Labor and Public Welfare, 1954), p. 19.

The accompanying figures show that the average Negro income increased more rapidly than white income between 1939 and 1949:

Sex and Color	Percentage Increase in Median Wage or Salary Income from 1939 to 1949
Male	
White	146
Nonwhite	197
Female	
White	140
Nonwhite	166

SOURCE: Elizabeth E. Hoyt *et al.*, *American Income and Its Use* (Harper, 1954), pp. 102–103.

The differentials in average income between the races varied considerably in different cities, as shown in Table 6. The median income of nonwhites, for example, was only 42 per cent of that of whites in Atlanta, Georgia, but it was 60 per cent in Washington, D.C.

TABLE 6

RELATIVE SIZE OF MEDIAN INCOME OF WHITES AND
NONWHITES IN 8 CITIES, 1949

City	Percent Nonwhite Median Income Is of White Income
Atlanta, Ga.	42.0
Birmingham, Ala.	47.2
Memphis, Tenn.	44.0
Nashville, Tenn.	43.1
New Orleans, La.	48.0
Norfolk-Portsmouth, Va.	43.2
Richmond, Va.	43.1
Washington, D.C.	60.0

SOURCE: U.S. Bureau of the Census, Preliminary Reports, Series PC–5, 1950.

Although the income of Negro families has been approaching that of whites, it is still true that "the Negro is identified with most of the economic problems faced by the poorest people in America. His low income is apparent in whatever comparison is made between whites and non-whites, whether in urban or rural areas." [37] It is small comfort to the Negro family which can afford only the darkest tenement that the wage differential between the Negro and the white earner is less now than it was a generation ago. The rats that infest the apartment bite babies as hungrily as ever. Being poor is still the common lot of Negroes.

HEALTH.   Before we turn to housing, a word about the relative differentials in health between Negroes and whites. In most indexes of health, as in other indexes, the Negro is still behind the white population; but here as elsewhere the important fact seems to be that he is beginning to catch up. In 1900–1902, for example, the average life expectancy at birth for nonwhite males (32.54 years) was only about two thirds that of whites (48.23 years); by 1944 it was nine tenths (58.30 years for nonwhites and 63.55 years for whites);[38] and in 1951 it was .89 (59.4 years for nonwhites and 66.6 years for whites).[39] Similar ratios obtained for females. It is interesting to note that, because of the more drastic selective forces operating among Negroes, once they have survived the hazards of early and middle life and attained the age of sixty-five years, their life expectancies probably exceed those of white persons of the same age. This is true for both men and women.[40]

Cancer and diseases of the heart are more common as killers among whites, but other diseases show higher rates among nonwhites. The death rate from tuberculosis has remained about two-and-a-half times as common among nonwhites as among whites since 1910.

Housing. Of all the indexes available, only those having to do with housing show no reduction of the status gap; and, in some respects, they show a widening of it. It is true that legal battles have been won. In 1948 the Supreme Court declared that covenants which forbade the selling or renting of property to Negroes could not be enforced in the courts. And many housing projects built with federal aid must be open to Negroes as well as to whites.

Much of the worsening of Negro housing in cities has been a by-product—a temporary one it is hoped—of slum clearance and urban redevelopment plans. As slums were cleared, no provision was made for those who were evicted; they therefore were more crowded than ever in the slums that remained.

> Slum clearance . . . acquired such political appeal and such irrepressible momentum that we simply could not stop tearing down slums. Under the public housing program nearly 200,000 substandard dwelling units were eliminated by June 30, 1953; 77 percent was accomplished through demolition, 17 percent through compulsory repair, and 6 percent by barring them to occupancy. Of the housing units built under the Housing Act of 1937, 89 percent were on sites from which old structures had been removed and only 11 percent on completely vacant land. . . . The urban redevelopment program provided no housing for [the underprivileged] and deprived them of the housing they had.[41]

Since at midcentury it was mainly Negroes, Puerto Ricans, Mexicans, and other low-status groups who lived in slums, they were the ones most affected by slum clearance projects. Overcrowding was far more serious among nonwhites than among whites, and it was greater in 1950 than it had been in 1940.[42] Although nonwhites constitute about a tenth of the population, they were three times more numerous than whites in the evicted population.[43]

For the lucky Negro families who could get into the new housing projects, the improvement was enormous. But the proportion who could was so small that the total picture of Negro housing was not greatly improved.

Improving the status of Negroes has met with much resistance. Although it is not our purpose here to review race conflict,[44] it is pertinent to review the violence which has marked the attempts of Negroes to improve their living conditions, especially in the field of housing.

Between 1945 and 1954 there were nine riots in Chicago. Between January 1951 and July 1952 there were forty bombings in the South.[45] In 1953 there were bombings in Houston, and arson, violence, or bomb-throwing in Kansas City, Atlanta, Chicago, East St. Louis, Cleveland, Indianapolis, and Los Angeles County.[46] In 1954 there were bombings in San Francisco, Louisville, and Norfolk County, Virginia.

Yet in the face of violence, slurs, and threats, the Negro continued pushing his way into the cities. He was there to stay. Racial covenants and mob action made things harder, but they could not force him back to the cotton and tobacco fields. He was establishing his new base. He was completing the migration he had put off while European immigrants had poured in. It was one of the momentous efforts of a subordinate race to rise to its place in the American sun. If it was met by resistance, prosecutions, terror, and violence, and left traumatic marks on the body politic, they were the price for the gains that were being achieved.[47]

The reasons for the resistance to Negroes in white residential areas are related to the implications of propinquity discussed above. People become frightened at the prospect of loss not only of property values, but also of status. That such loss is not inevitable is a lesson slowly learned and more slowly implemented. We may expect Negro housing to remain a difficult problem for some time yet.

Desegregation

THE CHURCH. For a long time white Christians justified the segregation accommodation between the races by Christian principle. By midcentury no Christian church was using this basis; the basis for the argument in favor of segregation, where it persisted, had been switched to social expediency.[48] Beginning in 1946 a series of resolutions and statements by the Federal Council of Churches and in 1952 by its successor, the National Council of Churches, established a policy of renouncing racial segregation in the church as elsewhere. And little by little attempts were being made to desegregate church activities.

There is rather general recognition on the part of the church membership that the churches have lagged in dealing with the pattern of racial segregation. In many quarters this recognition is serving as a stimulus to more forthright action. This is resulting in increased efforts to adjust the denominational practices as well as those of theological seminaries, camps, conference grounds and many other church-related organizations to facilitate desegregation and integration within church organizations.

An illustration of this type of adjustment by a denomination is the fact that the Colored Methodist Episcopal Church has changed its name to the Christian Methodist Episcopal Church, thereby eliminating a racial designation in its name. Along with this, the denomination has committed itself to "the principle and practice of inclusiveness in membership, and membership participation without racial or color discrimination." Also many local churches are serving persons on a racially inclusive basis as members of the congregation and/or as participants in the church program. In addition there are an increasing number of local churches in the process of achieving this type of service.[49]

In Connecticut in 1955 a congregation of white persons installed a Negro as their pastor.[50] The selection committee did not even mention his race during their deliberations.

Even in the South, Negro men of the cloth were slowly being accepted. In October 1955 a Negro priest said mass in a white Roman Catholic Church in Myrtle Grove, Louisiana, after he had been turned away from a church in Jesuit Bend. Archbishop Joseph Francis Rummel closed the church at Jesuit Bend and censured the men responsible for the incident.[51] And when three Catholic women attacked a woman who had been instructing a mixed group of Negro and white children in the catechism, they were excommunicated by their bishop.[52] Schools associated with the Roman Catholic Church had never remained segregated long where the law permitted them to be mixed.[53]

RECREATIONAL FACILITIES AND TRANSPORTATION. About a year and a half after the Supreme Court decision with respect to segregated schools was handed down, a decision based on the same reasoning was made with respect to public recreational facilities. On November 7, 1955, the Supreme Court said that Negroes could not be segregated at public parks and bathing beaches. Separate facilities were inherently unequal.

Following closely on the above decision was a decision by the Interstate Commerce Commission forbidding the practice of segregation—forbidden in interstate buses in 1946—on interstate trains. It said that "the disadvantage to a traveler who is assigned accommodations or facilities so designated as to imply his inherent inferiority solely because of his race must be regarded under present conditions as unreasonable." [54] The decision of this Commission did not, of course, have the same force as a Supreme Court decision, and it was taken for granted that it would be taken to court. But it was also taken for granted that the Supreme Court would agree with the Commission. In 1956 segregation in intrastate transportation facilities was also declared unconstitutional by a Federal Court in South Carolina.

THE ARMED FORCES.   Segregation was still in force in all branches of the military at the end of World War II. In 1948, Executive Order 9981 was issued, in which President Truman declared it to be the policy of the President "that there shall be equality of treatment and opportunity for all persons in the armed services without regard to race, color, religion or national origin. This policy shall be put into effect as rapidly as possible, having due regard to the time required to effectuate any necessary changes without impairing efficiency or morale." By January 1950, the Army had declared its policy to be one of full integration; but segregation continued until well into the Korean War. The Air Force began to implement its desegregation program in June 1949. The Navy had begun desegregation in July 1944, and by February 1946, all restrictions on Negro personnel were removed. The Marine Corps abolished segregation in June 1949. The Merchant Marine service has had a policy of nondiscrimination. The integration policy and its implementation in the last decade have been called a major reform,[55] although this policy has not always been uniformly successful.

There was resistance, however, to desegregation in the state military units. The southern states did not wish to admit Negroes into the National Guard reserves.

THE OTHER EDGE OF THE SWORD.   In discussions of desegregation we are likely to concentrate our attention on those who will gain by it wider and better opportunities. But there are some Negroes who may well lose by it. Business and professional personnel who have catered exclusively to a Negro clientele face at midcentury the danger of losing their protected clientele.

Teachers, for example, who had taught in Negro schools were by no means sure of retaining their positions in desegregated schools. The National Association for the Advancement of Colored People, anticipating this problem, set up a new section in its organization to advise teachers of their rights and employment status and to counsel them during the desegregation process. Fortunately the shortage of teachers at the time of desegregation protected them from dismissal.

It is not anticipated, in view of the tremendous overall shortage of teachers in the nation, that any appreciable number of qualified Negro teachers will be dismissed from their posts. Where legitimate consolidations occur and where seniority, tenure rights, and qualifications are taken into account, such teachers as are displaced will have aid in seeking new posts.[56]

White children in many schools were coming to accept Negro teachers as a matter of course.[57]

Negro businessmen also faced serious difficulties as segregation barriers began to crumble, making inroads on their markets. Some attempted to enter unprotected competition with white businessmen. In 1955, for example, Negro businessmen opened a brokerage company on Wall Street. But not all were prepared for such a step. Many had to decide at midcentury just what course they should follow.

The Negro is at the present time at a crossroad. The expansion of vocational and business education has brought forth a generation among whom are large numbers of Negroes excellently equipped for the business world and who, finding the roads seemingly blocked, turn toward a segregated economy. At the same time, the entire social trend in this country, from a long-range viewpoint, indicates that the forward-looking Negro has greater opportunities in business than ever before, not as a Negro businessman specifically, but as an American businessman.

Fundamentally, the dilemma thus resolves itself into one of outlook. If the Negro is at a crossroad, he finds paths leading in two directions. Standing at that point, a choice seems to be mandatory. Shall he think and work in terms of a separate economy, exploiting its possibilities, utilizing its advantages, prolonging its life? Or, shall the other pathway be taken, with the orientation toward integration, the overcoming of obstacles, the breakdown of separatist tendencies?[58]

Lest the above account of the narrowing of the status gap between the Negro and the white races be taken as an indication that nothing remains to be done, we point out here that enormous disabilities still remain, especially in the South. Opposition to Negro suffrage remains, for example, in spite of legal rights. In Mississippi "when a Negro tried to register he was required to take a test in which he had to read one of the most complex passages of the state constitution, and then spell a series of the most difficult words in that passage. If he did not falter in his reading and spelled all of the words correctly, he must then write an essay on Constitutional Government. . . . Few voters anywhere would pass the test."[59] Negroes who registered or signed petitions were publicized as trouble-makers, often losing their businesses, or their credit ratings, or even their homes, as a result.[60] The status gap is still enormous.

WHAT CAN LEGISLATION ACCOMPLISH? The status climb of Negroes and the progress toward desegregation which we have just reviewed are profoundly impressive. Why did they happen? To what can they be attributed? These are very important questions.

Foremost among the reasons, perhaps, is the impact of abundance on race relations.[61] It is doubtful if the position of Negroes could have been much ameliorated if a scarcity situation had existed at midcentury. The need for his skills was a vital force in upgrading the Negro.

But abundance does not operate mechanically or automatically. It works through policy. And here both crescive and legal norms have made themselves felt. The following analysis summarizes the manner in which legislation has guided the status climb of Negroes in the second third of the 20th century:

By legislative action, executive order and judicial decision, the race prejudices of Americans have been denied public sanction. Fair employment practices commissions, of national scope during the war and subsequently operative in a number of states and municipalities, integration of the Armed Forces, integration of many segregated schools, elimination of "white primaries" and removal of racial restrictions in many professional associations—all these have provided a living laboratory for the study of the impact of law on the mores.

At virtually every stage in the development, strong voices were raised to plead that morality could not be legislated, that an end to discrimination must await an unprejudiced public. Yet, the results indicate a high degree of compliance, some covert evasion, and only a few instances of violent resistance.

Moreover, it should be kept in mind that the success of desegregation laws or orders need not be measured against a hypothetical standard of 100 percent but against the usual standards of law enforcement. Even laws against homicide and rape, which have overwhelming community support, are occasionally violated.

But, while laws may restrain behavior, is there any evidence to indicate that attitudes are affected? Here the evidence seems clear: the law itself plays an important part in the educational process. . . . The key to analysis is the social situation.

Legislation and administrative orders which have prohibited discrimination in such areas as employment, the Armed Forces, public housing, and professional associations have brought people of various races together—often with initial reluctance—in normal day-to-day contact on an "equal-status" basis where the emphasis is on doing a job together. Contact of this kind gives people a chance to know one another as individual human beings with similar interests, problems and capabilities. In this type of interaction racial stereotypes are likely to be weakened and dispelled.[62]

These authors summarize the conditions under which legislation can be effective in group relations as follows: geographical dispersion rather than concentration of opposition; strong support by church leaders, journalists, trade unionists, businessmen, and politicians, who create a favorable climate of opinion; the degree to which sanctions can be administered; and the extent to which laws are actually enforced. Laws relating to private behavior, for example, can be enforced only with the greatest difficulty; but laws relating to community behavior— such as most desegregation legislation—are more amenable to enforcement. They conclude that:

> Although large-scale local considerations may call for special circumstances of implementation, the majesty of the law, when supported by the collective conscience of a people and the healing power of the social situation, in the long run will not only enforce morality but create it.[63]

So much, then, for the status problems of the Negroes at midcentury as they revealed themselves in the processes of desegregation. There were, in addition, two pockets of minority-group relations which posed serious problems, those of Puerto Ricans and of Mexican nationals and Mexican-Americans to other Americans. Because of the large admixture of Negro blood in many Puerto Ricans, and of Indian blood in so many Mexicans, these two groups are often treated as nonwhite by other groups. And many of their problems stem from this fact. We remind ourselves that it is not the biology of race which is important but its sociology. When people consider themselves colored or if they are treated as colored they have the problems of colored people.

The Puerto Ricans

In many ways the social and societal problems of the Puerto Ricans duplicate the problems which have arisen as each ethnic group has come to our shores. As one study points out, the comments being made at midcentury about the Puerto Ricans might well be those made about the Irish in the middle of the 19th century:

> The conditions under which they had been born and brought up were generally of the most squalid and degrading character. Their wretched hovels, thatched with rotting straw, scantily furnished with light, hardly ventilated at all, frequently with no floor but the clay on which they were built, were crowded beyond the bounds of comfort, health, or, as it would seem to us, of simple social decency; their beds were heaps of straw or rags; their food consisted mainly of buttermilk and potatoes, often of the worst, and commonly inadequate in amount; their clothing was scanty and shabby.[64]

With each wave of immigration, the same comments have been made. As early as 1797, Representative Otis of Massachusetts told his colleagues that "when the country was new it might have been good policy to admit all. But it is so no longer." [65] In 1837 the mayor of New York spoke of the streets "filled with wandering crowds of immigrants . . . clustering in our cities, unacquainted with our climate, without employment, without friends, not speaking our language. . . ." [66] Yet, given time, and protected from new waves, each ethnic group has managed to work its way out of the slums, becoming finally, as we saw above, in the third or fourth generation indistinguishable in every way from the old American families. It is in this early stage that most of the 226,110 Puerto Ricans in the United States found themselves at mid-century. There were 187,420 Puerto Ricans in New York City in 1950, 191,305 in New York State. They were largely concentrated in two areas, Spanish Harlem and Morrisania, considered by some observers to be among the worst slums in the world.

New York's Puerto Rican sections in 1953 probably ranked among the worst in the world. This was not because of the age or the exteriors of the buildings but because of the number of people crowded into small spaces—and because rents are so high that little is left for other needs. An American missionary described Harlem housing conditions as worse than what he had seen in China, the primary evil being the psychological collapse caused by overcrowding. It is not an overstatement.

In March, 1950, the writer saw a six-story, 25-foot wide tenement on East 100th Street into which 170 Puerto Ricans had been herded. Rents were about $16 a month per room; the apartments had to be shared and there were twelve people living in a single three-room apartment. Every hall window was broken. Splintered stair treads sank perilously with each step. Almost every toilet was out of order. Loosened plaster hung from the hall ceilings; great heaps of garbage rotted on the floor under the stairways; a dead rat lay on a landing. Gaping holes in the toilet walls served as passageways for the rats and one tenant said she kept two dogs and a cat to prevent them from attacking her children. There were 481 officially reported cases of rat bites in 1952, and since it is estimated that only 1 in 5 cases is reported, some 2500 human beings—mostly babies—are bitten by rats every year. Most of the cases are in the Harlem slums. . . . Housing conditions for the Puerto Rican migrants are far worse than they were for the nineteenth-century immigrants.[67]

Slum clearance meant only that those who remained had to crowd themselves into less and less space. By 1955 the Puerto Ricans were beginning to invade the lower East Side, and Spanish signs were replacing Yiddish ones in these old slums.[68]

As contrasted with earlier immigrant groups the immigrant Puerto Rican population was unique in that there were more women than men, the sex ratio—number of men per hundred women—for adults in 1950 being only about 92.3. Among the native-born of Puerto Rican parentage, however, the sex ratio was more nearly normal, that is, 102.2. The

More and more American families are moving into communities like Park Forest, Illinois, shown above. Most of the residents in such communities are young families. Since some of the adults grew up in deprived neighborhoods, or even slums, their new homes represent a heavy investment in improved socio-economic status. To those who grew up in neighborhoods of high socioeconomic status, their present homes represent, they trust, only the first rung as they climb the income ladder. But whatever their background, all the residents have in common a strong interest in protecting the middle-class status of their community.

There are no legal means—that is, no device that a court would sanction—for keeping Negroes out. But when a Negro family tries to buy a home, strong preventive protest follows—not bombs and physical violence, as in lower-class areas, but their verbal equivalent.

The parents of children in these "packaged suburbs" are often troubled by the school situation. No sooner is a new building opened than it becomes crowded, with children queuing up for admission. Where are the needed classrooms coming from? Where, even more urgently, can the additional teachers be found?

Every morning there is an exodus of men from communities like this. Unless there are two cars in the family, the wife may be stranded all day, for unlike older suburbs the new ones are not likely to be serviced by trains. Some of the women in these attractive homes feel as though they were caged.

In discussing the group cohesiveness of life in the new packaged suburbs, William H. Whyte, Jr., remarks that the residents sometimes "sense that by their immersion in the group they are frustrating other urges, yet they feel that responding to the group is a moral duty—and so they continue, hesitant and unsure, imprisoned in brotherhood."

This is one "design for living" in an age of abundance. Is it the best? What are some others? Are there others available which are to be preferred? *(Photo: Courtesy American Community Builders, Inc., Park Forest, Illinois)*

Puerto Rican immigrant group was unique also, as contrasted with European immigrant groups, in that a large proportion of it—8 per cent—was colored. The Puerto Rican immigrant problem, then, concerns one of the most vulnerable segments of the population.

The problems of Puerto Rican immigrants are compounded by certain status peculiarities. The colored Puerto Ricans tend "to consider American Negroes beneath [their] social status." [69] So long as Puerto Ricans retain their Spanish language they can maintain social distance between themselves and other Negroes; there is, therefore, not only less incentive to learn English, but a positive incentive not to learn it.

. . . there is a curious contradiction within American society which gives higher status to the foreign-born Negro, and particularly the non-English-speaking Negro, than to the native America Negro. Of necessity, the colored Puerto Rican is encouraged to maintain his identity as a "foreigner" rather than to blend himself in the world of the American Negro. Especially is this true for those in the intermediate colored group, the grifos, whose Caucasian features entitle them to a somewhat higher status on the island than the outright Negro or mulatto, but who in New York may lose that margin of privilege. These colored Puerto Ricans have less incentive and less opportunity to follow the pattern of Americanization than any other immigrants America has known. Only so long as they continue to remain conspicuously different from the American Negro can they improve their status in America.[70]

As a straw to clutch at, many of these Puerto Ricans come to identify themselves with other Spanish-speaking groups and take over their patterns rather than those of other groups in the United States. There are some rifts in the solidarity of these "Latinos"—as when some Cubans, let us say, who are in the country illegally claim to be Puerto Ricans and cast discredit upon the group—but by and large comfort is derived from this Latinism. It bolsters their self-confidence and improves their status.

What the growth of Spanish consciousness and the identification with it most accomplish for Puerto Ricans is a rise in their status. Their self-image is better served as Latinos than as Puertoriqueños. In their struggle to escape a minority position they can thus reach out and borrow prestige from some larger and more favored minority. If there are romantic elements in this image of themselves, if there is something of the posture in it, who can say but that such elements are a proud thing, and necessary in order to bear their kind of life? [71]

The status ambitions of the immigrants themselves are not high, but, like all immigrant groups which have preceded them, "an overwhelming number do aspire to white-collar or professional jobs for their children." [72] And if this seems unlikely when one observes the conditions under which these people live, one has only to recall that Irish, Italian, Polish, Jewish, and other immigrant groups have traveled this same route and emerged successful. Already we can catch a glimpse of the wave of the future by comparing the native-born children of Puerto Rican parentage with the immigrant generation itself. Among the native-born adults, that is, among those fourteen years of age and over, the average number of years of schooling was 8.2 as of 1950 in the United States, 8.1 in New York City. Those born in Puerto Rico have somewhat less than this—8.0 for all those in the United States in 1950 and 7.9 for those in New York City. But even in 1950, the native-born of Puerto Rican parentage were averaging almost two years of high school —9.8 years for the United States, 9.6 for New York City. These children of immigrants were on their way. They were about halfway between the total population of the United States and their parents so far as schooling was concerned. The wave of the future is also previewed in comparing young adults, aged twenty-five to forty-four, of the Puerto Rican immigrant generation with those who were native-born of Puerto Rican parentage. Although about the same proportion in both groups were employed and about the same proportion were laborers, at the other end of the occupational ladder, far more (28.5 per cent) of the native-born of Puerto Rican parentage than of the immigrant generation (17.6 per cent) were in professional, managerial, and clerical occupations.[73] As a result of their superior education, no doubt, and their higher occupational status, these native-born young men of Puerto Rican parentage had higher average incomes—$2,149 in 1950—than the comparable group of immigrants—$1,768.

As yet the native-born generation is very young, averaging only eight years of age in 1950, but by the time the small Puerto Rican children have reached their majority, most of the slums will have been cleared; like other ethnic groups they will lean over backwards to protect their children from the traumas of their own childhood; the third-generation Puertoriqueño will doubtless be almost indistinguishable from the third generation of any other immigrant group, with the exception that those who are colored will still be colored.

The role problems of these immigrants are similar to those of all people in this period of rapid change, but they are accentuated by the rapidity with which they appear. Among women, for example, almost three fourths—73 per cent—who are in the labor force, were not in the labor force in Puerto Rico.[74] In the United States "adjustment" involves getting a job rather than being a housewife, playing the role of gainful worker rather than that of homemaker. "Bourgeois society . . . thus turns the lower class woman into an agent of work rather than a housewife, thus rending family life—the center of the Puerto Rican world—in New York City." [75] The changes from a preindustrial type of social organization to an industrial type, which has been in process for almost two centuries, comes with stunning speed to these immigrants, with demoralizing impact on role definitions.

Freedom and psychic security are in tension. The tight social control of smaller communities is often a felt constraint, especially to those with new ideas or ambitions that go beyond the narrow limits; yet for many others control is a great comfort. This tension comes out strongly at the center of the Puerto Rican world; the family itself is in many instances disrupted. Children no longer get as much attention from the mother and may, in their freedom, feel rejected; women, as well as men, realize that they are no longer as dependent on each other as before. For many Puerto Ricans, New York may provide escape from rigid moral standards, but along with this there is the feeling of being lost in a large world where people do not know or care very much about each other. Guilt feelings are aroused in some migrants by actions which would not be countenanced at home; others may reject the new pattern completely and overemphasize their own rigidities.[76]

Looked at in cross section at any one moment, the problems seem almost insuperable. It is interesting to note that although students of this lowest ethnic and status group today recognize the similarity of pattern between them and the older immigrants, they nevertheless tend to feel that the prognosis is less good today than formerly. Thus it is felt that the Puerto Ricans are at a disadvantage because they have come at a time when—allegedly, but not demonstrably—upward social mobility has been slowing down and because they are handworkers in an increasingly mechanized economy.

It is difficult to believe, however, that the story will be so different in the second half of the century from that in the first half. The process may take somewhat longer now than formerly because of racial complications and because of the lack, as yet, of good leadership; but that the lowest group will in time climb and become middle class seems very likely.

The Population with Spanish Surnames in the Southwest

In 1950 there were 2,289,550 persons in five southwestern states—Arizona, California, Colorado, New Mexico, and Texas—who had Spanish surnames. Some of them had settled in their present areas—and this was especially true of those living in New Mexico—as long ago as the 16th century and had come into the United States under old treaties, as the land was annexed. These people are sometimes called Spanish-American or Spanish-Colonial, or Hispano, to distinguish them from more recent immigrants from Mexico and their children. These recent comers range from predominantly Indian to pure Spanish in ethnic background. Most of them—82.9 per cent—were native-born; 16 per cent were born in Mexico.

As a group, these people were young; the average (median) age was 20.6 years, ranging from 18.2 in Colorado to 22.7 years in California. Their schooling was meager. The average number of years of schooling was 5.4. In Texas it was only 4.3; in California it was 7.6.

Their living conditions are almost the worst in the country. Many of them are migratory workers, who are the lowest men on the totem pole and almost not in the social system at all. In earlier years the migratory worker was a single man—hobo or tramp—but at the present time he is likely to be a husband and father and to take his family with him, all of them working. His housing is inconceivably bad; the schooling of his children almost nonexistent; he shares few if any of the benefits of any of the welfare programs which have been established to protect most categories of workers.

The migratory worker has the worst housing. His low living standards make it unnecessary, in the farmer's opinion, to provide him with adequate shelter. He sleeps on the ground, in a cave, under a tree, or in a chicken house. He cannot bargain or protest. Water for washing, cooking, and drinking is frequently from a muddy irrigation ditch, and there are no sanitary facilities within sight.

The domestic Mexican or native Negro migrant worker has a better chance of getting some shelter from the elements, but even this is generally a ramshackle shed, tent, or cabin, or a ditch-bank camp of tents or canvas stretched across a pole with boxes, brush, or burlap across the end. This may be a squatters' camp or the land may be owned by the employer. Another type of house is the labor shack in the beet fields, built of rough lumber and covered with tar paper. It is not proof against the weather, has been frequently condemned by investigators and sometimes by an enlightened employer. In one case, a sugar company refused to contract for beets after seeing the housing provided for the field workers. "There is not much excuse for that sort of thing now after 25 years of beet-growing." But, though a quarter of a century has passed since then, conditions are no better in the beet fields and, in fact, have worsened considerably.[77]

Even in cities the housing of this group is bad. Yet they are fearful of slum clearance projects for when slums are demolished they are evicted, and have no place to go. Especially for those who are not citizens—11.6 per cent in 1950—and therefore not eligible for new housing, this can be calamitous. The infant death rate reflects the low living conditions; it was seven times as high in Imperial County, California, as it was in the state as a whole. Pellagra and even ordinary starvation occur; hardly any of the children in one Texas camp had had any milk for six months, while eight out of ten adults had not eaten any meat.[78]

The status of the lighter colored in this group is slightly above that of the Negro and native Indian; that of the darker ones, about the same as that of the Negro. One writer likens the status picture to a form of colonialism.

. . . in the case of the migrant Mexican, and to some extent other migrants, we have a unique kind of internal colonialism. The native laborer works hard for pitiful wages, suffers the social inferiority of a native in the eyes of his master and the community, and lives under the subhuman conditions so often characteristic of native colonial life. The difference between the traditional and the new colonialism is that our colonial natives are kept with us within distance when we want them—and then driven out of the community when no longer needed. They go back to the "colony" at the season's end, often under armed guard. In this novel system, a dual standard of capitalist morality has been constructed. We have on the one hand a minimum wage, a 40-hour week, social security, and a living standard that rates among the highest in the world. On the other hand we tolerate conditions as primitive as any that existed under feudalism.[79]

As in the case of immigrants in the 19th century and of the Puerto Ricans today, the picture looks very dark. As it was said of the earlier immigrants and as it is said of the Puerto Ricans, so also it is said of these people that "stratification has displaced evolution for those at the bottom. The process of enlightenment and upgrading through education does not function for them, nor even for their children." [80]

But when we look at the facts they do not look so discouraging. If, for example, we compare the average (median) number of years of schooling of those who were between fourteen and twenty-four in 1950 with those who were forty-five years of age and over, we find that the younger persons, males in this case, had about twice as much schooling. The native-born, age for age, had much more than the foreign-born. Half the native-born young group—except in Texas—graduated at least from elementary school; in California half were going on to high school. This is not a very high level as compared with the national average of high school graduation, but it is considerably higher than in the parental generation. The upward climb is beginning, slow as it may seem to impatient observers.

The same evidence of upward mobility can be found in the occupational distribution of the native-born of native parentage as compared with that of the native-born of foreign or mixed parentage or with that of the foreign-born. In California, for example, only a little more than half as many of the native-born of native parentage were in the unskilled laboring and service jobs (31.7 per cent) as were the foreign born (58.9 per cent). The native-born of mixed or foreign parentage fell in between (42.6 per cent). At the other end of the occupational ladder, 10.5 per cent of the native-born of native parentage in California in 1950 were in professional, technical, and managerial positions; 6.2 per cent of the native-born of foreign or mixed parentage and 6.2 per cent of the foreign-born were in these positions.

TABLE 7
AVERAGE NUMBER OF YEARS OF SCHOOLING OF PERSONS WITH SPANISH SURNAMES, 1950

Age	Arizona 14-24	45+	California 14-24	45+	Colorado 14-24	45+	New Mexico 14-24	45+	Texas 14-24	45+
Total	8.1	3.6	9.1	4.9	8.3	4.4	8.2	3.8	6.1	2.3
Native-born, native parentage	8.3	5.3	9.6	8.0	8.3	4.6	8.3	4.0	6.3	3.1
Native-born, foreign or mixed parentage	8.2	4.4	9.2	6.8	8.2	5.7	7.4	3.4	6.4	2.5
Foreign-born	5.3	2.9	5.2	3.8	—	3.1	6.9	2.0	2.8	1.9

SOURCE: U.S. Bureau of the Census, Special Report P-E, No. 3C, 1953. Persons of Spanish Surname, Table 6.

Income reflected this improved education and occupational upgrading. In California, Texas, and Arizona the median income for the native-born of native parentage was higher than that for the native-born of foreign or mixed parentage, and the income of the latter group was higher than that for the foreign-born. This was not true in Colorado or New Mexico, however.

The position of people with Spanish surnames has been complicated by the system whereby Mexican workers are imported (and then returned to Mexico) under contract for much of the agricultural labor required by the great commercial farms; it is also complicated by the so-called Wetbacks, or illegal entrants into this country from Mexico. A study of the attitudes of ranchers in one California community showed that almost half (48 per cent) considered the imported Mexican worker superior to the native or domestic worker; only 38 per cent considered them inferior. Domestic workers were considered less dependable; drinking was also noted as a problem.

The Wetback has apparently dropped out of the picture as a major problem because of tightened immigration inspection. Three reasons have been adduced to explain this: the McCarran-Walter immigration legislation of 1952, which provided for more careful scrutiny of immigrants and visitors to the United States; the new Social Security provisions of 1954, which require farmers to contribute to the old-age and survivors insurance fund of any employees earning more than $100 a year; and the greater ease with which Mexican citizens can be brought in.[81]

The author we have just cited suggests that perhaps the migratory worker is about to pass from the scene, to be succeeded by the seasonal worker.

Efforts are being made to get migratory laborers to select a given community as a home base and work out from this community to areas where crops need attention. Some of the seasonal industries, especially date processing, will not employ workers unless they have a permanent address. It may well be that California is beginning to witness the transition from migratory worker to seasonal worker. Permanent addresses where these workers can develop roots in the community may go far to remove some of the adverse reactions to them expressed by ranchers.[82]

The idea is to give the worker citizenship status in some community so that he will not be deprived of all his rights because of lack of residence qualifications.

The status relationships between the rancher and the Mexican national are simpler than those between him and the native worker. The Mexican national comes under a contract; there are no other ties than those specified in the contract. They are not fellow-citizens; they are not members of a community; there are no obligations other than those of a work relationship. The same is not true of the domestic workers. Here great social distance exists.

. . . considerable social distance exists between ranchers and domestic migratory workers. . . . The great chasm of social distance between rancher and "domestic migratory labor" may account for the steady demand that a large pool of Mexican nationals be maintained. Ranchers have come to rely on the Mexican national as a dependable source of labor in an area of fluctuating labor supply and perishable crops.[83]

So much, then, for the social problems associated with the stresses and strains of group mobility. The drive toward equality which abundance makes possible tends to reduce status differentials. But closing the status gap among ethnic and racial groups does not solve the problems of intergroup relations. It may, in fact, exacerbate them, as we saw, especially in the area of housing.

Housing and Group Relationships

We have noted the long shadow of slums all through our discussion of social problems. We spoke earlier of the slum-syndrome as comprising the major social problems of the 19th and early 20th century. We saw that most of the problem families with which welfare agencies have to deal live in slums. We have seen that many of the pathologies we discussed in Part IV have disproportionate incidence in slums. We noted that recorded juvenile delinquency occurs relatively more frequently in slums. And now we have seen that disadvantaged ethnic and racial groups also inhabit the slums.

The slum has weighed heavily on the minds of thoughtful students for a long time. Some concluded that it was an inevitable concomitant of urban development. Some concluded that slums were created by lazy and shiftless people. Some concluded that the slum was a temporary aberration in community development and that it could be eliminated.[84] The last-named theory is the one which now seems to prevail in governmental policy. We review here some of the trends in thinking and policy over the last century.

Changing Rationale in Housing Legislation

For the most part, with the exception of surplus commodity programs and school lunch programs, the responsibility of the government has not been interpreted as extending to the provision for individual families of consumer goods, as distinguished from general welfare services. But even here there has been a notable change in at least one area of consumption: housing. Originally the rationale for housing legislation lay in health requirements. Housing was a matter of public health concern from at least 1867, when New York passed its first extensive act dealing with tenements. A second major rationale for housing legislation was to further employment. Thus although the National Industrial Recovery Act of 1933 couched its objectives in terms of public health, it was designed primarily to furnish employment in a depression. When this Act was declared unconstitutional, the Public Works Administration Housing Division was set up to carry on a program of slum clearance instead.

In addition to reasons of health and employment, public housing programs have also been motivated by a concern with standards. The 1937 United States Housing Act stated its purpose to be: "the elimination of unsafe and insanitary housing conditions . . . the eradication of slums . . . the provision of decent, safe, and sanitary dwellings for families of low income, and . . . the reduction of unemployment and the stimulation of business activity." By 1949 the responsibility of the government for housing was no longer based on the necessity to furnish employment or to stimulate business activity; it was extended, however, to include remedying the housing shortage and aiding in urban development. Thus the 1949 Housing Act, which amended the 1937 act, stated the housing policy of the nation, as follows:

The Congress hereby declares that the general welfare and security of the Nation and the health and living standards of its people require housing production and related community development sufficient to remedy the serious housing shortage, the elimination of substandard and other inadequate housing through the clearance of slums and blighted areas, and the realization as soon as feasible of the goal of a decent home and a suitable living environment for every American family, thus contributing to the development and redevelopment of communities and to the advancement of the growth, wealth, and security of the Nation.

Status Reasons for Housing and Slum Clearance Legislation

Little by little status considerations creep into the rationale for housing programs and slum clearance. Implicit goals, such as the equalization of consumption patterns among classes, may be involved, even though not recognized. As one student of the subject has pointed out, we should probably distinguish between health and welfare goals and status goals.

It would be helpful to distinguish characteristics of housing important to physical health and increased productivity from those relating to status only. . . . It must be realized, of course, that one of the goals of individuals, of various groups, and of a society in general is a greater degree of equality for reasons independent of better physical health. There seems little reason to believe, however, that equality of housing is more important than equality of income as such.[85]

Status considerations have also crept in under the guise of health considerations. When mental—or role—and emotional health, as well as physical health, is included among the reasons for improved housing, the door is open for a wide extension of housing standards.

It is not always so clearly recognized that mental and emotional health is quite as important as physical health . . . the frustration which results from over-crowding, conflict between the desires and needs of various members of the family, fatigue due to the performance of household duties under unfavorable conditions—these are health menaces as serious as . . . poorly heated rooms and stairs without railings.[86]

As yet such clear recognition of status factors has not appeared in housing legislation, but it is beginning to appear in the administration of housing projects. Efforts are made to distribute and, if possible, mix families of different status rather than to preserve status differences in different areas.

Government responsibility for housing, then, was originally based on grounds of health, employment, and community costs; the trend appears to be toward basing this responsibility on grounds of status equalization among groups in at least one aspect of consumption, housing.

Although the ultimate result of housing and slum clearance legislation may be a reduction in status differentials, for the present the result has been just the opposite. As we saw in the case of colored ethnic groups, slum clearance has eliminated many substandard units, but the displaced persons have only been crowded more tightly into the remaining units. As contrasted, therefore, with the other criteria of status, housing differentials, especially for colored groups, have not notably decreased.

In Part VI we have surveyed some of the major group-generated social problems as they have emerged in our society in a time of abundance. We have seen that they tend to take the form of a status reassessment in which the differentials that used to characterize group relationships become less marked. The reduction in status differentials among white ethnic groups constitutes, we found, a stress factor which generates a considerable amount of anxiety both in those who rise and in those who, relatively, decline. As between the Negro and the white group, the narrowing—except in housing—of the status gap, involving as it does the undoing of an old accommodation based on segregation, has exacerbated many old role relationships. The Puerto Ricans and the populations with Spanish surnames of the Southwest, like other racial and ethnic groups who began at the bottom of the social structure, still have a long way to go, but intergenerational comparisons suggest that they, too, like others who have also begun at the bottom, are slowly climbing the status ladder and that the differentials between them and other groups in education, occupation, and income may in time be greatly reduced, even if not wholly eliminated. Throughout our discussion we have emphasized the importance of housing in group relations; many group-generated problems find expression in housing problems. Solutions are being sought in slum clearance and urban redevelopment projects.

Our focus so far in this volume has been on the social problems of an industrialized society, that of the United States. This is justified both practically, on the grounds that the student is most interested in these problems, and theoretically, on the grounds that the problems of abundance show in clearer focus in our society than in others. But our picture would be incomplete if we ended our study at this point. For the 20th century is seeing the emergence of social problems in so-called underdeveloped areas of the world also. And so, in order to round out the picture of social problems in the second half of the 20th century, we turn in Part VII of our study to a brief overview of some of the emerging social problems in other parts of the world today.

NOTES

[1] C. Wright Mills, Clarence Senior, and Rose Kohn Goldsen, *The Puerto Rican Journey, New York's Newest Migrants* (Harper, 1950), pp. 82–83.

[2] The old private schools, once the exclusive preserve of the wealthy, now allocate a large part of their resources to scholarships.

[3] David Riesman, *The Lonely Crowd* (Yale Univ. Press, 1950), p. 273.

[4] Retailers have been advised to give new gadgets to certain families in a neighborhood in order to stimulate others to buy them. There is, apparently, reluctance to exhibit competitive consumption. See William Whyte, Jr., "The Web of Word of Mouth," *Fortune*, November 1954, pp. 140–143, 204 ff.

[5] Richard Hofstadter, "The Pseudo-Conservative Revolt," *The American Scholar*, 24 (Winter 1954–1955), pp. 19–20; and Eric F. Goldman, "What Is Prosperity Doing to Our Political Parties?" *Saturday Review*, October 8, 1955, p. 36.

[6] Hofstadter, *op. cit.*, p. 17.

[7] *Ibid.*, p. 20.

[8] "Mr. Harper," in "After Hours," *Harper's*, March 1955, p. 80.

Doris Day	Doris Kapplehoff
Laurance Harvey	Larry Skikne
Tony Curtis	Bernie Schwartz
Karl Malden	Mladen Sekluovich
Marjorie Main	Marie Tomlinson Krebs
Tab Hunter	Arthur Gelien
Casey Adams	Max Showalter
Ginger Rogers	Virginia McMath
Mitzi Gaynor	Mitzi Gerber
Della Darvi	Bella Wegier
Ethel Merman	Ethel Zimmerman
Vic Damone	Vito Farinola
John Ericson	Joseph Meibes
Cyd Charisse	Tula Finklea
Frankie Laine	Frank Lovecchio
Dianne Foster	Dianne Laruska
Judy Holliday	Judy Tuvim
Rita Hayworth	
	Margarita Carmen Cansino
Aldo Ray	Aldo Da Re
Vince Edwards	Vincent Zoino
Jane Wyman	Sarah Fulks
June Allyson	Ella Geisman
Kirk Douglas	Issur Danielovitch
John Forsythe	John Lincoln Freund
Danny Kaye	David Kaminsky
Dean Martin	Dino Crocetti
Jerry Lewis	Joseph Levitch
Tony Bennett	Arthur Benedetto
Jill Corey	Norma Jean Speranza

Of course people change their names for other than status reasons. See, for example, Leonard Broom, Helen P. Beem, and Virginia Harris, "Characteristics of 1,107 Petitioners for Change of Name," *American Sociological Review*, 20 (Feb. 1955), pp. 33–39. Sometimes the new name is easier to pronounce or more alliterative. But this kind of verbal "passing" perpetuates anachronistic status patterns and, according to the author who compiled the above list, it actually does us harm abroad by concealing the success of the melting pot.

[9] Hofstadter, *op. cit.*, p. 21.

[10] Hofstadter, *op. cit.*, pp. 17–18. See also Harold Callender, "The Red Vote in France: A Study of Factors That Impel Non-Communists to Back Party," *New York Times*, January 9, 1956.

[11] Hofstadter, *op. cit.*

[12] Goldman, *op. cit.*

13 Maurice R. Davie, *Refugees in America* (Harper, 1947), pp. xvi-xvii.

14 A study of 219 men in Cambridge, Massachusetts, found that ecological measures, which include residence, were common to nineteen indexes of socioeconomic status. See Joseph A. Kahl and James A. Davis, "A Comparison of Indexes of Socio-Economic Status," *American Sociological Review*, 20 (June 1955), pp. 317-325.

15 J. H. S. Bossard, "Residential Propinquity as a Factor in Marriage Selection," *American Journal of Sociology*, 38 (Sept. 1932), pp. 219-224; Maurice R. Davie and Ruby Jo Reeves, "Propinquity of Residence before Marriage," *ibid.*, 44 (Jan. 1939), pp. 510-518.

16 But some of it has the effect of protecting the dominant group from competition of the minority group. See Jessie Bernard, *American Community Behavior* (Dryden, 1949), Chapters 16-20.

17 Charles Abrams, *Forbidden Neighbors* (Harper, 1955), pp. 269-271.

18 *Ibid.*, pp. 139-140.

19 C. Arnold Anderson, "Inequalities in Schooling in the South," *American Journal of Sociology*, 60 (May 1955), p. 547.

20 Eli Ginzberg and Douglas Bray, *The Uneducated* (Columbia Univ. Press, 1953).

21 Anderson, *op. cit.*, pp. 555-556.

22 *Ibid.*, p. 559.

23 *Negro Year Book* (Tuskegee Institute, 1952), p. 207.

24 *Ibid.*, p. 218.

25 *Southern School News*, June 1956, p. 3.

26 *Ibid.*

27 For example, footnote 11 of the decision specifies the following sources: K. B. Clark, *Effect of Prejudice and Discrimination on Personality Development* (Midcentury White House Conference on Children and Youth, 1950); Witmer and Kotinsky, *Personality in the Making* (1952), Chapter 2; Deutscher and Chein, "The Psychological Effects of Enforced Segregation: A Survey of Social Science Opinion," *Journal of Psychology*, 26 (1948), p. 259; Chein, "What Are the Psychological Effects of Segregation under Conditions of Equal Facilities?" *International Journal of Opinion and Attitude Research*, 3 (1949), p. 229; Brameld, "Educational Costs," in *Discrimination and National Welfare*, McIver, ed. (1949), pp. 44-48; Frazier, *The Negro in the United States* (1949), pp. 674-681.

28 Text of the Supreme Court Decision of May 17, 1954, delivered by Mr. Chief Justice Warren.

29 *Negro Year Book*, p. 15.

30 *Ibid.*, p. 15.

31 *Ibid.*, p. 12.

32 George Soule, *Men, Wages and Employment in the Modern U.S. Economy* (Mentor, 1954), pp. 41-42.

33 See L. C. Kisselman, *The Social Politics of FEPC* (Univ. of North Carolina Press, 1948).

34 In January 1954 there were twenty-five municipal agencies charged with reducing intergroup tensions; fifty other cities had Mayor's Committees or Civic Unity Councils performing essentially the same functions; and an additional twenty-six cities had commissions to promote or enforce fair employment practices. (*NAIRO Reporter*, published by the National Association of Intergroup Relations Officials, Jan. 1954.)

35 During World War II the migration of the Negroes was somewhat different from that of earlier years. Now the direction of movement was westward, and the people who moved were not rural persons but urban persons, not only from the Old South, but from the Southwest. "Between 1940 and 1944, the Negro population more than tripled in the San Francisco Bay area and nearly doubled in Los Angeles. Similar increases occurred in the Pacific Northwest. Westward migration continued after the war ended and the cities on the Pacific coast now have, for the first time, a sizable Negro population. This development is similar to that in northern cities after World War I. Of national interest is the departure from the traditional South-to-North route of Negro migration, and consequent redistribution of Negro population within the United States. The migrants came predominantly from the Southwest; more than half came from Texas and Louisiana, and a fourth came from Oklahoma, Arkansas, and Mississippi. Less than a seventh were from states outside the South. . . . Contrary to a widespread impression, the migrants were not primarily engaged in farming before coming to California. Less than a seventh reported their prewar occupation as in agriculture. More than a fourth were manufacturing workers and about a fifth were employed in service industries." (*Negro Year Book*, pp. 118-119.)

36 Soule, *op. cit.*, p. 118.

37 *Negro Year Book*, p. 125.

38 *Ibid.*, p. 162.

39 *Statistical Abstract of the United States* (1955), p. 66.

40 *Negro Year Book*, p. 162.

41 In New York City, for example, the Committee on Slum Clearance Plans in 1952 proposed the eviction of 6,000 low-income families to make room for private urban redevelopment projects which would rent for more than the evicted families could afford. The New York City Housing Authority proposed eviction of another 25,-000 families. It was argued that these dispossessed people always found some place to live. But "no study had ever been made of where they go. In practice, when a slum area is designated, the residents are warned, cajoled, made fearful of imminent dispossession, and under duress find shelter of some sort. A few are lucky, 5 per cent or so may move into a project on the site, but the bulk find less desirable quarters or double up." (Abrams, op. cit., p. 248.)

42 For nonwhite renter-occupied dwellings the proportion which were overcrowded —that is, which housed more than 1.51 persons per room—was 20.2 in 1940, 22.8 in 1950. (Negro Year Book, p. 174.)

43 Abrams, op. cit., p. 249.

44 For an analysis of Negro-white conflict, see Jessie Bernard, American Community Behavior (Dryden, 1949), Chapters 16 and 17.

45 Abrams, op. cit., p. 89.

46 "The monthly reports of Chicago's Commission on Human Relations in 1952 and 1953 began to read like field bulletins in a war. There was one incident after another of arson, attempted arson, property damage, vandalism, tension, threats, anonymous warnings, assaults, crowd gatherings, stone-throwings, hurling of fire-brands, anti-Semitic incidents, rumors, murder by 'nigger-hunters,' intimidation of workmen building Negro housing, and so on." (Ibid., pp. 116–117.)

47 Ibid., pp. 89–90.

48 J. Oscar Lee, "Protestant Churches and Public School Desegregation," Social Problems, 2 (April 1955), p. 212.

49 Ibid., p. 213.

50 New York Times, September 27, 1955.

51 Ibid., October 31, 1955.

52 Ibid., November 28, 1955.

53 In St. Louis an archbishop had once threatened to excommunicate a whole community if there was resistance to the admission of Negro children in a parochial high school. A similar incident occurred in Louisiana in 1956.

54 New York Times, November 26, 1955.

55 Negro Year Book, p. 146.

56 Roy Wilkins, "The Role of the National Association for the Advancement of Colored People in the Desegregation Process," Social Problems, 2 (May 1955), p. 203.

57 The story was told of a mother who, upon her first visit to school, found that her child's teacher was colored, and asked her child why he had not told her this fact. His reply was that it had never occurred to him. So far as he was concerned, there was nothing exceptional in her being a Negro. This story suggests that the overlap of generations sometimes causes older people to insist on the continued existence of problem conditions long after the current generation has mastered them. These might be called residual problems. Another example occurs at higher levels also. In some cases contemporary college and university students have never had anti-Negro attitudes or feelings. They want Negro fellow students in their clubs or fraternities. But the alumni members, who retain the attitudes and feelings of previous generations, prevent them from admitting them.

58 Robert H. Kinzer and Edward Sagarin, The Negro in American Business (Greenberg, 1950), quoted in Negro Year Book, p. 144.

59 New York Times, November 12, 1955.

60 Ibid.

61 See Jessie Bernard, op. cit., pp. 322–324, for a statement on the effect of scarcity or poverty on race relations.

62 John P. Roche and Milton M. Gordon, "Can Morality be Legislated?" reprinted from the New York Times Magazine, May 22, 1955, pp. 4 ff.

63 Ibid., p. 6.

64 Issac A. Hourwich, Immigration and Labor (Putnam, 1912), p. 73. Present quotation from Mills, Senior, and Goldsen, op. cit., p. 81.

65 Ibid., p. 81.

66 Ibid.

67 Abrams, op. cit., pp. 60–61, 63.

68 New York Times, June 24, 1955.

69 Mills, Senior, and Goldsen, op. cit., p. 89.

70 Ibid., p. 87.

71 Ibid., p. 138.

72 Ibid., p. 161.

73 Special Report P-E No. 3D, U.S. Bureau of the Census, Table 4, p. 13.

74 Mills, Senior, and Goldsen, op. cit., p. 189.

75 Ibid., p. 148.

76 Ibid., p. 123.

77 Abrams, op. cit., p. 53.

78 Ibid., pp. 54–55.

79 Ibid., p. 55.

80 Ibid., p. 55.

81 Edward C. McDonagh, "Attitudes toward

Ethnic Farm Workers in Coachella Valley," *Sociology and Social Research,* 40 (Sept.-Oct. 1955), p. 11.

82 *Ibid.,* p. 17.

83 *Ibid.,* pp. 17–18.

84 For a history of the theory of slums see Abrams, *op. cit.,* pp. 246–247. He quotes the 19th-century theory of slums in the words of a judge who, in 1897, said that slums were caused "to a very considerable extent, if not entirely, by the filthy habits of the people who inhabit them" (p. 246). As late as 1931, in spite of a quarter of a century of research, the President's Conference on Home Building and Home Ownership still defined a slum in terms of the people who lived in them as "the abode of half-starved, filthily clothed children, of diseased and crippled individuals; a place of poverty, wretchedness, ignorance and vice. We think of it as a recession from the normal standards of a sound society." (J. F. Dewhurst *et al., America's Needs and Resources* [Twentieth Century Fund, 1955], p. 490.) In 1933 *Webster's International Dictionary* still included a definition of a slum as a "foul back street of a city, especially one with a slovenly and even vicious population," although it also called it a "low or squalid neighborhood." New Deal legislation, however, laid no blame for slums on the people who lived in them. It defined them wholly in terms of dilapidation, overcrowding, faulty arrangement or design, ventilation, light or sanitation facilities or any combination of these features which were detrimental to safety, health, or morals—in terms of physical rather than moral factors. In 1941, the Committee on the Hygiene of Housing of the American Public Health Association said, in effect, that it did not make much difference whether ill health in slums was the cause or the result of people or of housing; it was certainly true that slums did breed illness. (C. E. A. Winslow, Chairman of the Committee on the Hygiene of Housing, "Health and Housing," *Housing for Health,* 1941, pp. 7–8.) At the present time there is little emphasis given to the kind of people who live in slums. Slums are explained in terms of such concepts as market forces, land use, inadequate planning, and the like.

85 Elizabeth E. Hoyt *et al., American Income and Its Use* (Harper, 1954), p. 189.

86 Committee on the Hygiene of Housing, *Standards for Healthful Housing: Planning the Home for Occupancy* (Chicago, Public Administration Service, 1950), p. v.

VII

ABUNDANCE
AND THE EMERGENCE OF
SOCIAL PROBLEMS IN
UNDERDEVELOPED AREAS
OF THE WORLD

"With a view to the creation of conditions of stability and well-being which are necessary for peaceful and friendly relations among nations based on respect for the principle of equal rights and self-determination of peoples, the United Nations shall promote:

a. higher standards of living, full employment, and conditions of economic and social progress and development;

b. solutions of international economic, social, health, and related problems; and international cultural and educational cooperation; and

c. universal respect for, and observance of, human rights and fundamental freedoms for all without distinction as to race, sex, language, or religion."—Article 55 of the United Nations Charter

WITH CHARACTERISTIC modifications, a pattern of social problems similar to that found in the United States might be said to exist in other industrialized societies also. Thus men and women from these societies who attend international meetings of criminologists, health personnel, social workers, and demographers find little difficulty in understanding one another's problems even when they do not share them. They can sometimes pool their experiences.

But this is not so for those who come from the nonindustrialized or so-called underdeveloped areas of the world. The problems of these areas are still to a very large extent, if not exclusively, those of sheer hunger, disease, and shelter. Many of these areas are in the beginning stages of industrialization, before abundance is achieved, and the characteristic social problems of slums in large cities as millions of people are uprooted from the land and deposited in them are as urgent as they were in the United States in the 19th century.

Interestingly, as the prospect of abundance opens up, as the possibility of adapting the new technology to underdeveloped areas grows, problems of status—this time among whole races and peoples—also appear. Technology brings role problems with it; new definitions are required of such age-old relationships as those of parents and children, owner and tenant. And, in addition, there are the problems involved in rapid population growth. These are the problems we shall deal with in Part VII.

One of the phenomena of the 20th century is the emergence of the concept of social problems in the underdeveloped areas of the world, some 150 to 200 years after it emerged in the more advanced nations. After millennia of accepting their lot with resignation, peoples in these areas are coming to see that something can be done about their suffering. In southern Morocco, for example, "the visiting doctors had demonstrated that trachoma was not 'an ailment which has to be accepted, as it had been for centuries, as the will of heaven.' " * Increasingly, therefore, these people are thinking in terms of seizing the initiative against fate and doing something about their problems.

In Chapter 23 we shall give some attention to a few of the groups —children, the aged, refugees, and women—that face special problems in the world today. Then in Chapter 24 we shall single out for discussion four major social problems: the problems of sheer physical survival: hunger, housing, and health; the problems of population growth which result from solving these primitive survival problems; the role problems involved in the industrialization required to increase productivity for the growing populations; and the problems of race—or status —relations, especially between the colored and the white races.

These problems fulfill all the requirements we have specified for social problems, as we shall presently show. In the past they were considered the concern primarily of private agencies—religious or industrial —but the League of Nations and later the United Nations assumed responsibility for them, and much that we shall now present is based on the work of the United Nations.

* *Newsweek,* October 3, 1955, p. 84.

23

Social Problems
on the
World Stage

The conditions in underdeveloped areas of the world today meet the three criteria which we have specified for a social problem. At this point we shall not apply the criteria from the point of view of the peoples themselves so much as from the point of view of people here at home. For although the people in underdeveloped areas are indeed beginning to understand the concept of a social problem—and it would be an interesting study in itself to document its emergence—as yet the concept is relatively new. Among the peoples of the West, however, the conditions in underdeveloped areas have been viewed as social problems for some time, and it is their viewpoint that is embodied here.

The Three Criteria Are Met

The Humanitarian Criterion

The Christian missionary has long been motivated by humanitarian sentiments. He went out to the back woods of the world to save

The Three Criteria Are Met

Widening Responsibility

*Children in Europe and in Underdeveloped
Areas of the World*

The Traffic in Women

The Aged

Refugees and Displaced Persons

souls, and soon found that one of the best ways to save souls was to help with health, diet, and technological problems. The medical missionary became a well-recognized figure. The agricultural missionary brought improved farming methods. Schools and hospitals were as much the concern of the missionary as were churches. He dealt with social problems as part of a religious program.

The humanitarian motive is still powerful in Christian appeals. One agency, for example, makes a direct appeal to the Christian conscience:

AM I MY BROTHER'S KEEPER? [1]

What sort of future has Sang Gi, crippled by a bit of shrapnel? What are his chances, begging on the streets of Seoul, with his homemade crutches? He has no home, no parents, no schooling. He has a good and intelligent face, but . . .

Is his future any business of mine? Should I be concerned with cripples and the needs and suffering of others? When I have enough to eat should I be worried because others don't, including little children? Should I care, when I was lucky enough to be born in America instead of India, where the majority of people do not get enough to eat and some are actually starving? What is the reason I was not born in Korea, like Sang Gi? There are still 35,000 homeless children in Korea. Why don't I live in a hut made of rubble, old tin cans and half rotten scraps of wood in Southern Italy, Hong Kong or in a crowded Austrian refugee camp? Why don't I happen to be a man with a job in Calcutta, working steady every day for long hours, who sleeps in the streets every night because my job does not pay me enough to share even a single room with a dozen other persons—a room without a stitch of furniture or protection from flies, swarming with bed bugs and without any sanitary arrangements whatever?

I am a Christian. Does that make me my brother's keeper? When my stomach is full must I be concerned about others, whose stomachs are empty? Must I? Am I *compelled* to think about these others? Or is it just, God helping me, that I *want* to think about them and because I have a heart, desire to help them?

In addition, other private, voluntary organizations make similar appeals on humanitarian grounds.

A Casualty in a War He Never Knew [2]

Robert has paid a price for freedom. Every small boy needs a father to mend his broken toys, to play with him, to see that he has warm clothes and enough to eat. Robert, who is not yet four, has none of these. A war 6,500 miles from France, half-forgotten already, took them away from him and left only loneliness and poverty. . . .

Private American foundations, notably the Rockefeller Foundation, have taken the health of the world as a major concern and have wiped out some diseases over whole areas of the globe. The International Red Cross views catastrophe anywhere in the world as its province. More recently the Ford Foundation has contributed to underdeveloped nations faced with "economic, social and political problems which affect their role in world affairs and are therefore of importance to free men everywhere." [3]

The Utilitarian Criterion

The administrators of empires have also concerned themselves with the social problems of the areas in which they worked. Sanitation, medical care, housing, and similar problems were assumed as part of "the white man's burden." Thus, for example, a British Royal Commission was appointed in 1953 to study the problems of the British colonial territories of East Africa. In 1955 it presented its report, including recommendations concerning land ownership, public health, education, and race relations. The low productivity of ordinary African labor was attributed not only to a lack of technical skill but also to malnutrition, poor physique, disease, and inadequate incentives.[4]

Industrial empires also undertook to deal with the social problems in areas where they operated. If they wanted to have efficient workers they had to supply medical services, housing, and schools. All over the world, therefore, American industrial firms were dealing with the social problems of underdeveloped areas as part of their programs. The motivation was quite frankly utilitarian, for, as a study of one industry put it: "In any society, the success or failure of a large-scale business organization is critically influenced by the way it handles its manpower and related social problems." [5] In the Middle East, American oil companies inaugurate programs in public health and medicine.

Local nurses, doctors, and medical attendants, trained in modern techniques in company hospitals, are making available medical attention of a character and on a scale not known before. Hospitals, constructed, equipped, and run by the oil companies, have provided patterns for community health centers under local supervision.[6]

And standards of living have been raised:

With new hospitals, schools, and factories, financed by oil, springing up everywhere through the ancient land, Arab living standards are rising at a jet-age pace.

The oil companies have contributed handsomely to all this progress merely by adhering to good business practices. They need well-trained, healthy employes—and in nations where medical and other facilities are limited, the firms have had to provide the services themselves. . . .[7]

Pharmaceutical, engineering, and manufacturing firms in India, Egypt, and Thailand face social problems among their workers which they have to deal with simply because they cannot afford not to.[8]

The Criterion of Dysfunctionality

It requires a high order of abstraction to see that the problems of Hottentots are part of our own problems. When the American government enters on a program of foreign aid it must justify itself, not on humanitarian grounds—that would lay it open to domestic criticism as "do-goodism"—but on grounds of self-interest. A limited mentality cannot see that the "pint of milk for every Hottentot" is not reckless philanthropy but a necessity in an interdependent world. The arguments in favor of such foreign aid are therefore often couched in terms which emphasize the danger to our system if we neglect the disadvantaged peoples of the world, or in terms which emphasize their military import. Thus, a great newspaper editorializes that humanitarian and military motives cannot be separated, although human welfare must always be important.

If we will do our thinking and planning at the rice-roots level we can get returns for expenditures not merely in a presumptive military safety for a threatened area but in terms of human betterment. We will be better off when the ratio of nonmilitary aid to military can be substantially increased.[9]

In connection with appropriations for the United Nations Refugee Fund, it was said:

. . . Administration spokesmen have pointed out that we "cannot afford to have refugees returning to Communist countries because, in view of their experience as refugees, they come to believe the conditions of living behind the Iron Curtain are better than in the free world." [10]

And a warning is given that unless we share with less privileged countries, we may lose out in the long run.

If we become increasingly the only fat duck in a hungry world—look out! This state of imbalance, projected into the next fifty years, will surely destroy the peace your generation is entitled to. . . .

The common man all over the world, knowing that it is possible to produce enough for all, is demanding his share as a right. If he fails to get it, he is willing to flirt with the devil. . . . If he doesn't get help from the United States, he will try to get help from the Soviet Union. If the great masses of Asia and Europe and Africa don't begin to get more of a share of the world's good things—in health, in security, in happiness—then I fear for the continued security of our unprecedented standard of living in the West.[11]

Widening Responsibility

From Local Parish to World Community

We have had occasion to make a distinction from time to time in our discussion between "social" and "societal," the first referring to the socius, or individual-in-his-group-relations, the second to the society at large. So long as human suffering and misfortune were viewed as "social" in the above sense they were viewed as the responsibility of the family or the church or the wealthy in the immediate vicinity. Even when these ills came to be looked upon as the responsibility of the state, as in England in the 17th century, it was the parish or local community to which this responsibility fell. Little by little the responsible unit expanded, but it was not until the 19th century that these ills came to be seen as "societal" as well as "social" problems, that is, as problems to the whole social order and therefore as a responsibility of the state. Most civilized nations today tend to assume responsibility for a wide gamut of social services to meet social problems.

All modern states now realize that the law must indeed take care of certain "private" economic needs, especially those which, as the direct product of modern industrial development, can properly be charged to the costs of industry.[12]

What is interesting and important now is that this trend in industrialized societies to enlarge the responsibilities of the government —sometimes called a movement toward a "welfare state"—is now extending even beyond national limits to include peoples everywhere. A "world society" has emerged and with it a world conception of social problems.

Acceptance of responsibility for the alleviation of distress has, during recent decades, begun to extend beyond the national community to the international or world community. Not only have governments used international organizations to help them develop their social policies, but also the international community has assumed responsibility for refugees and other persons rendered destitute by wars, political upheavals, and natural catastrophes, and for the most pressing needs of the more helpless members of the human family.[13]

Thus the same path in thinking that characterized industrialized nations in the 19th century has now been followed by the international community. The responsibility of the strong and wealthy toward the weak and poor, the assessing of the problems of one nation as the problems of all, the motive of self-interest—these ideas, with which we became acquainted in Chapter 5, are now applied on a world scale.

While modern science and technology—particularly the development of communication and transportation—have been drawing the different parts of the world closer together and making them more interdependent, a far-reaching change in out-look upon world social problems has been taking place. To an extent which might have seemed inconceivable even fifty years ago, there has come increasing recognition that 2,400 million people have somehow to contrive to live together, and share together the resources of the earth; that the general impoverishment of any area is a matter of concern to all areas; and that the technical experience and knowledge acquired in rapidly changing industrialized societies have somehow to be made available to those communities that are less advanced and less well-equipped. That this has come to pass is an historical and inspiring fact. Indeed, it has been suggested by a distinguished historian that, in the broad sweep, the twentieth century will be chiefly remembered in future centuries not as an age of political conflicts or technical inventions, but as an age in which human society dared to think of the welfare of the whole human race as a practicable objective.

In the basic ethics of all great religions, there has been the recognition that the better-endowed must help those who are less fortunate; but, developing from this deep impulse of human charity and consistent with voluntary help and personal giving, there is a new and wider concept: governments have accepted the principle that in the interests not only of their own communities but of the world in which these communities exist, they must organize and undertake mutual aid. This principle is valid on the material as well as on the moral plane; it is practical well-doing or "enlightened self-interest" on the part of countries that extend such aid to other areas; and countries that are raising their standards are helping to contribute to the equilibrium of world society. Amid the political tensions of the present day, this principle is universally avowed as a goal of international policy and a measure of international action.[14]

Social problems, in brief, are no longer viewed as local or national, but as international problems. Poverty in Indonesia or Chile or Timbuktu is coming to be seen as a social problem to the well-to-do nations of the world; malaria in Mexico, as a problem to all nations; inadequate nutrition anywhere, as the concern of the adequately fed everywhere. Housing, child labor, industrial exploitation, oppressive land tenure systems—these, in an increasingly integrated world, become social problems to the enlightened nations.

Unlike the tendency of the more mature industrialized nations toward leveling up and down within classes, the tendency of nonindustrialized nations has been to increase differences—greater poverty on the one hand and greater wealth on the other.

From the point of view of the distribution within countries of the goods produced, a certain levelling process appears to be under way in countries with relatively high and expanding national incomes: the poorer groups are receiving a larger share of the total income; wage differentials between occupational groups are narrowing; progressive labour legislation and systems of social security are defining minimum levels of welfare below which society does not permit individual members to sink—and these levels are being progressively redefined upwards.

In the less-developed countries, some recent improvements in the fields of large-scale industrial labour and plantation labour have likewise taken place. Yet, for the great masses of the people, who are illiterate peasants engaged in small-scale farming with primitive techniques, general poverty does not appear to have been substantially reduced in recent years—it has, in wide areas, quite possibly been aggravated as a result of declines in per capita agricultural production. Social security measures, labour legislation and various measures for the general welfare have had less effect upon these isolated and impoverished rural groups. In fact, it may be said that the peasants of under-developed areas have been the forgotten men of the twentieth century and have benefitted less from its changes than any other group. There is, however, growing recognition of their plight and increasing efforts, both national and international, to deal with it, as shown by the emphasis recently given to the importance of land reform and other agrarian measures.[15]

The governmental units assigned the responsibility for this international attack on world social problems have been the old League of Nations and, currently, the United Nations. Unless one makes a special effort to study the widespread and profound activities of the United Nations it is difficult to appreciate the extent of its impact. Today no one who is interested in social problems can afford to neglect the rapidly growing literature of the United Nations in this area.

The League of Nations and the United Nations

The ill-fated League of Nations assumed that it was part of its task to help solve the social problems of peoples everywhere. Standards of living, the traffic in narcotics and in women and children, and industrial problems were all part of its concern. It organized the International Labour Office to study the problems of industrial workers and to recommend ways for meeting them.

At midcentury the United Nations took over much of the work formerly done by the League of Nations. Article 55 of its charter states that it will promote, among other things, "solutions of international economic, social, health and related problems." There are many such problems. World War II saw the emergence of new ones, especially those of displaced persons, refugees, and stateless persons. Housing, health, the feeding of masses of homeless people, the reknitting of families all over Europe—these were among the social problems which were viewed as the problems of all nations.

Of special significance is the Economic and Social Council, which is directly responsible to the General Assembly of the United Nations. Consisting of eighteen members elected by the Assembly, it studies and prepares recommendations on human rights and on economic, social, educational, health, and other matters related to the welfare of mankind. It establishes *ad hoc* commissions on any of the subjects within its competence and coordinates the activities of various intergovernmental agencies; it also cooperates with private organizations. It is coordinate in importance with the Trusteeship Council and even with the Secretariat, indicating how much weight is attached to its functions.

The Economic and Social program of the United Nations is an innovation in international affairs. Breaking with the classical concept that such matters as the promotion of fundamental human rights, higher standards of living, or full employment have no place in an international agreement, the Charter of the UN has placed them among the main objectives of the broadest treaty ever signed.[16]

Among the commissions established by this Council are the Social Commission, commissions on narcotic drugs, on the status of women, and on human rights, with subcommissions on the protection of minorities and the prevention of discrimination. It is the Social Commission which deals most intimately with social problems.

The Social Commission, whose main task it was to report to the Council on social problems requiring immediate attention, had to begin by making definitions. First it had to define what was meant by the terms "social" and "social policy." In the past these terms were commonly associated with activities of a charitable nature based, according to the Commission, on "a condescending benevolence on the part of the privileged classes toward the poor, profoundly offending the dignity and the principle of democratic equality." The Commission has agreed that today, while there is still room for voluntary charitable activities, the main burden of securing an adequate standard of living for all must fall upon the community.

When the Commission came upon the term "standard of living" it had to define its meaning. It examined first of all the component elements of any standard of living, whether high or low. These elements are: housing, food and nutrition, clothing, health and medical care, education, and recreation. . . . It was obvious to the members of the Commission that this whole field is of such importance to the welfare of mankind that only a permanent body could deal adequately with the social task of the UN.[17]

Among the specialized agencies of the United Nations there are five which are of particular interest in any consideration of social problems in a world setting; they are the International Labour Organization (ILO), the Food and Agriculture Organization (FAO), the United Nations Educational, Scientific and Cultural Organization (UNESCO), the World Health Organization (WHO), and the United Nations International Children's Emergency Fund (UNICEF). The ILO, for example, promotes "improvement of labour conditions, especially where injustice, hardship and privation to large numbers of people exist, by furthering: regulation of hours of work. . . . the regulation of the labour supply; the prevention of unemployment; the provision of an adequate living wage; the protection of the worker against sickness, disease, and injury arising out of unemployment; provision for old age and injury; the protection of children, young persons, and women." [18] The FAO seeks to raise "levels of nutrition and standards of living of the peoples" and to better "the condition of rural populations." [19] UNESCO aims to secure for all full and equal opportunities for education. Of WHO and UNICEF we shall have more to say below.

United Nations publications cover such wide-ranging topics as human rights; refugees and displaced persons; tuberculosis; floods; land reform; social welfare administration; traffic in obscene publications;

family, youth, and child welfare; crime and correction; the physically handicapped; community organization and development; housing; demography; and dependent peoples. We shall rely heavily on these publications to tell the story of social problems in underdeveloped areas of the world today.

We shall single out for consideration here the problems of four special groups—children, the aged, refugees, and women—and in Chapter 24 we shall turn to an examination of more general and abstract world social problems.

Children in Europe and in Underdeveloped Areas of the World

A great many organizations are at work to help children in all parts of the world. We quoted above the appeals of some of them. In general it is easier for organizations to work with children than with adults and often it is considered that the investment of time and energy is more rewarding. Perhaps the greatest part of the work with children today is that undertaken by the United Nations International Children's Emergency Fund which was established in 1946 to care for the postwar emergency needs of children as the United Nations Relief and Rehabilitation Administration ceased its activities.

Refugee Children

Thus, refugee children and children who had lost their parents were the first major concern of UNICEF as well as of a number of volunteer relief organizations in the 1940's. The International Relief Organization and the Red Cross, as well as such private agencies as Save-a-Child, attempted to deal with them as available resources permitted. The refugee child no longer is an emergency problem, except, as we shall see below, in the case of the Arabs. But the shadow of these millions of erstwhile refugee children will hang over the rest of the 20th century, attenuated, no doubt, as the years pass, but present nonetheless wherever they live. In a study of repatriates and refugees in Switzerland, four fifths of the children and adolescents who had had to be hospitalized for personality disorders were cured or at least improved by 1949. But the horrors they had lived through in their early years had left a residue which Rorschach testing revealed as a "staggering filmstrip of the way they [had] lived." [20]

The Victims of the Mass Diseases

By midcentury the work of UNICEF with children had shifted from emergency care to assistance in dealing with long-standing problems of maternal and child welfare. Working closely with the World Health Organization, some ninety-one countries in 1951 were benefiting from UNICEF's programs. In talking about its work the individual child is lost in statistical masses, for UNICEF operates on a gargantuan scale. In 1955 alone, for example, some thirty-two million children in Asia, Latin America, and Africa were served in maternal and child health centers.

Lives of children in Asia, excluding China, were being saved at the cost of ten cents each in the 1950's. The death rate for children in their first year of life had traditionally been about 20 per cent— one in five. A mother took it for granted that she would lose every fifth child. Until recently the cost of the medical care required to save the children seemed prohibitive. Modern methods have reduced the cost of saving a child's life to ten cents. This is "mass production" in health work on an almost unheard of scale. In Indonesia, for example, UNICEF examined more than 10 million people for yaws, and treated more than 1 million. In Formosa 1.3 million children were tested for trachoma. In Burma 150 million people now have at least a year's protection against malaria. By 1954, 73.6 million children had been tested for tuberculosis, 32.5 million in one year, and there was a target of 37.5 million for 1955. Yet even on this unprecedented scale it was a close race with the birth rate; UNICEF was "testing the children only half again as fast as they . . . [were] being born; for the yearly crop of babies runs to about 25 million." [21]

Handicapped Children

In the past, even when children survived, in many areas of the world they suffered throughout their lives from the handicaps which illness left in its wake. The extent at midcentury of the problem of such handicapped children in the less-developed areas of the world is not known because factual surveys have not been made and because of the difficulties involved in establishing common criteria. What constitutes mental retardation in one society, for example, might not be so considered in another; degrees of handicap may also vary from society to society. A person with a partial visual defect might never know he had it in a preliterate society; he would know it as soon as he tried to read in a literate society. In general, however, more is known about physical handicap among children than among adults. We shall refer here to one kind of handicap, blindness, but the story would probably not be much different for other kinds.

The relative incidence of blindness is much greater in the under-developed areas of the world than in the Western countries. It is, for example, 250 to 500 per 100,000 in Algeria, Egypt, Union of South Africa, Cyprus, India, and Pakistan, and 500 to 1,000 per 100,000 in Libya, as contrasted with only 50 per 100,000 in the Netherlands and 175 per 100,000 in the United Kingdom and the United States; and the difference is probably even greater than this because of under-enumeration in the less developed countries. In Western countries, furthermore, blindness is associated with the older members of the population, whereas in the underdeveloped countries a large proportion of the people lose their sight as children. More tragic still is the fact that from 75 to 80 per cent of the blindness is preventable.[22]

The incidence of blindness has been proposed as a good negative index of the degree of economic and social development of an area, since ignorance and poverty constitute the fundamental reason for its prevalence. "It would seem, even when all possible reservations are made, that there are at least 6 million blind persons in the world today; that at least half of these need not have become blind; and that most of them could be helped by appropriate services to contribute to the raising of their own and their fellows' standards of living." [23]

As the work of UNICEF and WHO becomes increasingly pre-ventive in nature, one of the most fascinating chapters in human history is going to be enacted. Children of the underdeveloped areas of the world will be growing up without the stigmas of illness and disabilities; they are going to be literate, technically trained, eager to assimilate the new technologies. In many parts of the world children are already taller than their fathers and mothers. It is almost as though a new species were in process of emerging.

The Traffic in Women

Although it cannot be said to constitute a major world social problem, the traffic in women for exploitation as prostitutes has been considered serious enough by world powers to warrant international control. As early as 1904 there was an international agreement to suppress this so-called white-slave traffic. The work of the League of Nations on the problem resulted in three agreements, the last one in 1937. In 1949 the United Nations adopted a new convention, to go into effect in 1951, dealing with this problem.

The nature and direction of the traffic in women has changed markedly in the 20th century. At one time, for example, the major trade route was from Europe to South America; "the road to Buenos Aires" was synonymous with this marketing of women. At midcentury, North Africa and the Near East are the major markets. At one time the traffic in women was associated with violence, kidnapings, abductions, rape, and illegal detention. Today the picture is quite different. The men who recruit personnel are smooth businessmen who trap their victims with professional bait. They are, for example, theatrical agents, stage producers, bandmasters, ballet masters, cabaret owners. There is little force involved. "The cleverly conceived system is based on the principles of isolation from home and family; growing indebtedness, progressive degradation through drink, dope and abuse, legalistic chicanery and a methodical blocking of all possible avenues of escape." [24] In its modern form, the recruiting and trafficking in women are much more difficult to detect. The number of cases involved is not known, but one student believes more girls and women than ever before are being victimized.[25] One case will be enough to illustrate the methods used today in the international traffic in women. It is taken from the police files of Gelsenkirchen, a large industrial city of West Germany.

Early in July 1950, Anna Goelz, aged 19, took a job as a waitress in the restaurant Bertoloni at Bahnhofstrasse 17, Gelsenkirchen. There she met an Italian salesman, a traveler in textile fabrics, who induced her and four other young girls to emigrate abroad. They were last seen on German soil at Karlsruhe, Baden, on August 11.

From Karlsruhe, the girls continued towards Kehl, where they crossed the French border. All were in possession of passports issued by the "Combined Travel Board," Stuttgart. Anna Goelz, who gave her profession as "housemaid," was the bearer of a passport numbered 0347 911. Toward the middle of September, Anna Goelz was employed as maid in the household of one Julien Gance, a notary at Chartres, France. One month later, October 15, she quit this employment, going to Perpignan.

On January 9, 1951, Anna Goelz and six other alleged housemaids sailed from a port in Southern France aboard the liner *Georges-Luduc* for Oran, Algeria. The group was under the charge of an Italian named Amadeo Brazzano. . . .

[Several months later, the Oran Police Headquarters supplied the rest of the story, as follows:] Anna Goelz and four other German girls, to wit, Josephine Brandmaier of Rosenheim; Ingrid von Tessmer, of Berlin; Martha List, of Duisburg; and Anita Pfuhl of Bielefeld, have been identified as inmates of Algerian brothels. All have stated that they originally had been engaged as maids.

It has been further established that Andrea Brazzi, alias Amadeo Brazzano, is in a position to procure false identification papers. His ostensible occupation is that of a traveling salesman in textiles. He makes a practice of taking young women first to Karlsruhe, then across the border into France, where he places them in household service. Eventually, he withdraws them again for shipment to Oran, via Marseille.

Further investigation by the French Criminal Police has yielded the following results: Ingrid von Tessmer has committed suicide; Josephine Brandmaier has vanished without trace; Martha List is in a brothel in the interior of Algeria; Anita Pfuhl has returned to Germany in the company of a German formerly with the Foreign Legion.[26]

Similar cases are reported of women being transported for illegal purposes in all parts of the world. The markets change, but the traffic continues.

The white-slave traffic into the United States used to flourish; women were bought and sold for prices ranging from $200 to $2,000.[27] The decline in old-fashioned prostitution has been attributed to better screening of immigrants, the Mann Act of 1910, which forbade the transportation of women over state boundaries, the public scandal of Lucky Luciano's trial in 1936,[28] and to technological change.[29] But a great deal more is probably also involved. American girls have changed.

The modern American girl is not the type to fit the role of old-fashioned prostitute. The white-slave traffic is possible only when the old status relationship between men and women remains without the protection which the old status offered women. They were formerly economically dependent and subordinate to men. They took orders from men. In return they did not have to earn their living in the market. But when they did have to work outside the home and did not have the status which normally should accompany their role as worker, they remained subordinate and were easily exploitable, like Anna Goelz and her four friends.

Nowadays the American girl views the old-fashioned prostitute as naïve. The call girl may be considered technically a prostitute but her situation is more like that of the geisha girl; more is expected than sheer biological sex. There is a show of human interaction.[30] It approaches more nearly the kind of social life which is conventional except that the stakes are probably higher on both sides. In the conventional date a man may expect little more than petting in payment for the entertainment he provides; the customer of the call girl expects more and is prepared to pay more. She is less easily exploited either by her customer or by her "agent."

Perhaps only when the status and level of education of women everywhere have been raised to at least that enjoyed by women in the United States can we expect a notable decline in the international traffic in women.

The Aged

Because of the high death rates at all age levels in underdeveloped areas, a relatively small proportion of the people reach old age; hence the problems of older persons have not yet become acute. But as health is improved, the problems of the aged may be expected to resemble those of the aged in the Western countries. "In pre-industrial rural areas, society has traditionally made provision for the relatively small numbers of people who reach old age, usually according them a position of honour and leadership in the community and of security in the household." [31] It has been suggested that perhaps the underdeveloped areas may develop different patterns of location of industry, different kinds of housing, and different ways of making a living from those which evolved in the Western nations in the 19th century and which led to such serious problems for the older persons. They may, if they succeed, "preserve something more akin to their traditional type of family and social system." [32] Whether it is possible to industrialize, incorporating the values which go with industrialization, and at the same time to retain the family values which went with an agricultural society, is by no means certain. As yet, however, there are not enough aged in the underdeveloped areas to constitute a major social problem.

Refugees and Displaced Persons

Although our main emphasis in this chapter is on the social problems of other parts of the world, candor demands that we look first at the beam in our own eyes. In the American Indian are illustrated many of the problems of displaced persons anywhere and everywhere—demoralization and pauperization.

We referred incidentally on page 557 to the severe segregation which has cut the Indians off from the main currents of American life so that integration in their case is far more difficult than in that of Negroes. The history of the relations between the United States Government and the Indian tribes is one of so many and such major mistakes that any complete rectification of them seems all but impossible.

At midcentury a policy of permitting, if not actually of encouraging, the exodus of individual Indian families from tribal reservations was being experimented with. Families were allowed to sell their holdings and move into the outside world. Whether this policy was motivated, as some alleged, by a desire to acquire potentially oil-rich lands or by a genuine desire to improve the opportunities of the Indians to share in the abundance of American society, the consequences for many individual families were catastrophic. The ills of displacement are not easily undone. Without adequate preparation, without marketable skills, the Indian found himself in a strange world he could not cope with. Nor was there a chance to return to the reservation. His decision to leave was irrevocable. He was at an even greater disadvantage than the Negro, for he was a victim of a vast displacement that had made him a colonial in his own country. When we look at displaced persons in other lands, we should not forget those in our own land.

Extent of the Problem

Although the problems of refugees and displaced persons are very old, they have become acute in the 20th century, and especially in the aftermath of the two world wars, the Korean police action, and the several so-called brush wars. The importance of these problems today lies in the size of the populations involved "and the recognition of aspects of the problem as an international responsibility." [33] There were 6 million refugees and displaced persons in Europe at the end of World War II; over 5 million were finally repatriated. The civil war in Greece rendered 600,000 persons homeless. The partition of India in 1947 caused the migration of 14 million persons—9 million from India into Pakistan and 5 million in the opposite direction. The war in Palestine in 1948 resulted in the dispersion of about 1 million Arab refugees in the Middle East, of whom we shall have more to say below. The Korean police action produced $4\frac{1}{2}$ million refugees and displaced persons in South Korea.[34] The wars in Indo-China uprooted millions of families who fled to the south as Communist regimes took over in the north. Similarly there was a great exodus of Chinese to Formosa with the coming into power of the Communist government on the mainland. In 1956 the refugees from Hungary swelled the total number of homeless people by some hundred thousand. The sheer magnitude of such human uprootings is staggering, even to Americans who are accustomed to mobility.

Classes of Refugees

The refugee population is not homogeneous. It varies from place to place and from circumstance to circumstance. One study [35] has classified the refugee population of the 1950's as follows:

CLASSES OF REFUGEES

Group I: Prewar (White Russian, Armenian, and Spanish)	Group II: Repatriates	Group III: Displaced Persons Not Repatriated	Group IV: Anti-Communists from East Europe	Group V: Population Transfers (Indians, Germans, and Finns) of Postwar Settlements
Loss of homeland	No loss of homeland	Loss of homeland	Loss of homeland	No loss of homeland
Many years of moderate persecution	A few years of often severe persecution	A few years of often severe persecution	Short period of limited persecution, or none at all	Short period of limited persecution, or none at all
No specific claim on receiving country	Full specific claim on receiving country	No specific claim on receiving country	Slight claim on receiving political group	Full claim on government of country
Very long period of statelessness perhaps continuing	No real period of statelessness	Average of five years of initial statelessness perhaps continuing	Short period of statelessness to date, probably continuing	No period of statelessness
Usually no government resettlement	Usually no organized resettlement	Resettlement usually organized	Resettlement usually organized, but less than for displaced persons	Resettlement often government organized
Unstable home political background	Usually stable home political background	Usually very unstable home background	Usually very unstable home background	Home background variable

The problems of each of these classes of uprooted peoples are different to some extent. More is known about the displaced persons than about any other group. But what is known about them is probably true, in greater or lesser degree, about all the other categories also.

Effects of Displacement on Societies
and Individuals

The implications for world society of the presence of these uprooted people in many countries have been summarized as follows:

When populations are uprooted and moved to some distant land, the
process has lasting effects both on society and on the individual. We know a
good deal, for instance, about the importance in history of the migratory
hordes from Central Asia, and at the opposite pole we are learning much
today about the effect of voluntary migration on the health and stamina of
the individual migrant. But an important aspect of which we know much less
is that of the personal effects of forced migration. . . . The present time is
. . . almost the first occasion on which it has been possible for the personal
effects of flight and forced migration to be investigated.

The arguments for such an investigation were initially derived from
what we know about the general immigrant. We know that as compared with
native populations the latter shows higher mortality, suicide, and mental
hospitalization rates, that he tends to cling to the cities and eschew pioneer
situations, and that his children tend to show some cultural disintegration,
with increased criminality. All these effects are relatively small, but it is presumed that they are produced by certain strains associated with difficulties in
breaking away from an old culture and becoming established in a new one.
It is further presumed that refugees experience very similar strains, though of
a more severe nature. This leads us to expect that refugees will show to a
greater degree the same weaknesses as are found in general immigrants, and
the degree to which this is occurring has at least merited enquiry. More
recent studies, however, give us more positive grounds for disquiet. One of
the obvious points which distinguish the refugee from the voluntary migrant
is that the former is much more likely to have suffered hunger or starvation.
But starvation has for long been suspected of being able to produce permanent bodily and mental changes. . . . Since there is now . . . direct evidence that refugees suffer from some impairment of their ability to adjust to
new conditions, the question arises as to what extent the condition exists in
the world today.

It is a very difficult point to answer. . . . In the first place, there is the
question of the amount of disturbance needed to produce what, without
defining it, we may call the refugee state. . . . The next difficulty lies in how
long one is to choose to regard any group as refugees. . . . Our third difficulty . . . is that no matter what criteria are chosen, there are considerable
variations in the suggested figures.[36]

Bearing all these difficulties in mind, the author just quoted presents
the percentage of refugees in the total population of a number of
countries in 1952, ranging from 20.0 per cent in West Germany to 0.5
per cent in Greece.

As is usual in so many world social problems today, those involving physical care are far easier to deal with than those involving role

and status. There is probably no greater trauma to which human beings can be subjected than that of forced removal from homeland, from family and work group ties, and from their cultural milieu. All studies of refugees point up the deterioration of personality which they suffer; in some cases this may reach a point where the individual becomes merely an automaton.[37] There is no greater reminder of the dependence of personality, of the self, on the role network in which it functions. The disturbed refugee generation will leave its trace, in increasingly diluted form, wherever it is found. Years after the war, many refugees had not yet been located in permanent homes. Many countries accepted them in small numbers; many remained in camps, losing skills, losing morale, losing faith.[38] Literally they became a lost generation.

The Case of the Arab Refugees:
Political or Social Problem?

It is often impossible to draw a sharp line between political and social problems. The fine line separating world social problems from problems of policy is illustrated by the expression "the politics of hunger," referring to the impact which humanitarian or welfare activities in the underdeveloped areas of the world have in the Cold War's competitive race for the allegiance of these areas.[39] "Competitive coexistence" has come to involve an outbidding of one another by the contestants.

One illustration at midcentury of the way in which human beings may become pawns in this great game was the indeterminate number [40] —usually estimated at about a million—of Arab refugees living in some sixty camps in Lebanon, Jordan, Syria, and the Gaza Strip. They did not fall into any of the categories listed above. They left Palestine voluntarily at the time of the war in 1948, and since then leaders of the Arab League have continued to insist on their repatriation. Israel would not repatriate them, and the Arab League would accept nothing less. As a result, about a million people have become paupers. Unemployment—always a most demoralizing experience—was a perennial problem in the camps, for "even when satisfactory work projects are developed, it is often with great reluctance that the refugees are willing to participate and so give up their ration cards . . . [which] represent tangible evidence of social security." [41] When refugees did accept work, they accepted only the most transient accommodations or employment, fearing that a shift in status would prejudice chances of repatriation. By retaining their refugee status and also having the advantage of employment, they constituted a privileged class in the camps and caused resentment among the genuine hardship cases.

About half the population in these camps in 1955 were children under fourteen, who had lived more than half their lives in these camps. As we have emphasized and re-emphasized throughout this book, the problems of physical care are far easier to handle than those involving role and status. Difficult as it may be to feed, clothe, and house a million people, it is easier to do this than it is to prevent demoralization.[42] Observers continued to note "the disintegration, frustration and boredom of the refugee camp parents . . . [who] for nearly a decade . . . have been deprived of responsibility and have had decisions made for them." [43]

If the care of these people could have been approached as a strictly social problem the solution might not have been impossible; intertwined as it was, however, with political issues, it was considered by competent people to be unsolvable.[44] A request for 2,000 refugee farmers by Libya would, for example, be turned down on the advice of the Arab League, whose policy it was to "keep them as close to Israel as possible, whatever the conditions of life."

A firm policy on the part of the outside world might conceivably have found an accommodation to this impasse. But conflicts of principle and expedience nullified all efforts. And so the tens of thousands of healthy little children running around the camps, laughing, keen on sports, interested in their school work [45]—most of them could probably remember no other life—were indoctrinated to hate Israel. Time was not allowed to soften "the bitterness of separation and the prevailing sentiment of longing to return to their homes." [46] The fate of these little children was being decided in faraway cities by men who saw them not as human beings, but as trump cards in a political game with large stakes. What price, one might ask, health, education, and vocational skills in a world which permitted no functional role and put a premium on a dependency status? Social problems, inextricably entwined with economic problems through scarcity and abundance, are also closely enmeshed with political problems.

NOTES

1 Christian Children's Fund, Inc., advertisement, "Am I My Brother's Keeper?" in *Atlantic Monthly,* July 1955.

2 Save the Children Federation, advertisement, "A Casualty in a War He Never Knew," in *Harper's,* April 1955.

3 Report of the Ford Foundation for 1954, p. 57. The name of this report is "To Advance Human Welfare."

4 *New York Times,* June 10, 1955.

5 Eugene W. Burgess and Frederick H. Harbison, *Casa Grace in Peru* (National Planning Association, 1954), p. 61.

6 *Standard Oil Company (New Jersey) and Middle East Oil Production* (rev. ed., 1954), p. 29.

7 *Newsweek,* June 13, 1955, pp. 81–82.

8 Some of these enterprises were summarized in the *New York Times,* July 5, 1955.

9 *New York Times,* May 28, 1955.

10 *Ibid.,* June 24, 1955.

11 Gardner Cowles, in a commencement address reported in the *New York Times,* June 10, 1955.

12 Elizabeth E. Hoyt *et al., American Income and Its Use* (Harper, 1954), p. 49.

13 United Nations, *Preliminary Report on the World Social Situation* (United Nations, 1952), p. 128.

14 *Ibid.,* p. 3.

15 *Ibid.,* pp. 3–4.

16 Louis Dolivet, *The United Nations, a Handbook on the New World Organization* (Farrar, Straus, 1946), p. 58.

17 *Ibid.,* pp. 63–64.

18 United Nations, ILO, Constitution.

19 United Nations, FAO, Constitution.

20 H. B. M. Murphy *et al., Flight and Resettlement* (UNESCO, 1955), p. 166.

21 S. M. Keeny, "A Life for Ten Cents," *Atlantic Monthly,* June 1955, p. 30.

22 United Nations, *Preliminary Report on the World Social Situation,* p. 125.

23 *Ibid.,* p. 126.

24 From *Vice, Inc.* (p. 20). Copyright 1954 by Joachim Joesten and published by Ace Books, New York. All rights reserved.

25 *Ibid.*

26 *Ibid.,* pp. 9–10.

27 *Ibid.,* p. 123.

28 He is reported as having once said to one of his assistants: "Take joints away from madams, put them on salary or commission and run them like a syndicate—like large A & P stores. . . ." (*Ibid.,* p. 125.) He did just that.

29 "The call girl, like the ticket girl, is a typical American phenomenon. Both are, if one may say so, the daughters of technological progress" (*ibid.,* p. 125)—in this case progress means communication by telephone.

30 Polly Adler, *A House Is Not a Home* (Rinehart, 1953).

31 United Nations, *Preliminary Report on the World Social Situation,* p. 126.

32 *Ibid.,* p. 127.

33 *Ibid.*

34 *Ibid.*

35 Murphy *et al., op. cit.,* p. 19.

36 *Ibid.,* pp. 11–18.

37 In one case a boy in a concentration camp was left as dead; he believed himself dead. He was stacked with the corpses. When the liberators came and found him alive, he accepted their statement and believed himself alive. He made no judgments, even about his own body. He had been reduced to an automaton. (*Ibid.,* p. 41.)

38 The policy of the United States with respect to the admission of displaced persons became involved in security problems in the 1950's, and the number who came in was small. See Maurice Davie, *Refugees in America* (Harper, 1947), and Donald P. Kent, *The Refugee Intellectual* (Columbia Univ. Press, 1953).

39 For a brief statement of this kind of political competition, see Jessie Bernard, *American Community Behavior* (Dryden, 1949), pp. 643–646.

40 Marguerite Cartwright points out that there has been no accurate count of the number and that the United Nations administrator of the camps says one cannot be made. ("Plain Speech on the Arab Refugee Problem," *Land Reborn,* November-December 1955, p. 11.)

41 Quoted from a United Nations report, *ibid.,* p. 11.

42 "Many people in the camps seem materially better off than a majority of those living outside. In many ways, an amazingly good job has been done. . . . The health picture is an encouraging one. I myself saw and photographed scores of healthy looking groups of young people. . . . FAO investigators . . . found 'no

serious cases of mal-nutrition.' There have been no major epidemics . . . living testimony to the efficacy of mass immunization, maternal and child health clinics and cod liver oil capsules. . . . I also saw evidence of . . . solid achievement in education, with girls going to school—something hitherto almost unknown in that region. Elementary pupils were supplied with desks, blackboards, books and paper. There is reeducation and retraining of artisans and agricultural experts. . . . Only about 30 percent of the camp population lives in tents. Many live in the community, among the native residents, still collecting their rations from the Agency. . . ." (*Ibid.*, p. 13.)

43 *Ibid.*, p. 10

44 Henry R. Labouisse, the United Nations administrator of the camps, is quoted to this effect. (*Ibid.*, p. 13.)

45 Alexander E. Squadrilli, quoted by Harry Gilroy in the *New York Times*, October 3, 1955.

46 UNRRA report, quoted by Marguerite Cartwright, *loc. cit.*

24

Survival and Status

on the

World Stage

Problems of scarcity, of sheer survival, still persist in underdeveloped areas of the world today. At the same time, the coming of technological change is bringing with it the dislocations which destroy old role and status relationship. In this chapter we shall examine four major problems: those of sheer survival—hunger, housing, and health; the population problems which result from the survival of millions of people who would formerly have died at an earlier age—the race between the birth rate and technology; the social problems which accompany technological change—role disturbance, especially; and status problems among races and peoples.

Problems of Sheer Physical Survival

Hunger

To many well-fed Americans and Europeans, the lack of adequate nutrition in out-of-the-way places of the world seemed, until recently,

Problems of Sheer Physical Survival

Problems of Population Growth:
The Race between Population and Technology

The Social Problems Which Accompany Technological
Change: Role Disturbance

Status Problems among Races and Peoples

of no relevance. It was no concern of theirs. The exigencies of the Cold War, however, showed that there was a "politics of hunger" as well as a Christian or humanitarian obligation to feed the hungry. The existence of hunger, which could be exploited by Communism, was increasingly viewed as dysfunctional to the West. The elimination of hunger was seen as a tremendous weapon. To many people, therefore, the argument that hungry people are the best targets for Communist propaganda was decisive; it made a foreign-aid program palatable. But to many other Americans and Europeans, hunger is a social problem that should be overcome on humanitarian grounds; they do not like the idea of people going hungry, especially if means are available for helping them.

The Food and Agriculture Organization (FAO) of the United Nations is charged with the responsibility of studying the nutritional needs and resources of the world. In the early 1950's it measured the daily calorie consumption in different parts of the world against the estimated requirements, taking climate and activity into account, and found the following differences, expressed in per cent of requirements being met.[1]

FAR EAST		MIDDLE EAST		AFRICA	
Ceylon	−13.2	Cyprus	− 1.6	French North	
India	−24.4	Egypt	− 4.2	Africa	−20.9
Japan	− 9.9	Turkey	+ 1.6	Mauritius	− 7.5
Philippines	−12.1			Union of South	
				Africa	+ 5.0

LATIN AMERICA		EUROPE		NORTHERN AMERICA	
				AND OCEANIA	
Argentina	+22.7	Denmark	+14.9	Australia	+20.6
Brazil	− 4.5	France	+ 8.6	United States of	
Chile	−10.6	Greece	+ 5.0	America	+18.5
Mexico	−17.6	Italy	− 4.1		
Uruguay	+ 0.4	Norway	+10.2		
		United			
		Kingdom	+16.9		

For almost a decade after the end of World War II, the nutritional situation of the world deteriorated rather than improved. In the early 1950's, for example, for 80 per cent of the world population, the proportion consuming more than 2,700 calories daily had declined from the prewar level of 30.6 per cent to 27.8 per cent, while the proportion consuming less than 2,300 calories daily had risen from 38.6 per cent to 59.5 per cent.[2]

In 1955 the FAO reviewed food production in the first postwar decade. In 1945 agricultural production was down 5 per cent and the world's population up 10 per cent; there was a 15 per cent decline in production per capita. By 1954 this lag had been made up. Although food production did not continue to increase in 1954 and 1955, food availability per capita was still slightly above that before the war. But this improvement in the available food was not evenly distributed throughout the world. In many Far Eastern and in some Latin American countries, and in the Pacific Islands generally, food consumption was still below prewar levels, inadequate as these levels had been. In Pakistan there was 10 per cent less food per person than there was fifteen years earlier. In the Pacific Islands there was only 86 per cent as much food per capita as before the war. In China, also, there was less food per person in 1955 than before World War II.[3]

For those who inclined toward pessimism, the future looked no better. In most underdeveloped areas food production would have to be doubled in order to provide the inhabitants with the minimum FAO standard of 2,650 calories daily. The date 1987 was set by some as the year when it would no longer be possible to increase food production with currently known methods and techniques and when the people in more crowded poorer countries would begin to starve. Even for those who inclined toward optimism—hoping that new techniques would expand food production beyond 1987—the ideal of a world population adequately fed still seemed at midcentury a long way from realization.

The exploitation of new food resources such as algae and plankton was a possible source of food, but at midcentury production was still too costly. There were also suggestions for synthesizing algae-like foods by solar energy. As yet this was still only an idea.

Nor was the housing situation much better.

Housing

The 19th-century nature of social problems in the less developed areas of the world is particularly well illustrated in the housing situation. In these areas, as in the industrialized nations of the West in the 19th century, large numbers of rural people are inundating the urban communities, with resulting slum conditions.

The more conspicuous housing problems of the less-developed areas derive from the rapid expansion of their cities in recent years. Industrialization, migrations of peasants unable to support themselves on the land, and, in some areas—particularly of Asia—floods of refugees, have resulted in a mushroom-growth of city slums comparable to that accompanying the nineteenth century Industrial Revolution in Europe. The typical working-class family in most cities of Africa, Asia, and large parts of Latin America lives in a single room, frequently with no private cooking, bathing, or toilet facilities. The cities which have grown most rapidly are usually surrounded by slum suburbs of huts built of scrap material by their occupants—frequently squatters—and lacking even the most rudimentary system of water supply or sewage disposal. Often these huts are built by peasant migrants after the manner of their former rural dwellings which, inadequate enough in the countryside, are wholly unsuited to the congested conditions of urban life.[4]

In the great plantation areas of the world—Southeast Asia and the Caribbean region, for example—or where large-scale mining or refining operations take place, private corporations have traditionally provided housing for the workers. This housing is called estate housing. In the past it has been of low quality and without regard for the social needs of the workers.

Estate housing is frequently associated with dingy bachelor barracks, little consideration being given to the needs of the worker as the head of a family. Housing on many plantations consists of single rooms, usually built in rows of varying lengths. A number of families are crowded together under the same roof separated only by thin partitions. A building may contain twenty or more such dwelling units. In most of these "lines," the flimsy partitions dividing the units do not reach the roof, with the result that not only has the family no privacy, but smoke, noise, dirt and infection pass from one unit to another. Moreover, these units usually contain no facilities for cooking, bathing, washing, or storing of family possessions. The living space is extremely small, and adults and children sleep side by side in a row. Water and primitive sanitary facilities are in most cases available at one place only for the whole community.

Recently, there is evidence of a trend to deal with the housing problem of the worker on a long-term contract by facilitating the establishment of a normal family life in suitable surroundings. The building of family dwelling units is becoming a well-marked trend. In many instances, governments have enacted regulatory measures requiring (either by statute or by collective agreement) that the employer provide suitable housing for his workers or appropriate payment in lieu thereof.[5]

There are many difficulties in estate housing. The employing corporation may not know how long its operations are going to last; and even if it provides good housing, the worker may feel tied down and restricted, as workers did in the so-called "company towns" in the United States in the 19th century.

Rural housing in the underdeveloped areas of the world affects more people than urban or estate housing, since most of the people of the world are rural villagers. Lack of sanitary facilities and of safe water are only the most objectively measurable difficulties.

Despite the rapid growth of the cities and the development of large estates where housing is provided by the employers, the great majority of the population in most of the less-developed countries are rural villagers, living in houses built by themselves according to traditional patterns and from materials locally available without cost, such as mud bricks (adobe), or bamboo with roof of thatch. The relative habitability of such dwellings varies widely from region to region and from family to family. Many of them are one-room hovels where "ventilation and light are inadequate; floors are dirty or muddy, roofs are low, dirty and inflammable. Facilities for preserving and preparing food are usually painfully inadequate; cooking is a dark, smoky operation; and fuel for cooking may be difficult to get or it is wasteful of valuable resources. . . . Arrangements for washing persons and utensils are at best difficult. . . . The lack of sanitation is almost always dangerous. . . . Tuberculosis, pneumonia, and cholera cannot be controlled. . . . The water supply is inconvenient and frequently contaminated. Rodents and insects infest the huts. . . ."[6]

Crowded and insanitary shelter has been usual in many villages throughout the world, but it has worsened in modern times because of the pressure of increasing population, declining productivity of the land, war devastation, and natural calamities. Governments have come to view bad rural housing as a major social problem, but have found it useless to attempt to impose standards which are wholly impossible to meet in the present state of poverty and low productivity, and in the absence of technical skills. In the long run improved housing will have to wait for improved productivity. In the short run, schemes of "aided self-help" seem to be feasible. In these schemes, groups of prospective householders are organized and assisted—with funds, materials, equipment, and technical advice—so that they can help themselves.

The United Nations has taken cognizance of the seriousness of the housing situation in the world; the General Assembly has stated that "lack of adequate housing constitutes one of the most serious deficiencies in the standard of living of large sections of the population of the world . . . and the serious social problems originate in, or are aggravated by, the shortage of housing." [7] And not the least of these serious social problems originating in the shortage of housing is health.

World Health

Just as health became recognized as a social responsibility of the community in the middle of the 19th century, and disease as a burden of all, so the health of people in underdeveloped areas of the world has become recognized as a responsibility of the world community in the 20th century, and disease even in remote jungles as a burden to all. The World Health Organization was based on the recognition that "unequal development in different countries in the promotion of health and control of disease, especially communicable disease, is a common danger." [8] It is not merely a matter of protecting our own shores from plagues; it is a matter of increasing world economic productivity. Much of the poverty of the world has been attributed to the ill health of the people.

In Mymensingh, a district in East Pakistan, malaria control not only diminished infant mortality . . . but increased the production of rice by 15 per cent—from the same acreage . . . without any improvement in methods of cultivation or in the variety of rice. This increase was due to the fact that whereas in the past three out of every five landworkers had been sick of the fever at the critical seasons of planting and harvesting, five out of five were available for the manual operations when the malaria had been controlled. In other areas, removal of seasonal malaria has made it possible to grow a second crop. In still others, hundreds of thousands of acres of fertile land, which had been abandoned because of malaria, have been recovered for cultivation. People who are sick, ailing and incapacitated by disease lack the energy, initiative and enterprise needed to adopt new methods and improve their means of food production and so increase the yields from existing acreages.[9]

Exact morbidity statistics are lacking for most underdeveloped areas of the world, but that the rates are extremely high is definitely known. Millions of cases of malaria, tuberculosis, yaws, and nutritional diseases are known; there are doubtless many more that are not. Health researchers speak, therefore, of mass diseases.

We can . . . accept, by report from most countries and by statistics from others, that there are "mass diseases." That is a term here used merely as a convenience to describe diseases which are so widespread, and affect so high a proportion of the population, as to be a dominant factor in hindering the social and economic development of a country, and which, medically, mask other diseases to the point of making them clinically irrelevant until the mass disease is removed.

The mass diseases by this definition may be regarded as the tangle, the jungle undergrowth, of disease which has to be cleared before a country has a fair chance of development. When it is cleared, other forms of ill-health reveal themselves, as they have done in the highly-developed countries.

Mass diseases are: malaria, bilharziasis, yaws, hookworm, tuberculosis, trachoma, syphilis, gastro-intestinal diseases and nutritional diseases. Pestilential diseases—cholera, smallpox, bubonic plague, typhus, typhoid and yellow fever—would rank as "mass diseases" in epidemic form, since they would affect, kill or disable substantial proportions of the populations, but in endemic form they are localized and, in general, have been brought within the manageable limits of public health whereas the others, in underdeveloped countries, have not.[10]

The following description suggests the nature and incidence of the most serious mass diseases:

Malaria is almost certainly the mass disease which has the greatest effect on the greatest number of people. . . . It reaches its highest proportions in the densely populated, underdeveloped countries where, in some localities, e.g., Bengal, more than half the population are recurrently ill of the disease.

The *tuberculosis* death rate is probably higher than that of malaria and the disease is geographically more widespread, probably now universal. . . . *Syphilis* is also worldwide. Once it is introduced into an underdeveloped community, it often assumes extravagant proportions. In the Straits Settlements the rate of incidence was found in 1937 to be 494 per 100,000—thirty times that of England and seventy-five times that of Sweden. In the Ghund Valley (Simla, India) the whole population was clinically tested and showed 65 per cent positive cases. . . . *Bilharziasis* is widely distributed in parts of Africa, the Middle East, South America and China. It is a disease transmitted by a water-snail and is spread through bathing in the rivers and working in the irrigated fields. It has been estimated that it costs Egypt approximately £E20 million per year and decreases productivity by 33 per cent. About 10 million people are infected in Egypt. *Yaws,* a spirochaetic disease which is not spread venereally but by spirochaetic invasion of wounds and sores, is scattered through countries in tropical latitudes. *Hookworm,* spread through polluted water supplies, is found in practically every underdeveloped country. Control of the disease in one large tea plantation in India increased labour efficiency by 25 per cent. *Trachoma,* the eye disease leading to blindness, is most common in the arid zone, but is also found in wet tropical areas (India and Indochina have a high incidence). In Egypt it is widespread in the rural population, though not generally in its extreme forms. *Gastro-intestinal diseases* are due to many causes, but usually to unclean food or water. They are the cause of a high infant death rate and of general incapacity and deaths. Dysentery is the most common, but they include cholera and typhoid. Gastro-intestinal diseases are predominantly a problem of sanitation—and consequently expensive to control since sewers and clear water supplies mean heavy capital investment in public works.

Nutritional diseases—malnutrition short of starvation—derive from a complex of poverty and ignorance. In their clinical manifestations they are identifiable as beri-beri, pellagra, scurvy, rickets, a disease condition of increasing medical interest known as *kwashiorkor* and nutritional anaemia. But deficiencies in diet are a matter of degree and the individuals who end in hospitals, mental institutions or the grave as a result of text-book deficiency diseases are only a fraction of those who endure through life the miseries and disabilities of sub-normal health due to such deficiencies. For example, kwashiorkor is a disease manifested in children between the ages of 6 months and 6 years. It is characterized by a change in the pigmentation—a reddening or "rusting" of the hair and the skin—by retarded growth, fatty infiltration, the swollen stomach of oedema, cirrhosis of the liver and heavy mortality. The manifestations occur in populations where the child during the weaning and post-weaning period is put on to a diet deficient in animal and first-class protein. If he survives—and it is said that in many parts of Central Africa most children in the second or third year of life suffer from kwashiorkor—he is prone to develop later a primary cancer of the liver, as well as a chronic deterioration of health. Kwashiorkor, if not too far advanced, responds quickly to relatively small amounts of skimmed milk, but milk is one of the rarest foods in underdeveloped countries. Although self-evident forms of the disease are not so common outside Africa, there are signs of it in most underdeveloped countries. Apart from its clinical importance, the modifications of this disease (as of other deficiency diseases) must contribute to the poor health, lowered efficiency and premature deaths of millions in the protein-deficient underdeveloped countries.[11]

Because these mass diseases kill so many people in their early years, life expectancy is low. One World Health Organization officer has summarized some of the differences between developed and underdeveloped countries at midcentury as follows: [12]

	Developed Areas	Intermediate Areas	Underdeveloped Areas
Proportion of world population	⅕	Less than ⅙	⅔
Annual per capita income, in U.S. dollars	461	154	41
Food supply, calories per day	3,040	2,760	2,150
Physicians per 100,000 population	106	78	17
Life expectancy at birth, in years	63	52	30

Health services in the underdeveloped areas bring not only a reduction in the death rate, but also far-reaching changes in the economic and social life of the people. In Indonesia, for example, the contrast between villages in which yaws had been eliminated and those in which it had not, was spectacular:

. . . the houses are clean, the children well-cared for, and the crops and live-stock have improved. Because the people have found a new zest, farmers' clubs and rural extension courses have made headway; the peasants want to learn modern ways of producing better rice and developing better irrigation.[13]

It is as though a new race had been created; and, indeed, the difference between people chronically ill with the mass diseases and those who are free from them is far greater than the difference between people who have only racial differences to distinguish them.

The health services also put into motion forces which operate toward the emancipation of women, for disease cannot be attacked in one sex alone. "In countries where segregation of women is an intransigent problem for political reformers, the functional activities of doctors, nurses and health visitors are establishing contacts with women and helping to create among them a new spirit of inquiry and cooperation." [14]

The phenomenal achievements in the field of health are, of course, a feather in the bonnet of medical science. But there are unfortunate consequences as well. We saw above that there are great parts of the world where people are always underfed. And it is precisely in these areas that medical science is doing most to save lives. A second great social problem in the world community, then, and some people consider it the most urgent of all, is the unequal growth of food production and population.

Problems of Population Growth:
The Race between Population
and Technology

The humanitarian movements which are wiping out epidemics and famines, and which are lowering the death rate phenomenally, are also increasing population with astounding rapidity. The World Population Conference in December 1954 estimated that the population of

The Social Problems Which Accompany Technological Change: Role Disturbance

Technological change has a tremendous impact on both rural and urban living. Old social forms become modified; new ones take a long time to evolve. Personality suffers; families disintegrate; village ties disappear. Peoples are uprooted by the million. Cities are unable to receive them with decent facilities. It is difficult for people to face such profound social dislocations without traumas.

The problems in rural areas demand basic changes:

It should be noted that, while certain types of mortality reduction through control of mass disease may require only a consenting population (though good health requires much more), the increase of food production demands active and instructed cooperation, and in many cases it requires changes in deep-rooted customs and practices, resettlement, land reform, large-scale irrigation and conservation projects, and other far-reaching actions. The actual extent to which the food-producing capacity of the earth can be expanded by improved methods of cultivation, recovery of wastelands, exploitation of marine and inland waters and other means, poses a fundamental problem. . . .[20]

The social problems inherent in rapid urbanization, which struck the Western world so violently in the 19th century, are now striking the underdeveloped areas of the world. As peasant populations leave the soil and migrate to cities, this is what happens:

Congestion and slum conditions are especially noticeable in cities that have grown phenomenally during the last decade or so as a result chiefly of migration from the countryside. . . . Such cities in many less-developed countries now contain large floating populations of unskilled workers of peasant origin, beset by many problems and needs. This situation, together with underemployment, found very extensively among the rural peasantry, constitutes a tremendous waste of potentially productive manpower. The processes of change from rural subsistence economies to more complex market and monetary economies, with their greater mobility and urbanization, are giving rise to peculiarly urgent social problems among the transitional groups. Such support as was provided traditionally by mutual aid within the extended family and the local community becomes less and less available to the unfortunate—the sick, the unemployed, the handicapped, the aged, the homeless, the mentally afflicted.[21]

We discussed in Chapter 23 the social problems of some of these special groups, but here our chief concern is with a role phase of the social problems associated with technological change. We have already seen that industrialization tends to destroy old role relationships, to release individuals from age-old ties, and to confuse and disturb family roles and worker roles, in some cases resulting in *anomie,* or normlessness. Is such role anarchy inevitable? Must underdeveloped areas in the 20th century go through the same process of role disturbance as did the West in the 19th century? And if role modification is inevitable, can it be carried through with a minimum of casualties in the form of mental illness? Here is how one student describes the problem.

The words *technical change* have come to symbolize for people all over the world a hope that is new to mankind. Through the centuries most of the peoples of the world have lived close to fear—fear of hunger, of cold, of chronic illness, of ignorance. In those societies or at those periods which later have been called *great,* a small proportion of the population have been elevated above some of these fears; their food and drink, the care and protection of their children, their control over the knowledge that mankind had accumulated so far was assured. The others, ninety-nine per cent, remained relatively wretched; the most that the beneficent leader or monarch, priest or prophet, sage or artist could do was to alleviate their misery, giving them law or splendour, sacrament or messianic vision, wisdom or beautiful intricate form, within which life remained worth living in spite of hunger and thirst, cold and want. It is only very recently, actually only since World War II, that we have been able to share the hope that the peoples of the world need be hungry no longer.

But with the hope that misery can be prevented has come a new fear, a fear which is strongest perhaps in the small proportion of the human race who, exempted from the common misery, have been the custodians of the fine flower of human civilization, acutely aware of the patterns of culture—so fragile, so all of a piece—which they have guarded. If the abolition of hunger and want were to be bought only by industrialization, by urbanization, by mechanization, by westernization, by secularization, by mass production, would not the cost be too great? Of what use to introduce a tractor which made the yield of the grain fields greater, if in so doing the whole distinguishing fabric of life which had characterized a society would be ripped into shreds?

These questions have been asked by the literate and privileged in old societies where the majority of the population is illiterate and unprivileged; by the members of Western societies who, valuing the graciousness of their own past, recoiled before the crudeness of an as yet unrealized technical culture, by the specialist—the historian, the anthropologist—who warns how destructive contact has been in the past between technologically developed and technologically less developed cultures, how often the price of progress has been to turn proud, aristocratic nomads into pitifully limited factory workers, shorn of their own tradition and provided with no new values.

The conflict of these two points of view—between those whose imagination is caught by the possibility of releasing mankind from the spectre of famine and those who insist that man does not live by bread alone—finds its echo in the questions that are asked whenever technical assistance is mentioned. Eyes light up with the vision that is offered. For the first time in history there is a possibility that no man need go well-fed to his rest, knowing that his neighbour is hungry, that indeed so many of his neighbours are hungry and that though he broke the bread from his own table into a million pieces it would bring no real relief for a day, for an hour. But then faces fall, as people ask the second question: *How is it to be done*—in human terms? Granted that we know the technical answers: how to redistribute land in units which can support the use of modern agricultural machinery; how to locate industrial plants in relation to population and resources; how to utilize the local food supplies to provide a nutritional diet; how to reorganize town planning and water use so as to avoid the principal epidemic and endemic diseases in the world. Granted that we know all this, what will be the cost in terms of the human spirit? How much destruction of old values, disintegration of personality, alienation of parents from children, of husbands from wives, of students from teachers, of neighbour from neighbour, of the spirit of man from the faith and style of his traditional culture must there be? How slow must we go? How fast can we go?

This is the question which is repeated in the smallest village forum where people who were yesterday illiterate, today argue about how rapidly they dare change their age-old customs, and in the universities, in the halls of government, in the corridors of the United Nations, and in the specialized United Nations agencies. All over the world, this question has become a primary one as political leaders plan in terms of change or of resistance to change. . . .

The speed and constructiveness with which the peoples of the world can learn to share in the skills which will free them from their age-long fears is the measure of our right to hope. Upon our ability to hope will depend our willingness to act in the living present. Such reasoned belief must be based on knowledge. To think about the question, *How can technical change be introduced with such regard for the culture pattern that human values are preserved?* it is necessary to think about these patterns, these changes, and these considered attempts to protect the mental health of a world population in transition.[22]

In 1955 there were 65 UNESCO technical-assistance projects operating in 37 countries, with 130 experts in the field. In addition, as we saw above, many large corporations were operating their own "technical-assistance" projects. And although a large part of the national technical-assistance program was basically military, it also faced these role and status problems in underdeveloped areas. It is a matter of great concern that the role disturbance which is almost inevitable during the transition from an agricultural to an industrialized economy be kept at a minimum in order to preserve the mental as well as the physical health of the people involved.[23]

One Anatolian village—Balgat—has been described in the moment of transition from an agricultural to an industrialized economy by a social scientist who visited it in 1954. Four years earlier the community had been analyzed by another social scientist. Balgat is only five miles outside Ankara, in Turkey. In 1950 there had been no road. Almost everyone had been a farmer or a shepherd. It was little different from the way it had been for centuries. "Yet the story of the modern Middle East is summed up in the recent career of Balgat. Indeed, the personal meaning of modernization in underdeveloped lands everywhere is traced in miniature in the lives of two Balgati—the Grocer and the Chief." [24] In 1950 the Grocer had had the modern point of view, but he had been unique, and his status very low. He was "the only unfarming person and the only merchant in the village. . . . He is considered by the villagers even less than the least farmer." [25] The Chief, on the other hand, had typified the immemorial past. In 1954 everything had changed. There was a bus line to Ankara. There were no farmers left. "Most of the male population of Balgat was now in fact working in the factories and construction gangs of Ankara—*for cash*." [26] Role definitions had been completely revamped. Although the grocer was now dead, his occupational role, which had been so despised in 1950, was now being performed by—of all people—the sons of the old Chief, himself the embodiment of tradition. This is how the social scientist interviewing the Chief in 1954 described the change in role definition.

The new ways . . . were not bringing evil with them? "No, people will have to get used to different ways and then some of the excesses, particularly among the young, will disappear. The young people are in some ways a serious disappointment; they think more of clothes and good times than they do of duty and family and country. But it is to be hoped that as the *Demokrat* men complete the work they have begun, the good Turkish ways will again come forward to steady the people. Meanwhile, it is well that people can have to eat and to buy shoes they always needed but could not have."

And as his two sons were no longer to be farmers, what of them? The Chief's voice did not change, nor did his eyes cloud over, as he replied: "They are as the others. They think first to serve themselves and not the nation. They had no wish to go to the battle in Korea, where Turkey fights before the eyes of all the world. They are my sons and I speak no ill of them, but I say only that they are as all the others."

I felt at this moment a warmth toward the Chief which I had not supposed he could evoke. His sons had not, after all, learned to fight bravely and die properly. These two sons through whom he had hoped to relive his own bright dreams of glory had instead become *shopkeepers*.[27]

In this particular case there was perhaps a minimum of role dislocation because the men commuted back and forth between the city and their homes in the village. But in cases where they leave the village completely to live in the cities, the dislocation becomes severe.[28] We have already touched on some of the role changes with respect to women (in

Mexico) in our discussion of family roles (Chap. 15) and in our discussion of health, above.

Role redefinition is also accompanied by status problems. We shall not here discuss status problems within the underdeveloped areas, but rather the status problems which arise between them and the more advanced areas. For as the peoples of the underdeveloped areas come into contact with the West, as their leaders begin to dream of abundance for their peoples, and as industrialization begins to seem feasible to them, status problems become more acute. A fourth great social problem in the world today is, then, that of the relations among peoples and races.

Status Problems among Races and Peoples

It is difficult for people of the West not to look down upon the people of underdeveloped areas. From their vantage point in modern civilization, these backward people seem inherently inferior. The conviction of superiority in Westerners shows in their contacts with peoples of other color and culture. This attitude of superiority leaves a bad taste in the mouth of even those who benefit from Western assistance. As such it not only constitutes a social problem in many parts of the world but it also has serious political implications.

These status problems were considered so important that a discussion of them was included in a manual for personnel dealing with underdeveloped areas.

Much of the present phrasing of technical-assistance planning, and much of the present evaluation of change within a country, is conducted with explicit or implicit denial of the dignity of members of those countries which, while often the inheritors of much older traditions, have not been in the vanguard of those aspects of culture which stem from modern science. This is self-defeating, in that it arouses violent resistances and attempts at compensation and retaliation from those whose feelings of self-esteem have been violated; it is also contrary to the findings of modern psychiatric practice, which insist on the recognition of the patient's validity as a human being. Phrases which divide the world into the "haves" and the "have-nots" overvalue bread and plumbing and devalue music and architecture. Those whose status is defined as a "have-not" may come to repudiate the possibility of learning anything at all, or of sharing anything at all except "bread" with those who have so denigrated their cherished ways of life. Phrases like "under-developed," "backward," "simple"—to the extent that they cover a whole culture—are equally defeating.[29]

The stings of a thousand slights, of a thousand experiences of condescension, of a thousand relegations to inferior status finally accumulate and express themselves in political movements.

The Colored Peoples Vis-à-vis the White Races

The colored peoples of the world who endured the humiliation of colonialism until the middle of the 20th century are now rejecting the inferior status accorded them by the white races. They are now in process of asserting their political independence; but that is not enough. They remain extremely sensitive about the inferiority which has been imputed to them. They want more than political independence; they want more even than physical help. They want to be made to feel the equal of the white races. One thoughtful American observer has said that if we wooed the East and Africa with our political ideals of equality and of the dignity of man it might well be "more important over the years than our help in dollars and technology." [30] And another analyst of the situation comes to essentially the same conclusion.

> Precisely because our efforts to remove abuses and improve the conditions of living have been in some degree effective, the level of discontent is rising. We have been fostering a "revolution of rising expectations" that is being turned against us. People who have discovered, after millennia of hopelessness, that things can after all be changed will not be content with minor changes, small improvements. . . .
>
> We have been deluded by the notion of "stomach Communism"—the idea that all that men want is to fill their bellies and they will then pay no heed to the Communists. Our appeal is in this sense more materialistic than theirs. We try—largely in vain—to fill the stomachs of the hungry, while the Communists appeal to their sense of outraged human dignity, by promising to destroy those who have oppressed and humiliated them. The colored races, almost four-fifths of mankind, want above all else to eradicate the feeling of inferiority that has been imposed upon them. They will not be appeased by offers of bread.[31]

The yellow races have been the first to assert their equality. The black races, especially in Africa, are farther away from emancipation; they may have to wait until the 21st century. They have a long way to go until they are in a position successfully to challenge "white supremacy," especially in South Africa. The *apartheid* policy there, whose effect is to create separate and unequal facilities, will put a powerful brake on the upward status climb of the colored people. The depredations and terrorizations of the Mau Mau in Kenya were symptoms of the underlying social problems of contemporary Africa and, as one analysis of the situation summarized it, "*status* is the nub of the problem." [32]

It is not only among the underdeveloped areas of the world that status problems arise. The situation of the Soviet Union presents a special case, of such importance that it is presented here in some detail.

The Case of the Soviet Union

Russia has felt itself to be inferior to the West from at least the time of Peter the Great. The upper classes then began to look up to the West, to speak French, to read foreign books, and to assimilate foreign ideas. Perhaps it was this identification of Western culture with an upper class that gave it such prestige. At any rate, to this very day Russians seem incapable of shaking off this tendency to think of the outside world as superior to them. It is such a strong feeling that the Communist Party must make constant efforts to reassure Russians that they are just as good as, if not better than, anyone else. They are sensitive and defensive. In 1947 the Presidium of the Central Committee of the Trade Unions published a decree on Soviet patriotism, pointing out that many professional and state employees showed an unworthy adulation and servility to things foreign and to the "putrefying reactionary culture of the bourgeois West." [33]

This "harmful illness" was widespread among the least stable representatives of the intelligentsia, among whom, the decree contended, there were people capable of national self-degradation, in the loss of respect of Soviet citizenship and in the worship of bourgeois culture which was in a state of moral decay. These un-patriotic inclinations were explained by the fact that a certain portion of the intelligentsia was still in the grip of survivals of Tsarist Russia, when, according to this document, the ruling classes retarded the development of Russia out of deference to foreign interests. Servility, it stated, was also caused by the agents of imperialism who were seeking in every way to support and revive harmful survivals of capitalism. . . . The Presidium [therefore] decrees a number of measures designed "to inculcate a feeling of pride in the great achievement of socialism, to explain the superiority of the Soviet system over the capitalist system, to wage an irreconcilable struggle against all forms of unpatriotic acts, against the influences of reactionary decadent bourgeois culture and ideology.". . . Particular attention was to be paid to workers in the fields of art and medicine where, apparently, signs of servility to the West had been most widely detected. . . . The angry, exasperated terms in which some of its attacks on the "grovellers" were couched reintroduced a sharpness into Soviet polemics that had been absent for almost a decade. . . .

Attacks on servility towards the West as something incompatible with the dignity of the Soviet person and with Soviet pride continued through the winter of 1947–48. The roots of the sickness were seen as going back into the distant past. "The ruling classes in Tsarist Russia," wrote *Pravda,* "with no conception of national pride, forgetting even their native tongue, cringed before everything that came from abroad." The causes of this phenomenon were attributed to Russia's backwardness, providing conditions for the spread of admiration of Western culture. "But the situation has now changed radically. Every possibility now exists for the complete liquidation of servile admiration of the West." The ruling classes of Tsarist Russia, the argument ran, created the idea of the "inferiority" of the Russian intelligentsia. At the beginning of the 18th century Russia had been inundated with foreigners who behaved as if they represented a superior race. Everything French and later German was copied, and this had done infinite harm to Russian culture. Russian scientists had been plagiarised by foreigners. A discovery of Lomonosov had been wrongly ascribed to Lavoisier, the invention of the radio by Popov was ascribed to Marconi, and Yablochkov had not received credit for his invention of the electric lamp. . . .

Measures were taken to see that the schools and universities give suitable prominence to Russian achievements. *Pravda* protested in a leading article against the "tendency to belittle Russian scholarship both at home and abroad, recalling the anti-Slav theories of the school of historians who attribute the civilization of the Kievian Rus to Scandinavian influences brought by the Vikings, the outlook of Peter the Great who distrusted Russian discoveries, and the fostering of the Russian sense of inferiority by foreign capitalists." [34]

As a defense, history had to be rewritten to help prop up Russian self-feeling.

To a people which has always read the history of its land with excitement and interest, this new light on the past has been particularly illuminating. Working like a canker-worm at the heart of national self-respect the notion that Russian history began with the arrival of a foreign ruler had long weakened popular respect for the State and caused Russian patriotism to take the form of devotion to the community rather than to the state, an attitude which cannot meet with the approval of those who rule Russia today and who consider that it is the function of history to point a moral. . . . The Soviet people strongly resent any insinuation that their ancestors were an uncouth and backward people in relation to the rest of Europe, and in this the objective facts of history are on their side. . . . The Russian struggle to be culturally independent and the resentment of any implication that they were inferior to the foreigners in their midst, were no less characteristic of the 11th century than they are in our times. [35]

There has been great emphasis in recent times on Russian achievements—which undeniably are remarkable—in order "to get rid of that self-depreciation which has been a brake on Russian initiative in the past." [36] In 1947, *Bolshevik,* an influential Communist periodical, complained that Russians had been treated as an inferior people; many Russians, it alleged, remained obsequious to bourgeois culture; those who encouraged such attitudes were traitors to their country; everyone should defeat any tendency to be subservient or obsequious to foreigners. [37]

The theater was also used to point a moral of Soviet superiority,

especially in the field of science. A play by B. Romashov—*A Great Force*
—had for its theme the conflict between a patriotic Russian scientist,
Pavel Lavroy, and Milyagin, the Director of the Institute where he
worked, who had degenerated with success into a sharp businessman.
Here is part of the dialogue:

MILYAGIN. They have not yet been able to do this [even] in America. What
are you thinking of?

PAVEL. That's just it. That's the whole trouble. You are convinced that they
can do anything there . . . and I tell you that we can do far more. . . .
Our science cannot help being the most advanced in the world.

MILYAGIN. Our science? We have no science. Your science! Science belongs to
the entire world.

PAVEL. No, I shall never agree to that. What is dear to me is what is done in
my own country, by our hands.

.   .   .   .

PAVEL. You will forgive me. I, of course, am only an ordinary research worker.
. . . But I feel a sense of shame when I hear such self-debasing admiration of all things foreign. . . . I am simply ashamed. We are not such
ignorant and poor people as to walk along begging for help.

MILYAGIN. Pavel, no one is begging, but what is good is good.

PAVEL. Do we not intercept what is good? Are we not learning? We are most
respectful of advanced foreign technology and science. . . . The point
is that our people are vigorous, bold, progressive. . . . There is no need
for us to look through a peep-hole to see what is going on in European
culture. We ourselves are creating valuable things and can take pride in
our labour, our people and our young state! We have accomplished
something in science too and we shall accomplish a thousand times more.
There is no need for us to stand on tip-toes before European civilization!
I cannot but be interested in what goes on in the world. I am disturbed
by various new doctrines, by declarations in Fulton. All of this touches
me deeply . . . and it seems to me crazy that while the monopolists
abroad are making new blocks against our country, we still hear this
drivel about some sort of advantages of European culture. Of course,
we still have people who think that "we do not know how to live." . . .
They do not wish to understand, these people, that we are now on the
offensive. . . .[38]

After the death of Stalin a greater willingness to learn from the
West, especially technological processes from the United States, was
shown. But it seems still to rankle deeply in Russian minds that the
level of living there remains so low compared to that of other civilized
countries. They can explain it, but this does not seem to salve their
hurt pride. They can account for it by pointing out that their land has
been ravaged by war, that they have had—or have felt that they had—to
divert their productive energies into the manufacture of heavy goods
and arms rather than consumer goods. They have performed industrial
miracles, but they still suffer shortages in almost everything that caters

to the amenities of life. As contrasted with the West there is little glamour. To an outsider who knows Western culture, Russian life seems drab, colorless, without glitter or excitement. That the need of people for some such glamour is very real has been recognized by the government in its introduction of a cosmetics industry and in its encouragement of a fashion industry. Of course, the opera and the ballet —the best in the world, we are told—have for many years added glitter to Russian cultural life.

It is this long experience in feeling inferior which no doubt lends such drive to the Soviet appeals to colonial peoples everywhere. They can feel with the colored races and exploited peoples all over the world, for they, too, know what it means to feel unequal to the West in status.

NOTES

[1] United Nations, *Preliminary Report on the World Social Situation* (United Nations, 1952), p. 42.

[2] *Ibid.*, p. 41.

[3] Food and Agriculture Organization, *The State of Food and Agriculture, 1955* (United Nations, 1955).

[4] United Nations, *op. cit.*, p. 58.

[5] *Ibid.*

[6] *Ibid.*, p. 59.

[7] General Assembly resolution 537/(VI), adopted at the 371st plenary meeting, 2 February 1952.

[8] United Nations, *op. cit.*, p. 32.

[9] *Ibid.*, p. 36.

[10] *Ibid.*, p. 25.

[11] *Ibid.*

[12] *Ibid.*, p. 31.

[13] *Ibid.*, p. 22.

[14] *Ibid.*

[15] Reported in the *New York Times*, February 7, 1955.

[16] *Newsweek*, November 14, 1955, p. 53.

[17] United Nations, *op. cit.*, p. 4.

[18] A string of beads, like a rosary, was devised on which women were to calculate the "safe period" in the menstrual cycle.

[19] United Nations, *op. cit.*, p. 36.

[20] *Ibid.*, p. 4.

[21] *Ibid.*

[22] Margaret Mead, ed., *Cultural Patterns and Technical Change* (Mentor, 1955), pp. 5–7.

[23] The World Federation for Mental Health is attacking this problem of protecting peoples from social-psychological stresses and disorganization of family and community life; its aim is preventive rather than therapeutic. It was this organization which sponsored the manual, edited by Margaret Mead (quoted above), designed to prepare technical-assistance personnel for meeting the social and cultural as well as the technical problems involved in their work.

[24] Daniel Lerner, "The Grocer and the Chief," *Harper's*, September 1955, p. 47.

[25] *Ibid.*, p. 48.

[26] *Ibid.*, p. 53.

[27] *Ibid.*, p. 55.

[28] For a description of family disruption in China in the throes of urbanization, see Marion J. Levy, Jr., *The Family Revolution in Modern China* (Harvard Univ. Press, 1949); see also Martin C. Yang, *A Chinese Village* (Columbia Univ. Press, 1945).

[29] Mead, *op. cit.*, p. 299.

[30] Justice William O. Douglas, reported in the *New York Times*, May 28, 1955.

[31] Joseph H. Sigelman, "The Shift to the Initiative," *Harper's*, September 1955, pp. 42–43.

[32] Editorial, "Tropical Africa," *Atlantic Monthly*, December 1955, p. 10.

[33] Ralph Parker, *Moscow Correspondent* (SRT Publications, 1949), p. 159.

[34] *Ibid.*, pp. 159–162.

[35] *Ibid.*, pp. 188–189.

[36] *Ibid.*, p. 203.

[37] *Ibid.*, pp. 208–209.

[38] *Ibid.*, pp. 209–211.

L'ENVOI

If the problems today are different from those of the past, what can we expect them to be in the future? For the pessimist there are at least two views that may be held. One of these accepts the implications of abundance and sees it as existing in the future in all parts of the world. It raises the question, What then? It implies that abundance will have eradicated social problems and that as a result there will be only boredom and ennui. People who accept this view might echo William James's comments to his son after visiting a cooperative community, Chautauqua, in which the old problems did not exist. "The flash of a pistol, a dagger, or a devilish eye, anything to break the unlovely level of 10,000 good people—a crime, murder, rape, elopement, anything would do." [1] When examined, this point of view is genuinely sinister. It suggests that social problems are necessary to keep us amused, or at least from becoming bored. Those who espouse this pessimistic point of view raise the question, How can ordinary human beings fill eighty hours of leisure time a week with any satisfaction?

The implication that abundance will itself solve social problems is not, we believe, quite warranted. For, "contrary to the somewhat simple notion that prosperity dissolves all social problems, we see that prosperity brings in its wake new social groups, new social strains and new social anxieties." [2] No one need expect, therefore, that all social or societal problems will ever be solved. As old ones are conquered new ones emerge. We raise our sights, as we saw in Chapter 1, and find it as disturbing to lag behind higher standards as it was to lag behind lower ones. Nor will we ever eliminate all stress from human life; status pressures may be even more traumatic than those deriving from hunger, illness, or cold. Abundance does not spell Utopia.

A second pessimistic view of the future anticipates atomic and hydrogen-bomb warfare. We are daily reminded that mankind now has power to destroy the human species and all its works, and yet we are obliged to face the fact that war may come. Since we cannot as a species deliberately commit suicide we have to be as scientific about meeting the social problems of war as we are about other problems. It is often said of the military that they tend always to prepare for the last war rather than the next one. In a similar way we can prepare for the social problems which accompany war only in terms of past experience, no matter how anachronistic it may prove to be. We know that nuclear warfare would be more destructive than wars in the past and presumably more disruptive of customary patterns of living. We know also that distance, now conquered by supersonic planes and missiles, would no longer offer us protection, as it has in previous world wars. And we know that new kinds of illnesses—radiation illness and germ-warfare illnesses—would have to be provided for. But still we can plan specifically only in terms of past experience.

One study of social problems during World War II in the United States concluded that war merely intensified problems already present, but did not initiate new ones. Among those specified were the following:

The rate of . . . mobility was intensified, with 15 million civilians and 12 million soldiers and sailors on the move.

Social congestion was intensified in certain industrial and military centers.

The gradual decline in the traditional functions of the family was accelerated.

The trend toward the employment of women was intensified by the wartime shortage of labor.

Many of the tensions which lead to the peacetime disorganization of the family were increased.

Desertion probably increased.

The long-term trend toward a higher divorce rate and a greater yearly number of divorces was accelerated.

The emotional deprivation of children caused by the employment of mothers was increased.

Adolescence adjustment was complicated by the accelerated differences between the generations.

The trend toward increased sexual freedom was intensified by the war-time decline in the mores.

The number of illegitimate births increased, but not as fast as legitimate births.

Juvenile delinquency increased sharply, especially among girls.

Certain crimes against the person showed a considerable increase.

Various minor crimes and offenses against the public morality increased.

First admissions to mental hospitals for all psychoses increased.

First admissions to mental hospitals for certain organic psychoses of old age increased.

First admissions to mental hospitals for the functional psychoses showed a mixed trend, with manic-depressive psychosis decreasing slightly and dementia praecox increasing substantially.[3]

Some of these trends proved to be temporary; others, not. The high divorce rate, for example, subsided a few years after the war; the high rate of employment of women outside the home, however, continued.[4]

But it is doubtful if we can anticipate the social problems of an all-out atomic war on the basis of our past experience. At the very least we will have to study the experience of European countries in evacuating whole populations from urban centers, in separating children from parents, and in dealing with possible panic. The author quoted above may be quite correct in saying that our social problems during World War II were not new. But the same might not be true of an atomic war. Some students of atomic warfare conclude, in fact, that even Japanese experience may not be pertinent.

The following statement gives us some idea of the social problems that might be anticipated:

An evaluation of our knowledge of what we can expect of U.S. city-dwellers, assuming massive and saturating atomic attack, warning time from 0–6 hours, and evacuation the only civil defense measure available for minimizing death through action before the weapon explodes [suggests the following]:

Phase I, from the Yellow alert to the explosion: differences in conditions which will obtain (lack of practice and shelters) render data on European and Japanese responses to impending bombing attacks almost useless as a basis for prediction.

Phase II, from the explosion to a few hours after the explosion: there is evidence that the responses of the unwounded will range from disorganization to cogent activity; that persons in disaster areas are capable of helping others, especially family members; that mass depression or passively disorganized behavior rather than mass hysteria will be the more likely immediate response of the wounded. Intense upset, fear, and depression will probably be the major immediate result of witnessing casualties.

Phase III, from a few hours to a few days after the explosion: bombardment experiences (losing a loved one, being a near-miss) seem likely to produce a more or less persistent excessive state of anxiety, depression, and apathy. An increase is to be expected in neurotic disturbances.

Phase IV, from a few days to a few months after the explosion: food shortages are especially likely to engender considerable hostility directed to home agencies, who have failed to provide protection, not the enemy. Communal values will decay to some extent. Reuniting broken families, or at least providing definitive information on the whereabouts and health of missing members, seems closely related to morale and the recovery of psychological stamina. Data on prolonged morale effects of bombardment experiences are inconclusive.[5]

On the basis of studies of disaster behavior since 1950 we know that the major problems are not those of panic [6] but of role disorganization.[7] So long as a reasonable degree of role integration can be maintained, the social problems created by disaster—we are now referring specifically to war—may be manageable. But they will not be the same problems as those of past wars. And if, in addition to the above foreseeable problems which resemble those of the past with which we are familiar, we had new ones, or old ones in modern form, they would probably seem very different indeed from those of the past. Instead of simple mobility—as of workers or families of servicemen—we might have to provide for refugees or displaced persons or millions of bombed-out homeless people.

The sheer inability of most Americans to imagine the kinds of social problems that might accompany nuclear warfare is evidenced by the indifference or even apathy shown by most of them to the efforts of the Office of Civilian Defense to prepare them for attack. There is, fortunately, a mounting corpus of research data on disaster which may be applied if it should ever be required.[8]

Whether the social problems of atomic warfare will be merely an aggravated form of pre-existing problems or whether they will be wholly new, we do know that war leaves an aftermath of institutional debris no less palpable than the physical debris. Whole generations are devastated, as surely as are lands under a scorched earth policy, as our discussion of refugees intimated.

Between these two extremes of pessimism—one anticipating a time of endless boredom amid a plethora of gadgets and the other an atomic holocaust—there is room for at least a tempered optimism. As we saw above, the human species will never solve all its social problems. It will simply raise its standards and continue to have problems in meeting them. It is even conceivable that the results so far as war is concerned may eventually be judged not worth the cost. No one who has lived through the post-World-War-II period can help but be impressed by the resiliency everywhere displayed. And we have reason to believe that the human species is actually improving.[9] The species that is capable of creating atomic weapons seems also capable of defying them. It will survive.

NOTES

[1] *Letters of William James* (Atlantic Monthly Press, 1920), Vol. 2, p. 43.

[2] Daniel Bell, ed., *The New American Right* (Criterion, 1955), p. 4.

[3] Francis E. Merrill, *Social Problems on the Home Front, A Study of Wartime Influences* (Harper, 1948), pp. 230–231.

[4] See William Fielding Ogburn, ed., *American Society in Wartime* (Univ. of Chicago Press, 1943), Chapters 1, 2, and 10; see also Jessie Bernard, *American Community Behavior* (Dryden, 1949), Chapter 22.

[5] Abstract by S. L. Messinger of article by Donald L. Michael, "Civilian Behavior under Atomic Bombardment," *Bulletin of the Atomic Scientists*, 9 (May 1955), pp. 173–177, in *Sociological Abstracts*, 4 (Jan. 1956), p. 10.

[6] Charles E. Fritz and Eli S. Marks, "The NORC Studies of Human Behavior in Disaster," *The Journal of Social Issues*, X, 3 (1954), pp. 26–41.

[7] Lewis M. Killian, "Some Accomplishments and Some Needs in Disaster Study," *ibid.*, pp. 66–72.

[8] *The Journal of Social Issues*, Vol. X, No. 3 (1954) is devoted to disaster research.

[9] We have presented the evidence for this conclusion in earlier chapters. We know that health and longevity are improving (Chap. 8); as medical science learns to control the diseases which produce feeble-mindedness, the number so handicapped declines (Chap. 10); we seem to be on the verge of a break-through with respect to mental illnesses also (Chap. 13); the proportion of people who are problem drinkers seems to have declined, although the number who drink has increased (Chap. 11). Modern science is, in effect, pulling the human species up by its own bootstraps. There is even some evidence that people are improving so far as intelligence as measured by tests is concerned (Chap. 10).

INDEX

Abegglen, J. C., 68, 360, 508, 509
"abnormal," as concept, 134, 135
Abrams, C., 586, 587, 588
abundance, American character in age of,
  30–31, 389–393
  and change in class organization, 13-23,
    61, 442–443
    distribution of population, 29–31, 446
    occupational structure, 21
  and definition of parental roles, 376, 433
  evaluation of, 32–33
  ideology of, 13, 27–29
  and increase in anxiety, 285–287
  infectious diseases in age of, 185–186, 619,
    620
  nature of, 8–12, 635–636
  and rising standards of living, 12, 22, 23–
    27, 29
  and social disorganization, 174, 338, 510,
    537
  and standards of rehabilitation of handi-
    capped, 207–209
  and status of racial and ethnic groups,
    558–559, 572, 584, 629–631
  and stress, 73–74, 78, 79, 81
  and technology, 484
  and underdeveloped areas, 32–33
accommodation, of immigrant groups, 546–
  548
Ackerman, N., 335
Ackerson, L., 541
Adams, F. W. H., 444
Adams, S. H., 240
addiction, narcotics, 190, 259–264
addictive drinking, 248, 249, 251, 255, 258
adjustment, of aged, 468–470
  social, 44
Adler, P., 445, 528, 541, 612
Adlow, E., 406, 407, 444, 445
Adorno, T. W., 335
aged, characteristics of, at midcentury, 449–
  454
  degenerative diseases among, 186, 187–
    189
  dependency of, 453–459, 464
  factors in good adjustment of, 468–470
  family roles of, 454–455
  and group roles, 42
  health of, 451, 462–463, 468, 469
  as minority group, 466–467
  occupational degrading of, 405, 463–464,
    465, 470
  pathologies associated with, 180, 297, 298,
    446
  peer groups of, 451–452, 467, 468, 469

aged— (cont'd)
  political role of, 467–468
  rising standards in care of, 26–27
  rolelessness of, 49
  self-conception of, 451–452, 468, 469, 471
  status problems of, 457, 468, 469
  in underdeveloped areas, 606
  worker role of, 459–460, 466
aggregates, 57, 59, 69
aggression, 77, 417–418, 422
alcohol, exposure to, 253–256
alcoholics, and helping role, 42
  low status of, 58
  withdrawal symptoms of, 253, 269
Alcoholics Anonymous, 163, 249, 257
alcoholism, 190, 291, 506
  dependency as a factor in, 250–251, 257,
    329
  as expression of emotional disturbance,
    252–253, 268–269
  extent, trends, and incidence of, 244–247
  group forces as therapy for, 257
  legalistic approach to, 256, 258
  in Poland, 165
  as a social problem, 242–244, 255
  in Soviet Union, 164–166
  status dimension of, 58, 247–250
Allport, F. H., 153
Allport, G. W., 67
altruistic suicide, 312
Altschule, M. D., 305
amentia, 222
American character, 29–31, 389–393
amnesia, 292
Anderson, C. A., 586
Anderson, N., 120
Andrews, D., 508
Andrews, F. E., 175
Angell, R. C., 507
anomic suicide, 312
anomie, 142, 143, 313, 495, 626
Anslinger, H. J., 270
anti-intellectualism, 400, 553
antisocial behavior, effect of, on juvenile
  delinquency, 427
antisocial personality, 181, 331–333
anxiety, 47, 50, 51, 77, 81, 84, 306, 353
  absence of, in psychopathic personality,
    314–315, 320
  free-floating, 72
  increase in, 285–287
  related to status problems, 56, 279, 499,
    549, 551–553
  resulting from process of status equaliz-
    ing, 64–65

Monterrey

Merida
YUCATÁN

Mexico City
Vera Cruz

REVILLA GIGEDO
CLARION I.

Belize
BRITISH
HONDURAS

Guatemala
GUATEMALA
San Salvador
EL SALVADOR

HONDURAS
Tegucigalpa

NICARAGUA
Managua
San José

COSTA
RICA

Pa

PANAMA

COCOS I.

MEXICO
AND
CENTRAL AMERICA

SCALE IN MILES

0   200   400   600   800   1000

Base Map Copyright by HAGSTROM COMPANY, INC., N.Y.,

GALÁPAGOS IS.